PC User's Bible

John Ross and Kelly Murdock

BICENTENNIAL
1807
WILEY
2007
BICENTENNIAL

Wiley Publishing, Inc.

PC User's Bible

Published by
Wiley Publishing, Inc.
10475 Crosspoint Boulevard
Indianapolis, IN 46256
www.wiley.com

Copyright © 2007 by Wiley Publishing, Inc., Indianapolis, Indiana

Published by Wiley Publishing, Inc., Indianapolis, Indiana

Published simultaneously in Canada

ISBN: 978-0-470-08897-5

Manufactured in the United States of America

10 9 8 7 6 5 4 3 2 1

For general information on our other products and services or to obtain technical support, please contact our Customer Care Department within the U.S. at (800) 762-2974, outside the U.S. at (317) 572-3993 or fax (317) 572-4002.

Library of Congress Cataloging-in-Publication Data is available from the publisher.

About the Authors

John Ross has been working with and writing about computers and networks since the late 1960s. He has authored more than a dozen books about computers, networks, and the Internet for major publishers including Random House, Sybex, IDG Books, Microsoft Press, No Starch Press and Sunset Books, and has been a contributor to many others. He has also written technical manuals, white papers, and marketing material about network and telecommunications equipment, marine electronics, and broadcast equipment for many corporations including Motorola and AT&T.

As a sound archivist, John Ross works with broadcasters, music festivals, and folklore societies in the Pacific Northwest to restore, catalog, and preserve old audio-tape recordings and convert them to modern digital formats. He has also produced radio news and feature reports for National Public Radio, the BBC, Radio New Zealand, and other broadcasters around the world. On his own time, he collects folk music, restores antique toy trains, and makes hard cider. John Ross lives in a 100-year-old house in Seattle, which he is gradually restoring and updating to twenty-first century technology.

Kelly Murdock is the author of multiple titles including the *3ds Max Bible* (recently published in its seventh edition), *Adobe Creative Suite Bible*, *Maya Reveled*, and *Poser Revealed* (all in their second editions) along with numerous other graphics and Web-related titles including *Edgeloop Character Modeling*, *3D Game Animation For Dummies*, *Master VISUALLY HTML and XHTML*, and *JavaScript Visual Blueprint*.

When not writing computer books, Kelly works as a consultant and with his brother in the Logical Paradox Design studio that he helped found. He enjoys spending time with his family, playing basketball, mountain biking, and rock climbing.

The salesman says it's a machine that I need,
To organize my desk with accuracy and speed.
So I bought a computer and took it home,
To straighten up my office where papers freely roam,
So I unpacked the computer and put it to work,
By moving my papers just like a clerk.
I put all the critical papers next to the screen,
And under the keyboard the papers rarely seen.
Important papers are under the printer,
And next to the mouse are receipts from last winter.
The salesman was right, my computer is great,
But kind of expensive for a paperweight.
To Kerry and Donna, who know what it is like
to be organized, 2006

Credits

Acquisitions Editor
Courtney Allen

Project Editor
Chris Wolfgang

Technical Editors
Barry and Marcia Press

Copy Editor
Scott Tullis

Editorial Manager
Robyn Siesky

Business Manager
Amy Knies

Vice President and Executive Group Publisher
Richard Swadley

Vice President and Executive Publisher
Bob Ipsen

Vice President and Publisher
Barry Pruett

Project Coordinator
Erin Smith

Graphics and Production Specialists
Carrie A. Foster
Brooke Graczyk
Denny Hager
Jennifer Mayberry
Alicia B. South

Quality Control Technician
David Faust

Proofreading and Indexing
Techbooks, Kevin Broccoli

Wiley Bicentennial Logo:
Richard J. Pacifico

Acknowledgments

Thanks to the editorial and production staff at Wiley for converting our words and pictures into an attractive and well-organized book. The words are ours, but they have been polished and improved by Chris Wolfgang, Scott Tullis, and Marcia and Barry Press.

And thanks to Carole McClendon and the others at Waterside Productions for putting the project together. As always, the book would not have happened without their work.

Finally, thanks to all the people, corporations, and organizations that made the job easier by providing useful information, book images, and helpful explanations of complex topics and products on their Web pages. In particular, thanks to Amy Whelan at Pinnacle Systems, Mark Williams at Creative Labs, and Kelly Odle from Logitech.

Contents at a Glance

Contents

Contents

Contents

Contents

Contents

Contents

Contents

Contents

Contents

Contents

Part VIII: Security and Maintenance   773

Introduction

This book is a comprehensive reference for people who want to understand their Wintel computers inside and out, before and after they buy them. It contains advice about how to make informed buying decisions and how to use most of the features and functions supplied with your computer and the hidden tools and utilities in Windows XP that can make your computer easier to use. The book explains what most internal components, connectors, and external devices do, how they do it, and how all those pieces, parts, and add-on peripheral devices work together to form a computer.

By *Wintel computers*, we mean computers designed around Intel processors (and similar processors made by AMD), and the Microsoft Windows operating system. However, this is not a "How to Use Windows" book that covers every imaginable feature and function in the Windows operating system — there are other books in the Bible series for that. This book may have been specifically written about using your computer with Windows XP (with Service Pack 2 installed), but readers who run their computers with Linux or Unix and those who have upgraded to Windows Vista can also find a lot of useful information here.

As we wrote this book, we made some assumptions about our readers:

- You're probably not an absolute beginner, but you don't think of yourself as a hardcore computer geek either.

- You know how to turn on your computer and how to use Windows to do the basic stuff, like opening windows, using menus, and starting programs from the Windows desktop and the Start menu.

- You know something about Windows icons, files, and folders.

- You're comfortable moving your mouse around the screen, using both the left and right mouse buttons, and entering text and commands from your keyboard.

- You can send and receive e-mail.

- You also know how to use Internet Explorer or some other Web browser to find your way around the Internet. Throughout the book are pointers to Web sites that contain valuable information and useful utilities to download and install.

- Your computer has a lot of features and options that you have never used.

Icons

Like the other books in Wiley's Bible series, we have used icons to identify helpful comments, pointers, and suggestions:

CAUTION The Caution icon identifies possible problems or errors that may occur as a result of performing a step incorrectly.

CROSS-REF The Cross-Reference icon refers the reader to other chapters or sections within the book that are relevant to the topic being discussed.

NOTE The Note icon identifies important information that is tangential to the discussion.

TIP The Tip icon identifies special information or an insight.

What's in This Book

PC User's Bible contains eight parts:

Part I: Choosing Your Computer

This part offers guidelines for selecting and buying a new computer. It describes the relative advantages and disadvantages of laptop and desktop computers, explains where and how to buy the computer you really want or need, how to choose individual features and options, and how to evaluate the warranty.

Part II: Understanding Your Computer's Components

This part explains how a computer works and what each of the essential components contributes to the overall system. Among other things, it describes the central processor, the memory, the BIOS, hard drives, and many other components and how they all work together to move data around and perform useful work.

Part III: Using Your Desktop Computer

This part describes the appearance and locations of all the features and options inside and outside a desktop computer. It also explains how to control power consumption and how to increase the computer's operating speed by overclocking the CPU and the graphics controller.

Part IV: Using Your Laptop Computer

This part tells you how to choose a new laptop, what each of the controls and switches can do for you, and how to use the special keys that often appear in laptop computer keyboards. It also includes information about getting the most life out of your laptop batteries and how to use PC Cards and ExpressCards.

Part V: Improving Your Computer's Performance

This part contains a guide to setting up the computer for faster operation and improving the image on your monitor screen. It includes many tweaks that can make the difference between an adequate system and one that gives you the best possible performance. This part also contains information about adapting a computer for users with special needs.

Part VI: Putting Your Computer to Work

This part explains how to work with Microsoft Windows and how to use printers, scanners, projectors, and digital cameras with your computer. It also describes other operating systems as alternatives to Windows, how to set up automatic scheduling, and how to synchronize your data files between two or more computers.

Part VII: Using Your Computer for Communications

This part explains how to use the computer as a terminal for exchanging information with other people through a local network, a telephone line, and the Internet. It contains instructions for faxing through the computer, connecting to the Internet, and using virtual private networks.

Part VIII: Security and Maintenance

This part explains how to protect your computer against theft and how to install and use firewalls, antivirus and anti-spyware software. It also includes advice about preventive maintenance and a comprehensive guide to troubleshooting.

Part I

Choosing Your Computer

Chapter 1

Desktop or Laptop?

When it's time to think about buying a new computer, the very first question you must ask yourself (and the other people who will use the new computer) is the one in this chapter's title: Should I buy a desktop computer or a laptop?

This chapter should help you make that important decision; it explains how to evaluate the special features of each type and describe their benefits and drawbacks. Later in this book, you can find a lot more detail about using each of those features, but right now it's most important to decide whether the lightweight and compact design of a laptop is important enough to sacrifice the lower cost, flexible construction, and generally larger keyboard and screen in a desktop system.

IN THIS CHAPTER

Understanding the difference between desktop and laptop computers

Evaluating the way you plan to use your computer

Understanding the relative advantages of desktops and laptops

> **NOTE** In this book, the term desktop computer includes computers with both desktop (horizontal) and tower (vertical) cases, even if you normally place the case on the floor rather than a desktop or tabletop.

> **CROSS-REF** You can find more information about different kinds of cases in Chapter 3.

What's the Difference?

Before beginning a discussion on the pros and cons of each type, it might be useful to define certain terms.

A *desktop* computer usually has most of its components in a modular case, with a separate keyboard, video display, mouse, and speakers connected to the case through cables or wireless links. The case for a desktop computer might be either horizontal (with the widest surface sitting on the desk or table) or vertical (with a short face on the table or on the floor). Cases with their feet on the short surface are often called *tower* cases. A few specialty manufacturers offer compact designs that don't meet the industry standards (such as a computer with the processor and related parts built into the video monitor package), but most desktop computers resemble the ones shown in Figure 1.1.

FIGURE 1.1

A desktop computer is bigger and more flexible than a laptop.

A *laptop* computer is a self-contained, lightweight, portable unit that can operate on battery power. The most common laptop design is sometimes described as a *clamshell* because it opens up like a big bivalve, with the keyboard in the bottom half and the screen in the top. Figure 1.2 shows a typical laptop computer.

NOTE   The newest portable computers, known as *tablets*, have touch-sensitive screens that are often attached to the keyboard section with rotating hinges. This allows a user to write on the screen with a special stylus without opening the clamshell. Microsoft has designed support for tablets into the most recent versions of the Windows operating system.

FIGURE 1.2

Most laptop computers use a clamshell design.

How Do You Use Your Computer?

In most cases, the choice between a desktop and a laptop computer depends on the way you expect to use this particular machine. If you're planning to carry the computer with you when you travel for business, or if you want to take the computer on vacation with you to surf the Internet while your family surfs the waves on a beach, the choice is obvious: You need a laptop portable. On the other hand, if you are looking for an office machine that never moves away from your workspace, a desktop computer is the better choice.

To make a decision, think about the way you expect to work with your computer:

- Will you always use it in the same location, or will you carry it from one place to another?

- Do you expect to use your computer away from your own home or office?

- If you're in business, do you expect to use the computer in your clients' or customers' offices or on a job site?

- If you're a student, will you take the computer to class and use the same computer at home or in your dorm room? How about taking notes in the library or laboratory? Will you want to take this computer home during vacations?

- If you plan to use the computer at home, do you want to carry it from one room to another? If it's portable, will your children take it to their bedrooms and bury it under their toys or laundry?

- Are you buying this computer to share among two or more users who don't always work at the same location?

- Do you want to use this computer in places where AC power is not easily accessible?

- Will you have limited space in the location where you expect to use your computer?

- Is security important? Do you want to make sure that nobody else can use the computer when you're not there? Do you want to protect the computer (and the data stored on its drives) from theft and damage?

In general, you need a laptop if you expect to move the computer around. That might mean carrying it from one room to the next, or from one continent to another, or anything in between. If you plan to keep the computer in the same place all the time, a desktop computer is usually the way to go.

It's not always that easy. Sometimes, one type or the other might appear to be more convenient, but one or more specific features could drive your choice in the other direction. The rest of this chapter describes specific characteristics of each type that might contribute to your choice.

Pros and Cons of Desktop Computers

Desktop computers are the natural choice when a computer remains in the same place for all of its working life. The modular design of a desktop system makes it relatively easy to configure it with exactly the right set of features and functions for your specific needs. And if you expect to perform your own work, a computer in a desktop case is much easier to repair and modify than a laptop.

On the other hand, a desktop computer with its separate keyboard, mouse, monitor, and speakers is big, bulky, and awkward to move around.

Desktops cost less

When price is most important, a desktop computer is the better choice because a desktop computer almost always costs less than a laptop with comparable performance. Even after you add the price of a separate monitor, keyboard, and mouse to the basic system, the total is probably lower than a laptop with the same features. If you're looking for the least expensive computer you can buy, or the least expensive computer at a specific level of performance, a desktop system is the clear choice.

Of course, it is possible to spend more for a desktop computer than the price of a good laptop by choosing a super-fast processor and graphics controller, lots of memory, a large flat-panel monitor, and other high-end components and features, but that's not a fair comparison. The price of a desktop system is always far less than a laptop machine with similar specifications.

If you can assemble your own computer from parts, the savings can be even greater. Major computer builders such as Dell and Hewlett-Packard may offer very inexpensive models with limited performance (including slow processors, limited memory and low-capacity hard drives) for less than the cost of assembling a similar machine yourself, but if you want a system with better performance, you can often find higher-quality parts for less than the cost of an off-the-shelf product. Cases, motherboards, disk drives, expansion cards, and other standard parts for desktop computers are easy to find, so building your own system can be a practical alternative for people who have more time and assembly skills than ready cash, and who want something better than an entry-level system. But there are no widespread standards for the size and layout of laptop components, so it's not always practical to look for a generic laptop case, keyboard, video display, and motherboard that you can put together yourself.

CROSS-REF   See Chapter 4 for more details about motherboards, expansion cards, and other important parts of your computer.

Desktops use standard parts

As explained later in this book, the parts inside a desktop computer usually follow one or more design standards, so it's often possible to replace a component that fails with a new one from a different manufacturer. And when you want to add more memory, a larger hard drive, or maybe a second graphics controller and monitor to your system, you can be confident that you won't have to limit yourself to products from a single manufacturer. Just because the label on the case says Compaq or Gateway (or Ye Olde Neighborhood Computer Shoppe), you can still go to a big-box retailer such as Fry's or CompUSA or an online source such as Newegg and choose from among many different brands. This combination of modular design and competition is one reason that the prices of most desktop computer components are lower than the comparable, non-standard parts in a laptop.

In addition, the common parts specifications allow a repair shop to maintain a smaller inventory because they can use the same parts in many different desktop computer makes and models.

Desktops have a flexible design

Desktop computers are modular systems that make it easy to add or replace individual parts to meet each user's particular requirements. A computer intended for an illustrator or a computer-aided designer might have a higher-quality graphics controller and video display than the one in the next office, where a purchasing agent may not use anything more demanding (of computer resources) than a word processor and a spreadsheet. Most computer manufacturers let you order exactly the set of features and specifications that you want.

When your needs change, it's usually easy to open up a desktop case and reconfigure the system, unless your computer uses proprietary parts. You can be confident that the sockets on the motherboard and the mounting holes in the drive bays fit the new expansion card or disk drive, and the main printed circuit board that controls the rest of the system (the motherboard) works with the new parts.

Modular design also means that you can transfer some old parts to your new computer when you replace your Old Faithful machine that has finally become obsolete. For example, I wrote this book on an old Northgate keyboard that I have moved from one computer to the next for more than fifteen years; I like the way its keys respond to my typing. Northgate stopped making these keyboards many years ago (similar keyboards are still available from other makers, but they're very expensive), but the plug on the keyboard's cable still fits the socket on my current computer and it works just fine with a twenty-first century processor and motherboard.

Of course, there are some limits to this flexible design. You can't use a brand-new memory module or the latest disk drives with a 10-year-old motherboard because the designs have changed to accommodate newer and better processors and other devices.

Desktops are easy to upgrade

You can improve the computer's performance by adding new components and replacing existing parts with new ones that have faster speed, greater capacity, or more features. Once again, the desktop computer's modular design makes it easy to work inside the case. Of course, there's a point of diminishing returns where it's better and less costly to buy a new system, but just about every desktop computer has room for economical improvement.

The most common and effective way to improve a computer's performance is to add memory. In both desktop and laptop systems, the motherboard has one or more sockets for memory modules, so you can increase the total amount of memory by adding one or more new modules to the memory that is already in place. You can also remove the existing memory and replace it with the same number of modules with more memory on each module. Adding memory is easier in a desktop system because there's plenty of space inside the case.

Except for a few very small cases, all desktop computers have two or more internal drive bays. Therefore, you can add storage capacity by installing another hard drive to the system simply by mounting the drive in a vacant drive bay and connecting a couple of cables. It's not necessary to transfer the data already stored on the existing drive first.

The CPU chip in a desktop system — the central processing unit that controls everything else — is also relatively easy to remove and replace with a faster CPU with similar architecture, and that fits in the same socket. A new CPU can offer faster processing and better performance than the one that was originally supplied with the computer. Unlike most of the other integrated circuits on the motherboard, the CPU mounts in a special socket that uses a latching mechanism to hold it in place, so it's not necessary (or possible) to solder a new chip directly to the printed circuit board.

All of these upgrades are easy to perform, but they often require some changes to the computer's hardware or software configuration. Before you try an upgrade, consult the computer manual or the motherboard manual for information about jumpers or switch settings on the motherboard, and adjustments to the BIOS settings (the BIOS — basic input/output system — is the set of programs the computer uses to test hardware and load Windows or some other operating system).

CROSS-REF For more in-depth information about the CPU, the BIOS, and other PC components, see Chapter 4.

Desktops are easy to repair

Repairs and modifications to desktop computers are not difficult because there's more space inside the case. As a result, their designers could use larger parts that are easier to find and easier to handle. Cables, connectors, printed circuits, and hard drives are all big enough to find without a magnifying glass, and big enough for people with average-sized hands to work with.

The modular structure of a desktop computer also contributes to its ease of repair. The most common troubleshooting methods include swapping parts to identify a bad component, and moving expansion cards and cables from hard drives to a different socket. This may not be possible on a laptop system with only a limited number of sockets.

Even the screws that hold things together are bigger inside a desktop case than the ones inside a laptop. Bigger screws are often easier to insert and remove, and they're always easier to find when you drop one on the floor (especially on a carpet). And the full-size screwdrivers, pliers, and nutdrivers are far less fiddly and are easier to handle than the smaller versions that are often needed to disassemble a laptop computer.

Desktops take up a lot of space

Desktop computers do have some drawbacks. A desktop case with a separate keyboard occupies more physical space than a more compact laptop computer. For most of us, the space on our desks, worktables, or kitchen counters is prime real estate, so a computer with a smaller footprint is highly desirable. This may be less of an issue today than it used to be, because flat-panel monitors are much less intrusive than the old cathode-ray tube displays that were often 18 inches or more from front to back.

It might be possible to reduce the physical impact of a desktop system through careful design and planning. You could place the main processor case on the floor or on a shelf, and use longer cables to connect it to the monitor, keyboard, mouse, and speakers; but that big box has to go someplace, and sometimes you need to reach the controls on the front panel, so you can't just seal the thing permanently inside a cabinet. There's a whole branch of the furniture industry dedicated to designing and selling tables, cabinets, media centers, and other objects with the intent of placing computers and other electronic equipment on, within, or under them. Even a company such as E.A. Clore, which has been making chairs, tables, and cabinets since 1830, offers a fine "early-American" computer table (see Figure 1.3).

FIGURE 1.3

It's an ugly modern computer, but the table can still fit your décor.

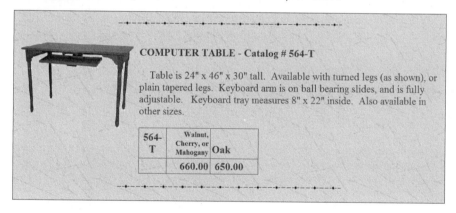

COMPUTER TABLE - Catalog # 564-T

Table is 24" x 46" x 30" tall. Available with turned legs (as shown), or plain tapered legs. Keyboard arm is on ball bearing slides, and is fully adjustable. Keyboard tray measures 8" x 22" inside. Also available in other sizes.

564-T	Walnut, Cherry, or Mahogany	Oak
	660.00	650.00

Desktops are difficult to transport

Desktop computers are big and heavy. If you ever have to move your desktop system with all its accessories and accouterments from one room to another, you probably want to use a cart with several shelves, or at least an office chair with wheels. Then you must find and attach at least half a dozen different cables to the back of the box or convince your local computer expert to do it for you before you can use the computer again. Moving a desktop computer is a complicated and time-consuming exercise.

 If you're planning on moving your desktop computer several times, take care. Moves are sometimes blamed for system crashes.

Sometimes you don't have any choice about moving your computer around. Maybe you're a teacher or a librarian who uses the same machine in different rooms; or possibly you're running a conference that includes PowerPoint presentations in several different places. If that's your situation, and you can't replace the system with a portable, your best bet is to find or build some kind of special computer cart that holds everything in place with all the cables connected. When you arrive at the new location, you can plug the power cord into the wall and hope that all the other cables haven't shaken loose from their sockets. The computer is still big and heavy, but it doesn't have to be quite as inconvenient to move.

Desktops require external power

The electrical circuits, fan motors, and disk drives in your computer use DC power from the power supply inside the case. On the other hand, the power supply, along with your video display and other external accessories, needs a source of domestic AC power (110 volts in North America and Japan, 220 volts in most other places). If there isn't a wall outlet nearby, you need some kind of generator, or a big battery with an inverter, or an extremely long extension cord.

It's possible to replace the usual AC power supply with one that uses a 24-volt or 48-volt DC input, but DC power supplies for desktop computers are expensive and uncommon. A DC supply might be practical in a location that uses solar power, or in a telephone switching center that already has a room full of batteries, but every off-the-shelf desktop system you're likely to find comes with an AC power supply. If you can't provide it with a continuous source of AC power, you're out of luck.

Pros and Cons of Laptop Computers

Laptop computers are compact, lightweight alternatives to full-size desktop machines. Your laptop is a self-contained system that can easily fit into a briefcase or backpack. When you arrive at your destination (or when you want to use the computer along the way), you can open up the clamshell case, turn on the power switch, and start working or playing a game just as soon as Windows completes its startup routine.

A laptop computer might be easy to carry around, but that convenience comes at a price in ease of use and repair, cost, and security. If you expect to move your computer often, a laptop is the obvious choice. But don't spend the extra money for a laptop until you consider the drawbacks of a portable system.

Laptops are portable

The whole point of a laptop computer is easy transport. If you're a frequent traveler, or if you expect to use a single computer at the office or school and at home, a laptop is far more convenient than a desktop system. A laptop weighs less than a desktop machine with similar performance, and it comes in a smaller package.

Because laptop computers can use batteries, you can use them almost anywhere. Combined with a wireless Internet link, you can work on your own computer or connect to the rest of the world without the need to find a source of AC power for a few hours.

Laptops have built-in keyboards and monitors

A laptop computer is a self-contained package. In addition to the central processor, memory, and data storage that are common inside a desktop case, a laptop computer also includes a keyboard, a video display, and a substitute for a mouse in the same convenient package. Therefore, you don't have to buy those devices separately, and you don't have to connect them to the case before you can start using your computer.

Laptops have design limitations

If laptop computers were better than desktop machines in every way, nobody would bother with a desktop system. However, the same small size and reduced weight that makes a laptop easy to move around often makes it more difficult to use.

Smaller screen

The screens on most laptop computers are no more than 15 inches from corner to corner, often as little as 12 or 13 inches. This compares to the most common desktop monitors, whose screens measure anywhere from 17 to 21 inches or more. When a desktop monitor and a laptop screen are set to the same resolution, the images on the laptop are always smaller. And the same text on the smaller laptop screen is almost always more difficult to read. A few laptops with larger screens — some more than 20 inches — are available, but they're extremely expensive, and a screen that big makes the whole computer less compact and portable.

Small keyboard

The size of a laptop computer's keyboard is limited by the width of its case. Except for a unique unfolding butterfly keyboard that IBM tried and abandoned in the mid-1990s, a laptop keyboard cannot be any wider than the lower half of the clamshell. Even though laptop keyboards don't include all of those extra keys that appear to the right of the traditional typewriter keys on a desk-top keyboard, the individual keys on a laptop are often smaller and closer together than those on a separate keyboard.

If you're a touch-typist who is used to a traditional keyboard, this can have a huge impact on your speed and accuracy. All those typing exercises in high school and all those years of text and data entry have conditioned your fingers to expect to find each letter in the same place on any key-board. You don't have to think about finding a letter; your brain automatically takes your fingers to that key. But when the keys' locations are slightly different, you either hit the wrong key more often, or you type more slowly in order to direct each keystroke to the right location.

Limited disk size

The standard hard drive in a desktop computer has one or more 3.5-inch platters inside the drive enclosure. A laptop has space for only a single 2.5-inch drive. Because the laptop's disks are smaller, they can't hold as much data. If you expect to use your computer to record audio or video or to store other very large files, this difference in capacity means that you must either connect a second, external drive to the laptop through a USB or FireWire port, or transfer the files to another computer for permanent storage.

Laptops are easy to steal

In an airport, a railway station, or a library, an unattended laptop computer can easily disappear within minutes. For all the same reasons that make laptop computers convenient to carry, they are also extremely attractive targets for theft. They're easy to grab and hide, and easy to sell to an unscrupulous bargain hunter.

Worse, the information stored on a laptop's hard drive can be even more valuable than the machine itself. Business records, thesis notes, and other information stored in data files can be difficult or impossible to reconstruct. And you've probably seen news reports about banks, credit bureaus, and government agencies losing confidential information when their laptops were stolen.

CAUTION Of course, you can and must take precautions to protect your laptop. If you travel with a laptop, you must never let it out of your sight. If you use it in a public location, use a cable lock to secure it to a table. If you leave it in a car, be sure to put it in the trunk where nobody can see it.

CROSS-REF Chapter 48 of this book offers many more ideas about keeping your computer secure.

Laptops are more expensive

When you buy a laptop computer, you pay something extra for the added convenience of a light-weight portable system. The price of a laptop computer is always higher than a desktop system with similar performance. That added cost is a combination of more expensive design (you can't just assemble a new model out of common components), non-standard parts, and an expensive battery in every computer. A laptop also has to be more durable than a desktop system.

Even though you can recharge it when you run the computer on external power, your computer's battery won't last forever. The life of a laptop battery depends on the way you use the computer, but you probably need a new one at least every couple of years.

Repairs are another potential expense. As the next section explains, a laptop computer is more likely to need service than a desktop machine, so that's one more item to add to the total cost of ownership. The alternative is an extended warranty, which is really a bet with the manufacturer that the computer will need service during the life of the warranty. If the computer breaks, you win the bet. If it works perfectly, you lose.

Don't forget to add the cost of essential accessories when you're estimating the cost of your new computer. At a bare minimum, you need some kind of carrier bag or a backpack for your laptop, and maybe some additional memory, and a cable lock or other security device.

CROSS-REF Chapter 25 describes many other accessories you might also want to use with your laptop.

TIP If you're considering a laptop because you want to carry it between home and work, but you don't care about portable operation, there's another possible option: Think about two inexpensive desktop systems and an external hard drive, instead of a single laptop. The total cost of the two desktops could easily be less than a single quality portable.

Laptops need repairs more often

It's easy to understand why a laptop computer is more likely to need repairs than a desktop machine if you consider the way people treat them. The owner of a laptop grabs it off the desk, drops it into a bag or a briefcase, and throws it over a shoulder or onto a baggage cart. Then it gets shaken around for a couple of hours, until the owner stops into a coffee shop and fires up the computer to check for e-mail. Oops! Was that hot coffee and warm milk you spilled into the keyboard? Oh well, use some napkins to soak it up and put it back in the bag.

On the other hand, a desktop computer in an office or at home is set up and assembled just once, and it sits in the same place for months or years at a time. Maybe a heavy-handed typist might wear out a keyboard, or a hard drive might crash, but most of the time the box just sits there without any serious abuse. If a keyboard or a mouse, or even an internal component fails, it's just a matter of unplugging the old one and installing a replacement.

Even if you handle your laptop computer carefully, it may still be exposed to more hazards than a desktop system: laptops run hotter, they are turned on and off more often, and they're subjected to more physical abuse.

Of course, a laptop machine is designed to absorb a lot more abuse than a desktop, but eventually, all that bumping and all those spills can take a toll. Some manufacturers and certain models have excellent track records for survival, while others are almost notorious for breaking down, so it's important to do some homework before you decide which one to buy. It's worth spending more for a reliable machine.

Laptops use proprietary parts

If a manufacturer controls the market for replacement parts, they can charge whatever they want. If you need that part, they have you over the proverbial barrel. A few laptop parts such as memory modules and hard drives are common among more than one manufacturer, but case parts, motherboards, mounting hardware, keyboards, and screens are all unique in just about every make and model.

Spare parts are often expensive, but if you stick to well-known brands, they should be easy to find. In order to identify the exact part your computer needs, you must consult a service manual, where you probably have to consult an exploded parts diagram. Your local computer parts emporium probably doesn't keep parts for every popular laptop type in stock, so you have to order the thing directly from the factory.

If you keep using the machine long after the manufacturer stops supporting it, you eventually have to venture into the world of used and surplus parts to keep it alive. There's probably somebody out there in an industrial park someplace who has a warehouse full of parts for your beloved machine. All you have to do is find the person (the Internet is your friend; search for the part number and you can probably find what you need). If you're very lucky, he or she won't insist on a minimum order of $150 when you only need a $3.75 circuit board.

Laptops are difficult to repair or modify

It sometimes seems as if the design of laptop computers is based on the Trash Compactor method. That's the one where you lay out all the parts on a big table and then squeeze everything down until it all fits into the case. The parts inside a laptop clamshell are tightly stacked and combined in order to fit all the same features and functions that are available inside a much larger desktop case.

This makes it a lot more difficult to work inside a laptop case. The parts are smaller and closer together, and they are often held together with teeny tiny screws and connectors that are easy to lose. It's often difficult to locate a disconnected cable or a loose screw because there's another component in the way. Without a detailed set of instructions from a service manual or a manufacturer's Web site, you might not even get the cover open without damaging something.

This also means that things that might have been on separate pieces in a desktop, such as the graphics controller and the sound card, are all integrated into the motherboard, so you can't upgrade or repair your laptop by simply swapping out an plug-in circuit board. Instead, you must either accept the original specifications or get yourself a new computer.

Of course, this might not be an issue if you don't expect to repair or modify your own computer. The major laptop manufacturers all encourage their users to send their computers back to a factory service center for repairs. Factory service can be expensive, but when the repaired computer comes back to you, the service center usually guarantees its work.

Choosing the Best of Both

There's a third alternative that might be worth your attention when you're trying to decide what kind of computer to buy. If you expect to use the computer in a single location most of the time, but you want the convenience of a portable when you take your twice-a-year business trips and on those rare evenings and weekends when you must take work home with you, consider using a laptop with a separate monitor, mouse, and keyboard. In the office, you have the functional benefits of a full-size keyboard and screen, but when it's necessary, you can pull a few plugs out of their sockets and take the computer with you.

Some manufacturers call this category a desktop replacement because the laptop takes the place of a conventional desktop processor case. Many laptops even include a special docking-station connector that takes the place of all those separate cables and sockets.

CROSS-REF Look for information about using a docking station, port replicator, or separate external devices in Chapter 22.

Summary

Desktop and laptop computers can provide similar performance in very different packages. When you're thinking about a new computer, it's essential to decide which type meets your specific requirements.

The most important advantages of desktop computers are related to economy and the size of the components inside and outside the case. Bigger keyboards and screens make it easier to use your computer, while the modular construction and extra space inside the box allow you (or your service technician) to repair or modify the computer more easily. On the other hand, those big cases and external devices are all heavy and bulky, so they're more difficult to move around.

Laptop computers are compact and easy to transport, but that also makes them harder to use and to service; the keyboard and screen built into a laptop are smaller than the separate units connected to a desktop computer, and less flexible when it's time to upgrade to a faster and better system.

Chapter 2

Evaluating the Warranty and Support

When you buy a new computer, you're also buying a relationship with the manufacturer, importer, or assembler of that computer. So the computer maker's ability to provide good, bad, or indifferent service and support should be an important part of your choice.

Just about everybody who owns a computer needs some kind of technical assistance at one point or another over the life of the machine. Therefore, the warranty and the support services supplied with a new computer are often just as important as the processor and the keyboard. It's entirely possible that the quality of service and support is the biggest difference between a brand-name computer and a comparable unit from a screwdriver shop.

In this chapter, you can learn how to read and evaluate a product warranty before you buy your computer, and how to deal with the world of customer support to help keep your computer working properly and to obtain answers to your questions.

IN THIS CHAPTER

Checking the terms and conditions of your computer's warranty

Evaluating service contracts

Getting the most out of formal and informal technical support

Obtaining repairs and upgrades for your computer

Read the Warranty

In the United States, the European Union, and most other countries, the manufacturers or importers of consumer products are required to provide a warranty that a product does what it is supposed to do, that it meets its published specifications, and that none of the parts are damaged or defective. If there's a problem during the life of the warranty the business that sold you the computer should promise to fix it at their expense.

That's easy enough if you're buying something simple, like a screwdriver. If it breaks, you take it back to the store, and the salesperson gives you a new one. But computers are a lot more complicated because they're assembled from a lot of individual parts. When something inside your computer fails, you can expect a repair or a replacement for that component. But you probably can't get a whole new computer. In most cases, the best you can expect is a new part.

It's important to understand what the manufacturer or dealer means when they tell you that the computer you're about to buy has a full warranty. Does that include parts and labor? Who performs the repairs? Does a service technician come to you, or must you take the computer to them?

Duration

A new computer should be covered under warranty for at least a year. The warranty is intended to protect you against defective parts and premature failures, but you should not expect it to cover normal wear and tear. So for example, if the letters printed on the keyboard's keys begin to wear off after a few months, you should have a legitimate warranty claim, but if the same problem shows up after five or six years, that probably counts as normal wear.

CROSS-REF   Fortunately, most electronic circuits that fail are likely to do so soon after they are placed into service, so a year is usually enough time to find and report problems. Chapter 27 contains detailed instructions for testing your new computer while it's still covered by the warranty.

Some of the parts inside your computer carry their own warranties, supported by the manufacturers of those parts. For example, many hard drives come with a five-year warranty, and most brand-name memory modules carry lifetime warranties. If a component has a longer manufacturer's warranty, the computer builder should extend that longer warranty to the purchaser.

Coverage

When you shop for a computer, don't believe a salesperson's verbal promises about the warranty without seeing something in writing or on a Web page. Before you make the purchase, be sure to read the printed warranty packed with the computer. If the warranty is posted on the seller's Web site, print a copy and keep it with the packing slip and other documents related to the computer.

Be sure you understand what the warranty covers. Some warranties include both parts and service for the first year, but only parts for an additional year or two.

The terms of your warranty also specify the type of service you can expect. Some include on-site service in your home or office, but others require you to carry the computer into a local service center or pack up the computer and ship it back to a distant factory or service depot.

Sometimes a company offers a warranty with better service or longer duration as an extra-cost option. For example, the basic warranty might include free access to telephone support, but if it's necessary to replace a part, the service center sends you the new part and expects you to perform the swap yourself, or you might have to send the computer back to a service depot. If you (or your IT staff) are comfortable working inside a computer, that might be all you need. The alternative could be a more expensive warranty that includes on-site repairs by a service technician in your office or home.

Look for exceptions or other terms and conditions that can limit the warranty's coverage. For example, if the warranty doesn't cover damage due to misuse or abuse, you might be out of luck if you drop your laptop, or when you spill a cup of coffee into the keyboard. And don't accept a warranty that doesn't allow you to open the case; if you ever upgrade a video card, add more memory, or even reattach a loose connector, the manufacturer might refuse to honor the warranty.

Service Contracts

A service contract or an extended warranty is a gamble between a consumer and a manufacturer or a third-party service provider. In effect, you're betting that your computer needs expensive service during the life of the contract. If your computer continues to work perfectly, you lose the bet.

Most home and office computers are pretty reliable. If they do require expensive service or repairs, it's probably within the first year, while the original warranty is in force (most product defects show up within the first couple of months). Remember, a computer is not like an office copier or a home furnace that needs periodic maintenance in order to continue working properly. And if you are reading a book like this one, you can probably do many computer repairs yourself, without the need for an expensive service call. Therefore, conventional wisdom tells us that most computer service contracts are a bad investment.

However, there are some cases where a service contract makes a lot of sense. For many users, a service contract is an investment in peace of mind. If you plan to use the computer in an environment where it is subjected to hard use such as a shop floor or a classroom, you can expect it to need frequent service. But if your business or school has its own computer support people, you may not need an outside service contract.

A service contract on a laptop computer is often a good investment for several reasons. Laptops often have more problems than desktop systems because most users handle them more roughly — opening and closing the cover, bumping them around when the computer gets moved from one place to another, and so on. And it's a lot more difficult for a typical user to repair a laptop without special tools and an inventory of parts.

Look for the same range of terms and conditions on a service contract that you found on the initial warranty. A low-cost contract might only include mail-in repairs and a limited number of telephone calls to the support center, while a more expensive contract could include on-site service and unlimited telephone support.

Tech Support

Technical support is closely related to warranty coverage, but they're not exactly the same. The warranty protects you against defective equipment, but tech support also includes help and advice about installing and using your computer's hardware and software. Even if the computer never requires any repairs, you still want access to a reliable source of support.

Finding decent support is an important part of deciding where to buy your computer. Bad technical support can often be worse than none at all.

It might be difficult to evaluate the quality of a computer supplier's technical support before you buy, but it's worth the effort. Ask friends and colleagues about their experiences and use the Internet to find other owners' reports.

Does your personal support team know this machine?

For most users, the first line of technical support is not the official support center provided by a computer company; it's that informal network of friends, relatives, and co-workers who know about computers and who answer questions and offer advice. It might be the Help Desk or IT department that provides support for your business. Don't forget about those people when you're choosing a new computer. Although it's true that most computers have similar designs, your personal technology advisor's experience with a particular combination of hardware and software makes it easier for him or her to help when you have a simple question or a more serious problem.

In a business or other organization that uses a lot of computers, the in-house support group probably keeps a small inventory of spare parts for quick repairs. If you depend on a friend or a relative for that kind of support, he or she probably has a junk box full of odd parts that can keep you going when something goes wrong. Either way, it's often a good idea to adopt one or two makes and models as a standard system. When a part fails, it's often convenient to install an existing spare and restore the computer to service without the need to send the bad one back to the service center and wait for the replacement to arrive.

When you're looking for a laptop computer, it's even more important to talk with your resident computer guru before you make a selection. Each make of laptop uses somewhat different keyboard layouts, special features, and controls, and each comes with a different set of bundled software. Somebody whose experience is limited to Hewlett-Packard or Dell laptops might not be able to offer as much help after you buy an Acer or a Sony.

And don't overlook the value of appealing to your friendly expert's ego by asking for advice before you get into trouble, rather than after you're knee-deep in digital quicksand. When your advisors encourage you to buy a particular computer make and model, they might feel an obligation to justify that recommendation by continuing to help keep the computer working properly.

Telephone support

When your local support system can't help you, it's time to move on to the official technical support centers provided by the builder of your computer and the companies that supplied individual parts and software. Some support centers accept questions by telephone, but others insist that you send your questions through e-mail.

A good telephone support center answers most incoming calls within a minute or less and connects callers to helpful agents and technicians who have been trained to recognize common problems and to use a knowledge base and other resources to find answers to more obscure questions. If you have consistently good experiences with a company's technical support services, you should seriously consider rewarding them with your repeat business.

On the other hand, a bad support center can be a nightmare for callers and a hellhole for the people working there. Fortunately, stories about such places circulate quickly through the Internet and in magazines. To find them, run a Web search for the name of the company with the words "review" and "support." If you discover that a company has a reputation for terrible technical support, don't buy its products.

NOTE If your computer comes with an OEM (original equipment manufacturer) version of Windows, you have to call the computer maker for Windows support. Microsoft won't take your calls. This is not as bad as it sounds, because the tech support of brand-name-computer makers should have the same kind of training and access to the same information resources as the people you reach when you call Microsoft directly.

Evaluating the quality of a computer company's support operation is a subjective process that can be extremely difficult before you have a problem. In many cases, the best you can do is talk to friends, colleagues, and other experts and look on the Internet for a pattern of praise or horror stories about a particular company (but don't become overly concerned about one or two complaints among dozens of positive reports. Everybody's entitled to a bad day). If this is not the first time you have purchased a computer, remember your previous support experiences; if a company has been especially helpful, you should encourage them with more business.

Free or paid?

Your new computer's warranty should include free access to technical support for at least the first year. After that, some companies continue to offer free support, and others charge a per-incident or per-minute fee. Although it would seem that every manufacturer really ought to provide unlimited free service for the life of their products, it does cost money to keep a support center going, and it's reasonable to pass that cost to the people who choose to call for help rather than reading the manual or searching the company's Web site. Because the alternative is to increase the cost of the product to all users, there is some logic to this approach.

TIP Many companies that charge for service calls after the warranty period is over waive the cost if you're calling about a problem that is their fault (such as a bug in a software upgrade). If you think you're being unfairly charged, it never hurts to ask for free service.

After the warranty has expired, you don't have to go to the computer builder's support center for help. If you're willing to pay, many independent service and support businesses are happy to answer your questions. If necessary, they might either send a service person to your home or office or accept walk-in customers at their local service center. Sometimes, these are the very same businesses that the computer makers use to provide on-site warranty service.

If your business has an assortment of computer equipment made by several different companies, an independent service center might be the best way to maintain your entire fleet. You don't have to worry about knowing which company to call for each system because the same people can fix any of them. You might save some money with a single service contract that covers all of them, because the repair folks can often combine calls for service on different brands into a single trip.

Can you get through easily?

One sign of a less-than-great technical support center is an inadequate number of telephone lines and staff to answer the calls. Most of the time, you should expect to reach a live support person within a minute or two. A support center that consistently forces callers to wait 15 minutes or more on hold (with or without a reassuring "your call is important to us . . ." message) does not deserve your business.

There are some exceptions. Certain days and times are busier than others at a support center, so you might have to wait longer on a Monday morning than a mid-week afternoon. But if it seems as though you can never get through to somebody without a long wait, the company you're trying to call has a serious problem.

Are the support people helpful?

Look for a computer company that stands behind their product with helpful support people. Excellent support and service is worth the extra cost it might add to the price of a new computer.

Working in customer support can be a rewarding and satisfying job if you enjoy helping people solve problems. Good technicians in a support center run by a company that believes in real customer service spend as much time as it takes to answer a question or solve a problem. They might even call or e-mail a day or two later to make sure the problem didn't reappear.

But many companies look upon their support operations purely as an unfortunate expense and an opportunity to reduce overhead instead of an opportunity to build good relationships with their customers. It's a lot faster to tell a caller to reformat a hard drive and reinstall Windows, instead of searching the Windows Knowledge Base (Microsoft's set of articles about known problems) to identify the real source of a problem and explain how to edit the Registry or install a new device driver to fix it. If they can convince the caller to order a $150 replacement for a motherboard or some other expensive part (with a big built-in profit) instead of searching for a loose connector, that's even better.

Working in one of those places is no fun at all. These are the support centers that tell their agents to work from a one-answer-fits-all-problems script, regardless of what the caller really needs. It's not fair to blame the people who give you bad support because they're also victims of their employers' poor attitude. But if possible, you should find a way to avoid dealing with those companies.

Online resources

Most computer companies and their suppliers offer information on Web sites and accept questions by e-mail as alternatives to live telephone support. By offering answers to frequently asked questions and public forums where you can read about other users' problems, companies can often supply useful information without the need to devote as much staff time and other resources to accepting telephone calls.

It's worth the time to explore a computer maker's online support services before you decide to buy anything from them. It's a very good sign if it appears that they are committed to providing as much information as possible in clear and easy-to-understand form. If there's an enthusiastic community of individual users who contribute to the support forums or news groups, you have probably found a company that takes good care of its customers.

But don't limit yourself to the official company Web sites. Many other Web sites are maintained by independent groups and self-appointed experts. On these sites, users share hints and tips without the filter that a company site might apply when irate customers turn against them. A Web search for a particular make and model number can often find pointers to both official and independent sources of helpful information.

Support by e-mail

Many companies prefer to receive questions from users via e-mail rather than by telephone. From the support center's point of view, e-mail is a much more efficient way to provide support because it allows them to let messages stack up without a customer tying up a telephone line. And a support technician can send the user a prepared answer without the need to talk them through a complicated procedure; while the user is trying the suggested fix, the tech can respond to several other questions from other people. Because a support center can handle several e-mail questions at the same time, many companies offer free support by e-mail, even if they charge for telephone calls.

A cost-effective e-mail support center may make sense for a computer maker, but it's not always in their customers' best interest. Some companies treat their e-mail support addresses as some kind of electronic black hole, where requests for help often disappear without a trace. Others can take several days to send a reply. Still others might reply quickly, but their answers don't contain any useful information. "This information is covered in your User's Manual" or "This is a known problem. We will fix it in a future release" is not what you want to hear from a support technician.

Beware of finger-pointing

Finger-pointing is another common method that computer support centers can use to avoid solving a user's problem. Whenever a customer calls with a new and difficult-to-fix problem, the support person tells you that it's not the support center's fault. If you're talking to a hardware company, they might blame it on the software. If they're a software developer, it must be a hardware problem. Or they might tell you that using the computer with a plug-in card they haven't approved cancels the warranty. Sometimes this is legitimate, but more often it's just a way to get you to go away and take your problem with you.

Computers are complex assemblies of hardware and software produced by several different suppliers. Your computer might have been assembled by Dell or Gateway, but it contains a motherboard made by a company based in Taiwan, with a video card from Malaysia, and a Korean monitor. The Windows operating system came from Microsoft in the suburbs of Seattle, and other software was produced by three different companies in California and by some shareware places you found on the Internet. When something goes wrong, it's not always easy to know exactly which component caused the problem, but you have to start someplace. The computer is still under warranty, so you call the computer maker's support center. Eventually, you reach an expert at fixing your particular make and model of computer. But they don't recognize the problem you describe, and there's nothing in this month's list of known problems. So they blame it on somebody else.

Don't let them get away with this. While it's true that every support center receives calls requesting help for somebody else's product, you shouldn't feel like the technician is just trying to get rid of you. Computers are supposed to work with a wide variety of hardware and software. If you have found a product that is not compatible with your computer (which is possible), a good support center wants to know about it. That way, they can either work with the other company involved to find a way to fix the problem or warn other users away from the offending program or gadget.

Once again, if you discover that a company has a reputation for frequent finger-pointing, you want to look elsewhere for your new computer.

Repairs and Upgrades

If you buy a computer through a Web site, by mail, or from a discount store, an office supply place, or some other national retail chain, remember to ask about repairs.

Obviously, it's a lot more convenient to have somebody come to you to perform repairs, but that kind of service is almost always an extra-cost option. Other options include taking the computer to a local carry-in service or sending it back to a factory repair center in another city. There are a few disadvantages to shipping out your computer. First, if you didn't save the original packing materials, you either have to order (and pay for) an empty shipping box, or run the risk of having the computer damaged inside an improvised container. Second, most companies expect you to pay for shipping, so repairs from a distant center are usually more expensive than local work. Finally, you can expect to be without your computer for a longer period of time because it may take several extra days for delivery.

Can you do your own repairs?

Fortunately, there are very few computer problems that make it necessary to return the whole system to a repair center. In most cases, the computer maker's technical support center can diagnose a problem by telephone or e-mail and send you one or more individual replacement parts. If you (or a member of your family or staff) can open the case, remove the old part and install the new one, you can often perform the repair yourself without the need to take the computer to a repair shop or call an on-site service technician.

Of course, you may want to let the authorized service people handle any repairs that may become necessary during the warranty period. But after the warranty has expired, you can save both time and money by handling routine service and upgrades on your own. If you do expect to do your own work, the type of service offered by the people who sold your computer to you may be less important than the quality of the information you can obtain from their support center.

CAUTION Don't think about repairing individual circuit boards; it isn't worth the time or effort to troubleshoot parts down to the component level. Most manufacturers simply replace bad motherboards and other printed circuits with new ones. You should do the same.

Also, don't try to repair your own video monitor, especially if it has a CRT display. The capacitors inside a video display can hold a lethal electrical charge, even if the unit is disconnected from AC power.

Remember, laptop computers offer a completely different set of problems. Just because you have successfully done work on one type of laptop is no assurance to expect the same kind of luck with a different make or model. You probably need specific instructions, just to get to the part you want to replace. Because most laptops use a combination of standard components (hard drives and memory modules) and proprietary parts (just about everything else), it may not be possible to do any repairs unless you obtain parts from the manufacturer.

CROSS-REF More particulars about the designs of laptop computers are discussed in Chapter 1 and in more detail in Part IV.

Finding a service manual

A service manual or some other source of detailed instructions is essential for many repairs. Without some kind of specific instructions for opening the case and removing various interior parts, you can sometimes spend more time trying to get the computer open than it takes to actually perform the repairs. This is common for most makes of laptop computers, but it can also be a problem for some desktop systems that don't use generic cases.

Fortunately, most of the major computer makers offer free service manuals on their Web sites. Many of the smaller computer builders use cases, motherboards, and other parts that come from third-party manufacturers who also offer free service manuals or other online documentation. For example, Figure 2.1 shows a Dell Web page that explains how to open one of their desktop cases.

If a service manual was not supplied with your computer, follow these steps to find one online:

1. Go to the computer manufacturer's Web site.

2. Look for a link to Support or Downloads and jump to that page.

3. Find the link to the specific model name or number of your computer.

4. At the page devoted to your computer, look for a link to a Service Manual.

The specific route from the home page to the Service Manual is different for every computer maker, but most lead you to a service document of some kind. If you can't find a service manual online, call or e-mail the company that built the computer and ask for the specific instructions you need.

If you can identify the original maker of your computer's motherboard, hard drive, or other modular part inside the computer, you can probably find a manual or other service information from that company's Web site. The name of the original equipment manufacturer (the OEM) usually appears on a label or printed directly on a printed circuit board.

FIGURE 2.1

Dell's online service manuals provide detailed information for opening their cases.

> **NOTICE:** Ensure that sufficient space exists to support the open cover—at least 30 cm (1 ft) of desk top space.

4. Lay the computer on its side so that the arrow on the bottom of the computer points up.

5. Open the cover:

   a. Facing the back of the computer, press the release button on the right side of the computer with one hand while pulling up on the top of the cover with the other hand.

   b. Press the release button on the left side of the computer with one hand while pulling up on the top of the cover with the other hand.

   c. Hold the bottom of the computer with one hand, and then pull open the cover with the other hand.

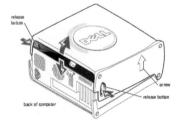

Are parts available?

Most desktop computers are assembled from common modular parts, so it's generally quite easy to find replacement parts for repairs and upgrades. When you need a replacement, you don't have to find an exact match for the original. As long as it has the right type of connector to fit a socket in the motherboard, it doesn't matter if the new part is the same make and model. For example, if you need a new video controller card, you can go to a computer store or an online retailer and choose any card with the same kind of connection to the motherboard that offers the performance specifications you want, even if it's a different brand from the original. When you're ready to upgrade the computer with an additional memory module or hard drive, you can choose the one that offers the best combination of price and performance, regardless of who made it.

But some computer parts, especially in laptop systems, are unique to a specific model. The only source for these parts is the original manufacturer. This should not be a problem if you need warranty service, but after a few years, some essential parts might no longer be available. By the time you have handed down the computer to the second or third child in the family, or relegated it to duty as a backup for low-priority use in your business, it could be extremely difficult to find a replacement for a worn-out switch or a damaged display screen.

Summary

The quality of a computer's repair and support services is not as easy to evaluate as the speed of the processor or the size of the hard drive, but it can be just as important. Any computer supplier that does not provide good support does not deserve to remain in business.

To find a computer with good support, read the warranty and any other service literature that comes with the computer, look for an extensive support area on the maker's Web site, and search for online comments about other users' experience with that company.

Chapter 3

Buying a Computer

Whether you ultimately decide to buy a desktop computer or a laptop (see Chapter 1 for help making that choice), your strategy for selecting exactly the right machine to fit your particular needs is the same: Look for the best combination of features, quality, performance, support, and price. This chapter tells you how to identify the features and options that your computer should include and how to evaluate the less tangible characteristics that make the difference between a cheap computer and a true bargain.

Cost

As in most retail, computer vendors do charge what the market can take. New features tend to cost more upon their first introduction to the public and decrease in price as the novelty wears off; fancy yet useless designs can also rack up the price a bit. But the largest part of a computer's cost is directly related to its performance and the quality of its components. Because the retail computer business is extremely competitive, computers with similar performance and features almost always have similar prices. A cheaper computer contains slower, cheaper parts. When you buy a new computer, you usually get what you pay for.

Unless you can find a special sale or rebate, it's probably not productive to choose a computer based exclusively on price. It's better to identify the features and options that make a difference to the way you use the machine. Let the performance and features drive your choice.

If one computer costs more than another, it probably has one or more of these features:

- The CPU has better or faster performance.
- The computer has more RAM.
- The hard drive is bigger.
- The graphics controller has more memory.
- The computer comes with a more expensive version of Windows.
- The optical drive plays and records DVDs.
- The computer comes with a more expensive monitor, mouse, keyboard, or speakers.
- The warranty is longer or it includes on-site service calls.
- The computer comes with one or more software utilities and applications.
- The manufacturer offers more or better technical support.

Quality

Quality in a computer is partially reflected in more durable, more reliable parts. Although it's possible to assemble a computer from premium-quality components, most manufacturers and screwdriver shops use less expensive parts that are still entirely adequate for most users. Most of the components inside your computer can last long after advances to the technology make them obsolete.

The Internet is full of detailed reviews and anecdotal reports about every imaginable piece of computer gear, from fully assembled systems to individual cases, motherboards, and plug-in cards. If a particular item has a history of failure or terrible factory support, you can be sure that a bunch of unhappy people have described their experiences online. A Web search on the make and model name or number plus the word "review" can probably direct you to sites that offer praise or warnings about the piece of equipment you're considering. Don't pay much attention to the glowing reports in the manufacturer's own site or those of their dealers, but look for independent reports, especially the ones in user forums and blogs. Don't worry as much about one or two negative stories among a lot more positives — even the best products get those. If you find a ten-page technical review, look for the subjective evaluations on the first and last pages.

There are a few places where a computer maker can cut corners. In a desktop system, the most common cheap parts are cases, power supplies, and memory modules. In laptops, the usual suspects are memory, video displays, and the fit and finish of the case itself.

A cheap desktop case might be constructed of thinner sheet metal inside and out with a less-than-perfect paint job. When you're shopping for a new desktop system, look for a solid case with close fittings between the top and the chassis. If you find rough edges inside the case, if the sheet metal seems a lot lighter than on other computers, or if the case or cover wobbles or flexes, find a different computer.

Shoddy power supplies are not common, but if its enclosure does not provide adequate shielding, a badly designed power supply can generate spurious radio frequency (RF) signals that can interfere with nearby radios, televisions, and even computer monitors. If your radio starts to hum or whistle when you turn on your new computer, or if you see a wiggling line moving up or down your TV or monitor's screen, and it stops when you turn off the computer, the computer's power supply is to blame. It may not be possible to identify this before you buy, but, assuming the computer is still under warranty, you should return it and insist on a replacement power supply from a different supplier.

> **NOTE** RF interference is regulated by the Federal Communications Commission (the FCC) in the United States, and by similar agencies in other countries, so you are within your rights to expect your computer to be properly shielded. It's the computer maker's responsibility to provide a power supply that doesn't create interference with other equipment.

Memory modules are small, printed circuit boards that hold several RAM integrated circuits. A brand-name module and a less expensive generic product might use memory chips from the same supplier, but the brand-name module maker pays more for chips that have been carefully examined and tested. Most brand-name modules are sold with a lifetime warranty. Cheaper memory chips might be just as good, but if they do fail after they have been in use for a year or two, you have to pay for the replacement module yourself. If you can't open up the computer and look for a brand-name label on the memory module, ask the sales person about the modules in the computer you are considering, or consult the maker's Web site for information about their warranty.

Flat-panel video displays in laptop computers and in stand-alone monitors can suffer from *dead pixels* that are always dark, or that always display the same solid color regardless of the image color on the screen. A very small number of bad pixels, especially at the outer edges of the display, might be acceptable, but if you discover more than about half a dozen of them, or if they're all in the same part of the screen, return the monitor or laptop and ask for a replacement.

> **TIP** Before you buy, ask what kind of dead pixel policy the seller can offer. Get it in writing.

Finally, the clamshell case of a laptop should feel solid, and the top and bottom should come together without any obvious gap. If the hinge that holds the two parts together seems loose when the computer is new, you can expect it to get worse after you've used the laptop for several months or years.

Another cost-cutting technique is to look out for computers assembled from obsolete or discontinued components. There's nothing wrong with buying a computer with last year's parts inside, as long as you know what you're getting and the price is right. If you can identify the motherboard and expansion cards, you can use the Internet to either confirm that they're current products or that the dealer isn't misrepresenting them. If the dealer seems defensive, or they won't tell you the makes and models of the components inside the box, don't buy it.

> **TIP** If you suspect that a computer contains obsolete parts, run a Web search on the names of the companies that made the motherboard and the graphics controller to find their Web sites. These sites almost always include a Products page that lists their current models.

If there's no obvious manufacturer's name on it, use the FCC's Equipment ID Search Page (`www.fcc.gov/oet/fccid`) to trace the ID code printed on the product.

Brand name or white box?

A handful of major computer makers such as Dell, Hewlett-Packard, and Lenovo (formerly IBM) add value to their products with custom software and special design features, but they and the vast majority of other desktop-computer makers use parts and components from the same suppliers. Many smaller companies assemble computers entirely from generic parts that are often equal in quality to the ones used by the big brand-name companies. Their products are often known as *white-box* computers because the packaging that surrounds the assembled computer does not always identify the company that put it together.

White-box computers (which are really beige or black more often than not) are assembled from standard cases, motherboards, and other parts by wholesalers and retailers as their house brands, and by Internet and mail-order dealers. They often carry an adhesive label with the assembler's name in an inch-square indentation on the front of the case and maybe a serial number on the back panel, but those are usually the only things that aren't completely generic. Assuming the computer has been assembled from high-quality parts, a white-box system is likely to be at least as reliable and perform as well as or better than one from a major manufacturer.

Laptop computers are a different story. Because it's not practical to assemble a laptop from generic parts, a house-brand laptop is really a preassembled unit from a manufacturer who allows the retailer to place their own name on the case. The dealer might plug a hard drive and an internal wireless network interface into some empty sockets, but that's about it. If you can identify the manufacturer's name and model number (look on the shipping box and on the printed material that comes with the computer), and if the collective wisdom of the Internet does not offer any tales of disaster about that model, a white-box laptop might be a bargain worth buying. But without more information, a brand-name laptop is a safer bet.

The biggest differences between a generic computer and a computer from one of the big international brands are the additional software supplied with the system and the quality of before-and-after-purchase support. The big manufacturers often include their own proprietary utilities for things like disaster recovery and online technical support preloaded onto the computer's hard drive, along with a customized version of Microsoft Windows that displays the manufacturer's name instead of a generic Windows logo every time you turn on the computer. Some of these programs are actually useful, but others just take up space. It's up to you to decide whether they're worth enough to justify a higher price.

CROSS-REF Some computer makers take their commitment to customer support far more seriously than others. Read Chapter 2 for advice about evaluating support services.

If you have been reading this section in order to find a definite answer to the question in its title, you're probably disappointed and a bit unhappy by now. The truth is that brand-name computers are not always better or worse than the ones that come in white boxes. If you know how to read the computer's specifications and lists of features and options, and how to evaluate the support supplied by the dealer and the manufacturer, either type can be a reliable system that can do all the things you want it to do.

Where to Buy Your Computer

In today's marketplace, you can buy a personal computer in almost as many places as you can buy a cup of expensive coffee. The big office-supply chains all offer computers and accessories in the next aisle beyond the paper clips and pencils, and the electronics retailers in every shopping mall are ready to sell you a computer along with your home entertainment system. Or if you prefer, you can go to a smaller computer specialty shop where they assemble each computer to order in the back room. And then there's the Internet, where dozens of manufacturers and thousands of retailers are waiting for your order. Are some of these places better than others?

Yes. Or at least maybe. It depends on how much you know before you walk into a store or fire up your Web browser, and whether it's important to take the computer home this afternoon. You can get a fine computer from any of those sources. But you can also end up with a system that is either wildly beyond what you and your business or family will ever use, or one that won't keep up with the everyday demands you place on it.

Big-box retail

There are at least five different kinds of big-box retail chain stores that sell computers:

- Office-supply stores, such as Office Max, Office Depot, and Staples
- Home electronics retailers such as Best Buy and Future Shop
- Discount clubs such as Costco and Sam's Club
- General merchandise places such as Wal-Mart and Target
- Computer specialists such as CompUSA and Fry's

These are all North American examples. You can substitute the names of similar chains in your own country.

Except for the computer specialists, these stores have two things in common: high volume and limited selection. If they have exactly the computer you want in stock, you can buy it at a fair price, take it home, and install it the same day. Most of them offer one or more national brands (such as Compaq, Sony, or Hewlett-Packard) along with their own less-expensive house brands.

What they don't always offer are knowledgeable salespeople who can answer all your technical questions. Even harder to find are sympathetic salespeople who understand that an elderly widow might only want to exchange e-mail with her grandchildren and maybe do some genealogy research on the Internet she doesn't need the same computer with all the latest bells and whistles that her 15-year-old grandson is using to play video games and download MP3 music files.

Because they're often working on commission, the sales people in big-box stores are often more interested in selling you something than learning what you really need. If a manufacturer is offering a cash kickback to the sales staff this month on every one of their computers sold, that's the make and model that is (surprise!) exactly the one the sales folks recommend.

So you should not expect any kind of useful assistance in one of these stores. But if you prepare yourself with the information in this chapter, and you don't allow the salespeople to "up sell" you to a computer with features you don't want or need, they can often be decent places to buy a computer, especially one made by a major manufacturer.

> **TIP** There are some decent salespeople out there. Working retail can be a tough way to make a living, and many stores don't provide adequate training to people trying to sell complex equipment. So you should be nice to them, even if you don't buy anything.
>
> When you do get a good salesperson, remember his or her name. If you decide later to go back to that store to buy your computer, make sure the original good guy (or gal) gets the credit and the commission on your sale. The salesperson appreciates it and will probably go out of his or her way to help if you have to return something for service or credit.

The big computer-specialty stores are a class of their own. They offer everything from fully assembled computers to obscure adapter cables and books like this one. Some of their sales people may know more about computers than their colleagues across the road at the discount store, but may still be working on commission and suffering from poor training. But you can usually find more choices in a specialty store, and many manufacturers offer attractive rebates that are not always available at other stores.

Screwdriver shops

Screwdriver shops are retailers who assemble desktop computers from parts. They are different from other businesses that sell computers because they are often small local operations, and because they are frequently flexible enough to build custom computers to meet their customers' specific requirements. When you want a computer with an extra graphics controller to support a second video display, an extra-quiet case, or an ergonomic keyboard, a screwdriver shop is the best alternative to assembling the computer yourself. And if you're buying multiple computers over time, a continuing relationship with a good screwdriver shop can be a huge asset to your business.

But remember that screwdriver shops can suffer from all the hazards of small businesses in an extremely competitive marketplace. Don't be surprised to discover that a shop that appeared to have been thriving six months ago has disappeared from the face of the earth because the owner received a better offer, or the competition from discount retailers has driven them out of business.

Screwdriver shops have lower overhead than the big chain stores, but they can't buy their stock in the same kind of volume. Therefore, the cost of a white-box computer is probably comparable through either channel. If a price seems unreasonably low, look for a reason; it could be either cheaper parts or inadequate service and support before and after the sale.

A screwdriver shop might be a one- or two-person business operating out of the owner's basement, or a somewhat larger operation with a dedicated sales force and a retail store in a strip mall. Even if you don't need a custom design, a good screwdriver shop can be an attractive place to buy a computer because it offers personal service from a local business. If you ask, the sales people can probably explain exactly why the shop has selected the particular motherboards and other parts they're using. If there's a problem, the service technician can easily consult with the person who put the system together in the first place. However, these are generally small businesses that can't always afford to provide the same kind of 24-hours-a-day support available from a major corporation.

To find a good screwdriver shop, ask friends and colleagues for their recommendations and look for advertisements in local computer publications. Before you buy, it's worth a telephone call to the Better Business Bureau to learn if the shop has a record of complaints from previous customers. In the end, it's important to trust your own instincts about whether or not you want to do business with them.

When you talk to sales people from a screwdriver shop, you should expect them to ask how you plan to use your computer and recommend a system that meets your specific needs. If you have done some homework first (meaning, you have read this chapter), you should be able to tell if the proposed package is right for you or if the sales person is loading it with features and options that you will never use.

Through the Web or mail

All the major computer manufacturers and many other suppliers sell computers through Web sites and mail-order catalogs. You can buy a brand-name computer directly from the maker or importer, or a white-box system from a dealer who can pack and ship the computer to you overnight or within a few days.

Ordering a computer from your home or office via catalog or Internet offers several advantages:

- **Access to more brands:** No retailer offers every one of the dozens of different makes and models that are available through the Internet. If you're located far from an urban center, your local options might be restricted.

- **Choice:** When you order a system directly from the maker, you can specify exactly the configuration you want. You're not limited to the features and options in a local retailer's inventory.

- **Special offers:** Web and mail-order dealers might offer bundled upgrades or accessories (such as extra memory or a bag for your new laptop) or discounted prices that are not available from local retailers. Many manufacturers also offer factory-rebuilt systems, often with full warranties, at substantial discounts.

- **Support:** When you buy directly from the factory, their customer assistance center is your first line of support. You don't have to take the computer back to a store, whose staff may or may not know how to help you.

- **Convenience:** When a manufacturer or retailer ships a computer to you, it is delivered directly to your door or your company's loading dock. You don't have to load it into your own car or truck and back out again.

The disadvantages of Web and mail order include:

- **Delayed gratification:** You have to wait for delivery after you order your new computer.

- **Added cost:** Most Web and mail-order places charge extra for shipping, which can increase the total by 10 percent or more, depending on the speed of delivery. If you can find a special free-shipping promotion, it can sometimes make a big difference.

- **What you see is what you get:** Unless you can find a similar item locally, it's not possible to examine a computer before you buy it through the Web. This is particularly important on laptops and the human-interface portions of a desktop system such as the keyboard, video display, and mouse. If you don't like the look and feel of a new computer, you have to pack it up and return it, which can be both costly and time consuming.

- **Difficult returns:** If part of your order has been damaged in shipping, or if a computer or component is defective or it's not the one you ordered, it's usually necessary to telephone or e-mail the seller, describe the problem, and request a return authorization. Depending on the company, you might have to pay for return shipping and wait until it arrives at the warehouse before they send out a replacement. If you're dealing with a particularly uncooperative (or dishonest) dealer, you could be in for a very long wait or worse.

When you're dealing with a distant business, it's even more important to take some time to investigate the company's reputation before you trust them with your order. Several independent Web sites offer ratings and comments from past customers, so a Web search on the name of the company combined with the word "ratings" or "review" usually produces pointers to useful information. Once again, the collective wisdom of the Internet can reduce the risks involved in buying by mail or through the Web.

Build your own computer

For some users, assembling your own computer from parts is a legitimate alternative to buying a preassembled system through any of the retail channels discussed here. If you have some experience and confidence working inside a computer case and if you are prepared to provide much of your own technical support, a home-built system can allow you to choose exactly the set of features you want and maybe reduce the cost of your computer without a sacrifice in quality or performance.

Building a computer from scratch is probably not worth the time and trouble involved if your only objective is to save money. You can probably find an inexpensive brand-name or white-box system at a local retailer or through the Web for about the same price as the total cost of all the parts you would have to buy. But if you already have an accumulation of usable spare parts or if you want to choose the particular components and features in your computer, a home-brew system might make sense. There are many more variations available in things like cases and graphics controllers than you're likely to find in any retailer's inventory. Once you move beyond the low end, you can often build a computer with better performance or special features for the same amount of money that an off-the-shelf system might cost.

For example, the manufacturers of desktop and tower cases offer many variations and options in their product lines, but most white-box assemblers limit themselves to one or two generic models. When you're building your own system, you can choose exactly the size, shape, and color you want. You can choose a compact case, or one with extra space for additional hard drives. If you want a silent computer, you can even choose an ultra-quiet case from Antec, Zalman, and several other suppliers.

When you compare the cost of buying versus building, don't forget the price of a new copy of Windows. Most store-bought computers include Windows as part of the package, but if you're building your own system, you have to buy the operating system software separately — you can't just install the same copy you already use on another computer. One reason the big manufacturers can offer such low prices is that Microsoft charges them a lot less than you must pay when you buy one copy of Windows at a time.

Assembling a new computer out of parts is not something you might ever want to try, but if you do, there's a special kind of satisfaction when you turn on the power switch for the first time, and — there it is! — data begins to appear on your monitor screen. But if it doesn't work, remember that you have to find and repair the problem yourself; you built it, so you get to fix it. Before you start, you may want to read a book about building your own computer, such as *Building a PC For Dummies, 5th Edition*.

CAUTION   **Building a usable PC is not usually a project for beginners. But if you enjoy that sort of thing, it can be a legitimate alternative to buying a new computer that has already been assembled and tested.**

Choosing a Processor

The CPU (central processing unit) is the core of your computer. It's the large integrated circuit mounted in a socket on the motherboard that controls all of the computer's other components. All of the actual computing inside your computer takes place in the CPU, so the choice of a processor dictates the computer's performance level and can have a significant impact on its cost.

Both of the major CPU manufacturers, Intel and AMD, offer several families of processors with somewhat different designs and feature sets. Within each family, the price of a CPU chip increases along with its speed and performance. Therefore, it's necessary to choose a particular brand, family, and performance level when you shop for a new computer.

Or is it? One of the great secrets of the consumer computer business is that most people buy computers with much more processing power than they really need. For the vast majority of computer users, the real differences between CPUs may not matter very much.

Even a relatively slow processor can provide as much computing power as most of us are likely to need in a desktop or laptop computer (unless you plan to play cutting-edge video games or do large-scale graphic design). For high-volume network servers that are constantly sending and receiving files or messages, and for systems in multimedia entertainment centers and other processor-intensive applications, a faster and more powerful CPU can provide a noticeable improvement in performance.

One reason to buy a better CPU than you need right now is to anticipate the next round of upgrades to your hardware and software. A mid-range or better processor might be inexpensive insurance that protects your computer from becoming obsolete too soon. If you buy a new computer with the least expensive CPU, you might not be able to use it a year or two from now when you want to install the latest gotta-have-it enhancement to your system, such as a new operating system, a popular new game, or a program for editing digital photos or sound recordings.

Intel or AMD?

The two major manufacturers of CPU chips are Intel and AMD (Advanced Micro Devices). Both companies make excellent products. Both companies would tell you that they are dedicated to advancing the technology to make all of our lives more rewarding. Both work hard to meet those goals. The competition between the two keeps prices low and encourages them to develop even faster and better processors in order to preserve and expand their shares of the market.

It's not possible to use one brand as a direct replacement for the other. The physical form and some of the low-level features of Intel and AMD processors are not identical, so each processor requires a motherboard that was specifically designed to operate with that type of CPU. But the motherboards for both brands follow the same specifications for dimensions, electrical requirements, and for input and output connectors and signals, so it's entirely possible to build similar computers with either make of processor. Windows works equally well on either one. Unless you go out of your way to run a diagnostic measurement program, you might never notice any difference.

Processor speed

Extra speed makes a difference when your computer runs very large programs or processes large amounts of data, and benchmark programs that produce bar graphs like the one in Figure 3.1 can be impressive. If you run a daily or weekly report that examines hundreds of thousands of records and evaluates every transaction, a faster processor can complete the job more quickly. But the improvement is far less visible during routine home and office tasks like word processing and Web browsing.

As their manufacturing processes improve and the technology advances, both AMD and Intel introduce newer and faster processors several times a year. When that happens, the prices of the previous speed demons drop, along with all the other members of the same processor family. And sometimes, the slowest version disappears from the list.

FIGURE 3.1

Faster processors can produce impressive results in benchmark tests.

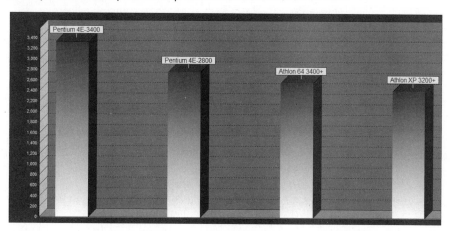

The difference in cost between the latest and greatest version of a CPU chip and a slower version that has been available for a year or two can be dramatic. A processor with a clock speed just 15 percent slower than the top-of-the-line version can reduce the cost of your computer by $200 or more. In most home and office settings, the apparent loss of performance is insignificant. On the other hand, buying the cheapest possible CPU is often false economy, because it may not have enough power for next year's new programs.

So the best strategy is usually to look for the best compromise between speed and cost, most often someplace close to the middle of the range. Unless you need to wring every possible bit of performance out of your computer, you probably don't need the fastest CPU.

The CPU's History of Speed

The speed and complexity of the CPU designs used in personal computers has grown almost unbelievably since Intel released the first microprocessor (the 4004) in 1971. Those early processor chips had a clock speed of 108 kHz (that's 108,000 cycles per second), and they contained the equivalent of 2,300 transistors. Today, the CPU inside a desktop computer might operate at 3 GHz (three billion cycles per second) or more and contain more than 200 million transistors. Moore's Law (named for its creator, Gordon Moore, one of the founders of Intel) predicts that the number of transistors within an integrated circuit of the same size will continue to double every 18 months, so you can expect the next generations of CPUs to be even faster and more complex than the ones that are available today.

Performance

Raw processing speed is not the only thing that contributes to a computer's performance. Other features of a CPU's internal design such as multiple processors and the amount of onboard cache memory can also help move data through the system more quickly. In some cases, those improved functions can compensate for a slower internal clock to produce faster overall performance.

Each processor family includes a different set of features. You can find detailed descriptions of each family and recommended processors for different uses at the Intel and AMD Web sites (www.intel.com/products and www.amd.com).

Memory

Every time you open a file or run a program, the computer loads commands and data into RAM (random access memory) chips located on memory modules mounted in sockets on the motherboard. The CPU exchanges data with these modules millions of times every second. When you save a file, the computer transfers the data from RAM to permanent storage on the hard drive or some other media.

In Windows and other modern operating systems, the CPU is often running one or more programs in the foreground and many other utilities and services in background. The computer is constantly moving programs and files between the RAM and a section of the hard drive reserved for use as additional virtual memory. Because the CPU can read data from RAM modules much more quickly than it can retrieve it from the mechanical, or *hard*, drive, a computer processes data faster if it has more RAM. Adding more RAM is often the single most cost-effective way to improve a computer's performance.

CROSS-REF Chapter 7 explains how memory works with the other components inside your computer, how to buy and install additional memory, and how to test your computer's RAM.

The specifications supplied by the manufacturer or dealer for every computer always includes the amount of RAM installed on the motherboard. The amount that your computer actually needs depends on the demands of the operating system and the application programs you expect to use. For Windows XP, the computer should include a bare minimum of 256MB; for better performance, increase the amount to at least 512MB or even 1024MB. For Windows Vista, the practical minimum is probably about 1024MB.

Those are minimums. For audio or video editing, graphic design, or other work that involves very large data files, and for games, adding an extra 512MB or more of memory makes the computer significantly more responsive and reduces the time necessary to open and close files. Even on less-demanding applications, additional memory can make a noticeable difference. In most cases, you can see a greater improvement in the computer's performance after you add more memory than with a faster CPU. But don't get carried away with adding memory. There's a point of diminishing returns where more memory doesn't make any more difference.

How Much Memory?

It's easy to become confused by the way memory size is described, because the names for large numbers of data bytes are based on multiples of 8. Therefore, 1 kilobyte (KB) is 1024 bytes (8 x 128), rather than 1000 bytes, 1 megabyte (MB) is 1024 kilobytes, and 1 gigabyte (GB) of memory is actually equal to 1024 megabytes. The most common sizes for memory modules are 256MB, 512MB, 1024MB (1GB) and 2024MB (2GB).

If you order additional memory along with your computer, instruct the dealer to install the new modules and test them in your system before they turn it over to you. Don't accept the loose modules as separate pieces that you have to install before you can use them, because loose modules may not have been tested before they were shipped to you.

If you add memory to an existing computer, run a memory test such as Memtest86 (available from www.memtest86.com/) after you install the new modules. If the test identifies any problems, remove the new modules and return them to your supplier for a refund or replacement.

Some types of memory modules must be installed in matched pairs. The manual for your computer or motherboard tells you if your system has this requirement.

Choosing a Hard Drive

Most new computers come with a single hard drive to store programs and data files. You can expect the dealer or manufacturer to format the drive and load Windows and other software before they deliver the computer.

The important characteristics of a hard drive are

- The amount of data the drive can hold (expressed in gigabytes)
- The speed at which the magnetic disks rotate inside the drive
- The buffer that stores copies of recently read data
- The type of interface between the drive and the motherboard

Before you buy your computer, it's a good idea to ask about the hard drive's capacity, speed, buffer, as well as its interface. It's quite possible that the salespeople, especially in a retail store, won't know the answers to your questions, but they should be able to tell you where to find out.

CROSS-REF Look for more information about hard drives in Chapter 9, including instructions for buying, installing, and using a second drive.

Capacity

A hard drive with a relatively small capacity costs less than a drive with more space, but when you calculate the cost-per-gigabyte, the larger drive might be more of a bargain. If you expect to store very large audio, video, or graphics files on your system, look for a computer with a big drive (at least 200GB for a desktop system). If you're buying a machine for your office that only needs to store relatively small text and data files, a smaller drive might be all you need. Hard drives for laptop computers are physically smaller than the ones inside desktop machines, so the maximum capacity is also smaller.

CROSS-REF   See Chapter 1 for more differences between laptop computers and desktops.

Don't assume that a home computer doesn't need a big drive. If you or your children play games with complex graphics or download MP3 music files and podcasts, the drive can fill up sooner than you think. And don't forget all those pictures that you transfer from your digital camera. It's a good idea to get a hard drive with a generous capacity in your new computer, but don't worry about underestimating your ultimate requirement. When the original drive comes close to filling up with data, it's easy enough to add a second drive.

Speed

Most new hard drives come with internal disks that spin at 7200 RPM (revolutions per minute) or more, but you might find a slower 5400 RPM drive in a less expensive computer. Obviously, faster is better, especially when you're working with very large files, because a fast drive takes less time to locate individual files. A computer with a faster drive loads Windows more quickly when you turn it on, and reduces the amount of time needed to open and store files and perform other common maintenance tasks.

Buffer

The disk cache, or buffer, is a temporary storage area on the drive that holds copies of data that the computer recently read, and expects to read again in the near future. When the drive reads data from the buffer, it is able to transfer it to the CPU more quickly because it doesn't have to spend time searching through the whole drive for the file that contains that data.

Most drives used in desktop computers have either a 2MB buffer or an 8MB buffer; some very large drives have 16MB buffers. A 2MB buffer is adequate for things like office work, e-mail, and Web browsing, but a larger buffer improves performance on video games and in servers that have heavy workloads. An 8MB buffer is a better choice for a laptop computer.

Interface

The interface is the system that the computer uses to exchange data with a disk drive. Your new computer should use either an IDE interface (also called an ATA interface) or an SATA interface. SATA drives were introduced more recently than the older IDE types, but the drive manufacturers still make both types. The computer's motherboard probably has sockets for both interface types if it's a desktop system.

If you have a choice, ask for an SATA drive, but don't worry if IDE is your only option. In today's computers, the difference in performance is insignificant, but SATA drives accommodate the faster processors and other improvements that may become available in the near future. In addition, SATA cables are more compact than the ones on IDE drives, so they make it easier to work inside the computer case.

CROSS-REF Chapter 9 discusses the difference between IDE (also called ATA) and SATA interfaces.

Inputs and Outputs

Today's computers have an almost overwhelming number of connectors and sockets that allow a wide variety of devices to exchange information with the processor. You can expect any new computer to have many of the inputs and outputs listed in Table 3.1 unless you're buying a very compact system with limited capabilities. However, some systems use several USB ports in place of the dedicated printer, mouse, keyboard, and other individual connectors.

The exact location of many connectors — front, back, or sides of the case — is purely a matter of convenience. As long as they work properly, the precise location of most connectors and controls makes no difference to the computer's performance. If you have a choice, look for a desktop computer with at least one or two USB connectors on the front panel; connecting and disconnecting portable devices like flash drives and digital cameras to the front panel is much easier than reaching around to the back of the case.

TABLE 3.1

Input and Output Connectors

Connector Name	Description
Power	AC or DC power input
Monitor	Output to video display
Printer, LPT, or Parallel	Interface to a printer, scanner, or other parallel device*
Serial or COM	Serial data interface*
Modem	Interface to the public telephone network
Ethernet or LAN	Interface to Local Area Network
PS/2 Keyboard	Input from keyboard*

continued

TABLE 3.1   (continued)

Connector Name	Description
PS/2 Mouse	Input from mouse or other pointing device*
USB	Input and output to Universal Serial Bus devices
IEEE 1394	Input and output to FireWire devices
Video	Output to a television set
PC Card	Socket for a PCMCIA card (most common on laptops)
Microphone	Audio input from a microphone
Line In	Audio input from a high-level source
Line Out (L & R)	Audio output to speakers (Left & Right)
Headphone	Audio output to headphone
Docking	Combined inputs and outputs to a docking station or port replicator (laptops only)
Infrared or I/R	Data port for infrared data transfer (most common on laptops)
Digital Media	Socket for one or more types of flash media card

* Many new computers use the USB ports in place of these connectors.

NOTE   There are no universal symbols to identify input and output connectors. A few are commonly used among different manufacturers, but you should look in your manual for the symbols on your computer.

CROSS-REF   Look for explanations of the devices that connect to all these connectors in Parts II, III, and IV of this book.

Choosing a Case

The first generation of personal computers were all true desktop systems because they were built into horizontal cases made to sit on a table or desk with the widest surface next to the tabletop. But it didn't take long for somebody to turn the case up onto one side and create a tower case with a much smaller footprint. Instead of placing the computer case on the table with the video monitor sitting on top, many users moved their tower cases down onto the floor or to remote corners of their desks. The choice of a desktop or tower case makes no difference to the computer's performance, but it could be a very big deal to some users. Many name-brand computer makers build all their systems in tower cases, but a screwdriver shop can probably accept your order for either type.

NOTE   In addition to desktop and tower cases, you might also find some other designs for special uses. For example, a computer for a child's bedroom might have pastel-colored plastic trim and an extra-durable keyboard and mouse. A computer for use in an engineering lab or a broadcast studio might have a 19-inch-wide front panel for mounting in a standard equipment rack.

Tower cases come in three basic sizes: full towers, typically about 2 feet tall; midsize towers, around 20 inches tall; and mini towers, about 15 to 16 inches high. As the case gets taller, there's more space inside and on the front panel for additional hard drives and other storage devices. You should choose a full- or mid-size tower if you expect to install several extra drives in your computer.

Some cases are heavier and built more solidly than others, but it's easy to find good examples of both shapes. However, many computer makers use inexpensive cases instead of increasing the prices of their finished products or cutting into their profit margins. If you don't expect to open up the case, you might never notice the difference between an inexpensive case and one that has more features and a better design.

Besides the choice between a desktop and a tower, other things to consider when you choose a computer case include:

- **Air flow:** A good case should have an exhaust fan near the back wall and vent holes in the front or sides. Air should move across the motherboard and the expansion cards to move heat away from the processor chip.

- **Noise control:** Some cases are designed to reduce the amount of noise and vibration that the computer produces.

- **Number of internal and external drive bays:** Internal drive bays provide mounting space for additional hard drives. External bays offer space for devices that must be physically accessible to a user, such as a CD or DVD drive.

- **Style and appearance:** Does the case fit into the décor or style of the room in which it is needed?

- **Color and finish:** A case might be painted with a flat or a glossy finish, black, beige or a bright color, or even unpainted metal.

- **Weight:** Aluminum cases are lighter and more portable than similar steel cases.

- **Ease of access:** Some cases include removable trays and sliding platforms for the motherboard and internal drives. These features make the computer easier to assemble and repair, but they make no difference to the day-to-day user.

- **Position of the controls and indicators:** The power and reset buttons, the pilot light, and the disk activity light are all normally located on the computer's front panel, but the exact position depends on the case design. Some users might prefer one layout over another.

- **Power supply:** If you're buying a separate case to assemble your own computer from parts, the power supply might be either be included with the case or sold separately. If it's included, is the power supply rated for enough watts to support all the internal parts without overloading?

Choosing a Graphics Controller

A graphics controller (also known as a video card or a graphics adapter) transfers the signal supplied by a computer's CPU to a video display unit called a *monitor*. A graphics controller takes over much of the control of the video signal from the CPU, so it carries its own special-purpose processor and memory. A faster graphics processor with more memory can send the monitor an image with more detail and more colors, and it can refresh the signal more often. If your monitor has a DVI (digital video interface) input connector, look for a controller card that provides a digital signal.

Every computer needs at least one graphics controller, but it's easy to choose a card that offers far more speed and performance than you really need. For the usual word processing, number crunching, and Web browsing, an inexpensive graphics controller often provides an entirely satisfactory image. Game players and graphic designers notice improvement with a more expensive card.

CROSS-REF Chapter 10 contains a detailed description of a graphics controller's features and functions.

Unlike many other features and functions of a new computer that are built into the motherboard, the graphics controller is often a separate expansion card. It's easy for a manufacturer or a screwdriver shop to substitute a different card for the one they include in their standard configuration. Don't expect to make this kind of swap if you buy your computer at a chain store, where the computers on the shelf are preassembled and ready for you to take home without any alterations.

If you're shopping for a computer in a retail store that offers computers with a choice of graphics controllers, ask to see the same image on identical monitors. If you can't see any difference on the type of programs you expect to use, buy the computer with the less expensive card. Don't buy a more powerful card just because it looks great on video games that are designed to take advantage of all that enhanced performance unless you expect to play some of those games.

A more expensive and more powerful computer often includes a more powerful graphics controller, but you might save a bit of money by choosing a different card. Or if you or your children will use the computer for graphics-intensive games, consider replacing the standard controller with one that has more memory and faster performance.

As a rule of thumb, an inexpensive graphics controller with 32MB or 64MB of on-board memory should be adequate for most Windows XP users. For Windows Vista, look for a card with at least 128MB and a DirectX 9 class graphics processor. For full 3-D video on games and interactive television, try a card with as much memory and as much speed as you can afford.

TIP In some computers, the fan mounted on the graphics controller card is the loudest thing inside the case, but you might not notice it in a noisy store. A card that provides the same performance with a big heat sink instead of a fan mounted over the graphics processor chip reduces the overall amount of noise that you computer produces.

High-performance graphics processor chips for game players often produce a lot of heat; the cards without fans are usually limited to the ones with slower and less powerful processors.

Refresh rate

The refresh rate is the number of times per second that the video controller wipes and replaces the image on the monitor screen. Faster is better for monitors that use CRT displays, up to about 75 or 80 Hz or more. For most LCD displays, the refresh rate is 60 Hz, so the higher rates don't matter.

Colors and maximum resolution

The image you see on a computer's monitor screen is a composite of many tiny dots called picture elements, or *pixels*. Resolution is the number of pixels that it takes to fill the monitor screen. The device driver software (the software that converts image information from the CPU to specific instructions for the graphics controller) supplied with your graphics controller can increase or decrease the resolution of the image that appears on the screen. The device driver also sets the maximum number of colors (each a slightly different shade) that the monitor can display. An image with more colors looks better because the different shades provide better definition.

The graphics controller must work harder to refresh an image with more colors or greater resolution, so a controller with more memory and a faster processor can produce a higher-quality image than one with fewer resources. In practice, this means that a card with more memory can accept a higher maximum resolution, refresh rate, and number of colors. In other words, look for a controller with more memory (up to 64 or 128MB) to produce a better-looking image. Cards with even more memory produce better results on games and other three-dimensional images, but they're not necessary for most other purposes.

Choosing a Monitor

Some computer retailers include a monitor as part of their standard computer package, and others sell the monitor separately. Even if the computer is sold with a monitor as a combined deal, it's always possible to choose "no monitor" as a lower-cost option. When you buy a new computer to replace an existing machine, you can save some money by moving your old monitor to the new system. If you're ordering your computer through the mail or online, you may want to consider shopping for the monitor locally. This way, you can evaluate the quality of the image before you buy.

Unless you have a limited amount of space for your monitor (such as a kitchen counter), a bigger screen is almost always better. Whether you use the added on-screen real estate to display bigger text and pictures or to view more than one window at a time, a large screen makes your computing experience easier and more pleasant.

Over the lifetime of your computer, you spend a huge amount of time looking at the monitor's screen, so it's worth the extra expense to buy the best monitor you can afford. Along with additional memory, buying a monitor with a clean, sharp image is the most effective way to upgrade your computer.

Unless a very low price is more important than anything else, your new computer probably comes with a flat-panel, liquid crystal display (LCD) monitor. Flat-panel monitors occupy less space than the traditional cathode ray tubes (CRTs), and they consume less power, so they cost less to operate. For most users, an LCD monitor is the better choice. However, some inexpensive LCD screens tend to smear colors when they display moving images such as DVD movies and animated Web pages. It's almost always worth the extra money to buy a better-quality monitor.

CROSS-REF Chapter 11 explains how monitors work and offers more advice about choosing the best monitor for your particular requirements.

TIP When you turn on a monitor, it might take some time for the image to stabilize. Don't try to evaluate a monitor in a store display unless it has been operating for at least 20 minutes.

Choosing an Audio Controller and Speakers

The audio controllers supplied with most new computers are entirely adequate for listening to MP3 files, podcasts, streaming Internet radio stations, and most of the other sound files that people play through their computers. They're also fine for recording MP3 files and Webcasts, and transferring vinyl records and cassettes to audio CDs, or storing them on a hard drive. With a good set of stand-alone speakers or a connection to a high-fidelity home entertainment system, you can enjoy sound from your computer that is comparable to FM radio or your audio CD collection.

Of course, the quality of the playback is limited by the technical quality of the source material; a heavily compressed MP3 music download doesn't have the same dynamic range or sound as the same song on a commercial CD.

TIP The audio processors on a typical computer motherboard or a Sound Blaster card are not as good as the equipment in a professional recording studio. For serious recording, and for archival-quality audio preservation, you want a separate analog-to-digital (AtoD) converter, either on a special expansion card or an external device that connects to the computer through a USB or FireWire port, or through a PC Card adapter.

Speakers for computer systems can range from inexpensive (less than $10) units with sound comparable to a table radio, to high-fidelity products that can cost $200 or more. Once you move beyond the low-end speakers, which may be just fine for speech and MP3 music downloads, the only way to make a rational choice is to listen to them and decide which ones you like best. Because the acoustics of your computer room contribute to the character of the listening experience, you should expect your dealer to let you try speakers on your own system and allow you to return them if you don't like the way they sound.

CROSS-REF See Chapter 13 for more detailed information about selecting and using a sound card and speakers for your computer.

Choosing a Keyboard

The choice of a keyboard for your computer is almost entirely a matter of personal taste. Some users are satisfied with generic keyboards, and others prefer a keyboard with a more responsive touch in the individual keys or a special layout designed to reduce stress or increase typing speed.

The inexpensive keyboards supplied with many new computers use a flexible membrane or a sheet with rubber domes under each key. When you press a key, the membrane or dome closes an electrical contact with a printed circuit board to send a set of codes back to the computer's processor. These keyboards have very few parts, so they're cheap to build and sell. More expensive keyboards use a separate spring-loaded pushbutton switch for each key.

Some keyboards use a short-range radio link to replace the cable that connects the keyboard to the computer case, or they include special function keys and controls along with the standard letters and numbers. And there's a whole world of specialty keyboards for left-handed typists (with the direction keys and the numeric keypad on the left side of the regular keys), keyboards for foreign languages, and keys with Braille key tops or high-contrast lettering. To find a special-purpose keyboard, search the Web for the one you want (such as "Russian keyboard" or "left-handed keyboard").

TIP Fortunately, many office supply stores and other computer retailers have a variety of makes and models on display, so you can try them before you commit yourself to a particular type. When you test keyboards in a store, try to place them at about the same height as your own computer table or desk.

If you already know what kind of keyboard you want to use with your new computer, you can often instruct the dealer to provide that make and model instead of their standard model. If not, go ahead and let them ship the computer with their generic keyboard. The additional cost is insignificant, and you can always keep it as a spare.

If you're happy with the keyboard attached to your old computer, it's easy to transfer that keyboard to a new system. Just turn off the old computer, pull the plug out of the case and plug it in to the new one. If the new computer doesn't have a socket that matches the plug on the old keyboard cable, you need an inexpensive PS/2-to-USB keyboard adapter that you can buy from a local computer supply store or through the Internet.

CROSS-REF See Chapter 12 for a lot more information about keyboards, mice, and other input devices, and Chapter 29 for information about special keyboards.

Choosing a Mouse or Other Pointing Device

Most of the same advice about choosing a keyboard for your computer also applies to choosing a mouse. You can settle for the simple inexpensive version that came with your computer, or you can replace it with your choice of additional features. Computer mice come in dozens of different sizes, shapes, and configurations. You can choose one that feels good in your hand, one with buttons, wheels, or other types of switches, and one with or without a cable.

If you don't want to drag a mouse around the table next to your keyboard, you can replace it with a big ball that you can move with your fingers (called a *trackball*), or a touchpad that moves the on-screen cursor as you slide your fingers. You can even use a set of foot pedals to do the work of the mouse buttons.

TIP   The generic mouse supplied with a new computer probably adds less than $10 to its total cost, so you might just as well let the dealer or mail-order supplier include it in the package unless they offer the particular model you really want as an option. It never hurts to have an extra mouse in your box of spare parts.

Summary

When you're ready to buy a new computer, consider several important things. The reputation of the company that manufactured the computer or assembled it from parts is crucial, and remember that the speed and performance of the CPU you need depends on the way you plan to use the computer. Also, the amount of RAM, the capacity of the hard drive, and the performance of the graphics controller are all integral to making your computer work the way you need it to. Don't forget about your preferences for monitor screen size and image quality, as well as the quality of the speakers. And if it's a desktop computer, decide whether you want a tower or a desktop case.

Finally, there are two other very important things to consider when you're choosing a new computer: the length of the warranty and the quality of the service and technical support supplied along with the computer. It's a sad fact that computers are complex machines that don't always work the way you expect. Just about everybody needs some kind of help setting up the system or using some of its features and options. When a component fails to work properly, it's essential to know that you can get the thing fixed or replaced.

Part II

Understanding Your Computer's Components

Chapter 4

Looking Inside the Case

Whether the computer in question is housed in a desktop case, a tower case, a portable clamshell, or some other less common package, every Wintel computer (*Wintel* systems are designed around the Windows operating system and Intel processors) contains the same basic set of components. These components might take different physical forms, but they're always there. An important first step in understanding how a computer works is to know where to find and identify the parts that combine to make up the whole.

This chapter describes each of the essential components, including the power supply, the central processing unit (CPU), Random Access Memory (RAM), and the motherboard. It also briefly explains what each piece does and how it works with the other parts of the system. You can find more detailed explanations of most of these components later in this book.

The Contents of a Case

The essential components that exist in every computer include:

- **Power supply:** The power supply converts AC power from a wall outlet to well-regulated DC power for all the other components in the system.

- **Central processor (CPU):** As the name suggests, the CPU, also known as the *chip*, is the computer's core data processing device. It accepts instructions (also called *commands*) from other components and responds to those commands by performing specific actions and sending the results of those actions to other components.

- **Chipset:** The chipset includes one or more additional circuits that support the CPU by acting as an interface with the other components in the computer.

- **Random Access Memory (RAM):** Memory modules store data and exchange commands and data with the CPU at high speed.

- **Basic input/output system (BIOS):** The BIOS memory circuit contains the instructions that the computer uses to test itself and load the operating system software.

- **Motherboard:** The motherboard holds the CPU, the chipset, the memory modules, the BIOS, and other electronic components.

- **Expansion cards:** Expansion cards plug into the motherboard and add specialized features and functions (such as control of sound or a video display) that the motherboard does not provide.

- **Data storage devices:** Storage devices are hard drives and drives for removable media, including compact disks and DVDs; older storage methods include floppy disks and tape cartridges.

- **Power cables:** Power cables move electricity from the power supply to other components.

- **Data cables:** Data cables transfer data between the motherboard and other devices.

- **Control cables:** Control cables carry signals between the inputs and outputs on the motherboard and the switches and connectors on the case.

- **Fans and heat sinks:** Fans and heat sinks are mechanical devices that move heat away from the CPU and other heat-sensitive components.

You might also find some additional components inside your computer, such as an antenna for a wireless data interface (in a laptop case) or acoustical insulation that reduces the amount of noise produced by the computer.

NOTE In this chapter, discussions of desktop cases refer to cases with the widest surface resting on a table, a shelf or the floor (as compared to tower cases that have a narrow surface on the bottom). In general usage, desktops and towers are both considered desktop computers, to differentiate them from portable systems or laptops. This is somewhat confusing, but in the world of computers, the word "desktop" has both meanings.

Opening the Case

Before you can examine the computer's internal components, you must open the case. There is no universal method for removing the cover because every manufacturer uses a somewhat different design. Computer case design is a compromise between appearance and function; the ideal cabinet looks good from any angle, but it's also easy to open and close.

If you're lucky, the owner's manual or other documentation supplied with the computer includes a detailed set of instructions for removing the cover, or there's a Web site with a short video or a step-by-step procedure. If not, you have to spend some time examining the computer in order to find the secret. Even if it's not immediately obvious, there is always a way to open the case — if

Safety Precautions

Before you open a computer case, you should take some precautions to avoid injuring yourself or damaging the components inside the case.

First, be sure to either unplug the power cable or turn off the switch on the back of the case before you remove the cover. Some components inside the computer remain "on," even when the computer is "off" — that's why you might see a lighted LED indicator on a motherboard when the computer is not running.

Second, don't try to open up the power supply or poke around inside it with a screwdriver or other tool; some of the components inside the power supply enclosure carry extremely high voltages that can cause injuries or even fatal shocks,

Next, ground yourself to prevent shocks caused by static electricity before you handle any components inside the case, with or without tools. Even if you can't feel a static shock, it can be powerful enough to damage internal parts. At an absolute minimum, place your hand on a metal part of the case before you touch a circuit board or other component. If possible, use an anti-static wrist strap or similar grounding system (available from electronics supply retailers) every time you open a computer case or handle other electronic components.

Finally, you can often save a lot of time and prevent confusion by taking some photos or making detailed drawings of the equipment inside the case and the individual jumper and switch settings on various parts, before you remove them. This makes it much easier to reassemble the computer and restore the original settings after you have finished your work.

there wasn't, the people who assembled the computer wouldn't have been able to install the parts inside the box.

Most cases use either sheet metal screws, thumbscrews, or some kind of latching mechanism to hold the cover to the case. The screws or latches are most often located on the back of the case, but sometimes you might find one at the front of a desktop case or on the side of a tower. If the case uses sheet-metal screws, you need either a screwdriver or a 1/4-inch nut driver to remove them.

 As you remove screws from the case, place them all in a little bowl where you can find them easily when you're ready to reassemble the computer.

Opening a tower case

Figure 4.1 shows common locations of the screws or latches that hold a tower case together. If the side of the case does not come loose after you remove the screws, try sliding it toward the back of the computer; sometimes there are sheet-metal tabs holding the side to the rest of the case. Move the side panel an inch or less and then lift up.

If the side of the case doesn't budge, take a close look at the front of the computer. In some designs, one or more screws are not visible or accessible until you remove the front panel.

FIGURE 4.1

Look for screws or latches at the back and side of a tower case.

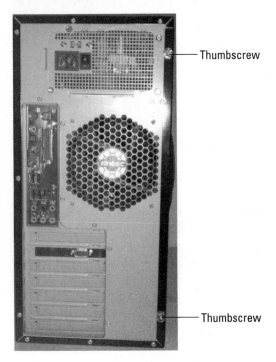

Thumbscrew

Thumbscrew

Most tower cases mount the motherboard on the right side of the case (looking at the front), so the piece to remove to examine the other components inside the computer is usually the left side panel. But it's inevitable that somebody, somewhere in the world makes a tower case that opens from the right. If you can't open the case from one side, or if you see nothing but a mounting tray or the bottom of a big printed circuit when you remove the side panel, try the opposite side.

Still other tower cases use a U-shaped cover that lifts upward off the cabinet. To remove a U-shaped cover, lift it up and away from the rest of the computer.

Opening a desktop case

The screws or latches that hold the cover to a desktop case are almost always located at the back of the case. Some case covers are flat panels attached to the top of the box, and others are bent sheet metal that cover the computer's top and sides. To open the case, remove the screws and slide the top toward the back or lift it straight up.

Providing Electricity: The Power Supply

The computer's power supply converts AC power from the domestic electrical service (power from a wall outlet) to the specific DC voltages that the CPU and other electronic circuits, and the motors of the disk drives, fans, and other mechanical devices, require to operate properly.

The power supply is usually located at the back of a tower or desktop case. Several sheet-metal screws hold the power supply to the case. The power supply often mounts on rails inside the case, next to a large hole in the back panel of the case that provides access to the AC power connector and the exhaust fan from the back of the computer. The back of the power supply might also include a small slide switch that selects the source voltage of either 117 VAC or 240 VAC, and a big master power switch that cuts off all AC power to the computer. Figure 4.2 shows the back of a desktop computer and identifies the power supply's location.

FIGURE 4.2

The power supply is located at the back of a computer's case.

 Power supply

Inside the computer, the power supply is a metal box with several bundles of wires connecting it to other components:

- The metal box is an essential part of the design because it keeps stray radio signals away from the rest of the computer and other nearby electronic equipment, and stray fingers away from lethal voltages inside the power supply.

- The power supply's DC outputs provide several voltages: +3.3 volts, +5 volts, –5 volts, +12 volts, and –12 volts, all relative to ground. These numbers are the specified values; in practice, the computer can work properly with voltage levels that are slightly higher or lower than the specification. The +3.3 v and +5 v outputs are used by the computer's electronic circuits; the motors in the disc drives, fans, and other mechanical components use +12 volts. The –5 v output was used by some older computers to provide power to floppy disk controllers and some other components, but it's now mostly obsolete. The –12 v output is used in some older serial port circuits, but it's not common in most modern computers. Both –5 v and –12 v are included to make new power supplies compatible with older components.

- The exact values of the power supply's output voltages are usually slightly more or less than the specified numbers. If the actual voltages are within an acceptable range (as shown in Table 4.1), the difference will not affect your computer's performance.

- The bundles of color-coded wires that come out of the power supply each have one or more standard power plugs that fit the power input sockets on the motherboard, the disk drives, the fans, and other components inside the computer's case. Each bundle of wires has a plastic connector at the end. Table 4.1 lists the industry-standard color codes for power supply wires.

TABLE 4.1

Power Supply Color Codes

Nominal Voltage	Acceptable Range	Color of Wire
+5 VDC	± 5%	Red
-5 VDC	± 5%	White
+12 VDC	± 5%	Yellow
-12 VDC	± 5%	Blue
+3.3 VDC	± 4%	Orange
Ground or Common		Black
Power Supply On indicator		Green

 Some power supplies, including those in Dell computers manufactured between 1996 and 2000, do not use the standard color codes.

The label on your computer's power supply (shown in Figure 4.3) includes these important items:

- The maximum number of watts and amps that the power supply can consume
- The individual output voltages
- The maximum current for each voltage

A power supply rated at 250–300 watts or more is probably adequate for most home and office users. However a server with four or more disk drives, a game machine tricked out with the latest and most powerful CPU and graphics controllers, or a high-powered sound card can consume as much as 500 watts or more. As a rule of thumb, if you replace an existing power supply, use a new one rated at the same or a larger number of watts.

FIGURE 4.3

The label on the power supply shows its maximum input and output ratings.

Supporting Everything: The Motherboard

Your computer's motherboard is the heart of the machine. Everything else is either mounted on the motherboard or attached to it through a cable. In a desktop computer, the motherboard is the big more-or-less-square printed circuit board at the bottom of the case. In a tower computer, it's usually mounted vertically along one side of the case. Figure 4.4 shows a typical motherboard.

The motherboard performs two major functions: It provides physical support for the CPU, the memory modules, the expansion cards, and a long list of input and outputs, and it carries digital data through its printed circuit board to and from all of the other components that make up your computer. Combined with the electronic components mounted on the printed circuit board, it performs all of the system's computing functions.

FIGURE 4.4

The motherboard supports all the other electronic circuits.

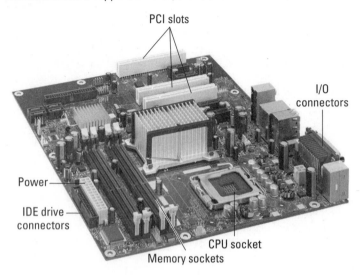

The personal computer industry has established standard specifications that define important characteristics of motherboards, such as the dimensions, the locations of mounting holes and input and output connectors, and the shape and arrangement of the power connectors. As a result, it's generally safe to expect any motherboard that meets the ATX standards to fit properly in an ATX case, and the power plugs coming from any ATX power supply to mate with the sockets on an ATX motherboard. The same thing applies to microATX and other standards. You can expect this even if the motherboard, the power supply, and the case were manufactured by three different companies. Table 4.2 lists the most commonly used motherboard standards.

TABLE 4.2

Standard Motherboard Form Factors

Name	Maximum Dimensions	Typically Used in
ATX	12 inches wide x 9.6 inches deep (30.48 cm x 24.38 cm)	Desktop and tower cases
MicroATX	9.6 inches wide x 9.6 inches deep (24.38 cm x 24.38 com)	Small cases
Mini-ATX	6.7 inches wide x 6.7 inches deep (17.02 cm x 17.02 cm)	Smaller desktops

Name	Maximum Dimensions	Typically Used in
FlexATX	9.0 inches wide x 7.5 inches deep 22.86 cm x 19.05 cm)	Mini-PCs Mini-desktops
BTX	12.8 inches wide x 10.5 inches deep 30.69 cm x 26.67 cm)	Tower PCs
MicroBTX	10.4 inches wide x 10.5 inches deep (26.42 cm x 26.67 cm)	Smaller PCs
PicoBTX	8 inches wide x 10.5 inches deep (20.32 cm x 26.67 cm)	Even smaller PCs and entertainment units

Unfortunately, a few large manufacturers sometimes use non-standard motherboards or other parts in their desktop computers; this ensures that users and repair people buy replacement parts directly from them, rather than use generic versions. If your computer uses one of these non-standard designs, the manufacturer's support center will be your main source of information about repairs and replacement parts.

The CPU: The brains of the outfit

As the name suggests, the central processing unit (CPU) is a relatively large (and expensive) integrated circuit mounted on the motherboard that exchanges instructions and data with all the computer's other components. The latest generation of CPUs used in personal computers can contain the equivalent of hundreds of millions of transistors, compressed into a space of just a few square inches or less. It's traditional to call the CPU and any other integrated circuit a *chip*, because the internal circuit is made from a thin slice (or chip) of silicon crystal.

The CPU chip mounts to the motherboard through a special socket permanently attached to the motherboard, with a lever mechanism that securely holds the CPU in place and provides a reliable electrical connection to each of the pins on the bottom of the integrated circuit. When the lever is released, it's possible to remove and replace the CPU without damaging the pins.

As the technology improves and changes, Intel and AMD, the two major CPU manufacturers, introduce new physical packages for their CPU products. The new packages make it impossible to mount a new CPU on an older, incompatible motherboard. The specification for every CPU includes the *socket type* that defines the CPU's package. Common Intel CPU packages include Socket 370, Socket 478, and Socket 775. AMD packages include Socket 754, Socket 939, Socket 940, and Socket AM2. Still other socket types become available as new CPU types are introduced. If you're assembling your own computer from parts, or if you want to replace a CPU chip with a faster and more powerful version to improve your computer's performance, make sure the socket type of the CPU matches the socket on your motherboard.

As electrical energy passes through the CPU, much of that energy converts to heat that can damage the chip's internal circuitry, so it's essential to control the physical temperature of the CPU. A metal or ceramic object called a *heat sink* conducts the heat away from the top of the integrated circuit. The heat sink has a very large surface area in order to disperse the heat as widely as possible. A cooling fan moves the heated air away from the heat sink and the CPU. Some computers have a heat pipe or an even larger heat sink in place of the fan, but the vast majority of PCs use cooling fans.

The combination of CPU, socket, heat sink, and cooling fan forms a large assembly that is usually close to the right side of the motherboard (when the input and output connectors are at the back). Figure 4.5 shows the location of the CPU on a motherboard.

CROSS-REF   Chapter 6 contains more details about the CPU.

FIGURE 4.5

The CPU is located directly under the heat sink, which is under the large cooling fan.

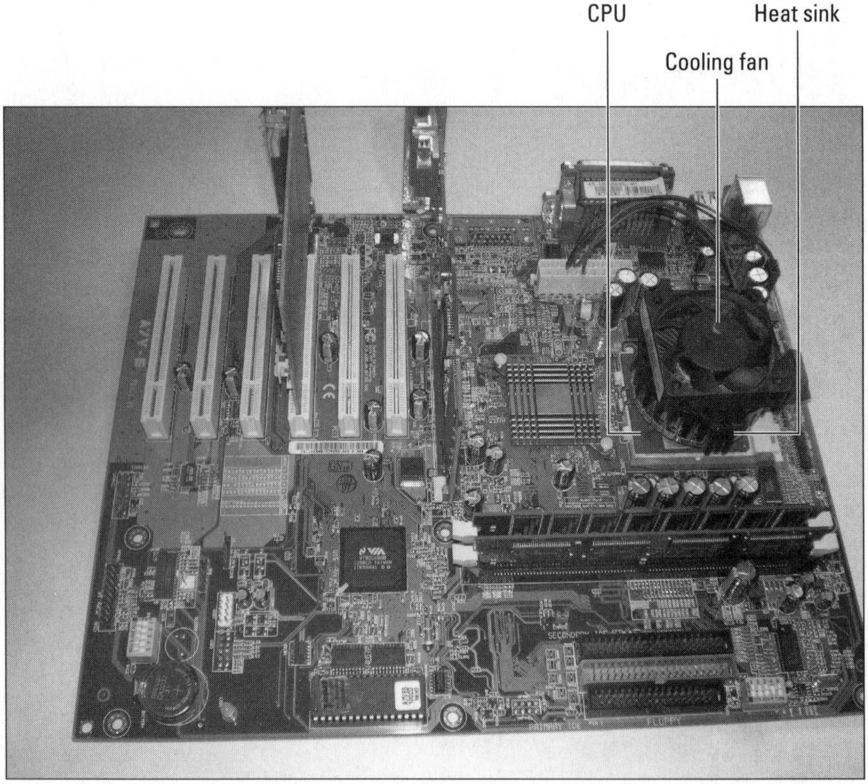

In a supporting role: The chipset

Even though the CPU itself contains all those millions of transistors, it still needs help before it can handle the very specific input, output, and control signals that it exchanges with the computer's memory and the input and output device. So every motherboard includes a set of circuits called a *chipset* that converts the generic CPU signals to and from the instructions and data that each component expects. The chipset also acts as a gatekeeper, directing inputs and outputs to the right locations at the correct speeds. Figure 4.6 is a simplified diagram that shows the way a chipset operates.

The design of the chipset and the other features and functions of the motherboard are closely related. Along with the CPU socket type, the specific chipset that the motherboard uses is its most important characteristic. Many motherboard manufacturers may offer several models that support the same CPU with different chipsets.

The design of the chipset and the other features and functions of the motherboard are closely related. Along with the CPU socket type, the specific chipset that the motherboard uses is its most important characteristic. Many motherboard manufacturers may offer several models that support the same CPU with different chipsets.

Most motherboard manufacturers (except Intel) don't make their own chipsets, so you may find similar chipsets on different makes and models. The two major producers of chipsets for AMD processors are NVIDIA and VIA Technologies. Intel makes chipsets for their own CPUs, and other chipsets for Intel CPUs are available from Silicon Integrated Systems (SiS) and VIA Technologies.

When you're reading chipset specifications, you may discover that many types use the terms *Northbridge* and *Southbridge* to describe their internal architecture. This design, which is used with both Intel and AMD processors, separates the controls into two parts: The Southbridge portion manages relatively slower devices such as the network interface and the USB ports, and the Northbridge handles higher-speed channels including communication with RAM and the graphics controller.

 See Chapter 6 for more information about the Northbridge and Southbridge parts of a chipset.

FIGURE 4.6

The chipset controls the motherboard's inputs, outputs, and memory.

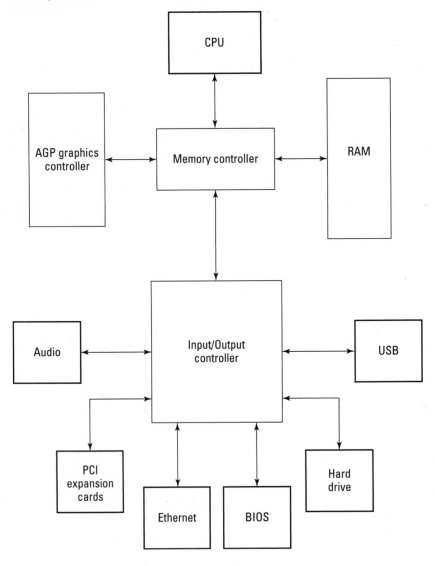

The BIOS: Starting the computer

The BIOS (basic input/output system) is a small set of software stored on a special memory chip. When you turn on the computer, it automatically runs the BIOS software, which includes a series of hardware tests, sets the system configuration, and runs the first of a series of programs stored on a hard drive or some other storage device. This series of programs eventually leads to Windows or some other full-featured operating system such as Linux or Unix that can run programs and perform other useful work.

CROSS-REF For more details about the BIOS, see Chapter 8.

Memory

Your computer uses random access memory (RAM) to temporarily hold the commands and data that the CPU is currently processing. Because the processor can read and write memory stored in RAM almost instantaneously, and because the memory modules are physically located close to the CPU and the chipset, the computer can process data in RAM much more quickly than it can handle data stored on a hard drive or another mass storage device.

Your motherboard has at least one socket (often two or more) for RAM modules like the one in Figure 4.7. Each module is a small printed circuit board with several integrated circuits mounted on it. A single module can hold up to two gigabytes of memory, but modules with smaller capacities (between 256MB and 1GB) are more common.

TIP Some older motherboards require matched pairs of memory modules, so it's always good practice to consult the manual for your motherboard or computer before you buy and install new memory.

CROSS-REF Chapter 7 contains more detailed information about selecting and using memory in your computer.

As processor speed and other characteristics of computer performance have improved, the capacity and speed of memory modules have also increased. Therefore, each generation of CPU requires a different type of module. In order to reduce the chance of conflicts, the memory sockets on your motherboard don't accept modules that are not compatible. The manual for your computer or motherboard should identify the specific type of memory to use.

Adding more RAM to your computer is often the single most effective way to improve the computer's performance. If the motherboard still has one or more empty memory sockets, install a new module in an empty slot; if all the sockets are already full, replace the old module that has the smallest amount of memory.

FIGURE 4.7

A memory module holds several individual memory chips.

Inputs and outputs

Without input and output devices, your motherboard is nothing more than an expensive printed circuit. The keyboard, video monitor, speakers, flashing lights, hard drives, network connections, and other components that connect to the motherboard are the media that send and receive electrical impulses and convert them to useful information.

Each connector on the motherboard is designed to work with a specific type of device, or with a whole category of devices—it might be a keyboard, a mouse, a network interface, or a simple LED indicator that lights when the computer is turned on. Some of those connectors are located on the edge of the motherboard where a user can reach them from the outside of the case, and others mate with wires or cables from other devices inside the case.

In general, the only time you have to worry about the input and output connectors that you can't reach from the back of the computer is when you are adding or removing a component, or after you have moved the case and one or more cables have shaken loose. Most of the connectors have a size and shape that mates with only one type of wire or cable. You can't accidentally plug your hard drive into the audio controller socket or attach the reset switch to a keyboard connector. But there are a few exceptions—many of the tiny connectors that control things like the reset switch and the power LED and attach to one or two pins on the motherboard are all identical, and they're easy to confuse. If you ever have to disconnect those wires, be sure you either have a copy of the wiring diagram for your motherboard, or draw your own diagram as you remove each connector.

TIP   Unfortunately, a few connector types allow you to install them upside-down or backwards. This is most common on older IDE and floppy disk drive connectors, but it can also happen with some other, less-common connector types. If it's possible to fit a connector into a socket more than one way, look for numbers (usually Pin 1) that identify one or more individual pins or holes on the plug, and matching numbers on or near the socket.

Over the last few years, many of the inputs and outputs that previously required a separate circuit board in an expansion socket that plugged into the motherboard have become standard features of new motherboards. The latest generation of motherboards include sound controllers and Ethernet network interfaces, along with all of the input and output connectors related to those services. Figure 4.8 shows the input/output panel attached to a typical motherboard, including connectors for the keyboard, the mouse, a printer, serial data, an Ethernet network cable, digital and analog audio, and several general-purpose USB ports. Some motherboards also include integrated graphics controllers, but they're not as common as the other inputs and outputs.

FIGURE 4.8

The motherboard's connector panel provides many inputs and outputs.

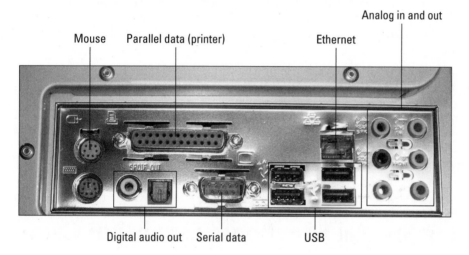

Other components on the motherboard

Along with the chipset and the sockets for the CPU, the memory modules, the expansion cards, and various data and control cable connectors, the motherboard also holds some other important parts of the computer. These include the clock battery, a reset switch or jumper, and sometimes another switch or jumper for adjusting the CPU's operating voltage and timing.

The computer takes power from its power supply. Why does it need a battery? The battery provides a constant charge that keeps the internal clock running (on an integrated circuit called the Real Time Clock) and maintains the computer's configuration settings, even if the computer is not connected to an external source of power.

A computer's clock battery typically lasts about five years. If the computer displays the wrong time and date every time you turn it on, even if you set the clock before you turned it off, or if the computer won't run the BIOS to start Windows, it's probably time to replace the battery.

CROSS-REF See Chapter 8 for more about how the BIOS starts Windows.

The reset switch on the motherboard is a last-resort method for restoring the internal configuration settings to their default values. You may never have to use this tool, but it can be a lifesaver if the motherboard suffers a power surge or other problem that scrambles one or more essential operations (like knowing where to find the keyboard or the drive that contains the operating system software). The computer manual or the motherboard manual (or the manufacturer's Web site) can tell you exactly where to find the reset switch or jumper.

 TIP If you don't know the make and model of your motherboard, use a utility such as Dr. Hardware (www.dr-hardware.com) to identify it.

On many motherboards, the reset switch is a tiny jumper between two pins or *headers*. To reset the configuration, remove the jumper for ten seconds and then replace it. If the motherboard doesn't have a separate reset switch or jumper, you can reset the configuration by removing and replacing the clock battery.

CAUTION Don't try to use the Reset switch or jumper unless you know exactly what you are doing. To avoid causing irreparable damage to the motherboard, read the instructions in the manual before you try to reset the BIOS.

Some motherboards also have a small numeric LED display that shows error codes when the BIOS detects a problem during startup. At least one manufacturer once offered a motherboard with a built-in vacuum tube audio circuit in order to provide high-fidelity sounds through the speaker outputs.

Adding Special Functions: Expansion Cards

Expansion cards are specialized printed circuit boards that add one or more features or functions to the basic set supplied by the motherboard. The most common expansion card in today's computers is the graphics controller that transfers images from the computer to a video display monitor, but many others are also available. Among many other things, an expansion card might contain a wireless network (Wi-Fi) interface, a higher-quality audio controller than the one on the motherboard, or a controller and connectors for additional inputs and outputs or hard drives.

The rear panel of the computer's case has a removable sheet metal cover over each expansion slot that keeps dust, fingers, and curious pets out of the case when no card is present. The sockets for expansion cards are connectors mounted on the motherboard that hold each card at right angles to the motherboard itself, with a sheet metal panel that replaces one of the removable covers. A machine screw attaches the cover or the back of the expansion card to the case.

 TIP Whenever you add an expansion card to your computer, it's a good idea to save the blank cover, just in case you ever remove the card.

The modular design of a PC makes the computer extremely flexible. It allows a user who needs some kind of specialized component to add that device on an expansion card without making the computer more complicated and more expensive for everybody else.

Interface types

The personal computer industry has used several standards for expansion cards. These standards specify the maximum dimensions, the number and arrangement of the electrical contacts on the surface that fit into a socket on the motherboard, and the signals supplied to each electrical contact. The sockets for different interfaces are not compatible with any other type, so each expansion card interface requires a matching slot on the motherboard.

Table 4.3 provides descriptions of the standard expansion card types used most often in desktop and tower computers.

TABLE 4.3

Motherboard Expansion Card Types

Name	Description
ISA (Industry Standard Architecture)	Black sockets. General-purpose ISA cards are common in older PCs. More recent motherboards might have one or two ISA slots to allow old cards to work in a new computer, but for all practical purposes, ISA sockets are obsolete.
PCI (Peripheral Component Interconnect)	White sockets. PCI devices can transfer data ten times faster than ISA cards. Widely used in PCs and other platforms. Compatible with Plug and Play devices.
AGP (Accelerated Graphics Port)	Usually a brown socket. High-speed interface for graphic controllers (video cards). Most motherboards have one AGP socket, located closest to the CPU. PCI Express will eventually replace these on new motherboards.
PCI Express	Black sockets. Very high-speed replacement for PCI and AGP cards. Many new motherboards use PCI Express instead of AGP for graphics controllers.

Installing expansion cards

Before you install a new expansion card, confirm that the computer's power supply is rated for enough power to support the new card along with all the existing components. The computer's manual and the specification sheets for each disk drive, CD/DVD drive, and expansion card lists the number of watts that each device requires.

To add a new expansion card to your computer, follow these steps:

1. **Unplug the AC power cable from the socket on the back of the computer.**

2. **Put an anti-static grounding strap on your wrist.** Connect into the computer's case or other electrical ground, as described in the instructions supplied with the strap.

3. **Remove the cover from the computer's case.**

4. **Find a socket that matches the type of card you want to install.** For example, if your new gizmo is a PCI device, find an unused PCI socket. If it's an AGP or PCI Express graphics controller, find the AGP or PCI Express socket and remove the existing card, if any.

5. **Use a 1/4-inch nut driver or a screwdriver to remove the screw that holds the cover plate next to the socket to the back of the computer.** Save the screw; you will need it to fasten the expansion card to the case.

6. **Remove the cover plate and set it aside.** If the cover doesn't fall off after you remove the screw, use a pair of long-nose pliers to pull it out. If necessary, loosen the screw on the next cover plate to make room for the one you want to remove.

7. **Line up and insert the expansion card into the empty socket.** Push it gently but firmly down into the motherboard to make sure the card is secure. If there's a latch holding the card into the socket, make sure it is engaged.

8. **Use the screw you removed in Step 4 to attach the expansion card's backplate to the computer's case.**

9. **Follow the instructions supplied with the card to connect any additional wires.**

10. **Replace the cover onto the case.**

11. **Plug the power cable back into the socket on the back of the computer and turn it on.**

12. **When Windows starts, it might report that it has detected the new card and offer instructions for installing a device driver.** Follow those instructions or the printed installation instructions supplied with the card instructions.

Holding the Drives: Drive Bays

There's one more major type of component inside your computer: the mass storage devices that hold your programs and data files. These include hard drives, floppy disks (these are very nearly obsolete), optical storage devices (CDs and DVDs), and drives for magnetic tape and other less common media. Desktop and tower cases have two kinds of supports for their storage devices: external drive bays for drives that use removable media, and internal drive bays for hard disk drives.

Drives and drive bays come in two sizes: big ones and little ones. The smaller drives are mostly used for 3.5-inch floppy disks. Larger drives, about 5.25 inches wide and 1 inch high, include hard drives, optical drives, and ancient 5-inch floppy disk drives. The dimensions and the location of the mounting holes on the top, bottom, and sides are the same on all drives intended for desktop and tower computers, so any drive should fit into any drive bay of the appropriate size.

External drive bays

External drive bays support drives that use removable media and other add-on devices with manual controls or visible displays. Floppy disk drives, CD and DVD drives, and PC Card sockets are common examples of external drives. Figure 4.9 shows a tower computer with a CD drive and a floppy disk drive mounted in external drive bays.

FIGURE 4.9

The drives are mounted in external drive bays.

The front panel of most desktop computers has spaces for both large and small external drives, with removable cover plates to fill unused holes. The drives that fit in those spaces usually slide into the computer from the front; some cases use metal or plastic rails that attach to the drives, and others use screws to fasten the drive directly to the sides of the drive bay.

CAUTION Don't throw away the blank covers when you install a drive or other device in an external drive bay. You might need it to fill a hole if you ever remove an external drive from the computer. Every manufacturer uses a different system to hold those covers in place, so you can't go to your neighborhood computer parts retailer to buy a generic cover; you have to go back to the company that built your computer or the maker of the case.

Internal drive bays

Just about every personal computer has at least one hard drive inside the case, and many include two or more. After a hard drive has been installed, there is no reason to remove it unless the drive fails or you replace it with a larger drive. Because it's not necessary to provide physical access to a hard drive during normal operation of the computer, the drive bays may be located deep inside the case.

So the internal drive bays can be just about anywhere: front, back, middle, at the top of the case or near the bottom. As long as the cables can reach the motherboard and the power supply, it doesn't make any difference. One of the challenges of designing a computer case is finding space for at least two or three hard drives without increasing the size of the case any more than absolutely necessary. Like Doctor Who's *Tardis* or Snoopy's doghouse, a computer case should be bigger on the inside than the outside.

If all the external drive bays aren't filled with drives that use removable media, it's easy enough to convert a vacant external bay to an internal drive bay by mounting a hard drive in the bay and replacing the original blank cover.

Moving Data Around: Internal Cables

The first thing you will probably notice after you open up your computer for the first time is that there are a lot of wires and cables inside, running in many directions. Fear not; there really is some kind of logic to this wiring.

There are several kinds of cables and wires inside your computer:

- Power cables that carry DC power from the power supply to the motherboard, the fans, the disk drives, and other devices. The power supply often includes enough cables and plugs to provide power to more devices than your computer currently uses, so there are often spare power cables and plugs that don't connect to anything; it makes the inside of the computer neater and easier to work with if you can use a cable wrap or even a short piece of string to tie the unused cables to a rail or some other part of the internal frame. That extra cable is useful when you want to add a new hard drive or other component to your computer.

- Data cables that move signals between the motherboard and the disk drives and other storage media.

- Audio cables that carry digital audio between the sound card (or equivalent on the motherboard) and the CD or DVD drive, and from the motherboard to the internal speaker inside the case.

- Control wires that extend switch contacts or LED indicators from the computer's front panel to the motherboard. Each of these wires has a connector at the end with a label that corresponds to a pin on the motherboard.

- Signal cables that extend data and control signals from the motherboard to connectors on the front or back of the case.

 **If you can't identify a wire or cable by looking at it or by looking at the device or socket connected to it, leave it alone; it's almost certainly doing something important. The best place to find explanations for all the wires, cables, jumpers, and other settings on your motherboard is the manual supplied by the manufacturer, or the manufacturer's Web site.**

Cooling and Air Flow

Earlier in this chapter, I talked about how the CPU and other components inside your computer produce a lot of heat. The fan attached to the CPU and heat sink move hot air away from the processor. The power supply also has a fan, but you still have to get that hot air out of the case and replace it with cooler air from outside. In other words, the computer must have some kind of ventilation system.

That's why your computer's case probably has some air holes on the front, back, or sides. There might also be one or more fans mounted inside, next to a hole in the cover. A fan can be either a *cooling fan* that pulls air into the case and across the sources of heat, or an *exhaust fan* that pulls warm air out. Some computers might have one or more of each.

Unfortunately, the same ventilation system that carries fresh air into the case also pulls in dust and dirt. So your computer case might have some kind of dust filter next to the air intake holes. If your case has a dust filter, remember to examine it every few months and clean it whenever it becomes clogged with dust or dirt.

If your case doesn't have a filter, there's probably a layer of dust and crud on the blades of the fan, the floor of the case, the motherboard, and every other horizontal surface. A computer can collect dust bunnies just as effectively as the space underneath your living room sofa. Anytime you have the top off the case, it's a good idea to remove as much dust as possible with a vacuum cleaner, a small brush, or a can of compressed air.

CAUTION **Make sure the power is not connected when you clean out the dust.**

The power and data cables inside your computer can also interfere with air flow. If you can, move as many cables out of the way as possible. This is especially true of the flat ribbon cables that connect disk drives to the motherboard — if you replace them with inexpensive round cables, you can allow air to circulate much more easily.

Controlling Noise

Your computer probably produces a moderate amount of noise whenever it's turned on. The CPU itself operates silently, but the fans and disk drives can produce enough noise to create a serious distraction when you're trying to concentrate. In many computers, the case itself can amplify the amount of noise created by vibrations from the fans and drives.

Therefore, the inside of your computer's case might contain some insulating material to absorb the sounds produced by spinning fans and vibrating disk drives. This could include foam or padding along the inside surfaces of the case, or special rubber or plastic supports and grommets to isolate vibrating fans and disk drives from resonant parts of the case. If you add your own insulation to the inside of your computer case, be sure you don't interfere with air flow.

CROSS-REF   Unfortunately, most case makers don't pay enough attention to sound reduction, so your computer probably makes more noise than it should. Chapter 27 offers some suggestions that can help silence a noisy computer, in spite of a bad original design.

Summary

Your computer case contains all of the essential components that it needs in order to operate. These components interact with external devices such as a keyboard, mouse, and video display to make the computer a useful tool.

Among the major components inside the case are the power supply and the motherboard. The motherboard holds the CPU, the chipset, the BIOS, and other electronic circuits. The case also holds expansion cards — these add specialized features and functions — and drive bays that hold hard drives and other storage devices. Also present in the case are cables for moving power, data, and signals through the computer; heat sinks and fans that move air through the case and control the computer's internal temperature; and insulation that reduces the amount of noise produced by the computer.

Chapter 5

How Your Computer Computes

In order to understand how the individual bits and pieces of your computer work together, it's helpful to start with the big picture of the computer as a set of logical blocks. Starting with a simple on/off circuit, this chapter builds from there to a computer that uses a complex operating system to control a keyboard, a video display, and many other peripheral devices.

The information in this chapter isn't enough for you to reconstruct the invention and evolution of the digital computer, but it should provide a decent foundation for understanding what's happening inside the computer on your desk.

From a Switch to a Bit

To understand how a computer works, look at a simple switch, like the one shown in Figure 5.1. When the switch is closed, the electrical circuit is completed and in this example, the light comes on. When the switch opens, the light goes dark.

FIGURE 5.1

A simple switch controls a light.

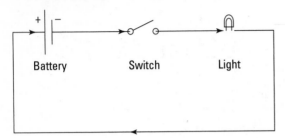

Battery   Switch   Light

Now substitute a choice of inputs for the switch and an output selector for the light and add a controller between the input and the output (see Figure 5.2). The controller receives an instruction from one of several possible sources that tells the circuit which input and output to use.

FIGURE 5.2

Instead of a switch and a light, this circuit can choose among several different sources and destinations.

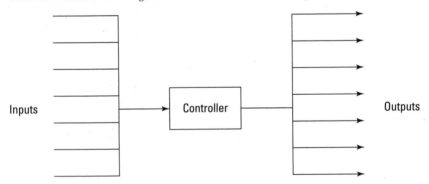

Inputs   Controller   Outputs

For example, an input device might have many individual switches. When a user closes a particular switch, the circuit sends a corresponding signal to the output. Congratulations! You've just invented a keyboard. Or the input might be a device that detects the presence or absence of a signal on an incoming communications circuit or at a particular location on a storage medium. It could also be an environmental sensor that triggers a signal when some physical condition changes, such as temperature or atmospheric pressure.

The output might be a light, a video display, a printer, a speaker, or an outbound communications circuit. In fact, it could be anything that can be directly or indirectly controlled by an electrical circuit.

By adding a device that can store the result of one instruction for the controller—a memory like the one in Figure 5.3—and allowing the circuit to use the memory as both an input source and an output destination, you can create a machine that uses the results of one action to determine a subsequent action.

FIGURE 5.3

Add a memory to the circuit to store instructions.

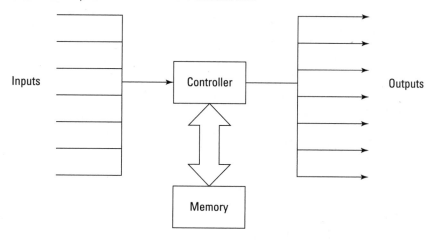

Finally, use a set of prepared instructions—a program—to instruct the controller how to respond to a series of input signals: either produce an output signal or send a new instruction to memory. Task Manager Window shown in Figure 5.4, shows the processes running at any given time.

This simple computer has a serious limitation: it can handle only inputs and outputs that have just two possible conditions. This is known as a *binary* system. If you want to do anything more complicated than turning a light on and off or counting to two, you have to deal with more than one circuit (or *bit*) at the same time.

FIGURE 5.4

A simple computer uses instructions from a program to drive the controller.

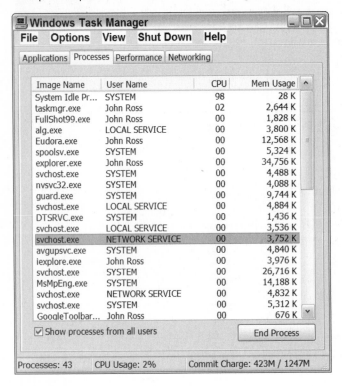

If you use two bits, the number of possible inputs and outputs doubles to four. Add one more and it doubles again to eight. Each additional circuit continues to double the total: 2, 4, 8, 16, 32, 64, 128, 256, and so on.

TABLE 5.1

How Bits Combine Into Bytes

Value	Bit 0	Bit 1
0	Off	Off
1	Off	On
2	On	Off
4	On	On

To use more than one circuit, we can either operate several parallel switches at the same time or examine a series of bits, one after another. A combined set of bits is called a *byte*. Today's personal computers use an 8-bit byte, which provides up to 256 different input or output conditions; more than enough to assign a unique value to each of the letters, numbers, and symbols on a keyboard, a printer, or a communications channel with enough left over for the Russian, Hebrew, and Arabic alphabets and more.

It's also enough to send one of 256 different shades of color to a video display, or the same number of other input and output conditions. In Windows XP, the computer processor handles four parallel 8-bit bytes, or 32 bits at a time. The latest generation of processors can handle 64 bits at one time. This increases the total number of possible input or output combinations from a couple hundred to several million or more.

The Parts of a Computer

The core of a computer has five parts:

- A set of instructions called a *program*
- The *central processor* that performs actions based on the instructions it receives from the program
- A *memory* that provides a workspace for the processor to read the program and hold the results of its work
- Inputs and outputs (known collectively as *I/O*) that allow the processor to communicate with the outside world
- A special type of I/O device called a *disk drive,* or some other storage medium that stores programs and data

Figure 5.5 shows how these five elements interact with one another. The computer processor performs work, specified by a program, on input signals and stores it in memory while it waits for the next instruction from the program. When the process is complete, the processor either sends a signal to an output, stores it on the disk drive, or both.

A modern personal computer can perform millions of processes every second. And it can handle either four or eight 8-bit bytes at a time (32-bit or 64-bit processing), so the total number of different I/O conditions is up in the hundreds of millions. This combination of high speed and extremely flexible I/O allows the computer to perform many types of work extremely quickly. But what does it take to move from processing bits to performing useful work?

FIGURE 5.5

A simple computer has five elements.

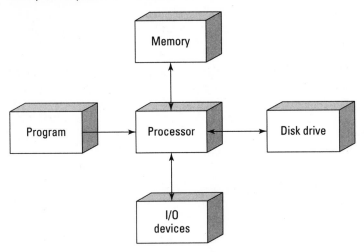

Computers: Structured in Logical Layers

Your computer uses a series of intermediate programs to move from simple data processing to specific tasks that allow you to edit words or music, send and receive messages, create graphic images, and save the planet from invading space aliens. You can think about each of these programs as an individual layer in a stack of digital pancakes. Each layer exchanges instructions with the ones above and below it in this logical stack. Figure 5.6 shows the logical layers that control your PC.

At the bottom of the stack is the hardware, or *physical* layer, which includes the central processor, the keyboard, mouse, video display monitor, and all the other I/O devices that perform some kind of physical work. These devices depend on the layers above them in the stack for instructions about how to do whatever they do.

Above the physical layer is the Basic Input/Output System, or the *BIOS*. The BIOS is a small block of code that tests and controls devices in the hardware layer, including a series of instructions that runs every time you turn on the computer. The BIOS tests the hardware and sets a number of configuration settings.

Next come several intermediate programs that prepare the computer to use the operating system. In Windows, there's a *boot loader* that tells the processor to expect 32 data bits at a time, a *boot program* that locates the operating system files, and a *detect* file that identifies and configures the I/O devices.

FIGURE 5.6

Each layer in this logical stack interacts with the layers above and below it.

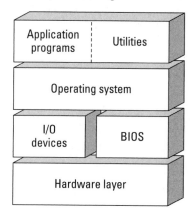

Above that, there's the *operating system*, such as Windows, which is the software that decides how the computer uses the central processor, memory, and other hardware resources to support and respond to application programs and utilities.

Finally, the *application programs* and *utilities* are at the top of the stack. The applications are your word processor, Web browser, MP3 player, and all the other programs that you use to perform actual work. Utilities are programs (many of which run in the background while you're using an application program) that control the way the computer works with peripheral devices, such as the appearance of information on the screen and the sounds that occur when certain events happen. Other utilities are maintenance programs that can make the computer run more efficiently (such as a disk defragmenter) or more safely (such as an antivirus program).

CROSS-REF To find out more about disk defragmenters and antivirus programs, see Chapters 48 and 49.

The physical layer

At the lowest level, the computer is a set of hardware devices, each of which performs some kind of action. The keyboard converts keystrokes to a set of specific electrical signals; the printer receives electrical impulses and places ink (or some other material) onto paper; and the disk drive writes and reads digital data to and from a magnetic disk. Even the central processor is just a collection of very fast and very complicated electrical circuits. Everything else that the computer does is ultimately reflected in some form at the physical level.

Before computers, many devices operated exclusively at the physical layer. For example, a piano has a direct mechanical linkage from each key to a felt-covered hammer that strikes a set of tuned wires to produce a sound at a specific frequency (a musical note). This is a relatively simple process, and there's a limited amount you can do with it. You can't press that same key to sound a note that's an octave higher—you have to press a different key.

At some very basic level, all of the components in your computer are like that piano—they do something in response to an impulse. But instead of your finger pressing a piano key, the impulse is usually some kind of electrical signal, or a combination of more than one signal. And most peripheral devices have an internal circuit that interprets that signal and converts it to a physical action.

For example, your computer's ink-jet printer has a nozzle that deposits ink on paper in the shape of each letter in the text you want to print. The internal circuitry in the printer receives each letter from the computer and instructs the ink nozzle exactly when to deposit ink on paper in order to create that letter. The same thing happens in your video monitor, which assembles each letter from tiny dots called picture elements or *pixels*.

All of the devices that make up the computer's physical layer do something similar. Each of them either converts an instruction from the computer to a mechanical or electrical action, or converts an instruction from outside the computer (in the form of a physical or electrical impulse) to a signal that the central processor can understand.

The BIOS

The BIOS (basic input/output system) is the bridge between the physical-layer hardware and the higher-level software. It's a set of relatively simple instructions that control the devices at the physical layer before the higher-level programs kick in. Among other essential actions, the BIOS provides the instructions that the processor needs in order to read code from the disk drive that contains the operating system software. The BIOS code is stored on a read-only memory integrated circuit mounted on the computer's motherboard.

The code in the BIOS performs several functions:

- **Power-On Self Test (POST):** The POST tests the most important components in the physical layer, including the processor, the memory, links to the graphics controller, the disk drive, the keyboard, and other inputs and outputs. If the POST detects a problem, or if it can't find some important piece of hardware at all, it displays an error message on the video display, unless the problem interferes with the display itself. If the POST can't display an error message, it triggers a series of coded beeps to identify the problem.

- **The Setup Utility:** The Setup Utility sets the computer's hardware to a condition where it's ready to perform useful work. If a component has more than one possible setting, the Setup Utility allows a user to select or change essential configuration options. One of these settings specifies the order in which the BIOS searches various storage devices (hard drives, a CD, floppy disk, USB flash drives, or some other medium) for the operating system software.

- **The System BIOS:** The System BIOS contains the instructions and settings that the processor uses to identify and control essential peripheral devices, and assigns priorities to each type of control. It also controls some low-level utilities, such as a temperature monitor. The processor uses some of these settings and controls as long as the computer is turned on, but it uses other settings only until the operating system takes control of them. Among others, the BIOS sets up initial controls for the clock, the keyboard, the serial and parallel data inputs and outputs, the video interface, and the disk drives. It also issues instructions that start the separate BIOS chips built into some peripheral devices, such as the graphics controller and some network interfaces.

- **The Boot Loader:** Finally, the BIOS sends an instruction to the next layer in the computer's operating structure to find and start a program that prepares the system to load the operating system.

Most motherboard manufacturers obtain their BIOS code (and the integrated circuits that hold that code) from specialist companies that work closely with Intel and AMD to produce core BIOS software for each type of processor. The motherboard makers add their own custom code to match the generic BIOS to the hardware on each of their motherboard models. The most widely used BIOSes come from American Megatrends (AMI) and Phoenix Technologies.

NOTE Some older computers might still have BIOS code produced by Award Software, which merged with Phoenix several years ago.

When a new version of the operating system or a new type of hardware comes to the marketplace, or if the motherboard manufacturer discovers a bug in the BIOS code, it is often necessary to install a new version of the BIOS software that recognizes those devices and programs. On most modern personal computers, the BIOS is stored on a form of memory called an *EEPROM* (electrically erasable programmable read-only memory) or *flash memory* that allows a user to install an update to the code by entering a special series of commands.

CROSS-REF Chapter 8 contains more detailed information about how the BIOS works, how to open and use the BIOS Settings Utility, and how to update the BIOS code to support new and improved hardware and software.

After the BIOS completes all of its testing and configuration activities, it starts a program called the *boot loader* that prepares the system to load the operating system. The boot loader for Windows XP loads some additional startup programs, it instructs the CPU to handle 32 data bits at a time, and it identifies the type of file system that the hard drive uses to organize and store data. When this is complete, the boot loader reads a file that lists the names and locations of the operating system files, and runs yet another program that takes over control of I/O devices from the BIOS. Finally, it loads the kernel of the operating system — the part that manages memory, input and output devices, and other system resources, and starts application programs — into memory.

In Windows XP, the operating system kernel is in a file called ntoskrnl.exe. When the boot loader successfully loads the kernel (along with a second file that contains some important hardware configuration information), it reads code from a database called the Windows Registry to finish the process of starting Windows.

The Operating System

An operating system, such as Windows XP or Linux, is a set of instructions to the hardware that manages the way the computer uses such resources as processor activity, memory, storage space, I/O devices, and interaction among multiple applications and utilities running at the same time. It also presents a consistent environment for programs and device drivers, so the same programs and I/O devices can run on computers with different processors, operating speeds, and amounts of memory and storage.

More specifically, an operating system performs these tasks:

- Managing the processor
- Managing memory
- Managing storage
- Managing generic I/O devices
- Providing an interface to application programs
- Providing an interface to the user

In practice, most operating systems (including Windows) come with a set of additional utilities and applications that use the application program interface and device drivers that support many specific I/O devices; but strictly speaking, these programs and drivers are not part of the operating system kernel, even if they are part of the operating system package.

Managing the processor

As the Windows Task Manager utility (see Figure 5.7) shows, the operating system can instruct the CPU to share its processing activity among several programs (or several processes within a single program) that appear to run at the same time. The Task Manager shows the percentage of the total processing time used by each program in the CPU column. The operating system acts as a broker that assigns a share of the processor's time to each program (called an *image* in the Task Manager) and switches among programs as efficiently as possible. If the computer has more than one processor, the operating system divides the total workload among all the available processors.

The operating system keeps track of all the programs that demand access to the processor and assigns CPU cycles to one of those programs, based on the order in which it receives the requests for access and the importance of each program. When the first program has used the amount of time assigned to it, the operating system copies and stores the current details of that program and immediately moves on to the next program in its queue. This sequence of events repeats many times every second, so it appears that all of the active programs are running at the same time.

FIGURE 5.7

In this example, Eudora.exe is using about two-thirds of the CPU's time.

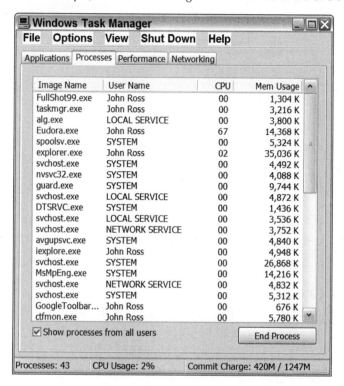

Managing memory

The computer reads instructions and data from memory and stores the results of its actions in memory. It uses other parts of memory to store configuration settings, such as the number of colors used by the video display and the actions assigned to each mouse button, and other information about the current condition of the computer. So the operating system must assign a separate physical location in memory for each active program, and other programs and services that may become active in the near future.

In order to operate as efficiently as possible, the computer stores data and programs in four different kinds of memory: one or more cache memories located on the CPU chip itself, RAM mounted on the motherboard, virtual memory located on a disk drive, and long-term storage on one or more disk drives and other storage devices.

The cache memory can communicate with the processor more quickly than other types of memory. This is why the computer uses a cache controller to select and place data in the cache that it expects the processor to use in the near future.

RAM is the set of memory chips that the operating system uses as its main memory. The operating system places programs and data files at specific addresses and instructs the processor where to find them.

Windows and other operating systems use virtual memory on a disk drive as overflow for active programs and data files that don't fit in RAM. Because it takes a lot longer to exchange data with a mechanical disk drive than an electronic memory module, adding RAM to a computer often improves the computer's performance and speed by reducing the number of times the operating system has to use virtual memory; if there's enough RAM in the system to avoid overflow into virtual memory, it won't be necessary to swap data back and forth between virtual memory and RAM.

Managing storage

The operating system moves program and data files between the processor and the disk drives (or other storage media). It uses information it obtains from the BIOS to identify the file structure used by each drive and to store files in the format that corresponds to that file structure.

Managing generic I/O devices

The operating system manages the exchange of input and output data between device drivers (described later in this chapter) and the CPU. It holds data from different sources in blocks of memory called buffers and relays the content of each buffer to the processor when the program or service that controls that data stream is active. When another activity takes control of the processor, the operating system continues to accept data and store it in a buffer.

Outbound data from the processor moves into a buffer, where the operating system releases it at a speed that the output device can handle. It also uses queues and buffers to hold incoming signals and pass them to the processor in an orderly manner.

Providing an interface to application programs

An application program interface (API) is a set of generic commands and responses that the operating system uses to perform specific functions. Application programs convert inputs from outside the computer to common API commands, and standard API outputs to specific visual, audible, or other forms (such as text or pictures on a screen, flashing lights or specific sounds) within the structure of that particular program.

For example, a graphics-communications program might let a user create a network by dragging and dropping icons and connecting links in an on-screen display. The program converts the specifications of the graphic network to a set of Network Services API commands that the operating system can use to assemble the network.

The Windows API includes these categories:

- **Base Services:** These provide access to core features of the operating system, such as memory, process and file management, and I/O devices. An application program can use these services to manage and monitor the computer's resources.

- **Common Controls:** These allow application programs to use the same appearance and control elements as the Windows shell (the look and feel of Windows). Common controls allow a user to expect a similar look and feel in programs produced by different software developers.

- **Graphics Device Interface:** Applications can use a consistent GDI to produce images for printers, video displays, and other devices.

- **Network Services:** These control communication between programs on different computers through a network.

- **User Interface:** This presents consistent visual images on the monitor, audible signals through speakers, requests for inputs, responses to mouse movement and keyboard inputs, and all the other ways that a user interacts with the computer. The Windows user interface also allows multiple programs to share the video display by placing information from each program in a separate window.

Providing an interface to the user

Finally, the operating system includes one or more *shells* that define the commands, graphic elements, and other properties of the interface between the computer and the people who use it. In Windows, the menus, the layout of the desktop, the mouse cursors, the shapes and colors of windows, and the sounds that play when certain events occur are all parts of the shell. Most people think of the operating system in terms of the user interface's look and feel, but it's often possible to use two or more very different shells with the same operating system.

Device Drivers

Windows uses a set of separate programs called *device drivers* to convert between the generic inputs and outputs in the BIOS and the specific set of input and output signals used by devices (such as a keyboard, a printer, or a disk drive) connected to the computer. By treating device drivers as separate files and not incorporating them in the core operating system, Microsoft has allowed the designers of new peripheral devices to make them compatible with Windows by creating a new device driver.

Each device driver provides an interface that converts the commands used by a device into the generic instructions that the operating system can understand. The device driver also converts generic output signals from the operating system into specific data and controls. In other words, a device driver for a keyboard would accept keystrokes, but a voice-command device for users who can't manipulate a keyboard might accept instructions through a microphone. Both device drivers would send the same commands to the operating system. Figure 5.8 shows how these two device drivers look the same to Windows.

FIGURE 5.8

Both of these device drivers present identical instructions to the operating system.

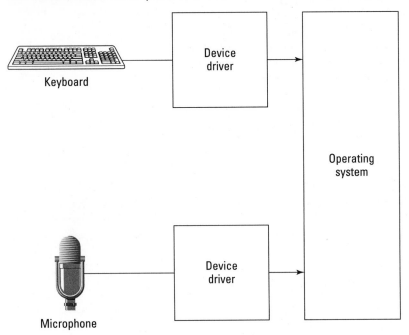

Device drivers also provide information about how the operating system communicates with the device (through a serial or parallel port, a USB port, or some other physical connection). They also communicate how the operating system should handle memory management and timing in relation to this device. Many device drivers also include a configuration utility that sets one or more options related to the performance of the device. For example, the control program for the keyboard includes options for different keyboard layouts used with different languages.

CROSS-REF   **When you install a new peripheral device in your computer, you must also load the corresponding device driver. Chapter 31 contains detailed instructions for finding and installing device drivers.**

In Windows and other complex operating systems, device drivers take over control of peripherals from the BIOS. When that happens, the device driver adds more features and options to the basic set supported by the BIOS, and it allows the device to work directly with other parts of the operating system.

Application Programs

Application programs are at the top of your computer's logical structure, and for most people, they are the whole point of using a computer. Applications are the programs you use to read and write letters, term papers and books, crunch numbers, listen to music, view Web pages through the Internet and movies from DVDs, create pictures, play games, and do everything else a computer does. As you know, there are thousands of application programs out there, each of which provides a unique combination of features and functions.

Applications relate to the operating system (which is the next layer down) through the Application Program Interface discussed earlier in this chapter. The command interpreter in an application converts the instructions you supply to the program into standard API commands.

Summary

A computer works with binary data in which every bit is either *on* or *off*. In order to handle complex data that can have more than two possible states, it combines several bits into larger groups of bits.

When the computer receives data from an input, it uses a set of instructions called a program to perform specific actions and return the results of those actions to an output. It uses a memory circuit as a workspace to read the program and hold the output data.

The modular operating structure of a modern personal computer extends to both hardware and software. Windows and other operating systems use a multi-level structure in which the software at each level interacts with the levels above and below it. In order to perform useful work, a personal computer uses several increasingly complex programs to start the computer and ultimately load the operating system that manages resources and supports application programs. Individual device drivers work with the operating system to take advantage of the specific features of peripheral devices, such as the keyboard, mouse and printer.

At the top of the computer's modular structure, application programs, including word processors, Web browsers, music players, games, and many other programs work with the operating system to perform the tasks that make a computer a useful tool.

Chapter 6

The Central Processing Unit

By now you have probably figured out that the processor (the CPU) is the physical heart and soul of your computer. Everything else in the system exists to support the CPU by exchanging power, commands, or data with it, or responding to instructions from the CPU. This chapter takes a closer look at the things that happen inside the CPU and explains how to read and understand the published specifications for a CPU chip.

But before looking at today's CPUs, consider how the CPUs used in personal computers have evolved.

History of the CPU

Before the days of integrated circuits, the earliest computers used electric relays and vacuum tubes in their processors. They were huge, expensive machines that cost a fortune to operate. The ENIAC, the ancestor of all modern computers, was built at the University of Pennsylvania in 1945. It weighed around 30 tons, and its 17,468 tubes consumed 150 kW of power. Between replacing burned-out tubes, the people who operated it (they were known as computers) had to set thousands of switches and plug in hundreds of cables to run a single program.

By 1952, computers were somewhat smaller and more efficient, but by today's standards they were still big and complicated, and they still used tubes. In one early demonstration, CBS News borrowed a pair of UNIVACs from Remington Rand to predict the outcome of that year's presidential election. They set up one in their studio on election night as a visual prop (with plenty of flashing lights and spinning tapes), while a second machine in Philadelphia actually analyzed the results. An hour after the polls closed in the east, UNIVAC predicted that General Eisenhower would win the election by a landslide, but the human analysts were expecting a closer race, so they didn't report the computer's estimates. By midnight, it was obvious that UNIVAC had it right. "The trouble with machines," reporter Edward R. Murrow told his TV audience, "is people."

At the same time that the mathematicians at several universities and corporate laboratories were building and using those early computers, another group of scientists at Bell Telephone Laboratories invented the transistor, which would eventually make vacuum tubes obsolete, because transistors could perform the same work in less space at lower cost. Transistor circuits were used in a computer for the first time in 1949.

Bell Labs started to license transistor technology to outside users in 1952, and transistors began to appear in hearing aids and portable radios within the next couple of years. By 1958, both Remington Rand and Philco had introduced all-transistor computers, which were much smaller, faster, and less expensive than the older tube monsters.

The new transistor technology led quickly to the next step in creating even smaller electronic circuits. W. A. Dummer, an English engineer, wrote in 1952, "With the advent of the transistor and the work in semiconductors generally, it seems now possible to envisage electronic equipment in a solid block with no connecting wires. The block may consist of layers of insulating, conducting, rectifying, and amplifying materials, the electrical functions being connected directly by cutting out areas of the various layers."

It took another seven years to move from Dummer's vision to the first true integrated circuit (known as a chip). By 1959, Jack Kilby built an integrated circuit at Texas Industries, and Robert Noyce at Fairchild Semiconductor developed a design for integrated circuits that could be mass produced. In 1968, Noyce and his partner Gordon Moore established NM Electronics, which soon became Intel.

One of Intel's customers was Busicom, a Japanese calculator company that wanted to build a programmable electronic calculator. Rather than building a new chip that was limited to Busicom's specific requirements, Ted Hoff, the Intel engineer on the project, designed a more flexible *microprocessor* chip that could be used for many purposes, depending on its programming. That first microprocessor, the Intel 4004, became available in 1971.

By today's standards, the 4004 was pretty primitive. It contained 2,300 transistors, and it could process only 4 bits and perform about 60,000 operations per second. But combined with three companion chips (a *chipset*) that provided memory support and I/O control, it was a fully functional, if limited, computer that fit on a single tiny circuit board.

Since that time, Intel has designed and produced a progression of increasingly complex and powerful CPU chips, as shown in Table 6.1. When IBM chose the Intel 8088 for their first PC, that design became the foundation for most of the personal computers that followed it. Intel's competitors have designed their own CPU families, but most of those chips are compatible with operating systems written for Intel products. The major exception was Apple, which used a Motorola CPU until recently, when they also adopted an Intel chip.

TABLE 6.1

Intel CPUs for Personal Computers

Name	Date Released	Number of Transistors	Maximum Speed
4004	1971	2,300	108 kHz
8008	1972	3,500	200 kHz
8080	1974	6,000	2 MHz
8086	1978	29,000	5 MHz
8088	1979	29,000	8 MHz
80286	1982	134,000	12 MHz
Intel386	1985	275,000	16 MHz
Intel80386	1987	1.16 million	33 MHz
Intel486 DX	1989	1.2 million	50 MHz
Intel Pentium	1993	4.5 million	233 MHz
Intel Pentium Pro	1995	5.5 million	200 MHz
Intel Pentium II	1997	7.5 million	450 MHz
Intel Pentium III	1999	28 million	1 GHz
Intel P4 Extreme	2000	178 million	3.8 GHz
Pentium Xeon MP	2002	286 million+	4 GHz+
Intel Itanium 2 (9MB Cache)	2004	592 million	

Intel's major competitor is AMD (Advanced Micro Devices), whose line of CPUs has evolved at a similar rate to the ones made by Intel.

In 1965, Gordon Moore predicted that the maximum number of transistors on an integrated circuit would double every two years or less. This has become known as Moore's Law. In microprocessors, the increased number of transistors is also reflected in the processing power, measured in millions of instructions per second (MIPS).

What the CPU Does

As integrated circuit technology has progressed and microprocessor designers have increased the number of transistors that they can fit into a chip, the speed, performance, and complexity of their CPUs has continued to grow. Some activities that had previously taken place outside the processor chip are now incorporated into them. As long as Moore's Law continues to drive the industry, you can expect future generations of CPUs to become even faster and more complex than they are today.

Therefore, any description of CPU operation is a snapshot of a moving target. The processors in this section represent current products that are available at the time this is written, in mid-2006.

CPU architecture

Figure 6.1 shows the internal organization of a typical CPU. This example happens to be based on an AMD design, but the same general principles also apply to Intel products.

FIGURE 6.1

The logical parts of a typical CPU

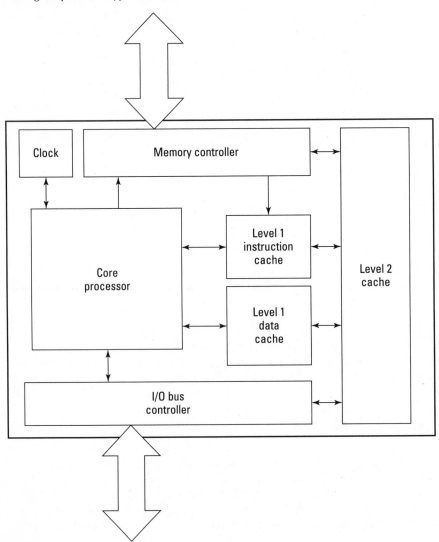

The CPU contains these elements:

- A clock circuit that produces a continuous stream of pulses at a regular interval.
- The core processor, which includes a control unit, an arithmetic logic unit (ALU), and other addressable registers. Each register is a group of memory bits that hold data that the processor will work with. The control unit in the core processor receives instructions from memory and tells the memory controller to move the necessary data from memory to the ALU.

  The ALU can perform three types of actions in response to instructions from the control unit:

  - It can perform mathematical operations on the data, such as addition or subtraction.
  - It can move data from one location in the computer's memory to another.
  - It can jump to a different instruction.

  After a string of instructions is complete, the control unit instructs the memory controller to send the results of those instructions to an output device such as a video display or a printer, or to external storage on a hard drive or other storage device.

- The memory controller, which exchanges instructions and data with the computer's RAM.
- The I/O bus controller, which moves data between the processor and the computer's input and output devices. The *bus* is the set of wires that carries the data.
- A Level 1 (L1) instruction cache memory, which holds frequently used commands before they move to the core processor.
- A Level 1 data cache memory, which receives data from the output of the core processor.
- A larger Level 2 (L2 or secondary) cache memory that acts as an intermediary between the L1 caches and the computer's RAM. In older processors, the L2 cache was a separate chip from the microprocessor.

Because the clock speed of a modern CPU is measured in gigahertz (billions of cycles per second), the computer completes each action much more quickly than it takes to describe them.

Multiple cores

Many of the latest CPUs have a *dual core* or *multi-core* architecture, with two or more parallel core processors that share the processing load. A single memory controller and I/O bus each coordinate communication with external devices and RAM. Because the computer can share the processing burden between the two (or more) cores, it can either handle more processing tasks within the same period of time, or reduce the amount of time needed to perform the same amount of work. In practice, a multi-core processor is particularly efficient for systems that run complex programs in background (such as searching a large database, rendering a 3-D image, or downloading large files), while a user runs other programs at the same time, and for running multiple tasks within the same program at the same time. As dual-core and multi-core processors become more common, many new application programs are being designed to take advantage of this feature.

Intel or AMD?

As mentioned earlier, the two major manufacturers of CPUs for personal computers are Intel and AMD. Intel has been the traditional sales leader, but by mid-2006, both companies owned healthy shares of the total market.

As active competitors, Intel and AMD have each developed their own product designs and manufacturing methods. The details of the two companies' CPU architecture are not the same, but they are both fully compatible with the Windows operating system (and other operating systems such as Linux). Both companies work closely with Microsoft to make sure their products continue to work with future Windows releases.

Of course, both companies support their products with aggressive marketing programs (remember those Intel Inside labels?), and each has customers who take the superiority of one or the other as a matter of faith. Both companies and their supporters can point to plenty of Web sites and benchmark tests that demonstrate that their favorite is the better performer.

The truth is that most users won't see any difference between the two. It's possible that some particular cutting-edge game might run slightly better on a top-of-the-line AMD processor than a comparable Intel CPU (or vice versa), and one brand might use a more elegant internal instruction set than the other, but it doesn't really matter that much to the way the average person uses a computer. Fast and reliable day-to-day operation is much more important than the numbers produced by a performance test. And since both companies introduce faster versions of most of their CPU models several times a year, this month's performance leader will be a mid-range version a year from now.

Within each product line, there are significant differences in clock speeds, cache memory sizes, number of core processors, and other features and functions (see Table 6.2). Both companies publish a tremendous amount of information about their products on their Web sites (www.intel.com and www.amd.com) and each can point you to the best processor family within their product range for your particular requirements.

TABLE 6.2

CPU Families

Manufacturer	Processor Type	Recommended Usage
Intel	Celeron	"Basic computing," e-mail, home computers*
	Celeron M	Laptop computers
	Celeron D	"Value-priced PCs"*
	Pentium 4	"Digital home and office applications"* Image processing, games and multimedia
	Pentium M	High performance laptop computers

Manufacturer	Processor Type	Recommended Usage
	Pentium D (Dual-core)	Multimedia entertainment, digital photo editing, running multiple applications, supporting multiple users
	Core Solo	Very-high-performance laptop computers
	Core Duo (Dual-core)	"Multiple demanding applications such as graphics-intensive games or serious number-crunching programs — while downloading music or running security programs in the background."*
	Core 2 Duo	High-performance energy-efficient desktop and mobile computers
	Xeon	Business applications, including Application servers, e-mail servers, Internet servers
	Itanium	"Business-critical computing . . . with mainframe-class reliability"*
AMD	Sempron	"Everyday computing with built-in security"*
	Athlon 64	"Leading edge performance with simultaneous 32-bit and 64-bit computing"*
	Athlon 64 X2 Dual Core	Running multiple applications simultaneously
	Athlon 64 FX	Running "the next generation of digital media and games"*
	Turion 64	"Optimized to deliver AMD64 performance in thinner and lighter notebook PCs"*
	Turion 64 X2	Multi-tasking, long battery life and compatibility with wireless and graphics technologies in high-performance laptops
	Opteron (multi-core)	Servers and workstations running simultaneous 32- and 64-bit computing

*Quotes are taken from the official Web site of the product listed.

CPU sockets

Most computer motherboards use a mounting socket to hold the CPU chip, rather than permanently attach it directly to the printed circuit board itself. This method offers several benefits:

- The very expensive CPU chip is not exposed to possible damage caused by heat from the soldering process during assembly.

- The computer builder can produce a common design for a range of products and install different CPUs to provide different levels of performance.

- The computer's user (or a service person) can remove and replace a damaged CPU or upgrade the computer's performance without using a soldering iron.

Both Intel and AMD offer processor chips designed for several different socket types, many of which can support more than one family of core processors. However, the CPU and the mounting assembly must share the same socket type, or the chip won't fit into the socket. Therefore, it's essential to identify the type of socket on your motherboard if you are assembling your own computer or if you have to replace or upgrade the CPU on an existing machine. The list of specifications in the owner's manual for your computer or motherboard should identify the socket type. The motherboard manufacturer's Web site should include the most recent list of compatible CPU models.

Most CPU chips are flat packages with their mounting pins on the bottom. Other processor chips mount into vertical sockets called slots.

The names of many socket types tell you how many pins (electrical contact points) are on the bottom of the chip. For example, an Intel Socket 478 Pentium 4 processor has 478 pins, and an AMD Socket 939 Athlon FX has 939 pins. However, you might also see some sockets that have arbitrary names or numbers, such as Socket 7 or Slot A.

Chipsets

It will come as no surprise to learn that a *chipset* is a group of one or more integrated circuits or chips. Remember those three other chips that the Intel 4004 needed for memory and I/O control? Today, the chipset on a personal computer's motherboard still controls the exchange of data among the CPU, memory, and the I/O devices that the CPU uses to communicate with the rest of the world. As Figure 6.2 shows, the chipset is the interface between the generic inputs and outputs on the CPU and the specific connections used by a particular type of RAM module, I/O connector, hard drive, and other devices.

FIGURE 6.2

The chipset converts between specific commands and data used by hardware and the generic instructions and data used by the CPU.

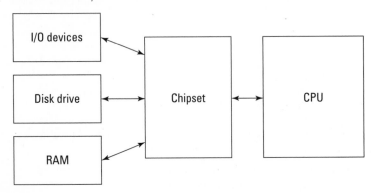

Integrated circuit technology has allowed the designers and manufacturers to squeeze more and more transistors into a smaller space. Some of the features and functions that had previously been located on the chipset have migrated to the CPU itself because data moves faster inside a single chip than from one chip to another. But there are still some good reasons to keep some actions separate. By keeping the controls for specific I/O devices on the chipset, you don't have to offer a lot of different models of expensive CPU chips; you can use the same processors with many different kinds of hardware, and you can use the same devices with more than one processor.

The chipset works closely with the BIOS. In fact, the code in your computer's BIOS was written to support a specific chipset; many of the instructions in the BIOS tell the CPU what signals to expect from the chipset. If a new chipset has a problem, the solution is often to install an updated version of the BIOS.

When Intel introduced the first microprocessors, they made their own chipsets to go along with them. It's still possible to use an Intel chipset with an Intel CPU, but they have also issued licenses to several other companies to make chipsets that are compatible with Intel processors. AMD, on the other hand, doesn't make their own chipsets, so their engineers and designers work closely with many of the same companies. As a result, it's often possible to find motherboards (and computers that contain those motherboards) that use the same Intel or AMD family of processors, but different chipsets.

Along with Intel, the other major chipset makers include NVIDIA, SiS, VIA Technologies, and ATI (which was purchased by AMD in 2006). In general, Intel's chipsets have a reputation for being extremely reliable from the first release; some of the others are often somewhat faster and they sometimes support new peripheral products sooner, but it might take a few months or more to wring out the bugs in their designs (that's not as bad as it sounds — if you have a buggy chipset, you can fix it by downloading and installing a free update to the BIOS).

Northbridge and Southbridge controllers

Most of today's chipsets have two major elements, called the Northbridge and the Southbridge. This has nothing to do with the *feng shui* of your computer room; it's left over from some old block diagrams that showed the relationships among various components in a computer system. They're called bridges because they provide routes for data. North and south are their traditional positions on the flow chart (see Figure 6.3). The chipset makers usually use two separate chips for the Northbridge and Southbridge, so they can replace them one at a time when they come up with new designs. In this case, two smaller chips are easier to manufacture than one bigger one.

The Northbridge is closer to the processor chip because it communicates directly with the CPU at high speed. It connects the CPU to the fast I/O ports including the RAM modules and the AGP graphics socket. The Southbridge handles the relatively slower devices like disk drives, USB ports, and old ISA expansion cards. It communicates with the CPU through the Northbridge.

Northbridge

The Northbridge handles the controllers for the computer's memory, the graphics controller (using either an AGP or PCI Express interface), and the interface with the Southbridge. If the computer supports disk drives or other devices that use a SCSI interface, the Northbridge also exchanges commands and data with the SCSI controller.

CROSS-REF For more information about AGP and PCI Express, see Chapter 9. Chapter 8 describes a SCSI interface.

FIGURE 6.3

A computer's chipset gathers input and output signals through controllers called the Northbridge and Southbridge.

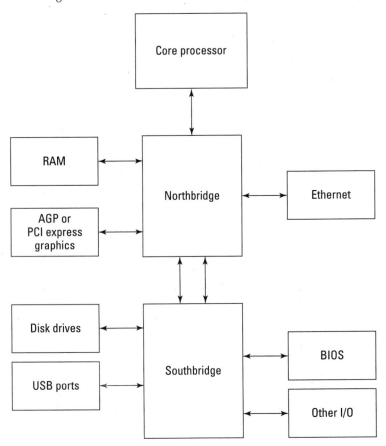

One of the Northbridge's most important functions is to direct data traffic as efficiently as possible among the cache memory on the CPU, RAM, I/O devices, and through the Southbridge to and from the computer's disk drives. It uses multiple buffers to hold small pieces of data from the CPU and RAM until it can lump them into larger strings that it can transfer to a disk drive more efficiently.

Southbridge

The Southbridge controls these inputs and outputs:

- ATA and SATA ports (for disk drives)
- USB and Firewire ports
- On-board audio
- On-board LAN (Local Area Network)
- PCI bus (for expansion cards)
- Real Time clock
- BIOS

The Southbridge exchanges data between the CPU (through the Northbridge) and all these sources and destinations, plus a few others (like an external keyboard and mouse controller) that all have one thing in common: They communicate more slowly than the sources that use the Northbridge, so the sources that use the Southbridge don't need to connect directly to the processor. To communicate between the two, the chipset uses several wires (called buses) to move data in each direction between the Northbridge and Southbridge. AMD and Intel use different methods to meet this requirement, but they both accomplish the same thing.

Summary

The microprocessor chip, or CPU, is the core of your computer's operation. Everything else — disk drives, keyboard, video monitor, and Internet connection, among others — is there either to provide instructions to the CPU, respond to data from the CPU, or both.

The CPU is a large and expensive integrated circuit that contains the equivalent of millions of individual transistors. It operates in response to stored instruction sets that it receives from one of several forms of memory.

Chapter 7

Random Access Memory

Every time your computer's processor performs an operation, it obtains instructions and stores data in memory. As the previous chapter explained, modern computers contain several types of memory, each in a different location within the system's logical structure.

This chapter concentrates on the Random Access Memory, or RAM, modules that store and forward commands to and from input and output devices such as the keyboard, the graphics display, and network links, and with permanent storage on disk drives, the BIOS, and removable flash drives. These modules are also called the computer's main memory or system memory.

First in the chapter is a very brief explanation of how these memory modules contribute to the computer's overall activity, then how to improve performance by adding memory, and finally how to confirm that the memory modules installed in your computer are working properly.

How Memory Works

The memory modules installed inside your computer contain RAM circuits that hold several hundred million memory cells. Each cell, made up of a capacitor and a transistor, represents one data bit (a capacitor is an electronic component that stores an electric charge; a transistor uses one electric charge or current to control the flow of another electric current). The memory circuit's control logic uses the transistor to read or change the charge on the capacitor. The charge state of the capacitor specifies the value of the bit assigned to that memory cell (on or off, 1 or 0, positive or negative).

The data bits are organized on each memory chip in an address system that allows the CPU to retrieve data from any address, thus Random Access Memory. Each bit in a computer's memory has a unique address, which is identified with a specific number. The bits are arranged in a rectangular grid of rows and columns, so the first part of the address identifies the row in which the bit is located, and the second part identities the column.

In order to preserve the memory's state, the memory controller must constantly refresh the charge on the capacitors. RAM that receives a refresh charge many times per second is called *dynamic RAM*, or DRAM.

The alternative to DRAM is static RAM, or SRAM. In SRAM, the circuit uses several transistors to set the state of each bit. Once the bit state is set, it does not change, as long as the transistors are continue to receive power, so there is no need for any refresh charge. The memory clears itself when the computer is turned off. Static ram is faster than DRAM, but it's also more expensive because it uses more transistors. The L1 and L2 cache in a CPU chip are normally SRAM because speedy access is the most important characteristic of cache memory, but it's less practical for the much larger main memory.

CROSS-REF   See Chapter 6 for more about L1 and L2 cache memory.

In the earliest personal computers, the individual memory-integrated circuits were mounted directly on the motherboard, but as the amount of memory that a computer could use increased, it became more practical to package memory chips on separate smaller printed circuit boards, or *modules,* that could mount onto the motherboard through a card-edge connector and a socket. This modular approach made it possible to fit more memory into the same amount of space on the motherboard and to easily increase the size of the system memory by adding or replacing one or more modules.

All of the memory modules that are compatible with your computer's motherboard have the same physical dimensions, so it's easy to remove a module with a small capacity and replace it with a bigger one (bigger capacity, that is), up to the maximum amount of memory your computer can use. The smallest memory modules you're likely to find for a new computer contain 256MB of RAM. The capacity increases in multiples of 256MB, with 512MB, 1GB (1024MB), and 2GB the most common. If you're upgrading a computer with an older motherboard, you might also find modules with 64MB or 128MB (but if your computer is that old, it might be more cost-effective to simply replace it with a new one — memory modules for those old computers are often very expensive).

How Much Memory Do You Need?

Unless you're an electrical engineer, it's okay to think about your computer's main memory as a big basket full of bits (if you are an electrical engineer, it's still okay, but you probably want to know more details about the activity inside the basket). When you start the computer and every time you run a program or enter a command through the keyboard, you temporarily take control of some of those bits. If the total demand for memory from all your active programs is greater than the total number of bits in the basket, the memory swaps data with another, slower basket called the *virtual memory*.

Every time the main memory has to go to the virtual memory, the computer's overall performance slows down because the virtual memory stores its bits on a mechanical disk drive rather than a purely electronic storage system. Therefore, your computer runs faster when it can work as much as possible from system memory. If you notice that the disk drive is running a lot when you aren't opening or saving a file — the disk activity light on the front of the computer flashes on and off, and the drive itself might make noise as it operates — you probably don't have enough RAM.

 The single most effective and inexpensive way to improve your computer's subjective performance is to add memory.

On the other hand, if you already have enough RAM to support all your programs without swapping back and forth with virtual memory, adding more won't accomplish anything except to consume more power and tie up some cash you could have spent on something else.

Unfortunately, there is no simple formula for calculating the optimal memory size for your specific combination of operating system, background utilities, and foreground programs. So the best approach is to learn from other users' experiences. Table 7.1 shows the amounts of RAM recommended by several memory manufacturers.

TABLE 7.1

How Much Memory?

If you want to do this:	You should have at least this much RAM:
Run Windows XP	256MB (bare minimum) 512MB (recommended)
Run Windows Vista	1024MB
Simple word processing and e-mail	256MB
General business use (word processing, spreadsheets, simple graphics, presentations, fax and simple Web browsing)	256-512MB
Databases, heavy Internet use, Web design, multimedia	1024MB
Graphics, computer-aided design (CAD), editing photos, editing video and audio	1024MB
Games	1024MB or more (up to maximum capacity)
3-D graphics design, animation	2GB
High-volume server applications	4GB or more

The makers of most commercial software often list a minimum amount of RAM in their specifications for each product. For example, Microsoft officially says that Windows XP can work with just 64 megabytes (MB), but they recommend using 128MB or more. Office XP needs another 8MB for each application program (Word and Excel for example) that runs at the same time. Those numbers are extremely low. It may be possible to run Windows XP with just 64MB, but you can be certain that nobody outside of a test lab likes the result. In the real world, you need at least 256MB for simple word processing and Web browsing, and 512MB or more for just about anything else.

The most extreme memory hogs are games, video editors, and other software that spends a lot of time updating the images on one or more monitor screens. If you're running those kinds of video-intensive programs, and your computer already has about 2GB of RAM, consider replacing the graphics controller with one that has more dedicated video memory before you add more general-purpose RAM.

To estimate the right amount of RAM for your computer, start by adding the recommended requirements for all the programs you expect to run at the same time, double the total, and then round up to the next multiple of 256MB.

Adding More Memory

Increasing the amount of memory in your computer is almost always worth the time and expense involved. A computer with enough memory to handle everything you want it to do can open and save files, refresh on-screen images, and respond to your commands more quickly than the same computer with a faster processor but not enough memory. Whether you do it yourself or pay a service shop to do it for you, you should start by learning how much memory is already installed in the computer, and what kind of memory modules your system uses.

How much RAM do you have?

To learn how much memory your computer has, follow these steps:

1. **From the Windows desktop, right-click the My Computer icon.**

2. **Choose the Properties command from the pop-up menu.** This command is usually at or near the bottom of the menu. The System Properties window appears.

3. **If it's not already visible, click the General tab to open the display shown in Figure 7.1.** The amount of memory installed in your computer appears near the bottom of the text on the right side of the window.

FIGURE 7.1

The arrow points to the line indicating that this computer has 512MB of RAM.

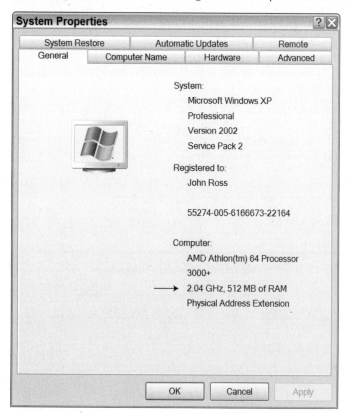

What kind of memory?

As computer processors have become faster and more complex, so has RAM. Your computer's chipset is designed to work with one or more specific memory designs:

- **FPM (Fast Page Mode):** FPM DRAM was used with the earliest Intel x86 processors. It's often identified just as DRAM. FPM memory locates and reads each bit before it starts to look for the next one. FPM memory is not used in computers that can run Windows XP or other recent operating systems.

- **EDO (Extended Data Out):** EDO memory is faster than FPM because it starts looking for each bit as soon as it has found the previous one, without waiting for the memory controller to read the first bit.

- **SDRAM (Synchronous DRAM):** The speed of an SDRAM module should match the clock speed of the CPU and performs one operation per clock cycle.

- **DDR SDRAM (Double Data Rate Synchronous DRAM):** DDR SDRAM performs operations on the rising and falling of the clock cycle or clock edges. It doubles the data transfer rate between RAM and the CPU.

- **DDR2 SDRAM (Double Data Rate 2 Synchronous DRAM):** DDR2 is an improved version of DDR technology that operates at higher speed while consuming less power and producing less heat.

- **RDRAM (Rambus DRAM):** Rambus modules, sometimes called RIMMs, transfer data 16 bits at a time through a high-speed Direct Rambus Channel. In some systems, Rambus memory is significantly faster than SDRAM. Because this approach produces a great deal of heat, RIMMs usually have aluminum heat spreaders covering the printed circuit board.

Before you buy new memory for your computer, it's essential to identify the type you need. Table 7.2 lists the most commonly used packages for RAM modules.

TABLE 7.2

Memory Module Types

Name	Dimensions	Number of Notches in Card Edge Connector	Usage
72-pin SIMM (single inline memory module)	4.25 x 1 in. 108 x 25.4 mm	1	Desktop computers (mostly 486 and early Pentium)
168-pin DIMM (dual inline memory module)	5.25 x 1.375 in. 133.35 x 34.92 mm	2	SDRAM in desktop computers (mostly Pentium and Athlon)
184-pin DIMM	5.25 x 1.25 in. 133.35 x 31.75 mm	1	DDR SDRAM in desktop computers
184-pin RIMM	5.25 x 1.25 in. 133.35 x 31.75 mm	2	Rambus in desktop computers
240-pin DIMM	5.25 x 1.18 in. 133.35 x 30 mm	1	DDR2 SDRAM in desktop computers
144-pin SODIMM (small outline dual inline memory module)	2.65 x 1.25 in. 66.7 x 31.75 mm	1	Notebook computers
200-pin SODIMM	2.625 x 1.25 in 66.7 x 31.75 mm	1	Notebook computers
144-pin MICRODIMM (micro dual inline memory module)	1.545 x 1 in 39.2 x 25.4 mm	0	Sub-notebook computers

Module types

Memory modules come in a confusing number of different physical sizes, speeds, and other characteristics. In order to make it impossible to install incompatible memory modules on a motherboard, the industry has established several different physical standards for modules and sockets. Each type has a specific number of electrical contacts on the socket and the module, a different size, and positioning slots in specific locations on the connectors. Figure 7.2 shows the relative sizes and shapes of several module types.

From top to bottom: 72-pin SIMM, 168-pin DIMM, 184-pin DIMM, 144-pin SODIMM, 200-pin SODIMM

Memory speed

The speed of a memory chip (or a module that contains several chips) is the minimum amount of time necessary for the memory to find and read each bit. The speed of older memory modules was rated in nanoseconds (ns), so a smaller number meant a faster memory. However, the speed of SDRAM modules is often listed in MHz (frequency, or millions of cycles per second), so faster SDRAM has a higher number.

SDRAM operates at the same speed as the CPU if it can, so it's important to use modules that are rated at the same or greater speed as your computer's clock. If you use memory that is rated for a faster speed than your computer can use, the actual access time is the system's internal clock speed. On the other hand, if you use memory that can't run as fast as the CPU, it can't synchronize itself with the processor, and the computer's overall performance suffers.

Unfortunately, each type of memory uses a different system to specify memory speed, so you must know which type of memory your computer uses *before* you choose the right speed for your system. Table 7.3 shows the speeds available for each type of memory module. In this table, *access speed* is the amount of time that it takes for a bit to move between RAM and the CPU, expressed in nanoseconds (ns); *system bus speed* is the maximum data transfer speed between the CPU and the L2 cache, expressed in millions of cycles per second, or megahertz (MHz); and *peak bandwidth* is the maximum amount of data that the CPU and RAM can exchange in one second, expressed in megabits per second (MB).

TABLE 7.3

Memory Module Speeds

Type of Memory	Typical Speed Ratings	Based on
FPM DRAM	50, 60, 70 ns (Nanoseconds)	Access speed
EDO	50, 60, 70 ns	Access speed
SDRAM	PC66 PC100 PC133	System bus speed in MHz
DDR	PC1600 PC2100 PC2700 PC3200 PC4000	Peak bandwidth in MB per second (for example, PC2700 = 2.7GB per second)
DDR2	PC2-3200 PC2-4200 PC2-5300 PC2-6400	Peak bandwidth in MB per second

Latency and other complications

Along with the type of memory and the speed, you may often see some additional numbers included in the description of a memory module. For example, one module's specification looks like this:

```
DDR PC2700   CL=2.5   Unbuffered   Non-ECC
```

A similar module from another company has these specifications:

```
PC2700 Latency: 2.5-3-3-7    Parity Unbuffered
```

Latency is the amount of time it takes for a memory module to respond to a command, measured in clock cycles. Some manufacturers show this value as CAS (Column Access Strobe) Latency, or CL.

Some memory specifications show latency as a series of three, four, or five numbers separated by dashes, like this: A-B-C, A-B-C-D or A-B-C-D-E. The B, C, and D values are based on the Row Access Strobe time, which is another element in the process of finding and reading a specific address in response to an instruction from the memory controller. In order, these values are:

- **CAS Latency:** The amount of time it takes for a memory module to respond to a command, measured in clock cycles.

- **tRCD (RAS-to-CAS delay):** The minimum number of clock cycles between the active command and the read/write command.

- **tRP (RAS precharge time):** The minimum number of clock cycles between the precharge command and the active command.

- **tRAS (Row Active Time):** The minimum number of clock cycles between activating a row and deactivating it.

- **CMD rate:** The minimum number of cycles after chip selection before a command can accept a command.

Normally, the BIOS sets these and other DRAM settings automatically during startup, but it's also possible to use the BIOS Setup Utility to change them.

Each of these values reflects part of a memory module's response time. To make sense of them, it's important to understand that each bit on a memory module has a physical location with a specific address, arranged in columns and rows. The memory controller uses a Column Access Strobe (CAS) and a Row Access Strobe (RAS) to find each bit. For most users, the important thing to know is that smaller latency values indicate faster memory performance.

Parity is an error-checking method that adds an extra bit to every 8-bit byte of data. In some systems, the parity bit is set to 1 when the number of binary 1s in the byte are even, and 0 when the number of 1s is odd. Other systems use the opposite values (the parity bit is 0 when the number of 1s is odd, and 0 when the number of 1s is even). When a memory module uses parity, the CPU counts the number of 1s in each byte and confirms that the parity bit is correct; if the parity bit is wrong, the CPU rejects the byte and instructs the memory module to resend it.

ECC (Error Correction Code) not only finds memory errors but fixes them as well. An ECC circuit attaches a series of ECC bits to the data bits and transmits them to the CPU along with the data. If one ECC bit is corrupted, the CPU corrects the error; if two or more bits are corrupted, it rejects the data.

Most desktop and laptop computers don't need memory with parity or ECC error checking, but they can improve performance in network servers and other high-volume systems. When you add memory to a computer, the new modules should have the same error checking and ECC specifications as the modules already in place.

Registered and *buffered* memory uses two or three register chips on each module to intercept and hold address and control signals. Registered memory is used in motherboards that have a relatively large number of slots for memory modules, such as the ones used for servers. Buffered memory works the same way, but it was used with older EDO and Fast Page Mode memory. On an unbuffered module, the signals go directly to the RAM chips. If the chipset on your computer's motherboard requires registered memory, it won't work with unbuffered modules; if it doesn't need them, the motherboard won't work with buffered modules. If you're not sure which type to use, consult the computer or motherboard manual, or the manufacturer's Web site.

> **TIP** The easiest way to find new memory is to use the selection tools that most major memory makers offer on their Web sites. Simply choose the make and model of your computer or motherboard, and the tool presents a list of compatible modules.

To find a new memory module, try the tools at these online locations:

```
www.crucial.com
www.corsairmemory.com/corsair/configurator_search.html
www.kingston.com
www.mushkin.com/doc/products/advisor.asp
www.pny.com/configurator
www.buffalotech/products/memory-configurator.php
```

Identifying your memory type

The Memtest86 program (you can download it from www.memtest86.com) is primarily a memory test, but it also displays the CPU type and clock speed, the sizes of the L1 and L2 caches, the amount of RAM installed in the computer, the chipset's make and model, RAM speed and type, and the memory's CAS values.

To run Memtest86, follow these steps:

1. **Place a formatted diskette in your floppy disk drive.** Run the install.bat program from the memtest86 folder. The program creates a boot floppy with the Memtest86 program on it.

2. **Leave the floppy disk in the drive and restart your computer.** The computer automatically loads Memtest86.

If your computer doesn't have a floppy disk drive, download the ISO image file from www.memtest86.com and follow the instructions supplied with the file to create a bootable Memtest86 CD.

Installing memory modules

Before you open up your computer, look in the computer or motherboard manual, or use one of the selector tools described earlier in this section to identify the type of memory modules that your computer uses. Either order one or more new modules directly from an online supplier, or buy them from a local retailer.

When you're ready to add more memory to a desktop computer, follow these steps:

1. **If you have a manual for your computer's motherboard, find it and open to the diagram that shows the locations of components.** If you don't have a manual, go to the manufacturer's Web site and download a copy. Print the page with the layout diagram.

2. **Turn off your computer.** Unplug the power cable.

3. **Remove the cover and put it aside.** If you have an anti-static grounding strap, put it on now and ground yourself to a metal part of the computer's case.

4. **Examine the motherboard to locate the memory module sockets.** At least one socket has a module mounted in it, as shown in Figure 7.3. If you can't find the memory sockets, refer to the diagram in the manual.

FIGURE 7.3

The memory modules mount in sockets near the CPU. This motherboard has two modules in place.

Plastic latch

Memory module

5. **To remove a module from its socket, move the plastic latch at each end away from the module itself.** Figure 7.4 demonstrates.

6. **If there are no empty sockets, remove all of the memory modules from their sockets.** Handle the modules carefully, holding them by their edges. Read the labels to identify the module with the smallest amount of RAM. That's the one you replace. If the computer or motherboard manual instructs you to replace modules in pairs, find the pair of modules with the smallest amount of RAM on each one.

7. **Line up the notches at the bottom of the first module and insert it into a socket.** Push each end of the module toward the motherboard until the latch on that end closes. Repeat for each additional module.

8. **Turn on the computer.** If the memory modules are properly seated in their sockets, the computer starts up normally. If the computer beeps as soon as you turn it on, the BIOS is producing an error code, either because the modules are not in the sockets correctly, or you're using one or more incompatible memory modules.

9. **When Windows has started, right-click the My Computer icon in the desktop.** Choose Properties from the pop-up menu. The System Properties window should show the new amount of RAM (go back to Figure 7.1).

10. **When you are convinced that the computer has recognized the new memory and is working properly, replace the cover.**

FIGURE 7.4

The plastic latches at each end of the memory sockets hold the modules firmly in place. Pull them away from the module to release a module from its socket.

Plastic latch

It's somewhat more difficult to explain how to add memory to a laptop computer because each make and model has a different design. Some provide access from the bottom of the case, and others place the RAM modules underneath the keyboard. Fortunately, most laptop makers offer their own detailed instructions in the manuals supplied with their products and on their Web sites. Don't try to open up a laptop case without instructions.

Testing Your Computer's Memory

Most memory problems appear as soon as you install a new module. However, several circumstances such as a power surge, can cause a RAM chip (one of the integrated circuits mounted on a memory module) or a whole module to fail. If that happens, you might want to run a diagnostic test. The Power-On Self Test (POST) tests the memory every time you turn on the computer, but sometimes it's useful to run a more detailed series of tests.

The Power-On Self Test

As part of its standard startup routine, the BIOS performs a complete test of the computer's RAM. Some BIOS menus allow the user to bypass the memory test to save time, and others might hide the results of the memory test behind a splash screen that fills the screen with the computer maker's name; but the POST can be a useful tool when you suspect that your computer has a memory problem.

 For more information about the POST and the BIOS, see Chapter 8.

Other memory tests

If your computer fails the POST memory test, or if you want more details about a possible memory problem, several other memory test programs are available.

Both Memtest86 (described earlier in this chapter) and Microsoft's Windows Memory Diagnostic program automatically load and run from a boot floppy disk or CD. They each perform a series of tests on the computer's RAM, and identify the addresses of any problems they find.

 You can download Microsoft's Memory Diagnostic program from this address: `http://oca.microsoft.com/en/windiag.asp`.

It's not possible to remove or repair the individual chips mounted on memory modules, so you must identify the module that contains the failed bits and replace it with a new one. If your computer contains only one module, there is no doubt that the bad RAM is on that module.

If the computer has more than one module, isolate the bad RAM by removing modules one at a time (or in pairs if the motherboard requires matched pairs) and running the test again. When the remaining modules pass the test, you know that the problem is in the one you just removed. The Microsoft program also includes a View Errors by Memory Module that identifies the physical location of a memory failure.

Summary

Your computer's CPU uses RAM as a workspace to temporarily hold active programs and data. If you don't have enough RAM, the computer offloads data to a virtual memory section of the hard drive. Therefore, adding more RAM improves the computer's apparent performance by reducing the number of times it has to swap between RAM and virtual memory.

The computer's motherboard holds RAM in individual sockets. When you add or replace memory modules, the new modules must be the type and speed that matches the chipset.

Chapter 8

Understanding the BIOS

When you turn on your computer, the CPU has no idea what to do with itself until it loads some kind of instructions. But it can't load an operating system, such as Windows, until it knows how to read the disk drive where the operating system code is stored. The BIOS (basic input/output system) is your computer's solution to the problem of starting itself without outside help.

The BIOS is a small block of software that your computer uses to test and configure its memory, disk drives, and other hardware, and to start the process that loads the operating system. Early computer designers called this process "pulling the computer up by its bootstraps," or *booting* the system.

The integrated circuit that contains the BIOS is an electrically erasable programmable read-only memory (EEPROM) that permanently stores the program until it receives a special command to erase and rewrite the program's code. This erasable function (also called *flash memory*) makes it possible to update the BIOS without physically replacing the BIOS chip. The BIOS EEPROM is mounted on the motherboard and communicates with the chipset (the set of integrated circuits that handles communication between the computer's processor and the other components).

Almost all BIOS chips contain code produced by two companies: Phoenix and AMI (American Megatrends). Award is another common brand, but that is owned by Phoenix. However, some large computer companies use private label versions that carry their name instead of the BIOS maker. The name of the BIOS maker usually appears on the BIOS chip, often with a version number. However, if the BIOS has been updated, the version number does not match the current version of the code stored on the chip.

This chapter discusses how the BIOS works, how to change the BIOS configuration settings, how to interpret the results of the Power-On Self Test, and also how to find and install updated versions of the BIOS software.

What the BIOS Does

As Chapter 5 explained, the BIOS performs several functions.

First, it reads the settings on a CMOS (complementary metal oxide semiconductor) memory chip that contains details about the computer's current configuration settings, including the current date and time, whether or not to use certain optional features (such as the audio and graphics controllers that are on many motherboards), and other options specified with the BIOS Settings Utility described later in this chapter. The computer uses a coin-sized battery to maintain a constant charge to the CMOS chip.

Based on the information in CMOS memory, the BIOS configures the chipset to work with the computer's hardware. Among other things, this includes the timing and latency of the RAM modules, and the order in which the BIOS searches disk drives and other storage devices for the boot loader software. These and other configuration settings are described later in this chapter, in the "Changing BIOS Settings" section.

Next, the BIOS loads interrupt handlers and device drivers. The computer's central processor (the CPU) uses these to exchange data with a limited number of I/O devices, such as the keyboard and the disk drives. When the CPU receives a request for access (an *interrupt*), it suspends and saves whatever it is doing and turns its attention to an interrupt handler that contains the instructions for responding to that type of interrupt. For example, when the processor receives an interrupt request from the keyboard, the interrupt handler converts keystrokes to code that the CPU can understand. After the interrupt is complete, the CPU returns to the task it was handling before it received the interrupt request.

Device drivers are similar blocks of software that supply details about I/O devices to the chipset and the CPU. Between the interrupt handlers and the device drivers, the BIOS provides the chipset with enough information to recognize and handle input and output signals from essential peripheral devices before the operating system loads.

After the device drivers and interrupt handlers have loaded, the BIOS starts the graphics controller that controls the video monitor. Many modern video controllers have their own BIOSes that they use to start the graphics processor in response to a command from the system BIOS. If the computer has more than one video card and monitor, the system BIOS loads only the one designated in the CMOS code as the primary; additional controllers wait for the operating system to start them.

Next, the BIOS runs the Power-On Self Test. The details of this test are described in the next section of this chapter.

The next step depends on the way the computer was turned on. There are two ways to start your computer. One is by simply turning on power (or pressing the Reset button on the front panel, which tells the processor, chipset, and other hardware to reinitialize themselves at a very basic level, and then restarts the computer), and the other is by entering a software command (the famous Ctrl+Alt+Del combination or a Restart command in Windows). Turning on power is a cold boot; restarting with a command is a warm boot. During startup, the BIOS looks for a flag in RAM (at address 0000:0472h) that identifies a warm boot. If it's a warm boot, the BIOS skips the memory portion of the POST. If it's a cold boot, the BIOS runs a read/write test on every memory address and displays the result on the monitor screen. When the memory test is complete, the BIOS tests the expansion cards connected to the motherboard.

At the end of the POST, the BIOS starts the graphics controller, which immediately displays some details about itself. Next, the BIOS reads some information about your computer from the chipset and displays it on the monitor. In most cases, this information scrolls up the screen faster than you can read it, but if you press the Pause/Break key, the BIOS routine stops and whatever information is visible on your screen at that moment remains on your screen. To restart, press the Reset button and follow any instructions that appear on the screen.

Finally, the BIOS searches for the boot loader program on a disk drive in the order listed in the Boot Sequence on the CMOS chip. If the first items in the Boot Sequence are a floppy disk drive or a CD/DVD drive (or some other drive with removable media), and there's no disk in the drive, the BIOS moves on to the next drive in the list. When the BIOS finds the boot loader, it starts the sequence of programs that leads to loading the operating system.

 **NOTE** If a boot drive has a disk without a boot loader program, or if the BIOS can't read the disk, the BIOS displays a message like this one:

```
Non-System disk or disk error
Replace and strike any key when ready
```

Or:

```
BOOT: I/O error reading disk
Please insert another disk
```

When you see one of these messages, make sure there are no disks in the diskette drive or the CD/DVD drive and push the Reset button. If the message appears again, there's a problem with the hard disk drive that holds the operating system software.

What Kind of BIOS Do I Have?

During day-to-day operation, it doesn't really matter which brand of BIOS your computer contains. But if you're trying to interpret the POST beep codes or use the POST diagnostic codes described later in this chapter, it may become necessary to know who produced the BIOS.

Here are several ways to identify the BIOS in your computer:

Before Windows Loads:

1. **Turn on the computer, or if Windows has already started, select Start ⇨ Turn Off Computer ⇨ Restart.**

2. **As soon as you see the splash screen that appears while the BIOS starts to load, or the first lines of text on your screen, press the key that opens the BIOS Settings Utility.** On most computers, this is either the Delete key or the F1 key, but it might be a different key on your computer — it's usually identified on the screen, and always in the manual. The first screen of the utility usually includes the name of the BIOS.

3. **If your computer does not show the type of BIOS in the Settings Utility, close the Settings program.** Allow Windows to load and use the "When Windows Is Running" method described below.

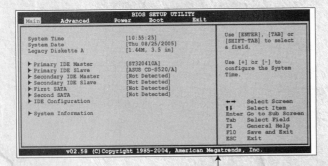

This computer uses an AMI BIOS . . .

When Windows Is Running:

1. **From the Start menu, select All Programs ⇨ Accessories ⇨ System Tools ⇨ System Information.**

2. **When the System Information window appears, look for the BIOS Version about halfway down the list of items in the System Summary.**

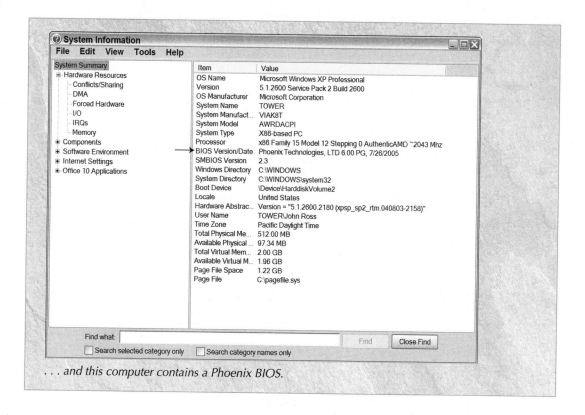

. . . and this computer contains a Phoenix BIOS.

The Power-On Self Test

The POST is a series of hardware tests that run on startup to confirm that the computer's essential components and processes are working properly. If the system fails any portion of the test, the BIOS stops before it loads the boot loader.

The POST includes these tests:

1. **The BIOS checks that the power supply voltages are within specification.**

2. **The BIOS inspects its own checksum to confirm that the BIOS code has not been corrupted.**

3. **The BIOS confirms that the CMOS checksum is correct.**

4. **The BIOS instructs the CPU to read and write every address in the computer's memory.** Many BIOSes have a fast memory test mode option in which they just check a few addresses per bank to verify the module is there.

5. **The BIOS tests the I/O controller.**

6. **The BIOS tests the video controller.**

When the POST memory test does not find any problems, it displays the amount of RAM it has tested as one of those lines of white-on-black text that appears for a few seconds before the computer begins to load Windows. If you concentrate, you might be able to read it, but it's not visible for long. If you're using a monitor with a cathode ray tube rather than a flat-panel display, the whole thing might be long gone by the time the monitor's picture tube has warmed up enough to display anything at all.

Don't worry about missing this information. If Windows starts, it's a safe bet that the memory passed the test. If there's a memory failure, the BIOS doesn't try to load Windows, and it either sounds a beep code or displays text that identifies the cause of the failure.

Beep codes

When the system fails any of these tests, the POST issues an error code and sounds an alarm. Because part of the POST runs before the BIOS has started the video controller, the alarms are a series of audible beeps in a specific sequence of long and short sounds (a series of beeps). If the system passes all of the POST tests, it may beep once or twice.

 **If the POST sounds a beep code to tell you that it has found a problem, it might catch you by surprise.**

If you do hear a beep code, try to replay the sound in your mind, and count the number of long and short beeps. If you can't remember the sequence, push the Reset button and count the beeps as they sound.

Each manufacturer uses a different set of beep codes, but there's no overlap among the codes, so you can't confuse them. Just count the number of long and short beeps and look up that code on one of the following Web sites in Table 8.1.

POST diagnostic codes

In addition to the beep codes, the BIOS also produces a series of two-digit POST status codes that identify the active process in the BIOS routine. Some motherboards include an onboard LED readout that displays the POST code, but if your motherboard does not have a built-in display, you need a special tool called a POST Code Diagnostic Card to read these codes. The diagnostic card plugs into one of the computer's expansion slots on the motherboard.

Each BIOS maker uses a slightly different set of codes. If there's a display on your motherboard, the motherboard manual includes the specific list that applies to your system. If you're using a plug-in diagnostic card, consult the BIOS maker's Web site at one of the addresses in Table 8.1.

TABLE 8.1	

BIOS POST Codes

BIOS	Web Address
AMI	`www.ami.com/support/doc/AMIBIOS-codes.pdf`
Phoenix	`www.phoenix.com/NR/rdonlyres/81E6C43C-93BD-4097-A9C4-62F05AAD6025/0/biospostcode.pdf`
Award	`www.phoenix.com/NR/rdonlyres/0835996A-6694-4F6D-8243-1030EE040D92/0/postcode.pdf`
Other Brands	`www.bioscentral.com`

Analyzing POST codes is definitely a form of advanced troubleshooting that goes beyond anything that a typical user ever needs. Most of the time, the beep code tells you enough to fix the problem. But if you do a lot of repair work, or if you're just curious about what's going on inside your computer's tiny brain during startup, the cost of a diagnostic card (typically in the US$50–$35 range) might be worth the expense.

Changing BIOS Settings

The BIOS Settings (or Setup) Utility is a configuration program that sets the options in the computer's CMOS memory. As explained earlier (in the "What the BIOS Does" section), the BIOS uses the information in the CMOS memory to instruct the chipset how to work with system hardware before the operating system loads its own set of device drivers.

To open the BIOS Settings Utility, start or restart your computer and immediately press the key that starts the utility program. On most systems, it's either the Delete key or the F1 key.

You can probably see an instruction on the screen that tells you which key to use on either the splash screen or the text that appears when you turn on the computer. If it goes past before you can press the right key, use Ctrl+Alt+Delete to restart the computer and immediately press the key.

If neither F1 nor Delete opens the Setup program, and the startup screen doesn't tell you which key to use, look in the computer manual or the motherboard manual.

Each BIOS maker organizes the settings and options in the Settings Utility differently, but they all include similar items. The manual supplied with your computer or motherboard usually includes a detailed explanation of every item in the Settings Utility, but unfortunately, many of those manuals seem to be bad translations of originals in other languages.

Almost every Settings Utility includes on-screen instructions for moving around the screen and for changing screens. Look for these instructions at the top, bottom, or right side of the screen. In most cases, you can use the left and right arrow keys to choose a screen, and the up and down arrows to move within a screen. The Enter key usually opens a list of options for the current item, and the F10 key closes the program.

WARNING   Don't change any BIOS setting unless you understand exactly what you are doing. Some of the more obscure settings might include options that could cause your computer to completely stop working.

The rest of this section explains the setup options that most users might want to change. For explanations of items not included here, consult your computer or motherboard manual.

NOTE   The names of many setup options are slightly different in utilities created by different companies. Don't be alarmed if the menu items on your screen aren't exactly the same as the ones listed here.

Date and time

The date and time settings control the calendar and clock in the CMOS memory. You can use the BIOS Settings program to change these settings, but it's easier to use the Date and Time Properties window in Windows. If you're connected to the Internet, use the Internet Time tab to synchronize your clock and calendar with an online time server that is tied to an international time standard.

IDE or ATA drive settings

For each disk drive installed in the computer, the BIOS must identify several technical details, including the capacity, the number of heads, and the number of sectors. All of these values are printed on a label attached to every drive, but most drives manufactured in the last ten years automatically report the necessary details to the BIOS. Follow the instructions in your BIOS Utility to run the auto-detect routine.

If you're installing an older hard drive that doesn't supply auto-detect information to the BIOS, copy the values on the drive's label before you mount it in a drive bay. After you reassemble the computer, open the BIOS Setup program and enter those values into the section that applies to that drive, one at a time.

The CMOS treats CD and DVD drives and other storage devices connected to the motherboard's IDE or SATA sockets the same way it handles hard drives. When you choose the auto-detect function for a drive channel, the Setup program should identify the type of drive on that channel.

Diskette drives

If your computer contains a floppy disk drive, the BIOS must instruct the CMOS which type of diskette that drive uses. The Drive A and Drive B settings include several obsolete types, along with the common 1.44MB, 3.5-inch and 1.2MB, 5.25-inch varieties.

Boot Sequence

The Boot Sequence is the order in which the BIOS examines disk drives and other storage devices during startup, when it's looking for the boot loader program. The usual sequence is:

1. **Floppy disk (if there's a diskette drive in this computer)**
2. **CD-ROM or DVD drive**
3. **Hard disk drive**

This sequence allows the computer to load an operating system or a startup program from a floppy disk or a CD when a disk is in one of those drives. However, if the drives are empty, the BIOS goes on to use the boot loader on the hard disk.

You must change this sequence if you want to use a USB device, such as an external disk drive or a portable flash drive to start the computer.

Hard Disk Priority

Hard Disk Priority specifies the order in which the BIOS searches for the boot loader when more than one hard disk drive is installed in your computer. The drive with the highest priority should be the one that contains the operating system software. This is normally the drive configured as the Primary Master or the Channel 1 Master.

NumLock Status

The NumLock key at the top of the keypad on the right side of your desktop keyboard (or a special key on a laptop keyboard) controls the functions of the numeric keypad. When NumLock is off, pressing each key enters the instruction printed on the bottom half of the key (up and down, left and right, Home, End, and so on); when NumLock is on, the NumLock LED indicator lights and each key sends the number printed on the top half of the key to the computer.

The NumLock Status option in the BIOS Settings program instructs the CMOS to turn NumLock on or off whenever the computer starts.

Power management

Some BIOS utilities offer one or more power management options that allow the computer to turn itself on automatically in response to an external signal from a network connection or a modem, or when a user presses a key on the keyboard. Consult your manual for specific details about the options available on your own system.

Unless you have a reason to want the computer to start up when it receives a telephone call (through the modem) or an attempt at a network connection, or in response to some other input, it's generally best to disable all of these automatic startup options.

Memory settings

Normally, the BIOS automatically detects the latency values of the memory modules installed in your computer, but some BIOS Utilities allow a user to change those settings. Don't mess with these settings unless you are instructed to do so by a qualified technician, such as a technical support representative from the company that produced the computer, the motherboard, or the memory modules.

Hardware monitor

Many motherboards have built-in temperature sensors that constantly monitor the amount of heat at the surface of the CPU and other locations inside the computer. If the temperature exceeds a preset level, the temperature monitor produces an alarm or shuts down the system. Another sensor reports the speed of each fan inside the system.

Many BIOS Setup Utilities include one or more options that display the current temperature and fan speeds, and allow a user to change the trigger value for an alarm. This can be useful when Windows produces fatal Stop errors (Blue Screen errors) caused by an overheated CPU. If there's no other obvious cause for the system to overheat, confirm that the fans are all operating properly and blow out any accumulated dust.

Another set of sensors measures the voltages produced by the computer's power supply. The BIOS Utility often includes a display that includes the actual value of each power supply output.

Default settings

If the BIOS settings become hopelessly muddled, the computer might not start at all, or if it does, it might not recognize one or more important components. If a well-meaning friend or relative tries to adjust the BIOS settings without knowing what he or she is doing (*you* would never make a mess of the BIOS settings), or if the CMOS settings become corrupted because of a power surge or some other disaster, the easiest way to restore the system to a usable condition is to load the default settings.

The default might not set every option exactly the way you want it, but it loads a configuration that allows the computer to start. After you have undone the damage to the BIOS settings, you can set the correct date and time and make the other changes necessary to restore your own preferred configuration.

If your computer's BIOS settings become corrupt, it saves time and reduces confusion if you have a copy of the settings that you can use to restore the system. Either copy each item in every screen of the BIOS Settings Utility with pen and paper, or take a picture of each screen, like the one shown in Figure 8.1.

Don't save the only copies of the digital photos on the same computer; you might not be able to open them when you need to restore the system. Print them out and keep them with the manuals and other papers related to your computer.

On some computers, you can print a copy of the current BIOS screen by pressing the Print Screen key twice. It doesn't always work, but it's worth a try.

FIGURE 8.1

Photos of BIOS Utility screens are helpful when you want to return to your CMOS settings.

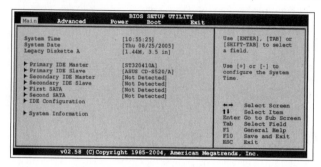

Clearing the BIOS Settings

As a last-resort method for restoring your computer's CMOS to a configuration that allows the computer to start, most motherboards include a way to clear the CMOS memory and reset the system to the original default settings.

As explained earlier in this chapter, a small battery keeps the data in the CMOS memory alive by providing a constant charge to the CMOS chip. If the CMOS loses that trickle charge, the RAM on the CMOS shuts down.

The design of the motherboard takes advantage of this by including a jumper (a removable wire or plug) in the signal path that connects the battery to the CMOS RAM chip. When you remove this jumper, you open the circuit, and the CMOS chip loses its trickle charge, which clears the CMOS settings. When you replace the jumper, the battery restores power to the CMOS chip. The next time you turn on the computer, the BIOS sets the CMOS to the default values.

Some motherboards don't have a Clear CMOS Memory jumper, so the only way to clear the CMOS is to physically remove the battery from its socket in the motherboard.

To clear the CMOS memory, follow these steps:

1. **Turn off the computer.**
2. **Disconnect the power cable from the back of the computer's case.** If you're working on a laptop computer, disconnect the external power supply and remove the battery pack.
3. **Remove the jumper or the battery.**
4. **Wait at least ten seconds.**

5. **Replace the jumper or the battery.** Make sure the battery is right side up.

6. **Plug the power cable back into the computer.** If it's a laptop, replace the battery pack.

7. **Turn on the computer.** Let it load Windows, just to confirm that it is working properly.

8. **Double-click the time in the lower right corner of the screen to open the Date and Time Properties window.**

9. **Set the date and approximate time in the Date & Time tab.**

10. **If the computer is connected to the Internet, open the Internet Time tab.** Click Update Now to set the exact time.

11. **If you want to change any of the other BIOS settings, restart the computer and open the BIOS Utility.**

Replacing the CMOS Battery

The CMOS battery is supposed to last at least five years, but many have failed more quickly. When the battery begins to fail the CMOS might lose its charge, so the BIOS can produce unreliable configuration settings. Therefore, it's a good idea to replace the battery after two or three years, but almost nobody remembers to do it until their computer begins to show the wrong date or it has other flaky settings.

To replace the battery, follow the instructions for clearing the CMOS, but install a new battery in place of the old one.

TIP When you're ready to replace the battery, remove the old one and take it with you to the store. Make sure the new one is the same type or part number as the old one. If you can't read the number on the old battery, consult the motherboard manual.

Updating the BIOS

The BIOS provides essential information to the CPU about the operating system and the I/O devices inside your computer. When a new operating system or a new version of an existing operating system adds new features, the BIOS must reflect those changes. When a new I/O device presents a different appearance to the BIOS from previous versions, the BIOS must know how to recognize and use the new interface. So the BIOS makers take advantage of the "programmable" feature of EEP-ROM technology to supply updated BIOS code to their users. Updated BIOS code also allows BIOS makers to distribute patches and fixes to bugs that might exist in early product releases.

As a general rule, there is no reason to replace or update your computer's BIOS unless you encounter a problem with the one that is already in place. You might need a new BIOS to support a new operating system or a piece of equipment that wasn't originally supplied with the computer (such as a DVD player/recorder), or to fix a problem that interferes with the computer's performance, but if the computer is already working, you won't see any improvement with an updated BIOS.

Because the BIOS code is slightly different for every chipset and motherboard, the BIOS producers encourage users to obtain updated versions from the computer makers and motherboard manufacturers. Don't try to replace your computer's BIOS unless you have exactly the right update package.

If you don't already know what kind of motherboard is inside your computer, the Dr. Hardware program available from www.dr-hardware.com can help. If your computer already has some other diagnostic program that can display the same information (such as the PC-Doctor program supplied with IBM computers), you can use that program instead.

To use Dr. Hardware to identify your motherboard and the current BIOS version, follow these steps:

1. **If you haven't already done so, install Dr. Hardware now.**

2. **Run Dr. Hardware.** The program's Overview screen appears.

3. **Click the Hardware icon in the Selection column at the left side of the Dr. Hardware window.**

4. **Click the Mainboard tab.** The window shown in Figure 8.2 appears. The top half of the window shows details for your motherboard; the bottom half contains information about the BIOS, including the date it was released.

Follow these steps to locate the latest BIOS version for your computer:

1. **Open your Web browser and go to the Web site maintained by your computer's manufacturer or by the maker of your motherboard.** If you don't have the address, look in your manual or use an online search tool such as Google.

2. **Find the link to the Support section of the Web site.**

3. **Follow the instructions to jump to the section dedicated to your specific model.** If there's a separate Downloads or BIOS section, jump to that Web page.

4. **Compare the BIOS date currently installed in your own computer with the most recent version available for download.** If a newer version is available, download it to a new folder.

5. **If the instructions on the Web page tell you to download a separate update tool or some other installation software, download that file to the same folder.**

6. **Look for specific instructions for installing new BIOS code on the Web page.** It might be a block of text, or possibly a downloadable text file. Either way, print a copy of the instructions and read them carefully.

In general, the procedure for installing a BIOS update is to copy the update software to a bootable floppy disk or a CD, restart the computer, and run the installation utility supplied with the updated code, but some suppliers (including Intel) offer utilities that allow you to update the BIOS while Windows is running. Read the specific instructions that apply to your system before you try to load the update, and follow them as closely as possible.

FIGURE 8.2

Make a note of the make and model of your motherboard and the BIOS date. You need this information to find an updated version of the BIOS.

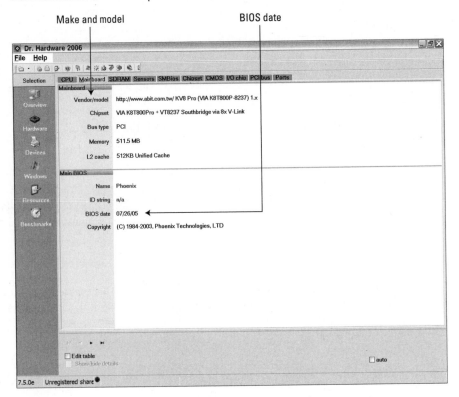

Make and model   BIOS date

Summary

The BIOS is the software interface between the CPU and the operating system. It runs a series of hardware tests when you turn on your computer, and it sets the configuration of the computer's memory and I/O devices.

This chapter has explained how the BIOS works and how to change the options in the BIOS Settings Utility. It also explains how to restore the BIOS to its default settings, how to replace the battery that keeps the CMOS memory alive, and how to update the BIOS software.

Chapter 9

Hard Drives and Other Storage Media

When the CPU is not working with them, your computer stores programs and data files on magnetic disks, optical disks, and other media. Unlike RAM, which loses data when power is turned off, the system's storage media can retain programs and files, even if the computer is turned off.

This chapter describes the various types of storage media commonly used in personal computers, and the interfaces that the motherboard uses to exchange data with them. It also explains how to install disk drives into a drive bay and how to connect external storage devices through a USB or FireWire port.

As a category, these devices that use storage media are known as *mass storage* because they can hold extremely large amounts of data. As far as the CPU is concerned, there's no difference among the different types of mass storage; the chipset handles the timing and the specific instructions necessary to find an address on each device.

Hard Drives

A hard drive (or more accurately, a hard disk drive) is a device that contains one or more magnetic disks, along with the mechanical components and electronic circuits required to spin the disk, read and write data, and convert between the magnetic impulses on the disc and digital data that the chipset can exchange with the CPU. Most new desktop computers come with one hard drive, and space for more. A typical desktop computer motherboard can support four or more hard drives (or other mass storage devices). In a laptop computer, there's usually space for just one relatively small hard drive.

IBM introduced the ancestors to today's hard drives in 1973. Because they contained two 30-megabyte disk spindles, they were widely known as *Winchester drives*, inspired by the famous Winchester 30-30 rifles. Since then, the industry has multiplied the amount of data that can fit in the same space many times, so the capacity of a modern hard drive might be as much as 750 gigabytes or more.

How hard drives work

Hard drives are digital recorders that use a recording technology related to an audio or video tape recorder: they use a thin coat of iron oxide (that's a fancy name for rust) or other thin-film metal media over a carrier to store millions of tiny magnetic bits. In a hard drive, the carrier is a polished metal platter.

A hard drive has several parts:

- One or more oxide-covered disks that hold the data.
- A motor that spins the disks at a constant rate of speed.
- A read/write head that hovers over each spinning platter and converts between magnetic bits and electronic signals.
- An arm for each disk that moves the read/write head to the physical location of each address on the disk.
- A sealed aluminum case that keeps dust, dirt, and moisture away from the disks and heads.
- A circuit board attached to the case that sends and receives instructions from the chipset and converts them to control information for the arms, and exchanges data between the read/write heads and the chipset.

There's an impressive amount of activity going on inside the case. The disks are rotating at up to 160 rotations per second or more, and the arms carrying the heads can change position hundreds of times per second as they move from one part of a disk to another. Unfortunately, you must to take my word for this because opening the case would contaminate the platters and heads, and effectively destroy the data stored on that drive. Figure 9.1 is a photo supplied by a drive manufacturer that shows a hard drive with its cover removed.

When the drive receives an instruction from the CPU, that instruction includes the address where the program or data file is stored. The logic circuits on the drive's circuit board translate that information into the physical location on one or more of the disks and instructs the arm to move the read/write heads to each location. When a head reaches its target location, it reads the data stored at that address or writes new data.

FIGURE 9.1

The read/write heads inside the drive are at the end of the arms.

Photo courtesy Seagate Technology

If you examine a hard drive, you may notice that the screws holding the case together require a special screwdriver, and some of the screws might be covered with labels that say "Warranty void if this label is removed." The drive manufacturers are serious about discouraging users from opening up a case. Don't take this as a challenge — you really will destroy the drive and lose all your files if you try to open it.

The disk drive uses tracks (concentric circles around each disk) and sectors (short segments of each track) to define addresses (see Figure 9.2). Before the drive leaves the factory, the manufacturer performs a low-level format routine that sets the physical locations of each track and sector. When you (or the computer maker) install the drive in a computer, you must run a second, high-level formatting routine that sets the file structure. The section Formatting and Partitioning a Drive later in this chapter offers more information about this.

Most drives have a separate head for each platter surface (front and back, or top and bottom), so the number of heads is double the number of platters.

The other unit of measure related to disk drives is a *cylinder*. You can think of each cylinder slicing through all the platters inside the drive, although it's purely a way to calculate the capacity of the drive, so there aren't any physical cylinders involved. The computer's BIOS uses the number of cylinders and the number of heads (one for each surface) to determine the physical location of each data address.

FIGURE 9.2

The dark circle is a track; the light gray block indicates a sector.

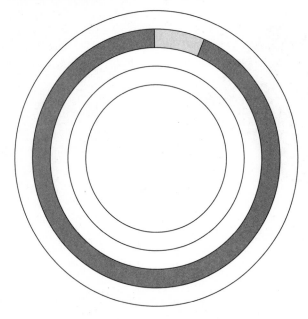

Choosing a hard drive

There are three reasons to buy a new hard drive:

- As part of a new computer
- As a replacement for a drive that has failed
- As an additional drive to increase your computer's storage capacity

In a new computer, you can be confident that the drive is fully compatible with the rest of the computer, so the only important thing to decide is the drive's capacity. You can never have too much storage space inside your computer, so a bigger drive is usually a better choice. But remember that you can always add a second drive to your desktop computer when the first one fills up, and the cost per megabyte a year or two from now will almost certainly be less than it is today.

If you're buying a laptop computer, look for the largest capacity that you can afford because you can't add a second drive inside the computer.

When you're replacing a damaged drive or adding a second (or third, or...) drive to an existing computer, the new drive's interface should be compatible with the motherboard (that is, if your motherboard only has IDE sockets, you must use an IDE drive; if the motherboard includes SATA sockets, you can use an SATA drive). Unless you really need an enormous capacity, look for the sweet spot that offers the lowest cost per bit. For example, you might find three drives on sale at your local retailer: a 100GB drive for $60, a 250GB drive for $90, and a 400GB drive for $175. In this case, the 250GB drive is the best choice.

Hard drives are bigger, faster, and more reliable than they were just a few years ago, and it's a safe bet that next year's models will be even better. All the major brands sell excellent quality products that should meet the needs of most users.

Size

The type of computer dictates the physical size of the hard drive. Drives for desktop computers are 4 inches wide and about 5.75 inches deep. Most desktop drives are 1 inch high, but some high-capacity drives with more platters inside are 1.63 inches high. Because these drives fit the same drive bays as a 3.5-inch floppy disk drive, you might see desktop drives described as 3.5-inch drives.

Most laptop computers use smaller drives that are 2.75 inches wide by 3.94 inches deep. The most common laptop drives are 0.75 inches (19 mm) high, but some very compact computers might use drives that are only 0.67 inches (17 mm), 0.49 inches (12.5 mm) or even 0.37 inches (9.5 mm) high. Based on the size of the platters inside the drive, these are known as 2.5-inch drives. Figure 9.3 shows the relative sizes of a laptop drive and a desktop drive.

Even smaller hard drives also exist, for use in sub-notebook computers, mobile telephones, and other portable devices. These tiny drives are not used as internal drives inside personal computers, but you might find one that fits a laptop computer's PC Card socket as a removable storage device.

Data capacity

The capacity of a hard drive depends on the number of platters inside the drive, the physical size of each platter, and the density of the data stored on the platters. As magnetic storage technology has improved, the maximum amount of data that a platter (and therefore a drive) can hold has increased, and the cost of storage has dropped.

Unfortunately, this increase in capacity has happened more quickly than the BIOS companies had expected. Because of the way the BIOS specifies addresses, there's a practical limit to the number of cylinders that it can use, even if the number of cylinders on the drive is greater than that maximum. In order to overcome this limit, you may have to either update the BIOS or use special translation software supplied with the drive. If the computer shows a significantly smaller capacity than you expect, look in the Support section of the drive manufacturer's Web site for instructions for bypassing the size barrier.

> **NOTE**   Don't let the difference between decimal kilobytes (equal to 1,000 bytes) and binary kilobytes (equal to 1,024 bytes) confuse you. Some drive manufacturers use the decimal capacity, but Windows and the BIOS utility reports that same capacity in binary, so a 200GB (decimal) drive might appear to have only about 180GB.

FIGURE 9.3

Laptop drives (right) are smaller than drives for desktop computers (left).

Speed

The specifications for a disk drive usually include several speed ratings; the two most important values are the average *seek time* needed for the drive to move a head from one address to another and the rotational speed of the platters.

Seek time is important because it reflects the amount of time needed for the CPU to request and receive data from the drive. Fast as it is, a drive with a seek time of nine milliseconds (ms) is exchanging data with a CPU that can perform millions of processes in that time. So a faster average seek time makes a huge contribution to the computer's overall performance.

As the name suggests, rotational speed is the rate at which the platters spin inside the drive, expressed in rotations per minute. The most common rotation speeds for new drives are 5400 RPM, 7200 RPM, and 9600 RPM, although some high-performance drives offer speeds up to 15,000 RPM. If you transfer a drive from an older computer, you might find one as slow as 3600 RPM, but those drives are probably at the end of their useful lives. Faster rotation is better, especially in servers and other high-demand systems, but it might not always be noticeable in home and office computers.

Cache buffer

The *cache buffer* is a RAM chip built into the disk drive circuitry that it uses as a buffer between the fast CPU and chipset and the relatively slow drive. It typically holds copies of the data that the drive has just transferred to the CPU or from the CPU to the buffer most recently, and one or more sectors adjacent to the one that moved most recently.

Even a small cache buffer improves the performance of a drive, but increasing the size of a buffer doesn't always provide a significant additional improvement. A 2MB buffer is enough for most single-user computer applications except games, streaming video, and multimedia editing, and an 8MB buffer should be entirely adequate for everything but high-usage servers. The difference in cost between a small cache and a larger one is often insignificant.

IDE, SATA, and SCSI Interfaces

The hard drive exchanges data with the CPU and chipset through a socket on the motherboard or on a plug-in expansion card. Most current computer models use either the IDE (Integrated Device Electronics) interface or the newer SATA (Serial ATA) interface. Some servers and older desktop computers might use the SCSI (Small Computer Systems Interface) system, but they are not common in new desktop and laptop machines.

 For more information about the CPU, chipset, motherboard, and expansion cards, go to Chapter 4.

IDE

For many years, the most common type in desktop and laptop systems has been the IDE interface. IDE is a parallel interface that transfers 16 bits (two 8-bit bytes) at a time, using control circuits located on each drive. The IDE standard is also called ATA (Advanced Technology Attachment), PATA (Parallel ATA) and EIDE (Enhanced IDE). Figure 9.4 shows a pair of IDE sockets.

The computer's motherboard normally has two IDE sockets that can accept cables from hard drives, CD or DVD drives, and other types of mass storage. Each IDE socket can support two disk drives or other IDE devices through a single cable, usually identified in the BIOS as Master and Slave. The position of a jumper on each drive identifies it as either a Master or a Slave. Figure 9.5 shows the connectors on an IDE drive. Table 9.1 lists the signals on each pin in an IDE connector.

FIGURE 9.4

This motherboard has two IDE sockets. The smaller connector at the bottom is for floppy disk drives.

IDE sockets

Connector for floppy disk drives

FIGURE 9.5

IDE drives use jumpers to identify themselves as Master or Slave.

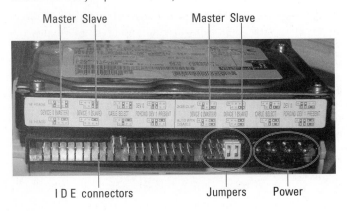

Master Slave   Master Slave

I D E connectors   Jumpers   Power

TABLE 9.1

IDE Connector Pins

Pin #	Signal Function	Pin #	Signal Function
1	Reset	2	Ground
3	Data 7	4	Data 8
5	Data 6	6	Data 9
7	Data 5	8	Data 10
9	Data 4	10	Data 11
11	Data 3	12	Data 12
13	Data 2	14	Data 13
15	Data 1	16	Data 14
17	Data 0	18	Data 15
19	Ground	20	Key
21	DMARQ	22	Ground
23	DIOW-	24	Ground
25	DIOR-	26	Ground
27	IORDY	28	CSEL
29	DMARK-	30	Ground
31	INTRQ	32	IOCS16-
33	DA1	34	PDIAG-
35	DA0	36	DA2
37	CS1FX-	38	CS3FX-
39	DASP-	40	Ground

SATA

The SATA interface has been introduced as a replacement for IDE, but the computer industry is still in a transitional period when both interfaces are widely used. Most new motherboards have sockets for both types.

Instead of the 40-pin IDE connector and cable, SATA drives use a 7-pin data connector. Each SATA socket supports just one drive, so there's no need for jumpers to identify Masters and Slaves. Table 9.2 lists the SATA pin connections.

TABLE 9.2

SATA Connector Pins

Pin No.	Signal Name	Description
1	GND	Ground
2	A+	Transmit +
3	A-	Transmit −
4	GND	Ground
5	B-	Receive -
6	B+	Receive +
7	GND	Ground

Figure 9.6 shows the connectors on an SATA drive.

FIGURE 9.6

SATA drives don't need jumpers.

Photo courtesy Western Digital

SATA is a serial interface, with a new design that offers several advantages over the older IDE drives:

■ SATA drives are easier to install because they don't require jumpers.

■ SATA drives don't produce as much heat.

■ SATA drives use smaller cables that don't interfere with airflow inside the computer case.

■ SATA drives can support faster data transfer than IDE.

That faster data transfer doesn't make much difference yet. In today's computers, IDE and SATA drives with the same specifications have similar performance. Up until now, there has been no reason to provide chipsets that could support a faster data transfer rate than the IDE drive design could handle. But SATA eliminates that bottleneck, so the next generation of motherboards and chipsets will support faster data transfer.

SCSI

The SCSI standard is a parallel interface that uses a single controller and a daisy chain of up to 15 internal or external devices. SCSI devices can include input and output devices (such as scanners) as well as storage devices. Each device in a SCSI chain has a unique ID number. A new, faster Serial Attached SCSI (SAS) standard is also available.

SCSI drives permit faster data transfer, and the interface can support more devices than IDE or SATA, so they're widely used in servers. However, they're not often used in modern PCs for home or office use. Most desktop and laptop computers don't work with SCSI drives unless you install a SCSI controller in an expansion slot or a PC Card socket.

Installing a new hard drive

Adding or replacing a hard drive inside your computer might seem like a major project, but it's not as difficult as it might appear. The drive bays in a desktop system have been designed to facilitate easy access.

Jumper settings

Each IDE controller can support two drives through the same cable: a Master and a Slave. Remember Figures 9.5 and 9.6? Before you install an IDE drive, you must configure the drive as either a Master or a Slave by moving the jumpers on the edge of the drive to the correct set of pins. SATA drives don't require any jumper settings.

Most drives have labels that show the different jumper settings that apply to that drive. If your drive has no label, consult the manual or the manufacturer's Web site.

The boot drive is normally the Master drive on the Primary IDE cable. However, each of the other drives in your system can be either a Master or a Slave, as long as you don't create a Slave drive on a cable that doesn't have a Master drive.

If you're replacing an existing drive, the new drive must have the same setting; if you're adding a drive, you need to know how the drives that are already in place are configured.

There are a couple of ways to identify a drive's settings. The easiest way is simply to look at the jumpers on the edge of the drive and compare them to the label on the top or bottom of the drive. Different brands of drives use different jumper arrangements, so there's no universal set of standard jumper settings.

The software CDs supplied with most new hard drives include a utility program that scans your existing drives and identifies their settings. If you don't have a CD, you can download the software from your drive manufacturer's Web site.

As an alternative, you can use the BIOS Settings utility to tell you which drives are assigned to each IDE channel and which are Masters and Slaves. This can often be easier than removing each drive to check the jumpers. To view the assignments, follow these steps:

1. **Restart the computer and press the appropriate key to open the BIOS Settings utility.**

2. **Go to the screen that shows all of the drives in this computer.** Depending on the type of BIOS, this might be the Main Menu, the Standard CMOS Features screen, the Drive Settings screen, or it might have some other name, but it has a list that includes:

   Primary Master

   Primary Slave

   Secondary Master

   Secondary Slave

   Or possibly:

   IDE Channel 1 Master

   IDE Channel 1 Slave

   IDE Channel 2 Master

   IDE Channel 2 Slave

3. **The list identifies the type of drive connected to each channel, including hard drives, the CD or DVD drives, and other IDE devices.**

If you're replacing an existing drive, find that drive on the list in the BIOS utility and note whether it's a Master or a Slave. Set the jumpers on the new drive to match the old one.

If you're installing a new drive, look for a channel with no drive in place. The BIOS utility might show a blank space for one or more channels, or it might say "No Drive Detected" or something similar. Note whether the unassigned space is a Master or a Slave and set the jumpers on the new drive to fill that space.

When you have set the jumpers on your drive, press Esc or F10 to leave the BIOS utility without making any changes. Let the computer restart and immediately use the Windows shut down routine to turn it off.

In a desktop

It's always helpful to read the installation instructions supplied with a new drive or any other computer part. If you discover that the manufacturer's instructions contradict the instructions in this book, follow the maker's advice.

TIP   Seagate (one of the major drive manufacturers) offers several videos that provide detailed step-by-step instructions for installing a disk drive. Even if you're using some other brand of drive, these video guides can help you understand how to do it. Look for the Seagate Online Multimedia Install Guide at `www.seagate.com/support/howto/install_guide`.

To install a disk drive into a desktop or tower case, follow these steps:

1. **Turn off the computer and unplug it.**

2. **Remove the cover from the case.** If you have an anti-static grounding wrist strap, put it on and ground yourself to the case.

3. **If you're replacing an existing drive, disconnect the cables from that drive and remove the drive.**

4. **Find an empty drive bay.** If you're installing a hard drive, look for an internal drive bay; for a drive with removable media, use one of the spaces in the front panel. Choose a space that allows air to flow around the drive, and make sure your data and power cables can easily reach the connectors on the new drive.

5. **Examine the mounting arrangement of the drive bay you plan to fill.** In some cases, you slide the drive into the bay, but in others, the drive mounts in a removable frame.

6. **Use at least four of the screws supplied with the drive to attach the drive to the frame.** If necessary, mount the frame inside the computer.

7. **Connect a power cable from the power supply to the power connector on the drive.** If you're installing an SATA drive and the power supply doesn't have SATA connectors, you need a power cable adapter (available from a computer retailer).

8. **If you're adding a Slave to a channel that already has a Master, find the unused connector on the data cable already connected to the Master and plug it into the new drive.**

9. **If you're installing a Master drive on the Secondary Channel, use the data cable supplied with the drive or buy a round replacement IDE cable.** Plug one of the data connectors into the drive. The cable connectors probably have labels that show which ones go to the Master, the Slave, and the motherboard.

10. **If it's not already connected, plug the other end of the cable (the motherboard connector) into the empty IDE or SATA connector on the motherboard.**

11. **Turn on the computer and immediately press the key that runs the BIOS Settings utility.**

12. **In the BIOS utility, move to the page that lists the IDE and SATA channels.**

13. **Choose the channel for the drive you just installed.** A new screen appears with details about the drive.

14. **Select the Auto-Detect line in the menu and press Enter.** This instructs the utility to identify the drive and reads the details into the BIOS.

15. **If the BIOS doesn't recognize the drive, make sure you have connected the cables and set the jumpers correctly.**

16. When the BIOS has accepted the drive details, use Esc or F10 to save the changes to the BIOS and restart your computer.

17. Replace the cover.

18. **Run the Drive Installation program supplied with the new drive to partition and format the drive.** There's more information about partitioning and formatting later in this chapter.

In a laptop

Installing a drive in a laptop is a different process because the computer has only one drive and it usually plugs directly into a connector on the motherboard. However, every laptop make and model is different, so there's no common method for opening the case and removing or installing a drive. Look on the computer maker's Web site for step-by-step instructions.

The designs of different laptop computers vary widely; in some computers, the disk drive is easy to remove and replace, but in others it's extremely complicated. If the instructions on the Web site or the Service Manual sound like they are excessively difficult, let a professional handle the project for you.

Any time you work on a laptop computer, remember to disconnect external power and remove the battery before you try to open the case.

Read the instructions supplied with the drive for information about jumper settings. The single drive inside a laptop computer is always the Master, but some drives still provide jumpers in case you want to install the same drive in a desktop machine (using an adapter that converts the laptop pin arrangement to the ones used in a desktop drive bay).

Don't try to remove or replace a laptop drive without specific instructions. In many computers, you might have to push, pull, or squeeze the drive or a mounting bracket in a way that's not obvious. If you have to force the drive to move it, you're probably doing something wrong.

Formatting and partitioning a drive

In addition to the low-level formatting that sets the locations of tracks and sectors on the drive's platters, a disk drive also requires a separate high-level formatting process that creates the drive's file structure and writes the boot files onto certain sectors. Because several different files structures are possible, the drive makers leave high-level formatting to the computer builder or user who installs the drive. In most cases, *formatting a drive* means performing a high-level format.

A new drive always requires formatting, and formatting can also be a last-resort method for repairing a drive with corrupted sectors or files. This corruption might be caused by a virus or by random corruption that happens for no apparent reason. Remember that formatting a drive can destroy all of the files stored on that drive, so it's always good practice to try other recovery techniques first. Some computer users (and some incompetent tech support advisors) suggest reformatting as a quick and easy way to fix an unknown problem, but there's almost always another, less destructive approach.

Partitions are separate sections of a physical drive that appear to Windows as different drives. For example, a disk drive with two partitions might show up in Windows as the D: drive and the E: drive. You can split a new drive into partitions when you format it.

As you know, Windows holds individual programs and blocks of data as files, which it stores in folders or directories. The file system is the structure that specifies the format of file names, and the way a drive stores and organizes those files. The operating system uses the file system to find and read files and folders. In Windows XP, the preferred file system is NTFS ([Windows] NT File System), but it can also recognize the older FAT16 (16-bit file allocation table) and FAT32 (32-bit FAT) systems.

The size of a partition was limited in some older file systems, so it was sometimes necessary to split large physical drives into two or more logical drives. This is not a problem with NTFS, so most users might want to create just one partition on each drive. However, separate partitions might be useful when two or more users share a single computer as a method for isolating each user's data files. Other users like to keep programs on one partition and data files on another, and still other use separate partitions to load more than one operating system (such as Windows and Linux) on the same drive.

The formatting tools supplied with new hard drives and the utility included in Windows XP offer all three files systems, but the NTFS system is almost always the best choice. The exceptions might be computers that can load more than one operating system (through a startup menu).

All of the major drive manufacturers supply formatting software with new drives unless they're sold in bulk OEM (original equipment manufactuer) packages. If you don't have a software CD for your drive, you can download the formatting program and detailed instructions from the manufacturer's Web site.

If you're adding a new drive to an existing system, you can use the Disk Management program supplied with Windows XP to format and partition the drive instead of the program supplied with the drive.

To format a drive with the Windows Disk Management tool, follow these steps:

1. **Complete the drive installation process described earlier in this chapter.**

2. **From the Start Menu, select Programs ⇨ Administrative Tools ⇨ Computer Management.** You can also open Administrative Tools from the Control Panel.

3. **Choose the Disk Management item at the bottom of the list in the left pane of the Computer Management window.** The screen shown in Figure 9.7 appears.

4. **Right-click the drive you want to format in either the list at the top right of the window or the bar graph in the lower right section.**

5. **Choose Format from the pop-up menu.**

6. **Follow the instructions as the program walks you through the formatting process.**

FIGURE 9.7

The Windows XP Disk Management tool can format and partition hard disks.

Disk Management

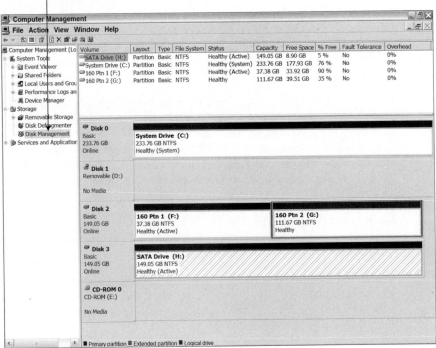

Floppy Disks

Floppy disks, also known as diskettes, are a form of removable magnetic media that used to be the universal form of storage and distribution for personal computer programs and files. They are gradually disappearing from new computers because of their limited capacity. In today's computers, rewritable compact discs fill the niche that used to be occupied by floppy disks.

Diskettes are called *floppy disks* because the actual storage media inside the envelope or plastic case are flexible plastic disks covered with magnetic material. The first personal computers used 5.25-inch floppy disks that were enclosed in flexible envelopes. Through the 1990s, these were gradually replaced by 3.5-inch diskettes in rigid plastic cases. Figure 9.8 shows both types of floppy disk.

Floppy disk drives use the same magnetic storage technology and track-and-sector structure as hard drives, but obviously, they're limited to the two surfaces of the disk. The HD letters on 3.5-inch diskettes stand for *high density*, which identifies the capacity of the disk as 1.44MB. Diskettes without the HD mark have a capacity of 720 kilobytes.

FIGURE 9.8

Larger 5.25-inch diskettes (top) have been rendered obsolete by 3.5-inch disks, which in turn are almost entirely replaced by rewritable CDs and other storage media.

5.25 inch diskette

PC card

CD

3.5 inch disk

The maximum capacity of a 5.25 disk was 1.2 MB, but some older disks could only hold 360 kilobytes. Windows has inherited the practice of assigning letters to disk drives from the earlier DOS (Disk Operating System) operating systems. Because many early personal computers had space for two floppy disk drives, the letters A and B have always been reserved for floppy disk drives. Drive A: was assigned to the boot floppy (the floppy disk that contained the operating system) and C: to the first hard drive.

Floppy disk drives connect to the computer's motherboard through a dedicated 34-pin connector that can support one or two drives. Some older floppy drives use a card-edge connector rather than a multi-pin plug and socket, so the ribbon cable that connects the drive to the motherboard might have both types of connectors. Some newer floppy disk cables are round rather than flat, and they might not include the card-edge connectors.

Floppy Disk Drive (FDD) cables normally have a twist inside the cable between the first and second set of drive connectors. This twist changes the wiring connected to the seven pins that identify each drive as either the A: drive or the B: drive. Therefore, the A: drive must connect to one of the connectors near the end of the cable. In the unlikely event that your computer has a B: drive, it should use a connector on the other side of the twist (the twist may not be visible inside a round cable, but those cables usually have prominent labels on each connector).

Floppy disk drives are almost obsolete. Many new computers, especially laptops, come without a floppy disk drive, but the newest motherboard models still have an FDD connector, so it's still possible to add a drive if you need one. You can probably live without a floppy drive, unless you have some old floppies that contain your only copies of some important files or programs. If you need to add a floppy disk drive to your system, go ahead and install a new internal drive. Or as an alternative, consider using an external drive that connects through the USB interface rather than an internal drive. This allows you to share a single drive among more than one computer, and you don't have to mess with the internal drive bays and cables.

CAUTION Over time, floppy disks can accumulate dust and dirt, develop bad sectors, or fail completely. They are not a reliable long-term storage medium. If you have some old floppy disks that contain valuable files, you should copy them to a hard drive or a CD for long-term storage.

TIP If you can't read a floppy disk, try rapping the edge of the disk on a table to loosen any dust or dirt. If that doesn't work, try another drive; the first one might be out of alignment or have dirty heads. If your drive frequently fails to read disks, pull the drive out and throw it away; you can buy a new internal floppy disk drive for less than $10.

CDs and DVDs

Compact discs (CDs) have replaced floppies as the universal medium for distributing programs and sharing data on personal computers. A CD drive (or a DVD drive that can also read and write CDs) is a standard part of every new personal computer. DVDs (Digital Video Discs or Digital Versatile Discs) are a newer type of optical storage media that are becoming common in new systems.

Both CDs and DVDs were originally designed as media for distributing commercially recorded entertainment. CDs began as media for music and other audio recordings, and DVDs for movies and other video programs. But they're both digital media, so it's just as easy to use them to carry computer programs and data files instead of rap singers or old sitcoms. As a side benefit, you can also use your computer's CD or DVD drive to play entertainment disks. The data formats are different for audio, video, and data, but the basic principles are similar.

The first CD drives for computers were CD-ROM drives — Compact Disc, Read-Only Memory — that could read CDs but couldn't create new ones. Today, almost all CD drives can also store data on recordable discs. Recordable discs come in two forms: CD-Rs (Compact Disc, Recordable) that can write data just once, and CD-RWs (Compact Disc, ReWritable) that can be erased and rewritten.

Data (or music or digital video) is stored on CDs and DVDs as pits in the surface of the disc, arranged in a spiral. The presence or absence of each pit corresponds to a digital data bit. The drive shines a very tightly focused light beam (a laser) at the disc and uses a photosensor to detect each pit. Because they use light to read the discs, both CDs and DVDs are known as *optical media*.

DVDs use a more advanced laser technology than CDs. The design and performance of the laser, the construction of the discs, and the format of the data are all more complex than the older CD technology. For most of us, the practical difference between CDs and DVDs is the amount of data that each disc can hold. Most data CDs have a capacity of about 700MB (or about 80 minutes of audio); DVDs can hold about 4.7GB today, but as the design evolves, the capacity of a single disc will continue to increase.

The original audio CDs were designed to spin at a speed that was adequate to convert the digital data on the discs to analog sound. There was no reason to increase the speed, because the music wouldn't sound any better if you moved it from the disc to a buffer more quickly. But when you're making your own recordings, and when you're reading and writing computer data, spinning the drive more quickly can reduce the time needed to complete the job. So CD drives for computers (and stand-alone audio CD recorders) use faster motors than audio CD players.

A faster CD drive can make a dramatic difference: at 1X (audio speed), it takes over an hour to fill a 700MB disc. At 8X (eight times faster), you can fill the same disc in nine minutes. And at 48X, the time to fill the disc is just 90 seconds. However, it's essential to use CD media designed for high-speed recording; look on the disc packaging to find the range of speeds that the discs can support, and use the options settings menu in your CD burning program to set a speed at or below the drive's maximum speed.

> **TIP** If you have a choice, don't try to record CDs at the highest possible speed your drive and media allows. Dropping the speed by about 10–20 percent often provides much more reliable performance, and reduces or eliminates the number of ruined CDs.

CD and DVD drives use the same data interfaces as hard disk drives: IDE, SATA, and SCSI. To install a new drive, follow these steps:

1. **Turn off the computer.**

2. **Remove the cover from the case.** If you have an anti-static wrist strap, put it on and ground yourself to the case.

3. **Remove the faceplate from an unused external drive bay.**

4. **Set the jumper on the drive to either Master or Slave (if it's an IDE drive).**

5. **Mount the drive in the bay.** Line up the face of the drive with the front of the computer case and use the screws supplied with the drive to secure the drive to the frame.

6. **Connect the power and data cables to the new drive.** If it's not already connected, plug the other end of the data cable into the motherboard. For best performance, connect the new drive to the Secondary IDE socket (the one that is *not* connected to the Primary hard drive).

7. **Turn on the computer and immediately press the key that starts the BIOS Settings utility.**

8. **Move to the BIOS Settings Utility's screen that lists the IDE and SATA drives and find the listing for the new drive.**

9. **Choose the Auto-Detect option.** The utility should identify the drive as a CD or DVD drive.

10. **Use the Esc key or the F10 key to close the BIOS utility and save your new settings.** Windows restarts.

11. **Windows should automatically detect the new drive.**

12. **If a software CD was supplied with the drive, insert the disk in the drive and run the Setup program.**

Other Removable Storage Media

Before recordable CDs became the common standard for removable storage of large files and programs, several other types of removable media were widely used in personal computers. These included several kinds of magnetic tape cartridges, and proprietary magnetic disk media such as the 100MB Zip disk shown in Figure 9.9.

FIGURE 9.9

Zip disks are smaller and more expensive than recordable CD-ROMs.

Today, these storage formats, and the drives that use them, are less common than they were in the 1990s, except for highly specialized archival storage applications. Zip drives and disks — which were promoted by Iomega, the company that produces them, as the replacement for floppy disks — have turned out to be far more expensive than recordable CDs. In addition, many users have reported drive failures that make the disks unreadable.

If you have some existing tapes or disks in one of these formats, you may need to find a drive to read them. Some are still in production, and others are available through surplus places and online auctions such as eBay.

Most of the drives that can read these old or uncommon types of storage media use either a SCSI interface or an IDE interface. If your drive has a SCSI interface but your computer does not, install an inexpensive SCSI controller card into one of the PCI expansion cards in the computer's motherboard.

USB Drives

The Universal Serial Bus (USB) standard is a specification for an I/O connection that can support many kinds of peripheral devices, ranging from simple things like mice and joysticks through keyboards and modems to complex devices like disk drives and other storage systems. Most personal computers and motherboards made since about 2000 include one or more USB ports.

USB was intended to overcome the proliferation of connectors that covered the back of most desktop computers and filled the edges of laptop machines. Before USB, most computers needed a serial port or two, a parallel port for the printer, PS/2 connectors for the keyboard and mouse, Ethernet ports for networking, and audio connectors for speakers, plus other, more specialized connectors for other input and output devices and services. USB replaced all of these with a standard connector that could support all of these services and more.

USB devices are supposed to be *Plug and Play*, meaning that the computer recognizes a USB device as soon as you plug it in (Plug and Play doesn't always work, but that's the goal). They're also *hot swappable*, so you can connect or disconnect a USB device without turning off the computer. To make connections even easier, the same cable that carries signal between USB devices and the computer can also supply power to those devices.

Some USB devices start working as soon as you connect them to the computer, but others don't work unless you have already installed the device driver or other software supplied with the device. Before you connect a USB device to your computer for the first time, read the installation instructions supplied with the device.

Most computers that have USB ports have at least two of them. Because each port can connect to a hub, it's possible to connect several separate devices to each port. The original designers wanted USB ports to support up to 127 devices, but the practical limit is closer to seven unless they're all relatively simple items like mice (not that you'd ever want 127 mice connected to the same computer).

Along with all those keyboards, mice, printers, sound controllers, and so on, USB can also connect one or more storage devices to a computer. These can be stand-alone disk drives, pocket-sized flash drives, or storage built into digital cameras and audio recorders.

Although every computer should have at least one internal disk drive to hold the operating system and other important software, separate USB drives can be a convenient way to increase the computer's total storage capacity. They make it simple to share data between computers at home and at school or between home and office, to back up your data, or to transfer data from one computer to another.

When a USB drive is connected to a computer, Windows detects the drive automatically (although it might take a minute or two), and treats it just like any other drive. It appears in the My Computer window and other drive directories with a temporary drive letter, with all the same features and functions as an internal disk drive.

Connecting a USB flash drive

USB flash drives are small storage devices that use electronic memory blocks (in integrated circuits) to hold up to several megabytes of data. Because they have no moving parts, flash drives can read and write data much more quickly than a mechanical disk drive.

Flash drives can be handy for carrying copies of important documents and other files wherever you go — your resume, family photos, even the manuscript of your novel-in-progress. The actual storage media are thumbnail-sized integrated circuits, which come inside a huge variety of packages, including pens, pocket-sized cases like the one in Figure 9.10, and thousands of novelty shapes, including small, plastic, glow-in-the-dark ducks (see Figure 9.11). Other USB flash drives double as tags for key chains or charms for necklaces.

FIGURE 9.10

Portable USB flash drives come in many forms, from simple and functional . . .

Photo courtesy Samsung Semiconductor, Inc

FIGURE 9.11

. . . to completely silly.

Photo courtesy www.i-duck.co.uk

To connect a USB flash drive to your computer, simply plug the USB connector on the drive into a USB port, or use a USB cable to connect the drive to the computer.

External USB disk drives

External USB disk drives are standard IDE or SATA drives mounted inside separate cases that can connect to your computer through a USB port (some drives can also use FireWire/IEEE 1394 connections in addition to USB). They are sold both as self-contained packages that include the drive and the case, and separate USB enclosures with mounting hardware and cable connections for loose drives. Unlike the smaller USB flash drives, these full-sized disk drives require a separate power connection.

CROSS-REF Chapter 14 covers more details about using FireWire and USB interfaces.

Halfway between full-sized disk drives and tiny flash drives, pocket-sized hard drives like the one shown in Figure 9.12 use 1-inch disk drives and retractable cables. They're slower than flash drives, but they often have space for more data.

FIGURE 9.12

Pocket-sized USB hard drives can hold a substantial amount of data in a small package.

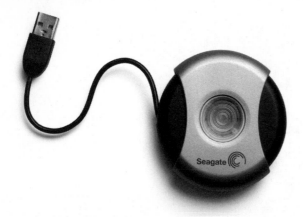

Photo courtesy Seagate Technology

Other Portable Drives

Flash drives and tiny hard drives are also available in packages that use other methods to connect to your computer. CompactFlash cards, Secure Digital cards, Sony Memory Sticks, and Microdrives are just a few of the forms that digital cameras and audio recorders use to store files. Other portable drives are mounted inside PC Cards that fit the PCMCIA sockets on most laptop systems. Like USB drives, Windows treats these media as removable drives with temporary drive letters, so you can also use them to read and write any other data files that you want to move between computers.

Some laptop computers come with built-in readers for flash media. For other computers, add-on readers are available as separate USB devices and as units that fit into an external drive bay in a desktop or laptop computer. Most readers have sockets for several popular types of flash media.

Summary

Your computer uses disk drives and other storage media to hold programs and data files when the computer is not reading or writing them. These include hard disk drives that store data on spinning platters covered with magnetic material, compact discs and DVDs that use a laser to read data encoded as pits over reflective material, floppy disks, and other forms of removable media.

All of these storage devices (except floppy disk drives) use IDE, SATA, SCSI, or USB interfaces to exchange data with the chipset and the CPU. The BIOS identifies each type of drive and sets the appropriate timing and signaling options.

Chapter 10

Understanding Graphics Controllers

Graphics controllers (also called video cards) are plug-in circuit boards that convert instructions from your computer's CPU into picture elements (pixels) that a video display (the monitor) uses to create images. The graphics controller is a secondary, specialized computer that has many of the same major elements as any other computer: a processor, a chipset, RAM, and an output interface. The video card usually connects to the computer's motherboard either through a dedicated AGP or PCI Express socket. In computers that use more than one monitor, additional graphics controllers can use one or more of the PCI sockets.

Some motherboards (especially the ones used in laptop computers) have an integrated graphics controller. These systems don't require a separate video card, but motherboards for desktop systems with on-board graphics controllers allow a user to disable the on-board controller and replace it with a separate card.

A graphics processor updates millions of pixels at least 60 times per second. It would be possible to perform all of this activity on the CPU and the motherboard, but that's less practical than using a separate processor; producing a high-resolution, full-color video image takes a lot of processing resources, so a graphics processor integrated into the computer's CPU would be a constant drain on the CPU's ability to do other work. Moving control of the video display away from the CPU allows users to choose a video card that matches their own particular requirements, without the need to pay for more performance than they need.

This chapter explains how a graphics controller converts data from the CPU to an analog or digital image, how to choose the best controller for your system, how to use Windows and other software to adjust the appearance of the image and the performance of the monitor, and how and why to use more than one monitor.

In order to understand how a graphics controller operates, it's helpful to think about the controller card and the video monitor as two parts of a single subsystem within the computer. Part of the job happens on the controller card and part within the monitor, but it's quite possible to move the controller into the monitor; that's how remote terminals work. For present purposes, this chapter treats them as two separate devices and talks about controllers in this chapter and monitors in the next.

What a Video Card Does

In the early days of personal computers, the graphics controller received nothing but text elements—letters, numbers, and a few other odd characters and symbols—so it didn't have much work to do. If you've been working with computers for a while, you might remember those old monochrome monitors that displayed everything in green or white or orange on a black background.

When color monitors and graphical user interfaces like Windows came along, the CPU suddenly had to handle a lot more graphics information. So *accelerators* were introduced that could offload much of that burden from the CPU. Instead of sending the graphics controller every detail of every pixel, an accelerator card already knew, for example, what many elements of a window looks like; the device driver would tell the accelerator, "Place a window in this location, with this information inside." The accelerator would then draw the window. This allowed the CPU to devote more of its time to other activities, while the video accelerator created images for the monitor far more quickly.

Today, Windows and other modern operating systems send much more complex data to the video subsystem, including text in a variety of typefaces, windows, icons and other graphic elements, still pictures, and moving images with thousands of shades of color and even the illusion of three dimensions on a flat screen. As the graphics controller has taken over more and more processing from the CPU, it has evolved into a second small computer system that assists the main processor. Graphics controllers have become a specialized part of the larger computer industry, dominated by a small handful of companies.

Figure 10.1 shows how a video controller moves graphic information from the computer's CPU to the display monitor. Like the computer's motherboard, the graphics card has a BIOS that contains instructions and timing information and also tests the card's inputs, outputs, and onboard memory in response to an instruction from the system BIOS. The graphics processor receives information from the computer's chipset and uses the BIOS settings to convert that information to a video image. After the operating system begins, the video device driver takes over control of the image from the BIOS.

If the controller is connected to an analog monitor, the video image passes through a digital-to-analog converter (a DAC or RAMDAC) on its way to the monitor. If the controller is connected to a digital monitor, the image goes directly to the monitor through a DV-I (digital video interactive) interface. Like the computer's CPU, the graphics controller uses RAM on the graphics card to hold incoming information from the CPU before the graphics processor can work on it and outbound images on the way to the monitor.

FIGURE 10.1

The structure of a graphics controller is similar to the overall operation of the computer.

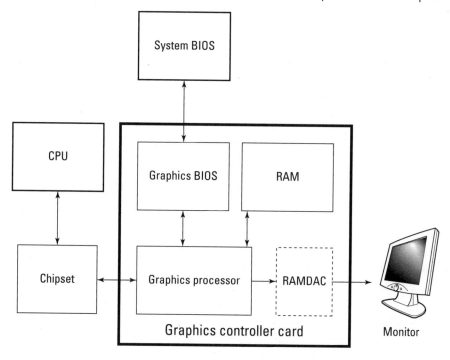

The monitor renews the on-screen image 60 or more times per second, but the graphics controller produces pixels more quickly than that, so the controller stores both the current image and the image under construction in part of the RAM mounted on the video card. The portion of video RAM that holds completed images is called the *frame buffer*.

Like the computer's CPU, video processors can handle data at very high speeds, which often produces a lot of heat on the surface of the processor chip. Therefore, most graphics controllers have heat sinks and fans to move heated air away from the surface of the printed circuit card. Unfortunately, the fans on many graphics cards are louder than CPU fans, so the video card is often one of the noisiest components inside the computer. If this is a problem in your office or home, you can replace the fan with a silent heat sink that uses copper fins or a heat pipe, like the ones made by Zalman and Thermaltake.

Selecting an Interface Type

Your computer's chipset supplies instructions and image data to the graphics controller through a dedicated AGP or PCI Express socket or one of the PCI sockets on the motherboard, or through.

Just about all recent motherboards include a video socket which can be either AGP or PCI Express, along with up to five PCI sockets. On almost all new motherboards, the video socket (AGP or PCI Express) is at the left of the PCI sockets as you face the back of the computer.

The latest computers, motherboards, and graphics controllers use the PCI Express interface, but the older AGP interface is still widely used. PCI graphics controllers (without the "Express" in the name) are much less common, but they are still available for users who want to add extra monitors to their systems. When you buy a new video card to support Windows Vista or some new and more demanding games, or because you want to use it with a new monitor with a very large screen, the new card must use the same kind of interface type as the one you want to replace, or it won't fit into the socket on your computer's motherboard.

CROSS-REF For more information about the chipset, see Chapter 6.

PCI

The PCI (Peripheral Component Interconnect) interface was created by Intel to define the system that connects expansion cards through sockets on the motherboard and a PCI controller to the computer's Southbridge chipset. The PCI bus can also support other devices and functions that are permanently attached to the motherboard, such as a USB controller or an on-board network interface. Data transfer between the chipset and the disk drives also moves through that same link from the Northbridge, so the link between Southbridge and Northbridge can become a major bottleneck in the computer's overall performance.

PCI cards and sockets have a total of 94 electrical contacts or *pins* (47 on each side of the card) on both sides of the plug-in circuit board, as shown in Figure 10.2. The locations of the key in the socket and the slots in the card edge identify the voltage used by each card.

By design, a video controller plugged into a PCI socket operates relatively slowly. The PCI bus moves 64 bits at a time between the expansion card and the motherboard, at speeds of 33 MHz, 66 MHz, or 133 MHz, depending on the device. This allows a maximum data transfer rate of up to 1GB per second, but of course, that's shared among all the devices connected to the PCI bus. In practice, the maximum sustained data transfer rate is less than 70MB per second. For typical home and office computing, that's fast enough to provide an excellent image, but it can be too slow to display images from video-intensive programs like games and high-definition movies on DVDs.

PCI video cards are also limited by the fact that the frame buffer ties up a substantial amount of the RAM on the card. This is not as big a problem today as it was ten years ago, when the maximum amount of RAM that could fit on a video card was about 8MB, of which at least 4MB would be used for the frame buffer. The remaining 4MB wasn't enough for complex 3-D moving images. Modern PCI video cards can hold as much as 256MB of RAM, so high-quality PCI video cards are widely available, but that data bottleneck to and from the Northbridge is still a potential problem.

FIGURE 10.2

A PCI expansion card has 47 electrical contacts on each side of the circuit board, and one or two positioning slots.

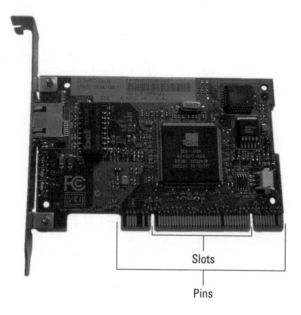

Slots

Pins

AGP

The Accelerated Graphics Port (AGP) specification was introduced in 1996 to overcome many of the limitations of using the PCI bus for a computer's video display. As Figure 10.3 shows, graphics controllers that use AGP sockets can operate more efficiently than PCI cards; this is because the AGP interface exchanges data with the Northbridge chipset, which is more than three times faster than the PCI interface, and because the interface doesn't have to share that data bus with other devices. AGP can also use part of the computer's system memory for processing video.

The AGP 1X specification moved data between the Northbridge and the video card at a maximum of 266MB per second. A year later, AGP 2X increased the maximum to 533MB per second. The current crop of AGP video cards support 4X and 8X, which kick the theoretical bandwidth up to more than 1GB per second and 2GB per second respectively. In practice, these numbers are somewhat greater than the actual performance of AGP 4X and 8X cards, but the actual number of bits moving through those cards is still extremely impressive.

AGP video cards are designed to be backward compatible, so an AGP 4X or 8X card works when you plug it into a motherboard with an AGP2 socket. The bandwidth is limited to the limits of the motherboard's AGP specification, but it will produce an image on your monitor.

FIGURE 10.3

The chipset sends data to an AGP card much more quickly than it sends data to a PCI card.

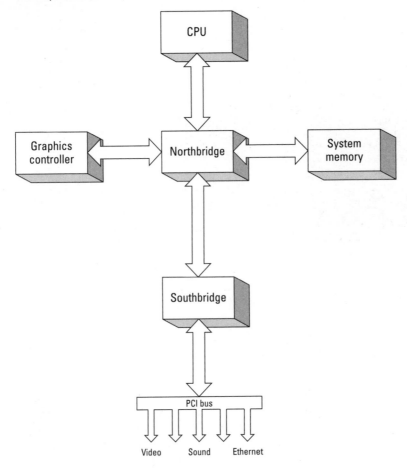

AGP cards and sockets have 132 pins, with a key gap between pins 21 and 26 that makes it easier to insert a card into a socket properly. A plastic latch on the end of the socket opposite the back of the computer holds an AGP card securely in place. Figure 10.4 shows an AGP video card.

FIGURE 10.4

AGP cards use a 132-pin edge-card connector.

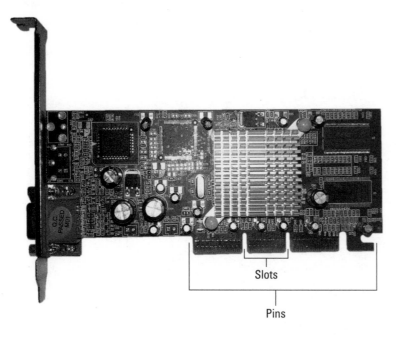

Slots

Pins

PCI Express

PCI Express is another, more recent approach to solving the I/O data bottleneck; PCI Express replaces the old shared parallel data bus (see Figure 10.5) with a set of dedicated serial, point-to-point *lanes* that can move data between a switch in the chipset and each PCI card, as shown in Figure 10.6. Because each PCI card has a direct connection to the chipset, the bandwidth isn't limited by the number of devices connected to a common connection.

Eventually, PCI Express cards will replace both PCI expansion cards and AGP video cards. Just as USB and FireWire connectors can replace many different external connectors on your computer, PCI Express may ultimately replace most of the internal I/O connectors on your motherboard.

FIGURE 10.5

Traditional PCI uses a shared parallel bus to transfer data.

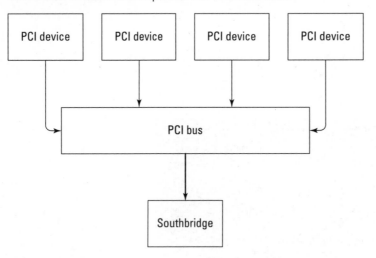

FIGURE 10.6

Each PCI Express lane can support 500MB per second, so an X16 video card can exchange 4GB per second in each direction.

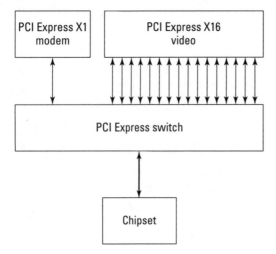

The number of lanes serving each PCI Express card is dictated by the amount of bandwidth it requires. So a device that doesn't need a fast connection (such as a 56 Kbps modem) might have only one lane in each direction (X1) for a maximum bandwidth of 250MB per second, while a video card would use many more lanes. PCI Express X16 video cards use 16 lanes to produce a useful bandwidth around 4GB per second.

As Figure 10.7 shows, PCI Express X16 video cards use 164-pin edge-card connectors and sockets. PCI Express cards with fewer lanes have fewer pins in their connectors.

FIGURE 10.7

PCI Express X16 cards have 164-pin card-edge connectors.

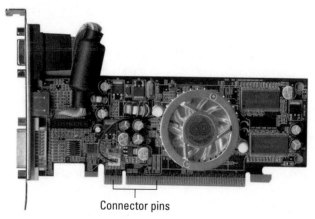

Connector pins

Photo courtesy Chaintech Corporation

As this is written, PCI Express video cards are the latest and greatest type of graphics controllers. They're faster than comparable AGP 8X cards, and they are the native design for most new high-end graphics controller cards. However, the difference between an AGP 8X card and a PCI Express X16 card may not make much difference when they're installed in today's motherboards (although any particular motherboard accepts only one type or the other). Both can be extremely fast and both work very well with anything short of a cutting-edge game or a very large monitor screen, but you may not notice the difference between one really fast video card and another card that's even faster than that. On the other hand, if you build your own computers and you expect to move the video card you buy today to a new motherboard two or three years from now, a PCI Express socket and card are the obvious choices.

Graphics Controller Performance

The performance of a video card is determined by several characteristics, including:

- Maximum screen resolution
- Bit depth (or color depth)
- Refresh rate
- Amount of memory
- Speed of the processor
- Bandwidth of the connection between the controller and the computer's chipset

Screen resolution

The resolution of a screen is based on the number of pixels it takes to fill the entire screen. When you increase the resolution, images on the screen become smaller because Windows defines their dimensions in pixels. On the other hand, if you use the same resolution on a bigger monitor screen, each pixel occupies more space, so the windows, icons, text, and pictures will all be bigger. Because the graphics controller doesn't know what size monitor is connected to it, a controller can support several different resolutions.

The same resolution is easier to read on a large screen. The text and pictures that are tiny on a 15-inch monitor at 1024 x 768 pixels will look fine on a 19-inch screen. In Windows, you can compensate for this difference by changing the DPI (dots per inch) setting in the General tab of the Advanced Display Properties window (Control Panel ⇨ Display ⇨ Settings ⇨ Advanced.

The best screen resolution for your monitor is a subjective choice, but Table 10.1 shows some commonly used settings. If you don't like the way the recommended resolution looks, try moving up or down to the next option that maintains the correct aspect ratio.

TABLE 10.1

Common Screen Resolutions

Screen Size	Resolution
15-inch	800 x 600
17-inch	1024 x 768
19-inch	1280 x 1024
21-inch	1600 x 1200

Most flat-panel displays (including laptop screens) perform best at one particular screen resolution. The manual supplied with the monitor or laptop should tell you the best setting for your screen.

Aspect ratio

In addition to the size of the screen, you should also consider the screen's *aspect ratio* when you set the resolution. The aspect ratio is the proportion of width to height, reduced to the smallest possible numbers. Because most CRT monitors used picture tube designs that were originally made for television, their aspect ratios are the same as traditional broadcast TV. Four units wide and three units high, or 4:3. 640 x 480, 800 x 600, 1024 x 768, 1400 x 1050, and 1600 x 1200 are all 4:3 aspect ratios.

When flat-panel monitors came along, their designers usually retained the same 4:3 aspect ratio. However, a few monitors have a slightly narrower 5:4 aspect ratio, so Windows often supports at least two 5:4 resolutions (1280 x 1024 and 1600 x 1280). Still other monitors (especially in laptop computers) use the wide-screen aspect ratio used by high-definition TV and DVD movies. If your monitor or laptop has a wide screen, it also supports a wide-screen aspect ratio.

Bit depth

Bit depth, also called color depth, is the number of bits needed to specify a different value to each shade. So the color depth of a black-and-white image is 1 bit, and a 256-color image has a color depth of 8. The maximum color depth on many computer graphics controllers is 32 bits, equal to more than 16 million colors.

Refresh rate

The screen refresh rate is the number of times per second the graphics controller renews the image on the screen. On a CRT, the refresh rate is the speed that the electron guns scan across the inside of the screen; on a flat-panel monitor, it's the rate at which the controller renews each pixel.

Every time the controller renews the image on a CRT screen, the image goes dark for a tiny fraction of a second before the new image appears. Your brain fills in the image during those dark moments, but if the refresh rate on a CRT monitor is too slow, you might notice that the screen appears to flicker rapidly, especially if you're working under fluorescent lights. To eliminate this problem, increase the refresh rate to 66 Hertz or more (explained later in this chapter).

Flicker is not a problem with LCD displays, so the best refresh rate is the native rate for that monitor. Most LCD monitors have a native refresh rate of 60 Hz, but some newer models might be faster. Consult your monitor's manual or specifications sheet to find the right setting for your monitor.

Because screen resolution, bit depth, and refresh rate all contribute to the number of bits that the controller must renew every second, the maximum values might be limited by the amount of memory on your video card. That's why the maximum refresh rate on a card with a limited amount of RAM drops as you increase the resolution; if you set the display settings to a high refresh rate, the card might automatically reduce the color depth.

Memory

In order to estimate the amount of memory your graphics controller needs, you must start by understanding how much memory it takes to create an on-screen image. For two-dimensional images, the minimum is equal to the resolution of the image, multiplied by the color depth.

To learn how much memory the graphics controller inside your computer has, follow these steps:

1. **From the Windows desktop, use your mouse to move the cursor away from any icon.**

2. **Right-click the mouse.**

3. **When the pop-up menu appears, choose Properties at the bottom of the menu.** The Display Properties window appears.

4. **Click the Settings tab.** The Settings screen shown in Figure 10.8 appears.

5. **Click the Advanced button near the bottom right corner of the screen.** A new properties screen for your graphics adapter appears.

FIGURE 10.8

The Settings screen in the Display Properties window controls graphics options.

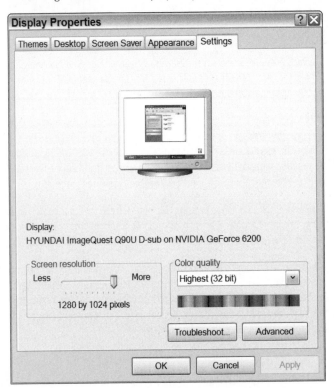

6. **Click the Adapter tab.** The screen shown in Figure 10.9 appears. The Adapter Information box in the middle of the window includes the make and model of the chipset and the amount of RAM on the graphics card.

FIGURE 10.9

The Adapter tab in the video card's Properties window identifies the chipset and shows the amount of RAM memory.

A graphics controller uses onboard RAM to hold several kinds of data:

- **The frame buffer:** This is the section of memory that sends the image to the monitor. It must be big enough to hold a complete image.
- **The back buffer:** The controller assembles the next image in the back buffer while the frame buffer feeds a completed image to the monitor. So the size of the back buffer must be equal to the size of the frame buffer.

Therefore, a two-dimensional display requires enough video memory to hold at least two complete bitmap images. So a 768 x 1024 image needs at least 3MB of video memory, 1024 x1280 needs at least 5MB, and 1200 x 1600 requires a minimum of 8MB. Video cards with more RAM than those minimums might produce somewhat better 2-D performance, but you can expect an old card with just 8 or 16MB of RAM to produce an adequate 2-D picture, although they might not support 32-bit color quality. But remember that Windows Vista uses 3D images, so you have to replace an underpowered video card when you upgrade your operating system.

Three-dimensional images require a lot more RAM because they have to support these additional elements:

- **The z-buffer:** In three-dimensional images, the z-buffer holds the data that places one item in front of another and creates the illusion of perspective. The depth of the z-buffer (most often 24 or 32 bits) defines the quality of the 3-D image. The size of the z-buffer is equal to the image size multiplied by the buffer depth.

- **Polygons:** Polygons are the shapes that contribute to the quality of a 3-D image. A graphics controller with more polygons produces a more realistic picture, but it doesn't necessarily require more memory.

- **Textures:** Textures are the shading, reflective patterns, and other characteristics of the surfaces of 3-D objects that give them a realistic appearance. A complex scene might include multiple textures. Complex textures can use large amounts of memory to support extensive amounts of detail.

In today's marketplace, even the most inexpensive low-end graphics controllers have 32MB, 64MB, or even 128MB of RAM. That's more than enough memory for any 2-D application. Three dimensions are a completely different matter. A 3-D image takes many times more RAM to hold all that additional information about each screen. That's why high-end graphics cards often have 256MB or even 512MB of RAM. 128MB is the bare minimum needed for games, Windows Vista, and other 3-D graphics.

Processor speed

The second important specification that describes the quality of a video controller is the clock speed on the graphics processor. Faster is better, especially for 3-D images, because a faster processor can render complete images more quickly. 250–300 MHz is plenty for non-gaming users; high-end 3-D video cards can reach 500 MHz or more. However, there's more to quality than just raw speed; some very fast video cards can produce images that are worse than the ones from other, slower cards.

In games and other 3-D programs, and for playing streaming video, the *frame rate*, or number of complete frames the processor can produce per second, is another indicator of the processor's speed. The frame rate is not the same as the refresh rate, because it measures the number of completely different images the controller can produce each second, rather than simply the number of times that the controller renews the same image.

The fastest graphics processor chips can consume a lot of power. In order to reduce the power drain on the PCI bus or the AGP socket, many high-end video cards have a dedicated power connector that plugs into a cable directly from the computer's power supply.

Bandwidth

Bandwidth is the rate at which the graphics processor and the controller card's on-board memory exchange data. The important bandwidth specification is the *memory interface*, which describes the number of simultaneous bits that move into the graphics card. Low-end cards use a 32-bit or 64-bit memory interface, but for high-performance operation, 128-bit or even 256-bit interfaces allow the graphics controller to produce much better images.

Graphics Processors and Chipsets

Many brands of graphics controller cards are out there, but almost all the core video chipsets — the integrated circuits that contain the graphics BIOS and processor — are made by a small number of companies. Like BIOS chips on motherboards, the make and model of the video chipset is often at least as important as the maker of the card. In general, two different graphics controller cards with identical chipsets and the same amount of memory have very similar performance, even if they were made by different manufacturers.

The vast majority of new video cards have chipsets from either ATI or NVIDIA. ATI makes their own branded video cards and also sells chipsets to other manufacturers, and NVIDIA is strictly a parts supplier to other manufacturers. Both companies offer a broad range of chipsets at many performance levels. ATI is now owned by the CPU maker AMD, but their graphics processors work equally well with Intel CPUs. A few other companies, including Matrox, VIA, and AGEIA, also make video chipsets, but ATI and NVIDIA products are the most common.

Most laptop computers and many desktop systems come with graphics controllers built into the motherboard. Some of these graphics processors are supplied by ATI or NVIDIA, but Intel and other chip makers also produce processors for this market.

Trying to understand the difference among different video chipsets is even more confusing than comparing different kinds of CPUs. As a general rule, the performance of both ranges improves as the model number of the chip increases, but there are exceptions. The best way to compare different types is to read the specifications on individual graphics controllers, consult the chip makers' Web sites (`www.nvidia.com` and `www.ati.com`), and read reviews in magazines and independent Web sites.

Digital or Analog?

Until flat-panel monitors began to replace the older cathode ray tubes (CRTs) in computer monitors, all monitors were analog devices that used a continuous stream of data to control a set of three electrons gun inside the CRT, which would scan across the phosphorescent surface of the screen to light selected areas (pixels) in red, green, or blue, which your eye combines into full-color images. This is the same technology that is used in traditional broadcast television. Because the computer and the graphics controller process the image as a series of digital signals, the controller must use a digital-to-analog converter (the RAMDAC) to create the analog signal.

In a digital monitor, the graphics controller sends a separate signal to control each pixel, so it's not necessary to include a RAMDAC in the path from the processor to the monitor. Flat-panel monitors are all digital, although some early ones had analog inputs to make them compatible with the analog outputs of existing video cards. Today, most flat-panel monitors have digital inputs, so the latest models of graphics controllers have digital outputs that bypass the RAMDAC. Many graphics cards include both analog and digital outputs on separate connectors.

If you have a choice, it's better to use a digital link between a graphics controller and an LCD monitor, because an analog connection requires conversion from digital to analog through the RMADAC, and then back to digital inside the monitor. Converting from digital to analog and back again slows down the transfer speed from the controller to the monitor and it might cause a slight reduction in the image quality.

The standard analog video output from a graphics controller is a 15-pin VGA (video graphics adapter) connector like the one shown in Figure 10.10. Most analog monitors have a captive VGA cable that is permanently connected to the case.

FIGURE 10.10

Analog monitors use 15-pin VGA connectors.

15-pin VGA connector

Digital outputs use a Digital Video Interface (DVI) cable, based on the Transition Minimized Differential Signaling (TMDS) standard. TMDS uses one or more transmitters in the graphics card to send data to an equal number of receivers in the monitor. A single link cable can support image resolutions up to 1920 x 1080. A dual link connection can increase the resolution to 2048 x 1536. DVI connections may be digital only (DVI-D), or DVI-integrated (DVI-I) that can support both digital and analog monitors. DVI connectors use three rows of eight pins or receptacles for the digital signal, and four isolated pins for the analog signal. Figure 10.11 shows single link and dual-link DVI-D and DVI-I connectors.

FIGURE 10.11

DVI connectors and receptacles come in four different configurations.

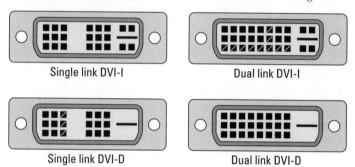

Single link DVI-I   Dual link DVI-I

Single link DVI-D   Dual link DVI-D

Some graphics adapters also have a third type of output connector, probably labeled *TV Out*. A cable from this output can connect to the S-Video or composite video connector on many television sets.

How Much Power Does Your Controller Really Need?

If you have been reading this chapter from the beginning, you already know what this section tells you: Unless you're using your computer for games, streaming video from DVDs or the Internet, or video editing, you don't need a state-of-the-art graphics adapter.

Older video cards

As long as the video card has enough RAM to support your screen resolution and enough power for a refresh rate of at least 66 Hz, it should be entirely adequate for word processing and most other office use, for e-mail and Web browsing, and for most of the other things that people do with their computers, *except* games, streaming video, and video editing. Just about every current make and model of graphics controller has more than enough power and memory for general home and office use. You might need a new and more powerful controller when you install the new Windows Vista operating system, but until then, the card you're currently using is probably okay.

On the other hand, if you buy an older video card with only 8MB of RAM or less at a swap meet or a surplus store, you're on your own. It will probably work well enough to send an image to your analog monitor, but it won't allow you to see a high-resolution image or more than a relatively small number of colors. Cheap video cards are a bad bargain; you can buy a new one with much better performance for just a little more money.

High-performance video cards

If you're a serious gamer, high-end graphic controllers make sense for your system. A high-speed processor, lots of memory, and a high-bit-rate memory interface all contribute to the quality of the 3-D images that make your favorite games so realistic. If you have a TV tuner in your computer, or if you watch a lot of DVD movies, you might not need the absolute best available graphics controller, but you see better image quality with a more powerful processor and more RAM than you might need for simple 2-D applications.

Upgrading your video card can make a tremendous difference to what you see on your screen. But remember that newer and even better video chipsets will be introduced in a few months, and the makers of new video cards want the early adopters to pay for most of their research and development costs. Today's top-of-the-line controller is next year's mid-range bargain.

Upgrading for Windows Vista

Microsoft's newest version of Windows includes a new and much more complex graphic environment than the one in Windows XP or any previous Windows release. In order to use all the features of this new package, Microsoft has announced a set of minimum requirements for Windows Vista's 3-D desktop, including at least 128MB of video RAM, support for DirectX 9 (a Microsoft specification for advanced multimedia performance) and a graphics processor that includes a pixel shader (a graphics function that can add shading, color and other details to individual pixels) and supports at least 32 bits per pixel. In other words, it probably needs a much more powerful video card than many non-gamers are currently using.

Each of the chipset companies has a Web site that lists their products that are compatible with Vista:

```
www.ati.com/technology/windowsvista/

www.nvidia.com/page/technology_vista_home.html

www.intel.com/business/bss/products/client/vistasolutions

www.microsoft.com/technet/windowsvista/evaluate/hardware/
entpguid.mspx
```

Vista requires more graphics processing power and memory than older Windows versions, but it's not necessary to spend hundreds of dollars for a super-deluxe video card designed for very high-performance games and multimedia editing programs — there are plenty of relatively inexpensive video cards that meet Microsoft's published requirements for Vista. When you're evaluating a new card, read the specifications carefully to make sure it has enough memory and it supports the other hardware and software requirements.

Changing the Display Settings

The appearance of everything on your monitor screen depends on the resolution, refresh rate, and color-quality settings that control the graphics controller's performance. To adjust the display settings, follow these steps:

1. **Right-click the Windows desktop and select Properties from the pop-up menu.** The Display Properties window opens.

2. **Click the Settings tab at the top of the window.** The dialog box shown in Figure 10.12 appears.

3. **Set the Screen resolution first.** Move the slider in the lower-left part of the screen to choose the resolution you want to use.

4. **Use the drop-down Color Quality menu to select the highest quality that your system accepts at the current screen resolution.** If you set the Color Quality too high, Windows automatically tries to reduce the resolution setting. If that happens, move the resolution setting back to the value you want and try a lower color-depth setting.

5. **Click the Advanced button.** An options window opens with settings that are customized for your monitor and graphics controller.

6. **Drag the custom window away from the Display Properties window so you can see both windows on your screen.**

FIGURE 10.12

Use the Settings screen to adjust resolution and color quality.

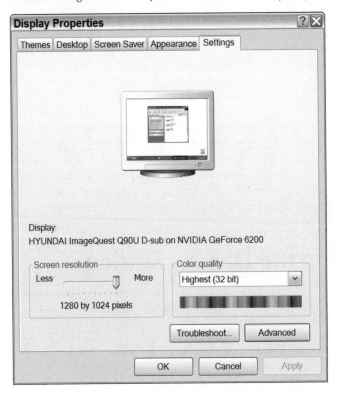

7. Click the Monitor tab to open a dialog box like the one in Figure 10.13.

8. Open the Screen refresh rate drop-down menu in the Monitor settings box.

9. **Choose the screen refresh rate you want to use.** For most users, a setting between 66 Hertz and 85 Hertz is fine. Click Apply to save your setting.

10. **Make sure the Screen Resolution setting doesn't change when you set the refresh rate.** If it does change, try a lower refresh rate.

12. **Click Apply to save your settings.** Windows asks you to confirm that you want to change these settings.

13. **Click Yes to make the changes. Depending on the way your system is configured, Windows might restart the computer.**

FIGURE 10.13

Use the Screen refresh rate drop-down menu to set the refresh rate.

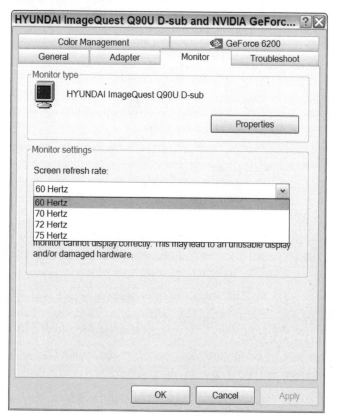

Supporting Multiple Monitors

It might sound like an extravagance, but adding a second monitor is one of the best possible ways to make your computer easier to use. If you have the space on your desk or worktable, two medium-sized (15-inch or 17-inch) monitors, or one large screen and one smaller one, can make you much more productive than a single large screen.

With two or more monitor screens, you can expand one program window to fill a screen, and still view other programs at the same time; you don't have to stack one active program on top of another and constantly click on the taskbar to switch programs.

Multiple monitors let you do many things that aren't possible on a single screen. Once you start to experiment, you may discover lots of ways to make working with Windows more convenient. For example:

- You can concentrate on a project in a word processor, spreadsheet, or other office program on one screen, while other programs, such as e-mail, an instant messenger, and a streaming Web site or a TV tuner are visible in the other screen.

- You can open documents, data files, or Web pages in one screen and take notes in the other.

- You can drag and drop text or artwork from a document, data file, or Web page in one screen to a new document in the other screen.

- You can edit a document or a Web page and automatically see what the changes look like as you work.

- You can expand the image in a graphics program or the text in a word processor to a full screen, and move the toolbars and other controls to the other screen where they don't get in the way of the image or document itself.

- You can extend an image beyond the limits of a single monitor for special presentations.

- You can take advantage of the multiple monitor features of games such as Microsoft Flight Simulator to display two or more views at the same time.

Adding a second monitor to your desktop system is not difficult. If your existing graphics controller doesn't include a dual output, simply buy and install a PCI video card (not PCI Express) into a vacant expansion slot and use the Display Properties window to configure it.

CROSS-REF   Chapter 28 contains detailed instructions for installing and using multiple monitors in both desktop and laptop systems.

If you're on a tight budget and you don't have a spare monitor, look for an inexpensive secondhand monitor — I've found completely functional, used, 15-inch CRTs for as little as $5 apiece in used-computer stores and places like Goodwill, where people have donated their old glass monitors after they replaced them with new flat-panel units. At that price, you can use the monitor until it dies (or the image goes out of focus), send it to the recycler, and get another one without a major investment.

Using the Software Supplied with Your Video Controller

The software CDs supplied with most graphics controllers usually include a configuration program that offers more sophisticated video settings and options than the ones provided with Windows. If you don't have the CD, you can download the software through the Internet from the maker of the graphics card or the company that supplied the video chipset.

Many of the added features and functions are things most people don't ever use (such as turning the image upside-down), but you might find something that improves the appearance or performance of your monitor, such as added controls for multiple monitors. If you decide that you don't need the add-on graphics tools, you can uninstall the program without sacrificing any of the graphics controller's performance.

Summary

The graphics controller in your computer converts data supplied through the chipset from the CPU to a bitmap image, and it sends that image to a video display monitor. Modern video controllers are single-purpose computers that offload the burden of creating images from the CPU.

For two-dimensional images, the graphics controller card needs enough RAM to hold two complete bitmap images, plus some extra for overhead. The number of bits in an image is equal to the screen resolution (width times height, in pixels), multiplied by the color depth. 3-D images consume much more RAM because they must include the z-buffer, polygons, and textures.

There are many makes and models of graphics cards, but most of them use chipsets supplied by either NVIDIA or ATI. All video cards with the same chipset and the same amount of RAM have very similar performance. Most of the features that make the difference between a relatively inexpensive graphics controller and a screamingly fast, high-quality 3-D card make little or no difference on anything except cutting-edge games, video editing, and streaming video from the Internet or DVD playback.

Chapter 11

Video Monitors

A computer uses a video monitor to convey information to you. Just about everything you do with the computer shows up on the monitor in some form. It would certainly be possible to use a computer without a monitor, but the experience would be completely different.

In simple terms, a computer monitor is a video display that shows the output of the graphics controller. So the monitor's only task is to receive bits from the controller and display them on a screen as actual images. Obviously, the operation of a monitor is closely related to that of the graphics card connected to it.

Until recently, the vast majority of desktop computer monitors used cathode ray tubes (CRTs) to display images. Like the televisions and oscilloscopes that preceded them, CRT monitors are big, bulky objects that were at least as deep behind the screen as they were wide. Because they had to be in plain sight (unlike the processor unit case that could be located on a shelf or hidden underneath a table), they required a tremendous amount of space on every user's desk. Today, the era of CRT monitors is almost over because they have been replaced by thin flat-panel displays that use liquid crystal technology instead of scanning electron guns.

Of course, millions of CRT monitors are still in daily use around the world, but the market for new CRTs is rapidly shrinking as one manufacturer after another announces that they are discontinuing them. Except for specialized applications that require very accurate color reproduction for publication, or very wide viewing angles, there's not much reason to buy a CRT monitor anymore except economy—new CRT monitors often offer very high-quality images at lower prices than flat panels (but they cost more to operate).

From the start, laptop computers have always used flat-panel displays — without flat panels, portable computing would be impractical; the early Osborne and Compaq portables that had CRT monitors were more like overweight suitcases than notebooks.

In this chapter, you can learn how both types of monitors work, how to evaluate and compare monitors before you buy one, and how to use the controls built into your monitor to adjust the appearance and performance of the display.

How CRT Displays Work

As Chapter 9 explained, CRT monitors are analog devices that use a continuous stream of electrons to create an image. The graphics controller uses a digital-to-analog converter (the RAMDAC) to generate an analog signal from the digital bitmap produced by the graphics processor.

A CRT monitor has three important elements: the *electron gun* at the back of the picture tube, a *shadow mask* or aperture grill, and a glass surface covered with phosphor dots. This is exactly the same technology used by traditional television sets with picture tubes.

To understand how this creates a picture, imagine a light bulb in a desk lamp or a ceiling fixture. When electricity passes through the filament of that bulb, the filament gives off a continuous stream of energy in the form of light and heat. In a CRT, the filament (also known as the cathode) also gives off energy, but that energy is a focused stream of electrons (that's the ray part). Because the cathode aims the rays at specific points, it's known as an electron gun. When those electrons strike the phosphors inside the glass screen, the phosphors, arranged in groups of red, green, and blue dots or bars, light up. The color that appears on that portion of the screen depends on the intensity of the electron stream and the way the red, green, and blue phosphors combine to create other colors. Figure 11.1 shows a cross section of a CRT.

The shadow mask (an opaque sheet with tiny holes in precise locations) or aperture grill (a set of thin vertical wires) is located very close to the screen. The holes or wires are aligned with the dots or bars to assure that each one has a precise shape. Without a mask, light from the beam could spill over to nearby dots and smear the image.

Now a beam illuminates one spot in the center of the CRT's screen. How does that beam scan across the screen from left to right and from top to bottom to create a complex picture? There are two coils of copper wires around the neck of the CRT that use magnetic fields to steer the beam — one coil for horizontal motion and the other for vertical motion. There's a precise combination of voltages to the two steering or deflection coils that corresponds to every dot on the screen.

The graphics controller breaks the image into red, green, and blue bitmaps and sends each image to the monitor through a separate wire in the cable that connects the controller to the monitor. Two more wires provide the horizontal and vertical synchronization signals. Circuitry within the monitor uses those sync signals to match the refresh rate and the screen resolution to the CRT's scan rate.

Put this all together and you have a beam that moves across the screen many times every second to relay the bitmap from the graphics controller to the surface of the CRT's screen. Your eye and brain do the rest, combining those millions of tiny dots into a coherent picture.

CROSS-REF Chapter 10 contains detailed explanations of the refresh rate and screen resolution.

FIGURE 11.1

The electron gun at one end of a CRT streams electrons at a screen at the other end. The coils around the neck of the tube steer the electron stream to cover the entire screen.

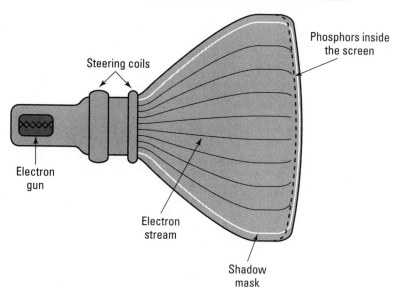

How Flat Panels Work

Flat-panel monitors are digital video displays that use backlit liquid crystal technology to produce images on a transparent plastic screen. Because they don't need an electron gun to shoot electrons through a big picture tube, a liquid crystal display (LCD) can be just a few inches or less from front to back. Flat-panel monitors occupy less space than CRTs, consume about one-third as much power, and produce brighter, sharper images.

A *liquid crystal* is a semiliquid substance with long parallel molecules (crystals) that respond to an electric charge by changing the way that light passes through them. When a layer of liquid crystal material is placed between a pair of polarizing filters at right angles, the presence or absence of a charge determines whether light is visible on that portion of the screen. Different materials have different light-passing characteristics, so monitors made with those materials can produce different images.

Figure 11.2 shows the layers of an LCD monitor. From back to front, an LCD monitor has these major elements:

- A source of light behind the screen. This is most often one or more fluorescent lights and a diffuser that spreads the light evenly through the entire surface of the screen.
- The first of two polarizing filters.
- An active matrix of thin-film transistors, each with a unique horizontal and vertical address that defines its exact location, mounted on a glass substrate that provides the charge to the liquid crystal material.
- The liquid crystal material.
- Another glass substrate.
- Three adjacent color filters, each of which can produce 256 shades, depending on the amount of light it receives. Combining the three colors (256 red x 256 green x 256 blue) can produce more than 16 million different colors.
- The second polarizing filter, at right angles to the first one.
- The surface of the monitor screen.

FIGURE 11.2

Light passing through a liquid crystal is controlled by a thin-film transistor matrix.

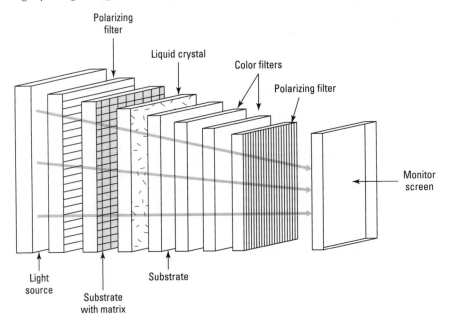

The graphics controller refreshes the image on an LCD monitor by scanning across the matrix of horizontal rows and vertical columns of thin-film transistors. Each address in the matrix corresponds to a pixel in the bitmap image supplied to the monitor by the graphics controller. The controller refreshes the entire image by moving through every row and column. Every pixel in the screen is made up of three adjacent sub-pixels, one for each color. The matrix receives instructions from the controller for one pixel at a time that tells it whether that pixel should be light or dark, and if it's light, which colors to use.

The source of light behind the LCD matrix is constant (unlike the pixels on a CRT that fade between scans), and the transistors in the screen remain open or closed until they receive an instruction to change, so an LCD screen does not produce the same kind of flickering image as a CRT at a low refresh rate. Therefore, most digital flat-panel monitors have only one refresh rate, usually 60 Hz.

Alternatives to LCDs

In addition to LCD, flat panel monitors can also use other technologies, including plasma, EL, OLED, LCoS, DLP, and LEDs.

A *plasma* or gas-discharge display uses neon gas between sets of horizontal and vertical (row and column) electrodes. When one electrode in each set receives an electric charge, the gas lights up at the intersection between the two electrodes.

EL (electroluminescent) displays use a phosphor layer placed between the horizontal and vertical electrodes. Like the neon gas in a plasma display, the phosphor lights up a pixel when the electrodes that define its address receive an electric charge.

OLED (organic light-emitting diode) displays use a thin film of luminescent organic material in place of the phosphor layer. Like plasma and EL displays, the luminescent material lights at the intersection of the row and column that define each pixel's address.

LCoS (liquid crystal on silicon) is a form of LCD display that uses a liquid crystal layer over an extremely reflective substrate layer. Because the switching circuitry and wiring is located underneath the reflective layer, there is no black space between pixels.

DLP (Digital light processing) uses a type of integrated circuit called a Digital Micromirror Device (DMD) chip. DMD chips contain a light source and millions of microscopic mirrors (one for each pixel) that switch toward or away from the light source to reflect light onto a screen in response to instructions from the graphics controller.

LED (light-emitting diode) displays use a set of individual electronic components that light up in a specific color when they receive a charge. In an LED display, each LED has address that identifies the row and column where that LED is located.

Response time is related to the refresh rate, because they both affect the amount of time needed for an image to change, but it's not the same thing. The response time is the amount of time needed for a liquid crystal to twist from one condition to another to pass light to a pixel, block light, and pass it again. This is defined in greater detail later in this chapter. The important difference between response time and refresh rate is that refresh rate originates in the graphics controller, and response time is a characteristic of the monitor.

Because it's not possible to physically change the number of pixels in an LCD display, each flat-panel monitor has a *native resolution* that produces the best possible image on that particular screen. Some monitors allow you to use other resolution settings by scaling the image and combining pixels, but the effect never looks as good as the same image at the monitor's preferred resolution.

Digital or Analog?

I said at the beginning of the last section that flat-panel monitors are digital devices. That's true, but many LCD monitors have analog VGA (Video Graphics Array) inputs, either as a companion to the digital input or as their only input connector. The analog connection allows users with older computers and graphics controllers to replace old CRT monitors without the need to open up the computer case and swap video cards. Because the only outputs on those older controllers are analog, the signal to the monitor's analog input passes through an analog-to-digital converter. If you're thinking that it's inefficient to convert from digital to analog in the controller and from analog back to digital inside the monitor, you're absolutely right, but it has allowed the monitor manufacturers to sell lots more flat panels.

CRT monitors are always analog. If you're shopping for a new LCD monitor, your best choice is one that has a digital input connector, even if your existing computer's graphics card is analog only. If you plan to use the new monitor with an older computer, the best way to take full advantage of the monitor's performance is to buy and install a new graphics card with a digital output at the same time. But if you can't replace the computer's existing video card, look for a monitor with both analog and digital input connectors.

CRT or LCD: What's the Difference?

In mid-2006, it's still possible to find new CRT monitors, but flat panels are rapidly becoming the universal choice. Is there still a good reason to buy a CRT?

Maybe. Consider the advantages and disadvantages of each type:

CRT monitors

Advantages:

- They're inexpensive. You can find a decent CRT with a 19-inch screen for less than $100 or a very good one for about $200. If you look around, you can probably find a usable secondhand CRT monitor for $20 or less.

- The color is more accurate on a CRT. This could be a very big deal if you're a graphic designer.

- Color depth and response time are better, so games, DVD movies, and TV shows may look better on a CRT (but LCDs are catching up).

- A CRT looks good from any viewing angle.

- CRTs can accurately display multiple resolutions and refresh rates.

Disadvantages:

- CRT monitors occupy a lot of desk space.

- A CRT monitor can weigh five times as much as an LCD with the same-sized screen.

- The phosphors inside a CRT eventually wear out; the image on a three-year-old monitor won't look as good as it did when the monitor was new.

- CRTs consume three times as much electricity as LCDs, so they cost three times as much to operate.

- Focus around the outer edges of the image is often less sharp than at the center.

- The image on a CRT is not as sharp as the same image on an LCD at the LCD's native resolution.

- Over time, a CRT monitor becomes less sharp that it was when new.

- CRTs are not as bright as LCDs. This can be important in a room with very bright lights or outdoors in sunlight.

- CRTs produce magnetic and electromagnetic radiation.

- CRTs produce a lot of heat.

LCD monitors

Advantages:

- Prices of LCD monitors are dropping rapidly.

- Flat-panel monitors weigh less and take up much less space than CRTs. You can hang one on the wall or put it on your desk and still have room for other things.

- Images on an LCD are sharp across the entire screen.

- LCD screens don't flicker.

- The image on an LCD screen is sharper and brighter than a CRT.

- Extended viewing is less fatiguing.

- LCD monitors are more energy efficient, so the cost of operation is lower.

Disadvantages:

- Fast-moving images on an LCD can smear.

- LCD screens look best at just one resolution; they don't look as good with non-native resolutions.

- LCD screens are hard to read when you try to view them from an angle (but newer monitors have wider viewing angles).

- The price of an LCD monitor is likely to be greater than a CRT with comparable quality.

So which is better? For must of us, the size and convenience of an LCD monitor makes it the obvious choice. The shortcomings in LCD image quality are rapidly disappearing, and the prices are dropping. But don't ignore CRTs, especially when price and color quality are important.

How Big a Screen Do You Need?

Bigger screens allow you to expand the size of text and pictures to make them easier to read, and they also make it possible to open more than one window at a time. Therefore, conventional wisdom says that you should get the monitor with the biggest screen you can afford. True enough, but there are some exceptions.

First, consider the trade-off between the size of a screen and the cost of the monitor. If you spend a lot of time sitting in front of your computer screen, a slightly smaller but higher-quality screen could be the better choice because the smaller screen could be sharper and brighter and less tiring to use. Buying the least costly big monitor you can find is often a poor way to save money.

There's a practical limit to the size of a monitor screen for home or office use. Anything larger than about 21 or 22 inches is likely to be extremely expensive, and more appropriate for a public display.

Second, think about getting two medium-size monitors instead of one big one. Or if you can afford it, add a second large monitor to your existing setup. Multiple-monitor operation can be a lot more flexible and productive than putting everything on a single screen.

CROSS-REF Chapter 28 explains more about setting up multiple monitors for your computer.

Third, a smaller monitor screen can have some benefits that have nothing to do with the performance of your computer. If you're setting up a computer on your kitchen counter, or in a corner of the living room or bedroom in a small apartment, you might not want a big screen to dominate the décor of the room.

Finally, remember that a laptop computer with a bigger screen must also be wider and deeper than one with a small display, even when it's turned off. A smaller laptop may fit into your briefcase or backpack more easily and it takes up less space in cramped areas like an airliner's fold-down tray table or a college lecture hall.

Understanding Technical Specifications

The best way to evaluate new monitors is to go to a local store and look at them to compare the images on many screens. But most retailers have a very limited number of makes and models, so it's extremely difficult to find out which monitor offers the best combination of appearance, features, and price. Many online retailers offer a wider range of monitors than any local retail outlet, but when you order by mail or through the Web, you can't preview a monitor before you order it.

Therefore, the independent reviews in magazines and Web sites can supply valuable, if subjective, information about currently available monitors. For more objective information, compare the lists of features and specifications for each monitor model.

If you can't evaluate a monitor before you buy it, make sure the seller offers a reasonable return policy. If you discover that you don't like the images on a monitor as much as you expected, you should be able to return for full credit or a refund within a reasonable period of time.

The most important specifications of an LCD monitor include:

- **Dimensions:** The size of a monitor is based on the diagonal measure of the screen, from the upper left corner to the lower right corner (or vice versa, of course). In an LCD monitor, the entire screen is visible, but the frame (also called the bezel) of a CRT monitor extends over the edges of the screen by almost an inch on each side. So the visible area of an LCD screen is bigger than the same-sized CRT. In practice, the difference means that an LCD monitor provides almost the same viewing area as a CRT with a screen two inches bigger.

- **Aspect ratio:** Aspect ratio is the proportion of the screen's width to its height. The most common aspect ratio for computer monitors and traditional TV screens is 4:3. Widescreen LCDs and HDTV screens use a slightly wider aspect ratio of 16:9.

- **Optimum resolution:** The optimum resolution is the native resolution of the monitor's screen in pixels. It might also be listed as recommended resolution. This is the resolution that provides the best appearance because it uses one physical screen address for each pixel. Any other resolution forces the monitor to scale the image.

- **Contrast ratio:** The contrast ratio is the difference between pure white and pure black. Larger contrast ratios are better, but it's more important to think about the relationship between a monitor's contrast ratio and its brightness; more contrast is possible in an image on a brighter screen.

- **Brightness:** The brightness of an LCD screen is the maximum amount of light a solid white screen can produce, measured in candelas per square meter (cd/m^2). Brighter screens are easier to use under bright ambient light, such as sunlight. Both brightness and contrast are adjustable, so it's always possible to reduce them when the screen is too bright for the space in which it is being used.

- **Pixel size:** Pixel size or *pitch* is the size of the individual dots in a CRT screen (smaller is better). In an LCD monitor, the pixel pitch is the same for all screens with the same size and native resolution.

- **Response time:** You may remember this from earlier in the chapter; response time is the amount of time in milliseconds (ms or msec) it takes a liquid crystal to change from blocking light to allowing light to pass through to blocking it again. Faster response time is better because full-motion video (games, DVD movies, and TV programs) can smear or produce ghosts if response time is too slow.

- **Viewing angle:** The viewing angle of an LCD screen is the maximum angle at which a user can see the image without losing brightness, color, or contrast. The viewing angle is expressed in degrees from extreme left to extreme right or from bottom to top of the range.

Other important features and functions include:

- **Analog or digital inputs:** The input connectors on your monitor must match the outputs on your graphics controller. If the monitor and the video card both have analog and digital connectors, use a digital cable to connect them.

- **Screen surface:** Some LCD monitors have matte-finish screens that reduce the amount of glare and reflected light from overhead lighting. Others use a more reflective surface that can enhance contrast. Neither is better than the other; the choice is purely subjective. Remember that where you place your screen makes a lot of difference with glare.

- **Bezel color:** The case that contains the monitor and the frame around the screen are usually either beige or black.

- **Built-in speakers:** Some monitor cases incorporate speakers into the frame that surrounds the screen. These speakers might be more convenient and less intrusive than separate speakers, but they also add to the cost of the monitor. If you're serious about using your computer to listen to high-fidelity music and other audio from DVDs, CDs, or streaming Internet sources, you want to use separate speakers that can produce better sound than the ones in a monitor.

Working with Your Monitor's Controls

The appearance of the image on your monitor's screen is controlled by the Windows Display Settings dialog box, the configuration program supplied with your graphics card, and also by the settings on the monitor itself. There's no standard location for the monitor's controls, but they're usually on the bottom of the frame that surrounds the display screen or along the edge of the frame. The specific set of controls changes from one make or model of monitor to another, so the best source of information about your own monitor is the instruction manual supplied with it (it you don't have one, look for a copy on the manufacturer's Web site).

Most monitors include controls that use on-screen menus and pushbuttons to change settings. Others can use software that allows a user to adjust the monitor with the computer's keyboard and mouse. Many of these controls are often awkward and somewhat confusing to use, but fortunately, most people don't have to change the monitor settings very often.

The most important monitor controls include:

- **Brightness:** The brightness control on an LCD sets the overall intensity of the monitor's backlight. The monitor's brightness is set correctly when black parts of an image appear as a true black.

- **Contrast:** Contrast is the difference between foreground and background items, or the difference between pure white and pure black. It's best to set the brightness first, and then adjust contrast, because you can produce a greater range of contrast on a brighter screen.

- **Horizontal position:** The horizontal position control moves the overall image to the left or right. Use this control if the image extends beyond the edge of the screen, or if there's a black line between the image and the screen's edge.

- **Vertical position:** The vertical position control moves the image up or down.

- **Horizontal size:** The horizontal size control increases or decreases the width of the image on a CRT screen. Use this control and the horizontal position control to center the image and fill the screen all the way to the right and left edges of the screen.

- **Vertical size:** The vertical size control increases or decreases the height of the image on a CRT screen. Use this control with the vertical position control to center the image vertically.

- **Color temperature:** The color temperature of your monitor specifies the relative warm (red) or cool (blue) level of the monitor's color balance. It has nothing to do with the thermal temperature of the monitor. The correct setting for your monitor depends on the spectral balance (the relative amounts of red, green, and blue light) of the other light sources in the room and your own personal preference. Most monitors offer two or more preset color temperature settings, either from the on-screen controls on in software. To set the color temperature, open the Windows Notepad program to display a window with a white background (Start ⇨ Programs ⇨ All Programs ⇨ Accessories ⇨ Notepad), try each of the monitor's preset values, and choose the one that produces the best-looking white background in the Notepad window.

- **Geometry:** The shape of the image on a CRT monitor screen can become distorted over time, so the monitor's controls offer settings that can correct the most common problems. When all of the geometry controls are set correctly, the lines on a grid should all be parallel, and the horizontal and vertical lines should be at right angles to one another.

The most common geometry settings are

- **Pincushion:** The pincushion control compensates for an image that is wider or narrower in the middle of the screen than at the top and bottom, like the shape of a pincushion.

- **Trapezoid:** The trapezoid control fixes images in which the top of the image is wider or narrower than the bottom.

- **Parallelogram:** The parallelogram adjustment corrects images in which the top of the image is shifted to the left or right of the bottom.

- **Rotate:** The rotate control shifts the image when the whole image is not absolutely vertical.

Figure 11.3 shows the shapes that each geometry setting corrects.

FIGURE 11.3

The geometry controls correct distorted shapes on monitor screens.

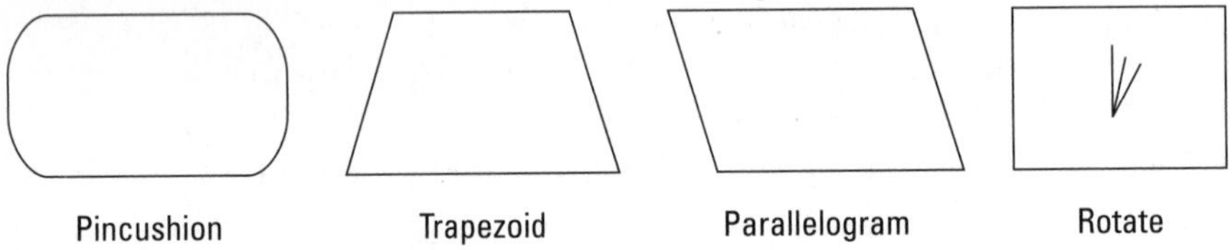

Pincushion   Trapezoid   Parallelogram   Rotate

Dead Pixels

If one or more of the thin-film transistors in an LCD monitor are defective, the spot on the screen controlled by those transistors remains dark or a solid color (depending on the design of the monitor) regardless of the signal supplied to it. These dead pixels can appear as small contrasting spots in the middle or edge of an image. A monitor with dead pixels is defective, but some manufacturers don't replace them unless there is more than some minimum number of dead pixels (often six or eight) on the screen. Depending on its location, a dead pixel can either be extremely distracting or easy to ignore.

If there are dead pixels in a new monitor, they usually appear when you turn it on for the first time, so it's important to examine your screen as soon as you receive it. If you discover dead pixels, contact the retailer and explain the problem. Even if you can't return it under warranty as a defective unit, consider sending it back for a refund under the seller's no-questions-asked return policy if they have one.

Repairing a Monitor

This one is simple: Don't even try to do your own repairs on a monitor. The capacitors inside a CRT can retain enough power to kill you if you touch the wrong contact points inside the case, and there's nothing inside a flat-panel monitor that you can fix easily.

Qualified service shops can still fix CRT monitors, but the cost of a repair will probably be more than the price of a new monitor. Even if you do spend the money to repair an old monitor, it is still an old monitor with an old CRT whose phosphors have begun to wear out. Don't mess with it. Spend the money to buy a new monitor instead.

Summary

Computer monitors use either cathode ray tubes (CRTs) or liquid crystal displays (LCDs) to display the output of a computer's graphics controller on a screen. CRTs were the most common type of monitor for many years, and millions are still in use, but LCDs have almost completely replaced them in the marketplace. Other flat-panel technologies, including plasma, electroluminescent (EL), and digital light processing (DLP) are also available, but they're mostly used in specialized applications.

LCD monitors have many advantages over the older CRT technology: they occupy less space and weigh less, and the images don't flicker at slow refresh rates. However, CRT monitors are still superior for graphic design and other applications that require accurate color displays.

When you can, the best way to evaluate monitors is to compare the images on their screens in person. If that's not possible, their published specifications can often provide useful information.

Chapter 12

Keyboards, Mice, and Other Input Devices

A computer's keyboard and mouse are its primary tools for receiving commands and data. Both devices take mechanical inputs from your hand and convert them to electrical impulses that the computer interprets as input signals to the processor.

The keyboard and mouse supplied with your computer are probably inexpensive models that are perfectly adequate, but they may not have all of the special features and functions that might be available on more expensive versions. If you use your computer a lot, it's worth the extra money to replace the generic devices with a keyboard that is more responsive to your personal typing style and a mouse that comfortably fits your own hand. Over time, a well-designed keyboard and mouse can reduce fatigue and even prevent physical pain in your hands and wrists.

This chapter explains how your keyboard and mouse work, and describes the features and options that allow you to customize their operation. The end of the chapter explains the use of alternative input devices, including bar code readers and handwriting tablets.

Using a Keyboard

On the surface, a keyboard seems pretty simple: You type text on the keyboard and it appears on your monitor screen. But of course, there's a lot going on underneath the surface. Your keyboard is really a small computer with its own processor, dedicated to interpreting keystrokes and sending them to the computer's CPU.

A keyboard is a set of pushbuttons that send coded signals to a computer, printer, or communications channel. Each pushbutton, or *key*, corresponds to one or more letters, numbers, symbols, or special commands. Underneath the key caps, each key might be an individual electric switch, a rubber dome with a conductive center, or part of a continuous membrane.

When you press a key, the keyboard sends a code to the computer's CPU that corresponds to the character printed on the key. When the CPU receives the signal, it accepts it either as part of a command or as text input.

That's the simple version. It's really a somewhat more complex process:

1. Underneath each key, a normally *open switch* (a switch that creates an electrical connection when you press the key) or a *capacitive switch* (a switch that changes the amount of charge between two points when you press the key) closes a circuit at a specific location on a printed circuit grid that has a contact point for each key.

2. The processor inside the keyboard (the keyboard controller) continually scans the grid. When you press a key, the processor notes the change in the state of the switch at that key's location and sends a scan code that identifies that location to the computer. If you hold down the key longer than some specified period of time (usually about half a second), the keyboard repeats the same scan code until you release the key.

3. The keyboard sends one scan code at a time to the computer's motherboard, through either a cable with a dedicated keyboard connector (called a PS/2 socket because it was first used in the IBM Model PS/2), a USB connector, or a wireless link.

4. Inside the computer, the BIOS or the keyboard device driver examines the scan code. If the keyboard is not using standard codes, the BIOS or device driver converts them to codes that the CPU understands.

5. The BIOS or device driver sends the scan codes to the keyboard buffer.

6. The chipset holds the incoming scan code in the keyboard buffer and notifies the CPU.

7. When the CPU accepts the request, it reads the oldest character in the keyboard buffer, converts it to a text character, and processes that character in the currently active program.

8. The keyboard buffer continues to receive additional characters from the keyboard and sends them to the CPU in the order it receives them (first-in, first-out).

Figure 12.1 shows the signal path from a keystroke to the CPU.

FIGURE 12.1

When you press a key, the keyboard sends a scan code to the computer's CPU.

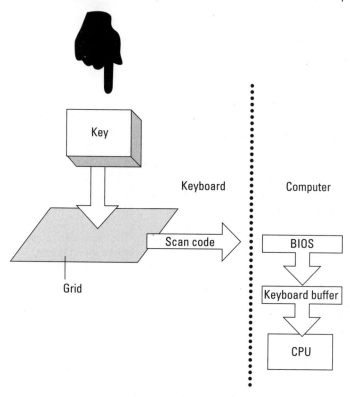

Scan codes

When you press a key, the keyboard sends the computer a scan code that the CPU converts to a specific letter, number, or symbol. Why doesn't the keyboard processor just use the standard ASCII codes and eliminate the need for conversion? Good question. If everybody in the world used exactly the same keyboard layout, that might be a great way to make the whole process more efficient.

However, the world is full of people who speak different languages and who use different alphabets and keyboard layouts. If you're American, you expect to find the # symbol on the Shift+3 key. But if you're in England, that key produces the £ symbol instead. If you're French, the top row of letters is azertyuiop instead of qwertyuiop. In Greek, it's ςερτυθιοπ.

Therefore, the computer sends the CPU generic scan codes that can mean anything you want them to mean. The Changing Languages and Special Layouts sections later in this chapter explain how to change keyboard layouts in Windows.

PS/2 vs USB vs wireless

As I mentioned earlier, the keyboard can use either a cable or a wireless link to exchange data with the rest of the computer. Most new keyboards with cables have a USB connector, and they come with a special adapter that allows you to use a PS/2 connector as an alternative.

USB I/O ports are supposed to replace all those confusing connectors on most personal computers with a single type of plug and socket that works with everything. Keyboards and mice were among the first devices to take advantage of the new standard, so most new ones have either a captive USB plug on the end of the cable (or the wireless receiver), or a converter that changes the cable from a PS/2 device to a USB device. There's no real difference in performance between the two connections (both can move data from the keyboard to the computer much more quickly than you can type), so your keyboard works equally well through either type of port.

PS/2 connectors have six pins arranged around a center positioning piece. The same connector is also used on mouse cables, so some laptop computers have a single PS/2 input connector that works with either a keyboard or a mouse. If you're using an older keyboard, it might still have a slightly larger five-pin AT connector (also known as a *big plug*) instead of the six-pin PS/2 connector (a *little plug*). Fortunately, both connector types carry signals on only four pins, so it's easy to convert from one to the other. To use a keyboard with a big plug, look for an AT to PS/2 adapter at a computer retailer or office supply store.

Wireless devices can use infrared or radio links such as a TV remote control unit or a Bluetooth connection. Either way, the wireless link uses a receiver that connects to the computer through a USB port. Because there's no cable from the computer to supply power, a wireless keyboard requires batteries to run its internal processor and the wireless link. Wireless keyboards and mice are more convenient and flexible than their wired cousins, but their price is often higher.

CAUTION If you're using a WiFi network connection or a cordless telephone that operates at 2.4 GHz, avoid using a wireless keyboard or mouse that uses Bluetooth. Both Bluetooth and WiFi use the same range of radio frequencies around 2.4 GHz, so the two signals can interfere with each other.

A tour of the keyboard

As Figure 12.2 shows, the standard keyboard for desktop computers has five groups of keys:

- The typewriter keys that send letters, numbers, and punctuation marks to the computer. This part of the keyboard was inherited from typewriters, which had a direct electrical or mechanical linkage from the keys to the mechanism that printed those characters on paper.

- The Function keys, with numbers from 1 to 12 (or 15) with the letter F in front of each letter.
- The arrow keys, with arrows pointing up, down, left, and right.
- The numeric keypad that has numbers arranged like a 10-key calculator.
- Special command keys.

FIGURE 12.2

A computer keyboard has several distinct groups of keys. This keyboard has the function keys along the left side instead of the top row.

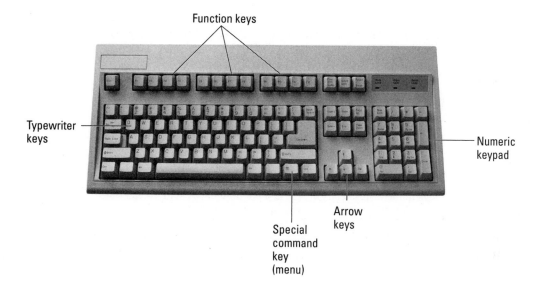

Typewriter keys

The typewriter keys with numbers and symbols all have at least two characters printed on them. When you press one of these keys, the keyboard sends the symbol on the lower part of the key to the computer. To send the upper symbol, you must hold down the Shift key while you press that key. The letter keys have only one character printed on them, but you can use still use them to send two different characters: the lowercase letter (that is, abcdefg) when you press a key by itself, or the capital letter (ABCDEFG) when you hold down the Shift key.

> **NOTE** The name of the Shift key is left over from mechanical typewriters, where every type element had two characters on it, and the Shift key physically shifted the paper to the upper one.

The computer keyboard also has a Caps Lock key that shifts all of the letter keys to capitals until you press Caps Lock again to release it. Caps Lock does not affect the number and symbol keys.

One big difference between an old-fashioned typewriter and a computer keyboard is that the computer keyboard has three different Shift keys: Shift, Ctrl (Control), and Alt (Alternate). The English-language keyboard doesn't use Ctrl or Alt for additional symbols (although some programs use them), but keyboards for some other languages do. In some languages, Windows treats the left and right Shift and Ctrl keys as separate functions, so the keyboard only shifts to the alternate set of characters when you press the Shift or Ctrl key on the right-hand side of the keyboard.

In Windows, many combinations of Ctrl or Alt plus another key are often shortcuts to specific commands.

Function keys

The function, or F#, keys send instructions to the computer that the operating system or a program interprets as a command. Windows uses these function key commands:

- **F1.** Open Help for the currently active program.
- **F2.** Rename the selected item.
- **F3.** Search for a file or folder.
- **F4.** Open the drop-down Address Bar list in My Computer, Windows Explorer, and Internet Explorer.
- **F5.** Refresh the active window.
- **F6.** Move to the next screen element in a program or the Windows desktop.
- **F10.** Activate the Menu Bar in the current program.
- **Alt+F4.** Close the currently active program.
- **Ctrl+F4.** Close the currently active document.
- **Shift+F10.** Open the shortcut menu for the active program (same as right-click).

The function keys were originally located in two vertical columns to the left of the typewriter keys. This was convenient for touch typists because many programs used commands made up of a function key and a nearby control key, such as Ctrl+F6, or Shift+F8. However, some programs would display the command that each function key would send to the computer along the bottom of the monitor screen, so IBM moved the function keys to the top of the keyboard where each key would be directly underneath the command on the screen. Of course, this meant that you couldn't enter a command like Ctrl+F6 with the fingers of one hand anymore, so some other keyboard makers either left the function keys along the left side, or provided two sets of function keys, like the one shown in Figure 12.3.

FIGURE 12.3

This keyboard has two sets of function keys: one set to the left of the typewriter keys and another set along the top.

Function keys

Control keys and status lights

The keys in the group directly to the right of the typewriter keys, along with the Esc (Escape) and Tab keys at the upper-left corner of the typewriter key group and Num Lock at the top left corner of the numeric keypad, send specific commands to the computer. Some of them talk directly to the BIOS before the operating system loads, and others send instructions to the operating system and individual programs. Three of these keys (Caps Lock, Num Lock and Scroll Lock) also instruct the BIOS to return a confirming signal to the keyboard that lights a status indicator when the corresponding function is active.

Wireless keyboards don't include the status indicator lights. When one of those functions is active, an indicator might light on the wireless base station connected to the computer, or a small notice might appear on the screen.

In the days before everybody had their own desktop computer, IBM sold a lot of remote terminals for use with mainframe computers that were usually located someplace else in the same building or campus. A remote terminal had a keyboard and a monitor screen, but the actual computer was usually a big mainframe system at the other end of a cable or telephone line. One of the first programs that many people used on their new IBM Personal Computers was a *terminal emulator* that let them use the new desktop computer as a remote terminal for the corporate mainframe. Therefore, the personal computer's keyboard included all of the special control keys that had been on the older remote terminals. Hardly anybody uses their personal computers as remote terminals anymore, but those control keys are still on everybody's keyboards.

Esc

Escape was a signal to a terminal that meant you wanted to escape from the connection to the mainframe and do something on the terminal itself, such as changing from a black screen with white letters to a white screen with black letters.

The Escape key sends an instruction to Windows and many programs to cancel the currently active task. Pressing the Escape key is often the only way to shut down a frozen or runaway program.

Tab

Tab is short for Tabulator, which was a name given by some long-forgotten typewriter maker for the key that typists could use to make tables. In Windows, you can use the Tab key to move forward from one option to the next in a window or a dialog box. In word processors, you can use it to jump to the next column or the next box in a table or list. Shift+Tab moves backward through the same options.

Alt+Tab opens a list of programs that are currently running on your computer, like the one in Figure 12.4. To see the names of each program, one at a time, keep the Alt key down and press the Tab key again. To move to the current program on the list, release the Alt key.

FIGURE 12.4

Use Alt+Tab to see a list of current programs. In this case, the programs are (from left to right) Internet Explorer, WeatherBug (an online weather forecast display program), a Time Synchronizer program, an e-mail program and Windows Explorer.

Backspace

Backspace instructs a text or numeric program to erase the character (or the selected group of characters) directly to the left of the cursor.

Print Screen/SysRq

In spite of its name, you can't print a picture of your monitor screen by pressing the Print Screen key. That's what it did on a remote terminal and in the old DOS operating system that was widely used before Windows was introduced, but in Windows, the Print Screen key is an instruction to copy the current screen to the Clipboard. To copy the active window (the window that you are currently using) only, press Alt+Print Screen. To use the image of the screen or window, open a document in a program and use the Paste command in that program.

It doesn't work on every system, but it's sometimes possible to print a copy of the current screen in the BIOS Settings Utility by pressing Print Screen twice.

The cryptic letters *SysRq* on the front of the Print Screen key stand for System Request. On a remote terminal, it was a signal to the mainframe that the terminal was active and the user wanted a command prompt. Today, unless you're using your computer as a remote terminal for a mainframe computer, it means nothing.

Scroll Lock

Scroll Lock is another one of those keys left over from the remote terminals that IBM used as models for their early keyboards. The only thing that happens when you press the Scroll Lock key is that the Scroll Lock indicator light will light. The computer keeps track of Scroll Lock's status, but it doesn't do anything with that information. Sounds useless, doesn't it? In fact, Scroll Lock would change the way the arrow keys worked in some old DOS programs, and it has a function in some spreadsheet programs and in the Opera Web browser, but that's about it.

Pause/Break

Pause was a command to a mainframe to suspend (or resume) the program that was currently sending data to the terminal. Break was an instruction to cancel the program now, before the job is complete, or to disconnect the communications link between the terminal and the mainframe.

If you press the Pause/Break key while the BIOS is still in control of your computer during startup, it interrupts the startup process. This can be useful if you ever want to read the text that scrolls up your screen before Windows starts.

The Break command (Ctrl+Break) instructs some programs to interrupt what they are doing and close the program.

Direction keys

The four arrow keys ($\rightarrow$, $\uparrow$, $\downarrow$, and $\leftarrow$) below the control keys move the cursor or some other object in the direction of the arrow in many programs.

Ctrl plus an arrow key or Shift plus an arrow key can have special navigation functions in some programs. For example, in many word processors and text editors, Ctrl+$\leftarrow$ or Ctrl+$\rightarrow$ moves the cursor to the left or right, one word at a time.

Other navigation keys

The Home and End keys move the cursor to the beginning and end of the current line of text in a word processor or the current cell in a spreadsheet or database. In many programs, Ctrl+Home and Ctrl+End move the cursor to the beginning and end of the current document.

The Page Up and Page Down keys move up or down one full page in a document or one full screen in a Web page.

Insert

The Insert key has no specific use in Windows, but in many programs it either controls the over-write function that types new letters over existing text, or it pastes an item from the Clipboard.

Delete

In Windows and many application programs, the Delete key removes the currently selected file, text, or other object from an open window. In many word processors and text editors, Delete removes the character to the left of the cursor.

The numeric keypad

The keys at the right end of the keyboard serve two purposes. When Num Lock is off, these keys duplicate the functions of the navigation keys and the Insert and Delete keys. When Num Lock is on, these keys perform like the keys in a calculator. When Num Lock is active, the Num Lock indicator at the top right corner of the keyboard lights.

TIP Some people like to have Num Lock active when the computer starts, but others prefer to keep it off until they need it. Many computers have a Num Lock Status option in the BIOS Settings Utility, usually in the Startup Options section.

Special Windows keys

Most new keyboards include two extra keys in the bottom row: one with a Windows symbol (⊞), and the other with a tiny menu. Table 12.1 shows the Windows keys shortcuts.

TABLE 12.1

Windows Key Shortcuts

Keys	Functions
⊞	Opens the Start Menu
⊞+E	Opens Windows Explorer
⊞+D	Minimizes or restores all open windows
⊞+F	Opens the Windows Explorer Find window
⊞+L	Locks Windows
⊞+M	Minimizes all open windows
⊞+Shift+M	Restores the minimized windows
⊞+R	Opens Run
⊞+Pause/Break	Opens System Properties
▤	Open the active item's right-click menu

Typematic delay and rate

If you hold down a key for more than about half a second, the keyboard's processor starts to repeat the scan code for that key, which sends multiple copies of that character to the keyboard buffer. In other words, it repeats the same character until you release the key. Windows and other operating systems call this the *typematic* function.

Windows offers two adjustments to typematic performance: the amount of time the keyboard waits before starting to send repeated characters (the delay), and the number of times per second that it sends the character (the rate). To change the typematic settings, follow these steps:

1. **Open the Windows Control Panel and choose the Keyboard icon.** The Keyboard Properties window appears.

2. **Choose the Speed tab.** The dialog box shown in Figure 12.5 appears.

FIGURE 12.5

Use the Keyboard Properties dialog box to change your typematic settings.

3. **Use the Repeat delay slider to set the typematic delay.** The best setting is a relatively long delay, because a short delay might not compensate for the time it normally takes for you to lift your fingers from the keys while you type. Use the test area in the dialog box to test your setting.

4. **Use the Repeat rate slider to set the typematic rate.** A moderate repeat rate is usually the best compromise between a slow rate that takes too long to complete and a fast rate that produces too many characters in a very short time. Use the test area to check your setting.

5. **Click OK to save your new settings and close the window.**

Extended character sets

The typewriter section of your keyboard has about 45 keys (not counting things such as Esc and Tab), which is more than enough for all the letters in the alphabet, with keys left over for numbers and punctuation marks. Holding down the Shift key gives you a second complete set of letters, characters, and symbols. But most type fonts include many more characters than that. The additional keys can include oddball symbols that don't appear in print very often (like ♥ and ♣), graphic characters (△), and even foreign-language alphabets. Depending on the typeface, an English-language font might also include the complete Greek, Cyrillic (Russian), Hebrew, Thai, and Arabic alphabets, or an assortment of Chinese, Japanese, or Korean ideographs.

You probably won't need most of these symbols very often (if ever), but sometimes they can be extremely useful. For example, if you're an American who uses the Internet to buy books or music from overseas, you might need to send an e-mail message or print a letter that includes the symbol for some kind of foreign money, such as euros (€), pounds sterling (£), Japanese yen (¥), or even Nigerian naira (₦).

Windows includes several ways to enter symbols that aren't on your keyboard:

The Character Map

The Windows Character Map shows all of the symbols and characters that are available in the current font and allows you to shift to a different font to find even more characters. You can select individual characters or create complete words or strings of symbols and copy them to the Windows Clipboard, or drag and drop individual characters directly into a document. To open the Character Map, use the Start Menu and select Programs ➪ All Programs ➪ Accessories ➪ System Tools ➪ Character Map. In the Classic Windows menu, use Programs ➪ Accessories ➪ System Tools ➪ Character Map.

Figure 12.6 shows the Character Map window. To see a larger version of any character, place your mouse cursor over that character and click once. To see more characters, use the scroll bar on the right-hand side of the map. To select a character, either double-click that character or click once and use the Select button. To find characters that are not available in the current font, open the drop-down Font list at the top of the Character Map.

Currently selected characters appear in the Characters To Copy field at the bottom of the window. You can use this field as a simple text editor, where you can add characters (and spaces) from the keyboard, or select one or more characters and drag them into a different order. To copy the selected characters into a document, either click the Copy button and then use the Paste command in the program where you want to place the characters, or drag and drop them.

NOTE Dragging and dropping doesn't work in all programs, but it's worth a try.

The Character Map utility uses the international Unicode character coding system that includes most of the world's written languages. Unicode assigns a unique four-digit code to every character and every symbol.

FIGURE 12.6

The Character Map allows you to enter many symbols and characters that are not on your keyboard.

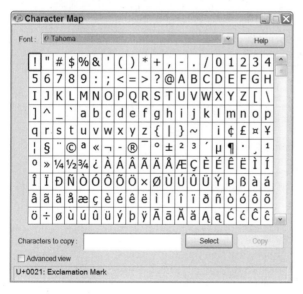

To use characters in less common languages, you might have to choose a different font and choose the option at the bottom of the Character Map window to use the Advanced view, as shown in Figure 12.7. For characters in widely used languages, open the Character set menu and choose the language you want.

To use type in a less common language, use a program called BabelMap (download it from www.babelstone.co.uk/Software/BabelMap.html) to identify the fonts that support that language.

After BabelMap tells you which font to use, follow these steps to open the font in Character Map:

1. Choose the font you want to use from the drop-down Font menu near the top of the Character Map window.

2. Select the Advanced View option to open the expanded Character Map window.

3. Open the drop-down Character set menu and choose Unicode.

4. Open the drop-down Group by menu and select Unicode Subrange. A new Group By window will open next to the Character Map window.

5. Scroll down the Group By list to find and select the language you want to use. If the current font supports that language, you will see the character map for that language.

For Chinese, Japanese, and Korean characters, use the Group by menu to choose a style. For a list of languages and other character subsets, choose the Unicode Character set and Group by Unicode Subrange.

In this example, I want to use characters in the Malayalam language, which is used by almost 30 million people in South India. Different fonts include character sets for different languages, so you might have to try more than one font before you find the language you want. You can scan through the fonts by selecting the Font field and using the up and down arrow keys.

FIGURE 12.7

Use the Character Map's Advanced view to search for a character.

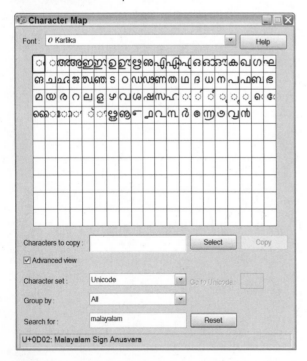

Keystroke codes

Many relatively common characters that don't appear on your keyboard have special keystroke codes that allow you to enter them directly from your keyboard. If there's a keystroke code assigned to a character, it appears at the bottom right of the Character Map when you select that character.

To enter a keystroke code, make sure Num Lock is on and then hold down the Alt key while you use the numeric keypad to enter the code. For example, the keystroke code for the yen sign (¥) that was shown in Figure 11.6 is Alt+0165.

 Don't try to use the numbers across the top of the typewriter keys when you want to enter a keystroke code. They won't work for this.

Shortcuts in programs

Some programs have their own methods for adding characters that aren't on the keyboard. In Microsoft Office programs, there's an Insert ⇨ Symbol command that opens a different version of the Character Map. In Microsoft Word, there are some keyboard shortcuts that are somewhat more intuitive than the Unicode system.

For example, you can enter the copyright symbol (©) in Word by typing Ctrl+Alt+C, or the Euro symbol (€) with Ctrl+Alt+E.

Changing languages

Alternate symbols and Unicode keystrokes are fine for entering occasional symbols, but if you are typing in Russian, or French, or Arabic, or any other language, you shouldn't have to use the same keyboard that an American uses to type in English. The layouts of computer keyboards are very different in different parts of the world. In most cases, your copy of Windows has been localized for your own country, including the standard keyboard layout for your language and alphabet. And the physical keyboard supplied with your computer should have keycaps with letters in your language.

 American keyboards are sometimes called QWERTY keyboards, after the letters in the top, left-hand row.

But if you have imported your computer from another country, or if you're working in a foreign language, you might want a way to change keyboard layouts from one language to another. Microsoft has anticipated this problem, so Windows allows you to shift keyboard layouts quickly and easily.

To add another keyboard layout in Windows, follow these steps:

1. **Open the Control Panel and select Regional and Language Options.**
2. **When the Regional and Language Options window appears, choose the Languages tab.**

3. **At the top of the Languages tab, find the Text services and input languages box and click the Details button.** The window shown in Figure 12.8 appears.

4. **The Installed services box shows all the keyboard layouts that are currently available on your computer.** To load a new keyboard layout, click Add.

FIGURE 12.8

Use the Text Services and Input Languages window to add or remove a keyboard layout.

5. **In the Add Input Language dialog box shown in Figure 12.9, choose the new Input language from the drop-down menu.** The program automatically recommends a keyboard layout. Unless you have some kind of specialized keyboard (such as the Brazilian keyboard used in Brazil), go ahead and accept the recommended layout.

6. **Click OK to save your choices and close the dialog box.** The list of Installed services now includes the new keyboard, as shown in Figure 12.10.

FIGURE 12.9

Choose the type of keyboard you want to add from the menu.

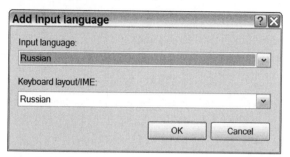

FIGURE 12.10

The Russian keyboard layout has been loaded.

7. If you want to change the keyboard layout that Windows loads when you turn on the computer, use the menu in the Default input language box at the top of the window.

8. Click OK to add the new keyboard layout and close the window.

Notice that there's now a two-letter code in the taskbar at the bottom of the screen. This code identifies the currently active keyboard layout. To change keyboard settings, click the language symbol and choose the new layout from the pop-up menu.

CAUTION Don't try to swap keyboards while the computer is running; that could damage your motherboard. To install a different keyboard, turn off the computer, replace the keyboard and turn the computer back on again.

Unless you're an excellent touch-typist who never looks at the keys when you type, you will probably want to swap keyboards when you change layouts. Typing on a QWERTY keyboard into a computer set to accept an AZERTY layout is guaranteed to confuse and distract almost anybody. If you normally use two different layouts, you might want to find a bilingual keyboard like the one shown in Figure 12.11.

FIGURE 12.11

This keyboard has both English and Russian characters on its key caps.

Special layouts

In addition to the keyboard layouts for most of the world's languages, Windows can also recognize some alternative keyboards that have been designed for improved typing speed and other designs for users who can only use one hand.

The best-known alternative layout in English is the Dvorak keyboard, developed by Dr. August Dvorak of the University of Washington around 1930. On a Dvorak keyboard, the most commonly used letters are in the middle *home* row of keys in an order that Dr. Dvorak selected to make typing in English as efficient as possible. All the vowels in a Dvorak keyboard are under the left hand, and most of the consonants under the right hand, so a typist alternates hands when typing many words in English.

After World War II, an American military officer who had lost his right arm asked Dr. Dvorak to consider the needs of people who could only use one hand. Dvorak developed two more special keyboard layouts: one for the right hand and a different layout for the left hand. On these keyboards, the most commonly used letters are close to the center, and the least common letters are out at the edges.

 **Windows includes all three Dvorak keyboards among its English Language layouts.**

Other special keyboards are available for left-handed typists. These keyboards have moved the traditional typewriter keys to the right, and the navigation keys and numeric keypad to the left. The keys within each group are still in the normal order, but the groups are closer to the user's left hand. These left-handed keyboards don't need a special configuration or special driver software; the CPU receives all the same scan codes as from a conventional system.

Customizing the keyboard

If you want to add some special symbols that aren't on the standard keyboard, you can use Microsoft's free Keyboard Layout Creator program to define your own keyboard layout. You can download the program from www.microsoft.com/globaldev/tools/msklc.mspx.

Increasing the size of the keyboard buffer

If you're an extremely fast typist, it's possible that you send characters to the keyboard buffer in the computer more quickly than the CPU can read them, especially when the computer is performing other jobs that have a higher interrupt priority. This is not common, but if the computer beeps at you while you're typing, your buffer is probably full.

CAUTION **Don't change the buffer size unless you're having a problem. It probably won't make any difference unless you can type at least 100 words per minute.**

To solve this problem, increase the amount of memory that the computer dedicates to the keyboard buffer:

1. From the Start Menu, choose Run and type regedit. Click OK.
2. When the Registry Editor opens, select HKEY_LOCAL_MACHINE\System\Current Control Set\Services\Kbdclass\Parameters.
3. In the left side of the screen, right-click on KeyboardDataQueueSize and choose Modify from the pop-up menu.
4. Change the number in the Value data field from 64 to c8 (equal to decimal 200). Click OK to save your change and close the dialog box.

5. Confirm that the entry in the Data column now reads 0x000000c8 (200).

6. Close the Registry Editor.

7. Restart your computer.

Using an ergonomic keyboard

Many special keyboard designs have been introduced to make the process of typing more comfortable. Some are just simple changes to the standard design, but others are completely different physical arrangements. If you have pain in your hands, arms, or wrists when you use a keyboard, one of these special designs might help.

Microsoft, Logitech, and other keyboard makers all offer *ergonomic* keyboards like the one shown in Figure 12.12 that attempt to move the keys closer to your fingers. If they aren't enough to solve a problem, you might want to look for a more exotic design. A Web search for "ergonomic keyboard" can provide links to many specialist manufacturers and dealers.

FIGURE 12.12
_____

Many ergonomic keyboards split the typewriter keys to make them easier to reach.

An exotic keyboard can cost 10 or 20 times more than an off-the-shelf standard model. This might seem excessive, but if you spend hours pounding keys every day, the expense can be justified. You wouldn't buy a pair of shoes that don't fit properly just because they're cheap; you shouldn't use an inexpensive keyboard that makes your wrists hurt either.

Sometimes it's possible to accomplish the same kind of relief from painful typing without the need to replace your keyboard. Most keyboards have adjustable feet that can raise or lower the back of the keyboard enough to change the angle of bend in your wrists. Your goal should be to keep your wrists as straight as possible.

TIP The U.S. Occupational Safety & Health Administration (OSHA) recommends the use of a wrist or palm rest in front of the keyboard to reduce stress to the nerves and tendons. The wrist rest should match the width, height, and slope of your keyboard, and it should be at least 1.5 inches (3.8 cm) deep.

CROSS-REF See Chapter 29 for more information about ergonomic keyboards and other ways to be more comfortable while using your computer.

Special keys in laptop computers

Because the size of a laptop computer is limited, there isn't enough space for all of the keys that you normally find on a desktop keyboard. So the separate navigation keys and the numeric keypad are gone, and many of the other keys have more than one use. Unfortunately, this is one more feature that different makes and models handle in various ways; you might easily find that one computer works quite differently than another.

The Fn key

The Fn (or Func) key is yet another shift key that changes the performance of many of the keys on a laptop. To use one of the Fn functions printed on a key cap (often in a different color from the main function of the same key), hold down the Fn key and press the control or function key.

When you hold down the Fn key, many of the function and control keys have special uses that don't exist on a desktop computer. Some of the special Fn keys on a laptop run services that are closely related to battery-powered portable operation. For example, one of the keys might open a battery display, and another turns the built-in wireless networking interface on or off. Your computer's online Help and the User's Guide supplied with the computer are the best places to find explanations of the computer's specific Fn controls.

The numeric keypad

As I explained earlier in this chapter, there are a few applications that treat the number keys in the numeric keypad differently from the numbers across the top of the typewriter keys.

In many laptops, the numeric keyboard is available as a secondary function for a group of type-writer keys, arranged so that the top row of the keypad (the 7, 8, and 9) use the same numbers on the typewriter keys, and the rest of the keypad numbers and arithmetic keys match a keypad as closely as possible (see Figure 12.13). The keypad numbers appear on the lower part of each key cap.

To turn on the numeric keypad, use the Num Lock key. On many laptops, Num Lock is a secondary use for one of the F# or control keys. To activate Num Lock, hold down the Fn key while you press the Num Lock key.

TIP   The numeric keypad function on a laptop is OK for occasional use, but if you use your laptop for a lot of numeric data entry, you should seriously consider using an external 10-key keypad. USB 10-key numeric keypads are widely available from computer retailers and online sources.

FIGURE 12.13
_____

The numeric keypad is combined with the typewriter keypad.

Using the On-Screen Keyboard

The On-Screen Keyboard shown in Figure 12.14 is exactly what the name suggests: It's a Windows utility program that displays a keyboard on your monitor. When you click a picture of a key, Windows treats it as if you had pressed a key on the physical keyboard. The On-Screen Keyboard is intended primarily for computer users who can move a mouse or some kind of alternative input device more easily than they can enter text and commands through a traditional keyboard, but it could also be useful in some special situations, such as a computer where the keyboard has been lost, broken, or stolen, or a setting where the sound of clicking keys might be intrusive.

FIGURE 12.14

The On-Screen Keyboard replaces mouse clicks for keystrokes.

To open the On-Screen Keyboard, select Start ➪ All Programs ➪ Accessories ➪ Accessibility in the Windows XP menu or Start ➪ Programs ➪ Accessibility ➪ On-Screen Keyboard in the Classic Windows menu. If you prefer, you can open Start ➪ Run and type osk in the Run field.

CROSS-REF The On-Screen Keyboard is just one of a wide variety of special tools that can make a computer more accessible to users with limited mobility or other special needs. Chapter 31 describes many tools and utilities that you can use to make your computer more accessible.

Using a Mouse

Your computer uses a mouse or other pointing device to follow the movement of your hand, and convert that motion into instructions. These instructions enter commands and move a cursor on the monitor screen. A mouse or some alternative is an essential part of the Windows graphical user interface.

Like the keyboard, a mouse is a simple computer that exchanges information with the main CPU in a computer through a controller in the computer's chipset. Most mice include these elements:

- A motion sensor, most often either a light-emitting diode (LED) and optical sensor or a rolling ball that moves along the surface of a table or other flat surface.

- A pair of mechanical devices that convert the horizontal and vertical motion detected by the motion sensor into digital data. This data specifies the direction and speed that the mouse is moving.

- One or more electrical switches (usually two or three) that respond to pushbuttons on the surface of the mouse.

- A small processor that accepts input data from the motion sensor and the state of the switches (open or closed). The processor relays that data to the mouse controller in the computer through either a cable or some kind of wireless link.

Many mice also include a wheel (most often on top of the mouse, between the buttons) that a user can rotate or twist to send another set of instructions to the processor.

When the mouse controller receives data that the position of the mouse has changed, or that a pushbutton's switch has been pushed or released, or the wheel has turned, the controller sends that information to the CPU. The CPU uses instructions from the mouse device driver software to interpret the data and respond according to the device driver's configuration settings.

In practice, this means you can do several things with a mouse:

■ When you move the mouse along a table or other surface, an arrow or other indicator) on your screen (the *cursor*) follows that motion or performs some other action.

■ When you push or click one of the buttons or rotate the wheel, Windows performs an action specified by the mouse configuration settings program.

Choosing a mouse

You can choose among several hundred different computer mouse models, not counting touchpads and alternative tracking devices built into keyboards. The major differences among all these mice include:

■ Size and shape

■ Number of buttons

■ Connection type

■ Tracking method

■ Sensitivity and performance

■ Color or other decoration

Fortunately, most new mice are not expensive, so you don't have to settle for the generic model supplied with your computer. In most cases, the best mouse is the one that offers the shape, size, and combination of buttons and other features that makes it a comfortable extension of your hand. Therefore, the best way to shop for a new mouse is to go to one or more retail stores, try all the mice on display, and choose one that feels best in your hand. There's no good reason to settle for an uncomfortable mouse.

Ball or optical tracking?

Most early mice used a small rotating ball that rolled along the table and turned a pair of rollers to transmit motion. A few new mice still use balls, and old ones still work well, but many new models use an optical sensor with an LED or a laser in place of the ball. In most applications, both types work equally well, but manufacturers claim that optical mice offer more precise motion tracking and longer life because they have no mechanical parts.

On the other hand, if you don't abuse it, and you clean out the accumulated gunk every few months, a mouse with a ball inside can last for many years. And if you prefer one of those "upside down" mice that uses a big ball that you rotate with your fingers instead of moving the whole mouse across the table, a trackball is your only choice.

TIP If you do use a mouse with a ball in it, place a mouse pad under it to prevent scuffs or other damage to the table top.

The feel of a mouse in your hand is much more important than the technology that it uses to translate motion on the table to motion on the screen. Unless you need extremely precise operation, either type can give you more than adequate performance.

Wired or wireless?

Wireless mice are more flexible than mice with cables because you aren't limited by the length of the cord, and you don't have to deal with cables that tangle or catch onto objects between the mouse and the computer. If you like to lean back in your chair while you browse the Internet, or if you want to use the mouse for public presentations where you're more than six feet from the computer, a wireless mouse is the obvious choice.

But if you share the computer with other users, or if it's in a public location, a wireless mouse will probably disappear into a desk drawer or somebody's pocket within a short period of time. Even worse, some mice use the same 2.4 GHz radio frequencies as Bluetooth and Wi-Fi devices, as well as many cordless telephones and microwave ovens, so radio interference can be a serious problem. If you can't use an RF (radio) mouse, consider one that uses the same kind of infrared signaling as a TV remote control unit.

TIP Wireless mice need batteries, and batteries can die at the most inconvenient times. Unless you have a spare battery when the battery wears out (and you remember where to find it!), your computer will be out of commission until you can find a replacement. To avoid this kind of problem, it's a good idea to keep a spare wired USB mouse (and a set of batteries) in your desk-drawer collection of emergency computer parts.

Performance and responsiveness are similar for both wired and wireless mice. If the convenience of using a wireless mouse outweighs the potential risks of loss, theft, and interference, go ahead and try one.

How many buttons?

Windows requires mice with at least two buttons: left and right. You use the left one for clicking items to select them and the right button for opening context-selective menus and other right-click functions.

Many mice also include a third button, often combined with a wheel that can scroll text up or down the screen without using the scrollbar at the side of the window, whose performance is set by the mouse configuration utility. Some of the most common uses for the middle button include double-clicking (which sends two left-clicks to the processor), opening a menu, or saving the current document or job. To open the Mouse Properties utility, open to the Windows Control Panel and click the Mouse icon.

If two buttons are good, and three are better, why not four or five buttons, or even more? Some specialized mice offer that option. Additional buttons can be programmed to enter commonly used text strings (such as your name or password), or to enter fast-trigger commands in games and other programs. Don't forget to try a multiple-button mouse before you buy it; if a button doesn't fit easily under one of your fingers, you probably won't ever use it.

PS/2, USB, or serial port

The mouse cable or the wireless receiver connects to the computer through either a USB port or a dedicated mouse port that uses the same kind of input connector as a PS/2 keyboard cable. Most new mice use USB connectors, but many come with an adapter for the PS/2 mouse port that is still present on most computer motherboards.

Both USB and PS/2 mice can work equally well. However, a mouse is an extremely low-impact device, so it generally doesn't matter one way or the other.

Other important specifications

Just about any new mouse can meet most users' needs, but gamers and other performance geeks might want to examine some other specifications. These include:

- **Refresh rate:** An optical mouse's motion sensor detects new images at regular intervals (up to 500 reports per second in the most sensitive mice). The refresh rate is the number of samples per second. Microsoft calls this the *imaging rate*, and Logitech calls it the "report rate." When the refresh rate is higher, the cursor on the monitor screen tracks the motion of the mouse more precisely.

- **Resolution:** Resolution is the number of dots per inch (dpi) that the optical sensor crosses as you move the mouse. For most users, 400 to 800 dpi is good enough, but a game that requires more sensitive mouse motion for precise placement of the cursor might benefit from resolution as high as 1600–2000 dpi.

- **Speed.** If you move the mouse across the table too quickly, the cursor on the screen might move farther and faster than you want it to move. The mouse configuration utility often includes an adjustment that can change the maximum tracking speed. When you reduce the speed, you can control the cursor with more precision.

Handheld mice, trackballs, touchpads, and other alternatives

Sometimes it's easier to hold a pointing device in your hand or move a ball with your fingers rather than move the whole mouse around a tabletop. Several manufacturers offer handheld mice with a ball that you can control with your thumb, trackballs, and other alternatives to conventional mice. Still others use a touchpad that tracks the motion of your finger across a surface that detects the electrical charge between your finger and the pad. The signal supplied to the computer's mouse controller from an alternative pointing device is identical to the signal from an ordinary mouse. The only differences are the physical motions by your hand that trigger those signals. If they're designed well, alternative pointing devices can do everything that a mouse can do.

But consider this: Over the last 20-plus years, many alternatives to traditional mice have come and gone because they didn't feel good in *anybody's* hands. (Trust me on this. My box of junk computer parts is full of them.) If you find something that works for you, go ahead and use it, but don't expect some pointing device that somebody designed on their kitchen table and sold through an obscure Web site to be better than the mouse you can buy at your local office supplies store.

 For information about using touch pads and pointing sticks in laptop computers, see Chapter 20.

Tweaking your mouse

Every new mouse comes with a device driver and a configuration utility that loads into the Windows Control Panel. If you're trying to install an old mouse into a new system, look for the control software that you can download from the mouse maker's Web site. If you can't find any product-specific software, use the software supplied with Windows.

There's also a set of generic mouse configuration software built into Windows. But unless you're using a two-button Microsoft mouse, you get better performance and more features with the specific program designed for your own mouse's make and model. To open the configuration utility for the mouse installed on your computer, open the Windows Control Panel and choose the Mouse icon.

Each configuration program is slightly different, but many include these options and settings:

Device type

The major mouse makers, including Microsoft and Logitech, use the same mouse configuration utility for mice that may have quite different sets of features. Therefore, the first thing to do when you configure the settings for a new mouse is to choose the specific model you're using from the Device menu. If you don't know which model you're using, look for a label on the bottom of the mouse.

Buttons

The Buttons settings assign specific functions to each of the mouse's buttons and other controls. For example, the window shown in Figure 12.15 sets the settings for a three-button mouse.

FIGURE 12.15

Use the Buttons settings to assign a specific use to each mouse button.

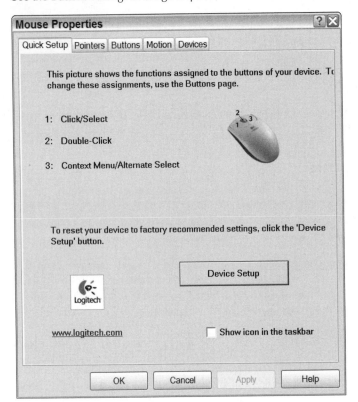

Pointers

Pointers are the cursors and other symbols that Windows uses to show the current location of the mouse on your monitor screen. The Pointers menu offers several different sets of symbols, so you can select one that's easy to see against the background of your Windows desktop and other on-screen items. For example, the Windows Default pointers use a white arrow as the normal cursor, which is great for a screen with a dark background. But if you use a lighter background, such as the one shown in Figure 12.16, a black arrow is often a better choice. Other schemes can include a larger cursor that's easy to find, but which can sometimes cover text or other details in a document or a Web page.

Some mouse utilities also include several novelty pointer schemes along with the more utilitarian cursor sets. If you or your children are easily amused, consider installing one of these schemes. However, be wary of cursors and other mouse programs that you find as free downloads on the Internet; they're a notorious source of spyware and adware.

FIGURE 12.16

Choose a cursor scheme that contrasts with the background of your Windows desktop.

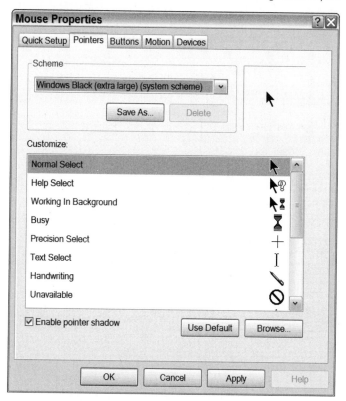

Motion or pointer options

The Motion dialog box, shown in Figure 12.17, includes several options that affect the way the on-screen cursor responds to mouse motion. For most users, the best Pointer speed is someplace in the middle of the range, and the other options are matters of personal taste.

The best way to set the cursor speed and other settings in this dialog box is to change one setting at a time, click the Apply button, and see how the new setting feels. When you have set each option to the response you want, move on to the next one.

FIGURE 12.17

Use the Motion tab of the Mouse Properties dialog box to adjust the way the cursor moves across the screen.

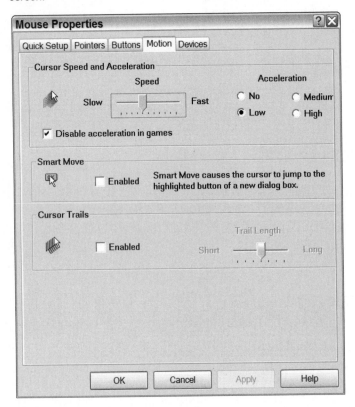

Using Pen Tablets and Digital Notepads

A pen tablet is an input device that allows a user to draw or write directly onto a flat surface with a stylus and transfer an image of the drawing or handwritten text to a computer. When a compatible program is active, it displays the words or pictures as soon as you create them. You can also use a tablet as an alternative to a mouse by moving the stylus to move the cursor, and tapping the stylus on the tablet's surface to click an icon or other object on the screen.

A digital notepad is similar, but it can store and display the drawings or text within the notepad and allow the user to transfer them to the computer later. Therefore, you can use a notepad just as you would use pen and paper to make handwritten notes at a meeting or lecture without the need to carry a computer.

Many tablets and notepads use a grid under the writing or drawing surface with a unique address for each point on the surface that corresponds to a pixel on the monitor screen. When the tablet or pad detects pressure from the stylus at a specific location, it either sends that information to the computer through a USB port or stores it in local memory inside the notepad for later transfer. After the CPU receives the information, it uses instructions from the device driver to interpret the location of the stylus (and a command, if any) and relays it to the active program, which displays a mark on the screen or performs the command.

Tablet computers do something similar, but they use a special monitor screen that has a layer beneath the surface that can sense stylus pressure rather than a separate drawing pad. A special version of Microsoft Windows, called Windows XP Tablet PC Edition, includes the device drivers and other programs necessary to incorporate the Tablet PC functions into Windows.

Tablets and notepads are not the same as the touch pads that many laptop computers use as an alternative to a mouse. The touch pad is a separate surface; touch-sensitive notepads and tablets accept inputs directly onto the computer's display screen.

Tablets and notepads offer more precise control of a cursor for drawings and handwritten notes because the stylus duplicates the familiar motion of a pen, pencil, or brush. It's possible to use a pen tablet as a replacement for a mouse, but it's often easier to have both: a tablet and stylus for drawing, and a mouse for the usual cursor controls.

Using Bar Code Readers

Bar codes are those rows of black lines that seem to show up on everything from soup cans to library books to tracking labels on packages. Anytime there's a need to assign a very large number (more than about four or five digits) to identify something, it's usually easier to use a bar code instead of copying the number by hand. The familiar 8- or 12-digit bar code on most consumer products is called the *Universal Product Code*, or UPC.

A bar code reader is not standard equipment for most computer users, but they can be useful for things like inventory management or cataloging your collection of books, CDs and DVDs. The UPC Database Web site (www.upcdatabase.com/itemform.asp) can translate UPCs to the products that each UPC identifies.

Most bar codes use groups of vertical lines of different widths to indicate the binary value of each number or other character in the code. About a dozen different bar code structures exist, but it's possible to use the same readers (with different software) for just about all of them.

TIP   If you're interested in learning how to interpret many common bar codes, take a look at the Barcode Island Web site at www.barcodeisland.com/symbolgy.phtml.

A bar code reader is a light pen or laser that detects the thickness of each bar and converts the sequence back to a specific number, which it transmits to a computer. Depending on the size and shape of the object that carries the bar code, the person using a bar code reader might move a portable reader across the object, or he might move the object past a stationary reader. The computer searches for that number in a database that contains detailed information about the item assigned to that number, such as the name and price of the soup, the title of the book, or the shipping details of the package.

A bar code reader has two parts: a scanner that reads the bar code and converts it to electrical impulses, and a decoder that converts the signals from the scanner to a code number and transmits it to a computer.

Many older bar code readers use a wedge that plugs into a computer's keyboard socket and sends bar code numbers to the computer as key scans. Some wedges have a second keyboard connector, so it's possible to use both the bar code reader and a traditional keyboard or a 10-key keypad at the same time. Today, readers with a USB interface instead of a wedge are more common.

To use a bar code reader with your computer, simply plug the PS/2 cable from the wedge or the USB cable from the decoder into the appropriate connector on the computer and load the device driver software supplied with the reader. Once again, different makes and models of bar code readers have different feature sets, so the installation instructions and User's Guide are your best source of specific information.

Summary

Your computer's keyboard, mouse, and other input devices are the primary channels that you can use to send commands and data to the CPU. Both the keyboard and mouse contain small, self-contained computers that convert electrical impulses to data and transmit that data to a buffer inside the computer.

Because you use the keyboard and the mouse so often, it's extremely important to find models that fit comfortably under your hands. Using the wrong ones for your particular needs can literally become a very painful experience.

Other input devices are also available, and they might be better choices for some users. These include touchpads, graphics tablets, and even bar code readers. But for most of us, the mouse and the keyboard will be the most common physical interface between you and your computer.

Chapter 13

Sound Cards, Speakers, and Other Audio

The sounds produced by the earliest personal computers were limited to occasional beeps and clicks through the speaker inside the case. There were programs that could make high beeps and low beeps, and some really goofy programs that made the computer talk like one of those robots in a bad science fiction movie, but the sounds produced by those computers were really just audible signals.

It didn't take long for *sound cards* to appear as plug-in expansion cards that could play recorded sounds in games, educational programs, and other software. These sound cards used external speakers that sounded a lot better than the little ones built into the case, so music and speech could actually sound like something produced by human beings (or in many games, by aliens from outer space).

This was all happening at about the same time that digital recordings on compact discs were beginning to replace the older analog vinyl records and cassette tapes. As these two trends (computer sound and digital audio) evolved, it was inevitable that personal computers would make more extensive use of sound. Today, millions of people use their computers to store and play music and other recorded sound.

Sound cards aren't limited to playing recordings that were created someplace else. The same cards also have input circuits that can record and store sound from microphones and other sources. As the performance of computer-based sound has improved, most radio stations and recording studios have replaced their old tape recorders with high-quality sound processors connected to computers.

225

A sound card, or a sound controller built into the motherboard, is now standard equipment on most new personal computers, and Windows uses a long list of prerecorded sounds. Audio has become an essential part of the overall computing experience.

Built-in Speakers

Almost all computers still have a small speaker mounted inside the case. This speaker is adequate for the audible signaling that Windows and other software produces to warn you when some important event has occurred. The computer's BIOS also uses this speaker to produce the beep codes that sound when the Power-On Self Test detects certain types of system problems.

Because those beeps and other alarms are intended to attract your attention rather than to entertain you, small cheap speakers are entirely adequate for this use. But when you want to listen to the sounds that come to you through the computer, you want something better.

When Windows detects a sound controller on the motherboard or a separate audio device, it re-directs alarm sounds from the built-in speaker to the sound controller. You can use the BIOS Setup Utility to disable the sound controller and use the built-in speaker instead.

How Sound Cards Work

The sound you hear all around you is produced when a physical object — such as the strings of a gui-tar or violin, the brass surface of a bell, or the vocal cords of a bird or a human being — moves within a range of frequencies between about 15 and 18,000 times per second (15 Hertz–18 kilohertz). This vibration causes the surrounding air to vibrate, which transmits the sound to the membranes in your eardrums and causes them to vibrate at the same frequencies.

This is called *analog* sound, because your eardrum vibrates at the same rate and volume as the object that produced the original sound. Analog sound travels to your ear or through an electronic circuit in a continuous stream.

In a computer, recorded sound is *digital,* because that continuous stream of vibrations has been broken down into thousands of separate numeric values every second. Digital sound must be con-verted back to analog and played through a speaker, earphones or some other similar device before you can hear it.

A computer's sound controller performs these activities:

- It receives digital data from the CPU and converts it into an analog signal.
- It amplifies the analog signal and sends it to two or more speakers.

- It receives analog sound directly from a microphone or from some other source and amplifies it if necessary.

- It converts the analog signal to digital form and sends the digital data to the CPU.

Some sound controllers use separate analog-to-digital converters (ADCs) and digital-to-analog converters (DACs). Lower-quality controllers perform both kinds of conversion in a single circuit called a CODEC (COder/DECoder).

In order to convert analog sound to digital form, the processor on the sound card slices the analog audio stream into tiny pieces, and it measures the volume and frequencies of the sound in each piece. The quality of a digital recording depends on two elements: the number of slices per second (the *sampling rate* or *sample rate*) and the number of digital bits the processor uses to store each sample (the *bit depth*).

A sound controller can play existing files, and it can also instruct the CPU to create new sound recordings and store them on the computer's disk drive.

The combined sampling rate and bit depth is often described as the *bit rate* of a recording; the quality of the recording improves as the sampling rate and bit depth increase. For example, the bit rate of a commercial audio CD is 16 bits and 44,100 samples per second, or 16-bits/44.1 kHz, but many recording studios and sound archivists create and store their digital master recordings at 24-bits/96 kHz, or even 24-bits/192 kHz. Of course, there's definitely a point of diminishing returns where most listeners can't hear any improvement, but a higher bit rate also allows an audio engineer to perform more precise processing on a recording to reduce noise or add special effects.

If you're acquainted with the way your computer handles video, the rest of a sound controller's operation might sound familiar: a specialized processor called the digital signal processor (DSP) controls the conversions between analog and digital sound, and exchanges instructions with the computer's central processor. The CPU treats the sound controller as one more source and destination for data to and from active programs.

CROSS-REF See Chapter 10 for more information about understanding video in a computer.

Some programs, such as Windows Media Player and RealPlayer, act as readers for sound files and incoming data streams. When you want to listen to an audio file stored on your disk drive, a CD, or a streaming Internet service, one of these programs reads the data in the file or stream and sends it to the sound card. Other programs can send sounds directly to the sound controller, without the need for a separate program in between. For example, when America Online produces its well-known "You've got mail!" message, the audio goes directly to the sound controller.

Choosing a Sound Card

Sound cards and processors on motherboards in today's new computers are commodity items: Unless you go out of your way to find a cheap one, you can expect the audio controller supplied with your system to provide entirely adequate performance for listening to music in two-channel stereo from CDs, movie soundtracks on DVDs, and streaming audio from the Internet. The quality you hear depends on the quality of the original recording or the bandwidth of the Internet feed, but you can generally expect the sound through your computer to be at least as good as a local FM radio station or a decent CD player.

The basic feature set includes:

- Stereo (two-channel) recording and playback
- Analog line-level input
- Microphone input
- Analog output for stereo speakers
- Headphone output
- Minimum CD quality (16-bit/44.1 KHz) bit rate

Many motherboards and sound cards have additional features that build on that minimum. These include:

- Surround sound outputs (at least 5.1, which means five speakers plus a subwoofer)
- Digital inputs and outputs that bypass the ADC and DAC converters
- Support for DVD movies
- 96 KHz or 192 KHz maximum sampling rate
- 24-bit bit depth
- MIDI (Musical Instrument Digital Interface) input for connecting keyboards and other instruments to the computer
- Support for 2-D and 3-D audio in games and other accelerated video

Some audio engineers believe that a sound controller inside a computer case, on either a motherboard or an expansion card, should never be used for serious recording because the computer's power supply and other components can produce electronic noise. Therefore, many professional recording interfaces are in a separate enclosure that connects to the computer through a USB or Firewire port.

Sound Blaster and other standards

The Sound Blaster range of sound cards made by Creative Technology has been the dominant brand in consumer-level audio controllers for many years. As a result, some salespeople describe controllers on motherboard and sound cards from other manufacturers as "Sound Blaster compatible."

In fact, Sound Blaster cards have evolved and improved over time, so it's entirely possible for a competing card to be "Sound Blaster compatible" because it matches the features and functions of an old and long-obsolete Sound Blaster model; but that's no guarantee that it's as good as a current-model Sound Blaster (or a current card from some other company).

The real standard for sound controllers in personal computers is the joint Intel-Microsoft *PC 2001 System Design Guide* that includes the technical guidelines for expansion cards and peripheral devices that work with Windows (you can download a copy from www.microsoft.com/whdc/system/platform/pcdesign/desguide/pcguides.mspx, but it's not particularly exciting reading). Any new sound controller you're likely to find probably exceeds the *Design Guide's* specifications, so there is no longer any reason to worry about whether or not a sound card is "Sound Blaster compatible."

Higher quality sound cards

As I said earlier in this chapter, the sound controllers supplied with most new computers are fine for day-to-day listening and occasional recording, but like everything else attached to a computer, it's also possible to replace them with high-end versions that offer improved performance. Like just about everything else inside your computer, one of the most common reasons to buy one of those high-end sound controllers is to play the latest generation of computer games. However, high-end audio cards also have some other uses.

High-quality sound controllers fall into several quite different categories: sound cards for games, surround sound for home entertainment systems, and interfaces for professional-quality recording. Each of these applications requires a specific type of audio product; it's not possible to install an all-purpose, high-end sound controller.

Sound for games

As you know, many new games place extremely heavy demands on a computer's CPU, RAM, and other components. Audio is no exception, so a sound card designed specifically for games enhances the game-playing experience.

The design goals for a game-player's sound card include:

- 2-D and 3-D positional effects that create the illusion of individual sounds coming from specific directions that may track the images on one or more screens. The best positional audio effects work either through speakers or headphones.
- A DSP that offloads as much audio processing as possible from the CPU.
- Dedicated audio RAM that leaves more system memory for other activity.
- High definition (24-bit) audio conversion to enhance sound quality.

Surround sound

The objective of a modern home theater system is to reproduce the experience of watching a movie in a theater, with speakers located all around the seats. Unlike a concert hall (or traditional two-channel stereo) where the sound is spread across an aural stage in front of the listener, a surround sound system places you right in the middle of the action.

Surround sound requires at least four speakers (two in front and two in back), but the most common setups add a fifth center-front speaker. In addition, most surround systems include a separate speaker for very low frequencies called a *subwoofer*. A system with five main speakers and a subwoofer is identified as a 5.1 system. Some systems also add a pair of side speakers between front and rear to create 7.1 sound.

Therefore, an audio controller for a surround sound system has enough output connections for all of the main speakers. These might be separate sockets for each speaker or a big multi-pin plug that mates to a special breakout cable.

Many DVDs and audio files include soundtracks already encoded for surround sound; a surround sound audio controller can also synthesize surround sound from a file with only two channels.

Professional recording

For serious recording, a sound controller must create and store digital audio files that are the most accurate possible copies of the original analog or digital source material. Those sources can include an amplifier, a microphone connected directly to the sound card, or the analog or digital output of a mixing desk. The same sound card's outputs are often used to convey digital audio from the computer to a professional environment such as a radio station or a recording studio.

To accomplish this, a professional-quality recording interface usually has these features:

- Balanced analog input and output channels that are less sensitive to hum and noise
- Very low internal noise and distortion
- High sample rates and bit rates (at least 24-bit/96 kHz)
- Digital inputs and outputs
- Support for the ASIO (Audio Stream In/Out) specification for multi-channel recording
- Clock synchronization with digital inputs
- Flexible control software (see Figure 13.1)

FIGURE 13.1

The control software for a professional audio interface offers many options and settings.

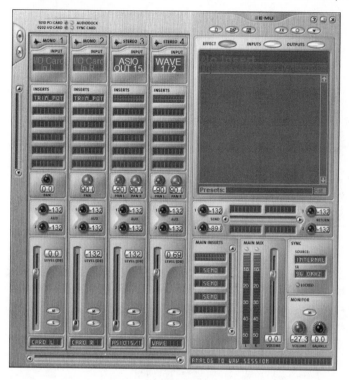

External sound controllers

The alternative to an internal sound controller is an audio interface in a separate enclosure that exchanges data with the CPU through a USB or Firewire port. An external sound controller can be anything from a simple adapter like the one shown in Figure 13.2 that simply converts input signals to digital format and passes it to the computer, to the full-featured mixing desk in Figure 13.3 that includes multiple microphone and high-level inputs, audio equalization and many other features.

FIGURE 13.2

An external sound controller can be quite simple . . .

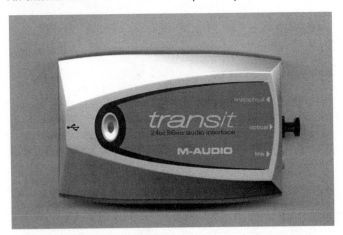

FIGURE 13.3

. . . or extremely complex.

External sound controllers can offer these benefits:

- Lower exposure to hum and noise generated inside the computer case
- Hardware controls for input and output channels
- Higher-quality microphone channels and other audio circuits
- More flexible operation

Configuring Windows for Your Sound Card

The configuration software for the sound controller installed in your computer includes several settings and options that affect the way you play sounds. The Sounds and Audio Devices Properties window is the first place to look for these controls. To open the Properties window, open the Windows Control Panel and click the Sounds and Audio Devices icon.

The Properties window normally has five tabs. The exact appearance of each tab may be different from the ones shown here, because your sound controller's device driver might have a slightly different feature set.

Volume

The Volume tab (see Figure 13.4) contains a master volume control for your speakers. Move the Device volume slider to the right to make the speakers louder or to the left to turn them down. This is the same control that appears in the Volume Control window that you can open from the Windows taskbar.

If there's a volume control knob on your speakers, that control is located after the Properties control in the audio chain. In other words, if you send a loud signal to the speakers, you can use the volume control on the speaker to turn it down, but if the speaker volume is turned down, you can't turn it up from the Windows Volume Control.

When the Mute option is turned on, no sound goes to the speakers. The Advanced button in the Volume tab opens the Volume Control window.

FIGURE 13.4

The Volume tab controls the output playback level from your sound controller.

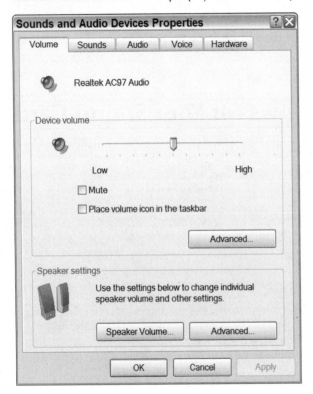

The Speaker Volume button at the bottom of the screen opens another dialog box (see Figure 13.5) where you can set the individual volume for each speaker. In most cases, you want to keep all the speakers at the same level, but this can be useful if you are sitting closer to one speaker than the other (or your hearing is impaired in one ear) in a two-channel system, or if you want to balance the relative level of the front, back, and side speakers in a surround sound system.

FIGURE 13.5

Use the Speaker Volume controls to balance the relative levels of your speakers.

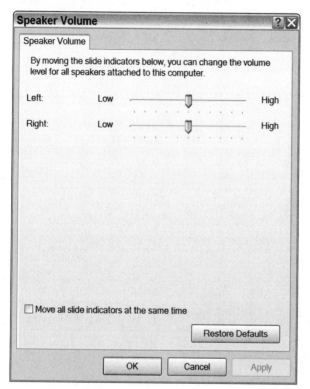

The Advanced button in the Speaker Settings box at the bottom of the Volume tab opens yet another window with several tabs. The Speakers tab (see Figure 13.6) offers a long menu of speaker arrangements; choose the one that most closely resembles your own system to optimize the sound quality for that layout.

FIGURE 13.6

Use the Advanced Audio Properties window to optimize sound playback for your speakers.

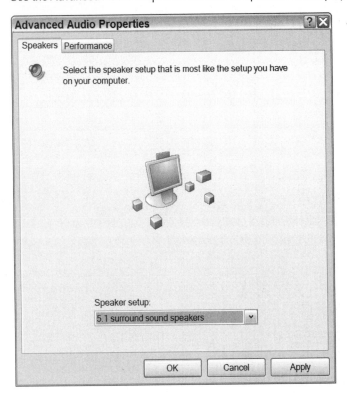

The Advanced Audio Properties Performance tab changes the way Windows allocates sound processing activity between the CPU and the sound controller. Unless you're having a problem with sound playback, move both sliders to the extreme right. Unless you're using certain games, you probably won't ever need to change these settings.

Sounds

The Sounds tab (see Figure 13.7) controls the sound effects that Windows and many other programs play when certain events occur. To change the set of sounds, use the drop-down Sound scheme menu. To completely turn off those sounds, choose the No Sounds scheme.

If you're amused by odd sound effects, you can replace the entire Windows Default scheme or any individual sound with other sound files.

FIGURE 13.7

Use the Sounds tab to change Windows sound effects or to turn them off completely.

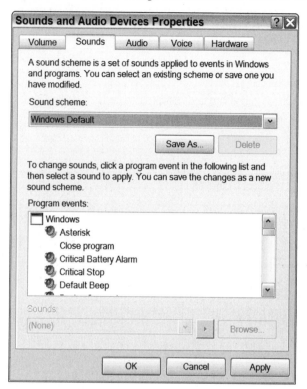

Audio

If there is more than one sound controller connected to your computer, the Audio tab (see Figure 13.8) is the place where you can tell Windows which one to use as the default for recording and playback, and for playing music through a MIDI device. You don't ever need this control unless you have two or more sound controllers or MIDI controllers attached to your computer at the same time.

If your computer does have two or more sound controllers (such as an internal sound card and an external recording device) connected through the FireWire or USB port, use the drop-down menus to choose the sound controller you want to use as your default playback, recording or MIDI controller.

Notice that these are default settings. Many sound editors and other programs that record and play audio include their own option settings that can override this default.

Voice

The Voice tab controls the input and output levels for the text-to-speech features in Windows. If you have a microphone connected to the computer for voice-input commands, or if you use Narrator or another program that converts text to sound, use the two Volume buttons to set input and output levels, or use the Test hardware button to run a configuration wizard.

Hardware

The Hardware tab has no configuration settings. It provides shortcuts to the Properties windows for each hardware device that plays a part in audio input or output.

FIGURE 13.8

Use the Audio tab to select the sound controller that it uses as the default for recording and playback.

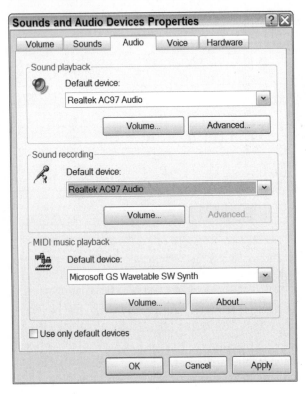

Other Audio Control Utilities

Many audio device drivers also include their own control software that sometimes includes control settings that aren't available in the Windows Sounds and Audio Devices Properties dialog boxes. These programs often try to imitate the appearance of a stereo amplifier or some other piece of audio hardware. Some controls do exactly the same things as similar settings and options in the Sounds and Audio Devices Properties window, but others can change the character of the sound by altering equalization (relative level of high and low frequencies) and adding echo to the sound. For example, the SoundMax utility's main screen, shown in Figure 13.9, duplicates the controls in the Windows Volume Control window. However, the SoundMax Preferences window (see Figure 13.10) offers settings that can imitate many different acoustic environments and compensate for the different hearing ranges of adults and children.

FIGURE 13.9

The SoundMax control panel duplicates the Windows Volume Control.

In most cases, any configuration setting that changes the equalization or *environment* is more likely to degrade the sound rather than improve it. Go ahead and experiment with these options, but remember that the *None* options probably sound better than any other adjustment.

CROSS-REF See Chapter 42 for information about using your computer to play, record, and edit sound.

FIGURE 13.10

SoundMax includes many settings and options that are not accessible from Windows.

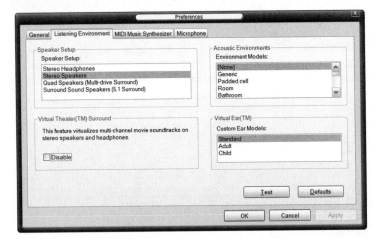

The Windows Volume Control

The most common adjustment you may want to make on audio playback or recording is the volume level. You can open the Volume Control window shown in Figure 13.11 from the Start menu (Start ➪ Programs ➪ Accessories ➪ Entertainment). The Options ➪ Properties command opens a window where you can add additional volume sliders to the Volume Control window for individual sources and destinations, such as a microphone or a CD player.

FIGURE 13.11

The sliders on the Volume Control window set input and output levels for audio signals.

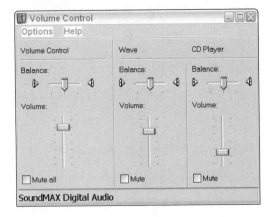

The horizontal Balance sliders in each column control the relative level of the audio to or from the left and right channels.

Adding a Subwoofer

A subwoofer is a special speaker that enhances the low-frequency bass response of a music reproduction system. Because low frequencies demand more power from an audio amplifier than other parts of the audio spectrum, many speakers are designed to ignore extremely low frequencies. This may be fine for listening to speech and many kinds of music, but anything with significant deep bass content sounds much better with a subwoofer to restore the bottom end. Rock-and-roll bass lines, pipe organs, and even bluegrass or jazz are all more realistic if you add a subwoofer to your system. If you're looking for realistic sound in games and DVD movies, a subwoofer is just about essential.

Subwoofers are an essential part of a multichannel surround sound environment, but they also enhance the quality of a simple two-speaker system. A matched set of speakers and subwoofer usually produce more pleasant sound than a random combination. Many mid-range and better computer-speaker makers offer subwoofers that are matched with their other speakers; the bottom end of the regular speakers' sound overlaps with the top of the subwoofer's range, so the subwoofer extends the main speakers' low end.

If you can't find a matched set, try to test several different subwoofer makes and models with your new or existing speakers. It's best to choose the main speakers first and then find a sub that sounds good with it.

No matter how many regular speakers you're using, you need only a single subwoofer. Unlike the mid-range and treble sounds that your ear can locate very accurately, sounds at those low frequencies are not directional: Wherever you place the sub, the bass sounds fill the room.

Different makes and models of speakers and subwoofers use different connection methods. The instructions supplied with your sound controller and the subwoofer itself are your best sources for specific instructions.

Using a Microphone

A microphone is an important part of a computer's sound system. Many programs, including instant voice messaging, voice-over-Internet Phones (VoIP), podcasts, and voice commands use speech as a source of commands or content.

Unless you're using a sound control interface intended for professional recording, you don't need to spend a lot of money on a microphone for your computer. All the fancy features that can make a microphone sound wonderful in a studio or on a stage can actually create bad sound if you plug the microphone into a computer.

It may look similar to the microphones you see on a stage, but the one plugged into your computer is there for just one reason: To make your voice easy to understand. For speech, the best place for a microphone is between six inches and a foot away from the speaker's mouth. If you're too close, the microphone distorts your voice; if it's too far away, the other noises in the room (including echoes from the walls and ceiling) overpower it. Yes, it's true that many singers work a lot closer, but their microphones are designed to eliminate the distortion known as *proximity effect* that occurs when an announcer or vocalist is too close (or emphasize it, if that's what they want). Look for a microphone with a table stand that can sit on the table close to your keyboard.

Summary

Your computer uses a sound controller to convert analog audio from a microphone or some other source into digital data that it can store as files, and from digital files to sound that plays through speakers. Most computers use either a sound card that plugs into one of its PCI sockets, or a controller built into the motherboard. Special high-performance sound controllers are available for game players, for surround-sound home-entertainment systems, and for professional recording studios and broadcasters.

Your computer treats sound as one more type of data that it uses to warn users about certain events, stores on disk drives, and processes through an I/O controller. The Windows audio configuration settings and options are accessible through the Control Panel.

Chapter 14

Using USB and FireWire Interfaces

If you can do it without moving a lot of furniture around, take a look at the back of your computer. You can see a bunch of mismatched connectors that all require different kinds of cables. There's probably a serial data port or two and a printer socket, plus assorted other connectors for the keyboard, the mouse, the monitor, the speakers, the network, and maybe a telephone line. Except for the keyboard and mouse sockets, every one of those connectors was originally designed for some other purpose and tacked onto personal computers when somebody decided that their systems needed to connect to something or other.

But it didn't stop there. Still other devices came along that needed a way to connect to a computer. These included external storage devices such as Zip drives and tape drives, and new kinds of input sources such as scanners and digital cameras. Some of these products used the existing serial or parallel port connectors and others came with their own special expansion cards that added yet another type of connector to the mixture.

This all happened gradually, as each generation of computers added a few more connection types, but by the mid-1990s, some of the biggest players in the personal computer business (Microsoft, Intel, Hewlett-Packard, Compaq, and NEC among them) began to recognize that enough was enough. The solution to the problem of too many connectors was the Universal Serial Bus (USB), which could use the same connector for many purposes. The original USB specification had a maximum data transfer speed of 12 Mbps. A few years later, the USB 2.0 standard increased the maximum to 480 Mbps.

At about the same time, Apple Computer extended its FireWire high-speed serial data transfer method from internal hard drives to external peripheral devices. The Institute of Electrical and Electronics Engineers (IEEE) adopted the FireWire specification as a standard for both Macintosh and Windows computers, which it called IEEE 1394. Sony was the first of many camcorder makers to use IEEE 1394 as a way to transfer video to computer (they called it i.LINK). The maximum data transfer speed through a 1394 interface is 400 Mbps, but even faster FireWire 800 (800 Mbps) interfaces are beginning to appear on some new computers and motherboards.

> **NOTE** Strictly speaking, FireWire is Apple's trademark for its use of the IEEE 1394 specification; any use of that standard that does not involve either a computer or a peripheral device made by Apple should be called an IEEE 1394, or a 1394 connection, or device, or port, or whatever. In practice, this is widely ignored, and the two names are used as if they are interchangeable.

From a user's perspective, the greatest benefit of both USB and IEEE 1394 is that they allow you to simply plug a cable into a socket — any socket — on the front or back of the computer and expect the computer to automatically recognize the gadget on the other end of the cable. If you're using a new device for the first time, Windows might tell you to load some device driver software, but after that, it's all automatic. And the hot-swap feature means that you can connect and disconnect your camera or telephone or portable flash drive (or anything else) without the need to shut down the computer first.

More than ten years after the first USB ports appeared on motherboards and assembled computers, they still haven't completely replaced all those other inputs and outputs, but the industry is definitely moving in that direction. FireWire connections are less common, but they have become a standard for many multimedia devices and applications. By the time you're ready to replace the computer that's on your desk today, it's entirely possible that the new one will use USB and IEEE 1394 connectors for everything except the digital cable for your video display.

In this chapter, you can learn how the USB and FireWire standards work, and how to use them in Windows-based computers.

How USB Works

This section explains how the USB bus recognizes new connections and how it moves data to and from your computer. This is probably more detail than you want or need to connect your printer and your mouse to the computer.

The simple version

When you plug a new device into a USB connector, Windows automatically recognizes the device and starts to exchange data with it. If you haven't used the device on this port before, Windows might ask you to load a device driver first. If you want to disconnect a USB device, just unplug the cable. If all the USB connectors on your computer are full, you can add more by using a *hub* that shares the signal among two or more connections. A hub can be a stand-alone unit with several USB connectors, or it might be built into another device, such as a keyboard or the base of a monitor. The hub normally connects to a computer's USB port through a USB cable.

That's it. That's all you need to know about the way USB works. Now you can skip to the section about cables and connectors later in this chapter. Of course, everything is not that simple. If you want to know how USB's internal plumbing works, keep reading.

The complicated version

The current USB specification (USB 2.0, introduced in 2000) has these design objectives:

- Support for up to 127 separate devices on a single port through one or more hubs
- Data transfer at up to 480 Mbits per second, shared among all devices connected to the same host computer
- Plug and Play operation — Windows automatically recognizes new devices
- Hot swapping — connect or disconnect a USB device without shutting down the computer
- Support for three kinds of data transfer:
  - **Interrupt mode** for low-volume devices like a keyboard or a mouse (up to 1.5 Mbits per second)
  - **Bulk mode** for devices such as a printer or a scanner that transfers data in blocks and verifies the integrity of each block (up to 12 Mbits per second)
  - **Isochronous mode** for continuous streams of data to or from the computer in real time, such as speakers or a Webcam without taking the time for error correcting (up to 480 Mbits per second)
- Transfer DC power from the computer to small peripheral devices

Hubs and expansion cards

A single USB host controller can support multiple client devices through one or more hubs that can share a single host connection. The most common hubs split the connection four ways, but you can also find two-way hubs and others with seven ports or more. To connect more devices than that, simply connect additional hubs in series with the first one.

Each USB host controller is supposed to support up to 127 separate devices, but that's somewhat misleading. It can be done if you connect 127 mice (or other very low-bandwidth interrupt-transfer devices) through the same host, but if you add something like a speaker or a network router to the mix, you will have trouble supporting more than six or eight other devices.

Fortunately, most new computers have more than one host controller. Your computer's chipset includes a USB controller that exchanges data with the Southbridge. Depending on the specific chipset on your motherboard, it can support six, eight, or ten USB hosts, although many motherboards have fewer physical connectors than that. Each USB host connector on the motherboard can connect to one connector on the case.

If the motherboard (or the case) doesn't have enough USB host connectors for everything you want to plug into them, either add a USB hub, or install one or more additional USB controllers on expansion cards in the computer's PCI sockets. If it's a laptop computer, use a hub or a USB controller on a PC Card.

Power distribution

In addition to data exchange, a USB host can also supply electric power to a peripheral device such as a mouse or a keyboard, as long as the maximum power drain is less than about half an amp (500 mA). Larger peripherals like printers normally have their own power supplies.

A USB port can have one of several power modes:

- **Root port:** Power to a root port comes directly from the USB Host Controller. A computer that runs on external power must supply at least 500 mA to each port. A battery-powered computer may supply either 100 mA or 500 mA.

- **Bus-powered hubs:** A bus-powered hub draws all of its power from the host or from a hub between this one and the computer. An external device connected to a bus-powered hub can draw a maximum of 100 mA.

- **Self-powered hubs:** A self-powered hub, or simply a *powered hub*, gets its power from an external power supply or an internal battery rather than the USB host. A hub with external power must supply up to 500 mA to each port. A battery-powered hub may supply either 100 mA or 500 mA to each port.

Therefore, when you shop for a hub, you must choose either a bus-powered hub or a self-powered hub, depending on the type of peripheral devices you plan to use with it. For general use, a self-powered hub is the better choice because it can support more than one bus-powered USB device at the same time. A bus-powered hub may not provide enough power for multiple bus-powered devices, especially with a laptop or other system that uses batteries instead of external power.

Enumeration

When a USB host starts, it detects all of the devices connected to it. This process (called *enumeration*) in which the computer assigns an address to each device includes these steps:

1. **The USB host detects one or more devices and sends a reset command.**

2. **The host requests a series of descriptors from each device.** These descriptors identify the type of device — interrupt, isochronous, or bulk, terms defined later in this chapter — along with the amount of bandwidth each device requires, and other configuration information.

3. **After the host controller receives the descriptors, it assigns an address to each device.**

4. **Windows asks for a device driver.**

5. **Reserving 10 percent of the total bandwidth for bulk transfers and control packets, it continues to accept and enumerate additional devices until the entire maximum bandwidth (480 Mb per second) has been claimed.**

If the host detects a new interrupt device or isochronous device (because a user has plugged another device into a hub), it adds that device to the enumeration, unless the host is already supporting its maximum bandwidth. When a user unplugs a device (or turns it off), the host removes that device's load from the enumeration.

The purpose of enumeration is to identify each device and to allow the USB host to keep track of the maximum bandwidth that all the devices connected to it can use. When the demand exceeds that maximum, the host won't accept any more connections.

Data transfer

Remember that a USB host can handle three different kinds of data: interrupt, isochronous, and bulk. During enumeration, the USB host notes the address and data transfer mode for each connected device. When more than one device connected to the same host wants to transfer data at the same time, the host uses a combination of priorities and shared bandwidth to fulfill the demands it receives from each device.

> **NOTE** USB data transfers take place at different speeds, depending on the requirements of each device and each type of data. Just because one transfer is considered slow compared with another, it's still zipping along; we're talking about the difference between tenths of a second and milliseconds.

Interrupt transfers

Almost all messages that move between interrupt devices and the USB are extremely short: things such as a single scan code from a keyboard or an instruction to light an indicator on the device. Because they don't use much bandwidth, the USB controller can move interrupt transfers without interfering with more time-sensitive isochronous transfers.

When one or more interrupt devices are connected to the USB host, the host conducts a periodic poll of each device to learn if a device has placed an interrupt request in its (the device's) buffer. When the host detects an interrupt request, it transfers the request from the buffer to the CPU and sends an acknowledgement back to the originating device. If the host does not receive the data successfully, it returns a failure message and the originating device tries a resend.

When the host originates a transfer to an interrupt device, it begins by sending the device an "attention" message, followed immediately by the message.

Isochronous transfers

Isochronous transfers are continuous streams of digital data that often require transfers at relatively high speed, such as audio or video. The host or originating device initiates the transfer with a series of control messages; but because it's more important to maintain the ongoing stream of bits to or from the computer, the USB host doesn't bother to take up bandwidth with acknowledgements or other handshaking data after the transfer begins.

Bulk transfers

Bulk transfers are used for *bursty* data which moves in occasional spurts rather than continuous streams, such as a page of data to a printer or an image from a scanner or a digital camera. Because accuracy is more important than speed, the device and the USB host apply extensive error correction to every data packet.

Both interrupt transfers and isochronous transfers have priority over bulk transfers, so a bulk transfer might be slower than normal when it shares a USB port with an active isochronous transfer. A bulk job uses the spare bandwidth left over after the host controller has allocated bandwidth to other transfers. It also uses that 10 percent of the total bandwidth that the host reserved during enumeration. In other words, a print job might take longer than usual if you try to print while you're listening to music through USB speakers.

Therefore, it's often possible to optimize the performance of all the USB devices connected to your computer by connecting devices that use bulk transfers and isochronous transfers to separate USB connectors on the computer, rather than connecting them through the same hub.

How FireWire Works

IEEE 1394 is another method for transferring data between computers and external peripheral devices. A 1394 connection includes these features:

- Data transfer speed up to 800 Mbits per second
- Support for up to 63 devices
- Plug and Play operation
- Support for hot swapping
- Support for peer-to-peer data exchange

Considering that they do very similar things, it's not surprising that the internal operation of an IEEE 1394 connection is very similar to a USB link. Both systems use enumeration to identify devices connected to the bus and to allocate bandwidth, but 1394 was never intended to be a one-size-fits-all solution like USB. It doesn't include the interrupt transfer method for mice, keyboards, and other low-impact devices.

Like USB, FireWire is a Plug and Play system: To connect a new device, just plug in the cable and Windows sets up the connection. To disconnect, pull the plug.

A single 1394 bus can support up to 63 devices through a single connection to a host computer. Many 1394 devices have two connectors, which makes it possible to connect several 1394 devices in a daisy-chain configuration; however, it's often better to use a multi-port 1394 hub because a hub allows you to disconnect one device without losing the rest of the chain. The total number of cables in an end-to-end chain should not exceed 16 cables or about 236 feet (72 meters).

Because an IEEE 1394 bus doesn't require a controller, it's also possible to connect two or more devices together without a host, in a peer-to-peer configuration. This can be useful for duplicating CDs or DVDs or copying from one camcorder or portable music player to another, or from one to many; just connect the source player and one or more destination recorders together. A 1394 link can also connect two or more computers as a network.

In theory, it should also be possible to use 1394 links to share a peripheral device among more than one computer. For example, you might want to read and write files on a hard drive from two different computers. However, Windows does not include controls for shared disk drives or other storage devices. If you have to share access to a disk drive, it's better to connect through a network.

IEEE 1394 uses two data transfer methods: isochronous and asynchronous. It can also support network connections among two or more computers.

Isochronous transfers

FireWire uses isochronous transfers for high-volume, time-sensitive streaming data from sources such as networks, DVDs, camcorders, and interfaces from audio production equipment. The IEEE 1394 standard assigns priority to isochronous data services in order to let the data move at a constant rate.

In an isochronous transfer, the data moves as a continuous stream, without error checking or other tests that could interrupt the transmission with re-feeds of corrupt data.

Asynchronous transfers

FireWire uses asynchronous transfers for load-and-store applications that don't require a continuous data feed, such as disk drives and printers. In an asynchronous transfer, the originating device holds data in a buffer until enough bandwidth is available to perform the transfer.

Network connections

In Windows XP (and Vista, when it becomes available), IEEE 1394 also supports local networking. 1394 is not as flexible as a traditional Ethernet network; but it's quick and easy to set up and use. This can also be a convenient way to connect a second computer to the Internet through a host computer that is already connected.

CROSS-REF For more about establishing a 1394 network, see Chapter 44.

What's the Difference?

USB and IEEE 1394 are similar technologies designed to perform similar tasks. The most important differences are the data transfer speeds and the way they connect peripheral devices to a computer.

In terms of raw speed, the maximum bandwidth of a USB 2.0 bus is 480 Mbps, and FireWire is 400 (or 800) Mbps. However, USB uses more of its bandwidth for handshaking and other overhead between the host and the other devices on the bus than 1394, so the effective maximum data transfer speed of a 1394 link is faster.

But that's the maximum speed that each bus can handle. If you're only connecting a single high-speed USB or FireWire device, it might not use up all the available bandwidth, so either type can provide acceptable performance.

As for the connection structure, the differences are more technical than practical. USB uses a bus architecture that uses the host computer to control all the bandwidth arbitration and data transfer. On the other hand, IEEE 1394 specifies a peer-to-peer arrangement in which each device can set up a data exchange with any other device on the bus, without intervention from a host.

So which is better? In most cases, a FireWire connection is the better choice for multimedia devices and maybe for disk drives, but USB is usually the only option for printers, keyboards, mice, and other low-volume devices. In practice, most new computers and motherboards include both USB and 1394 connections, so you can choose devices that work with either one. If your own computer does not include the interface you need, look for an expansion card for your desktop system or a PC Card for your laptop with an add-on USB or IEEE 1394 interface.

Connectors and Cables

USB cables move power and data in both directions, so it's important to make sure that the pin that carries an output at one end connects to an input at the other end. Therefore, a standard USB cable has a Type A connector at one end and a Type B connector at the other end. (Figure 14.1 shows both cable connector types. Figure 14.2 shows the matching sockets.) The Type A cable connector normally plugs into a computer's USB port, and the Type B connector fits the USB port on a peripheral device. USB hubs have one Type B port for the connection to the host, and two or more Type A ports, for cables to peripherals or additional hubs.

FIGURE 14.1

USB cable connectors: Type A (left) and Type B (right)

A   B

FIGURE 14.2

USB sockets: Type A (left) and Type B (right)

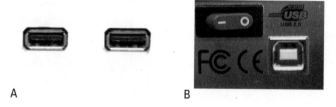

A   B

However, there are exceptions to that rule. Many small USB devices, including digital cameras and mobile telephones, use a smaller mini-USB connector that takes up less space than the Type A version (as shown in Figure 14.3), so they need a special mini-to-Type-A cable. Most USB flash drives are designed to plug directly into a Type A socket, so they have Type A plugs.

FIGURE 14.3

Many digital cameras use mini-USB connectors.

Are you confused yet? It's not as bad as it sounds. Fortunately, most USB devices use standard Type A to Type B cables, and the devices that require a non-standard cable include one with the device. If you need a replacement cable, make a note of the type at each end before you head for the store or begin your online shopping.

FireWire/1394 cables are easier because they use the same kind of six-contact connector at each end of the cable. Figure 14.4 shows a 1394 connector and socket.

The practical limit to the length of a USB cable is a maximum of about 16 feet (5 meters) between full-speed devices, or about 9.75 feet (3 meters) for low speed devices. If you need to place a device farther away from the computer (up to about 80 feet or 25 meters), add one or more powered hubs in series to extend the total distance. For greater distances, use a second computer and connect it to the first one through a network.

The maximum cable length for a single FireWire cable is 14.85 feet (4.5 meters). The maximum number of chained cables is 16.

FIGURE 14.4

IEEE 1394 plug (left) and socket (right)

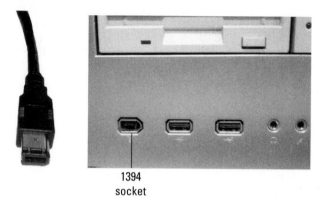

1394
socket

Connecting to a Windows Computer

When you connect a new USB or FireWire device to a computer for the first time, Windows displays a Found New Hardware message in a bubble near the lower right corner of the screen, and automatically installs the device. If Windows has never seen this device before, it asks for a pointer to the device driver software.

If you have the software CD supplied with the new device, place it in the computer's drive. If you don't have the software, look for a downloadable version on the manufacturer's Web site. Either way, use the Browse button to point Windows to the device driver software. Windows installs the device driver and loads any related control programs from the CD or download.

That's all there is to it. Your new USB or FireWire thing is ready to use.

After the first installation, Windows treats the device just like any other peripheral. If it's connected when you turn on the computer, its device driver loads along with everything else. If you plug in the cable or turn on the device's power switch after Windows is already running, Windows recognizes the device immediately.

Summary

Both FireWire and USB seem to be computer services that the designers have gotten right. When you plug a cable from either type of interface into your computer, you can realistically expect the device connected to that cable to work.

A USB interface can control just about everything from a simple input device like a mouse or keyboard that transfers just a few bits at a time, to a multimedia player or network connection that streams several megabytes per second. Each USB host can support several simultaneous USB connections.

FireWire (IEEE 1394) is used most widely with camcorders, audio consoles, and other high-bandwidth multimedia devices, but it can also connect disk drives, printers, and other peripherals. Unlike USB, a 1394 bus does not require a controller in a host computer; each device controls its own connection.

Chapter 15

Using Bluetooth

In spite of the name, *Bluetooth* is not a second-string pirate captain or a particularly bizarre dental malady. It is, in fact, a short-range wireless communications technology. The original Harald Bluetooth was a tenth-century Danish king who united parts of Norway and Denmark into a single Viking kingdom. Modern Bluetooth technology was named in his honor because it was intended to unite the worlds of portable computers and mobile telephones. Today, Bluetooth has become an industry standard for wireless connections among computers, printers, and other peripheral devices, along with mobile phones, headsets, and even wearable items with built-in wireless data exchange.

In general, Bluetooth is intended to replace wired connections between electronic equipment. Ultimately, the designers of Bluetooth hoped to completely replace the confusing tangle of wires and cables behind many computers with a single wireless interface module. More important, Bluetooth makes it possible to use external peripherals (including keyboards, mice, and printers) or transfer data to a computer without the need to find and attach a cable first.

Bluetooth is used for many kinds of wireless connections, including:

- Connecting a keyboard and mouse to a computer
- Connecting one or more computers to a printer
- Connecting a cordless telephone to a base station or a computer
- Connecting a mobile telephone or PDA to the Internet
- Connecting two computers or a computer and a handheld PDA, for data transfer
- Connecting to a Personal Area Network (PAN)

IN THIS CHAPTER

Understanding Bluetooth operation

Connecting a Bluetooth adapter to your computer

Loading Bluetooth control software

Setting up a Bluetooth connection

- Connecting a headset or earpiece to a mobile telephone
- Connecting headphones to a computer, a stereo, or other home entertainment system

Bluetooth's maximum data transfer speed is only 700 Kbps, which is a lot slower than some other wireless data transfer technologies, so it's not the best choice for every application. It's fine when you want to connect one or more peripheral devices to a computer, but not as a replacement for high-speed Ethernet or WiFi connections.

Because Bluetooth uses radio signals that can interfere with medical equipment and aircraft navigation systems, it's best not to use it in certain situations. Therefore, it's always a good idea to carry cables or alternative, non-Bluetooth devices (such as a headset that connects to your computer through a cable) that you can use in places where you can't use a Bluetooth connection.

How Bluetooth Works

Bluetooth is a short-range, frequency-hopping spread spectrum (FHSS) radio service that operates in the same unlicensed 2.4 GHz frequency range as WiFi networks and many cordless telephones, microwave ovens, baby monitors, garage door openers, and other wireless products. *Frequency-hopping spread spectrum* means that a Bluetooth transmitter splits the radio signal into very small segments and hops among 79 different frequencies 1,600 times per second to reduce interference and fading.

Because a Bluetooth radio is both a transmitter and a receiver, it's sometimes known as a *transceiver.* In order to further reduce the likelihood of interference, Bluetooth transmitters use very weak signals. The output power of the most common Class 2 Bluetooth radios is just 2.5 milliwatts (0.0025 watts) or less, which gives the signal a range of about ten meters (30 feet) in free space. By comparison, a cellular mobile telephone typically transmits at .6 watts or 3 watts. More powerful Class 1 Bluetooth radios with a maximum range of about 100 meters (320 feet) are also available.

Computers, peripherals, and other Bluetooth devices within range of one another form a *piconet* (*pico* is Greek for "really small") that includes one master device and one or more slaves. The master sets the frequency-hopping pattern and clock, and sends a synchronizing signal to all of the slaves, so the master maintains a two-way communications channel with each slave; individual slaves can't communicate with each other, except through the master. The channel is divided into time units called *slots* that carry data from one device to another between frequency hops.

Each device identifies itself with an address that lets other Bluetooth devices know what it is. For example, all keyboards have addresses within one range, and telephone handsets have addresses in another range. When a host or base station creates a new piconet (or adds a device to an existing piconet), it only communicates with devices whose addresses are within the right range (in Windows, the Bluetooth Properties dialog box specifies the types of slave devices). When a second Bluetooth host communicates with a different address range (say, a mobile phone and headset), it creates another piconet that uses a different frequency-hopping pattern. Most of the time, the two frequency-hopping patterns don't overlap, so the two piconets don't interfere. If they do try to use the same frequency at the same time, both masters back off and try different frequencies. Each piconet is limited to a master and seven slaves, but there's no practical limit to the number of piconets that can run in the same area.

When one Bluetooth device wants to communicate with another device on the same piconet, the master and slave exchange control signals in a format called the *link manager protocol* (LMP) or *access control list* (ACL). These signals specify the target device to which the signal is directed and the action that the originating device wants the target to take.

All of this radio communication is invisible to a user. Once you set the Bluetooth configuration options in Windows, the computer should automatically detect nearby Bluetooth devices and automatically establish communication links with them. If there are other Bluetooth devices in the same room, the computer ignores them because their addresses identify them as the wrong type of device.

TIP Not every wireless peripheral uses Bluetooth technology. Even if they use 2.4 GHz radios, many keyboards, mice, and other small peripherals communicate with some other kind of wireless link. If you're trying to use a Bluetooth interface on your computer, make sure the peripheral devices all carry a Bluetooth logo.

Installing Bluetooth in Your Computer

Many new laptop computers include built-in Bluetooth transceivers. If yours does not, or if you want to add Bluetooth to a desktop system, you can add Bluetooth by connecting a Bluetooth adapter to one of the computer's USB ports or a plugging a PC Card into a PCMCIA socket. The most common Bluetooth USB adapters are small modules (sometimes called *dongles*) like the one shown in Figure 15.1, with a Type A connector that plugs directly into a Type A socket on the computer case.

CROSS-REF For more information about USB, see Chapter 14. For information about PC Cards and PCMCIA sockets, see Chapter 24.

When you connect a Bluetooth adapter to your computer for the first time, Windows automatically detects the adapter and installs a device driver, either from the software supplied with Windows, or from the software disk that came with the adapter.

The Bluetooth software provided with your adapter might include a configuration program with more features and options than the program supplied with Windows. For example, the software supplied with WIDCOMM adapters includes the Bluetooth Setup Wizard shown in Figure 15.2. If you have a Bluetooth software disk, install it before you try to use Windows to set up your connections.

FIGURE 15.1

USB Bluetooth adapters are often plug-in modules.

FIGURE 15.2

The software supplied with many Bluetooth adapters includes more features than the generic Windows driver.

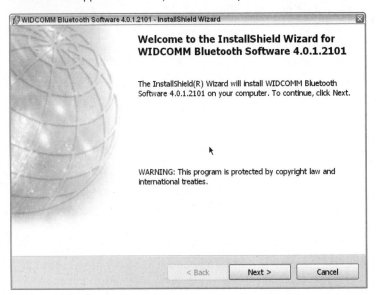

TIP If you don't have a CD for your adapter, look for a device driver at the manufacturer's Web site.

After you have installed the device driver, follow these steps to set up a Bluetooth connection:

1. **If it's not built into your computer, connect your Bluetooth adapter to the computer.** A Bluetooth logo like the one in Figure 15.3 appears on the screen in the system tray, next to the clock.

2. **Turn on the Bluetooth device that you want to use with your computer.** Follow the instructions supplied with the device to make it discoverable (or visible). If you're using a mouse or keyboard, press the button on the bottom.

FIGURE 15.3

The Bluetooth logo appears on adapters and other Bluetooth devices and on the Windows System Tray.

3. **Right-click the Bluetooth logo and choose Add a Bluetooth device from the pop-up menu.** The Welcome screen of the Add Bluetooth Device Wizard, as shown in Figure 15.4, appears. If you're using software supplied with your Bluetooth adapter, you might see a different screen, but it instructs you to perform similar actions.

4. **If you're using the Add Bluetooth Device in Windows, click the box next to My device is set up and ready to be found.** Click Next.

5. **The wizard searches for your Bluetooth device.** When the wizard finds the device, it establishes a wireless connection.

FIGURE 15.4

Use the Add a Bluetooth Device Wizard to connect a Bluetooth device to your computer.

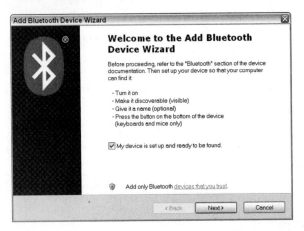

Some Bluetooth devices such as PDAs and mobile telephones perform a process called pairing (or bonding) to authenticate the connection. When you set up the connection for the first time, each device will ask you to enter a PIN (or passkey) that must be the same on both devices. The devices will convert the PIN to an internal *link key*, which they can store in their memories. On subsequent connections, you can either enter the passkey on both devices, or allow them to exchange the link key automatically.

Letting other hosts find you

Sometimes you may want to configure your computer as a slave on a piconet with another device as the master. For example, you might want to use Bluetooth to exchange files with another computer or a handheld Personal Digital Assistant (PDA), or communicate between your computer and a mobile telephone.

To make your computer visible to other Bluetooth devices, follow these steps:

1. Double-click the Bluetooth icon in the system tray to open the Bluetooth Devices window.

2. Click the Options tab to open the dialog box shown in Figure 15.5.

3. In the Discovery box, select the Turn discovery on option.

4. In the Connections box, turn on both the Allow Bluetooth devices to connect and the Alert me options.

5. Click OK or Apply to save your choices.

FIGURE 15.5

Use the Options tab to make your computer visible to other Bluetooth hosts.

Using Bluetooth as a COM port

Some Bluetooth devices (including many PDAs) treat a Bluetooth connection to your computer as a substitute for a wired connection through a serial data port. In order to transfer data via Bluetooth to one of these devices, you must assign a COM port number to the Bluetooth link. The instructions supplied with your PDA or other Bluetooth device tells you if you need to use a COM port to connect to your computer.

CROSS-REF See Chapter 16 for an explanation of serial data ports.

To assign a Bluetooth device to a COM port, follow these steps:

1. **If it's not already open, double-click the Bluetooth icon in the system tray to open the Bluetooth Devices window.**

2. **Open the COM Ports tab.**

3. **If the device you want to assign to a COM port does not appear in the list, click Add.** The Add COM Port window shown in Figure 15.6 appears.

4. **If this computer is supposed to be the master in your piconet, choose the Incoming option.** If some other device is the master, choose the Outgoing option.

FIGURE 15.6

Use the Add COM Port dialog box to assign a Bluetooth device to a COM port.

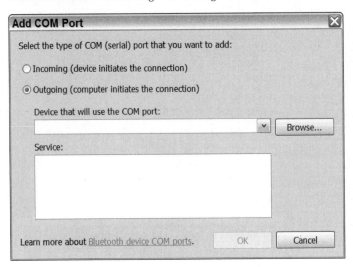

5. **If you specify Incoming, the master device detects your computer.** If you specify Outgoing, use the Device that will use the COM port field to choose a Bluetooth device. If it's not in the drop-down menu, use the Browse button to detect nearby Bluetooth signals. After you choose a device, select the service you want from the list in the Service list.

6. **Click OK to save your choices and close the Add COM Port window, and again to close the Bluetooth Devices window.**

Using Bluetooth Devices

After you set up your Bluetooth piconet, your computer automatically detects the other devices on the piconet and makes the same kind of connection that would occur if the other devices were linked to your computer with cables. If the Bluetooth connection is configured properly, it should be completely transparent.

If your computer can't find the other device, take a close look at that device and read the instructions supplied with the device for setting up a Bluetooth connection. Is the power switch turned on? Is Bluetooth active? Is the battery good? On a keyboard or a mouse, push the button on the bottom of the unit to make sure Bluetooth is on.

Summary

Bluetooth is a short-range wireless communication technology that can replace many of the cables that connect your PC to peripherals such as a keyboard or mouse, and to other electronic equipment including mobile telephones, headsets, home entertainment systems, and PDAs. Many laptop computers include internal Bluetooth transceivers; if yours does not, you can attach an inexpensive interface adapter through a USB port. When you connect a Bluetooth interface to your computer, Windows automatically detects the interface and loads the appropriate device drivers.

To exchange data between your computer and other devices via Bluetooth, you must create a piconet that includes a master and at least one slave. To assign your computer to a piconet in Windows, use the Bluetooth Devices dialog box.

Many Bluetooth interfaces come with proprietary configuration software with more options and better features than the standard Windows utility. If you have a choice between the Windows utility and the one supplied with your Bluetooth adapter, the proprietary program is often the better choice.

Part III

Using Your Desktop Computer

Chapter 16

Exploring Your Desktop Computer

A desktop computer is usually a box with a lot of electronic circuit boards and storage devices inside. The box might sit on its wide surface or on one of the short sides, but it operates the same either way.

This chapter describes all the bells and whistles on the outside of your computer, including the switches and pushbuttons that you use to operate the machine, the lights that tell you what's happening, and the sockets to connect peripheral devices to the system. There's no universal standard for the external layout of a computer case, but Figure 16.1 shows a typical system. The front panel of your computer probably includes most of these features:

- A large pushbutton power switch
- A reset pushbutton
- An LED indicator that lights when the computer is on
- An LED indicator light that shows disk drive activity
- Two or more large drive bays for CD drives, DVD drives, and other devices
- One or more small drive bays for floppy disk drives and other devices
- One or more air intake vents

Many computers also have some or all of these connectors on the front panel:

- One or more USB sockets
- An IEEE 1394 (FireWire) socket
- A headphone output connector
- A microphone input connector

IN THIS CHAPTER

Identifying the controls on your computer

Starting the computer

Shutting down the computer

Recognizing input and output connectors

Working with parallel and serial data ports

Setting up a game controller

FIGURE 16.1

A desktop computer's front panel includes several controls and indicators.

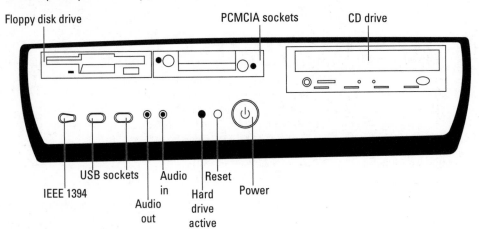

Figure 16.2 shows the rear panel of the same computer. The rear panel usually includes these features:

- A connector for a removable AC power cable
- Several removable cover panels for AGP, PCI Express or PCI expansion cards
- An assortment of input and output connectors:
  - One or more USB connectors
  - One or more IEEE 1394 (FireWire) connectors
  - An Ethernet network connector
  - A 15-pin analog VGA video output connector
  - A DVI digital video output connector
  - An S-video connector
  - Various audio input and output connectors
- An exhaust vent for the internal fan

Several other connector types are gradually being replaced by USB sockets, but you might still find some of them on your computer. These include:

  - A PS/2 mouse connector
  - A PS/2 keyboard connector
  - One or more 9-pin serial port connectors
  - A 25-pin parallel port connector
  - A 15-pin Game port

FIGURE 16.2

The rear panel provides access for most of the external inputs and outputs.

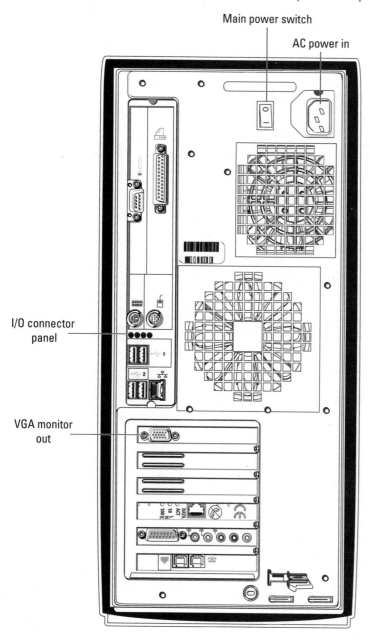

Main power switch

AC power in

I/O connector panel

VGA monitor out

Almost every new motherboard gathers all of its I/O connectors into a group at the left end of the board (as you look towards the rear of the board) that fits the cutout holes in a cover plate. When the motherboard is mounted in a case, the cover plate snaps into an open space in the case's rear panel. On older motherboards and cases, each connector mounts in an individual hole in the rear panel or a separate piece that fits in one of the expansion slots, but this arrangement is increasingly uncommon.

Turning the Computer On and Off

Most of us start our desktop computers by pushing the On/Off pushbutton on the front panel. It would appear that the pushbutton is a simple power switch, but there's more to it than that.

Whenever the computer's power supply is connected to AC power (and the master power switch on the back panel is turned on), it sends a +5-volt *soft power* signal called +5 VSB (or + 5 volts standby) to the motherboard, which is enough to keep some components in a standby condition. On many motherboards, a green LED indicator lights whenever soft power is alive.

When a user pushes the On/Off pushbutton, it's an instruction to the motherboard to send a signal back to the power supply to turn on all of the power supply's other output voltages. After the motherboard receives these additional voltages, the BIOS to begin the startup routine described in Chapter 7.

In many computers, the BIOS offers several additional startup options. When these options are active, the BIOS automatically sends the startup signal to the power supply when the motherboard detects one of these events:

- An incoming signal from a network connection
- An incoming telephone call through a modem
- Any keyboard activity or a specific "hot key" entry from the keyboard
- Any motion or pushbutton activity on the mouse

If you discover that your computer appears to mysteriously turn itself on without warning, one of these startup options is almost certainly to blame. To enable or disable these auto-start functions, open the BIOS Settings utility and look for a list of startup or power management options.

Configuring the power button

When the computer is off, pushing the power button on the front panel turns it on. But if you push the same button when the computer is already running Windows XP, the computer will take the action specified by the current setting of the Power Options Properties dialog box. Your choices include:

- Do nothing
- Ask for instructions

- Stand by
- Hibernate
- Begin the Shut Down routine

If you hold down the power button for more than four seconds, the computer will turn itself off, regardless of what it is doing at the time.

To change the Power Button setting, follow these steps:

1. **From the Windows Control Panel, open the Power Options window.**
2. **Choose the Advanced tab to open the dialog box shown in Figure 16.3.**

FIGURE 16.3

Use the Power Buttons options to control the On/Off button.

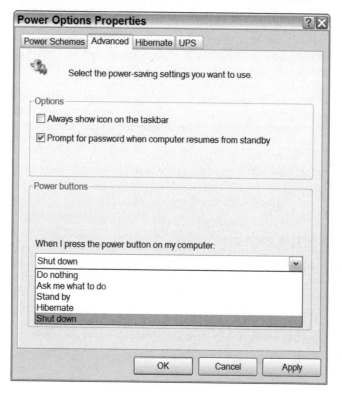

3.   **Open the drop-down menu in the Power Buttons box in the lower half of the dialog box.** The options are

■ **Do Nothing**

■ **Ask Me What to Do**

■ **Stand By:** In standby mode, the computer turns off the monitor and hard drives to save power. When you restore from standby by pressing a key or moving the mouse, the computer returns to exactly the same condition it was in before it went into standby.

■ **Hibernate:** When the computer hibernates, it saves a copy of the data currently in memory to a disk, and then it shuts down. When you restore the computer, it reads the data from the disk and returns to the same condition it was in before it went into hibernation.

■ **Shut Down:** When the computer shuts down, it systematically closes all active programs and services, and then turns off the power (except the +5 volt soft power).

The reset pushbutton

The reset pushbutton on the front of your computer is a normally open switch. When you push it, it turns off the computer and starts it up again. This is known as a *hard reboot* because it immediately shuts down all activity without saving anything and restarts from scratch.

Reset is a last-resort method to shut down or restart the computer when the computer has frozen, or if it has gone into some kind of runaway process and nothing else works. Before you push it, try the Escape key, or press the Ctrl+Alt+Del combination and choose Turn Off or Restart from the Shut Down menu.

Some recent computers don't have separate reset buttons. If yours is one of those, you can turn off the computer by pushing the power button and holding it down for about four seconds. To restart the computer, release the power button and push it again.

Windows shut down

One of the greatest mysteries of the Windows design is the fact that you click the Start button to shut down the system. It must have seemed logical to somebody, so the rest of us have to put up with it. When you have ended your session using Windows and you're ready to turn off the computer, the most common method is to follow these steps:

1.   **From the Start menu, select Turn Off Computer at the bottom of the menu.**

2.   **When the Turn Off Computer window appears, choose Turn Off.**

The Turn Off Down command instructs Windows to end things in a systematic manner by closing all the active programs and services and storing all the settings it needs the next time you turn the computer back on. If any active programs have open files, those programs may offer to save the files before Windows closes the program.

Windows has at least three other ways to perform a systematic shut down:

- Press the Ctrl+Alt+Delete keys to open either the Task Manager window or the Windows Security window (depending on whether or not the Welcome Screen is active in Control Panel ⇨ User ⇨ Accounts ⇨ Change the way users log on or off).

  If you see the Windows Security window, choose Shut Down. If you see the Task Manager, select an option from the Shut Down menu.

- Right-click the taskbar which is usually at the bottom of the Windows desktop, select Task Manager from the pop-up menu, and then select an option from the Shut Down menu.

- Set the Power Buttons option to Shut Down and press the Power On/Off pushbutton.

The Restart command

The Restart command in the Shut Down window and the Task Manager's Shut Down menu instructs Windows to perform a systematic shutdown and then immediately restart the computer. There's one important difference between a hard boot from the On/Off pushbutton or the reset pushbutton and a *soft* reboot with a Restart command: when you use a Windows command to restart the computer, the BIOS does not reset a marker in memory that tells another part of the BIOS to run the complete Power-On Self Test (POST). As a result, the overall startup time on a soft reboot can be up to a minute or two faster than a hard reboot.

If nothing else works . . .

In the unlikely event that you can't shut down your computer with Ctrl+Alt+Delete or the reset pushbutton, there's one more thing you can do that should always work: pull the plug. It might seem obvious right now, but in a panic situation when there's smoke coming out of the power supply and nothing else responds, it's more important to cut your losses and turn everything off than to worry about a systematic shutdown.

If possible, pull the plug out of the computer's rear panel first so you don't pull out some other cord by mistake, but if it's easier to reach the wall outlet, go ahead and pull that one before you try to move the computer or other furniture to get to the back of the computer.

Sending and Receiving Data: Inputs and Outputs

The number and variety of input and output connectors on the back of your computer is enough to confound anybody except a truly dedicated geek. In another five or ten years, many of those connectors will be replaced with USB ports, but today, most computer and motherboard makers provide both the general-purpose USB connectors and a dozen or more specialized connectors.

In this section, you can find similar explanations of the older types of input and output connectors that you might still find on a desktop computer.

CROSS-REF Interested in USB and IEEE 1394/FireWire? Check out Chapter 14.

In order to reduce confusion, the joint Intel-Microsoft PC design specification includes a color code for most of the common types of computer connectors. Most computer and motherboard makers use plastic shells and sockets or labels of the appropriate colors to identify each socket, and the makers of many peripheral devices use the same colors for the plugs at the ends of their cables. When the system works, choosing the right connector is as simple as matching the colors on the plug and the socket. Table 16.1 lists the common connection types with their standard color codes and a description of each connector.

TABLE 16.1

Computer Connector Color Codes

Color	Description	Connector
Green	Mouse	6-pin round PS/2
Purple	Keyboard	6-pin round PS/2
Burgundy	Parallel printer port	25-pin D
Teal or Turquoise	Serial port	9-pin D 25-pin D
Blue	Analog VGA video	15-Pin D
White	Digital video	DVI
Yellow	S-video	6-pin round DIN
Yellow	Composite video	RCA plug
Pink	Analog microphone input	3.5 mm audio plug
Light Blue	Analog line-level input	3.5 mm audio plug
Lime Green	Analog line-level outputs for headphones or speakers	3.5 mm audio plug
Brown	Analog line-level surround sound speakers	3.5 mm audio plug
Orange	S/PDIF digital audio output speaker or subwoofer output	3.5 mm audio plug
Gold	Game port or MIDI	15-pin D
Black	USB port	USB Type A
Grey	IEEE 1394/FireWire port	IEEE 1394
None	SCSI, telephone, Ethernet	Various

PS/2 mouse and keyboard sockets

Keyboards and mice both use identical round 6-pin plugs and sockets that carry power from the computer to the keyboard or mouse, and data in both directions. The mouse plug and socket are generally green, and the keyboard connectors are purple. Both have been widely replaced by USB connections. They are called PS/2 connectors because they were first used on IBM's PS/2 computers. Figure 16.4 shows the PS/2 sockets.

FIGURE 16.4

Many desktop computers still use PS/2 connectors for the keyboard and the mouse.

Keyboard connector

Mouse connector

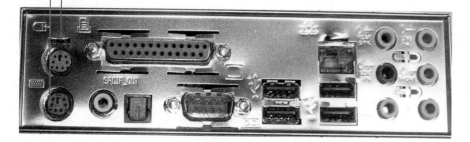

Parallel (printer) port

Parallel data transfers, in which each of the 8 bits in a byte uses a separate wire, are fast and efficient over short runs, but the cable that contains all those wires becomes extremely expensive when they are used over long distances. In personal computers, a parallel connection had been used most often for data transfer to and from a printer, but most new printers use USB connections, either as an alternative to the parallel cable or as the only connection.

The cable that carries the data from your computer to a printer is more than a bit odd. The connector on the computer is a 25-pin type DB25 socket, but the "matching" socket on the printer is a 36-pin socket called a Centronics connector. Centronics was a very early printer company that was in the right place at the right time to have their choice of parallel printer connectors adopted by the rest of the industry. Unfortunately, the rest of the industry, including such giants as Hewlett-Packard, IBM and Epson also took over the printer market, and Centronics had disappeared by 1988. However, the 36-pin Centronics connector lives on as the standard parallel printer socket.

Other uses are increasingly rare, but if you're working with peripheral devices that are more than eight or ten years old, you might discover some equipment that uses your computer's parallel port, including scanners, external storage systems, and scientific data gathering devices.

Just about every personal computer still has one parallel printer port, although some new machines have eliminated them in favor of a USB port. If you need an extra parallel port, you can install one on an inexpensive PCI expansion card.

Parallel port standards

Those parallel ports on early computers moved data on each pin in only one direction. Pins 2 through 9 carried data from the computer to the printer, and the remaining pins either sent control information to the printer or they returned acknowledgements and status information (such as "paper out") back to the printer. But as printers became more complex, and as other devices began to use the parallel port, the connection was redesigned to allow data to move in both directions. And of course, what had been a single universal standard evolved into a set of incompatible connections that all used the same plugs and sockets.

The first of these new parallel connections was the Standard Parallel Port (SPP), which used automatic switching inside the computer and the destination to reverse the direction that the data bits would travel through the cable.

SPP improved data transfers to a printer, but it wasn't good enough for other devices like disk and tape drives that demanded even more speed in both directions. So the Enhanced Parallel Port (EPP) specification was introduced. At about the same time, faster and better printers were appearing (this was the era when laser printers were replacing the old dot matrix machines that used dot matrixes and film ribbons), and a separate industry group developed their own set of improvements on the SPP design, called Extended Capabilities Port (ECP). And of course, ECP wasn't compatible with EPP. When the dust settled, the IEEE (the same industry standards group that later adopted the FireWire specification as IEEE 1394) developed a single specification called IEEE 1284 that included both EPP and ECP.

Most parallel printers, plotters, and other devices that use the parallel interface made in the last ten years automatically identify themselves to the computer as either EPP or ECP. If yours does not, you'll have to use the BIOS Settings utility to change the Parallel Port Mode setting to match the device connected to your computer. The usual options are

- **Normal** or **Printer:** This is the original configuration used by printers made before about 1988.
- **SPP:** In this mode, the printer or other device returns rudimentary status information back to the computer.
- **EPP:** In this mode, data moves through the parallel data port at higher speed.
- **ECP:** In this mode, additional status information moves through the parallel port in both directions.
- **EPP+ECP:** In this mode, the BIOS automatically detects and uses the same mode used by the device at the other end of the cable. Unless your printer or other parallel device specifies some other mode, or you're using a very old printer, this is the best choice.

Alternatives to the parallel port

If your printer has both a parallel data connector and a USB port, you can use either one to connect the printer to the computer. Both types of connection move data to the printer as fast as the printer can produce printed pages, but the USB connection might support some diagnostic tests and other functions that aren't always possible through the slower parallel port.

In many home and small business networks, a printer is connected directly to the network as an independent device, rather than through a computer, so it can accept requests to print directly from all of the computers on the network. In this kind of setup, Windows directs print commands through the network rather than either the parallel port or a USB port.

Serial ports

In a serial data transfer, the bits in each byte move through a single pair of wires, one bit at a time. Before USB ports were introduced, the serial data ports on the rear panel were the primary I/O ports for transferring data through an external modem or other communications device, and for connecting many peripheral devices to a PC. Today, high-speed Ethernet and USB connections on new computers and external peripherals have almost completely replaced the older and slower serial data ports.

Serial data communication ports can have either 9 pins or 25 pins. The smaller 9-pin connector is most common on personal computers, but you might see a system with a 9-pin connecter designated as COM 1, and a second 25-pin connector as COM 2. The performance of both types of connector is identical, so you can use either size with any external device; an external modem that uses a serial data port usually comes with a "modem cable" that has a 9-pin female plug on one end and a 25-pin male plug on the other. The outline of the shell that contains both the 25-pin and 9-pin connectors looks vaguely like a letter *D*, so the plugs and sockets are sometimes called D-sub connectors. If your new computer doesn't have a built-in COM port, you can add one on a PCI expansion card.

The original specification for serial data communication is a relic from the 1960s, back in the days of steam-powered computers. The most common use of this specification was to define the connection between a computer and a remote terminal through a telephone line or other communications circuit. It was adopted in the United States by the Electronics Industry Association (EIA) as RS-232 (Regular Standard No. 232), and in the rest of the world by the International Telecommunications Union as Recommendations V.24 and V.28. Because the earliest personal computers were widely used as remote terminals for mainframe computers, the serial data interfaces on PCs have always followed the RS-232 standard for 25-pin serial data connections. 9-pin connectors follow the EIA 574 standard.

Figure 16.5 shows a serial data link between a terminal and a host computer through a modem and a telephone line. Each pin on an RS-232 serial port carries data in only one direction, so the outputs on each end of a serial data link must connect to the inputs on the other end. Because the cable that connects the terminal to the modem ties Pin 1 to Pin 1, Pin 2 to Pin 2, and so on, the connections on the terminal are not the same as the ones on the modem.

FIGURE 16.5

A remote terminal connects to a computer through a modem and a telephone line.

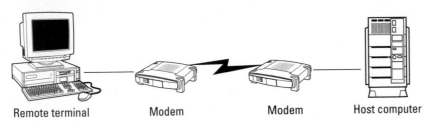

Remote terminal   Modem   Modem   Host computer

Therefore, the RS-232 standard calls for two kinds of serial data ports: Data Terminal Equipment (DTE) and Data Communications Equipment (DCE). The computer, remote terminal, and any other device that originates or receives data uses RTE connections, and the modems, network interfaces, and other intermediate devices use DCE.

Null modem cables

This all works very well until you try to connect two terminals (or two computers) together without any DCE devices in between, as shown in Figure 16.6. You might want to use an RS-232 connection to transfer files from one computer to another, or to set up a point-to-point communications link.

FIGURE 16.6

If you try to connect two DTE serial data ports to each other, no signal goes anywhere.

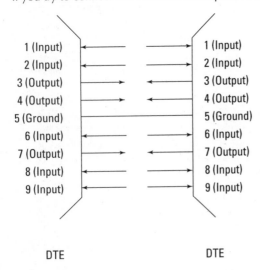

DTE   DTE

When you connect Pin 2 (the data output) of one DTE serial port to Pin 2 of another DTE port, the two devices both try to send data, but neither knows how to receive it. And when you connect Pin 3 (the input) to Pin 3, both ports wait forever for a signal. The same thing happens on all the other pins that send and receive control signals. Figure 16.7 demonstrates what a correct connection should look like.

FIGURE 16.7

When you connect a DTE port to a DCE port, all of the signals pass from one to the other.

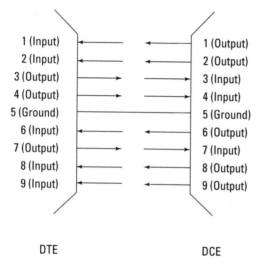

The solution to this problem is something called a *crossover cable* or a *null modem* that connects each output pin to the corresponding input. Any time you try to set up a direct connection between the serial data ports on two computers, you must use a null modem cable or a null modem adapter like the one shown in Figure 16.8.

NOTE   By today's standards, communication through the serial data port is slow and inefficient. If you have a choice, it's almost always better to use a network or an IEEE 1394 link.

FIGURE 16.8

When you connect two DTE serial data ports to each other, you must use a null modem adapter or cable.

Changing the serial port settings

Before Windows passes data through a serial data port, it encodes each character into a series of bits in a specific order that had originally been defined for sending text through telegraph lines to mechanical teleprinters. In addition to the data bits that define each letter, number, or symbol, the character sequence also includes a handful of additional bits that identify the beginning and end of each sequence.

The character sequence includes these elements:

- A *Start* bit that notifies the device at the receiving end that a new character is beginning.
- A series of 5, 6, 7, or 8 bits that represents a letter, number, or other character. The number of bits depends on the specific type of code it uses.
- A *Parity* bit that provides a simple form of error checking.
- A *Stop* bit that allows the mechanical printer to return to its idle state before the next character sequence begins. The duration of the Stop bit depends on the amount of time the printer needs to coast to a complete stop. In electronic data communications, the end of the Stop bit defines the beginning of the Start bit.

Figure 16.9 shows the format of a serial data character sequence.

FIGURE 16.9

Every serial data character uses a standard format.

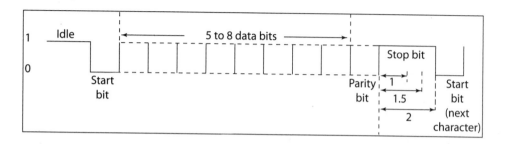

The only thing you really have to know about the data format used by a serial data port is that it must be exactly the same at both ends of a link. If you were using modems ten or fifteen years ago to transfer data to and from your computer, you might remember the ritual of setting the data bits, stop bit, and parity for each connection and confirming that the person on the other end of the line was using the same settings. Today, it's assumed that just about everybody uses 8 data bits, no parity, and 1 stop bit, so it's almost never necessary to change them.

However, it is possible to make changes if you're using your computer with some kind of oddball device that doesn't like the standard settings. In addition to data bits, parity, and stop bits, you can also adjust the data transmission rate and turn *flow control* (the procedure for suspending transmission when the receiver's buffer is almost full) on or off. If you're using a terminal emulator program or a control program for an external device that connects to your computer through a serial data port, use that program's configuration settings to adjust the data format.

In the unlikely event that you have to change the default settings for a serial port, follow these steps:

1. From the Windows desktop, right-click My Computer and select Properties from the pop-up menu.

2. In the System Properties window, choose the Hardware tab.

3. Click the Device Manager button to open the Device Manager window shown in Figure 16.10.

4. Scroll down to the bottom of the Device Manager window and double-click the Ports listing. Sub-listings for the Communications Port and Printer Port appear.

FIGURE 16.10

Use the Device Manager to open the COM port properties window.

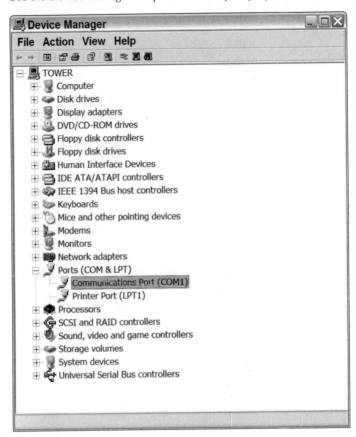

5. Double-click the Communications Port item to open a Properties window.

6. Choose the Port Settings tab to open the dialog box shown in Figure 16.11. Each of the items in the Port Settings dialog box is a drop-down menu. To change a setting, open the menu for that setting and choose the new value to match the setting at the other end of the serial communications link.

Most Windows users don't know that it's possible to change these settings. If you don't have a good reason to change them, leave them alone.

Use the Communications Port Properties dialog box to adjust the default configuration settings.

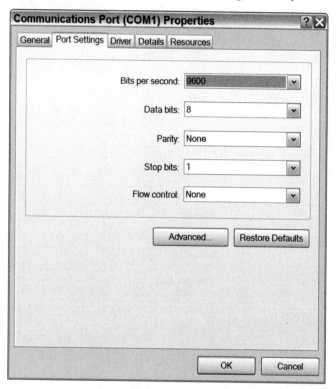

Testing a game controller

When you install a new game controller, you can use Windows to test each of the controls, including the joystick, buttons, wheel, yoke, or pads. If your controller comes with its own test and setup software, use that program instead of the generic windows utility.

To use the Windows utility to test the controller, follow these steps:

1. **From the Control Panel, choose the Game Controllers icon.** If your Control Panel is divided into groups, look in Printers and Other Hardware. The window shown in Figure 16.12 appears.

FIGURE 16.12

The Game Controllers window shows the currently installed controller.

2. **Click Add.** A list of controllers appears in the Add Game Controller dialog box shown in Figure 16.13.

3. **Choose either a description of your controller or the specific make and model.** Scroll down the list to find the specific types.

4. **Click Properties to test the controller.** Select the Test tab to open the dialog box shown in Figure 16.14.

FIGURE 16.13

Choose your controller to test its functions.

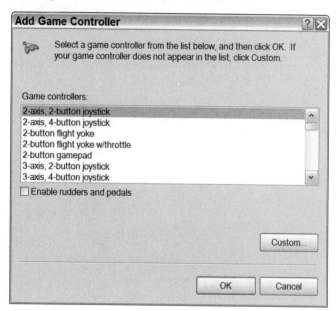

5. **Move the joystick or other navigation control in all possible directions.** The + marker inside the box should follow the joystick and reach all four edges of the box.

6. **Test each of the controller's pushbuttons, one at a time.** One of the numbered items in the Buttons box should respond when you push each button.

7. **If any of the controls appear to be working improperly, try calibrating the controller.**

Use the Test dialog box to test the individual controls on your game controller.

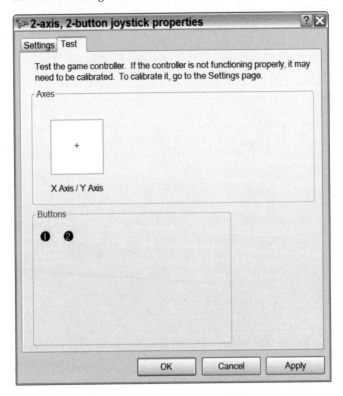

Calibrating your game controller

If your game controller didn't perform the way you expected it to when you ran the tests in the last section, follow these steps to calibrate it:

1. **Click the Settings tab in the controller properties window you used to test the controller.** The screen shown in Figure 16.15 appears.
2. **Click Calibrate.** The Game Device Calibration Wizard opens.
3. **Follow the instructions in the wizard to adjust the way Windows receives commands from the controller.**
4. **When the wizard closes, it returns you to the Test tab.** Confirm that the + symbol is now in the center of the Axes box, and that it follows the motion of the joystick.
5. **If you're satisfied with the controller's performance, click the OK buttons until you have closed all the open windows.** If it still isn't working the way you want it to, try calibrating the controller again.

FIGURE 16.15

Open the Settings tab to calibrate your game controller.

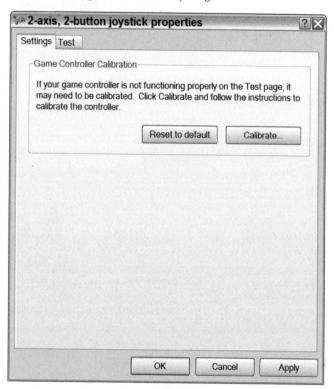

Summary

Every desktop or tower computer case includes a set of standard controls, indicators, and connectors. On the front of the case, these usually include the on/off pushbutton and a reset pushbutton, a power LED indicator and a disk activity indicator, and possibly one or more audio, USB, and IEEE 1394 connectors. The front panel also provides space for access to several external drive bays.

On the back of the computer, the computer has an assortment of I/O connectors including parallel and serial data ports, USB and IEEE 1394 ports, and specialized connectors for audio, video, and specific input devices. On some newer computers, many of these ports have been replaced with additional USB ports.

Chapter 17

Managing Power on a Desktop Computer

Every computer requires electric power to operate the CPU and other electronic circuits, the video display, and the motors inside the disk drives and other storage devices. Most modern computers don't require a huge amount of power, but in today's era of increasingly expensive energy, it's in everybody's interest to do whatever you can to consume as little as possible without reducing the computer's performance.

This chapter explains how to use the power options in Windows and other tools and techniques for controlling your computer's power consumption.

Setting Windows Power Options

Depending on the motherboard and the BIOS, Windows can support either of two power management schemes: the Advanced Configuration and Power Interface (ACPI) or the older Advanced Power Management (APM). Both of these specifications were created in order to control the way a computer consumes power, but each takes a different approach. In ACPI, the operating system is in control; APM places that control in the BIOS.

In general, APM does not run on desktop computers because it is primarily concerned with monitoring battery status in portable computers. In ACPI, Windows (or another operating system) uses a *power policy* to specify the devices to turn off when they are not in use, and when to place the whole computer in a low-power condition. In most cases, the power policy for each device is implemented by the device driver.

IN THIS CHAPTER

Using the Power Options in Windows

Saving power with Standby and Hibernation

Consuming less power

Protecting your system with an uninterruptible power supply

Running your computer on DC power

Under ACPI, devices within the computer that consume power, including the CPU, the disk drives, the graphics controller and monitor, and the network interfaces work closely with Windows to provide full power when necessary, but to shift to a reduced-power mode when they're not in use. For example, if the computer is idle, the operating system can reduce power to the hard drive. AMD's Cool'n'Quiet and Intel's SpeedStep fan controls are similar power-saving features.

Much of this power control happens automatically, but there are a few optional settings explained later in this chapter.

To learn if your computer is using ACPI, follow these steps:

1. **From the Windows desktop, right-click the My Computer icon and choose Properties from the pop-up menu, or choose System from the Control Panel.** The System Properties window opens.

2. **Click the Hardware tab and then click the Device Manager button.** The Device Manager window shown in Figure 17.1 opens.

3. **Double-click Computer near the top of the list of devices.**

FIGURE 17.1

If ACPI is active, it appears under Computer in the Device Manager.

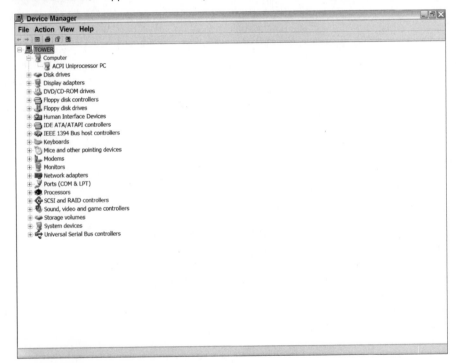

If there's an active ACPI item listed under Computer, Windows is using ACPI. The exact name of the item might be slightly different from the text in the figure.

If you don't see an ACPI item, look in the BIOS Settings utility to confirm that ACPI is active. If you can't find an ACPI setting, look for a BIOS update. After you update the BIOS, you have to reinstall Windows to turn on ACPI mode.

CROSS-REF See Chapter 8 for information about finding and installing a new BIOS version.

Standby and hibernation

When the computer goes into standby mode, it stores the details about the current state of the system, including active programs, network connections, and so on in RAM, and then it turns off most of the circuits and devices. When the computer returns to the active state, it uses the data stored in memory to return to the computer's condition when it went into standby. Because the standby data is stored in RAM, the computer loses that data if the computer loses power while it's in standby.

When the computer goes into hibernation, it stores the current system information on the hard drive and turns off power. When it comes out of hibernation, the computer restores all the programs and network connections that were active when hibernation began.

To enable or disable hibernation, follow these steps:

1. **From the Control Panel, choose Power Options.** The Power Options Properties window appears.

2. **In the Power Options Properties windows, choose the Hibernate tab.** The dialog box shown in Figure 17.2 appears.

3. **Use the Enable hibernation option to turn hibernation on or off.**

4. **Click OK to save your choice and close the properties window.**

To restore the computer from either standby or hibernation, either push the power button or (on a laptop), open the lid of the computer. If you're using the computer in a location where unauthorized users might try to gain access to the system when you're not there, you can set it to require a login and password to restore itself from hibernation or standby.

FIGURE 17.2

Use the Hibernate tab to turn hibernation on or off.

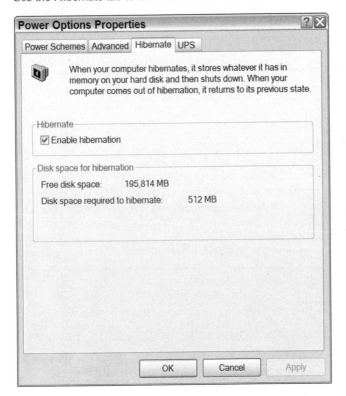

To turn password control on or off, follow these steps:

1. **From the Control Panel, open the Power Options window.**

2. **Choose the Advanced tab to open the dialog box shown in Figure 17.3.** You don't see the Sleep button or Close the lid options unless your computer has those features.

3. **To require a password, click the box next to the Prompt for password option.**

4. **Click OK to save your change and close the Properties window.**

If the wake-on options in the BIOS are turned on, the computer can also restore itself from standby or hibernation when it receives a telephone call through the modem or an incoming request for access through the network interface. These wake-up functions don't require a password, so turn them off if security is an issue.

Don't try to connect or disconnect a peripheral device (including USB flash drives) while the computer is in standby or hibernation. If you do, the system may not be able to return to normal operation properly.

To restart the computer when it refuses to come out of standby, use the reset button or the power button on the front of the computer to restart the computer.

FIGURE 17.3

Use the Advanced tab to enable or disable password control.

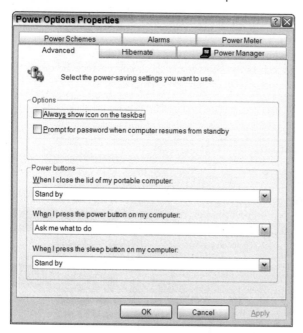

If the computer fails to come out of hibernation, the Hiberfil.sys file that contains the contents of the computer's memory is damaged. You will see this message or something similar:

```
Delete restoration data and proceed to system boot menu
```

Press Enter to delete the Hiberfil.sys file and perform a normal startup.

Power schemes

Windows organizes its power management settings into *power schemes* that specify the amount of idle time before it turns off the monitor and disk drives, and until the computer enters the standby and hibernation states. After you have created a scheme for your office or home computer that uses AC power, there's usually no reason to change it. In a laptop or other portable, you may want to use different schemes for battery operation in different situations (such as a long flight where you want to maximize battery life, or an office or hotel room where you have unlimited access to AC power).

> **TIP** If you're using your computer in a display or presentation, you might want to change to the Presentation scheme in which the monitor never goes dark and the computer never shifts to standby mode.

Because it takes longer to read data from a disk drive than it does to read the same data from RAM memory, the usual arrangement is to go to standby first, and then wait a bit longer before it goes to hibernation.

To change to a different power scheme, or to create a new scheme, follow these steps:

1. **Open the Windows Control Panel and select the Power Options icon.** If you use the Category View, look for Power Options in the Performance and Maintenance window. The Power Options Properties window shown in Figure 17.4 appears.

FIGURE 17.4

Use the Power Schemes tab to create or change a power scheme.

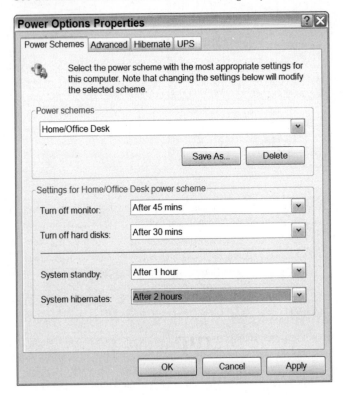

2. **Use the Power schemes drop-down menu to choose the power scheme whose name comes closest to the way you are using this computer.** For example, use Home/Office Desk for your desktop system, or Always On to keep the system running all the time.

3. **If you want to change one or more of the settings for the scheme you choose, use the drop-down menus in the Settings section.**

4. **If you have made any changes to the standard settings, click Save As, assign a new name to your scheme, and then click OK to save the scheme and close the Properties window.** If you're using a standard scheme, just click OK.

Reducing Power Consumption

The ACPI functions in Windows XP can reduce the amount of energy that your computer consumes, but they don't drop consumption all the way to zero. Even if the computer is off, it's still consuming a small amount of electric power. Add the amounts consumed by external peripheral devices such as the monitor, printer, and modem, and you're probably using enough energy to make a small but noticeable difference on your monthly electric power bill.

Therefore, it's worth the time and trouble to pay some attention to the way your computer (and your TV and other electronic equipment) use power, even when they're not running. For some devices, the convenience of instant-on operation might be worth the pennies it costs to provide standby power, but in other cases, it's just wasted money and energy. For example, there's really no good reason for your monitor, printer, or Internet modem to continue drawing power when the computer is off.

The easiest way to attack this problem is to plug your computer equipment into a power strip or an uninterruptible power supply with a switch that cuts off power to all of its outlets. When you're ready to use the system, turn on the main switch power first; when you're done for the day, shut down the computer normally, and then turn off the master power switch.

But that's not always the most efficient way to operate your equipment. In many cases, the computer and other devices consume two or three times as much power in an initial surge immediately after you turn them on as they use during normal operation. So that surge might use up more power than you have saved by cutting off standby power. It's probably not cost-effective to turn off the master power switch if you expect to use the equipment again within a few hours.

Using an Uninterruptible Power Supply

In theory, the AC power that comes from the wall outlet near your desk provides a constant, reliable voltage without any surges or drops, at exactly 60 (or 50 outside of North America) cycles per second (Hertz). But the truth is that your house current is subject to many kinds of interference, caused by anything from a nearby refrigerator or air conditioner motor overloading the line, to a falling tree branch cutting it off completely. An uninterruptible power supply (UPS) is a battery-powered device located between the AC outlet and the computer that evens out the AC power source. It also monitors the incoming AC line and automatically switches to the battery back-up when a power failure occurs.

One major maker of UPS products, American Power Conversion (APC), has identified several types of power problems that can affect a desktop computer:

- **Transient impulses** are very brief (less than 50 nanoseconds) events that raise the voltage or current. These impulses can be caused by lightning, poor grounding, electrostatic discharge, or problems at the electric utility. Transient impulses are also known as spikes or power surges. Lightning strikes (or near misses) are usually the most damaging form of transient impulse.

  Other forms of transient problems can occur when a sudden change to the load alters the steady-state condition of the power supply. For example, this can occur if a large motor (such as a refrigerator's compressor) on the same AC circuit starts or stops.

- **Interruptions** completely cut off voltage or load current. Interruptions are caused most often by damage to the power utility's grid. The duration of an interruption can be anywhere from a few cycles to several minutes or more.

  When your computer sustains a power interruption longer than a fraction of a second, it immediately shuts down, and all of the open files are lost, along with any work performed since those files were saved.

- **Sags** and **undervoltage** occur when AC voltage drops for less than a minute (sags) or for a longer period of time (undervoltages or brownouts). Sags can happen when a machine draws a heavy startup current (up to six times its normal load). This is similar to the effect on your household water pressure when somebody starts the washing machine while you're taking a shower.

A UPS addresses these problems by placing a surge suppressor and a filter between the AC power source and the computer's power supply, along with a transfer switch that automatically shifts to a battery backup when the AC power fails (see Figure 17.5). When AC power is available, the UPS uses it to charge the backup battery. In some designs, the surge suppression and filtering are incorporated into the inverter that converts from DC to AC.

In most cases, you know that a power failure has occurred because all of the lights go dark and the other electrical appliances around you suddenly stop. When the UPS shifts to battery power, it also sounds an alarm. If the alarm sounds, but the other power in the room is still on, it's possible that somebody has accidentally pulled the plug that connects your UPS to the wall outlet, or a circuit breaker or fuse has blown. If the UPS sounds an alarm for just a few seconds, the alarm was probably caused by a transient surge or interruption.

When your UPS shifts to backup power, don't assume that the computer will keep going until the power returns. Most UPSes used with desktop computers have relatively small batteries that can't keep the computer going indefinitely, but they provide enough extra time for you to save your work and perform an orderly shutdown.

296

FIGURE 17.5

Uninterruptible power supplies provide clean AC power and a battery backup to your computer's power supply.

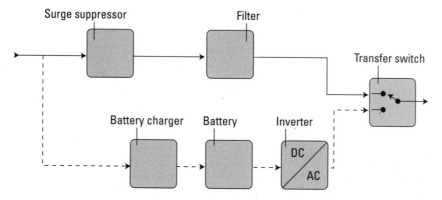

Choosing a UPS

When you shop for a UPS, remember that you want to provide power to some external peripheral devices along with your computer itself. At a minimum, you should choose a UPS with enough power and additional AC outlets to provide back-up power for your monitor and network modem or Internet router. If you store your data on an external disk drive, that drive should also take its power through the UPS.

Most UPS manufacturers offer detailed recommendations about the best size of UPS for specific combinations of run time and computer power consumption. Before you buy a UPS, look for a data sheet or Web site that shows the ideal combination for your own requirements.

In a business or another setting where the computer is performing essential work, your UPS should obviously be more powerful and more reliable, so you can keep the computer running on battery power until your emergency standby generator can kick in.

Using a UPS with Windows

If your UPS has a serial data port or a USB port, Windows can monitor the condition of the UPS; Windows either performs an automatic system shutdown or it goes into hibernation after a power failure while the UPS battery still has enough power to keep the computer alive.

APC and other major UPS manufacturers provide proprietary UPS interface software with their products that often have more and better features than the Windows utility. If your UPS came with software, you should use that program instead of Windows.

To configure the Windows UPS interface, follow these steps:

1. **Install the UPS according to the instructions supplied with it.** Turn on the UPS and the computer. If the UPS came with a software disc, run the installation software now.

2. **From the Control Panel, double-click the Power Options icon to open the Power Options Properties window.**

3. **Click the UPS tab to open the dialog box shown in Figure 17.6.**

4. **Click the Select button in the Details box.** The dialog box shown in Figure 17.7 opens.

5. **Choose the manufacturer and model of your UPS from the drop-down menus.** If the UPS is connected to your computer through a serial data port, make sure the On port option shows the correct port number.

FIGURE 17.6

Use the UPS tab to configure and monitor the state of your UPS.

FIGURE 17.7

Use the UPS Selection dialog box to identify your UPS to Windows.

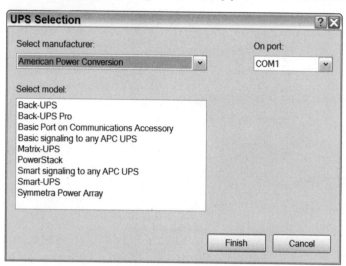

6. Click Finish to save your choices and close the window.

7. In the Power Options Properties window, click Configure to open the dialog box shown in Figure 17.8.

8. Click OK in the UPS Configuration window and again in the Power Options Properties window to save your settings and close the windows.

When a power failure occurs and the UPS shifts to battery power, the Status box in the Power Options Properties window changes its display to show the Current Power Source as On Battery. If the UPS can provide additional information, the Status box also shows the estimated remaining life of the UPS battery and other useful information.

FIGURE 17.8

The UPS Configuration window controls what happens when a power failure occurs.

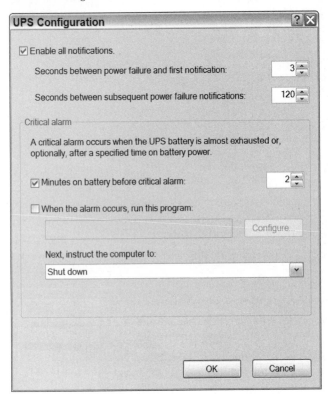

Using a DC Power Supply

Most desktop computers operate on domestic AC power, but in some specialized situations, you might want to replace your computer's power supply with one that uses a DC power source. For example, a DC-powered desktop computer can be useful if you're using it aboard a boat or truck that doesn't have access to AC, or if you're obtaining power for the computer from batteries or solar power. DC power supplies that fit the same space in your computer case as the conventional AC power supply are available from several suppliers.

Before you replace the power supply in your computer with a DC supply, be sure you consider the alternatives, including a separate DC-to-AC inverter, and a laptop or other portable that normally uses DC power. A power unit for a laptop that plugs into a car's cigarette lighter or some other DC source is likely to be less expensive and more flexible than a desktop computer that can only run on DC power.

Whether you use a DC computer or an inverter, don't overload your power source or the wiring between the power source and the computer. You can't run a 250 watt computer and monitor through a cigarette lighter, or connect the computer to the power source with tiny wires.

And remember that in these situations you also need a monitor that can use DC power — they're out there, but they're not common.

If you do decide to install a DC supply in your desktop computer, simply remove the original AC supply, put the DC unit in its place, and connect the output cables to the motherboard, disk drives and other components inside the computer case.

Summary

Windows includes several features and options that control the way your computer consumes electric power. The Advanced Configuration and Power Interface (ACPI) scheme works with the power policies in individual device drivers to reduce the amount of power each device uses when the device is not in service. Windows also uses Power Schemes, specified in the Power Options dialog box, to specify the amount of idle time before the monitor and disk drives shut down and the entire computer enters either the standby or hibernation state.

Uninterruptible power supplies provide a battery backup that allows you to shut down your computer in an orderly manner when your AC power fails. The UPS tab in the Power Options window contains settings that specify exactly how a UPS responds to a power failure.

Finally, in certain specialized situations, replacing the conventional AC power supply in your desktop computer with a DC power supply can offer some significant benefits. However, a laptop or other portable is often the better solution to the same set of problems.

Chapter 18

Overclocking Your Computer

O verclocking is a method used to push the performance of a computer's components — the CPU, the chipset, the RAM memory, and
the graphics controller — beyond their rated limits in an attempt to
make the system run better and faster than the designers' specifications. The
most common techniques for overclocking include increasing the processor
speed and increasing the system bus speed.

Depending on your point of view, you can think about overclocking as either
the computer equivalent of fine-tuning a car to wring out every possible bit
of performance, or as a somewhat obsessive practice that might cost more
money on extra cooling and other components than it would cost to achieve
the same performance with a faster processor.

In other words, overclocking is one of those activities that has less to do with
using a computer as a tool for performing other work, and is more of an end
in itself; most overclockers aren't concerned about making their computers
work better for word processing or Web browsing, but they are delighted
when they can increase the score that the computer achieves on some benchmark test of raw computing speed.

Overclocking is almost exclusively a sport for owners of desktop computers;
the close quarters inside a laptop case make it almost impossible to increase
the cooling needed by an overheated CPU.

Reasons to Overclock

Why would you want to overclock your computer? The most practical reason is to improve the performance of an older computer so that it can run

IN THIS CHAPTER

**Understanding the benefits of
overclocking**

Evaluating the risks

Speeding up your CPU

**Cooling down your overheated
CPU**

**Increasing the speed of your
graphics controller**

newer games or applications that need more power than the computer was designed to provide. If you're on a very tight budget, overclocking might allow you to keep that old clunker in service until you can afford to replace it.

But for some people, that's less important than the simple challenge of pushing the CPU, motherboard, and other components to their absolute limits, and the opportunity to announce on an Internet newsgroup that you are running your system 37 percent faster than the processor's rated speed. And if you're an enthusiastic gamer, it's possible that even a tiny improvement in performance can make some of your games run noticeably better.

In the end, the best reason to try overclocking your computer is for the pure joy of the exercise, rather than any kind of practical application. If hot-rodding a computer sounds like fun, and you don't depend on that machine for reliable day-to-day use, go ahead and try it. But don't assume that you can just move a few jumpers on a motherboard and magically turn your antique computer into a rock-solid state-of-the-art screamer.

Reasons Not to Overclock

Before you try to improve your computer's speed and performance by overclocking, take some time to consider whether the potential benefits outweigh the risks. Unless you're working with a spare system that you don't use for important work, it's important to understand that an overclocking failure can cause enough problems to do some serious damage.

It's entirely possible that your overclocked system could work flawlessly. But these are some of the major things that can go wrong:

- **You can destroy the CPU.** Worst case, the processor doesn't work at any speed after you try to boost its speed. This is uncommon, but it can happen.

- **The system could slow down.** If you choose the wrong jumper settings, or if the settings you use create a wrong configuration, the overall performance of your system may actually degrade, even if the CPU is running faster.

- **The system can become unreliable.** An overclocked system may appear to start and run faster than it did before, but you might see some other problems, including system crashes, hardware or software conflicts, and intermittent POST failures.

- **You can reduce the life of your system.** Even if the computer appears to work properly at a higher speed, the CPU produces more heat and added stress on the system that can gradually break down its internal circuitry.

- **You can lose data.** When you restart your computer after overclocking, the processor and chipset might have trouble working with your hard drive. A serious conflict or other problem could damage the drive's boot files or data files. And when Windows tries to load, the CPU's unpredictable performance can corrupt the system registry.

- **You can void the warranty.** If your computer or any of its components are still covered by the manufacturer's warranty, overclocking the processor violates its terms. If you fry a CPU or damage a hard drive, don't expect to get a free replacement.

- **You can damage other components.** When you increase the speed of the system bus, you're also forcing everything connected to the motherboard to run faster, even if some of those components can't handle the higher speed. Your computer's RAM, the chipset, the graphics controller, and the expansion cards plugged into the PCI sockets are all at risk.

Overclocking is often promoted as an economical alternative to buying a new computer or replacing the CPU and motherboard. However, that's not always true; if you have to spend money to replace the CPU's heat sink or install additional input and exhaust fans to compensate for the increased amount of heat inside the case, you might end up spending as much or more than the cost of new components. If the computer breaks down as a result of your overclocking efforts, you have to buy or build a replacement—that's a just-about-perfect definition of a *false economy*.

In many cases, the improvements produced by overclocking may not make any real difference. Most of the time, even a 20 percent increase in speed is not enough to notice. Unless you're running test programs rather than real applications, the practical benefits are minimal. If you're serious about making your computer run faster, buy a faster computer. Even a new mid-range processor and motherboard almost certainly performs better than a five-year-old system pushed to its limits.

Finally, overclocking has potential impact on the other people who use the computer. A server that supports dozens or hundreds of individual users should be as reliable as possible and not subject to downtime caused by a flaky processor or an enthusiastic overclocker trying to push the machine beyond its published limits.

Methods

The actual process of overclocking your CPU is simple: Just change the clock speed, the Front Side Bus (FSB) multiple, or both, on the motherboard. The clock speed is the rate (in millions of cycles per second, or megahertz) at which the CPU's internal oscillator operates—when you increase the clock speed, the CPU runs faster. The FSB connects the CPU to the main memory and the chipset, so increasing the FSB multiple reduces the amount of time the CPU needs to communicate with the memory and chipset.

Depending on the motherboard's design, you can sometimes change these values by either moving a jumper, changing a switch setting, or editing the BIOS settings. Other systems, including most Intel CPUs and motherboards have the speeds locked, so overclocking may not be possible on systems that use those components.

The User's Manual for your motherboard should contain specific instructions for setting the clock speed, so you must have a copy of the manual before you proceed. If you can't find the manual, look for a copy to download from the motherboard maker's Web site.

You won't find a section in the manual called "How to Overclock," but the information is probably there if it's possible to change the speed. For example, the instruction sheet shown in Figure 18.1 explains how to change the switch settings on an older ASUS A7V333 motherboard.

Some brand-name computer makers don't encourage overclocking, so they don't include the necessary information in their manuals. If you have one of those systems, your best source of information will be the Web sites dedicated to overclocking.

On more recent motherboards, the BIOS sets the clock settings instead of depending on switch or jumper settings. For example, one of my computers has an Overclock Tuner option in the BIOS Settings utility.

In addition to the manual, the other source of valuable information about overclocking your particular combination of CPU and motherboard is the online community of enthusiasts. If other people have tried overclocking a computer with the same components, there's a good chance that they have described their experience in one of the overclocking forums or newsgroups, or in a users' forum sponsored by the motherboard manufacturer.

FIGURE 18.1

Change the switch settings on this motherboard to set the clock speed.

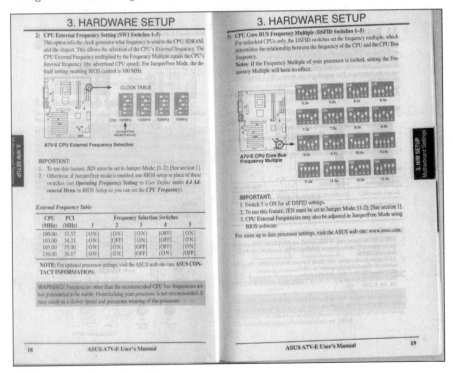

It's worth the time and trouble to search for information before you try to modify your own system. It's always cheaper to learn about potential disasters from somebody else's experience. If there's a potential hazard or pitfall, you want to know about it before you fry your own CPU chip; if there's a particular combination of settings that work best, you want to know that, too. To find online information, use Google or some other Web search tool to search for your motherboard make and model.

> **TIP** Before you start to experiment with overclocking, be sure to make a complete backup of all the essential files on your hard drive. This way, if your overclocked processor damages the contents of the drive, you can restore your data from an offline copy.

If your motherboard uses jumpers or switches to change the clock settings, unplug the power cable from the computer before you do anything else. Use an antistatic wrist strap to protect your computer from static electricity.

When you have found and read everything available about overclocking with your motherboard, try increasing the settings, one step at a time. Don't go immediately to the highest possible numbers, but do things gradually. After each change, turn on the computer and watch closely as the BIOS runs the POST and Windows loads. Before you run any other software, use the system monitor utility supplied with your computer or motherboard, or a diagnostic program such as SpeenFan (download it from www.almico.com/speedfan.php) or Motherboard Monitor (http://mbm.livewire dev.com/) to measure the CPU's temperature. If everything appears to be working, try running a game or some other program that consumes a lot of system resources while you watch for the temperature to rise.

> **TIP** The Dr. Hardware diagnostic program can tell you exactly how fast your CPU is running, and run some benchmark programs that show you how your performance has improved. You can find Dr. Hardware at www.dr-hardware.com

If the system seems to do everything you want it to do, let it run for an hour or two to allow heat to build up and make sure there isn't a problem that wasn't obvious at startup. Then turn off the computer and increase one of the overclocking settings by one more step. Repeat the process, one step at a time until Windows doesn't load, or the temperature monitor tells you that the CPU or other components are too hot, or you get a blue-screen failure, or the system doesn't start at all. At that point, either you have pushed the system to its current limits, or the CPU is overheated, so you should either drop the settings by one step, or try to increase the amount of cooling with a bigger or more effective heat sink (see the next section in this chapter for more about cooling your system).

As you run tests on your newly overclocked system, remember that you're trying to get the system to fail; that's the only way to find the highest settings that your system tolerates. In effect, you're cranking up the speed until something breaks, and then turning things down until they work again.

Your system has at least two speed settings that work together: the clock and the FSB multiple. You can try increasing just one setting, and leave the other one at the standard value, or try changing both values, one at a time. You may discover that certain combinations work better than others.

Keeping Things Cool

High-speed operation doesn't usually cause your overclocked CPU to fail. It's heat. When you increase the clock speed, you also increase the amount of energy that the processor consumes; much of that energy ends up as heat. The cooling fan and heat sink supplied with your computer's CPU are adequate for normal operation, but once you start overclocking, you're going to need a more effective cooling system. Eventually, the CPU might reach a clock rate that it can't handle, but the system will probably overheat before it gets to that point. Your local computer parts retailer might have a few kinds of CPU coolers in stock, but if you're really serious about overclocking, you should go to one or more of the specialist retailers who sell high-performance cooling products through the Internet.

Along with the retailers, the Internet can also take you to Web sites created by dedicated overclocking enthusiasts, who have tried all of the standard (and many unusual) cooling techniques. Before you replace your existing CPU cooler, it's worth the time to explore the Web sites that have tested dozens of different cooling products and published the results.

The most common CPU cooling method is a two-step process: a conductive metal object with a large surface area (a heat sink) dissipates the heat from the CPU chip, and a fan blows the heat away from the heat sink. The standard-issue heat sink is usually made of aluminum, which is moderately conductive. To create a more effective heat sink, you can increase the surface area, replace the aluminum with a more conductive metal such as copper or silver, or a combination of both a bigger surface and a different metal.

The main alternatives to a simple heat sink and fan are water-based coolers and thermoelectric modules called Peltier elements. A water cooler works like the radiator in your car: a small pump circulates water through a set of tubes and hoses between a conductive block next to the CPU and a radiator that dissipates the heat. Thermoelectric elements are heat pumps that use an electric current to transfer heat between two different conductive materials. This heat transfer is called the Peltier Effect.

Both water cooling and Peltier cooling are a lot more effective than a simple heat sink and fan, but they do have their own drawbacks. Water-cooled systems are essentially small plumbing systems that add a whole new set of complications to your computer. Peltier devices are very effective at pulling heat away from a CPU, but they need their own heat sinks and fans to dissipate that heat and move it out of the case; and they can consume as much power as the CPU itself. If your computer's power supply isn't adequate to support a Peltier element, you may have to replace it with a more powerful unit.

Another potential problem with a Peltier system is condensation. The cooling element can become cold enough to pull moisture out of the surrounding air and form water droplets on the CPU and other nearby surfaces. This is not something you want inside your computer, so you probably need a gasket or other insulation around the Peltier cooling surface.

By the time you install a water cooling system or a Peltier element, you've probably spent almost as much on cooling as you would have paid for a faster CPU that didn't require all this tweaking. At this point, we're rapidly moving into the world of the obsessive hobbyist, where economy is no longer relevant. Like most hobbies, it's entirely possible to carry supercooling to extremes. It's not uncommon for the truly dedicated overclocker to try things like immersion in liquid nitrogen and external refrigeration systems to cool down their processors. Whatever it takes to drop the temperature a few more degrees or boost the speed a few more percent is fair game. For links to descriptions of many cutting-edge overclocking and supercooling projects, run a Web search on CPU overclocking, CPU supercooling, and extreme overclocking.

Overclocking Your Video Card

Many graphics controllers also allow users to increase their clock speed. A faster video display probably won't make a lot of difference on office applications or Internet browsing, but it could improve the quality of a high-performance game.

Overclocking a graphics card is easier than overclocking a CPU because it's done in software — either the control program supplied with your graphics card or a separate program such as RivaTuner (download from `http://downloads.guru3d.com/download.php?id=13`).

If your graphics controller has an NVIDIA processor that supports overclocking, the NVIDIA Display Control Panel is the logical choice. To change the controller's processor speed, follow these steps:

1. **Open Device Manager (Control Panel ⇨ System ⇨ Hardware and click the Device Manager button).**

2. **In the Device Manager window, double-click Display adapters.** The name of your graphics processor appears.

3. **Download the latest version of the driver software for your graphics card from the NVIDIA Web site** (`www.nvidia.com/content/drivers/drivers.asp`).

4. **Install the driver software and reboot.**

5. **When the installation is complete, open the NVIDIA Display Control Panel.** Click the arrow at the left side of the control panel to open the menu shown in Figure 18.2.

6. **Look for the Clock Frequency Settings option.** If your graphics controller supports overclocking, select the option to open the dialog box shown in Figure 18.3.

FIGURE 18.2

Choose the Clock Frequency Settings option to increase the graphics processor speed.

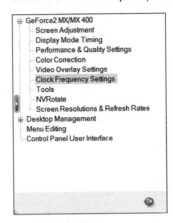

FIGURE 18.3

Use the clock frequency sliders to overclock your graphics controller.

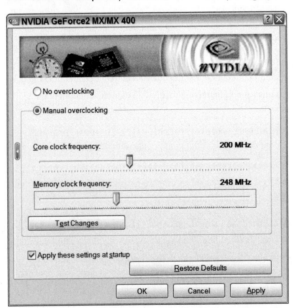

7. Select the Manual overclocking option near the top of the dialog box.

8. **Use the sliders to change the Core clock frequency and Memory clock frequency settings.** Don't push the settings all the way to top speed. Try increasing the settings by about 10 percent of the original value.

9. **Click the Test Changes button to let the program test your new settings.** If the system works at the new settings, wait at least an hour to let the card heat up, and then try increasing them by another 10 percent at a time until the Test Changes routine fails.

10. When you reach the speed you want to use, turn on the Apply these settings option and restart the computer.

CROSS-REF Chapter 10 includes more details about NVIDIA graphics controllers.

To increase the speed of an ATI card to what ATI considers an optimal level, use the Catalyst control program supplied with the card. From the Catalyst Control Center, choose ATI Overdrive, and turn on the Enable ATI Overdrive option. The ATI Overdrive function uses a sensor to monitor the temperature of the graphics processor, and automatically drops the clock speed if the processor overheats.

The RivaTuner utility also works with some ATI controllers, so it's worth a try. To use RivaTuner, use the Web site mentioned earlier and follow these steps:

1. **Start the RivaTuner program.** The dialog box shown in Figure 18.4 opens.

2. **Under the Main tab, click the Customize option at the right side of the description of the video controller.** A pop-up group of icons appears.

FIGURE 18.4

Use RivaTuner if your graphics card's control software does not support overclocking.

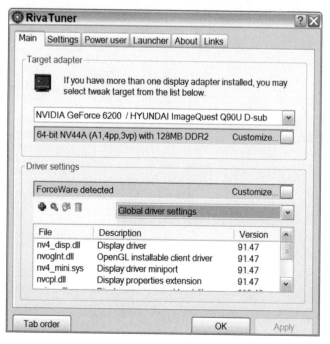

3. **Choose the icon that looks like a video card, at the extreme left of the group of icons.** The dialog box shown in Figure 18.5 appears.

4. **Turn on the Enable low-level hardware overclocking option.**

5. **Set the Core clock and Memory clock sliders to the new values you want to use, and click the Test button at the bottom of the window.**

6. **If the new settings pass the test, turn on the Apply overclocking at Windows startup option.** If they don't pass, use the sliders to reduce the speeds and test them again.

7. **When you are happy with the settings, click OK to save your settings and close the window.**

8. **Click OK in the main RivaTuner window to close the program.**

If RivaTuner doesn't support your ATI graphics controller, try another program called ATITool, as shown in Figure 18.6 (the version in the figure is a beta version, released for testing. By the time you read this, it will probably be the production version of the program). You can download ATITool from www.techpowerup.com/atitool/. Before you try to use the program, read the ATITool instruction manual at www.techpowerup.com/wiki/doku.php/atitool/start.

FIGURE 18.5

The Low-level system tweaks dialog box includes overclocking controls.

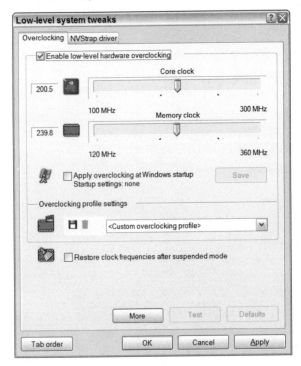

FIGURE 18.6

ATITool is a quick and easy tool for overclocking graphics controllers with ATI chipsets.

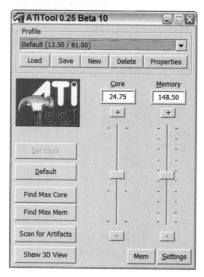

Summary

Overclocking is the process of increasing the speed of your computer's CPU or other processor. Overclocking can improve the way the computer performs in benchmark tests and games, but it may have less obvious effects in other real-world applications. The best reason to try speeding up a computer is for the pure fun of it, if that's your idea of fun. On the other hand, overclocking does carry some risks, including damage to your CPU and other components, and lost data. If problems do appear, you're on your own; the warranty doesn't cover damage caused by a failed attempt at overclocking.

If you do try overclocking your CPU, the two best sources of instructions are the motherboard manual and the overclocking enthusiasts' Web sites. It's always cheaper to learn about potential disasters from somebody else's experience. To overclock a graphics controller, use either the Nvidia control panel software, or a third-party program such as RivaTune or ATITool.

Part IV

Using Your Laptop Computer

Chapter 19

Choosing a Laptop Computer

Shopping for a laptop computer is not the same as choosing a desktop system. Along with the performance issues that drive the choice of a desktop computer, you must consider several additional factors when you buy a laptop. Screen size, weight, battery life, and ease of use are just a few of the things that can affect your choice.

In this chapter, you can learn how to evaluate these and other features that make the difference between an excellent laptop and one that's just adequate or worse.

Before you begin to evaluate a computer's features and options, it's essential to think about the way you plan to use it: every user has different needs, so no single laptop computer is the universal choice. The answers to these and similar questions should contribute to your selection:

- Where will you use the computer?

- Do you plan to carry it on your shoulder or in a backpack for long periods of time, or just move it between your office or home and your car?

- Do you plan to use the computer in a classroom, a conference room, or any other location where you must depend on battery power?

- Will you use the computer aboard airplanes or trains, where space might be an issue?

- Do you expect to watch DVD movies and videos on this computer?

- Do you need the fastest possible CPU and graphics?

Your choice of a new laptop computer should balance the size of the screen, the weight of the machine, and the life of the battery.

IN THIS CHAPTER

Evaluating laptop features

Evaluating the tradeoff between weight and screen size

Extending the life of the battery

Deciding on a CPU and other components that affect speed and performance

Protecting your laptop from loss or damage

Evaluating the computer's warranty

Understanding inputs and outputs

Storing and reading data on disk drives, optical drives, and flash media

Bringing your laptop up to date

Screen Size and Appearance

Laptop computer design is a trade-off between screen size and weight: as the size of the screen increases, so does the weight of the computer. If you want a big screen, you have to accept the added weight. Conversely, an extremely lightweight computer probably has a smaller screen.

New laptop computers are available with screens that range in size from about 12 inches up to 20 inches or more, measured from corner to corner, as shown in Figure 19.1. Up to a point, the rule of thumb is bigger-is-better, but that point is somewhere around 15.4 inches. A laptop bigger than that is more of a desktop replacement than a true portable computer — it's extremely heavy, and the screen consumes a lot of power, which translates to limited battery life. For example, Acer's Aspire laptop with a 19-inch screen weighs more than 16 pounds, as compared to a typical 6-pound, 15-inch laptop.

FIGURE 19.1

The size of a computer's screen is measured from corner to corner.

15.4 inches

The other exceptions to the bigger-is-better rule are extra-lightweight portables that often come with 12.1-inch screens. Here again, the balance between size and weight is the reason; a compact laptop can weigh as little as three pounds. The processing speed, maximum disk drive size and other performance characteristics of a lightweight model might be somewhat less than a larger and heavier computer, but those differences are less important than the weight and screen size.

NOTE Some lightweight laptops don't include a CD or DVD drive, so you have to carry a separate external drive to read those discs — including emergency boot discs and recovery discs — so that three-pound weight is somewhat misleading; by the time you add the extra hardware, you're approaching the weight of a laptop with a bigger screen and a built-in drive.

Bigger screens are certainly easier to read, but the difference may not be as much as you might think. If you're planning to use the computer for taking notes or writing reports, a smaller screen might be all you need; you can always increase the size of the display fonts.

TIP Using larger fonts limits the amount of text that can fit on your screen at one time, which makes it more difficult to refer back to earlier notes. Besides, some text-entry software doesn't handle non-standard font sizes well. Before you use your laptop in a critical note-taking situation, be sure to try the software in advance.

Not all laptop screens have the standard aspect ratio of four units wide by three units high (4:3). Dell, Lenovo (formerly IBM), and other manufacturers also offer wide-screen laptops with an aspect ratio closer to the 16:9 format used by high-definition television (HDTV) and many DVD movies. If you plan to use your laptop as a multimedia device, a wide screen could be a good choice.

If possible, compare the appearance of the computers' screens before you buy. Like stand-alone LCD monitors and graphics controllers, the screens in different laptops have different brightness levels, contrast ratios, and other performance characteristics that can affect their subjective appearance.

Weight

In general, a laptop computer should weigh as little as possible, provided it includes all the features you want or need. When you have to carry your computer across a college campus or through those long airport concourses, an extra pound or two can make a huge difference.

When you're comparing the weights of different computers in published specifications, make sure they're all describing a computer with the battery pack in place — the battery could account for as much as 15 percent of the total weight or more.

Remember that you probably won't carry the computer all by itself. By the time you put the computer into a carrying case and add all the extra cables, AC power unit, adapters, and other goodies to the case, the total weight of your five-pound laptop might end up closer to nine or ten pounds. If you can, try carrying a fully loaded case on your shoulder to make sure you can comfortably haul it around.

Weight may not be as much of an issue if you don't expect to carry the computer around very much. Those extra pounds don't make much difference when you're only moving the machine from your home office to the kitchen, or from home to work in the trunk of your car.

Battery Life

A laptop battery should be small and lightweight, but it should also last as long as possible between charges. Unfortunately, longer-lasting batteries are usually heavier than the ones that need more frequent recharges, so the ideal battery provides a balance between operating time and weight.

Most new laptops use lithium-ion (Li-ion) batteries, which are more costly than older nickel-cadmium (NiCad) and nickel-metal-hydride (NiMH) types, but they offer several advantages:

- They carry more energy in the same space.
- They weigh less than older types.
- They don't require periodic discharge.

Some laptop models can accept two different battery packs: one with six battery cells that can last up to two or three hours on a charge, and larger nine-cell packs that extend the battery life by several hours. The larger (and heavier) nine-cell battery packs may be worth the extra expense if you want to use your laptop on coast-to-coast or transatlantic flights.

Another approach to extending the battery life is used in laptops with a modular drive bay that can hold a second battery in the space that normally holds the DVD drive. With both batteries in place, the computer can run for almost twice as long, and it's not necessary to suspend the system to replace a battery.

The other way to extend a computer battery's life is to reduce the amount of power the computer demands. Therefore, the battery in a computer with a slower CPU or a smaller screen lasts longer.

Processor Performance and Memory

Within the same family of models, price of a laptop computer increases along with the speed and processing power of the CPU and the amount of RAM. For most business and home users, the difference in performance between a middle-of-the-pack CPU and a faster and more expensive processor is not important enough to justify the added cost.

If you have the extra money to spend, you see a much more dramatic improvement in performance if you spend some of that money on additional RAM, especially if you expect to upgrade the operating system to Windows Vista. Your new laptop should have at least 512MB, with space for expansion to 2GB.

Ease of Use

Other features and functions of a new laptop are more subjective than screen size, weight, and battery life, but they can be equally important; if the computer isn't easy to use, it can become a source of irritation every time you turn it on. If you possibly can, try typing on the keyboard, moving the cursor with the touchpad or pointing stick, and testing the other controls on each of the laptops you're evaluating. If you're buying the computer by mail or online, look for a dealer or manufacturer that offers a satisfaction-guaranteed right to return the computer within a week or two (30 days at Lenovo) if you don't like it.

CROSS-REF If reliability is more important than convenience, see Chapter 1 for help in making the choice between a desktop and a laptop.

Keyboard

The size of a laptop's keyboard is usually related to the size of the screen: a small screen means a narrow clamshell case, with less space for the keyboard. If the screen size is less than 13.75 inches (measured on the diagonal), the keyboard might be narrower than the standard 11-inch typewriter section of a desktop keyboard, which forces the individual keys closer together. If you're an experienced touch-typist, this could mean that the keys aren't exactly where your fingers expect them to be.

In addition to key spacing, look for a keyboard whose keys are responsive to your particular style of typing: if you pound on each key, it should provide some solid physical feedback; if you're a light-fingered typist (no, that doesn't mean you steal keyboards), the keys should accept less force to enter each character.

TIP Almost all laptops have a PS/2 connector or a USB port that accepts an external keyboard. If you use your laptop in one or more fixed locations (such as an office or a college dorm room), consider buying a separate keyboard that you can unplug and leave behind when you move the laptop.

CROSS-REF In addition to convenience, separate keyboards also allow you to use the computer more comfortably. See Chapter 29 for more about improving the ergonomics of your computer workstation.

Mouse, touchpad, or pointing stick

Just about every laptop computer has a built-in pointing device that fulfills the same purpose as a mouse on a desktop system. The most common are touch-sensitive pads that follow the motion of your finger, but some laptops also include a movable pointing stick embedded in the keyboard. Neither of these tools is as easy to use as a separate mouse, but they can be tolerable after a little practice. The choice between a touchpad and a pointing stick is purely subjective; if you like one method better than the other, choose a laptop that offers that option.

The alternative is to use a traditional mouse or trackball with your laptop. If weight and size are a concern, look for one of the mice designed for notebooks that are about one-third the size of the standard desktop versions.

Control keys and buttons

You won't use them as often as the keyboard and cursor control, but the extra control buttons on your new laptop are an important part of its user interface. These controls usually include the pushbutton that turns the computer on and off, the volume controls for the built-in speakers, a brightness control for the video display, and possibly a switch that controls the built-in wireless networking interface. Some controls, like the power switch, are obvious and well-labeled, but others are camouflaged as secondary uses for a function key.

It seems as if every computer designer treats these controls as a necessary evil that's less important than making a laptop with an attractive physical appearance. It's often close to impossible to find all the controls without a guide.

The best way to learn about these controls is to consult the manual or quick-start guide supplied with the computer. Fortunately, the computer makers all offer downloadable versions of those manuals and other documents through their Web sites. It's worth the time to skim the instructions for any laptop computer you're considering in order to find the location and use of each control before you buy it. This enables you to choose the machine whose design you like best, and to avoid making an expensive mistake.

Battery replacement

If you travel often with your computer, or if you use the laptop frequently at meetings and lectures where AC power is not available, you may want to acquire a spare battery and an external recharging unit. If you have a hot spare, you can remove and replace the battery from your computer in just a few minutes, without the need to recharge the battery inside the computer.

Even if you don't use an external recharger, you eventually need to remove and replace the battery. The typical useful life of a modern Li-ion battery in a laptop computer is less than two years, so you almost certainly have to replace it with a new one long before you're ready to replace the computer.

Either way, the design of a new laptop should allow a user to remove an old battery and install a new one without major surgery to the computer's case. The battery should either be accessible from the outside of the case, or it should be under an easy-to-remove access panel.

Fit and finish

Look for a laptop whose maker appears to have paid attention to good design and careful construction. Good quality should include these features:

- The two parts of the clamshell case should fit together easily, without any obvious gaps.
- The hinges should operate smoothly, and the screen should remain in position.

- Access panels and other removable parts should fit solidly.
- Switches and control should work easily.
- The case should have no sharp edges or excess trim.

Security Features

All of the same things that make your laptop easy to carry around also make it an attractive target for thieves. Still others are damaged when they drop onto a solid floor or bang against a desk or other hard surface. Therefore, it's absolutely essential that you take steps to make your own laptop safe and secure.

Most new laptop computers come with special security features and software, but many of those features do more to protect the data stored on the computer than the computer itself. It may be reassuring to know that a thief can't read your private files, but that doesn't recover your stolen machine.

Look for these security features on a new laptop computer:

- **Universal Security Slot:** Most laptops have a security slot near one of the back corners of the computer (some makers call it a *security keyhole*). This slot is a receptacle for a cable lock that you can use to attach the computer to a table leg or other solid object while it's in use, or when it's unattended in a hotel room or other location.

- **Motion sensor:** In some new laptops, an accelerometer detects sudden motion that occurs when you drop the computer, or somebody trips over a cable and pulls it off the tabletop. When this occurs, the built-in protection system immediately stops the disk drive and locks the heads to reduce the threat of damage from a sudden impact. This won't protect your computer against damage to the case or the screen, but it can probably keep the data on the drive intact.

- **Fingerprint reader:** Several laptop makers offer an optional fingerprint reader as an additional security feature, and others are available as external devices that connect through a USB port. When a fingerprint reader is active, a user can pass one finger across a built-in scanner; if the security software recognizes the fingerprint, it automatically enters a matching user ID and password to the Windows login or any other program or service that requires password access.

- **Encrypted disk drive:** At least one disk drive manufacturer offers a drive for portable computers that stores all data in encrypted form. The drive requires a password before a user can gain access to any of the data or programs stored on it.

CROSS-REF Look for more about protecting the physical security of your laptop computer in Chapter 48.

The Warranty

Because laptop computers receive more rough treatment than computers that remain in one place, they are more likely to suffer from hardware problems. Therefore, it's important to evaluate the warranty on your new laptop computer.

If you order your new computer directly from the manufacturer, you may have a choice of warranties at different prices. The major differences among various offerings are the length of coverage and the location where the service is provided.

The best warranties include *on-site* service, which means that the manufacturer sends a technician to perform the repairs at your location. On-site service is convenient, but it can be twice as expensive as a warranty that includes repairs done at a service depot. *Depot service* often includes pickup and delivery by a courier, so the only real difference is the amount of time the computer is out of service.

CAUTION   If you do send your laptop away for service, be sure to look into various security features to keep your data safe while it's out of your hands. Some of these features are discussed in the previous section.

If you travel overseas with your laptop, be sure your warranty includes service in all the places you normally visit. Some warranties include local service in many countries, but others may require the owner of the computer to return it to the country where it was purchased.

If you bought your computer from a local store (especially if it's a big-box retailer), the salesperson might pressure you to buy an extra-cost service contract or protection plan. Don't do it. Retail service contracts are huge profit centers for the stores, but they're a bad deal for the user — you can get better coverage for less money directly from the manufacturer.

Conventional wisdom says that extended warranties and service contracts are a bad investment, because problems appear most often during the initial warranty provided with the computer. However, extended coverage (provided by the manufacturer) could be worth the additional cost if you carry the computer around a lot, or if you run your entire life and business out of your computer.

TIP   If you pay for your new computer with a credit card, you might be eligible for extended warranty coverage from your credit card company. MasterCard, Visa, and American Express all have programs that offer up to a year of additional coverage after the manufacturer's warranty expires. You might need a free upgrade to your credit card account (to MasterCard Gold or Platinum, or Visa Signature, for example), so you should talk to your credit card supplier or consult their Web site before you buy the computer.

Unless you're buying a white-box laptop from a screwdriver shop, the warranty on your new computer also includes technical support for the Windows operating system. Microsoft provides the same technical resources to their resellers that their own tech support centers use, but some companies provide better support than others. If software support is important to you, check the reviews of manufacturer's tech support centers in magazines and online.

 For more details about warranties, see Chapter 2. If you need more information to make an informed choice about where to buy your computer, or if you simply want to know what a white-box computer is, check out Chapter 3.

Inputs and Outputs

Much of the time, you will probably use your laptop computer without anything connected to it. However, you should still make sure it has all the input and output connectors that it needs to connect to the Internet or a local network, and to peripheral devices such as a printer, an external mouse, monitor, keyboard, and various USB devices.

A new laptop should include these connectors discussed in the sections that follow.

USB and FireWire ports

Many new computers use USB connectors as replacements for the older serial data port, printer port, and PS/2 keyboard and mouse sockets, so your laptop should have at least two or three USB sockets. The exact number of sockets is not particularly important because you can always use a USB hub to connect additional devices to the computer.

If you expect to use the computer with a video camera, audio production console, or other multimedia equipment, you also want an IEEE 1394 (FireWire) socket on your laptop. One is enough because the 1394 specification allows daisy-chain connections of multiple devices.

CROSS-REF For a more detailed explanation of the USB and IEEE 1394 interface standards, see Chapter 14.

Ethernet and modem ports

Your new laptop should have a high-speed Ethernet socket that can connect the computer to a local network or an Internet gateway, and a 56 Kbps modem port for connecting to the public telephone network.

Wi-Fi

A built-in Wi-Fi wireless networking transceiver is a standard feature of most new laptop computers. In most cases, the antenna associated with the Wi-Fi radio is built into the case, usually along one side of the monitor screen.

As wireless networking has evolved, several new versions have appeared, each with a different letter suffix. Many laptops use an Intel network adapter on a removable module that is compatible with all three Wi-Fi standards, 802.11a, 802.11b, and 802.11g. At a minimum, the Wi-Fi interface supplied with a new laptop should use the 802.11g standard, which is also compatible with 802.11b base stations.

Yet another Wi-Fi standard will probably be introduced sometime in 2007, with faster data transfer speed and greater signal range than the current versions. The working designation is 802.11n, but that might change when the standard is adopted by the IEEE and other industry groups. When 802.11n becomes available, it will be possible to remove the existing Wi-Fi module inside your laptop and replace it with a new one. In the meantime, several manufacturers offer "Pre-n" wireless routers and network adapters that use what the makers expect to be the new standard.

If you're not using a Wi-Fi connection when the computer is running on battery power, it should be possible to turn off the internal Wi-Fi transceiver to reduce the drain on the battery. Your new laptop should have either a dedicated switch or a Function key that can turn the Wi-Fi adapter on or off.

An internal Wi-Fi adapter inside your laptop is not absolutely essential. Separate Wi-Fi adapters are widely available on PC Cards.

CROSS-REF   See Chapter 44 for more information about configuring and using a Wi-Fi network.

Audio connectors

Along with all those data connectors, a laptop computer usually has two audio sockets: a stereo output jack for headphones and an input plug for a microphone. This is probably adequate for listening to CDs, DVD movies, streaming radio from the Internet, and MP3 music files, but you want to use a separate USB or FireWire audio input device for serious recording.

PCMCIA (PC Card) and ExpressCard sockets

PC Cards are credit card–sized modules that follow the PCMCIA specifications. PC Cards can contain network adapters, storage media, audio adapters, and dozens of other types of peripheral devices or interfaces for mobile computers. Before the USB interface was introduced, the PCMCIA socket was the main channel for connecting an add-on device to a laptop. PC cards are still handy for many applications, including TV tuners and GPS (global positioning system) receivers because they don't take up a lot of space outside the computer's case.

PC Cards come in three sizes: Type I is 3.3 mm thick, used mostly for memory cards; Type II is 5.0 mm thick, used for network interfaces and other I/O devices; and Type III is 10.5 mm thick, used for rotating disk drives (new Type III cards are extremely rare because flash media and thinner disk drives have replaced the older drives). A new laptop computer should have at least one PC Card socket, with enough clearance for a Type II card.

ExpressCards are the latest generation of PC Card technology. An ExpressCard is about half the width of a PC Card. Many laptops combine a PC Card socket and an Express Card socket in the same space.

CROSS-REF   For more about using PC Cards and Express Cards, see Chapter 24.

Mouse and keyboard connectors

Some new laptops might still include PS/2 sockets for an external keyboard and mouse, but the latest generation of mice and keyboards come with USB plugs, so the PS/2 sockets are gradually disappearing. If your new computer doesn't include them, either use a USB mouse and keyboard, or find a couple of USB-to-PS/2 adapters.

Video monitor output

An external video output connector isn't as important as it was in the days of laptops with 10-inch screens, but most new computers still include a VGA socket, a DVI socket or both. They're still useful for dual-display setups. If your monitor can accept only a digital input cable, make sure your new laptop has a DVI output connector.

CROSS-REF Dual-display setups are discussed in more detail in Chapter 28.

Docking port

A docking port is a single socket on the back or bottom of your laptop that connects to a separate connector panel where you can plug in the cables from an external keyboard, mouse, video display, and network access. If you use your laptop with those external peripherals in one location, but you also disconnect all those cables every time you travel with the computer, a docking port can save you some time and trouble.

Serial and parallel data ports

The traditional multi-pin serial and parallel data ports that were the standard I/O ports on early personal computers are rapidly becoming obsolete. They're still common on desktop computers, but they're missing from many new laptops. Most of us won't miss them.

If you have to connect an old printer or some kind of serial device to your laptop, you need a serial or parallel adapter that plugs into a USB port or a PCMCIA socket.

Data Storage

Every laptop computer should include a hard disk drive and at least one drive for removable media. Today, the removable drive is usually a combined CD/DVD drive that may or may not support recordable DVDs. In some systems, the CD/DVD drive is a removable module that a user can replace with an optional floppy disk drive or an extra battery. Many laptops also include readers for flash media.

Hard disk drives

The hard disk drive inside your laptop computer is physically smaller than the ones in desktop systems, which means that the maximum capacity for data storage is considerably less than in a desktop system with a physically larger disk drive.

Many manufacturers offer the same or similar models with more than one drive size. If you have a choice, it's probably worth the extra money to order a computer with a bigger drive, especially if you expect to store music files or videos on it. However, the drives with the largest capacity also cost more than smaller drives, so the best choice is probably someplace in the middle of the range. When you run out of space on the internal drive, you can always add a second, external drive through a USB port.

CD and DVD drives

Lower-priced laptops generally include an optical drive that can read and write CDs, but can only read data DVDs and play videos—more expensive drives can also store data on DVDs. If your computer does not come with DVD player software for movies and videos, you can download a free player from www.cliprex.com or http://xinehq.de/, or use the same RealPlayer or Windows Media Player programs that you use to listen to audio through the computer.

Flash drives

At some point, you may want to transfer files from the flash memory cards in your digital camera, sound recorder, and other digital device to your computer. You can connect the camera or recorder directly to your computer through a USB or FireWire cable, but it's often more convenient to remove the flash card and let the computer read the files directly. Some laptops include built-in sockets for the most popular flash card formats; if yours does not, you can use an inexpensive card reader that connects to the computer through a USB cable, or an adapter on a PC Card. Unfortunately, flash media come in about half a dozen different shapes and sizes, so it's essential to make sure you choose a card reader that supports the type of cards you use.

Upgrading the Computer: Now or Later

Even if you buy a new computer with all the latest features and options, it's inevitable that you will want to improve it within a year or two. You might decide to add more RAM or install a new and bigger disk drive, or maybe the next generation of DVD drive or wireless network interface. Your computer's modular design should allow you (or your in-house support person) to replace existing components quickly and easily without professional help.

Therefore, you should confirm that simple upgrades are indeed simple, and they don't require special tools or incredibly complicated procedures. You might need professional help for major repairs, but it ought to be possible to remove and replace major modules yourself. Before you settle on a particular make and model, look for detailed instructions for adding memory, changing the drives, and performing other simple upgrades on the manufacturer's Web site.

Summary

When you're shopping for a new laptop computer, the three most important characteristics are the size of the screen, the weight of the computer, and the amount of time the computer runs on its battery. For most of us, the best choice offers a balance among the three. Before you make your own choice, think about the way you expect to use the laptop and select the features that support that use.

Chapter 20

Finding Your Way Around Your Laptop Computer

The layout of a laptop computer sometimes seems to be a product of the Trash Compactor School of Industrial Design. Everything is there, but it's all squeezed into a very tight space.

This chapter describes and explains how to use the most common features and functions in laptops. There is no standard location for many of these features, so you should consult the manual and other documents supplied with your own computer as you read the descriptions here.

Controls and Switches

Most of the controls for your laptop computer are located on the same surface as the keyboard.

Power button

When the computer is off, the power button turns on the computer. When the computer is on, the Power Options Properties dialog box shown in Figure 20.1 specifies the function of the power button: either shut down the computer, put it into standby or hibernation, or display a menu of options.

If the computer freezes and it does not respond to any keyboard input, hold down the power button until the computer turns itself off. To restart, count to ten and push the power button again.

FIGURE 20.1

The Advanced Power Options settings dialog box controls the response to pushing the power button.

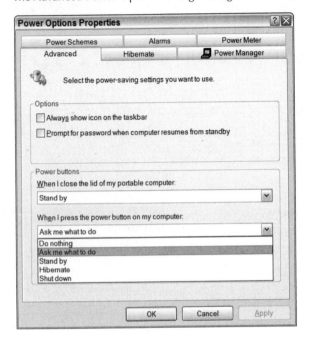

Audio controls

The volume control buttons increase and decrease the volume level of the computer's audio output through the built-in speakers or the headphone output.

The mute button turns off the audio output. To restore the sound, press one of the volume control buttons or push the mute button again.

The Fn Key

The Fn (Function) key is an extra shift key that converts the functions of several keys on the computer's keyboard. Some of these functions duplicate some of the control keys on a conventional keyboard (such as Num Lock), and others perform special functions that are unique to a laptop computer.

Each computer maker assigns a different set of functions to Fn+N combinations (where N can be any other key), but they all label the keys that work with Fn, as shown in Figure 20.2. The symbol on the lower half of the key, in the same color as the *Fn* on the Fn key (usually blue), identifies the command that you enter when you hold down the Fn key and press that key.

FIGURE 20.2

The keys that perform special functions when you hold down the Fn key have additional symbols printed on them.

The touch pad

Most laptop computers include a touch-sensitive pad located between the bottom of the keyboard and the front of the case. The touch pad is a pointing device that follows the motion of your finger across its surface and displays that motion with the cursor on the monitor screen.

The touch pad accepts these commands:

- To move the cursor, slide your finger along the touch pad.
- To select an object, move the cursor over that object and tap the pad.
- To double-click, move the cursor over an object and tap the pad twice.

The buttons under the touch pad perform the same functions as the buttons on a mouse.

Some laptop makers provide a configuration program that allows users to adjust the sensitivity of the touch pad and control other options. If your computer includes such a program, it's accessible through a tab in the Mouse Properties window, which you can open from the Control Panel.

The pointing stick

Many laptops have a pointing device embedded in the keyboard and a set of buttons directly below the space bar as an alternative to the touch pad. If your computer has one, it's the colored object about the size of the eraser at the end of a pencil, located directly above the *B* key, as shown in Figure 20.3.

 Different companies use different names for the pointing stick. For example, Dell calls it the *Track Stick*, and IBM/Lenovo calls it the *TrackPoint*.

FIGURE 20.3

The pointing stick is the flexible object directly above the B key.

Pointing stick

To move the cursor, place your finger over the pointing stick and push it in the direction you want the cursor to move. The buttons under the space bar perform the same functions as the buttons on a traditional mouse. Some pointing sticks, including the IBM/Lenovo TrackPoint, also include a Press to Select feature that allows you to push or tap the top of the pointing stick to select an object on the monitor screen.

To adjust the way the pointing stick responds, open the Mouse Properties window from the Control Panel and use the tab that contains the options that control the pointing stick. The exact name on the tab is different on different computer brands because it's part of the software supplied by the manufacturer.

Over time, the colored cap on your pointing stick may wear out or become very dirty as it picks up oil and grime from your finger. Replacement caps are available directly from your computer's manufacturer or from a repair shop or an on-site service technician. To remove the existing cap, just pull it straight up and off. When you replace the cap or install a new one, make sure it is firmly seated on the post. If the cap extends beyond the surface of the keyboard, it can damage the screen when you close the case.

Wireless power switch

If your laptop has a built-in wireless network (Wi-Fi) or Bluetooth interface, it probably also has a switch to turn the radio transceivers off. The switch is often located on the front edge of the case. When you're not using a wireless connection, turn the radio off to reduce the drain on your computer's battery and to assure that an intruder can't gain access to the data stored in your computer.

Indicator Lights

Most laptops have a row of status indicator lights directly under the monitor screen. In many computers, these are backlit symbols that light when the associated function is active. On some computers, a second, more limited set of indicators is visible from the top of the case, near the hinge.

Unfortunately, every manufacturer uses a somewhat different set of symbols, so it's not always obvious what each light means. The most common indicator lights include:

- **Power On:** The Power On indicator lights when the computer is turned on. It blinks when the computer is in standby or hibernation.

- **AC Power Status:** The AC Status indicator lights when the computer is connected to an external power supply.

- **Battery Status:** The Battery indicator lights when the battery has an adequate charge, and blinks when the battery needs a recharge.

- **Disk Activity:** The Disk Activity indicator lights when the internal disk drive is reading or writing data.

- **Wireless Activity:** The Wireless Activity indicator lights when the wireless network interface is active.

- **Bluetooth Status:** The Bluetooth indicator lights when the Bluetooth interface is active.

- **Network Activity:** On some computers, an LED indicator next to the Ethernet port flashes when the computer is sending or receiving data.

- **Caps Lock:** The Caps Lock indicator lights when the Caps Lock key is active.

- **Scroll Lock:** The Scroll Lock indicator lights when the Scroll Lock key is active.

- **Num Lock:** The Num Lock indicator lights when the Num Lock option is turned on and the computer uses the alternative 10-key numeric keys on the right side of the keyboard.

Your computer might not have all of these lights, and it might include one or more others. Your best sources of information about the lights on your own computer are the manual and the online Help screens.

Inputs and Outputs

The computer's input and output connectors are located along its back and side edges. Most of these connectors are similar to the ones on the back of a desktop system, but the laptop also has a few others that are not common on desktops.

The most common connectors include:

- **Video monitor output:** The video monitor output is a VGA or DVI connector that can provide a signal to an external LCD or CRT video display monitor. Some laptops include separate VGA and DVI connectors. The video output is also the connection point for a projector or other display device.

- **S-Video output:** The S-Video output connects to a television or a video recorder.

- **Modem connector:** The modem connector is an RJ-11 telephone jack that can connect to the public telephone network through a standard modular telephone cable.

- **Ethernet connector:** The Ethernet connector is an RJ-45 jack that can connect to a data network or an Internet router through a standard CAT 5, CAT 5e, or CAT 6 data cable.

- **USB connectors:** The USB connectors are I/O connectors for external peripheral devices (see Chapter 14 for more about USB).

- **IEEE 1394 connector:** The IEEE 1394 connector is an interface for external FireWire devices including video cameras, hard drives, or audio controllers.

- **Mouse and keyboard connectors:** Some laptops still include PS/2 connectors for an external mouse and keyboard. However, these connectors are rare on new computers because most new mice and keyboards use the USB interface.

- **Serial data port:** The serial data port is a 9-pin serial I/O connector for external peripheral devices (see Chapter 16 for details about serial connections). Many laptop manufacturers have stopped including a serial port on their computers.

- **Audio input and output connectors:** The audio connectors are sockets that connect to cables with 3.5 mm plugs from a microphone and a pair of headphones or earpieces.

- **PC Card and ExpressCard sockets:** PC Cards and ExpressCards are credit-card-sized interface adapters and peripheral devices that can add new I/O functions, portable storage, security, and other functions to your computer. In some computers, the sockets for the two types of cards are combined in a single space with two multi-pin connectors inside the computer; in others an ExpressCard requires an adapter. To install a card, insert it into the socket until it is firmly mated to the connector. To remove a card, push the mechanical release button next to the socket.

- **Power input:** The power input connector connects to an external source of DC power, such as an AC power adapter or a cigarette lighter adapter in a vehicle. Be sure to use a power adapter that provides the correct number of volts and watts for your computer. See the section Power Supplies for Laptop Computers later in this chapter for more details.

- **Infrared port:** The Infrared port is a transmitter and receiver for IrDA wireless communication with other IrDA-equipped computers and digital cameras. This is the same technology used by many handheld remote control units. To configure your computer for IrDA communication, open the Control Panel and select the Wireless Link icon (if you use Category View, Wireless Link is in the Pointers and Other Hardware category).

- **Digital media socket:** Some laptops include a socket for one or more of the most widely used flash media formats, including CompactFlash, Secure Digital, or Memory Stick. To use a compatible media module as an additional storage device, or to transfer data, images, or sound files from a digital camera, portable audio or video recorder, or another computer, simply insert the module into the socket.

- **Docking connector:** The docking connector is a multi-purpose I/O connector that mates with a port replicator, base, or dock that provides access to an external mouse, monitor, keyboard, and network interface. It's often located on the bottom of the computer, under the keyboard. If you use your laptop as a replacement for a desktop computer, you can connect it through the docking connector.

Figures 20.4 and 20.5 show the connectors on the sides of a typical, closed laptop computer.

FIGURE 20.4

From left to right: Air vents, VGA video connector, RJ-11 Modem connector, RJ-45 Ethernet connector, audio input and output connectors, IEEE 1394 jack, PC Card/ExpressCard socket

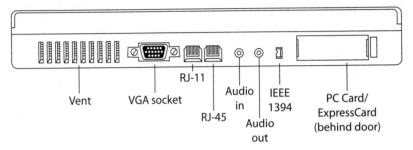

FIGURE 20.5

From left to right: S-Video output connector, DVD drive, and two USB connectors

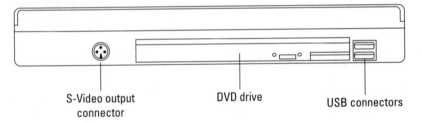

Looking Inside the Case

Laptop computers include the same components as their desktop cousins, but those components are squeezed into a much smaller space. Many of the parts that would be easy to find and replace in a desktop case or a tower are either hidden under an access panel, buried under the keyboard, or integrated into the motherboard.

The internal components are in different places in just about every make and model of laptop computer, so a universal roadmap is simply not possible. In most instances, you need specific instructions just to find your way around, let alone to remove and replace anything.

CAUTION Don't try to get at the internal components of your laptop without the service manual or the procedures on the manufacturer's Web site. The manuals for most major laptop brands (available through their Web sites) include very detailed step-by-step procedures for finding and replacing what are often called Customer Replaceable Units (CRUs) or Field Replaceable Units (FRUs), such as the battery or a disk drive.

If you do have to perform your own emergency repairs on a laptop computer, it will probably be when you're away from your home base. You might want to keep a paper or CD copy of the service manual and a small screwdriver in your computer bag.

Power Supplies for Laptop Computers

Power supplies for most laptop computers are divided into two sections: an external power unit that converts AC house current to DC (most often either 12 volts or 20 volts), and a separate circuit inside the computer that drops the incoming DC power to the lower DC voltages that the electronic and mechanical components require. The internal power supply can take power from either the computer's internal battery or an external DC power unit. When the external power unit is connected to a laptop computer, it charges the internal battery at the same time that it provides power to the computer.

This approach provides several benefits for a portable machine. First, it reduces the weight of the computer by moving the power unit to a separate package that you can leave behind when you're operating the computer on the internal battery, and it also moves a significant source of heat away from the other components.

The label on an external power unit shows much of the same information as the internal power supply inside a desktop computer. As Figure 20.6 shows, the label identifies the AC input voltage and the DC output voltage, along with the maximum amount of power the unit can handle.

CAUTION Don't try to use a power unit with the wrong voltage or a lower maximum current rating than the values specified for your laptop; the computer doesn't work properly with too little power. Too much power can damage the internal circuitry.

FIGURE 20.6

A laptop computer's power unit provides DC current to run the computer and charge the battery.

Input: 100-240V
Output: 20V

Adjusting the Monitor

The video display on your laptop occupies most of the top half of the clamshell case. Because it's an LCD screen, it looks best within a limited range of horizontal and vertical angles; if you look at the screen from outside that range, the images will be a lot less clear.

Therefore, it's important to move the screen on its hinges for the best viewing angle whenever you use the computer. The hinges that hold the screen to the keyboard section of the computer should hold it in any position, from flat on the table to almost closed.

The brightness and contrast of the screen are the other adjustments that make the display easy to see. On a desktop system, you can often set the levels for the amount of light in the room and forget about them, but if you use your laptop in different locations, you will sometimes move from one place with a lot of background light to another where the lights are dim. Some laptops have a light sensor that automatically adjusts screen brightness to meet the needs of the current location; if yours does not, you should use the computer's manual brightness controls to adjust the screen for the best appearance.

A brighter screen consumes more power, so you can extend the time between battery charges by reducing the brightness. Some laptops include Power Schemes for maximum battery life with reduced brightness. Other power schemes can reduce the brightness after the computer has been idle for a specified period of time.

Cooling the Innards

The CPU and other electronic components inside any computer produce heat as they perform the work they were designed to do. In a desktop computer case, the heat sinks mounted on the CPU and other chips, and the cooling fans inside the case, move the overheated air away from the chips before it can damage the components. Obviously, there's much less space inside a laptop computer, but the same problem remains: the heat has to go someplace.

Most laptops use two methods to dissipate the heat produced by the CPU: they have one or more air vents in the case that allow the heat to escape (helped by small fans), and they have a metal plate inside the bottom of the case that conducts heat from the motherboard to the case itself. You know how effective that heat-spreading plate is if you have ever actually used your laptop on your lap.

Because space is so tight inside the laptop case, it's not possible to add extra cooling fans to reduce the heat; the best you can do is to make sure there's nothing blocking the air flow. The air intake vents are usually located on one or both sides of the computer case, with the exhaust vents on the bottom, so cool outside air comes in through the sides and warm air exits through the bottom. You should take these preventive steps to keep your laptop from overheating:

- Some laptops have a filter inside the intake vents to keep dust and other crud out of the case, so it's essential to make sure the dust doesn't accumulate in front of the filter. Use a small artist's brush or a can of compressed air to remove dust from the vents.

- Be sure there's some free space underneath the bottom of the computer so the heated exhaust air has someplace to go. If the computer has flip-up feet, use them. If it has permanent feet attached to the bottom, they should be adequate if the computer is on a solid surface like a tabletop.

- Don't use the laptop on a soft surface such as a bed or a couch: the weight of the computer could be enough to block the exhaust vents.

- Don't use the computer when it's still in its case unless the case allows some free space for airflow to and from the vents.

Summary

A laptop computer is a wonder of modern industrial design; it incorporates all the features and functions of a high-performance personal computer into a relatively lightweight portable package. Many laptop controls may have more than one function, so you should take the time to examine your own computer with the user's manual in one hand.

One of the most common controls on a laptop computer is an extra shift key called the Function (Fn) key that changes the performance of many other keys. The exact set of keys that the Fn key changes is different on each make and model of computer, but those keys usually have Fn printed on them in blue or some other contrasting color. Other features include the touchpad or pointing stick that replaces the mouse, and a set of indicator lights that tell you when certain functions are active.

Unlike desktop computers, the AC power supply for a laptop computer is a separate unit that connects to both an AC wall outlet and the laptop's power input connector. When the computer is connected to AC power, it automatically recharges the battery until the battery is at full capacity.

The inside of a laptop computer's case has much less space than a desktop case. Because of this, it's essential to move heat out of the laptop as efficiently as possible. Along with a metal plate inside the case, most laptop cases include air intake vents on one or two sides, and an exhaust vent on the bottom. Therefore, it's important to allow some free space underneath the computer; most laptop cases have feet that can do the job, as long as you don't place the computer on a soft surface like a bed or a couch.

Chapter 21

Managing Power on a Laptop Computer

A laptop computer can run on electric power from an external source or it can use an internal battery. This makes it possible to use the computer in places where AC power is not always available, such as your back yard, or the seat of an airplane or train.

Any time the computer detects external power, it automatically uses that source. If the battery is not already fully charged, the computer recharges it at the same time, whether the computer is turned on or not.

This chapter explains how your laptop works with both battery power and external power, and how to use the Power Options in Windows to optimize power consumption and extend the life of the battery.

Working with the Battery

Since the first portable computers were introduced more than 20 years ago, battery technology has continued to evolve. The lithium-ion (L-Ion) batteries supplied with today's laptops are lighter, more powerful, and more reliable than the older nickel-cadmium (NiCad) and nickel-metal hydride (NiMH) types.

If you're using an older laptop, the battery may be one of the older types that can suffer from a memory effect that reduces the useful time between charges, so it's necessary to let them run down completely and then recharge them to full capacity for best performance. Newer Li-Ion batteries don't suffer from memory effect, so you can recharge them at any point in the discharge cycle.

If you don't know what kind of battery your computer uses, look on the battery's label. As Figure 21.1 shows, just about every battery's label identifies its type and capacity.

FIGURE 21.1

The label on your computer's battery should identify its type, as the arrow indicates.

Watching usage and power drain

It's absolutely essential to keep track of the remaining time available before your laptop's battery runs down; both Windows and the bundled software supplied with your laptop include programs that monitor and display the battery's condition.

Power Meter

In Windows, the Power Meter program displays an icon in the task bar whenever the computer is using its battery. The color of the icon shows the general condition of the battery. When you position the cursor over the icon, the Power Meter displays more detailed information in a pop-up balloon.

To see a constant view of the battery's condition, double-click the battery icon. The Power Meter window shown in Figure 21.2 doesn't add much to the information in the pop-up, but it's easier to read.

FIGURE 21.2

The Windows Power Meter shows the current status of the battery.

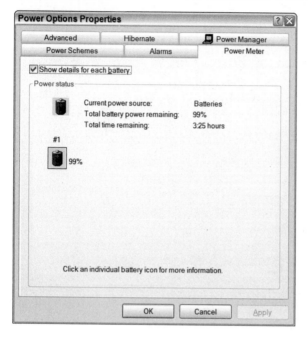

Battery alarms

The power meter can trigger alarms at two levels: a Low Battery alarm and a Critical Battery alarm. Normally, the Low Battery alarm occurs when the battery is down to about a 10 percent charge, and the Critical Battery alarm occurs with about 3 percent remaining. To change these settings, follow these steps:

1. **From the Control Panel, choose Power Options.** The Power Options Properties open.

2. **Choose the Alarms tab to open the dialog box shown in Figure 21.3.**

3. **Use the sliders in the Low battery alarm and Critical battery alarm sections to set the thresholds for the two alarm conditions.**

4. **Click the Alarm Action buttons to open either the Critical battery alarm dialog box or the dialog box shown in Figure 21.4.** Here you can specify the actions that each alarm condition triggers.

FIGURE 21.3

Use the Alarms tab to set the battery levels that will produce alarms.

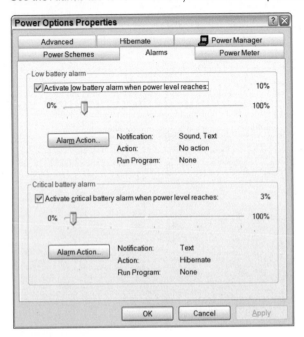

FIGURE 21.4

The Low Battery Alarm Actions dialog box sets the actions that take place when an alarm occurs.

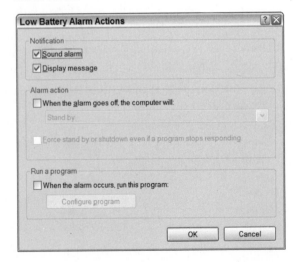

Just about every laptop maker also supplies its own battery alarm program as a supplement to the one in Windows. For example, the IBM/Lenovo ThinkPads place a second, larger battery-level icon in the taskbar, and they include a Power Manager window with more information than the Windows Power Meter provides. Figure 21.5 shows the Battery Information window in the ThinkPad Power Manager.

FIGURE 21.5

IBM/Lenovo ThinkPads include additional battery information that is not available from Windows.

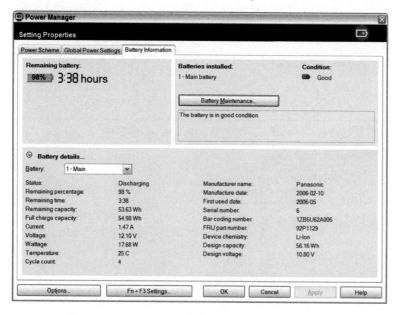

Don't be surprised if the percentages shown by Windows and the proprietary battery meter are slightly different. The two programs might use different methods for estimating the amount of power left in the battery, so they may produce different results.

Multiple batteries

Many new laptops can use a second battery in the drive bay that otherwise holds a CD/DVD drive. Like the internal battery, the battery in the drive bay automatically recharges when the computer is connected to external power. The second battery, combined with the one built into the computer, should provide several additional hours of operation between charges.

Two batteries operating in parallel last longer than letting one battery run down and then installing the second one. Therefore, if you have a second battery for your computer, both batteries last longer if you install both batteries at the beginning of your session, rather than waiting for the first one to run down.

Charging the battery

The battery supplied with a laptop computer is rechargeable, which means that it can "refill" itself to a full charge from an external power source. You can recharge your computer's battery while it is mounted in the computer, or recharge it in a separate charging unit.

Inside the computer

To recharge your computer's battery, simply connect the computer to the power unit supplied with the computer or a compatible replacement power unit. The computer automatically recharges the battery, even if the computer itself is turned off. On some laptops, the charging process takes less time when the computer itself is not running.

When the battery is recharging and the computer is on, the Windows Power Meter shown in Figure 21.6 shows the progress of the charge.

FIGURE 21.6

The Power Meter shows the amount of power currently available in your laptop's battery.

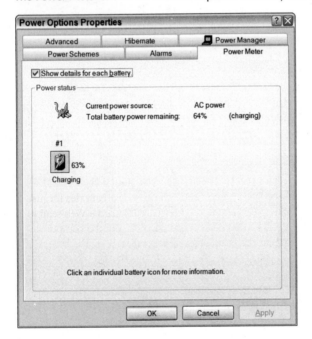

Outside the computer

Many laptop users need more time away from an AC outlet than a single battery can provide. The solution to this problem is to carry a second battery and use an external charger to keep it charged. Separate stand-alone chargers are available from most laptop manufacturers and from independent battery dealers. When you buy a battery charger, make sure it's the right model for your computer's battery. The packaging for most chargers includes a list of compatible makes and models.

To change to a *hot spare*, a charged battery, shut down the computer and remove the old battery. Install the new one in its place and turn the computer back on.

Adding a spare battery to your computer bag increases its weight, but it's often worth the trouble when you're traveling a long distance or you're facing an entire day of meetings or lectures. When the battery in your computer is almost drained, you can suspend the computer and swap batteries. When you get back to your home or office, you can throw the spare into the charger until you're ready to travel again. On the road, you should connect the power pack to the computer until the first battery is fully charged (usually about three hours for a Li-Ion), and then swap it for the second one and charge that one.

Replacing the battery

At some point, you may want to buy a new battery for your computer; either the original battery has worn down, or you want to carry a spare. Whether you use it or not, the battery in your laptop eventually reaches a point where it can no longer accept a recharge. The total lifetime of a computer's battery depends on the type of battery, the number of recharges, and the battery's overall age. As Figure 21.7 shows, the internal circuit within the battery pack notes the dates that the battery was manufactured and placed into service. Even if the battery is sitting on a shelf, unused, it eventually wears down as the electrolyte inside the battery decays. A Li-Ion battery is generally good for about 375 charges, or two to three years.

What to look for

Every laptop manufacturer sells replacement batteries for its laptops through its Web sites and often through the same retail channels that sell the computers. You can also find batteries for just about every laptop ever made through specialist Web sites and battery dealers (run a Web search on laptop batteries to find them). If you don't order the new battery directly from the computer maker, look for the make and model of your computer on the battery package or on the battery dealer's Web site.

A replacement battery should be exactly the same size and shape as the one that was supplied with your computer. The exceptions to this rule are some new laptops that can accept either a relatively small battery pack that mounts flush with the computer's case, or a larger package that extends a few inches beyond the back. The bigger battery packs are heavier than the more compact units, but they also provide more operating time between recharges.

FIGURE 21.7

The internal "clock" in your computer's battery starts when it leaves the factory.

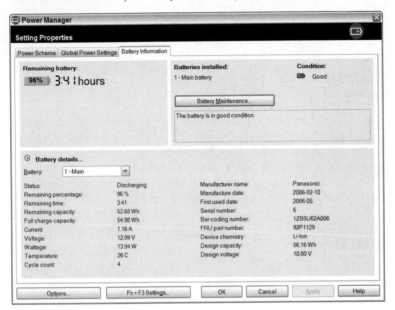

The power-handling capacity of a computer battery pack is shown on the battery itself and the product specification in the Web site or packaging. As a general rule, if the voltage is the same, you can expect a battery with more milliamp hours (MaH) to last longer.

Because Li-Ion batteries begin to wear down as soon as they are assembled, you should follow these guidelines for buying them:

- Check the date of manufacture when you buy a new battery pack.
- Don't buy old stock, even at bargain prices.
- Don't buy Li-Ion batteries until you need them.

Removing the old battery and installing the new one

To replace the battery from your computer, follow these steps:

1. **Turn off the computer or place the computer into hibernation mode.**
2. **If the computer is connected to an external power unit, disconnect it.**
3. **Follow the manufacturer's instructions for removing the battery.** You might have to lift the keyboard, remove an access panel, or release a latch before you can get to the battery itself.

4. **Before you install the new battery, read any instructions supplied with it, or look for a protective cover over one or more of the electrical contact points.** If necessary, remove the cover before you install the new battery.

5. **Insert the new battery in the space where you removed the old one.**

6. **If necessary, replace the cover or access panel.**

Disposing of old batteries

The materials inside some batteries can be hazardous to the environment unless they are handled properly when you remove them from service. Mercury, cadmium, and other heavy metals are just a few of the potentially dangerous contents of many household batteries, including the ones in laptop computers. They can also contain toxic lead. Many towns and cities have very specific requirements for treatment and disposal of old batteries as hazardous waste.

Before you drop your old batteries into the trash, check with your local garbage or solid-waste agency to find their recommended procedures. If you prefer, you can take your old batteries to a nearby retailer that participates in the Rechargeable Battery Recycling Corporation's Call2Recycle program. You can find lists of drop-off sites in the United States and Canada at the RBRC Web site (www.rbrc.org/call2recycle/dropoff).

Using an AC Adapter

Every new laptop computer comes with an AC power adapter that converts power from an AC wall outlet to the DC power required to run the computer and charge the internal battery. The input voltage and the type of AC connector or power cable must be correct for the domestic AC supply in the country where you expect to use the computer.

When local AC power is available, you should use the power adapter to run the computer. If you're paying for it, AC is considerably cheaper than battery power, and the supply doesn't run down after a few hours.

If you use the same computer in one or more semi-permanent locations, it can be convenient to buy extra power adapters. This allows you to keep one adapter plugged into the wall behind your desk (or wherever you use the laptop most often), and keep the other one in your computer bag for temporary use in the library, in a coffee shop, or a hotel room.

Choosing your adapter

Retailers and Web sites that sell batteries and accessories for laptop computers often offer power adapters at lower prices than the ones sold by the computer's manufacturer. Before you buy one of these third-party adapters, be sure it is intended for your particular make and model. The output voltage and the cable connector should be exactly the same as the one that came with your computer, and it should be rated for at least the same number of watts and amps. Be sure the adapter carries the certification mark from Underwriters Laboratories (UL) or the comparable testing agency for your own country or region.

Adapters for foreign travel

Before you try to use your computer's power adapter in a place that uses a different AC voltage from your home country, read the adapter's label carefully to be sure it is rated for the local power source. If it's not, or if the local AC power outlets at your destination use a different kind of plug, ask the manufacturer's technical support center or look on their Web site for information about ordering a different adapter or cable.

The alternative to a replacement cable or AC adapter is a simple AC plug adapter. These are widely available from airport shops, luggage stores, and other retailers who specialize in products for travelers.

TIP When you plan to travel overseas with your laptop computer, take the time to find the adapter or cable needed at your destination before you leave home. Unless you can visit someplace like Singapore's Funan Mall (where you can probably find just about any kind of computer part), you could waste a lot of time in an unfamiliar city if you have to search for a computer part.

Using External DC Power

Even if you're not close to an AC power outlet, it may still be possible to connect your laptop to an external power source. Adapters that take DC power from the cigarette lighter socket in a car or the in-seat power outlets on some airliners to the voltage used by your computer are also available.

DC adapters work just like the AC adapter supplied with your computer: just plug the output connector into the computer's external power socket, and connect the input plug to a power source. Like an AC power unit, it's essential that you use a DC adapter that provides the right voltage and uses the correct power plug for your particular laptop.

They're far from universal, but a growing number of airlines offer power points for laptop computers and portable entertainment devices on the armrests of some seats, especially in the first-class and business-class sections of their airplanes. The best place to learn which airlines offer this amenity, and which of their seats have power points is the SeatGuru Web site at `www.seatguru.com/articles/in-seat_laptop_power.php`.

Reducing Power Consumption

When you're running your laptop on battery power, it's often important to make the battery last as long as possible. The best way to extend the amount of time you can get before you need to recharge is to reduce the amount of work you're demanding from the computer.

This section offers some specific suggestions for reducing the amount of power the computer consumes. Some are more effective than others, but if you follow all of them as you use your laptop, you should see a noticeable increase in the run time of your battery.

Remove PC Cards not in use

If you use them frequently, it's very convenient to leave a flash memory or network interface card in your computer's PC Card or ExpressCard socket all the time. It's right there when you need it, so you don't have to dig it out of your computer bag and install it before you can use the card.

However, every PC Card or ExpressCard consumes power whenever it's in the socket. If you're not using a card, pull it out.

Turn off optional services

The Wi-Fi radio transmitter and receiver built into most new laptops can operate whenever the computer is on, unless you take specific action to turn it off. If the computer has an internal wireless interface, it probably has a switch that can turn it off.

Even if battery life is not an issue, you should use the switch to turn off the wireless interface when you're not using it. An active radio can be a hidden gateway for sophisticated eavesdroppers and snoops to gain access to the files stored on your disk drive. Most people who connect to Wi-Fi networks without permission are probably just looking for free Internet access, but this kind of silent break-in is possible.

Other services and optional functions can also use up the battery more quickly. If you're trying to maximize the battery's run time, unplug the network cable and any USB devices that you're not using. If there's a CD or DVD in the computer's drive, remove it.

Adding memory can also increase battery life because a larger system memory reduces the number of times the system must swap data between the system memory on RAM and the virtual memory on the disk drive. The additional RAM consumes more power, but not as much as the drive uses to spin up to speed more frequently.

Turn down the video screen

The backlight behind the video monitor screen is another potential power hog. To extend the run time of the battery, use the function switches on the keyboard or the control next to the screen to reduce the screen's brightness to the lowest level you can view comfortably.

Use Windows Power Options

The Windows Power Options icon in the Control Panel is a link to the Power Options Properties window shown in Figure 21.8. The Power Schemes tab offers a range of preset schemes that define the amount of idle time the computer waits before it turns off the monitor and disk drive, and before the computer enters the standby and hibernation states. The Maximum Battery Life and Max Battery schemes shut the system down within minutes, rather than the longer times that may be more convenient and less distracting.

FIGURE 21.8

Use the Windows Power Schemes to reduce the battery's power consumption.

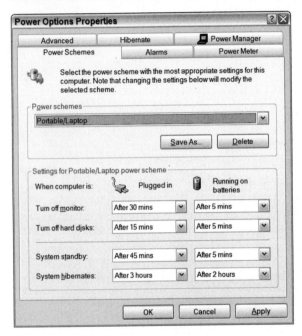

Some laptops come with more sophisticated power management features than the Windows utility provides. For example, the ThinkPad Power Manager program supplied with IBM laptops (shown in Figure 21.9) includes schemes that automatically reduce the screen's brightness, drop the CPU's processing speed when the computer is running, and decrease the monitor's display rate when the system has been idle for more than a few minutes. Other laptop brands may have different combinations of power-saving options, but almost all of them include features that are more effective than the Windows Power Schemes.

FIGURE 21.9

The ThinkPad Power Manager is a more aggressive power-conservation program than the one supplied with Windows.

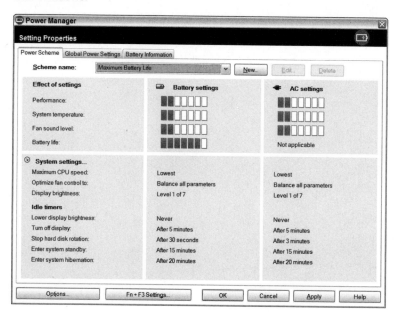

Summary

Your laptop computer can use power from either a battery or an external power source. When it's using the battery, Windows and the proprietary software supplied with the computer monitor the state of the battery's charge and issue a series of alarms when it reaches critical levels.

The Li-Ion battery used by just about every new laptop has a useful life of about two to three years or less, depending on the number of times you recharge it. When you shop for a replacement, look for a fresh battery with as many milliamp hours (MaH) as possible.

When the computer is connected to external power, the battery recharges, whether the computer is turned on or not. If you buy a second AC power unit, either as a replacement or a spare, be sure it provides the same voltage and at least the same amount of power (in watts) as the one supplied or recommended by the computer manufacturer.

In order to expend the amount of time between recharges, reduce the amount of power that the computer consumes; disconnect or remove all unnecessary peripherals and accessories. Also, use the Windows Power Schemes and proprietary energy-saving programs to shut down the disk drive, and monitor screen and other internal components when they're not in use.

Chapter 22

Using External Devices with a Laptop

A laptop computer is a self-contained system that can operate without any additional equipment connected to it. But it can also act as the core of a computer system that uses additional devices to improve the experience by adding features and functions that are not available from the laptop itself.

This chapter describes the major add-on peripherals and accessories you can use with a laptop, and explains how to configure your computer to make the best use of them.

Using a Separate Keyboard

The design of a laptop computer is a triumph of efficient packaging over comfort. You can't change the distance between the screen and the keyboard, so you can either place the computer where you can comfortably view the screen, or where you can use the keyboard without stretching your arms. You can't do both at the same time.

The solution is to separate either the monitor, the keyboard, or both from the computer itself, so you can place the keyboard at your fingertips and the monitor at eye level, where the likelihood of eyestrain and fatigue is reduced. Of course, this isn't possible when you're using the laptop on the road, or in a conference room or lecture hall, but when you set up the computer in a semi-permanent location such as an office or college dorm room, that extra keyboard or screen can make a huge difference to both your comfort and your productivity. When you take the computer to another location, you can unplug the keyboard and screen (and a mouse and a power adapter) and leave them behind.

357

If you're on a tight budget, the obvious first choice is to buy and install a keyboard that connects to your laptop through a USB port. Keyboards are relatively inexpensive, and a full-sized keyboard with all the control keys, navigation keys, and the numeric keyboard located in separate groups is a huge improvement over the one built into a laptop, where everything is jammed together.

The latest generation of laptops has eliminated the PS/2 connectors that had previously been used for keyboards and mice; most new keyboards and mice are compatible with the computer's USB inputs. If you're using an older keyboard that has a PS/2 plug with your new laptop, you can try using a PS/2-to-USB adapter, but don't be surprised if the keyboard doesn't support USB connections. If your laptop has a PS/2 keyboard input and you want to use an older keyboard, don't worry about an adapter; go ahead and use the PS/2 input.

If you have a very old keyboard, it might have a large 5-pin plug instead of the smaller 6-pin PS/2 plug. In this situation, you need a 5-pin-to-PS/2 adapter to use it with a PS/2 socket. Don't expect it to work through a USB port.

If you're connecting the keyboard through a USB input, you can plug it into the computer at any time; but if you're using a PS/2 input, you must make the connection before you turn on the computer. Either way, the computer should automatically detect the new keyboard and load any new drivers that aren't already installed. Once the drivers are in place, the computer should automatically begin to accept inputs from the keyboard. After the first time, the keyboard works as soon as Windows loads. Don't try to connect or disconnect a keyboard with a PS/2 plug while the computer is running.

Laptop computers are also prime candidates for wireless keyboards. In place of the usual cable, a wireless keyboard uses radio or infrared signals to transmit keystrokes from the keyboard to the computer and acknowledgement signals from the computer to the keyboard, so you can locate the keyboard anywhere within a couple of feet (or about one meter) or more away from the computer. A wireless keyboard can use either Bluetooth or a proprietary transmission system; if the computer does not have a built-in Bluetooth interface, a non-Bluetooth wireless keyboard uses a small transceiver module (supplied with the keyboard) that connects to the computer through a USB port.

CROSS-REF   Take a look at Chapter 15 for more information about Bluetooth.

Using an External Monitor

Now that the screens on many laptop computers are as big as a small desktop monitor, there is less reason to use an external monitor than there once was. However, it's still possible, and there are still good reasons to use one:

- If you're using one of those lightweight laptops with a 12-inch screen, text on a bigger screen is much easier to read.

- You can place the monitor at eye level.

- On some laptops, you can place the external monitor next to the laptop's screen for a dual-screen desktop.

- You can use a larger display for games or graphic design programs.
- A full-size (19-inch or bigger) monitor provides more working space than the built-in screen on all but the biggest laptops.

To connect an external monitor to your laptop, simply plug the VGA or DVI plug on the cable from the monitor into the matching connector on the side or back of the computer. Plug the monitor's power cable into an AC outlet and turn on the monitor before you turn on the computer.

Most laptops use one of the Fn shift key functions to switch between external monitor options. The specific key and the descriptions of the options are different on different brands of computers, but the most common options include:

- Switch the desktop between the laptop screen and the external monitor (the other screen goes dark)
- Display the same images on both screens
- Display an extended desktop across both screens

The configuration settings for both screens are located in the Settings tab of the Display Properties window (accessible from the Control Panel), as shown in Figure 22.1. Set the second monitor to one of these settings:

FIGURE 22.1

The Settings tab in Display Properties controls the way Windows handles multiple monitors.

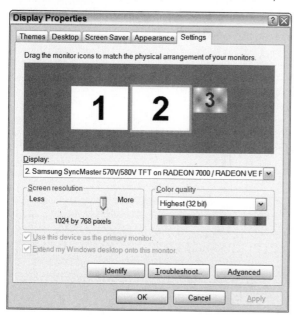

- To create an extended desktop, select Display No. 2 (the external monitor) in the diagram in the top part of the window, and turn on the Extend my Windows desktop option.

- To display the same image on both screens, turn off the Extend my desktop option.

- To use the external monitor and turn off the laptop screen, turn on the Use this device as primary monitor option, and turn off the Extend my desktop option.

CROSS-REF For detailed information about using multiple screens, see Chapter 28.

If you're not sure which display number applies to which screen, click the Identify button to superimpose a big number over each screen, like the one shown in Figure 22.2.

To connect more than one external monitor to your laptop, consider using the Matrox DualHead2Go or TtipleHead2Go expansion modules, or the SideCar range of display extenders (www.digital tigers.com/sidecar.shtml) that can support up to four additional monitors through a PC Card adapter. A SideCar adapter can cost more than a middle-range laptop computer, but under the right circumstances, it could be worth the expense.

FIGURE 22.2

The Identify command in the Settings tab places a big number over each screen.

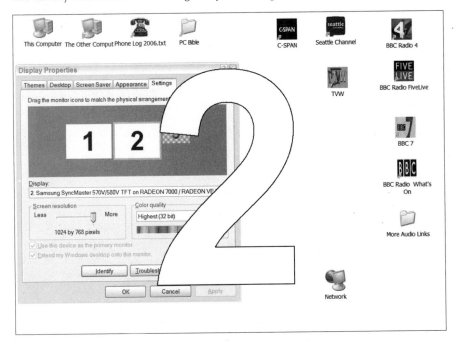

Using a TV as a Monitor

If your laptop has an S-video (for Super-Video) output connector, you can use it to connect the computer to a TV with an S-video input connector. S-video is a method for moving video images that splits the image's brightness and color signals, and transmits them separately. S-video cables are widely available from electronics and home entertainment retailers.

To set up an S-video connection, follow these steps:

1. **Turn off the computer and the television.**

2. **Connect the cable between the S-video connectors on your computer and your television set.**

3. **Turn on the television.**

4. **Turn on the computer and wait for Windows to load.**

5. **From the Windows desktop, move the cursor to an empty spot and right-click.**

6. **When the Display Properties window appears, choose the Settings tab.** The dialog box in Figure 22.1 (see the previous section) appears.

7. **Windows treats a television connected through an S-video cable just like any other second monitor,** but many laptops can produce only a copy of the main image through the S-video connector. Follow the instructions in the previous section to use the television as an extended monitor, a duplicate of the laptop screen, or a single monitor.

Using a Mouse or Other Pointing Device

Neither the touchpad nor the pointing stick on most laptop computers is a really good substitute for a traditional computer mouse or trackball. Unless you're using the laptop in a very limited space, an external mouse connected to the computer's USB or PS/2 mouse port is easier to use than the internal pointing devices.

To connect a mouse to a PS/2 port, plug it in before you turn on the computer. You can connect a USB mouse at any time. Windows should automatically detect a new mouse and run a configuration program that assigns commands to the buttons and allows you to choose other options. After the configuration is complete, Windows uses that configuration whenever a mouse is plugged into the computer. On most computers, the external mouse and the internal touch pad or pointing stick (or both) work at the same time, so you don't have to tell the computer which device you want to use.

If you travel with your laptop computer, you may want to use one of the smaller mice that take up less space in your computer bag. Look for a mouse with a model name that includes the words *compact*, *notebook*, or *mini*. If you travel by air, don't use a wireless mouse; most airlines won't allow you to use radio transmitters in flight.

Using External Storage

The hard drives built into most laptop computers have smaller capacities than the ones in new desktop computers because there is limited space on the platters inside the drives. Therefore, the drive inside your laptop will probably fill up relatively quickly with program and data files.

It's possible to replace the original drive with a new one that has more space, but moving Windows and all your other programs to a new drive on a laptop is a major project because it requires a special adapter to transfer files from the old drive to the new one. So the best way to increase the amount of storage your computer can use is to connect a second, external drive to the computer through a USB or IEEE 1394 (FireWire) port or a PC Card.

For large data files, such as the ones that you might create during an audio or video recording project, and for files you don't use when you're away from your home base, a full-sized hard drive is the better choice. On the other hand, if you want to offload a few text or data files at a time, you can use a pocket-sized flash drive or hard drive. Both types can be convenient for using the same data files with more than one computer.

When you connect an external drive to your laptop, Windows should immediately recognize it and add it to the list of drives in My Computer and the finders that appear when you use the Save As command in many programs. As far as Windows is concerned, the external drive is just another place to store and read data; you can treat it the same way you treat the computer's internal drive.

Hard drives

External hard drives are sold in two forms: preassembled ready-to-run Plug-and-Play drives, and enclosures that hold standard IDE or SATA drives. If you don't mind spending a few minutes to mount a drive inside an enclosure and run the formatting program supplied with the drive, a do-it-yourself enclosure can be the more economical approach; but if you prefer a simple and convenient hookup, the preassembled version is the obvious choice.

Flash drives

Flash drives are compact modules that store data in nonvolatile memory and that connect to your computer through a USB connector or a PC Card or ExpressCard socket. Because many flash drives are small enough to fit on a key ring or a chain that you can wear on your wrist or around your neck, they're a good way to carry extremely sensitive or confidential information that you don't want to store on the computer's disk drive, or to carry data files from one computer to another (for example, from home to office, or from your own computer at home to a public computer in a library or classroom).

Both USB drives and PC Cards are hot-swap devices, so you can connect or disconnect them without the need to turn off the computer.

Port Replicators and Docking Stations

Port replicators and docking stations both perform similar functions: they provide a central connection point for external devices that you can use with a laptop computer. If you use the laptop as a part-time substitute for a desktop computer, with an external monitor, keyboard, and mouse, you can connect them permanently to the port replicator or docking station along with a network connector, external speakers, a printer, and other external devices. A laptop mounting in a docking station can offer all the flexibility and ease of use that you expect from a desktop computer, with the added benefits of a portable system.

When you want to take the laptop with you, all you have to do is lift out the computer, or unplug a single connector; everything else remains in place. Many docking stations also have a security lock that requires a key to prevent unauthorized removal of the laptop from the dock.

Port replicators and docking stations are usually designed to match a specific make and model of laptop computer. The computer fits into the base and automatically mates the docking port connector on the back or bottom of the case with a connector built into the base unit, so it's essential that the dimensions of the case and the exact location of the docking connector are correct. The alternative is a universal port replicator that uses all of the laptop's input and output connectors.

Port replicators and docking stations may both use the same multipurpose connector, but there are some differences: a port replicator extends access to input and output connectors to a separate package that remains in place when the computer itself has been removed; a docking station can include space for built-in expansion cards (such as a video controller or a sound card), a CD or DVD drive, and an extra disk drive.

If you're using your laptop with an external monitor, some docking stations offer an important advantage: you can choose a graphics controller card to drive the monitor, instead of settling for the one built into your computer. If you're using the computer for intensive graphics or for high-performance games, this can make a big difference to the quality of the images on your monitor screen.

Most laptop manufacturers sell the docking stations designed for their computers through their Web sites or mail-order catalogs. You might also find a few makes and models at a large computer superstore.

Summary

A laptop computer trades compact design and easy transport for comfort and ease of use. The package that incorporates the keyboard, screen, and pointing device into a single, self-contained case is a compromise at best, and an ergonomic disaster at worst. Any time you can connect external peripheral devices to your laptop, you make the computer much easier to use.

Common external laptop accessories include keyboards, mice, and video monitors. In addition, the USB ports on laptop computers make it possible to connect external hard disk drives, audio, and video recording equipment and other devices.

When you use a laptop as a part-time replacement for a desktop computer, a docking station can be a great time-saver when you're ready to disconnect the laptop from its accessories and take it on the road. Some docking stations are designed to work with a single make or model of laptop, but others can work with any system that uses standard input and output connectors.

Chapter 23

Connecting Your Laptop to the Internet

For most of us, a portable computer is as important as a communications device as it is for running individual programs. Many laptop computers come with built-in Ethernet and Wi-Fi network interfaces, but those interfaces are only useful when the computer is within range of a wired data network (a local area network, or LAN) or a Wi-Fi base station. In places where your laptop can't connect to a wired LAN or a Wi-Fi network, many mobile telephone services offer high-speed cellular data services that provide wireless access anywhere their digital mobile telephone service is available.

This chapter explains how to connect your laptop to wired and wireless networks, and how to configure Windows to send and receive data.

IN THIS CHAPTER

Wired connections for your laptop to access the Internet

Wireless connections, including Bluetooth, Wi-Fi, WiMax

Connecting via cellular

Wired Connections

Connecting a laptop computer to a wired LAN or directly to an Internet service provider is easy: just connect a data cable from the computer's Ethernet jack to the network. If your laptop doesn't have a built-in Ethernet port, use a network interface adapter on a PC Card. The point of connection to the network might be a pre-wired wall outlet, a switch, hub, or router in the same room, or directly to a cable or DSL modem. It's all the same to the network interface inside the laptop; high-speed (10, 100, or 1,000 Mbps) serial data moving to and from the computer.

If you don't have access to a LAN or a broadband Internet connection, use a dial-up connection to an Internet service provider through a modem. Most new laptops come with built-in modems, but if yours does not, you can use a modem on a PC Card.

Many laptops come with proprietary software that can create and manage more than one network connection profile; when you move your computer, you can select that location's profile and quickly reconfigure the computer's network settings. For example, IBM ThinkPads use a program called Access Connections, shown in Figure 23.1, that can manage access to both wired and wireless networks. If a network management utility wasn't included with your system, you can use a program such as MultiNetwork Manager (www.globesoft.com/) to do the same thing.

FIGURE 23.1

The Access Connections program changes all the configuration settings needed to switch between network connections.

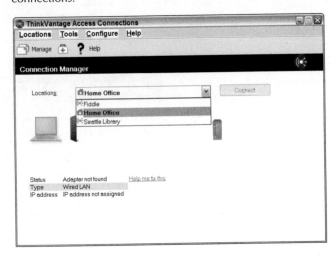

In this example, the owner of this computer has created two location profiles: one profile for a 100 Mbps wired (Ethernet) network called Home Office, and a second profile for a wireless network called Fiddle. The computer is currently connected to the Home Office network. The brick wall in the path between the laptop on the left and the network host on the right indicates that a firewall is protecting the laptop from unwanted attempts to read or write files through the network. To use the Connection Manager, choose the name of the network you want to use from the drop-down Locations menu and click the Connect/Disconnect button (which is currently showing the Disconnect option).

CROSS-REF   If your laptop does not include a profile management program, use the New Connection Wizard in Windows to configure your Internet connection. See Chapter 46 for detailed instructions.

Wireless Options

Some wireless connections to the Internet can be slower than connections through a high-speed wired Internet connection (such as a LAN or a DSL or cable modem service), but they're much more convenient when you're away from home base. However, there are several types of wireless network access, each of which has its own set of benefits and drawbacks.

Table 23.1 shows the signal range and data transfer rates of the most widely used wireless services.

TABLE 23.1

Wireless Data Services

Service	Maximum Signal Range	Maximum Data Transfer Rate
Wi-Fi (802.11a, 802.11b, 802.11g)	300 feet	Up to 54 Mbps
Wi-Fi (802.11n) -- due in 2007	1,500 feet or more	100+ Mbps
WiMAX	4–6 miles per cell	72 Mbps
Edge	1–5 miles per cell	384 Kbps
1 x EV-DO	1–5 miles per cell	2.4 Mbps (typically 300–600 Kbps)
UMTS	1–5 miles per cell	2 Mbps
Mobile Phone Modem	1–5 miles per cell	56 Kbps
Bluetooth	30 feet	720 Kbps

The most common wireless services include Bluetooth, Wi-Fi, WiMAX and several digital cellular data technologies. EDGE (Enhanced Data rates for GSM Evolution), 1xEV-DO (Evolution-Data Only), UMTS (Universal Mobile Telephone Service, also called WCDMA, or Wideband Code-Division Multiple Access) and 1xRTT (Radio Transmission Technology), are all methods for sending data through a cellular mobile telephone network.

With a few exceptions, the data transfer rate decreases as the coverage area increases; in other words, you can exchange files and Internet services faster through a nearby Wi-Fi hotspot than through a cellular data service that covers an entire metropolitan area. The exceptions are a mobile modem, which uses the mobile voice network, and WiMAX, which is not yet available in most locations.

Eventually, the radios and network interfaces that support wireless access to the Internet will automatically find the type of signal that can handle the fastest data transfer to and from your current location, and set up a link to your computer. In the future, when you're in an airport waiting area or a coffee shop, the computer will find and use a fast Wi-Fi service; but when you're visiting your elderly aunt, it will use one of the slower cellular data services instead. Today, that kind of seamless handover is not yet possible so you must set up each type of link separately.

Bluetooth

Bluetooth was designed to replace the short cables that connect a desktop or laptop computer to peripheral devices such as the keyboard and mouse. If both your computer and your mobile telephone have Bluetooth adapters, it's possible to establish a Bluetooth link between them and place calls to an Internet service provider (ISP). The maximum range of a Bluetooth connection is about 300 feet (100 meters), at a maximum data transfer rate of about 720 Kbps. In most cases, this kind of Internet connection is not worth the trouble to set it up; it's mostly useful for uploading ringtones and other data to your phone or downloading text files or voice messages to your computer, rather than connecting the laptop to the Internet.

One possible use of a Bluetooth link between a mobile telephone and a laptop computer might be in a car or truck where a navigator (not the driver!) uses it to obtain directions. However, a self-contained GPS (global positioning system) can do the same job more easily.

CROSS-REF For more information about Bluetooth, see Chapter 15.

Wi-Fi

Wi-Fi (Wireless Fidelity) is the wireless equivalent to a local area network (LAN). It's fast and relatively easy to configure, and it's built into most new laptop computers. If your laptop doesn't have an internal Wi-Fi adapter, look for an inexpensive Wi-Fi interface on a PC Card. When your computer is within range of a public Wi-Fi network, or you have an account on a nearby private network, Wi-Fi is your best choice.

CROSS-REF For information about installing a Wi-Fi module and configuring your computer to use it, see Chapter 44.

WiMAX

WiMAX (Worldwide Interoperability for Microwave Access) is a broadband wireless alternative to wired DSL and cable modem services for Internet access. Like cellular mobile telephone services, it will provide coverage from multiple towers and rooftop antennas to serve an entire metropolitan area or major transportation corridor. As this is written, WiMAX networks are still in the planning and financing stages; the first widespread public systems will probably become available in late 2007 or early 2008. A few test systems might be online sooner.

Digital cellular services

Most major mobile telephone companies offer one or more cellular data service options. These wireless wide area network (WWAN) services are slower than a local Wi-Fi hotspot, but they can reach places where Wi-Fi is not available. Each of these services uses one of several new technologies, including EDGE, UMTS, 1xEV-DO and 1xRTT, that are constructed on top of the particular type of digital cellular telephone service that each company uses. The companies that offer these services can supply a cell data modem on a PC Card that plugs into the PCMCIA socket on your laptop, along with the necessary software that you need to send and receive e-mail, data files, and other Internet services.

The choice of technology is less important than the quality of the signal in the places where you are likely to use the service. Each company that offers data service can give you a coverage map that shows the area where the service is available. If you already have a mobile telephone, ask your service provider about a package deal that adds data to your existing account.

After you have loaded the device drivers, Windows automatically detects that card and configures the computer to connect to the service provider's network when you insert a cellular data card into your laptop. After the connection is in place, it is transparent, just like a connection through a LAN or a Wi-Fi hotspot.

Connecting through your cell phone

If your digital mobile telephone has an accessory connector port or a Bluetooth interface, you can probably use it to connect your laptop computer to the Internet or directly to another computer through the public telephone system. Data calls through a mobile phone are a lot slower than dedicated wireless data networks, but they don't require a costly separate data account.

Different makes and models of cell phones use different connectors, so you must find the correct cable for your own phone. Data cables are available directly from the maker of your cell phone, or from many large electronics retailers and telephone stores. If you can't find the right cable locally, look for it on the manufacturer's Web site. Don't confuse the manufacturer of the phone (such as Motorola, Nokia, or Samsung) with your cellular service provider (such as Verizon, T-Mobile, or Telus) — it's quite possible that the mobile phone service has no idea how to set up one of these connections.

Most new data cables use one of the computer's USB ports, but you might also find an older cable that uses a serial port. Be sure the cable package includes a software disk with the device driver and software that allows you to place a telephone call from the computer's keyboard. If you're using a Motorola phone, you might have to buy their TrueSync software separately.

CAUTION Cheap cables are often available through eBay and other cut-rate suppliers, but those cables are often less reliable than the ones sold by the phone manufacturer, and they probably don't include the device driver software necessary to set up the connection.

In order to use your cell phone as a wireless modem, you must have a dial-up account with an Internet service provider (ISP), or dial-in access to your company's network. If you usually connect through a DSL, cable modem, or other broadband service, ask your ISP's tech support center or your network help desk for a dial-in telephone number, login name, and password. Remember that most mobile telephone services don't charge extra for long-distance calls, so there's generally no need to keep a list of separate numbers for different locations.

At least one mobile telephone service provider in the United States, Sprint, offers direct Internet access through their dial-up network. Rather than dialing into a separate ISP, Sprint subscribers can dial 777 to create an Internet connection. To learn if your own cell-phone company offers a similar service, talk to a sales person or customer service representative.

To set up a dial-up connection, follow these steps:

1. **Attach the cable to the phone and the computer.** If the phone is not already on, turn it on now.

2. **Install the software supplied with the cable on your laptop.** When the program is ready, it detects your phone and displays the model number in a window like the one shown in Figure 23.2.

In this configuration, the Motorola software has detected a Series 60c phone.

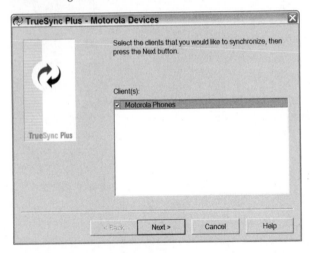

3. Close the configuration program.

4. From the Start menu, open Settings and select Network Connections.

5. Select the New Connection Wizard.

6. When the wizard asks how you want to connect to the Internet (see Figure 23.3), choose the Set up my connection manually option.

7. When the Getting Ready window appears (as shown in Figure 23.4), choose the Set up my connection manually option.

FIGURE 23.3

Choose the Set up my connection manually option to set up a dial-in connection.

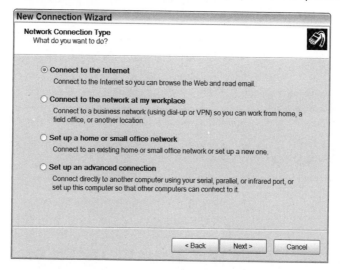

FIGURE 23.4

Use the Set up my connection manually option.

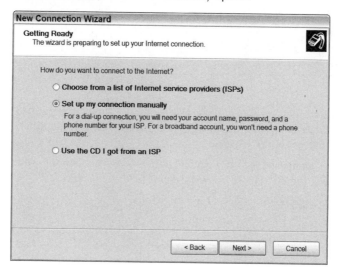

8. In the Internet Connection window, choose the Connect using a dial-up modem option.

9. In the Connection Name window, type the name of your service provider in the ISP Name field.

10. Next, the wizard asks for the telephone number of the ISP. Type the number provided by your ISP in the Phone number field, as shown in Figure 23.5.

FIGURE 23.5

Type your ISP's access telephone number (or the mobile telephone company's Internet access number) in the Phone number field.

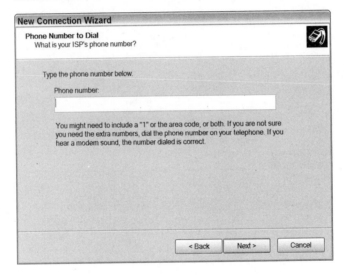

11. In the Internet Account Information window (shown in Figure 23.6), type your login name and password, and turn off (remove the checkmarks) all of the options at the bottom of the window.

12. In the Completing the New Connection window, turn on the Add a shortcut option and click Finish to close the wizard and save your choices.

13. Close all the open windows on your screen.

14. **Test the configuration by double-clicking the connection shortcut on your desktop.**
Windows should call your ISP through your mobile phone and automatically send your
login name and password. When you see a "Connected" message, your computer can use
your Web browser, e-mail program, or other Internet client.

After the configuration is complete, you can follow these steps to connect your laptop to the Internet
through your mobile phone:

1. **Connect the cable between your laptop's USB or serial port and your mobile telephone.** If the phone is not already on, turn it on now.

FIGURE 23.6

Enter the login name and password for your dial-in account.

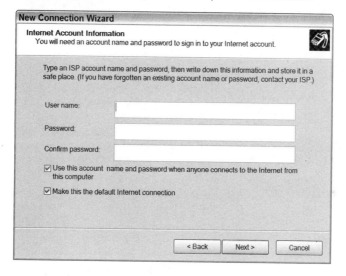

2. **Double-click the desktop shortcut to your dial-in connection.** A Connect dialog box
appears, with your login name and password, and the ISP's telephone number already in
place, as shown in Figure 23.7.

3. **Click Dial.** Windows calls your ISP and automatically enters your login name and
password.

FIGURE 23.7

Use the Connect dialog box to connect to your ISP.

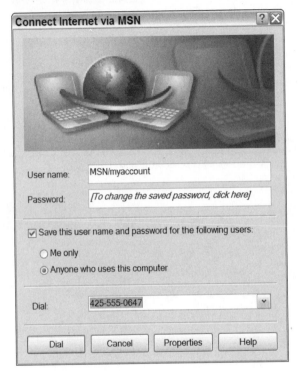

Summary

You can connect your laptop to the Internet or a local network through a wired LAN, a wireless Wi-Fi connection, a dial-up Internet service or a mobile-telephone company's wireless data service. Each type of connection requires a different kind of network interface adapter, and an account with a different service provider.

A laptop can establish a wired connection to the Internet through its Ethernet port (or a separate network interface adapter), or through a modem to a telephone line. Wireless connections can use a Wi-Fi access point, or a wireless data service; many laptops have built-in Wi-Fi radio transceivers, but each cellular data service requires a separate adapter that plugs into the computer's PC Card socket.

Regardless of the technology you use to connect, Windows can create a Network Connection profile that sets up your access to the Internet. Many laptops come with network management utilities that can allow you to select the profile you want to use for each session; if yours doesn't include one of these programs, several commercial programs can perform similar actions for you.

Chapter 24

PC Cards and ExpressCards

P C Cards are compact devices that meet the standards of the Personal Computer Memory Card International Association (PCMCIA). ExpressCards are even smaller devices that follow a more recent set of PCMCIA standards. Both PC Cards and ExpressCards can carry a wide variety of features and functions, including data storage, input and output connectors, and network adapters, among other things. Because the PCMCIA sets the standards and specifications for PC Cards, you may also see them described as PCMCIA cards.

Sockets for PC Cards have been a standard feature of just about every laptop computer for more than a decade. The cards that fit in those sockets allow a laptop computer owner to provide features and functions that were not built into the computer itself. Like the expansion cards that fit into PCI sockets on a desktop computer's motherboard, PC Cards can add a wide variety of services to your portable computer.

Many of the features that once required a PC Card have become standard parts of new laptop computers — these include modems that connect the computer to a telephone line, Ethernet adapters, Wi-Fi adapters, and USB ports — but plenty of other applications and services are still available on PC Cards that can either add new functions to your laptop, or provide better performance than the built-in adapters and interfaces.

Because it's easy to insert a PC Card into the socket on your laptop, they are a fast and effective way to add services that may not yet have been available when your computer was new, such as new and more advanced wireless data standards.

This chapter describes the PCMCIA standards for PC Cards and the newer ExpressCards that will eventually replace them, and explains how to use them with Windows XP.

The PC Card Standard

As Figure 24.1 shows, most PC Cards are 54 mm (2.126 inches) wide and 85.6 mm (3.37 inches) deep, with a 68-pin connector on one of the short edges. Some cards, especially those that contain wireless data network interfaces, AM/FM and TV tuners, or other types of radio transceivers, extend to about 115 mm (4.5 inches) deep, in order to allow the antenna inside the card to extend beyond the edge of the computer's case.

The PC Card standard specifies three thicknesses (as shown in Figure 24.2): Type I (3.3 mm), Type II (5.0 mm), and Type III (10.5 mm). Type I is most often used for memory cards; Type II is the most common size for I/O cards and other network interfaces; and Type III is used almost exclusively for cards that contain rotating disk drives. All three types use the same 68-pin connector, so a Type III socket can accept all three types, and a Type II socket can accept both Type I and Type II.

 Many laptops have Type II PC Card sockets, so they can use only Type I and Type II cards. Before you buy a disk drive on a Type III card, make sure your own laptop can accept it.

FIGURE 24.1

PC Cards are about the same size as a credit card.

FIGURE 24.2

From left to right: Type I, Type II, Type III, and an extended Type II card

Voltages

PC Cards take their electric power directly from the computer, through the PC Card socket. The connector inside a PC Card socket provides 3.3 volts and 5 volts on separate pins, so each card can use either voltage (or both). The designers of each PC Card choose the voltage they need for their particular design, so each card automatically draws the correct voltage.

CardBus Cards and slots

The original PC Card specification was limited to 16-bit connections and services. In 1995, an enhanced standard called CardBus was introduced for 32-bit hosts and applications. CardBus PC Cards always have a gold grounding strip on the top of the card, next to the 68-bit connector, often with eight small metal bumps across the strip. 16-bit PC Cards work in a CardBus socket, but older 16-bit sockets don't accept CardBus cards.

Just about every computer with a PC Card slot made after 1997 should support both 16-bit PC Cards and 32-bit CardBus Cards, so the difference between the two should not matter on a computer that can run Windows XP or Windows Vista. But if you're using an older laptop, it might not accept CardBus Cards — if you try to insert a 32-bit card into a CardBus slot, the card won't go all the way into the connector.

 If you plan to install a PC Card socket in your desktop computer, make sure it supports CardBus cards.

Uses for PC Cards

The PCMCIA Association, the agency that sets standards for PC Cards, has identified a long list of applications that use the PC Card standard, including:

- Ethernet adapters
- Analog-to-digital converters

- AM/FM radio tuners
- Bar code readers
- Biometrics cards
- Bluetooth adapters
- Cellular data (WWAN) interfaces
- Global Positioning System (GPS) cards
- Hard drives
- Game controller (joystick) interface cards
- Flash memory cards
- Memory module adapters
- Modem cards
- Parallel port interfaces
- SATA host adapters
- Serial port adapters
- SCSI adapters
- Security tokens
- Sound cards
- Analog and digital TV tuners
- USB adapters
- IEEE 1394 adapters
- Video (VGA) adapters
- Video capture/frame grabber cards

This list is far from complete. The PC Card specification is flexible enough to support many other even more specialized services and applications. Except for a few very early cards, you can safely expect just about any product on a PC Card to work with your laptop, as long as it fits into the socket.

However, many of the same products and services are also available with a USB interface that is often faster and less expensive than a PC Card. Because your laptop almost certainly has both a PC Card socket and at least one or two USB ports, you can use either one to add features and functions to the computer.

ExpressCards

ExpressCards are smaller, lighter, and faster plug-in cards that were introduced by the PCMCIA people in 2003. In addition to all the services available through PC Card sockets, an ExpressCard socket can also support the latest USB and PCI-Express connections. As Figure 24.3 shows, ExpressCards exist in two sizes, 34 mm wide and 54 mm wide. Both sizes use the same 26-pin connectors, so an ExpressCard/54 (54 mm) socket accepts both types. ExpressCards are not yet common, but many laptop manufacturers, including Fujitsu, NEC, Sony, Lenovo, Toshiba, and Dell have all begun to include ExpressCard slots in their new laptop computers.

FIGURE 24.3

ExpressCards are shorter and narrower than PC Cards.

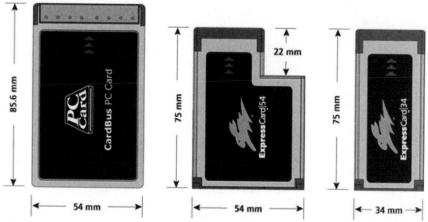

Illustration courtesy of PCMCIA.

If your laptop does not include an ExpressCard socket, don't worry (yet); it should be possible to find a PC Card or a USB device that performs the same function as any currently available ExpressCard. Or if you prefer, you can look for an external ExpressCard reader that connects to your computer through a USB port.

Installing and Removing Cards

Figure 24.4 shows an ExpressCard inserted partway into a socket on a laptop computer (there wouldn't be much to see if it was all the way in because the edge would be flush with the side of the computer). A PC Card looks about the same from the outside of the computer. Windows automatically detects a PC Card or ExpressCard as soon as you insert the card firmly into the socket, and displays a "Found New Hardware" message at the lower right corner of your screen. If Windows recognizes the card, it immediately loads the device driver and activates the service on the card.

FIGURE 24.4

ExpressCards fit into sockets on many new laptop computers.

Photo copyright PCMCIA

When Windows has loaded the device driver, it displays a Safely Remove Hardware icon in the System Tray, next to the clock in the lower right corner of your screen, as shown in Figure 24.5. This is the same icon that appears when a removable disk drive is installed in your laptop.

FIGURE 24.5

The Safely Remove Hardware icon indicates that one or more PC Cards or other removable hardware devices are active.

Before you physically remove a PC Card or ExpressCard from its slot, you must instruct Windows to disable the card. Follow these steps to remove a card:

1. **Click the Safely Remove Hardware icon in the system tray.** A list of all currently active removable devices appears.

2. **Choose the name of the card you want to remove.** The Safely Remove Hardware window shown in Figure 24.6 appears.

3. **Select the name of the card you want to remove and click the Stop button.** Windows asks you to confirm your request.

FIGURE 24.6

Use the Safely Remove Hardware window to disable a PC Card or ExpressCard before you remove it.

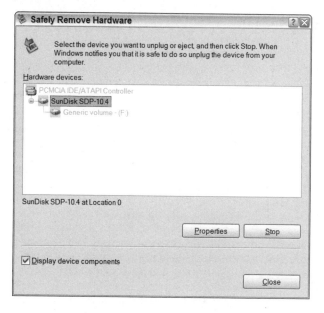

4. **Click OK to confirm that you want to remove the device.** When Windows has finished uninstalling the device, it displays a "Safe to Remove Hardware" message in a balloon near the Safely Remove Hardware icon.

5. **To physically remove the card, push the eject pushbutton next to the slot.** This pushbutton is linked directly to a mechanical latch that disconnects the card from the socket and forces it out of the slot. Grab the card between your thumb and forefinger to pull it the rest of the way out, or gently use a pair of pliers. On some computers, you might have to push the button to engage it before you can push it a second time to separate the card from the connector.

Adding a PC Card Reader to a Desktop Computer

To use a PC card in a desktop system, you must install a PC Card reader in your desktop machine.

This PC Card reader (also called a socket) can take one of three forms:

- An external USB device
- An internal PC Card socket that mounts in one of drive bays on the computer's front panel
- An internal PC Card socket on an expansion card that mounts in a PCI connector, with the slot on the computer's rear panel

Adapters for all three of these types are available with slots for either one or two cards. If you expect to use a PC Card as a more-or-less permanent part of your computer (such as a wireless network interface card), a rear panel slot is probably the best choice because the PC Card in the slot is out of sight and out of your way when you're trying to do something else. But if you plan to add or remove the card more than once every few months, a PC Card slot adapter in a front-panel drive bay or on a table next to the main computer case will be much easier to reach.

Some PC Card readers for desktop computers are still limited to only accepting 16-bit cards. Even if you don't currently use any 32-bit CardBus PC Cards, don't even consider a reader that doesn't accept both 16-bit and 32-bit cards. The difference in cost is insignificant, and there's always a chance that you may want to use a CardBus device sometime in the future.

Any PC Card reader should come with device driver software for Windows XP. If and when you upgrade your computer to Windows Vista, either Microsoft or the maker of the card reader should offer new software in the Vista package or through their respective Web sites.

NOTE   The only reason to use a PC Card in a desktop system is to use the same device that you're already using with your laptop. If you're buying a new accessory exclusively for your desktop computer, you'll get better performance from a USB device.

Summary

Just about every laptop computer includes one or more slots for PC Cards. Most new laptops also have slots for the more recent ExpressCard specification. Both 68-pin PC Cards and 26-pin ExpressCards are small and easily transportable storage media, network adapters, and other peripheral devices for personal computers.

To install a PC Card or ExpressCard, simply insert it into the slot. To remove it, click the Safely Remove Device icon and follow the on-screen instructions.

PC Card readers are also available as add-on adapters for desktop computers. If you buy one to install in your system, make sure it supports both 16-bit PC Cards and 32-bit CardBus cards.

Chapter 25

Laptop Accessories

Traveling with a portable computer is sort of like traveling with a baby: every time you take it anywhere, it seems like you need a whole bag of accessories. There's a whole industry out there that makes and sells add-on items for laptop users. Some, like an AC power adapter and some kind of physical security, are all but essential; many others, like an external mouse and a cleaning cloth or brush, just make your computer easier to use.

In earlier chapters, I talk about a few common accessories for laptop computers, including external keyboards and mice, AC and DC power adapters, and flash drives and PC Cards. This chapter describes some other accessories for laptop computers that may be more obscure but can still be useful. You probably don't want to carry every one of these items with your laptop every day, but you might discover one or more that become essential parts of your computer kit.

Bags and Cases

Any time you carry the computer any farther than the next room, you should use a carrying case to protect it from the weather and make the computer easier to carry and less obvious to potential thieves. Carriers for laptop computers can range anywhere from inexpensive canvas bags all the way to hand-tooled leather cases with individual compartments for everything you might ever want to carry with your computer. Of course, the case should be comfortable when you carry it in your hands, hang it on your shoulder or across your back, or when you wheel it through an airport concourse.

The design of a computer case or bag is a combination of fashion and function. It should look good (whatever that may mean to your particular sensibility), and it should also protect the computer, make it easy to carry, and provide space for all the other stuff you want to carry along with the computer itself.

The first and most important characteristic of any computer carrier is its size; the case should be wide enough to hold the computer, but not so big that the computer slides around while you're carrying it. The label or tag on a new bag should show the maximum screen size that it can hold. Even so, it can be helpful to note the dimensions of your own computer and carry a small tape measure when you're shopping for a new bag. A well-designed computer bag or case should also have internal straps or other restraints to keep the computer from sliding around.

Computer carriers come in several forms: briefcases, backpacks, travel cases with space for a change of clothes, and messenger bags that fit over one shoulder. Still others resemble attaché cases, ladies' large purses, and traditional luggage. If you expect to carry your computer through public places like airports and hotel lobbies, you may want to seriously consider a case that does not look like it contains a computer. Carrying a standard computer case can be like attaching a big sign to your luggage that says "This bag contains valuable equipment. Please do not steal." A bag that looks like it contains nothing more than three changes of underwear and a couple of clean shirts is a lot less attractive to would-be thieves.

Most of the major laptop computer manufacturers offer bags, backpacks, and other carriers that fit each of their laptop models through their Web sites. Or if you prefer, Targus, one of the biggest makers of laptop carriers, offers an online tool that can identify matching bags for many makes and models. You can find the Case Configurator at www.targus.com/us/compatibilitysearch.asp.

In addition to space for the computer itself, a computer case should include:

- Pockets for accessories, including a power adapter, mouse, PC Cards, cables, and so on

- Space for a notepad and several pens or pencils

- Compartments for blank CDs, flash drives or other removable storage, and emergency software

- Pockets for anything else you might carry with the computer, such as manuals, airline tickets or a supply of business cards

Security Tools

It's an unfortunate fact that laptop computers are attractive targets for thieves. Any time you carry your computer, and any time you use it in public, you must protect the computer against dedicated criminals and light-fingered passers-by. A lost or stolen laptop computer can represent a tremendous loss, not only of the equipment itself, but also the data stored on its disk drive; losing confidential business data, or the only copy of an important document, can easily be more valuable and difficult to replace than the computer that contained it.

So it's absolutely essential to do whatever you can to protect your laptop computer and your files. There are several categories of tools and services that can discourage thieves and help recover the computer after somebody tries to steal it:

- Locks and cables can keep the machine from disappearing.
- Alarms can let you know when somebody is trying to run off with it.
- Tracking software can use the Internet to send a "here I am" message to a recovery service.

As for your files, you should have two goals: preserving the data and keeping them away from unauthorized eyes. The best way to reduce the impact of lost data is to make backup copies frequently on a flash drive, a recordable CD, or on another computer's hard drive. Keep the copies separately from the computer itself—at home or in your office, or in a pocket, purse, or briefcase. To keep other people from reading confidential files on a stolen computer, use a fingerprint scanner and encrypt your files.

 See Chapter 48 for more about encryption techniques and other ways to protect confidential data.

Locks and cables

Any time you must leave your laptop out of your immediate reach, use a security cable and lock to attach your computer to an immovable object such as the leg of a desk, a heavy table, or a chair that is fastened to the floor. This might not be practical at an airport security barrier, but it's essential when you're using your computer at a library or a coffee shop.

Most laptop security cable locks are built like bicycle cables, with one end designed to fit the security socket built into the computer, and a lock that uses either a padlock, a combination lock, or a cylinder lock. The cable itself is armored or reinforced to make it extremely difficult to cut with anything short of a blowtorch or a very large bolt cutter. If your computer does not have a security socket, look for a lock that comes with a metal eye or loop attached to a pad with a special adhesive that makes the pad impossible to remove.

Of course, just about any lock can be picked, and any cable can be cut if somebody has enough time and the right tools. But an effective cable lock can encourage a computer thief to move on and look for a less difficult target.

Alarms

Alarm devices that sound a very loud signal when a thief tries to walk away with your computer take several forms, but they all operate on a similar principle: they're motion detectors that use either software or a set of input switches or pushbuttons to arm and disarm the alarm. Some of these products fit the security socket or attach to a cable lock, and others are PC Cards. Either way, they produce enough noise that you and everybody else close to the signal will immediately notice; the thief will probably drop the computer and run away.

Of course, when you carry one of these alarms, there's always the risk that you might forget to disarm it when you try to carry your own laptop away with you. Depending on your location, this can be either an embarrassing nuisance or an opportunity to explain yourself to a police officer or an airport security inspector.

Tracking and recovery software and services

Tracking services are an effective form of insurance, especially for travelers and students.

Several companies offer services that can help you find and recover your laptop after it has been stolen. The tracking service provides a small (and difficult to remove) piece of software that returns information to the tracking service about the computer's location (the IP address, the location of the wireless host, or the originating telephone number) any time the computer is connected to the Internet.

When you report a theft, the tracking service captures the locator information from your computer and notifies appropriate law enforcement authorities, who can obtain a warrant and often recover the computer. Some services can also send your computer a command that locks the hard drive, so the thieves can't read or use your confidential data files. Among others, Computrace (`www.compu trace.com`) and The CyberAngel (`www.sentryinc.com`) offer laptop tracking services

Reading Light and Flashlight

A small lamp can provide extra light for your laptop's keyboard and screen in places where it's otherwise too dark to work, like a darkened airplane or conference hall. Some new laptops come with a built-in work light, but if yours does not, you can use a worklight that takes power from the computer's USB connector.

Most of these lights use low-power LEDs that don't draw a lot of power from the computer's battery; one maker, Kensington, claims that their version uses only about 90 seconds of battery charge per hour. The light is mounted on a flexible shaft that you can place exactly where you need it.

In addition to the USB light, you might also want to carry a small flashlight in your computer bag to cast light on the back and sides of the computer when you're connecting cables and USB accessories, and for finding things inside the computer bag. The tiny lights that are common giveaways at trade shows, like the ones shown in Figure 25.1, are ideal for this kind of use. If you can't find a freebie, look for a small flashlight at a hardware store or office supplies retailer.

FIGURE 25.1

A small, LED-base flashlight can be a useful accessory for your laptop computer.

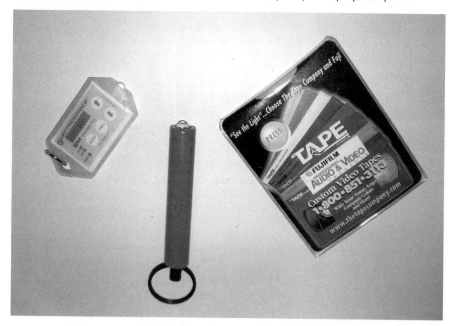

Earphones

There are several reasons to use headphones with your laptop; among others, playing music, DVD movie soundtracks, or audio from a streaming Internet site through speakers can be very intrusive to the people around you, and the sound quality of the speakers on most laptops is mediocre at best. So playing audio through headphones can improve your own listening experience while you avoid irritating your neighbors.

If you carry an iPod or other portable music player along with your computer, you can use the same earphones for both devices.

Headphones and earpieces come in several forms at a huge range of prices. The rule of "you get what you pay for" generally applies, but there's definitely a point of diminishing returns: a $75 set of headphones will sound a lot better than a pair of $15 ear buds, but the additional improvement when you move to $300 headphones is considerably more subtle.

The best way to shop for headphones is to listen. Take your laptop and an audio CD that you know well to a retailer where you can compare the performance of as many makes and models as possible, using your own equipment. Look for these characteristics:

- **Comfort:** How do the earphones feel when you're wearing them? Do you prefer earpieces that fit inside your ears, over your head, or under your chin? Does the weight of the earphones become unpleasant over time?

- **Sensitivity:** Some earphones are more sensitive than others. Can you play music or speech through the earphones at the volume level you want to hear without distortion?

- **Sound quality:** Can you hear high and low frequencies without distortion, or does it sound like you're listening through a telephone? Does your CD sound the way you expect it to sound?

- **Weight:** Big over-the-head earphones are much heavier and bulkier than compact earpieces. Do your headphones add significant weight and take up space in your computer bag?

Portable Desk

They're called *laptops*, but your lap is far from ideal as a platform for your portable computer. When you operate a computer on your lap, the keyboard is in the wrong place for comfortable typing, the screen is far from eye level, and the temperatures produced by the heat shield and battery are enough to produce serious discomfort or even burns on your upper legs. At least one study has even identified a potential connection between prolonged use of laptop computers on men's laps and male infertility.

The obvious solution is to operate the computer on a table, counter, or other surface, instead of your lap. When that isn't possible, you can use a collapsible platform that provides a working surface for the computer at a comfortable height (either sitting or standing). These *portable desks* come in several forms, so you can choose the one that offers the best combination of size, stability, and weight for your particular needs.

Some portable computer desks are simply padded boards that lift the computer away from your legs, but they don't move it to a position for more comfortable use. When you place your laptop on one of these boards, the keyboard is still too close to your body, and the screen too low to view without crooking your neck.

Privacy Shield

A privacy shield for a laptop computer is a folding cover that extends forward from the top and both sides of the screen, to prevent people sitting nearby from reading the data on your monitor display. As a side benefit, the shield also reduces or eliminates screen glare when you're using the computer outdoors on in bright artificial light.

When you shop for a privacy shield, make sure it fits over your computer's screen, and that it folds down to a size and shape that fits into your computer bag.

Cleaning Supplies

After you have been using your laptop for more than a few weeks, it will probably begin to accumulate dirt and crumbs in the keyboard and a light haze over the screen. It's not your fault; you probably handle the computer extremely carefully, but we all live in a world with lots of environmental crud all around us.

You could wait to clean the computer until you return home, but a few simple cleaning supplies don't add much weight to your computer bag. A small artist's brush, a soft cotton cloth, and maybe a small plastic container of all-purpose cleaner are enough to remove dirt and spills from the keys and the case. To clean the screen, wipe it with a soft lint-free cloth lightly moistened with water or isopropyl alcohol.

TIP As an alternative, look for cleaning sheets in sealed packets, specifically designed for LCD screens, such as No. CL360 Notebook Screen Cleaning Wipes from 3M, or Surface Guardian® Wet/Dry Cleaning Wipes from Kensington.

CAUTION Don't use ethyl alcohol, acetone or other solvents, or any glass cleaner that contains ammonia on your laptop's case or video display; these chemicals can permanently damage the surface of the screen and the material that makes up the outer case.

What to Carry with Your Laptop

The specific contents of your computer bag reflect the way you use the computer and the places you take it. Here's a list you can use as a starting point:

- Your computer's AC power adapter
- A cube tap or other AC power splitter
- A spare battery (if necessary for long trips)
- One or two pens and a small notebook or note cards
- A cable lock and alarm
- One or two USB or PC Card flash drives
- An Ethernet cable (at least 8–10 feet or 3 meters long)

- An Ethernet interface adapter (if not built into your laptop)

- A Wi-Fi adapter (if not built into your laptop)

- A modem on a PC Card (if not built into your laptop)

- A modular telephone (modem) cable

- Earphones

- Copies of the computer's User's Manual and Service Manual, preferably on a CD

- An emergency startup CD or USB drive including antivirus and antispyware software

- A Windows installation CD or the restoration CD recommended by your computer's manufacturer

- Several blank CDs

If they're appropriate for your particular needs, you might want to add these items:

- A pocket-size AC line tester

- Adapters for foreign AC power outlets

- An external mouse

- A small flashlight

- A reading light

- An external 10-key keypad (if you do a lot of numeric data entry)

- A USB cable

- A USB Bluetooth adapter (if not built into your laptop)

- A cellular data interface PC Card (if you have an account with a cellular service provider)

- A cable for connecting your laptop to your cellular telephone

- A FireWire (IEEE 1394) cable

- A parallel printer cable or a USB-to-Centronics adapter cable

- A privacy shield

- A pocket-size screwdriver with both flat and Phillips head blades (leave this out if you're traveling by air)

- Any special tools you need to perform minor repairs on your computer

- Long-nose pliers

- A spare pointing stick cover (if your computer uses a pointing stick)

- A small plastic bag or box for odd spare parts

After you have been using the computer for several months, take a quick inventory of your bag's contents. If you find bits and pieces that you haven't ever used (except for obvious emergency resources like the boot disk and the manual), leave them out.

For obvious security reasons, there are some things you should not carry in your computer bag:

- Credit cards
- Keys
- Driver's license and other personal ID
- Checkbook
- Large amounts of cash
- Passport
- Prescription drugs
- Anything else that would be difficult or impossible to replace on short notice

Many computer bags include a special outside compartment for your mobile telephone. Before you drop your phone into that pocket, think about the impact on your daily life if you lose both your computer and your portable telephone at the same time.

If possible, you should also carry some information outside the computer bag, in a pocket or brief-case (this should all fit onto a single sheet of paper). If your computer is lost or stolen, the items on this list will help you connect to the Internet from another computer:

- A list of important telephone numbers, including:
  - Your company's tech support center or help desk
  - Your Internet Service Provider's support center
  - Your tracking and recovery service's hotline
- Information about your Internet access account, including:
  - Dial-in telephone numbers
  - Domain Name Server (DNS) numeric addresses
  - Step-by-step instructions for going online
  - Information about your company's virtual private network, if any
- A list of important Web site addresses
- The make, model, and serial number of your computer, so you can report them to the police.
- A list of essential e-mail addresses

Summary

Unless your laptop remains in one place all the time, you should use some kind of carrier bag to transport the computer from one location to another. Computer bags come in a wide range of sizes, shapes, and colors; you should choose one that is big enough to hold the computer and its accessories, and that does not call attention to itself as something valuable. A carrier that resembles a backpack, a traditional briefcase, or a lady's large purse are better choices than obvious computer cases.

Along with the computer itself, you want to carry some essential or useful accessories in your computer bag. These can include the AC power adapter, a security cable and lock, a reading light, a set of earphones, an external mouse, supplies for cleaning the computer's keyboard and screen, and all of the cables, adapters, and interfaces you need to connect your computer to the Internet and local area networks, a printer, and other peripheral devices. You should also carry enough information on paper and on a CD or flash drive to recover from common computer problems.

Chapter 26

Traveling with Your Laptop

S ome of the challenges related to traveling with a laptop computer have very little to do with the computer's features and functions. Others involve finding a place to take advantage of those features when you're away from your own office or home.

This chapter describes several of the most common challenges for laptop computer users, including carrying a laptop computer through airport security, using the computer from a seat in an airplane or train, finding public access to the Internet through a Wi-Fi hotspot, finding a place to print your documents, and sending copies of your data back to your home or office.

IN THIS CHAPTER

Using your computer en route

Finding Wi-Fi hotspots

Using other Internet connections

Finding a place to print

Sending data home while you're away

Moving Through Airports

In today's environment of tightly enforced airport security, carrying your laptop presents two challenges: protecting it against grab-and-run thieves, and convincing the security personnel that your computer really is a computer.

One insurance company reports that more than half-a-million laptop computers are stolen every year, at least 10 percent of them in airports. To avoid adding your own computer to that statistic, take some common-sense steps to discourage thieves:

- **Never let your computer out of your sight.** Even better, keep the computer bag on your shoulder, or place the strap around one leg when you have to put it down at a ticket counter or even a restroom stall. While you're seated in the boarding area, keep one hand on the bag or the strap.

■ **Disguise the computer.** Don't use a distinctive computer bag or one with the manufac-turer's logo on the side. Computer carriers are available in many forms of camouflage, including briefcases, backpacks, tote bags, and ladies' large purses.

■ **Use a cable lock.**

■ **If possible, use a small padlock to secure the compartment that holds the computer.** This will discourage a thief from trying to remove the computer while leaving the bag behind.

■ **When it's time to send the computer through the security X-ray machine, make sure the people in front of you aren't creating a delay.** Don't place the computer on the belt until you can walk directly through the machine. In one common technique, one person holds up the line after you place your computer on the conveyor belt, and then a partner grabs it after it passes through the machine before you can get to it. If this happens to you, shout "Stop thief!" as loud as you can and hope the security people can help.

■ **Pack your AC adapter and cables separately from the rest of the gear in your bag, and if possible, send them through the security machine separately.** A jumble of odd parts can be difficult for an inspector to identify.

■ **Tape your business card or engrave some kind of identification on the bottom of the computer case.** This assures that you take your own computer from the security area — remember that you have to send the computer and the bag through the X-ray machine separately. While you're at it, place some kind of identification inside the computer's case in a place where it's not visible from the outside.

■ **Subscribe to a tracking and recovery service.**

Except in extraordinary situations, every airline allows you to carry your laptop on board their air-craft instead of checking it through as baggage. However, the airport security people might often instruct you to remove the computer from the bag and send it through their X-ray machines sepa-rately, or to turn on the computer to demonstrate that it's not just a shell disguising something more dangerous.

Here are a few things you can do to speed up this process:

■ **Before you leave your home or office, start the computer and place it in Hibernation mode.** When an inspector asks you to turn on the computer, you can start it in just a few seconds, instead of waiting for the whole tedious Windows startup routine to run. Hibernate consumes a very tiny amount of the battery's charge, so you still have most of the battery's power available to use the computer in flight.

■ **Make sure your computer's battery has a reasonably full charge.** It can be a huge nui-sance to search for an AC outlet when you need to turn on the computer for an inspector.

■ **Before you leave home, make sure your computer bag doesn't contain anything that isn't allowed in a carry-on bag.** This could include a small knife or other pointed object, and even a small plastic bottle of screen cleaning fluid. For the latest list of items and materials that are allowed and prohibited on flights to, from, or within the United States,

see the Transportation Security Administration's Web site at `www.tsa.gov/travelers/`
`airtravel/prohibited/permitted-prohibited-items.shtm`. For flights
originating in Canada, see the Canadian Air Transport Security Authority's site at
`www.catsa-acsta.ca/engilsh/travel_voyage/list.htm`. For the very
latest word, call your airline.

Using Your Computer on Trains and Airplanes

After you make it through the security barrier and on to your airplane, you might want to use your
computer during your voyage. On a short flight, you may be able to use the computer's internal
battery, but if you're traveling from coast to coast or overseas, the battery probably won't last as
long as your flight. The security issues aren't as extreme when you travel by train, but you might
face many of the same short-battery-life problems on an extended rail trip.

Some airliners and passenger trains have power outlets for personal computers and other electronic
devices at many seats, especially in premium class sections. If you can find one of these outlets,
you can use your laptop for the entire duration of your trip. Of course, you're still obligated to
cooperate with requests from the flight crew to shut down electronic equipment during take-off
and landings. When you reserve your seat, ask about access to a power outlet.

> **TIP** To avoid conflicts with other passengers for access to a limited number of outlets, carry
> a three-way cube tap outlet adapter.

If you can't use AC power at your seat, carry a spare battery. Some recent laptops can accept extra-
large batteries with longer charge time than the ones supplied with the computer; they're somewhat
heavier, but they might be ideal for a longer trip.

Other portable batteries connect to the computer's external power input connector. Some are less
than an inch thick, so they can fit in the bag next to the computer itself. Many of these external
laptop batteries are quite expensive, but they can run your computer for an additional three hours
or more. Before you buy an external battery, make sure it provides the correct output voltage for
your computer.

Computer security doesn't stop when you pass your laptop through the X-ray machine. Don't leave
your computer in plain sight when you leave your seat, or it might not be there when you return.
If your computer is stolen, notify a flight attendant or conductor immediately.

Finding and Using Wi-Fi Hotspots

In most urban and suburban districts, Wi-Fi hotspots — publicly accessible base stations with
connections to the Internet — seem to be almost everywhere. Coffee shops, airport waiting areas,

public libraries, and college campuses all seem to offer Wi-Fi access to customers, students, and random passers-by. Many of these service providers require a paid account or a membership (or maybe a library card or student ID), but some might still be free to anybody with a network interface in their computer.

Some laptop computers (most notably certain Dell models) have a built-in sniffer tool that searches for Wi-Fi signals and lights an LED indicator when it detects one. In practice, this is not as useful as it may first appear because the sniffer can't always tell you whether the signals it has located are encrypted or require a password for access.

The Microsoft Wireless Network Connection tool and the similar tools supplied by the makers of your wireless network interface adapter and your computer are more useful because they let you know which Wi-Fi signals are protected with WEP encryption. As Figure 26.1 shows, two of my neighbors have active Wi-Fi networks, but they're both protected, so I can't use either network to connect to the Internet unless I have a network key.

FIGURE 26.1

Both of these Wi-Fi networks are protected by passwords.

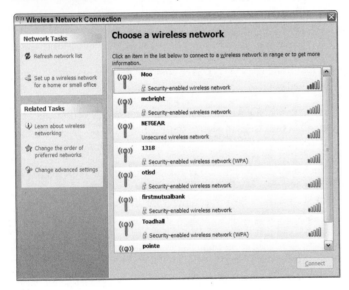

When a Wi-Fi signal is accessible (or if you have the network key code needed to use a protected network), the Microsoft tool displays details about the network like the one that is highlighted at the top of the list in Figure 26.2. To use a network, select it from the list and click the Connect button. The Connection Window places a star next to the signal-strength bars when a connection is active.

CAUTION Many unprotected private sites are also active and accessible, even if their owners don't know that they are providing free access to anybody within range of their signals. Remember that stealing Internet access is illegal; people have been arrested for it

FIGURE 26.2

In this location, Windows has identified five networks, two of which are configured for open access.

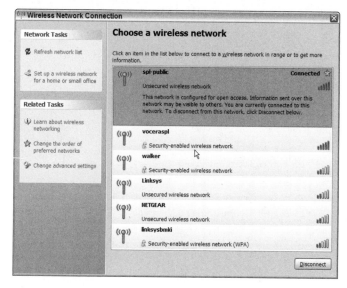

Both the software supplied with your Wi-Fi network interface and your computer's proprietary software also include search tools for detecting nearby Wi-Fi signals. For example, the internal Intel Wi-Fi adapter inside many laptops uses the search screen shown in Figure 26.3. Figure 26.4 shows the software supplied with IBM ThinkPad computers.

FIGURE 26.3

The software supplied with the Intel wireless network interface detects more signals than the Microsoft tool.

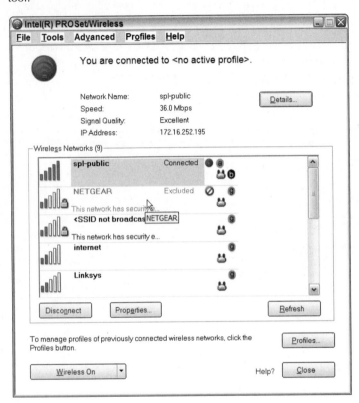

I ran all three of these programs with the same Wi-Fi hardware from exactly the same location. As you can see, each of them detected a slightly different set of hotspots: The Microsoft program found five hotspots, the Intel program found six, and the ThinkPad utility identified nine, including two hosts that use more than one channel apiece (but it missed one that the Intel program detected). Obviously, some Wi-Fi scanner programs are more sensitive than others, and each uses a different format to display information about nearby hotspots. Therefore, when you're searching for an accessible hotspot, you might want to try a different program if the first one doesn't find a network you can use.

The Wi-Fi program provided with IBM/Lenovo ThinkPads includes a graphic display of nearby Wi-Fi hotspots.

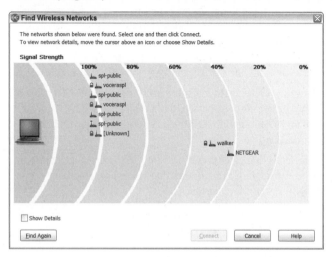

Other Internet Connections

Wi-Fi is not your only option for connecting your laptop computer to the Internet when you're away from home base. If you have an account with a cellular data service, you can set up a connection anywhere in most major metropolitan areas and transportation corridors. And when you're visiting a friend or another office within your own company, it might be possible to plug a cable into a wired home or office LAN.

CROSS-REF For more details about setting up a cellular data connection, see Chapter 23.

Finding a Place to Print

It's entirely possible to carry your own small portable printer along with your laptop computer, but it's generally not necessary unless you're traveling to an extremely isolated location. In most places, you can find an existing printer service that probably produces better quality at the same or lower per-page cost.

Among the likely places that can print your reports, proposals, and other documents are

- **Airport business centers:** Just about every major airport has one or more commercial business centers in the departure area, with computers, Internet access, and related services available at a nominal cost. If the business center's location isn't immediately obvious, ask at an information booth or look for it on one of those "You are here" directory panels. Because travelers often have no other choice, airport business centers are often more expensive than other places that can provide similar services.

- **Airport club lounges:** Many airlines offer private waiting areas and other services for members of their VIP clubs and premium-class passengers. If you're a member of one or more of those clubs (or if you are traveling in first or business class), ask if they can provide business services at your destination.

- **Hotel business centers:** Most hotels that cater to business travelers can provide computer support to their guests. Look in the book or brochure that describes available hotel services or ask the concierge or the front desk for assistance.

- **Conference and convention centers:** Business services are often available at venues for conferences, conventions, and other business meetings. The event staff or reception desk can tell you where to find them.

- **Print and copy shops:** Most print shops, copy shops, and office supply superstores can print documents from a CD or a flash drive. Several major chains, including FedEx Kinko's, OfficeDepot, and OfficeMax can accept document files through the Internet and either hold the job for pickup or deliver it to you.

- **College and university libraries or print centers:** Many students don't have their own printers, so print centers are common in educational institutions. Some of these centers can only provide service to students and faculty, but others happily take anybody's money.

- **Public libraries:** Most public libraries have computers and Internet access for on-site patrons. Many also offer free Wi-Fi service. Ask the librarian if they have a printer for public use.

- **Friends or business colleagues:** Within limits, you can sometimes convince friends or colleagues to let you print your documents on their home or office printers. If you're making more than a handful of pages, you might want to offer to replace the paper and pay for the ink you consume with your print job.

If you can't transfer a document to a print service through the Internet, the easiest way to print is to copy the document file to either a USB flash drive or a CD and open the file from a second computer connected directly to a printer. It's a safe bet that the people who work in the copy shop or business center do print jobs all the time, so they know exactly how to do it for you.

Checking Documents for Errors

It's always a good idea to carefully proofread a copy of your printed document for errors, even if you have used your program's spell checker and double-checked it on your computer's screen. If possible, ask the copy shop or business center to print one copy for proofreading before they print multiple copies for distribution. Don't forget to check every word on the title page and headlines. There's nothing more embarrassing than spelling your own name (or your client's name) wrong in 36-point type.

If you're concerned about protecting confidential information in Microsoft Office programs, open File ⇨ Properties to be certain that there's nothing in any of the tabs that you don't want other people to see.

Sending Backup Data Home

Any time you're on the road for more than a day or two, it's a good practice to send home copies of each day's notes, documents, and other important files. If your computer is lost or stolen, or the disk drive crashes, you will still have copies of your recent work.

If you have access to the Internet, the easiest way to send copies of your files back to your home or office is to send them to yourself or to an assistant or associate as e-mail with attached files. Or if your company has an FTP server or a virtual private network (VPN), you can use one of those methods for moving files instead of e-mail.

When you send files through the Internet, it's always good practice to use a compression tool that can combine several large files into a single smaller one, even if you're only sending a single file. Not only do compressed files reduce the size (and therefore the transmission time) of the transmission, but they also include error-checking, so you can be certain that the received file is an accurate copy of the one you sent. Windows includes a compression utility that uses the .zip file format.

 Some file types, including many graphics and sound files, are already compressed, so you won't see any significant reduction in size when you add them to .zip files.

To combine multiple documents and other files into a single compressed file (also known as a *zip file*), follow these steps:

1. **From the Windows desktop, open My Computer and create a new folder called "AttachMail [date]."**

2. **Copy each of the files you want to send into the AttachMail folder.**

3. In the AttachMail folder, open the Edit menu and choose the Select All option.

4. Right-click one of the highlighted items in the folder and select Send To ⇨ Compressed (Zipped) Folder. A compressed folder appears.

5. Rename the compressed folder with today's date (M-D-Y or D-M-Y).

The alternative to electronic transmission is to copy each day's files to a CD and mail it to yourself. If you expect to use this approach, remember to include a set of blank (or rewritable) CDs and a padded envelope for each day of your trip, along with the other supplies in your computer bag. If possible, you can save time by pre-addressing each envelope and attaching postage before you leave home (be sure to use the correct stamps for each country).

Summary

Traveling with a laptop computer presents a set of practical challenges that aren't all related to operating the computer. If you travel by air, remember to prepare the computer and the related materials for a security check at each airport, and do whatever you can to avoid attracting attention to yourself or your computer to prevent theft.

While you're away from home, you may want to find a way to connect your computer to the Internet, or to print one or more files or documents. There are plenty of public Internet access points, commercial copy shops, and business centers that can provide the services you need.

Part V

Improving Your Computer's Performance

Chapter 27

Setting Up Your Computer

The default configuration settings that come up when you turn on a new computer for the first time are far from ideal. They include a lot of on-screen links and shortcuts to programs and Web sites that you might never use, options and settings that don't do anything useful, and even more that seem to be optimized for some mythical user who wants automated access to every bell and whistle that Windows can supply.

This chapter explains how to set up a new computer or reconfigure your existing computer to do the things you want it to do, and how to change or eliminate the things you want to avoid.

Install the Device Drivers

Almost every new computer reaches you with Windows and all of the computer's features and functions installed and tested. The computer should work the first time you turn it on, although it might ask you for some setup and configuration information (such as your Internet connection settings) before it allows you to begin real work. If this describes your computer, you can skip the rest of this section.

However, if you assemble your own system, and when you reinstall Windows after a system crash, you must install the device drivers for your network interface, graphics controller, sound controller, and other devices and services immediately after you install the Window operating system. Windows automatically detects and installs many of these devices, but others don't work until you load them separately.

The CDs supplied with your computer, your motherboard, and each add-in expansion card and USB device contain the drivers and control software for that device. Immediately after you install Windows, remember to load all of the drivers and control programs for the built-in services on the CD supplied with your motherboard, and then each of the CDs that came with other expansion cards and USB devices.

Even if Windows recognized and installed a device driver for one or more of these devices, go ahead and install the versions on the CD; the versions provided by the manufacturers often include useful control programs and other utilities.

If you don't have the original CDs, look for downloadable versions of the drivers and software on each manufacturer's Web site.

Install Security Programs

Because it's never safe to connect your computer to the Internet without protection against intruders, viruses and spyware, you should install security utilities on your computer immediately after Windows starts running.

 See Chapter 48 for information about firewalls, antivirus programs, and anti-spyware programs.

Download and Install Windows Updates

Microsoft releases updates, bug fixes, and security patches for Windows at least once a month. Some are substantial changes to the operating system, such as Service Packs 1 and 2, and others are repairs for newly discovered bug and protection-against-security problems. After installing or re-installing Windows onto your computer, you should complete the installation by loading all of the available updates.

If you have a high-speed connection to the Internet, updating Windows is easy and relatively fast. But if you must use a dial-up Internet service, the initial software download might take a very long time. As an alternative, you can order Service Pack 2 on a CD directly from Microsoft at www .microsoft.com/windowsxp/downloads/updates/sp2/cdorder/en_us. This is an English-language Web page, but you can also use it to order update disks in many other languages.

If you don't have any access to the Internet through this computer, you can use another computer to order the update disk. For additional updates, use a temporary Internet connection through a USB modem.

To update Windows through the Internet, follow these steps:

1. **If your system doesn't have a permanent Internet connection, connect it now.**

2. **Turn off all active programs.**

3. **From the Windows Start menu or the Tools menu in Internet Explorer, choose Windows Update.** Your Web browser opens and connects you to the Windows Update or Microsoft Update Web page.

4. **The first time you connect, the site offers to install an ActiveX program.** Follow the instructions on the site and in the yellow band across the top of the Web page to download and install the program. When the installation is complete, the Web site (shown in Figure 27.1) offers a choice between an Express installation that automatically downloads and installs all available updates, and a Custom installation that allows you to choose the updates you want.

5. **Click the Express button.** The Web site uses the ActiveX program to inspect your computer to identify the updates that have not yet been installed. At the end of the inspection, all available high-priority updates download and install themselves, while the status window shown in Figure 27.2 is visible on your screen. Some updates may force the computer to restart, but this should all happen automatically.

6. **When the updates have all been installed, return to the Windows Update site.**

7. **This time, choose the Custom option.** After the site inspects your system, it shows three types of updates in the left-hand column of the Web page (see Figure 27.3): High Priority, Optional Software, and Optional Hardware, with the number of available updates in each category.

FIGURE 27.1

Choose either Express or Custom downloading to install new Windows Update files.

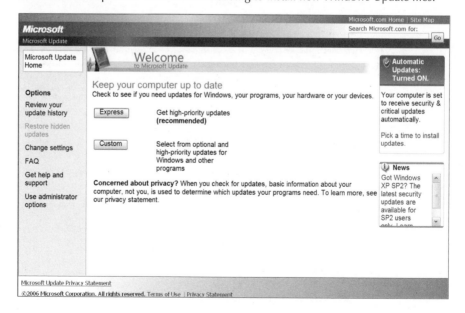

FIGURE 27.2

The Windows Update utility displays the status of downloads and installations.

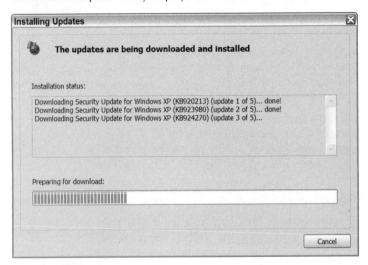

FIGURE 27.3

The Custom update option shows three types of updates: High Priority, Optional Software, and Optional Hardware.

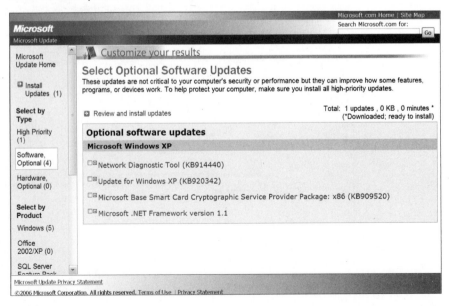

8. **The number next to High Priority should be (0), because you just installed all the available High Priority updates.** If there's a number greater than (0) next to either of the Optional types, click that number to see a list of available updates, with a description of each one.

9. **Read the description of each optional software and hardware update and choose the updates you want to install.** The optional software updates are not critical to Windows operation or security, but many of them can improve the operating system's performance. However, some optional software updates might only apply to programs or services that you never use. Optional hardware updates are new versions of device drivers that Microsoft has agreed to distribute on behalf of hardware manufacturers.

10. **Click the Review and install updates link.** The update software downloads and installs the updates you have selected.

Test Everything While It's Under Warranty

Every new computer comes with a warranty, so it's in your best interest to test every possible hardware feature and function while you can still return it for free repair or replacement. During the first month after you get a new computer, try to run it through an exhaustive series of tests.

As you use your computer, make a note of anything that does not appear to be working properly. Try all of the computer's optional features and functions, including the things you don't normally use. If you discover a problem, note the programs that were running and the actions you took when the malfunction occurred.

In addition to your regular use of the computer, run some diagnostic tests on the computer's memory. These memory diagnostic programs are available at no charge through the Internet:

- **Windows Memory Diagnostic:** http://oca.microsoft.com/en/windiag.asp
- **Memtest86:** www.memtest86.com
- **Memtest86+:** www.memtest.org

These three programs are all memory tests that can confirm that none of the computer's memory modules are defective. They're used most often to test and diagnose memory problems when the POST fails or Windows produces memory-related error messages, but they're also helpful for testing a new computer. All three programs perform similar tests, so you only need to run one of them.

Any new computer should pass these tests with no problems. If you discover that your system fails a test or a component does not appear to work properly, contact the retailer or manufacturer immediately and let them know that you have a problem. A reputable company should do whatever might be necessary to fix your computer at their expense.

Checking the BIOS Settings

The BIOS is a block of software that your computer uses before it loads Windows or some other operating system. Every time you turn on the computer, it performs a series of tests and sets a number of options that control the computer's performance.

The default BIOS option settings usually provide a configuration that works under most conditions, but many of them are not always the best choices for every user. When you're setting up a new computer, you may want to change one or more of these settings.

To open the BIOS Setup utility, restart your computer and immediately press the key that interrupts the startup process.

CAUTION   Some of the settings in the BIOS Settings utility are critical to the operation of your computer. Don't change any BIOS settings unless you understand exactly what you're doing and why you're doing it.

CROSS-REF   See Chapter 8 for more details about the BIOS.

Optimizing Windows

If you dig deep enough, it's possible to change every element of the Windows user interface — the look and feel of the operating system. If you carry this to extremes, you can make your system completely unrecognizable; but short of that, you can and should tweak the out-of-the-box configuration settings to satisfy your own taste and to make the computer easier to use. Remember, it's almost always better to adjust Windows to match the way you want to work, rather than to change the way you work to match the way Windows is set up.

Turning sound on or off

The first thing to change after you turn on your computer for the first time is the set of sounds that Windows and many other programs produce to accompany many actions. You turn off all the standard sounds, turn off individual sounds, or even substitute other sound effects for the ones Windows provides.

Each set of links between sounds and the events that produce them is called a *sound scheme*. If you don't like the default Windows sound scheme, you can alter an existing scheme, create a completely new scheme, or turn off sounds completely.

To change the sound scheme, follow these steps:

1. **Open the Control Panel and select the Sounds and Audio Devices item.** The Sounds and Audio Devices Properties window opens.

2. **Click the Sounds tab to open the dialog box shown in Figure 27.4.**

FIGURE 27.4

The Sounds tab controls the Windows sound scheme.

3. To turn off all sounds, choose No Sounds in the drop-down Sound scheme menu.

4. To turn off a sound associated with a specific event, highlight that item in the list of Program Events, and choose (None) from the drop-down Sounds menu.

5. Click OK to save your changes and close the Properties window.

You don't have to limit yourself to the sounds supplied with Windows and your other programs. If you prefer, you can use short musical sound clips, sound effects, or even record your own voice describing each event.

 You can find links to thousands of free downloadable sound effects at www.stonewashed .net/sfx.html.

 Like any other downloads, scan the sound effects files you obtain through the Internet for viruses and spyware before you install them on your own computer.

To assign a new sound to an event, follow these steps:

1. **Choose the sound clip you want to use.** If it's not already in that format, convert the audio file to the WAV file format. If you don't already have a conversion program, you can use the free Audacity program (http://audacity.sourceforge.net) to convert from other audio file formats (open the audio file in Audacity and use the File ➪ Save As command to save it in .wav format).

411

2. Move a copy of the WAV sound file to the C:\Windows\Media folder.

3. In the Sounds tab of the Sounds and Audio Devices Properties window, highlight the Program Event that you want to associate with the new sound, and open the drop-down Sounds menu.

4. Choose the new sound file from the list of files.

5. **Click the play button next to the Sounds field to listen to the sound file you have selected.** Click OK to confirm your choice and close the Properties window.

Display settings

Now that you have either changed or eliminated those irritating sounds, you can concentrate on customizing the rest of the performance and appearance of Windows. The changes that will have the widest impact are controlled by the Display Properties window.

To open Display Properties, right-click the My Computer icon on your desktop and select Properties from the pop-up menu or open the Control Panel and select Display. As Figure 27.5 shows, the Display Properties window has at least five tabs. This section describes these tabs in order of subjective importance, rather than the order in which they appear on the screen; the Themes tab, at the extreme left, is the one that saves the settings you create with the other tabs.

FIGURE 27.5

The options and settings in the Display Properties window control the appearance of just about every visible element of Windows.

The Settings tab

The Settings tab controls the performance of the graphics controller (the video card) and the display monitor. As part of your initial setup, you want to set the Screen Resolution and Color Quality for optimal appearance and performance.

If you're using a CRT monitor, follow these steps to adjust the Screen Refresh Rate:

1. From the Settings tab screen of the Display Properties window, click the Advanced button in the lower right. A secondary Properties window opens.

2. Click the Monitor tab to open the dialog box shown in Figure 27.6.

3. Open the drop-down menu under Screen Refresh Rate, and choose a refresh rate of at least 70 Hertz.

4. Click OK to save your choice and close the secondary Properties window.

FIGURE 27.6

The Monitor tab includes a setting for Screen Refresh Rate.

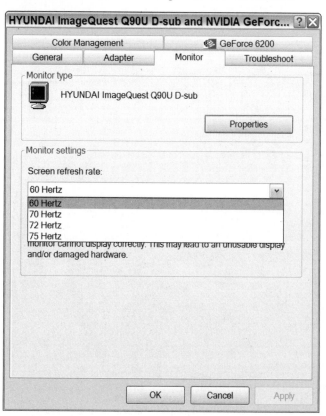

5. **Confirm that Screen Resolution has not changed.** If it has, go back to the Screen Refresh Rate and drop it down to the next lower value.

6. **In the Settings tab of Display Properties, click Apply.** If Windows asks to restart the computer, choose the option that changes the settings without restarting.

 **CROSS-REF**   For more details about video cards, see Chapter 10. Read Chapter 11 to learn more about the monitor.

The Desktop tab

The first time you turn on Windows, you see a background image that was chosen either by Microsoft or by the maker of your computer. Some of these images are blatant advertisements, and others are pleasant pictures that were selected to avoid offending anybody.

You are under absolutely no obligation to keep that image on your screen. You can replace it with a picture or abstract image of your own, or use a live Web page or a screen with nothing but a solid color background. For example, the screen shown in Figure 27.7 uses an early television test pattern as a background image.

FIGURE 27.7

This computer uses a 1940s TV test pattern as its background image.

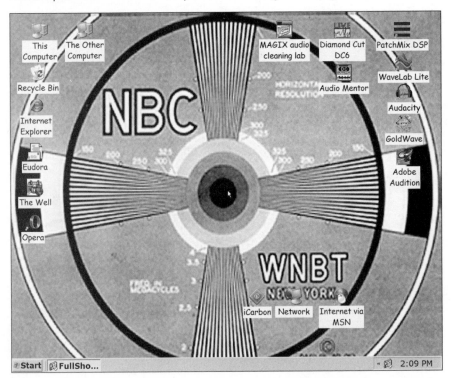

To change one of the background images supplied with Windows, open the Desktop tab in Display Properties and choose an item from the list of Backgrounds. To use any other image file, follow these steps:

1. **Use the Windows Picture and Fax Viewer program to open the file.** If the Viewer doesn't open when you double-click the file icon, right-click the icon and choose Preview from the pop-up menu.

2. **Right click the image in the Viewer program.** Choose Set as Desktop Background from the pop-up menu, as shown in Figure 27.8.

3. **From Control Panel, open Display Properties and the Desktop tab.**

4. **Use the Position drop-down menu on the right side of the window to set the new background image as a full-screen image, a smaller centered image, or a mosaic of multiple copies of the same image (Tile).**

FIGURE 27.8

Use the Set as Desktop Background command to use an image on your desktop.

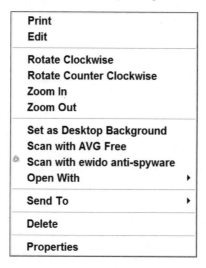

To place a Web page on your desktop, click the Customize Desktop button and choose the Web tab.

The background image can fill the entire screen with a large version of the image, appear only in the center of the screen, or fill the screen with repeated copies of the image. The drop-down Position menu specifies the way the image appears.

To create a desktop with no background image, choose (None) at the top of the list of Backgrounds.

To change the background color, use the drop-down Color menu at the right side of the Desktop dialog box. As a general rule, lighter colors present better contrast under icons and shortcuts.

The Screen Saver tab

Screen savers were invented in the days of monochrome monitors, when a constant image (such as a block of text) would eventually burn a ghost image onto the phosphors inside the screen. In order to preserve the monitor, a *screen saver* program would automatically replace the active text or image on the screen after a preset period of time — often 10 or 15 minutes. The replacement image would move around the screen rather than staying in one place, so the danger of a burned-in image was eliminated.

What began as a practical necessity quickly became an opportunity to place an entertaining set of images on millions of computer screens. Abstract geometric figures, tropical fish, and the hugely popular Flying Toasters were on screens all over the world.

On today's monitors, burn-in is no longer a problem, so there's no practical need for a screen saver any more. Modern LCD and CRT screens can display a constant image for months on end without any danger. And it's a lot more practical to automatically shut down a monitor when it's not active because a blank screen doesn't consume nearly as much power. But the fact remains that screen savers amuse many people, so Windows continues to offer them as an alternative to the energy-saving power schemes.

The Screen Saver tab in the Display Properties window shown in Figure 27.9 controls the way Windows uses screen savers. To turn them off completely, chose (None) from the drop-down menu. To change the default image to a different screen saver, choose the one you want from the drop-down menu. The Wait field specifies the number of idle minutes that Windows waits before it starts to run the current screen saver.

WARNING Screen savers are among the most common method for viruses and spyware to enter your computer. Don't try to download or install a new screen saver unless you have up-to-date antivirus and anti-spyware programs running.

If you do use a screen saver, don't limit yourself to the default version. Take a look at the Settings options to see how the designers of the screen saver program allow you to customize the characteristics of the images that appear on your screen.

FIGURE 27.9

The Screen Saver tab specifies the image that appears when the computer is idle.

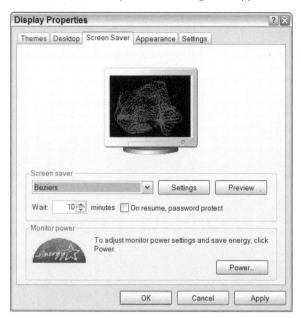

The Appearance tab

The settings in the Appearance tab control the typefaces, colors, sizes, and other characteristics of the text, icons, and windows that appear on your screen. Windows includes about two-dozen pre-set color combinations, of which at least half are seriously ugly, but those schemes are just a start; the Advanced Appearance dialog box makes it possible to change every element of the Windows desktop one at a time.

The Appearance dialog box, shown in Figure 27.10, shows the current appearance settings in the top half of the window, and offers three sets of drop-down menus:

- The Windows and buttons menu offers a choice between Windows Classic style, with sharp corners, and Windows XP style, with rounded corners.

- The Color scheme menu offers a choice of preset color combinations. The Color scheme menus are different for Windows Classic style and Windows XP style.

- The Font size menu offers a choice among Normal, Large, and Extra Large fonts. After you choose a font size, you can alter individual font sizes in the Advanced Appearance window (see the next section).

FIGURE 27.10

The options in the Appearance tab control fonts, colors, sizes, and other characteristics of every item on your screen.

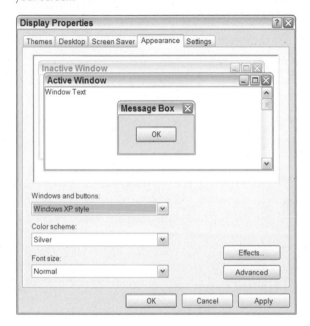

When you select an item from any of the three menus, the samples in the top half of the window change to show the new selections. To use the current selections, click Apply or OK. To discard your selections and keep the current scheme, click Cancel.

Advanced Appearance options

The Advanced button in the Appearance tab opens the Advanced Appearance window shown in Figure 27.11. To change the characteristics of an item in the sample box in the top half of the window, click that item, and notice that the name of the item appears in the Item field. The Size, Color, and Font settings all contain the current values for that item.

Several items are included in the drop-down Item menu that do not appear in the sample box. These include:

- **Icon:** The Icon setting controls the size of the icons and shortcuts that appear in the Windows Desktop, the My Computer window, and other windows that show the contents of drives and folders. The Font settings set the typeface and size of the icons' captions, the Address fields in My Computer and Internet Explorer, and other text elements in Windows Explorer and Internet Explorer.

FIGURE 27.11

The Advanced Appearance dialog box controls the appearance of individual screen elements.

- **Icon Spacing:** The two Icon Spacing options set the vertical and horizontal distance between icons in My Computer and other lists of files and folders. The (Horizontal) setting also sets the width of each line of text in icon names on the desktop, so a higher number allows for more characters; if the setting is too low, the entire name of a program or shortcut won't be visible.

- **Palette Title:** This is easily the single most obscure setting in the entire Display Properties set. Palettes are the free-floating versions of the toolbars that are most often located directly under the title bar in program windows, and in the taskbar at the bottom of the Windows screen. Figure 27.12 shows Microsoft Word with two toolbars displayed as palettes. The Palette Title option sets the size and typeface that Windows will use for the title of a palette.

- **ToolTip:** ToolTips are those little balloon-like objects that pop up on the Windows desktop to offer brief explanations of some features and functions. The ToolTip option in the Advanced Appearance dialog box sets their background color and typeface.

FIGURE 27.12

In this window, the Standard toolbar and the Reviewing toolbar are floating palettes.

Effects options

The Effects button in the Appearance tab opens the Effects dialog box. These options control the way Windows displays menus, ToolTips, screen fonts, shadows under icons, and other items that Microsoft has defined as "effects."

Most of these options are purely subjective; choose the ones that you like and ignore the rest. The exception is "Use the following method to smooth edges of screen fonts," which makes some very subtle changes to the typefaces that appear on your screen. For the clearest text, Microsoft recommends that you choose Standard for CRT monitors and ClearType for laptops and other LCD screens.

The Themes tab

Themes are stored sets of all the options specified in all of other the Display Properties tabs, except the Settings tab. When you select a theme from the drop-down menu, Windows changes everything at one time. It's a convenient way to switch between different combinations.

After you have chosen the set of appearance options that you want to use on your computer, you should save that set as a new theme. Click the Save As button and assign your name to the new theme. This gives you an easy way to return to your preferred settings after you try one or more alternate options.

If you share your computer with one or more other users, each of you can create your own theme, which automatically loads when you log onto the computer.

CROSS-REF   For more information on themes, see Chapter 28. To learn more about sharing your computer with other users, go to Chapter 34.

NOTE   Windows has an irritating bug that automatically returns the sound scheme to Windows Default every time you change display themes. Don't be surprised when the computer begins to make noises after you open a theme. To return to your preferred sound scheme (or to No Sounds), see "Turning sound on or off" earlier in this chapter.

Visual Effects List

A very long list of additional options related to the appearance of many screen elements is hidden in the Performance Options window (Control Panel ⇨ System ⇨ Advanced ⇨ Performance Settings).

The descriptions of most Visual Effects options are clear, but one near the bottom of the list, Use drop shadows for icon labels, is not. When the Drop Shadows option is turned on, in some fonts the labels under all the desktop icons use outline letters instead of solid letters. Most people think the drop shadow fonts look awful, so you should know how to get rid of them if you (or somebody else messing with your computer) turn them on by accident.

This desktop icon is shown with the Drop Shadows option turned on . . .

. . . and with Drop Shadows turned off.

Setting your mouse options

After you have set up the layout and appearance of your screen, use the Mouse Properties window to set the characteristics of your mouse or other pointing device.

CROSS-REF See Chapter 12 for detailed information about adjusting the mouse's controls and response.

Customizing the taskbar

The *taskbar* is the colored bar that normally appears at the bottom of the Windows desktop. It contains the Start button at the extreme left, and the clock at the extreme right. When a program is running or a folder is open, a button appears in the taskbar that identifies that task; if you minimize a window in the desktop, the button remains in the taskbar.

To move the taskbar to the top of your screen, or to the right or left side, move your cursor to either the middle of the taskbar or the clock and drag it to the border of the screen where you want it to appear.

Several other optional features are also accessible through the taskbar. Each of these features is a *toolbar* within the larger taskbar. To add or remove a toolbar from the taskbar, follow these steps:

1. **Move your cursor to a blank space in the taskbar and right-click.** A pop-up menu appears.

2. **Choose Toolbars from the menu to open a submenu that contains a list of toolbars.**

3. **To open a toolbar, click its name in the submenu.** A check mark appears next to the name.

4. **To close a toolbar, click the name of the toolbar to remove the check mark.**

If you use more than one toolbar, or if you have a lot of icons in a toolbar, you can expand the taskbar to make more space for icons and links. To increase the amount of space that the taskbar occupies, move the cursor to the edge of the taskbar. When the cursor changes to a double-ended arrow, drag the edge toward the center of the screen.

The toolbars supplied in a standard Windows installation include:

- **The Address Bar:** The Address Bar is a duplicate of the Address toolbar in the My Computer and Internet Explorer windows. When you type the address of a file or folder on your own computer or a computer connected to your computer through a network, or the URL (the Web address) of a Web site, Windows opens the default program for that item and loads the file or folder at that address.

- **Links:** The Links toolbar duplicates the options list of Links in the Internet Explorer toolbar. Because it comes from Microsoft, all but one of the shortcuts in the list open Web pages that advertise Microsoft products, so it's mostly a waste of time and space. You can either turn off the Links toolbar and ignore it (see below), or delete each button (right-click the button and choose Delete from the pop-up menu) and add new ones by dragging their addresses from the Address field in Internet Explorer or My Computer.

  In practice, the Links toolbar does nothing that you can't do just as easily from the Quick Launch toolbar.

- **Desktop:** The Desktop toolbar contains a button that corresponds to each of the shortcuts on the Windows desktop. Clicking, double-clicking, or right-clicking one of these buttons has exactly the same effect as performing the same act on the desktop icon.

  Placing desktop shortcuts on the taskbar offers several possible benefits:

  - When an active program fills the entire desktop, you can use a link in the taskbar to open a second program without minimizing the original program.

  - When you fill the desktop with a live Web page, you can hide the desktop shortcuts to make the contents of the Web page easier to read. To hide desktop icons, move your cursor to a blank spot on the desktop, right-click, and turn off Arrange Icons By ➪ Show Desktop Icons (see Figure 27.13).

FIGURE 27.13

The Show Desktop Icons option hides or displays shortcuts on the Windows desktop.

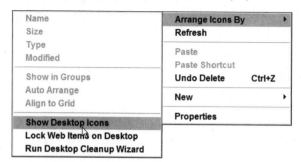

- **Quick Launch:** The Quick Launch toolbar is an alternative to the desktop that displays icons linked to individual programs, Web shortcuts, and other resources. Some programs automatically add links to the Quick Launch toolbar, and others offer to add a link during the installation process.

  To add an item to the toolbar, drag and drop the icon from the desktop, the My Computer window, or the address field of Internet Explorer.

  To remove an item from the Quick Launch toolbar, right-click the icon and choose Delete from the pop-up menu.

- **Language bar:** If more than one Input Language has been installed on your computer, the Language bar provides an easy way to choose a language. To change languages, click the symbol in the Language bar and choose the new language from the pop-up list, as shown in Figure 27.14.

FIGURE 27.14

The Language bar displays a symbol for each installed input language.

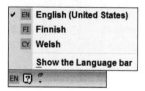

When speech recognition or handwriting recognition is active, the Language bar contains buttons that perform specific tasks and open controls such as the Writing Pad window.

■ **Windows Media Player:** The Windows Media Player toolbar contains a set of controls for the Media Player, including a Start/Pause button, advance to the beginning or end of the current track, a mute control, and a volume control, as shown in Figure 27.15. To use the Windows Media Player control, turn on the toolbar and minimize the Windows Media Player window.

FIGURE 27.15

The Media Player toolbar offers a set of controls for Windows Media Player when the program window is minimized.

In addition to the standard toolbars supplied with Windows, some additional programs can add useful toolbars to the taskbar. Some of the most useful add-on toolbars include:

■ **Virtual Desktop Manager:** The Virtual Desktop Manager program creates up to four separate virtual desktops, with different windows open in each one. This provides a quick and easy way to switch among up to four different programs without the need to save or minimize one program before you can view the next one. The Virtual Desktop is available as a free download from Microsoft at www.microsoft.com/windowsxp/downloads/powertoys/xppowertoys.mspx.

Figure 27.16 shows the Virtual Desktop Manager's Preview Mode, with smaller versions of all four screens.

■ **Taskbar Magnifier:** The Taskbar Magnifier toolbar, available from Microsoft at www.microsoft.com/windowsxp/downloads/powertoys/xppowertoys.mspx, creates a tiny magnifying window in the toolbar that shows an expanded version of the area surrounding the cursor.

To expand the Magnifier window, drag the double vertical line to the left, and drag the top of the toolbar upwards.

 Check out Chapter 30 for more details about the Taskbar Magnifier.

FIGURE 27.16

Virtual Desktop Manager can display active programs in up to four separate screens.

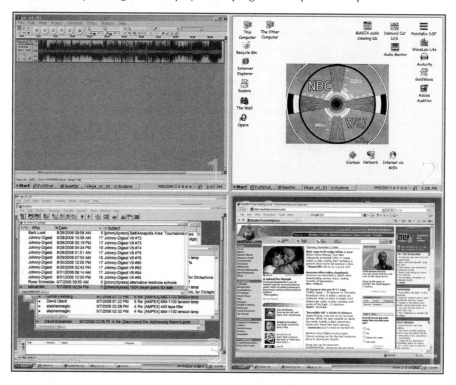

Optimizing the System Tray

The *System Tray* (also called the Notification Area) is the box at the extreme right side of the taskbar (if your taskbar is at the bottom of your screen) that contains the clock and may also include one or more icons linked to active programs.

Setting the date and time

The Time & Frequency Division of the National Institute of Standards and Technology (NIST) in the United States and other standards agencies around the world maintain a worldwide system of timeservers that allow computer users to synchronize their clocks through the Internet. The NIST offers extensive information and free software through their Web site at `http://tf.nist.gov/timefreq/service/its.htm`.

If your computer is connected to the Internet, you can use the Date and Time Properties programs in Windows to synchronize the calendar and clock in your computer with a time server linked to an International Time Standard service.

To set your clock to the International Time Standard, follow these steps:

1. **Double-click the time display in the system tray.** The Data and Time Properties window appears on your screen.

2. **Click the Internet Time tab to open the dialog box shown in Figure 27.17.**

3. **Turn on the Automatically Synchronize option.**

4. **Choose a time server from the drop-down Server menu and click the Update Now button.** The default servers are time.windows.com, a time service maintained by Microsoft for Windows users, and time.nist.gov, operated by the National Center for Atmospheric Research in Boulder, Colorado.

   In practice, it doesn't matter which server you choose because they are all linked to the primary time standard, so they are equally accurate (within milliseconds of the exact time). If neither server responds to your request (probably due to excessive demand), close the drop-down menu and type **pool.ntp.org** in the Server field. This connects you to the next available system among a worldwide pool of time servers. For a directory of additional Network Time Protocol (NTP) servers, go to the list at http://ntp.isc .org/bin/view/Servers/WebHome.

5. **Make sure the Automatically Synchronize option is active.** This instructs Windows to synchronize your computer's clock to a time server once a week.

6. **Click OK to close the Time Properties window.**

FIGURE 27.17

Use the Internet Time tab to set your computer's clock to the exact time.

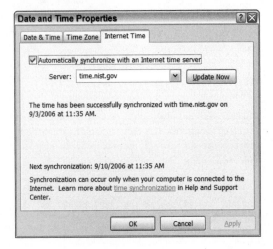

Hiding inactive icons

The icons in the System Tray are useful as indicators that a program is active in background, or that the status of a program has changed; but when you have several icons in the tray, the information supplied by each icon can get lost in the visual clutter. It may be helpful to hide the icons that don't provide any important information.

For example, your antivirus and anti-spyware programs probably place icons in the taskbar to let you know that they are working in the background. When one of these programs detects a problem, it probably changes color or shape at the same time that it displays an alarm message on your screen. But because the alarm is enough to attract your attention, you can safely hide the taskbar icon.

Therefore, Windows allows you to hide each icon when the program is not active, or to hide it permanently. To change the way Windows displays each icon, follow these steps:

1. **Right-click the Start button and choose Properties from the pop-up menu.** The Taskbar and Start Menu Properties window opens.

2. **Open the Taskbar tab to display the dialog box shown in Figure 27.18.**

3. **Turn on the Hide inactive icons option at the bottom of the dialog box, and click Customize.** The Customize Notifications window shown in Figure 27.19 appears.

FIGURE 27.18

The Taskbar tab in the Taskbar and Start Menu window controls the contents of the System Tray.

FIGURE 27.19

Use the Customize Notifications control to set the configuration for each icon.

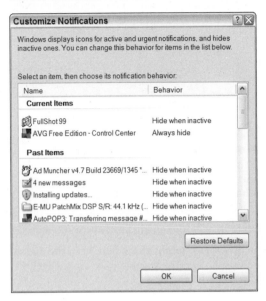

4. **To change the way Windows handles each type of icon, click the instruction next to that item in the Behavior column.** A drop-down menu appears with three options:

   ▪ **Hide when inactive:** When an icon is set to Hide when inactive, it only appears in the System Tray when the program associated with that icon is performing some kind of action.

   ▪ **Always hide:** When an icon is set to Always hide, that icon never appears in the System Tray.

   ▪ **Always show:** When an icon is set to Always show, it's visible in the System Tray whenever the program is running.

   To view hidden icons, click the double chevrons («) at the left side of the tray.

5. **Click the OK buttons in both the Customize Notifications window and the Taskbar and Start Menu Properties window.**

Tweaking Windows

When you first install Windows, or when you start a pre-installed version for the first time, it includes a huge number of obscure features and options, and almost as many features that are of no real value. So it's a very good idea to spend some time adjusting and deleting things.

Delete the stuff you don't need

First, eliminate the programs and shortcuts that you never use. These include the links on the desktop and the Start menu to Internet Service Providers, advertisements for services and Web sites that you don't need or want, and programs that you will never use.

Start with the desktop. Double-click each shortcut, just to see where it takes you. Unless you believe you will use that shortcut a lot — at least a couple of times every month — get it off your desktop. You can either drag the shortcut to the Recycle Bin icon located on your desktop or right-click on a shortcut and choose the Delete option from the pop-up menu.

Next, open the Start ⇨ All Programs (or Start Programs) menu and look for junk shortcuts. Anything that seems to be a link to an advertisement should go.

Finally, look for pre-installed programs that you don't need or want. Follow these steps to remove unnecessary Widows programs:

1. **Go to Start ⇨ Control Panel ⇨ Add or Remove Programs.** Click Add/Remove Windows Components on the left side of the window to open the Windows Component Wizard shown in Figure 27.20.

2. **Start at the top of the list of Components, and select the first item.** After you select a Component, click Details in the lower right corner to open a subsidiary list of categories or individual components.

FIGURE 27.20

Use the Windows Components Wizard to remove Windows programs that you don't need.

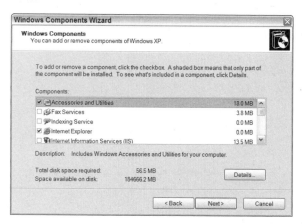

3. **Select the first item in the list of Subcomponents.** If there's another Details button, click it to drop down one more level. When you get to a list of individual programs, examine each item, one at a time. If you don't expect to use this program, remove the check mark from the listing. If you want to remove every item in a category (such as Games), remove the check mark next to the name of the category.

4. **Continue this process until you have evaluated every item in every category and subcategory.** Remove all the items that you don't expect to use.

5. **After you have worked through the entire list, click Next.** Windows deletes the items you removed and completes the wizard.

6. **Click Finish to close the Wizard.**

 The Indexing Service program is a notorious waste of processing time. Turn it off.

Tweak UI

Microsoft offers a free tweak program that is essential for fine-tuning the look and feel of your Windows system. Download and install TweakUI from www.microsoft.com/windowsxp/downloads/powertoys/xppowertoys.mspx.

Figure 27.21 shows the TweakUI window. Each of the items in the tree structure on the left side of the window opens a dialog box that controls a different part of the Windows user interface and a description of the controls and options on that screen.

FIGURE 27.21

TweakUI includes a huge set of options and settings that affect the look and feel of Windows.

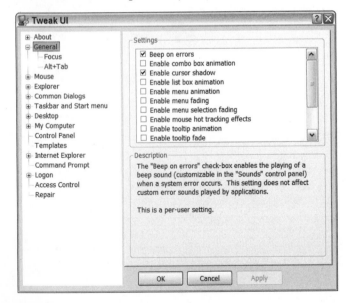

After you install TweakUI, run the program and work your way through each screen in the tree structure, including all the second-level items. Some options are more useful than others, so you may want to ignore many of them. Examine each option and read each description, and use the ones that make useful-sounding changes. Don't forget to click on the + symbol in the list of screens to see additional sub-screens, and to scroll down through the lists of options and settings that extend beyond the bottom of the list box.

Some of the most useful TweakUI options include:

- **Explorer:** The Explorer settings are options that change specific appearance characteristics and other features of the Windows desktop, the Start menu, and other parts of Windows. If you don't use things like the list of Recent Documents in the Start menu, you can disable them from the list of Explorer Settings. If you use the Classic Windows Start Menu, be sure to scroll down the list to see options that apply to that menu format.

- **Desktop:** The Windows desktop normally includes five icons: Internet Explorer, My Documents, My Network Connections, Recycle Bin, and My Computer. If you never use one or more of these icons (such as My Documents), you can use this TweakUI screen to remove it from the desktop.

- **My Computer ⇨ AutoPlay ⇨ Types:** Windows normally runs programs and/or plays music and videos automatically when you insert a CD or DVD in your computer's drive. Use this option to disable to AutoPlay feature.

- **Templates:** In the Windows desktop and in Explorer and My Computer windows, when you right-click a blank space, a pop-up menu appears that includes a New submenu. You can use the Templates screen in TweakUI to add or remove items from this list.

- **Logon:** The list of Settings in the Logon screen allows you to add or remove accounts from the Welcome screen that appears when you turn on the computer and start Windows.

- **Logon ⇨ Autologon:** If only one person normally uses this computer, or if all users share a single account, you can use the Autologon screen to automatically open that account every time you turn on the computer. To start Windows without a password, click the Set Password button and make sure that the password fields are blank.

Choosing Startup Programs

Every time you turn on your computer, Windows automatically runs a set of secondary programs and services before it allows you to do anything from the desktop. Some of these programs and services are useful utilities, but many others are there because some software developers want you to use their programs as often as possible, or because loading a program during startup might make it open a few seconds more quickly when you actually want to use it.

There are about half a dozen different ways to tell Windows to automatically load a program during startup. However, the System Configuration Utility picks up most of them and displays them in one place, so you can remove unwanted autostart programs without digging through all those other lists.

Follow these steps to use the System Configuration Utility:

1. **From the Start menu, choose Run and type** msconfig **in the Open field.** Click OK to enter the command. The System Configuration Utility opens.

2. **Click the Startup tab to display the dialog box shown in Figure 27.22.** The programs listed in this dialog box are the ones that run on startup on your own system, so it probably includes a different set of items from those shown here.

FIGURE 27.22

Use the System Configuration Utility to disable autostart programs. Your list may be slightly different from what is shown here.

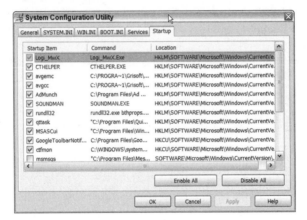

3. **Examine the name and Command text for each item in the list of Startup Items.** If you can identify an item as something you don't want during startup, remove the check mark from the box next to the item's name.

4. **Make a written list of each Startup Item whose name you don't recognize (or use Notepad and print it out).**

5. **After you have unchecked the items you want to remove from your list, click OK.** When Windows offers to restart the computer, go ahead and restart.

6. **After the computer restarts and Windows loads, the Configuration Utility displays an information window, warning that it has made changes to the Startup routine.** Turn on the Don't show this message option and click OK to close this window and instruct the program not to open it again.

7. **Use a Web search tool to find an explanation of each item on the list you made in step 4.** Note the ones that you want to remove from the list of Startup Items.

8. Return to the Configuration Utility and the Startup tab.

9. Turn off the items you identified in step 7.

10. Click OK to save your changes, and let the Utility restart the computer one more time.

When you restart the computer, you should notice that it takes less time for Windows to reach the desktop. If the computer fails to restart, or if some important service is missing, go back to the Configuration Utility (Start ➪ Run ➪ msconfig) and re-enable each of the programs that you disabled, one at a time.

Activating Windows

When you turn on your computer for the first time, Windows might display a very insistent request to activate the operating system. This is an anti-piracy tool that is designed to discourage people from buying a single copy of Windows and installing it on more than one computer.

You won't see Windows Product Activation if your computer came from a major manufacturer with an OEM version of Windows, or if your company has a volume licensing agreement with Microsoft. But if you bought your copy of Windows XP at retail, or as an upgrade from an earlier version, you must run the activation routine within 30 days after installation. You might also see a request for authentication if you replace several major components (such as the motherboard and CPU) at the same time. If you don't activate your copy of Windows, it stops working after a month.

Product activation might appear to be a serious intrusion on your privacy, but it really isn't that bad. Microsoft may conduct some aggressive and even offensive business practices, but product activation is not usually one of them. They have a legitimate right to enforce the product license that limits each copy of Windows to a single computer. If you run Windows on two or more computers, you must buy a license for each one.

> **TIP** Microsoft does offer a small discount on licenses that allow you to install your copy of Windows on additional computers. Each license includes a new Product Key and the right to use Windows on a separate system. For information about additional licenses, go to www .Microsoft.com/windowsxp/pro/howtobuy/addlic.asp. The discount is based on the full retail price, so you might find an even lower price from a computer superstore or office supply retailer, especially when they're running a special sale or promotion.

Many people suspect that product activation is a thinly disguised attempt by Microsoft to collect personal information about you and your computer. However, nobody has found any evidence that they're doing anything but trying to thwart software pirates. Their official line is "At no time is personally identifiable information secretly gathered or submitted to Microsoft as part of activation. Product Activation is completely anonymous."

If your copy of Windows requires product activation, Windows uses the unique Product Key code supplied with the software CD to create an activation ID code and a *hardware hash* code during installation that contains information about these components:

- The type of CPU
- The CPU's serial number
- The amount of RAM
- The type of graphics adapter
- The IDE controller
- The SCSI adapter (if any)
- The MAC address of the network adapter
- The make and model of hard drive
- The hard drive's volume serial number
- The type of CD or DVD drive
- Whether the computer includes a docking station or a PC Card socket

During Setup, Windows offers to run the activation process, but unless you have already configured your Internet connection or your modem, you probably can't make the connection yet. You have 30 days to complete the activation, so it's okay to skip it until you have finished the setup process; Windows will keep reminding you to activate.

You can activate your copy of Windows through the Internet, or by making a voice telephone call to Microsoft. If you have an Internet connection, choose the online method; it's much easier than reading a 50-digit code to a service representative and typing a 42-digit installation ID code into the computer by hand.

If Product Activation sends Microsoft an ID code that has already been used, it compares that ID code with the hardware hash of the earlier activation. If everything matches, there's no problem, and they accept the new activation. If four or more components have changed, or if it has been less than three months since the last time you made major changes, Microsoft rejects your request for activation.

When the online activation rejects your request, it displays a telephone number and asks you to call with an explanation. If you have a reasonable story, the customer service agent who takes your call may believe you and tell you how to activate. But if you try to use the same Product Key to activate two or more completely different systems within a week or two, or if you use the same code on a dozen different machines, they will probably refuse to help.

TIP It's important to understand that product activation is not the same as registration. You must activate your copy of Windows, but registration is purely optional. If you don't want to tell Microsoft who you are and how you use Windows, you don't have to register.

Making Recovery Disks

Almost all major computer makers ship their computers with a customized version of Windows already installed on the hard disk drive. In too many cases, they don't bother to include a separate copy of the operating system and other preloaded software; they leave it to new computer's owners to make their own recovery disks.

You need a set of recovery disks to reinstall Windows and other software if the primary disk drive fails, or if you want to restore the contents of the hard drive to its original condition. On a laptop computer, you can also use the recovery disks to restore Windows and other software when you replace the original disk drive with a larger one.

Recovery disks are a last resort tool for restoring your computer after a major failure has occurred. When you use them, you wipe everything from your hard disk drive and reconstruct the drive from scratch. Don't use your recovery disks unless every other problem-solving method has not worked.

NOTE If your copy of Windows came directly from Microsoft, or if you received a Windows XP CD with your computer, you don't need recovery disks. You can use the Windows XP CD to reload Windows and ignore the information in this section.

Because a disk drive can fail without any advance warning, it's important to make a set of recovery disks soon after you start using your new computer.

To create your recovery disks, look in the Start ⇨ Programs menu for a submenu of special programs supplied by the computer's manufacturer. On IBM ThinkPad computers, this is called ThinkVantage; on HP and Compaq computers it's PC Help & Tools. Your own system may use a different name, but it's probably buried someplace in the Programs menu. If you can't find it, consult your manual.

When you run the Create Recovery Disks command, the program displays instructions for inserting CDs in the drive and recording the individual disks. Don't forget to label each disk after it comes out of the drive. Keep the recovery disks in a safe location, along with all of your other software disks and manuals.

If you lose your recovery disks, or if the hard disk breaks down before you get around to making your recovery disks (too many computer owners never bother to make them), you can probably obtain a set of disks directly from your computer manufacturer's technical support center. Look on their Web site for ordering instructions.

CAUTION If the drive that failed also contains important data files (and you don't have backup copies), you should buy and install a new disk drive as your boot disk and load Windows from the recovery CD onto the new drive (set the old drive as a secondary drive, at least until you can rescue your files). Either that or use a data recovery program such as GetDataBack (use another computer to download it from www.runtime.org/) before you use your recovery CDs. If you ever have to use your recovery disks to restore your hard drive, follow these steps:

1. **Place Disk No. 1 in the computer's drive.**

2. **Restart the computer.** The computer should automatically load the recovery software directly from the CD before it tries to load Windows from the hard drive.

3. **If the computer can't find the CD drive, restart the computer and use the BIOS Settings Utility program to use the CD drive as the first boot device.**

4. **Follow the additional instructions as they appear on your screen.**

When recovery is complete, you have to completely reconfigure and personalize your system.

Install Your Application Programs

Finally, after you set all the configuration settings and options, turn off the services you don't want or need, and install security utilities, it's time to install the programs that you plan to use to perform real work or play with your computer.

Most programs that are on CDs have an automatic installation routine that either run automatically or when you open the CD. Programs that come to you through Internet downloads usually have a setup program. It's always a good idea to read the Getting Started or Quick Setup section of the manual (or any other installation instructions) supplied with any program before you begin to install it.

 Be sure to scan every program you download or obtain from any other source you don't trust for viruses and spyware before you install them.

Summary

Installing Windows on a new computer, or reinstalling the operating system after a major system failure is only the first step toward making your computer work the way you want. Before you can put your computer to work, you often must install some additional device drivers and control programs, and adjust some of the Windows configuration settings that are not necessarily the best possible choices. These include sounds, display settings, mouse options, and the performance of the System Tray and the taskbar. You should also disable the Windows utilities and programs that you never plan to use.

While you're at it, you might also want to change some of the options in the BIOS Settings utility, but don't change anything in the BIOS that you don't understand.

Windows and other programs often load automatically during startup. You can use the System Configuration utility (msconfig) to disable startup programs that you don't actually need. After your Windows installation is complete, you must protect your computer with antivirus, anti-spyware, and firewall software. As further protection, you should download and install all of the security updates and software patches that Microsoft offers at no charge through their Windows Update Web site.

Your new computer is covered by a warranty, so it's a very good idea to test the system and all of its components while somebody else would have to pay for new parts and service. During the first 30 days of use, you might also have to run the Windows activation routine.

If your new computer came from a major manufacturer, it probably has a proprietary version of Windows already installed and no Windows software CD. To protect against losing the pre-installed software, you should make a set of recovery CDs and store them in a safe place. You can use these disks to restore Windows if the original version on the computer's hard disk becomes damaged.

After all this setup and tweaking, there's one more thing to do before you can start using the computer: install each of the programs that you plan to use to perform actual work.

Chapter 28

Enhancing the View

M ost users spend many hours looking at their computer screens, so it's worth the time and expense to do everything possible to improve the appearance and performance of your monitor. In addition to the Display Properties settings described in the previous chapter, it's also possible to make even more extensive changes to the Windows desktop and other on-screen objects, and to improve your productivity by using more than one monitor.

This chapter describes some tools and techniques for changing the appearance of the images on your screen, and several methods for using more than one screen with your computer. Before you try any of these changes, read the Display settings section of Chapter 27 to understand the basic elements of a Windows screen and how to change them. If you have already used the Display dialog boxes to customize your screen, be sure to save your settings as a new theme so you can return to those settings as a baseline configuration after you experiment with other themes, skins, and individual settings.

IN THIS CHAPTER

Creating and using themes to change the look and feel of Windows

Extending the display to extra screens

Using a separate screen with a laptop

Adding more control and features with MaxiVista and UltraMon

Using two or more monitors with the same image

Themes

A *theme* is Microsoft's name for a set of configuration settings that control the appearance of the desktop, the Start menu, most windows elements (such as type size, and shapes of menus, windows and boxes) and other visual elements of Windows. Some themes also include sound schemes. After you set your Display Settings preferences, you can use the Themes tab in the Display window to save them as a new visual theme or return to one that you have previously saved.

TIP   After you have adjusted the display settings in Windows to your own liking, save the set-tings as a theme, with your name or initials as the name of the theme. If you ever make temporary changes to one or more settings, you can use the theme to return quickly to your base line configuration.

Microsoft and other suppliers offer pre-assembled themes that change many elements of the Windows display around a specific topic, or a more-or-less consistent abstract design. For a list of currently available themes from Microsoft, go to www.microsoft.com/downloads, and search for "Windows themes."

For example, the screen shown in Figure 28.1 is Microsoft's Ontario theme — the background image shows native animals from that Canadian province, and some of the icons are pictures or designs related to Ontario. Note in the upper left corner that the My Computer icon is the provincial coat of arms.

FIGURE 28.1

Microsoft's Ontario theme changes the background and icons on the Windows desktop.

The San Fermín theme shown in Figure 28.2, also distributed by Microsoft, makes even more changes. In addition to the image on the desktop and the icons, this theme also uses distinctive mouse cursors (that's the rocket near the upper-left corner), sounds, and a unique screen saver that shows an underwater running of the bulls.

FIGURE 28.2

The San Fermín theme celebrates the Running of the Bulls at Pamplona. It's available from Microsoft in English and Spanish.

In addition to pre-assembled packages, available from Microsoft and other sources, themes are also useful for distributing a standard configuration to all the computers in a large organization. To create a new theme, follow these steps:

1. From the Control Panel, click **Display** to open the Display Properties dialog box.

2. Use the **Desktop, Screen Saver** and **Appearance** tabs to set the display settings you want to include in your new theme.

3. If you want to include a new mouse pointer scheme in your theme, open the **Mouse Properties** dialog box from the **Control Panel** and choose the **Pointers tab.** Choose a pointer scheme from the drop-down Scheme menu.

4. **To include a sound scheme in your new theme, open Sounds and Audio Devices from the Control Panel and choose the Sounds tab.** Choose a Sound scheme from the drop-down menu and click OK.

5. **Return to the Display Properties dialog box and open the Themes tab.** Click the Save As button to save your new settings as a theme.

6. **In the Save As window, type the name you want to use for this theme in the File name field and click the Save button.**

After you save your theme, follow these steps to distribute it to other users:

1. **If there's a My Documents shortcut on your desktop, open it.** If not, open My Computer and use the Up command in the toolbar to move to the Desktop folder, and open My Documents.

2. **Copy the [*name*].theme file you want to distribute.**

3. **Close the My Documents window.**

4. **Open My Computer and move to your C: drive.**

5. **Create a new folder called My Theme, open the folder, and paste the theme in that folder.**

6. **Use the copy of your .theme file in the new folder to make copies for distribution either through e-mail, on a file server, or any other distribution channel.**

If your new theme includes a custom background image, sound scheme, pointer scheme or screen saver, remember to distribute those files along with the .theme file.

To install a .theme file, simply treat it like any other file: double-click the icon to load the theme into the Display Properties window. Use the Save As button to add the new theme to the Themes drop-down menu.

Using More Than One Monitor

Most people connect just one monitor to their computer, or they use the screen built into their laptop. But if you have the space on your desk or worktable, adding a second screen can make your computer much more flexible and easier to use.

Using two or more monitors with your computer can offer these benefits:

■ You can work on a document or other project on one screen while background programs, such as e-mail, a streaming Internet news feed, or the output of a video camera, run on another screen. It's much easier to glance over to the second screen to see if there's any activity than to move the background tasks on top of your current project window.

- You can move toolbars and palettes in an application program out of the active window to create more space for the project in the window. For example, Figure 28.3 shows a Visio project with the project window in one screen and the stencils in the other.

- You can eliminate overlapping windows and the need to move them around your screen.

- You can view a text editor or other programming tool in one screen and immediately see the effect of your work in a second screen. For example, a Web designer could use an HMTL editor in one screen and a Web browser in another screen. To view changes, simply save your work in the editor and refresh the image in the browser. This is much easier than switching between windows on a single screen.

- You can use information (such as a document or a Web page) in one screen as source material while you write, draw, or perform other work in another screen.

- You can expand a single image to fill two or more screens.

- Some games can provide two or more simultaneous images when multiple monitors are available.

Windows can support up to a maximum of ten monitors, but after the second or third screen, most users reach and exceed a point of diminishing returns. However, a truly massive multiple-screen set-up can create an impressive display for a trade show, a multimedia show, or some other form of public presentation.

CAUTION If you do try to use multiple screens for a public presentation, make absolutely sure that it works properly with the actual equipment you will use during the show. *Rehearse, rehearse, and rehearse again.* Nothing loses the confidence of your potential customers (or the general public) more than a multi-screen program that has turned into nonsense because one screen is a step behind everything else, or the screens are not arranged in the right order.

After you install a second screen, it becomes second nature to drag icons and windows from one screen to another, and to create your own uses for the extra on-screen real estate that has become available to you.

If you have the table space, adding a second monitor doesn't have to be expensive. Secondhand monitors, especially monitors with CRT screens, are out there at giveaway prices. Remember that your second screen doesn't have to be as fast or as large as the primary (two 15-inch monitors give you more useful screen area than a single 19-inch monitor; two 17-inch or 19-inch screens are even better), so you can get along with an older 15-inch screen and a controller card with only 16MB of graphics memory or less. In an urban area with a decent secondhand computer retailer, the whole project could cost less than $20. If you have an old computer that you no longer use taking up space in your basement or storage closet, you can probably recycle the graphics card if it has a PCI interface. Of course, a new monitor and graphics controller will almost always provide a better-looking image, but they cost a lot more than inexpensive secondhand equipment.

You can connect multiple monitors to your computer in several ways:

- With a separate graphics controller card for each monitor
- With a single graphics card that supports two or more monitors
- With a combination of both

FIGURE 28.3

Moving controls and tools to a second screen creates more space for the actual project.

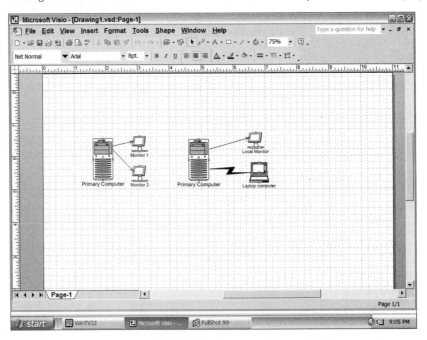

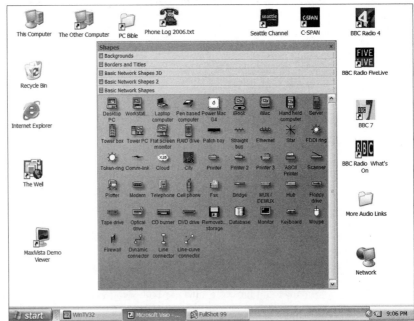

Multiple video controller cards

To use more than one graphics controller in a desktop computer, each card must be either an AGP, PCI-Express, or a PCI device. Assuming your computer's existing graphics card is an AGP or PCI-Express card, this means that your additional card (or cards) must be a PCI card. If you're shopping for graphics cards in the junk-parts bin at a secondhand computer store, you should take this book along and use the photos in Chapter 10 to identify the interface used by each card. Generally, the card-edge connector on an AGP card has an L-shaped tab at the end farthest from the backplate; on a PCI card, the edge connector has no tab.

If you're buying a new graphics card, make sure it has the correct interface. Most new graphics cards use either AGP or PCI Express interfaces, but many manufacturers still make PCI video cards; they are available at larger computer retailers, but probably not at electronics stores or office supply places that don't have extensive inventories. If you can't find one locally, order it from an online retailer.

If your existing graphics controller is built into your computer's motherboard, use PCI cards for the additional controllers.

If you're using a secondhand graphics card, try to identify the make and model before you install it. If the card doesn't have a label, find the FCC ID number on the controller board and look it up through the Internet at the Federal Communications Commission's Equipment Authorization Search page (`https://gullfoss2.fcc.gov/prod/oet/cf/eas/reports/Generic Search.cfm`). When you have the make and model number or name, go to the manufacturer's technical support Web site and download a copy of the latest Windows XP device driver. Save the device driver file in a new folder on your hard disk drive called *Device Drivers*.

Follow these steps to connect one or more additional monitor to a desktop computer through more than one graphics card:

1. **Turn off your computer and disconnect the power cable.**

2. **Open your computer case.**

3. **Find an unused PCI or AGP slot on your motherboard.**

4. **Remove the filler backplate next to the empty slot.** Save the screw.

5. **Insert your graphics card into the empty slot.** Push it down (toward the motherboard) at the front and back to make sure it's firmly seated.

6. **Use the screw that held the filler plate to attach the graphics card's connector panel to the back of the computer.** You might have to loosen the screws on adjacent backplates to fit the graphics card's connector plate solidly against the mounting rail.

7. **Plug the video cable from your second monitor into the VGA connector on the newly installed graphics controller.**

8. **Plug in the power cable on the new monitor and turn both monitors on.**

9. **Plug the power cable back into the computer and turn it on.** Windows displays a "Found New Hardware" message and installs a device driver for the new graphics card. If

Windows doesn't automatically find the device driver software, use the Browse button to identify the driver on the CD that came with the card or that you downloaded from the manufacturer's Web site.

10. **Move your mouse cursor to a blank spot on the desktop and right-click.** The Display Properties window opens.

11. **Choose the Settings tab.** A dialog box like the one in Figure 28.4 appears.

FIGURE 28.4

The Settings tab in the Display Properties dialog box controls multiple monitors.

12. **Turn on the Extend my Windows desktop onto this monitor option and click Apply.** The second monitor comes to life, with the same background color and picture as the primary monitor.

13. **If the software supplied with your new graphics card (or that you downloaded from the manufacturer) includes additional programs, run the setup program now.**

Cards with multiple heads

Many new graphics controllers have separate VGA and DVI output connectors. If you connect monitors to both connectors, the same card controls both displays. When a single graphics controller drives two monitors, it shares its on-board memory and other resources between them, so the card's response to commands and mouse travel might be slightly slower than the same card can provide with just one screen (but not enough to notice unless you're using the computer for graphics-intensive programs).

To use a second monitor, follow these steps:

1. **Turn off the computer.** Make sure power is connected to both monitors.

2. **Plug the cable from the second monitor into the extra connector on your graphics adapter.** If necessary, use a DVI-to-VG adapter.

3. **Turn on the computer and both monitors.** You see the Power-On Self Test (POST) information on both screens, but when Windows starts, the desktop is only visible on one screen.

4. **Right-click in an empty spot on the Windows desktop to open the Display Properties window.**

5. **Open the Settings tab.** The box at the top of the dialog box shows outlines of both screens, with one in white and the other gray.

6. **Click inside the gray outline.** The Display field identifies this outline as Display No. 2.

7. **Turn on the Extend my Windows desktop onto this monitor option and click Apply.** The second screen comes to life with the same background image and color as the original monitor.

Configuring Windows for multiple monitors

Whether you use a single graphics card with two or more connectors or a separate controller card for each monitor, the Settings tab in the Display Properties window controls the performance of each monitor and the relationship between or among the screens.

Configuring the new screen

After you connect a monitor to each graphics controller, or each output on a dual-head controller, you must configure each screen to work as part of a multiple-monitor system. Follow these steps to adjust each screen:

1. **Place each monitor on your desk or work surface in the locations where you plan to use them.** Turn on all the monitors.

2. **Click the Identify button at the bottom of the Settings dialog box to display a big number on each screen.** This number corresponds to the number of that screen in the drop-down Display list.

3. **Choose the screen number of the monitor you want to configure.**

4. **Set the Screen Resolution and Color Quality for that screen.**

5. **Click the Advanced button to open the secondary properties window and choose the Monitor tab.**

6. **Choose the Screen Refresh Rate for this monitor.** Use 60 Hz for LCD screens, or at least 70 Hz for CRT screens.

7. **Click OK to close the secondary window and confirm that the Screen Resolution and Color Quality haven't changed.** If they have, go back to the Advanced ⇨ Monitor tab and reduce the refresh rate.

8. **Repeat the process for each additional screen.**

9. **Click OK to close the Display Properties window.**

Positioning the screens

The box in the upper half of the Settings dialog box shows outlines of each screen connected to your computer. Depending on the combination of controllers and monitors, it might also show one or more additional phantom screens in solid gray, but you can ignore them.

In order to move your cursor and drag objects between screens, it's important to match the images in the Display Properties window with the physical positions of the screens. To move an on-screen image, follow these steps:

1. **Click the Identify button near the bottom of the window.** A large number appears on each screen that identifies that screen in the drop-down Display list. If you're using more than two monitors, you might want to place some kind of removable label on each monitor. A Post-It note works well for this.

2. **Treat the No. 1 screen as a fixed position.**

3. **Click the image of the No. 2 screen and hold down the mouse button.** The name and number of the monitor appears in the Display field.

4. **Drag the outline of the No. 2 screen to a position similar to the location of the physical monitor screen.** Release the mouse button and click Apply.

5. **Slowly move the mouse from one screen to the other.** As the cursor jumps across the boundary, notice how it moves. If the mouse motion between screens is not continuous, drag a screen up or down or from side to side to correct the problem. Click Apply after each move, and try moving the mouse cursor again.

The control software supplied with video cards that use either NVIDIA or ATI graphics chips often includes additional features and options for multiple-screen operation. For example, Figure 28.5 shows the NVIDIA Multiple Display configuration tool that offers several display choices:

- Just one display
- The same image on all screens
- A single desktop that extends horizontally over all available screens to allow multiple-screen images

- A single desktop that extends vertically over all available screens to allow multiple-screen images

- Traditional multiple-screen display, with different resolution, color depth, and refresh rate settings for each screen, if necessary

If your NVIDIA Control Panel does not look like this one, you can download new Control software and updated drivers from www.nvidia.com/content/drivers/drivers.asp.

FIGURE 28.5

The NVIDIA Control Panel program offers additional multiple-monitor options.

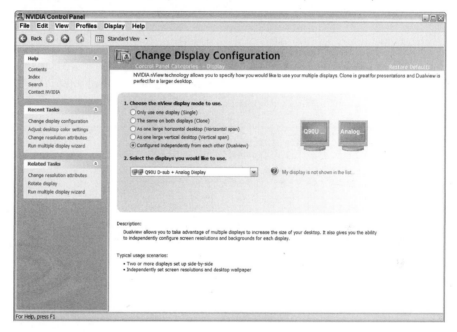

The most recent versions of ATI's Catalyst Control Center include a similar program, as shown in Figure 28.6. If the software supplied with your ATI graphics controller doesn't include this feature, you can obtain a newer version from http://ati.amd.com/support/driver.html.

FIGURE 28.6

ATI's CATALYST Control Center also includes support for multiple-monitor operation.

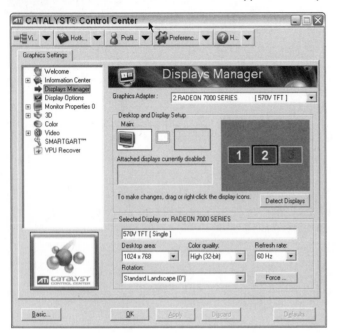

Connecting a Monitor to a Laptop Computer

A separate monitor connected to a laptop can either replace the screen built into the computer's case, or act as a second screen in a multiple-monitor configuration. To connect a separate monitor to a laptop computer, plug the cable from the monitor into the VGA or DVI connector on the side or back of the laptop, or in the back of a docking station. For more than one external monitor, you can use a graphics controller on a PC Card.

When a single controller, such as the graphics controller in a laptop computer, drives two screens, Windows XP uses a utility called Dualview to control the separate displays on each screen. When Dualview is active, it takes its instructions from the Settings tab in the Display Properties window. The functions are exactly the same, except that Dualview doesn't let you choose the primary display — in a laptop, the No. 1 screen is always the one built into your computer's case.

Many laptop computers that use Intel CPUs also contain Intel's Mobile Graphics Media graphics controller chipset. The driver software that controls the Intel chipset, shown in Figure 28.7, offers additional controls, including assignment of the Primary screen to either display. Like the ATI and NVIDIA programs for desktop systems, the Intel software provides a more flexible way to configure multiple screens than the Microsoft utility. Similar control programs are included with other laptop graphics controllers.

FIGURE 28.7

The Intel Graphics Media control program can configure a dual display from a laptop computer.

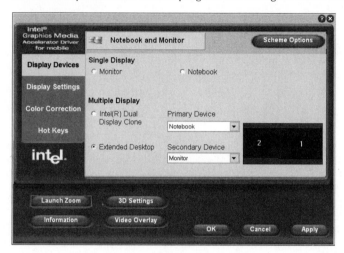

Using Multiple Screens through a Network with MaxiVista

MaxiVista is a program that can use the monitor connected to another computer through an Ethernet, IEEE 1394 (FireWire), or wireless network as an additional screen for the primary computer. Instead of using two monitors connected to the same computer, it uses a second computer to provide the second screen. For example, if you have a desktop computer and a laptop, you can use the laptop's screen as a second display for the desktop machine. Figure 28.8 shows the difference between multiple monitors on a single computer and multiple computers using MaxiVista. A free demonstration version of MaxiVista is available from www.maxivista.com.

If you don't normally use your laptop when working at your desk, or if you have a spare or retired laptop in the back of your storage closet, you can use MaxiVista to convert it to a second monitor screen for your main desktop computer. When you want to take the laptop with you, just turn off MaxiVista, turn off the laptop, disconnect the network cable, and go.

MaxiVista provides several useful services:

- It allows use of a laptop computer as a second screen for a desktop computer (or another laptop).
- It allows you to control up to four computers with a single mouse and keyboard.
- It can send a copy of a computer's screen (and access to the programs, menus, and short-cuts on the screen) to another computer on the same network.
- It allows you to place text or other data in the Clipboard on one computer and move it to the other computer.

Obviously, there's often a practical limit to the number of monitors you can place on your desk or worktable. If you already have a desktop computer and a laptop, or any other combination of two or more computers in front of you, you might not have enough space for yet another monitor; MaxiVista lets you obtain all the benefits of multiple monitors without adding more hardware.

The MaxiVista package include two separate programs: the *Server* program that runs on the computer that controls the images on all the screens (the PrimaryPC), and the *Viewer* program that runs on the computer that provides the added display (the Secondary PC).

FIGURE 28.8

Windows can support two or more monitors from a single computer (left); MaxiVista uses the monitor from a second computer as the second screen (right).

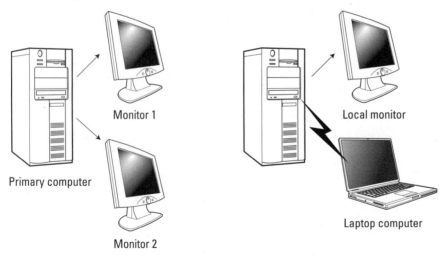

When both the Server and Viewer programs are running, Windows treats the computer running the Viewer program as an added monitor on the Server. The same Settings dialog box in the View Properties window controls both multiple monitors and monitors connected through MaxiVista. In fact, if you connect a second computer to a system that already uses multiple monitors, you can use both at the same time, as shown in Figure 28.9. MaxiVista uses exactly the same Display Properties dialog box that Windows uses for other multiple monitor systems.

In Remote Control mode, MaxiVista doesn't take over the secondary computer's screen. Instead, it allows a user to move the mouse cursor from the primary PC to the secondary PC's desktop, and use the Primary PC's keyboard on programs running on the Secondary PC.

FIGURE 28.9

This computer has two monitors (screens 1 and 2) connected directly, plus two more connected through MaxiVista (screens 3 and 4).

Managing Multiple Screens with UltraMon

UltraMon is a utility for multiple-monitor users that adds many useful features and controls that are not available through the Windows Display Properties window. Some of the same functions are provided in the free control software supplied by NVIDIA and ATI, but UltraMon includes many more services, and it's not tied to a specific type of graphics controller card. If you use multiple monitors, UltraMon may be worth its moderate price. You can download a free demonstration version from www.realtimesoft.com/ultramon/.

UltraMon includes these major features:

- A taskbar on every screen, rather than just the Primary screen. The taskbar on each screen can be limited to the programs running on that screen, or it can include all tasks.
- New controls in the Windows title bars, as shown in Figure 28.10. One button moves the active image to the other window; the other button expands the current window to fill all screens. The same commands may also be available in one of the menus.

FIGURE 28.10

UltraMon can add Move and Expand controls to the Windows title bar.

Expands window to fill all screens

Moves image to other screen

Showing the Same Image on Two or More Screens

In certain situations, it can be useful to feed the same display to more than one monitor. This could include a classroom, a customer service center or office where you want to show the same information to people on both sides of the counter or the desk, or a trade show or other public presentation. This is called a *clone* or *mirror* display.

Unfortunately, the Display Properties tools supplied with Windows do not include a clone display, so you must either use a program from another source, or connect the monitors to the computer through a video splitter.

For example, the NVIDIA Control Panel program includes the Change Display Configuration dialog box shown in Figure 28.11. To display the same material in more than one screen, choose the "same on both displays" option.

In the Intel Graphics Media control program, choose the Dual Display Clone option to show the same display on both screens. Similar control programs for other laptop graphics adapters include their own forms of the same commands.

Video splitters are simple hardware devices that duplicate the same input display on two or more outputs. The least costly versions are simple splitter cables, but more expensive splitters contain a distribution amplifier that boosts the strength of each output signal. For fulltime installations, a VGA or DVI splitter is generally the best and most reliable approach, especially with more than two screens. For short-term temporary use, a simple inexpensive splitter cable could be quite adequate.

FIGURE 28.11

The NVIDIA Control Panel includes a "same on both displays" option.

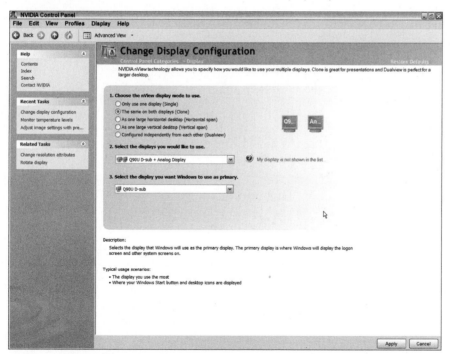

Summary

Several tools can make radical changes to the appearance of a Windows display, and extend the image to more than one screen. Themes, visual styles, and skins are all methods for altering every possible element of the Windows user interface.

Adding a second monitor to a computer is an inexpensive way to make the computer more flexible and easier to use. The Settings tab in the Display Properties window provides basic controls for multiple monitor operation; other programs, including MaxiVista and the programs supplied with many graphics controller cards, can also enhance multiple monitor operation. The third-party UltraMon program adds many more useful features and options.

Chapter 29

Ergonomics: Making the Most of Bad Design

There's another very important component involved in operating your computer: your own body. The human body can do a lot of things very well, but spending hours at a time staring at a screen and operating a keyboard is not one of them.

The physical arrangement of your computer's keyboard, monitor, mouse, and other parts of your workstation in relation to your hands, eyes, and posture can have a tremendous effect on your comfort and productivity. In extreme cases, locating your computer improperly, sitting in the wrong kind of chair, or lighting the keyboard and screen badly can cause pain, fatigue, eyestrain, or even permanent damage to your wrists or your vision. This chapter offers solutions to many of these potential problems.

Your working environment is a combination of several elements, including the furniture that holds the computer, the chair that supports your body, the distance from your eyes to the monitor screen, the way you hold your hands and arms over the keyboard, your posture, and the source of light on the keyboard and screen, among others. Sometimes, it's just not possible to place everything in exactly the right place, but it's important to know what contributes to safe and comfortable computer use. Your own computing environment might not be perfect, but it should not be worse than it has to be.

This chapter concentrates on the parts of your computer that interact directly with your hands and eyes: primarily the monitor, mouse, and keyboard. Unless you're using a laptop computer where the keyboard and screen are integrated, it generally does not matter where you place the main computer case. For the sake of convenience it ought to be within easy reach, so you can turn it on easily, and you can insert and remove CDs, DVDs, and other media, but the exact location is not critical.

Locating Your Equipment

Choose the locations and positions for your computer's keyboard, monitor screen, and mouse carefully, along with the placement of any other input or output equipment. Each should be at the correct height for comfortable operation without the need to keep your head, hands, and arms in an awkward or uncomfortable position.

The keyboard

When you bring your chair close to the table or work surface, the keyboard should be within easy reach, with your upper arms close to your torso and your forearms or elbows resting on the armrests of your chair. Your wrists should be in a neutral position: not bent up or down. You should move your fingers rather than your wrists when you type. If necessary, raise the front or back of the keyboard with a piece of wood or a rolled-up cloth in order to avoid bending your wrists upward or downward. If you sit upright, you might want the keyboard flat or with the space bar slightly higher than the home row; if you type from a reclined position, the back of the keyboard (the number row) should be slightly higher than the space bar.

> **NOTE** Many keyboards have adjustable rear feet that can raise or lower the top row of keys, but the angle of the keyboard with the feet extended is often too high for comfortable typing because it forces you to bend your wrists backward. Use a ruler or a couple of ¼-inch-thick erasers instead of extending the feet.

Your chair's armrests should keep your wrists about an inch above the surface of the table, at approximately the same height as the tops of the keys on the keyboard, as shown in Figure 29.1. When you reach for a distant key, move your whole hand in that direction, instead of just extending one finger. And don't hold the base of your palms against the table with your wrists bent upward. If necessary, use a wrist rest along the front of the keyboard to keep your hands and wrists level.

FIGURE 29.1

Type with your hands level. Don't bend your wrists upward or downward.

If you can't find a comfortable position using a traditional flat keyboard, try one of the many *ergonomic* designs, like the ones shown in Figures 29.2 and 29.3. Some of these keyboards offer curved or contoured surfaces modeled after the shape of your hands, split key rows to reduce the need to twist your wrists, and adjustable heights and angles for different groups of keys. A few simple ergonomic keyboards made by Microsoft and Logitech are widely available through computer and office supply retailers, but many other, more exotic types are sold by specialist suppliers; search on the Web with the keywords "ergonomic keyboard."

If you're left-handed, and you frequently use the directional keys and numeric keypad that are normally located to the right of the standard character keys, you might find a left-handed keyboard, with the additional keys on the left side of the character keys, more comfortable and efficient. If you share the keyboard with right-handed users, consider adding a separate numeric keypad on the left side of a traditional keyboard, or use a keyboard with a separate keypad. Run a Web search for a left-handed keyboard to find suppliers of special keyboards and add-on keypads.

FIGURE 29.2

Microsoft's Natural Ergonomic Keyboards have a Comfort Curve design that reduces the need to twist the wrists while typing.

Photo courtesy of Microsoft

FIGURE 29.3

The Kinesis Contour Keyboard is a more extreme design that was created to optimize comfortable typing and reduce repetitive strain injuries.

Photo courtesy of Kinesis Corporation

The mouse

Your mouse should be close to your keyboard, within easy reach of your dominant hand — on the right side if you're right-handed, the left if you're left-handed — resting on the same surface as the keyboard. Don't place the mouse (or trackball) in a location where you have to extend your arm to reach it; place it at about the same distance from the edge of the table as the keyboard's spacebar. When you're using your mouse as much or more than the keyboard, shift your chair toward the mouse to reduce the distance you have to reach. Depending on the size and shape of the mouse or trackball, you may want to use a wrist rest that's slightly thicker than the one you use with the keyboard.

Mice and other pointing devices come in a wide variety of sizes, shapes, and types, so you shouldn't have to settle for a design that doesn't comfortably fit your hand. Try the samples in a local store, or order online from a place that allows you to return a mouse you don't like for a full refund.

The monitor

Place your monitor in a location where the top of the screen is at or slightly below your eye level. The screen should be perpendicular to your line of sight, as shown in Figure 29.4. Normally, this means that the screen should be tilted back slightly because you're looking down toward the center of the screen. The best angle is about 15 to 20 degrees below your eye level.

FIGURE 29.4

Keep the top of the monitor screen at or below eye level.

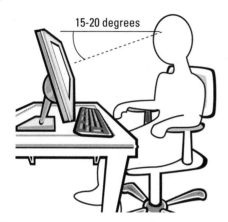

15-20 degrees

Your monitor's screen should be located between about 20 and 40 inches (50 to 100 cm) from your eyes. That's typically about arm's length or a little more. When the monitor is closer than that, you can have more trouble focusing on the text and images on the screen; if it's too far away, most people tend to lean forward, which means that you lose the support from your chair's backrest. If you have trouble reading text at that distance, increase the DPI setting in the Display Properties ⇨ Settings ⇨ Advanced ⇨ General dialog box.

The exact height of your monitor depends on your own height and the height of your chair. To place the top of the screen at eye level, use a shelf or riser to lift it up from the surface of the desk or table. If you're using a computer with a horizontal desktop case, the case can double as a riser for the monitor, but don't try this with a vertical tower case — the top of the case would be too high. If nothing else is available, you can use a couple of big-city telephone directories (you can always look up numbers through the Internet).

CAUTION If you do set your monitor on top of a horizontal desktop case, be careful to not block any air vents that might be on top of the case. ·

Now that LCD monitors don't weigh as much as the older CRT versions, movable monitor arms or platforms that attach to the edge of a table are more practical than they used to be. As you move around in your chair, you can also pull the screen closer or push it away from your head.

If you're using multiple monitors, either place one directly in front of you and the others at a slight angle, as shown in Figure 29.5, so each monitor is facing you; or keep them all in the same plane and place your chair at a center point where you can see all the screens.

> **TIP** If you normally wear eyeglasses, you might have difficulty focusing on a computer screen because it's located too close for your distance glasses, but not close enough for reading glasses. Your optometrist can use your regular prescription to produce special computer glasses for you, with the focal range optimized for the distance between your eyes and your computer screen.

FIGURE 29.5

Place multiple monitors in positions where you can look directly at each screen.

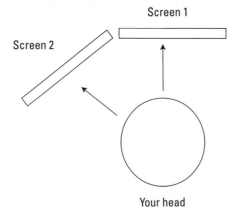

> **CAUTION** If the screen is at eye level, don't use bifocals that force you to look at it through the lower portion of your lenses. This makes you tilt your head backward, which can create fatigue and pain in the back of your neck. The alternative is to place the monitor on the table (rather than six inches or more above the surface) and tilt the screen backward, so you can look down at the screen without tipping your head.

Telephones and copy holders

If you use a telephone at the same time you use the computer, place it next to the keyboard, on the opposite side from your mouse. The dial and other pushbuttons should be within easy reach without stretching your arms, and the caller ID or other readout should be easy to see. If you spend a lot of time on the phone, use a speakerphone or a headset — don't try to cradle the handset between your head and your shoulder while you type and talk.

When you're reading text from a book, notepad, or loose papers while you type into the computer, use some kind of copy holder that places the pages upright, rather than flat on your desk. Depending on the space available, the copy holder can be at one side of the screen or between the screen and the keyboard. A copy holder that attaches directly to the frame of the monitor can hold the papers at the same eye level as the screen.

Choosing the Right Furniture

The locations of your keyboard and monitor depend on the table or desk that supports them; that, combined with the importance of the chair that supports your body, means you should think seriously about the furniture that you use with your computer. Rather than just placing the computer on a convenient space on your desk (or your kitchen counter) and pulling up the nearest chair, think about the height and distance between your body and the machine, and support for your back and your arms.

Table or work surface

Begin with the table, countertop, desk, or other work surface that holds your computer; whichever you choose, this surface should be dedicated to the computer. Don't try to squeeze the monitor, mouse, and keyboard onto an already cluttered space, because it will probably force you to adopt an awkward position to use the computer.

The work surface should be deep enough to place the monitor screen at least 20 inches (50 cm) from your eyes, with the screen directly in front of you. As mentioned earlier in this chapter, remember to keep the screen perpendicular to your line of sight (don't place the screen at an odd angle). You need additional clearance behind the screen if you're using a monitor with a CRT screen; if necessary, you can often create more room for a CRT monitor by moving your desk or table away from the wall.

CAUTION Don't try to make more room for a big CRT monitor by placing it in a corner, unless you can place your chair and your keyboard in a position where you're looking directly at the screen. Don't put it in a place where you have to twist your neck or tilt your head to see the screen.

The keyboard and mouse should fit comfortably under your hands, with your wrists at the same level or slightly below your elbows. This allows the height of the surface to be closely related to the height of your chair. If you can't raise and lower the chair, find a way to adjust the height of the work surface.

Underneath the surface, you should have open space for your feet and knees without obstructions. In other words, your knees should not bump up against a solid horizontal or vertical surface. If the surface is too low for you, consider placing the desk on solid risers (such as wood blocks), or remove the center drawer from a traditional desk to create additional clearance. If it's too high, raise your chair, and use a footrest to support your feet.

In general, the height of a work surface for a keyboard and mouse should be about four inches lower than a typical desk designed for reading and writing, so the ideal office workstation often has a split surface or a separate adjustable tray for the mouse and keyboard.

Chairs

The function of any chair, especially a chair used for work, is to support your upper body without placing any more strain on your spine than absolutely necessary. It should also provide support for your arms at the correct height and position for operating a keyboard.

A chair used at a computer workstation should have these elements:

- A *seat* at the right height to let you keep your feet on the floor or on a footrest, and your knees slightly higher than the seat of the chair. The seat should be wide enough to accommodate your hips, and deep enough to let you change your posture over time.

- A *backrest* that supports the shape of your spine as you change position. In most cases, this means a chair with adjustable lumbar (spinal column) support that fits the small of your back, and which allows you to lean back at least 15 degrees from vertical. As you lean back, the chair should support the weight of your upper body. The relative positions of the back and the seat should let you sit with your spine against the backrest without hitting the inside of your knees against the front of the seat.

- An *armrest* that can support your lower arms (below the elbows), while keeping the upper part close to your body and your shoulders relaxed. Your wrists should be at about the same level as your elbows or a little lower. The armrests should be comfortably padded with no sharp edges.

- A *base* that provides solid support, regardless of your position. The best office chairs have five horizontal legs to prevent tipping, with casters that allow you to move around the floor.

The height of your chair depends on the height of your keyboard and your monitor. If you're sitting in front of a raised drafting table or counter, you should use a stool with a footrest at the correct height to keep your knees at or slightly below your hips and your forearms level.

They're rare, but you might find a chair or stool that has all of these elements in exactly the right places to fit your body. If you find such a wonder-chair, buy it. But don't count on finding that chair. Because people come in so many sizes and shapes, most chairs for computer workstations offer adjustable settings for height, back support, and armrests. If possible, try sitting in a chair before you buy it and try more than one type before you make a decision.

Watch Your Posture

Your typing teacher probably told you that you should always sit up straight when you use a keyboard. Your piano teacher agreed. That's fine in theory, but most of us move around in our chairs when we use a computer for more than a few minutes at a time. Relax. If you're not comfortable in your chair (or standing up), you won't hold that position for more than a few minutes.

These days, the experts at the Occupational Safety and Health Administration (OSHA) say, "Regardless of how good your working posture is, working in the same posture or sitting still for prolonged periods is not healthy. You should change your working position frequently throughout the day." They recommend moving around by:

- Making small adjustments to your chair or backrest occasionally.
- Giving your hands and arms a good stretch.
- Standing up and walking around for a little bit.

So good posture doesn't always mean sitting absolutely upright, with your feet, knees, hips, and elbows all at exactly the right angles, and your eyes looking directly ahead of you. As you use your computer, your goal should be to find a series of positions that don't twist your arms, wrists, shoulders, and neck into painful or unnatural angles. Things to avoid include sitting sidesaddle in your chair and working at an odd angle to the keyboard and screen, dangling your feet or curling them up under your backside, and sitting on the front edge of your chair without any support for your lower back. Basically, if it feels awkward, don't do it.

Your goals should include:

- Keep your hands, wrists, and forearms straight, and roughly parallel with the floor.
- Your head should be upright, or bent slightly forward, directly above your shoulders.
- Relax your shoulders and let your upper arms hang naturally.
- Don't hold your elbows away from your sides.
- Place your feet on the floor or on a footrest.
- Let your chair support your back, thighs, and hips.
- Sit up straight or lean back into the back of your chair.
- Keep your knees at about the same height as your hips, or a bit lower.

That sounds like a lot to think about, but you shouldn't have to think about it at all. After you go through that checklist two or three times, it ought to become automatic.

Notice that there's nothing in that list about sitting up straight and rigid, like a Marine standing at attention. It's entirely okay to shift around from one position to another. You can sit upright or even slouch a little, lean back 15 or 20 degrees in your chair, or stretch your legs forward. Over the course of your time in front of the computer, you might adopt all of these positions and find a few more of your own.

It's also possible to stand up while you use your computer. Keep your head, neck, torso, and legs vertical, with your arms hanging down and your forearms extended, as shown in Figure 29.6. If you like, you can place one foot on a footrest or a rail, but don't lean on the work surface with your arms or elbows. Of course, your keyboard and monitor screen should be higher when you're standing than when you're working from a chair, so you might be more comfortable standing when the computer is on a countertop or a shelf.

FIGURE 29.6

When you use a computer standing up, keep your body vertical.

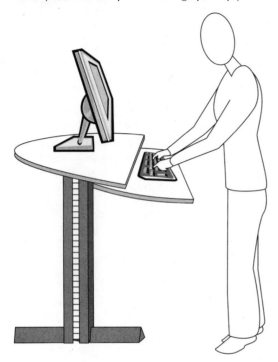

Take Frequent Breaks

No matter how comfortable you might be in your carefully designed and properly adjusted chair, sitting in front of your computer at exactly the right height and position, you should still take short breaks to rest your body and your brain, rather than perform exactly the same activity for hours on end.

A healthy computing routine should include these breaks:

- Change your working posture frequently.

- Take your hands away from the keyboard, look away from the screen, and breathe deeply four or five times every 10 minutes.

- Get out of your chair and stretch your arms and legs three or four times every hour.

- Move your chair away from the table; roll your head up, down, left, and right; twist your upper body from the waist; and flex your wrists and fingers every 10 or 15 minutes.

- Take a 10- or 15-minute break every couple of hours. Walk away from the computer, go fill your coffee cup (or make a cup of tea), chat with a co-worker, or go look at a bulletin board; anything to provide an excuse to move around and think about something different.

- If you job allows it, alternate between computer work and other tasks, in order to use different muscle groups.

- If you can, take occasional drinks of water, juice, or other liquids while you work. Not only does this keep your body hydrated and move your hands away from the keyboard, but the need for frequent bathroom breaks gives you an excuse to get up and walk away from the computer.

NOTE The need for breaks applies to all kinds of computer use, not just productive work. It's easy to enter a semi-trance state when you're playing a computer game that can keep you going for hours at a time. Because games often require a very limited range of hand movements, they can cause damage even more quickly than most other keyboard-and-mouse activity. Remember to stop and stretch, or take a walk between games; those space aliens will still be there when you get back.

Preventing Repetitive Strain Injury

As the name suggests, *repetitive strain injury* (RSI) is a class of physical damage caused by performing the same awkward, prolonged, or forceful physical action many times. Medical professionals call this a *cumulative trauma disorder* (CTD). It can appear in the hands, neck, shoulders, or arms as pain, numbness, weakness, or loss of motor control.

RSI hurts. The symptoms are not always the same — they could be sharp pains in your shoulders or forearms, sore or numb hands, or loss of fine motor control, among other things — and can appear while you're using the computer or hours later. The best-known type of RSI is *carpal tunnel syndrome*, which appears as numb or tingling fingers and a painful wrist, but other forms of RSI can affect other groups of nerves, tendons, and muscles. Depending on the specific form, the pain can be severe enough to wake you in the middle of the night.

Obviously, this is something you want to avoid if you possibly can. The best way to prevent RSI is to understand its causes:

- **Constant muscle contraction:** Typing, clicking mouse buttons, and dragging a mouse, as well as sitting in one position for prolonged periods of time, all keep your muscles contracted, and keep them from receiving fresh blood when they are relaxed. Over time, your muscles adapt by remaining in the contracted position. This forces your tendons to stretch, which causes pain and inflammation.

- **Cumulative trauma:** As you repeat the same motions for hours, days, and months, your muscles, tendons, and other tissue wear because of friction and excessive motion. When this starts, the damage is slight and your body can repair the damage with rest and relaxation. But if you repeat the same activity before you have recovered from the original injury, the damage builds upon itself and becomes susceptible to even more damage.

467

- **Poor posture:** If your body is twisted into an awkward position, you're forcing it to work harder and to move your muscles in potentially damaging ways. Even good posture, if kept in one position too long, can be detrimental.

- **Excessive force:** When you grasp your mouse or pound on a keyboard harder than necessary, or if you hold the keys down too long with too much pressure, you can decrease the circulation in your fingers and increase the tension in your muscles.

- **Pressure against a nerve:** Leaning a wrist or elbow against the edge of a table, or even wearing a tight wristwatch, can compress certain nerves that run close to the skin.

This is all frightening stuff. You can reduce the likelihood of RSI by following the advice earlier in this chapter. But many of us are creatures of habit, and it's often difficult to remember to keep your wrists up and your feet on the floor if you have been doing things differently for years.

So if you do happen to wake up some morning with early symptoms of RSI, talk to your doctor as soon as possible. It's a lot easier to treat RSI before it becomes more intense. If you don't take steps to reverse or eliminate the problem, it continues to get worse until it becomes a major disability. At that point, you may be facing an extended period away from your computer, combined with drug treatment and a long schedule of physical and occupational therapy.

CAUTION With some exceptions such as carpal tunnel syndrome, most forms of RSI do not respond to surgery. Before you agree to any surgical procedure related to your RSI symptoms, get at least one second opinion.

If you obtain any kind of alternative treatment for RSI, such as acupuncture, exercise devices, or home ultrasound therapy, be sure your physician knows about it. These methods might be effective, but they could also conflict with the treatment provided by your medical team.

CROSS-REF For information about special keyboards and other computer equipment for people with RSI, see Chapter 30.

Optimizing Your Lighting

Your working environment should have enough light and a minimum of glare to let you see the keyboard, screen, and nearby papers and documents but not so bright that the contrast between the screen and the rest of the room makes text on the screen difficult to read.

If possible, the room where you work on your computer should have a combination of well-distributed ambient light and direct task lighting (usually from a table lamp) aimed at the keyboard and the surrounding table. Place the light sources in a position where you can't see glare or direct reflections on the screen. The monitor screen provides its own light, so it's not necessary to point a task light at it.

If there's a window in the room, the best location for the computer screen is perpendicular to that window, so the bright outside lighting during the day and the darkness at night doesn't produce a distracting contrast to the amount of light coming from the screen. If the monitor is opposite the window, the sun can shine directly onto the screen, which makes it extremely difficult to read text or view images. Curtains, window shades, or blinds can often help with this.

If lights in the room use fluorescent bulbs, the flicker on a CRT screen can become very distracting, especially if the refresh rate is set to 60 Hz. The display is far less unpleasant to use if you increase the refresh rate to at least 70 Hz. LCD monitors don't have this problem, so the native 60 Hz refresh rate is usually the best choice.

Use the controls on your monitor to adjust the image to the best combination of brightness and contrast in your particular environment. If the room becomes dimmer or brighter, or if the amount of light coming through the window changes, adjust the monitor settings to a comfortable level for the new conditions.

Don't forget to clean your monitor screen frequently. There's no excuse for looking at the screen through a layer of dust and grime that reduces both clarity and brightness.

Reducing the Noise

Most computers are relatively quiet, but there's usually plenty of room for improvement. Several noisy computers in the same room can become loud enough to break your concentration and add to your stress level.

If you're building a computer from scratch, you can choose a case, fans, and other components that are designed for minimal noise and vibration. If you're working with an existing system, many of the same techniques can make your work environment a lot more pleasant. Search the Internet using the keywords "quiet computer" for specific products and techniques.

The main sources of computer noise are

- **Fans in the power supply, and the case:** A computer with an exhaust fan in the back of the case is quieter than one with an input fan in the front. If the case fans make a lot of noise, replace them with quieter versions that are the same size and operate at the same speed. If you can find them, install fans that use magnetic levitation (made by SilenX and Sunon) instead of ball bearings.

- **Blowers mounted on heat sinks on the CPU and the graphics controller card:** Look for a "silent" CPU cooling fan and a graphics card with a passive heat sink or replace the original noisy fan with a low-noise cooler (such as the ones made by Zalman and Thermaltake).

- **Vibration transmitted from the power supply fan to the case:** Add silicon grommets between the power supply and its mounting rails.

- **Vibration transmitted from hard disks through the rigid portions of the case**: Use rubber grommets to mount the drives and physically isolate them from the case. Place insulating foam along the sides of the case to further reduce vibration and noise, but don't block any of the air holes or vents.

CROSS-REF For more information about reducing computer noise, see Chapter 4.

Working with a Laptop Computer

As far as ergonomic design is concerned, a laptop computer is a disaster waiting to happen. If you place the screen far enough away from your eyes to minimize eyestrain, reaching the keyboard requires an uncomfortable stretch. If you place the keyboard directly under your hands, the screen is too close for comfort.

The best you can do with a laptop is a compromise between comfort, function, and attention to the positions of your hands, arms, shoulders, and head. If you can use a separate keyboard or screen, keep them far enough apart to position them correctly. If not, do the best you can to place the screen at an angle where you can look directly at the image, and keep your arms loose and your hands level. Take more frequent breaks to stretch your arms and hands, and shift position whenever you think about it.

The other potential physical problem with a laptop computer occurs when you're not using it: when it's in its case and hanging from your shoulder. Try to eliminate any unnecessary weight from the computer bag, and move the bag from one shoulder to the other often. If you have the option of using a bag with wheels instead of a shoulder bag or backpack, that may be a much better choice.

CROSS-REF   See Chapter 25 to read about accessories that can make using your laptop more comfortable.

Summary

You can't operate your computer effectively when your hands, arms, shoulders, or neck are fighting with you. Painful muscles and nerves are your body's way of telling you that you are doing something wrong.

To prevent repetitive strain injury, take frequent breaks, and pay attention to your posture and the way you hold your hands over the keyboard. Keep your wrists level, and your hands in a neutral position. When you use the keyboard, move your entire hand and arms to distant keys, instead of just reaching with your fingers. Choose a chair that supports your lower back and arms, at a height that allows you to move your knees under the keyboard. Place the monitor screen at eye level, and adjust the contrast and brightness for the most comfortable levels relative to the ambient light in the room.

Chapter 30

Accessibility

The design of desktop and laptop computers presents special problems and challenges for people whose bodies work differently from the majority of users. Impaired vision, hearing, dexterity, or mobility can make a standard off-the-shelf computer difficult or impossible to operate. Therefore, Microsoft and the designers of many computer peripheral devices and software offer a variety of products that can make a computer more accessible. These include:

- Options and programs that can make objects on the computer screen easier to see

- Features that can make the sounds produced by the computer easier to hear, and programs that display captions and visual warnings as alternatives to sounds

- Text-to-speech and voice-operated input tools

- Adjustable mouse and keyboard options

- Alternative keyboard layouts for users who type with one hand or one finger

- Alternative input devices that do not require use of the hands, or which don't require fine motor skills

- Keyboard shortcuts for many application programs

- Programs for people who have difficulty with reading and writing

This chapter describes many of these features and options and explains how to find and use them.

Using Windows Accessibility Features

Windows XP and Windows Vista include a long list of accessibility features and utilities that can make your computer easier to use. These include adjustments and alternatives to the standard display, sounds, keyboard, and mouse performance, and a utility that accepts inputs from a pointing device or a joystick.

Using the Accessibility Wizard

The Accessibility Wizard combines many of the Windows accessibility features into a single sequence of dialog boxes. You might find a few additional combinations if you set the options one at a time, but the wizard makes the whole process a lot faster and easier.

TIP Before you run the Accessibility Wizard, save the current theme using the Display Properties dialog box. If the result of the wizard isn't what you want or need, it's easy to get back to where you started.

To run the Accessibility Wizard using a mouse, open the Start menu and choose All Programs (in the Windows XP Start menu) or Programs (in the Classic Start Menu) ➪ Accessories ➪ Accessibility ➪ Accessibility Wizard. Using a keyboard, press Ctrl+Esc or the Windows logo key, and then press the R key and type accwiz in the Run window.

Following the introductory screen, the next two dialog boxes in the Accessibility Wizard offer several options for changing the appearance of the Windows desktop. The Text Size screen, shown in Figure 30.1, offers to increase the size of the on-screen text, but it doesn't change the size of text embedded in graphic images. Choose the smallest text that you can easily read and click Next.

Next, the Display Settings dialog box (shown in Figure 30.2) offers more options to change the size of many screen elements.

When you click the Next button, Windows immediately makes the changes you requested and ask if you want to keep them. If you don't like the changes, click Cancel to return to the Display Settings dialog box and disable the option you don't like.

FIGURE 30.1

Use the Text Size dialog box to increase the size of type and windows.

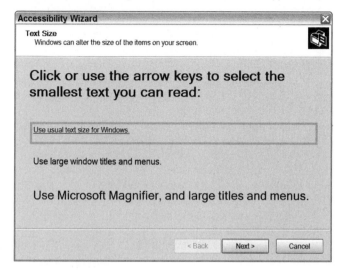

FIGURE 30.2

The Display Settings dialog box includes more options to make things bigger on the screen.

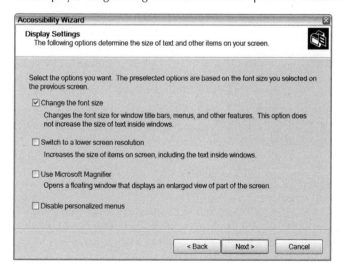

The next screen (Figure 30.3) asks you to choose the options that describe your requirements.

When you click Next, the Wizard moves on to the specific set of options and adjustments that apply to the special requirements you specified. Choose each of the settings that best fits your own specific requirements and move through the Wizard.

The last option on the list applies to administrative options. If you choose this option, the wizard opens a dialog box that offers to turn off the accessibility features after the computer has been idle for a specified period of time. This might be useful if you share your computer with other users, but you have to re-load your enhanced options as a theme when you return to the computer yourself.

If you prefer, you can change display settings and turn on other accessibility utilities one at a time. The next few sections explain what each of them does and how to use them.

FIGURE 30.3

Choose the options you want to adjust in this dialog box.

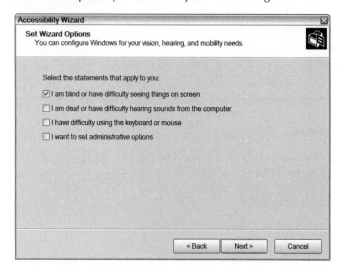

Adjusting the display

The same Display Properties options that allow you to customize the appearance of your Windows desktop and other on-screen elements also make it possible to optimize the display for users with impaired vision. Additional tools can make Web pages easier to read and magnify on-screen images.

CROSS-REF For more about adjusting the display, see Chapter 28.

Changing the desktop

Users with impaired vision can change the appearance of objects on the screen to improve visibility. When you change such elements as the size, style, and colors of text, icons, and images, and by changing the cursor's size and blink rate, these objects can be much easier to see. For example, the screen shown in Figure 30.4 shows a very high-contrast color scheme with extra-large fonts.

To set the screen elements for maximum readability, follow these steps:

1. **Move the cursor to an empty spot in the desktop and click the right mouse button.**

2. **Choose Properties from the pop-up menu, or select Display from the Control Panel.** The Display Properties window opens.

3. **Choose the Appearance tab.** The dialog box shown in Figure 30.5 appears.

4. **To create a high-contrast color scheme, open the drop-down Windows and buttons menu, select Windows Classic style, and choose one of the High Contrast options from the Color scheme menu.** Each High Contrast option is optimized for a different type of limited vision, so you should examine all four before you settle on one of them.

FIGURE 30.4

This scheme uses high-contrast colors and enormous fonts to make the screen elements easier to see.

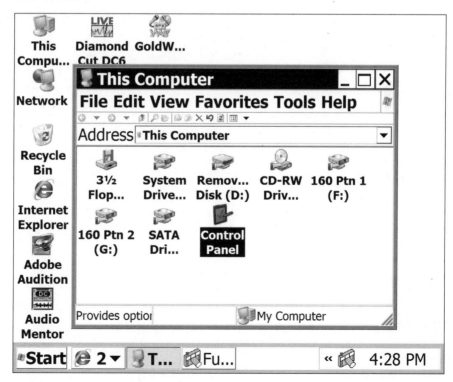

5. To increase the size of the on-screen fonts, choose either Large or Extra Large from the Font size menu.

FIGURE 30.5

Use the Appearance tab to select more visible screen elements.

Using Magnifier

Magnifier is a Windows utility that creates a magnified version of the regular desktop (including all open windows) either in the top part of the screen or in a floating window. Figure 30.6 shows a magnified screen. To turn on the Magnifier, select Start ➪ All Programs ➪ Accessories ➪ Accessibility ➪ Magnifier.

CAUTION   Using the Magnifier changes the locations of some icons on your desktop. You may have to look around to find a particular program that has moved from where you had it before changing your display.

FIGURE 30.6

The Magnifier utility displays a larger version of part of the Windows desktop and open windows.

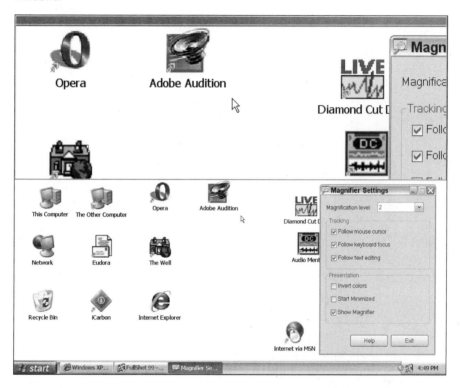

The Magnifier Settings dialog box, shown in Figure 30.7, controls the Magnifier options:

- The Magnification level menu can increase or reduce the size of the magnified image.
- When the Follow mouse cursor option is active, the magnified image moves when you move your mouse.
- When Follow keyboard focus is active, the center of the magnified image moves as you use the Tab key to choose an option or change the active window.
- When Follow text editing is active, the magnified image moves as you type, so the current text stays within the magnified window.
- When Invert colors is active, the magnified image uses a reversed color scheme within the magnified window. The inverted colors often provide higher contrast than the original color scheme.

- When Start Minimized is active, the Magnifier program opens as a button in the taskbar at the bottom of the screen instead of an open window.

- The Show Magnifier option opens the magnified window. To hide the window, disable Show Magnifier, or right-click within the magnified window and choose Hide from the pop-up list.

FIGURE 30.7

Use the Magnifier Settings dialog box to adjust the performance and appearance of the magnified image.

To increase or decrease the size of the magnified image, drag the bottom of the magnified section of the screen up or down. To move the magnified image into a floating window, position your cursor inside the magnified image, click, hold the button, and drag it toward the bottom of the screen.

As an alternative to the Magnifier program, Microsoft also offers a free Taskbar Magnifier program that can display a magnified image of part of the desktop in the taskbar, as shown in Figure 30.8. This program is available for download at `http://download.microsoft.com/download/whistler/Install/2/WXP/EN-US/MagnifierPowertoySetup.exe`.

FIGURE 30.8

The Toolbar magnifier displays an expanded version of part of the Windows desktop. Move your mouse to move the magnified section.

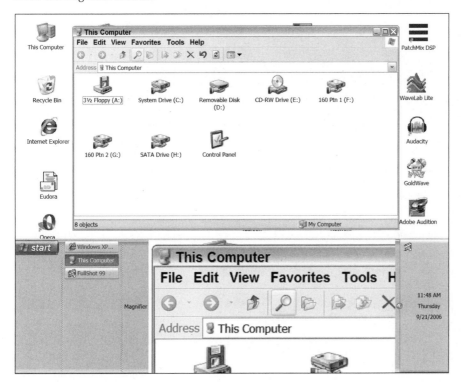

Changing Web pages

The most recent version of Internet Explorer (IE 7) includes a Zoom option that can magnify the size of the image within the browser window, as shown in Figure 30.9. Microsoft includes a free upgrade to IE 7 as part of the Windows Update program; if you have an earlier version of Internet Explorer, run Widows Update from the Internet Explorer Tools menu now.

To change the image, click the arrow next to the current percentage number in the lower right corner of the browser window, and choose the amount of magnification you want. To rapidly change among 100 percent, 125 percent, and 150 percent, click the current number. If your mouse has a scrolling wheel, you can also zoom in and out by holding down the Ctrl key and moving the wheel up or down.

FIGURE 30.9

Use the Internet Explorer Zoom feature to increase or decrease the size of Web pages.

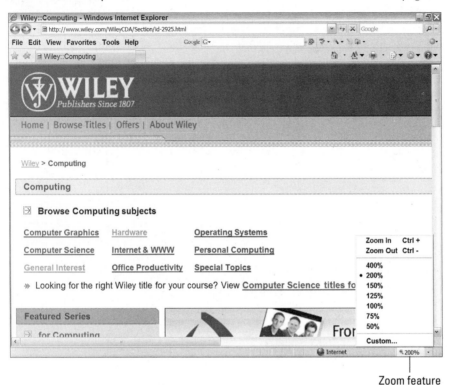

Zoom feature

Most Web sites use fonts that have been specified by the designer of each page. To override these settings and instruct Internet Explorer to use a large, easy-to-read typeface for all text (except text embedded within a graphic image in a Web page or an e-mail message), follow these steps:

1. **Open Internet Explorer.**

2. **Click the Size icon in the toolbar.** The submenu shown in Figure 30.10 appears.

3. **Choose the Larger or Largest option from the Text Size submenu.**

4. **Open the Tools menu (with the gear icon) and choose Internet Options.** The dialog box shown in Figure 30.11 appears under the General tab.

FIGURE 30.10

Use the Text Size option in the Tools menu to change the type size in Internet Explorer.

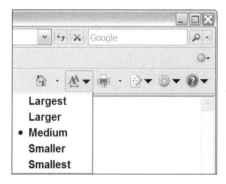

FIGURE 30.11

The General tab of the Internet Options window controls several elements of the browser's display.

5. **Click the Accessibility tab at the lower right part of the dialog box.** The Accessibility dialog box shown in Figure 30.12 appears.

6. **Turn on the Ignore font styles and Ignore font sizes options, and click OK.** The Accessibility window closes.

7. **Back in the General tab, click the Fonts button at the bottom of the window.** The Fonts dialog box shown in Figure 30.13 appears.

FIGURE 30.12

Use the Accessibility options to override font sizes and styles in Web pages.

FIGURE 30.13

Choose the fonts you want to see in Web pages.

8. **Choose the fonts you want the browser to use from each of the font menus.** When you select a font, a sample appears in the box directly below that menu; select a font in each column that is easy for you to read and click OK.

9. **In the Internet Options window, click OK to save your changes and close the dialog box.**

On-screen cues

Some users might have difficulty seeing the LED indicator lights in the keyboard that light when Caps Lock, Num Lock, or Scroll Lock are active. The ToggleKeys utility sounds an audible signal when a user turns one of those functions on; and another signal, an octave higher, sounds when the user turns it off.

To turn Toggle Keys on or off, hold down the Num Lock key for five seconds. When ToggleKeys activates, an information window appears that asks you to confirm that you want to keep the utility on.

Text-to-speech translation

Windows includes a relatively simple text-to-speech program called Narrator that can read items in several on-screen items, including the Windows desktop, Windows setup, Notepad, WordPad, Internet Explorer, and many Control Panel programs.

To turn on Narrator, select Start ➪ Programs ➪ Accessories ➪ Accessibility ➪ Narrator. To use a different voice, or to change the speed, volume, and pitch of the voice, click the Voice button to open the Voice Settings window.

Several more sophisticated text-to-speech programs are available from third-party sources, including:

CoolSpeech	www.bytecool.com/dlcoolspch.htm
TextAloud	www.nextup.com/TextAloud
NaturalReader	www.naturalreaders.com
2nd Speech Center	www.2ndspeechcenter.com
Aldo's Text-to-WAVE	www.aldostools.com/text-wav.html
ReadPlease	www.readplease.com

Many of these programs use Microsoft's Speech Application Program Interface (SAPI 5.1) and speech engines made by Lernout & Hauspie or AT&T. If a text-to-speech program requires additional software, you can find links to sources on its Web site. The AT&T Natural Voices in particular are much less artificial-sounding that the Microsoft Sam voice supplied with Windows.

Adjusting or replacing sounds

Windows and many application programs associate sounds with many actions and conditions, including alarms and notices of incoming messages through the Internet or a local network. Users with hearing impairment and users in noisy environments may have difficulty hearing those signals, so Windows provides visual alternatives to audible signals and messages. These include special sound schemes, on-screen captions, and visual signals.

Turn up the volume

In some cases, the only thing necessary to make sounds from your computer easier to hear is to make the sound louder. The Windows Volume Control (Start ⇨ All Programs ⇨ Accessories ⇨ Entertainment ⇨ Volume Control) and the physical volume control knob on the external speakers connected to your computer both provide ways to turn up the volume.

Sound schemes

A sound scheme is the set of sounds that Windows and other programs produce when specific events occur. For example, the vaguely musical sounds that play when Windows starts and ends, and the famous AOL "You've got mail" alert, are all part of sound schemes. If you (or another user of your computer) have hearing limitations that make sounds within a limited range of audio frequencies easier to hear than others, you can use an audio recording and editing program to create new WAV files to replace the ones in the Windows Default Sound Scheme.

 See Chapter 27 for step-by-step instructions for creating a new sound scheme.

ShowSounds and SoundSentry

ShowSounds and SoundSentry are Windows utilities that display signals on the screen when audible signals occur. ShowSounds displays text for speech and sounds, and SoundSentry flashes the active caption bar, window, or the entire desktop when the system produces a sound.

To turn on ShowSounds, SoundSentry or both, open the Control Panel, select Accessibility options, and choose the Sound tab.

SoundSentry only works when the computer's internal speaker is in use, so it's necessary to turn off the sound card or sound controller that drives external speakers. To disable the sound controller, follow these steps:

1. **From the Control Panel, open Sounds and Audio Devices.**

2. **In the Sounds and Audio devices dialog box, choose the Hardware tab.**

3. **In the list of devices, select the name of the sound controller and click Properties.**

4. **In the sound controller Properties dialog box, choose the Properties tab.**

5. **In the list of Multimedia devices, open the Audio Devices submenu and select the sound controller.** Click the Properties button at the bottom of the dialog box.

6. **In the new Properties dialog box, choose the General tab and select Do not use audio features on this device.**

7. **Click the OK buttons in all the open dialog boxes to close the boxes and save your changes.**

Mouse options and alternatives

Windows and the utilities supplied with many mouse drivers include several options that can make a mouse, trackball, or other pointing device easier for people with limited fine motor skills to use. To use these options, open the Mouse Properties window from the Control Panel. The specific set of options is different for different makes and models, but the most common ones include:

- **Double-Click Speed:** Set the double-click speed to Slow to allow more time to complete the sequence of two clicks.

- **ClickLock or DragLock:** This option allows a user to click an item and drag it without holding down a mouse button.

- **Pointer Speed:** This sets the rate at which the mouse cursor moves across the screen.

- **SnapTo or SmartMove:** This automatically moves the cursor to the default button in a new dialog box.

- **Cursor or Pointer Trails:** This adds shadow images behind the cursor, which makes it easier to follow as it moves across the screen.

- **Pointer Schemes:** This changes the set of on-screen cursors and pointers. Options include high-contrast and extra-large pointers.

- **Reverse Left and Right Buttons:** This swaps the functions of the left and right mouse buttons. Because the left button is used most often, it should be under the strongest finger.

MouseKeys

Windows also includes the MouseKeys utility that allows a user to control the mouse pointer with the numeric keypad at the right side of most desktop keyboards, and the numeric keypad option on a laptop keyboard.

To turn on MouseKeys, follow these steps:

1. **From the Control Panel, choose Accessibility Options.**

2. **Open the Mouse tab.** The dialog box shown in Figure 30.14 appears.

3. **Activate the Use MouseKeys option and click the Settings button.** The Settings for MouseKeys dialog box shown in Figure 30.15 opens.

4. **Set the options to control the way you want MouseKeys to respond.** Click OK to close each window. Notice that there's now an image of a two-button mouse in the system tray.

FIGURE 30.14

Turn on MouseKeys to control the mouse pointer with your numeric keypad.

To use the numeric keypad as a replacement for your mouse, press the Num Lock key. If the icon in the system tray shows a slash through it, push Num Lock again.

MouseKeys accepts these commands from the numeric keypad:

- Press one of the arrow keys to move the pointer in the direction of that arrow.
- Press the 1, 3, 7, or 9 key to move the pointer diagonally.
- Press the 5 key to click.
- Press the + key to right-click
- Press the Ins and then an arrow or diagonal key to drag an object such as a desktop icon.
- Press the Del key to release an object.

FIGURE 30.15

Use the Settings window to control MouseKeys options.

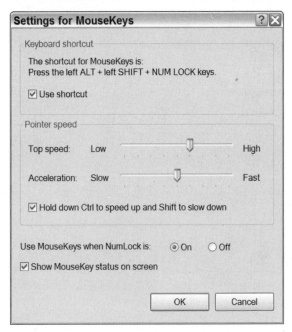

Alternatives to conventional mice

Many alternative devices are available for users who have difficulty using conventional mice and trackballs. These include touch screens, joysticks, foot pedals, puff switches, and cameras or infrared devices that follow eye movements or head movements. For more information, run a Web search using the keywords assistive technology or start at the Microsoft guide to assistive technology products at www.microsoft.com/enable/at.

Keyboard options and alternatives

Several Windows utilities can assist users who have difficulty operating a keyboard. These include StickyKeys, which allows a user to enter multiple-key commands by pressing one key at a time; FilterKeys, which instructs Windows to ignore keys held down for an extended period of time; and an On-Screen Keyboard that allows a user to enter keystrokes with a mouse.

To run StickyKeys or FilterKeys, open the Control Panel and select Accessibility Options. The Keyboard tab in the Accessibility Options window, shown in Figure 30.16, contains the controls for both programs, along with ToggleKeys (described earlier, in the "On-screen cues" section).

FIGURE 30.16

Use the Accessibility Options control to turn StickyKeys and FilterKeys on or off.

StickyKeys

StickyKeys allows people who have difficulty pressing two keys or more at the same time to enter keyboard shortcuts and other commands that use multiple keys, such as Ctrl+F4, Alt+Esc, or Ctrl+Alt+Del. StickyKeys makes it practical to use these commands with one finger, or with a head stick or mouthstick.

To turn StickyKeys on or off, press either Shift key five times. When you turn the program on or off, you will hear a series of tones. When StickyKeys is active, pressing Shift, Ctrl, Alt, or the Windows Logo key once latches that key down until you press some other, non-latching key. If you press a latching key twice, it stays down until you press the same key one more time.

FilterKeys

Erratic motion tremors, slow response time, or other random hand or finger motion can produce unwanted inputs, so FilterKeys can disable the keyboard input features that would otherwise respond to rapid or prolonged keystrokes.

FilterKeys includes two options: RepeatKeys, which can adjust or disable the repeat rate, and SlowKeys, which instructs the computer to ignore rapidly repeated keystrokes. To configure FilterKeys, click the FilterKeys Settings button in the Keyboard tab of the Accessibility Options window.

When FilterKeys is active, you can turn it on or off by holding the right Shift key down for five seconds. (The Settings dialog box says eight seconds, but on some computers it might turn on or off after five seconds. Go figure.)

On-Screen Keyboard

The On-Screen Keyboard included in Windows (Start ⇨ All Programs ⇨ Accessories ⇨ Accessibility ⇨ On-Screen Keyboard) shown in Figure 30.17 can accept mouse clicks or commands from a joystick or other pointing device. Microsoft admits that On-Screen Keyboard is a klunky program (they call it a *limited solution*) that does not lend itself to daily use, but it does have its uses.

FIGURE 30.17

On-Screen Keyboard accepts inputs from a mouse or other pointing device.

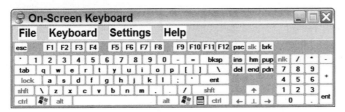

Several third-party on-screen virtual keyboards offer more and better features for users who can't use a physical keyboard. Each has a somewhat different feature set, so you need to examine all of them before you install one. For more information, see the developers' Web sites:

WiVik On-Screen Keyboard Software	www.wivik.com
SofType	www.orin.com/access/softype
OnScreen	http://imgpresents.com/onscreen/onscreen.htm
MiloSoft Virtual On-Screen Keyboard	www.march-of-faces.org/resources/vkt.html
REACH Interface Author	www.ahf-net.com/reach.htm
The Grid	www.zygo-usa.com/grid.html
Gus! Access Keyboard	www.gusinc.com/accessbrd.html

Alternative keyboards

In some cases, replacing the conventional QWERTY keyboard with a keyboard designed for users with special needs can be all that is necessary. This category can include traditional keyboards with big keys or large, high-contrast letters printed on the keys; keyboards with special layouts; keyboards for one-handed users; and keyboards for one-finger, head stick or mouthstick typing.

For links to sources for these keyboards, search the Web using the keywords adaptive keyboards or assistive keyboards.

Making Public Computers More Accessible

Microsoft's Shared Computer Toolkit (described in Chapter 34) includes features that allow users with special needs to turn on one or more accessibility utilities on a computer in a public location such as a classroom or a library, without changing the settings for other users.

Summary

Personal computers should be accessible to everybody. The Accessibility features and options in Windows are designed to overcome many of the difficulties that confront users with special needs. These include utilities that produce sounds to accompany on-screen information for users with limited or impaired vision, utilities that display information on the screen for users with difficulty hearing, and still others for people who are unable to use a mouse or keyboard.

Microsoft also cooperates with other hardware and software developers who produce more specialized adaptive and assistive products that meet the needs of users with specific requirements.

Part VI

Putting Your Computer to Work

Chapter 31

Working with Microsoft Windows

The first piece of software that is added to a computer is an underlying framework that allows all other programs to be easily accessed and configured. This underlying framework is called the *operating system (OS)*.

A computer's operating system controls all the communications between the system's software and its hardware. Its tasks include managing memory and device requests, saving and recalling data files, and enabling networking and security.

For PCs the most popular choice is the Windows operating system created by Microsoft. This chapter looks at the history of the Windows operating system, explains the installation process, loading device drivers and software, and concludes with a look ahead to the Vista version of Windows.

Understanding Operating Systems

Much of the book thus far has focused on *hardware,* which are the physical components that make up the computer. Hardware includes the computer itself, its keyboard and mouse, and any connected devices such as printers, scanners, and even your iPod.

Another important element of computers is the software. The term *software* means the programs loaded onto the computer to enable it to do things like send email, view a Web page, compose documents, calculate taxes, and make presentations. Software usually comes on a CD-ROM or a DVD and needs to be installed before it works on your system.

Operating system functionality

In between the hardware and software is an important piece known as the operating system (OS). The operating system has several important tasks that it does including:

- **Managing memory:** The operating system controls and manages all the requests for system memory.

- **Controls input/output devices:** The operating system handles all data coming from input devices like the keyboard and mouse and all documents being output such as print jobs.

- **Prioritizes system requests:** When several hardware requests are made at the same time, the operating system decides which request gets answered first and keeps track of the lower priority requests.

- **Networking:** Access to networking systems is made possible through the operating system.

- **Security:** Operating systems also include security measures that keep the data safe from unauthorized users.

- **Organizes data and files:** All data and files that are written to the hard drive are done through the operating system. This includes writing files and reading them back.

Although the core level functionality of an operating system includes the low-level operations required to do the things listed above, many operating systems also include a host of utility programs that provide an added level of functionality. These utilities can include simple programs such as a calculator, a day planner, and more advanced utilities like file managers and virus checkers.

CROSS-REF You can learn more about the available operating system utilities in Chapter 49.

Operating system options

Some operating systems have text-based interface, but recent operating systems such as Windows, Mac OS, and Linux use a Graphical User Interface (GUI). These interfaces let you interact with the operating system by manipulating graphical icons and controls using a mouse device.

Several different operating systems exist, including Windows, Linux, Unix, and Mac OS. Some of these choices are built to operate on a specific computer system. For example, Mac OS is designed to work on Macintosh computers, but others like Linux are *system agnostic*, meaning they can run on any hardware.

CROSS-REF You can read more about the other available operating systems in Chapter 33.

Most PCs come pre-configured with the Windows operating system, but even within the Windows operating system, there are many different versions available. Software is designed to work with only a specific operating system, so if you purchase a copy of Microsoft Office for Windows, it will not work on a Macintosh system and vice versa.

Choosing a Version

If you look closely at the current version of Windows, you can find several different flavors. Different users need different sets of features. This section provides a glimpse at the various iterations in the Windows evolution.

Windows evolution

Throughout Microsoft's history, several different versions of Windows have appeared, with each new version building on the successes of the previous versions.

 In between each new version, Microsoft typically makes regular updates available as Service Packs. These Service Packs include fixes and improvements to the current system.

DOS

Microsoft's first operating system was a text-based system of commands known as the Disk Operating System, or DOS for short. It worked by allowing users to type in specific commands that could manage the hard drive data and files.

After several versions of DOS, Microsoft branched into a new visual user interface that relied on a unique device known as a mouse to move a cursor around the screen. A similar interface had been used on the popular new Macintosh computers that appeared around the same time.

Windows 3.1

Early versions of Windows were problematic, but offered a uniquely different operating system that didn't require users to memorize all the DOS text commands. Windows 3.1 marked a stable version release that was adopted extensively by business users. It allowed common users access to an operating system that was easy to use and efficient.

However, this version of Windows ran on top of the stable DOS system, maintaining support for those users that had mastered the skill of working with DOS. It also allowed any problems with the Windows software to be quickly remedied using the underlying DOS system.

Another huge advantage of Windows 3.1 was all the applications that shipped with the system. Right out of the box came utilities such as a calculator, WordPad, a paint program, and even games.

Windows 95 and 98

In 1995, Microsoft released a new version of Windows that was completely redesigned. The new version was called Windows 95 and it was quickly adopted by the home market. Three years later an updated version named Windows 98 was released that was much more stable and robust.

Windows NT

About the same time that Windows 95 was dominating the consumer market, Windows NT was making inroads into the higher-end workstation and business markets. Windows NT differed from Windows 95 in that it was no longer built on top of a DOS system, but was instead a native operating system. This gave Windows NT additional security features that made it work well for businesses.

Windows 2000 and ME

Windows 2000 was an updated version of Windows NT aimed at the business market. It included many of the security features that made Windows NT so popular, but it also was streamlined, allowing access to the trickier functions like the Windows Registry without confusing the non-technical user.

For the home market, Microsoft released Windows Millennium Edition (ME).

Windows XP

In 2002, Windows XP was released, taking the operating system to a new level. Windows XP was redesigned to be more efficient than its predecessors while including many of the Windows NT advancements in networking and security.

There are several different versions of Windows XP available, each with its own unique set of features. These versions include the following:

 **There are also several different flavors of Windows Server that aren't included here.**

- **Windows XP Home Edition:** The Home Edition is focused for home computers.
- **Windows XP Professional Edition:** The Professional Edition includes additional security features and the ability to remotely access the system.
- **Windows XP 64-Bit Edition:** The 64-Bit Edition has a larger data pipeline for using software optimized for 64-bit architectures.
- **Windows XP Tablet PC Edition:** The Tablet PC Edition is designed specifically for Tablet PCs that includes support for writing commands instead of typing them.
- **Windows XP Media Center Edition:** The Media Center Edition includes support for television and stereo systems so programs can be recorded and saved using hard drive space.

Windows CE

About the same time as Windows XP was being developed, a new version of Windows called Windows CE was released. This version was made for PDA devices and provided the familiar Windows tools on a smaller system.

Windows Vista

The latest desktop version of Windows, named Windows Vista, is right around the corner and Microsoft promises that it will be the best version yet. See the "What's New in Windows Vista" section later in this chapter for more details on Windows Vista.

Determining which version you have

If you're unfamiliar with the subtle differences between the various versions of Windows, there is a simple utility that you can run that tells you the current version of Windows that you're running.

To determine which version of Windows you're running, follow these steps:

1. **Select the Start ⇨ Run menu to open a dialog box where you can execute commands.**
2. **In the Run dialog box that appears, type** winver **and press OK.**
3. **An information dialog box, shown in Figure 31.1, appears.** This dialog box shows the current version number and any service pack that is installed. It also lists the amount of memory available on the computer.

FIGURE 31.1

The About Windows dialog box lists the version number for the current version of Windows.

Loading Windows

For most PCs, the task of loading Windows happens automatically at the plant where the computer is assembled. A large majority of computer-makers preload the latest version of Windows on new computers.

New computers often ship with an installation CD of Windows that can be used to reinstall Windows if any problems arise.

 If your computer doesn't ship with a separate installation CD, you can contact Microsoft and they will send you an installation CD for a nominal fee.

If you ever need to reinstall Windows on your computer, follow these steps:

1. **Insert the Windows installation CD into your computer's CD-ROM or DVD drive.**

2. **Before you can install Windows on a computer, you need to get access to your computer's CD-ROM or DVD drive.** You can set the computer hardware to boot from a CD using the BIOS settings. When you first turn the computer on, a message appears stating how you can access the BIOS. Within the BIOS menu, look for an option that lets you boot from a CD and enable it. Save the changes.

 Some computers recognize and run the inserted CD without having to change the computer's BIOS.

3. **A note appears asking if you want to boot from the CD.** Type the letter *Y* to okay this action. The basic operating system features load and the installation process begins.

4. **Follow the installation steps to start the installation.** One of the installation steps lets you choose which Windows components to install.

CAUTION While Windows is installing, it first searches for an existing installation of Windows. If one is found, Windows offers an option to repair the current version instead of installing the entire OS again. However, during the installation process, some files may be erased or the entire hard drive may be formatted, which erases all the data on the hard drive. Be sure to back up all data that you want to save before installing (or repairing) Windows.

5. **After all the selected components are installed, the computer automatically restarts.** You are greeted with a Windows welcome screen.

Understanding Device Drivers

An operating system is not only the underlying system for accessing and working with software applications installed on the computer; it also provides a framework for the peripheral devices connected to the computer to work.

When a new piece of hardware is connected to the computer, it requires that a piece of software be included that allows the hardware to communicate with the existing operating system. These pieces of software are called *device drivers*, or *drivers* for short.

New pieces of hardware usually come with a CD-ROM or disk that includes the device driver on it. Some installation CDs include their own installation programs, or you can use the Windows process to install the device drivers.

NOTE For devices that don't ship with a device driver CD or disk, Windows has quite a number of generic drivers that can be used.

Over time, hardware companies release updated device drivers that fix existing problems and provide better integration with your system. Some hardware automatically detects and installs these updated device drivers, or you can manually install them yourself.

 Some simple devices such as a mouse or a keyboard are fine using the generic drivers, but other devices such as video graphic cards can benefit greatly from updated drivers.

Adding new hardware to your system

The latest versions of Windows include a Plug and Play feature that allows the computer to detect when a new piece of hardware has been connected to the current system. When detected it automatically begins the process of installing the necessary device drivers. During the installation process, the computer asks that you insert the installation disk where it can load the device driver.

If the new hardware doesn't have an installation disk, then you can install the new hardware using the Add Hardware Wizard, shown in Figure 31.2. You can access this wizard from the Control Panel. The first step of the wizard searches your system for any newly installed hardware. If a new hardware device is found, the wizard asks you to load the CD or disk that contains the new device driver.

FIGURE 31.2

The Add Hardware Wizard lets you install and troubleshoot new hardware.

Using Device Manager

If a hardware device starts to work improperly, it could be that the device is starting to fail or that the device driver has become corrupt. You can replace or upgrade device drivers using the Device Manager. You can open the Device Manager by double-clicking the System icon in the Control Panel. This opens the System Properties dialog box. To open the Device Manager, select the Hardware tab and click the Device Manager button.

The Device Manager window, shown in Figure 31.3, shows all the installed hardware for the current system. If you select a specific hardware device from the list and open its Properties dialog box, you can see specific information on the selected hardware.

FIGURE 31.3

The Device Manager shows all hardware installed on the current system.

The Properties dialog box for the selected hardware includes several tabs. The General tab, shown in Figure 31.4, shows the hardware's type, manufacturer, and installation location. There is also a status field that explains if the hardware is having any trouble.

The Driver tab of the Properties dialog box, shown in Figure 31.5, displays the current driver version and date. It also includes buttons to get more details about the driver, update the current driver, roll back the current driver, and uninstall the driver.

FIGURE 31.4

The Properties dialog box displays the details about the selected hardware.

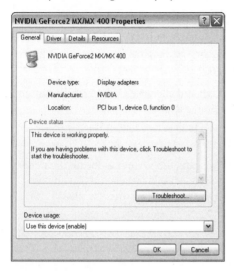

FIGURE 31.5

The Driver tab of the Properties dialog box has an option to display the details about the selected hardware's device driver.

To update a hardware device driver, follow these steps:

1. Select Start ➪ Control Panel to open the Control Panel.

2. Double-click the System icon in the Control Panel.

3. Select the Hardware tab and click the Device Manager button.

4. In the Device Manager, select the hardware device that you want to update and choose the Action ➪ Properties menu command.

5. In the Properties dialog box, select the Driver tab and click the Update Driver button. This opens the Hardware Update Wizard, shown in Figure 31.6.

6. If you have the updated device driver on CD or disk, select Install the software automatically and click Next.

7. The next step of the Hardware Update Wizard scans the system to locate the new device driver. If the device driver is found, it is automatically installed. If it cannot be found, you can go back in the wizard and try to locate the device driver manually.

FIGURE 31.6

The Hardware Update Wizard guides you through installing new device drivers.

 Before accessing the Hardware Update Wizard, download the new updated device driver to the desktop where it can be easily located.

Finding and Installing Patches, Service Packs, and Upgrades

Even though software is released, development teams continue to work to improve the software and to track and eliminate bugs that can hamper the software. When a fix to a bug is found, the software company informs the registered users that a fix is available.

> **NOTE** When you register a purchased software product, most software vendors offer an option to request software update information as it becomes available.

These incremental updates are frequently called *patches* because they don't reinstall the entire piece of software, only the file or files that are in error. Software patches are generally small and can install quickly to fix existing problems.

When several important patches are combined together into a larger package, they are commonly called *service packs*. Service packs in general are much larger and take a considerably longer time to install, usually requiring the software or even the entire computer to be restarted.

An upgrade can be small or large, but it typically denotes a new feature that is available for you to add to the software.

Whether you're working with a patch, a service pack, or an upgrade, the methods for installing the fix are all about the same. The new files need to be installed using an installation routine. You can do this via a CD-ROM, a floppy disk, or via a downloaded file from the Internet.

Using Automatic Updates

Several software packages including Windows XP can automatically locate and install software updates using the Internet. Using the Automatic Updates option, you can select to check for updates daily or weekly; or you could set Windows to automatically download or notify you when updates are available without installing the updates.

To enable Automatic Updates for Windows, follow these steps:

1. Select Start ⇨ Control Panel to open the Control Panel.
2. Double-click the Automatic Updates icon in the Control Panel.

> **TIP** You can also access the Automatic Updates panel from the System Properties dialog box.

3. In the Automatic Updates panel, shown in Figure 31.7, select the Automatic option and choose an update time when you computer is likely to be idle. Click OK.

FIGURE 31.7

The Automatic Updates tab lets you select an option that searches for Windows updates on a daily basis.

CAUTION If you're concerned about letting Microsoft install updates for you automatically, you might want to consider selecting the Download updates for me but let me choose when to install them option or the Notify me but don't automatically download or install them option instead of Automatic.

What's New in Windows Vista

As the evolution of Windows continues, the next version of the popular operating system is Windows Vista. Vista is intended to be an even easier system than ever before. With Vista, the key is being able to visually manage and organize your data more efficiently than in previous versions. To accomplish this, Vista allows you to see the content of files without having to open them, and includes more wizards that make difficult tasks easy.

To help you quickly locate what you're looking for, Vista's new Instant Search lets you type a word or phrase, and the file is quickly located and able to be launched. The new Windows Flip feature displays all open applications as thumbnails, and Flip 3D lets you use the mouse scroll wheel to quickly move between open documents.

Vista's new security features are focused on keeping malicious software, including viruses, off your computer. These features also keep the Internet a safe place to browse.

You can position the Vista Sidebar off to the side of the screen where it can display mini applications such as weather reports, movie clips, or music files.

Vista includes several new features that take advantage of flash memory to improve performance, save battery power, and load files quicker. Vista's new Restore and Backup features provide several layers of backup, insuring that you can recover quickly from system crashes without losing any data.

Windows Vista includes a powerful Speech Recognition engine that lets you dictate documents and control basic commands by speaking them in lieu of typing commands on the keyboard and using the mouse. The result is a system that is much more efficient, allowing you to work quicker.

CAUTION Even though Vista promises to be another leap forward in productivity, many companies are wary of the new OS until it has had time to be proven in a business setting. If you're concerned about how Vista might impact your computer, you may want to wait until the system is proven.

Summary

A computer's operating system is the framework that enables the installed software to communicate with the computer's hardware to get work done. The operating system is responsible for managing memory, reading and writing data to the hard drives, and controlling the input and output requests from the various connected devices. There are several different operating systems available.

Continual development and improvement have resulted in the Windows versions used by millions of people throughout the world. Windows typically comes preinstalled on new PCs, but you can choose to reinstall it using the Windows CDs.

Device drivers are software that let the operating system control the connected system hardware. You can update these drivers using the Device Manager; updating a driver can improve the performance of a problem device.

Software updates can include simple patches or more comprehensive service packs. Some software, including Windows, can automatically search for and install updates using the Internet.

Vista is the next-generation version of Windows and offers PC users a new level of efficiency.

Chapter 32

Essential Software

Computer hardware by itself doesn't allow you to do much, but when coupled with the proper software, the system can run businesses, control your finances, and provide endless entertainment.

There are several categories of software; some are essential for maintaining a safe, functioning computer environment, others are productivity based, and others are simply fun.

The software that you include on your computer system depends on your budget and how you want to use the computer. This chapter provides a guide to some software to consider when setting up, buying, or updating a system.

IN THIS CHAPTER

Learning software for Internet access

Using Utilities software

Discovering the available application software

Playing computer games

Software for Accessing the Internet

The software for connecting your computer to the Internet is meant to be used in conjunction with an access account. So, there are actually two key decisions that you need to make in order to access the Internet. The first question deals with selecting an Internet service provider (ISP), and the second question deals with the software that you use to surf the Web.

An ISP is a company that has powerful dedicated computers (called *servers*) connected directly to the Internet. These servers provide features such as e-mail and hosting Web content, but before you can access these functions, you need to be connected to the Internet, and you need to pay the ISP in order to establish a connection.

CROSS-REF   You can learn more about the details of locating an ISP and connecting to the Internet in Chapter 46.

Selecting a Web browser

Once you have access through an ISP, you can turn your attention to the software that you need to browse the Internet. The main piece of software used to view Web pages on the Internet is a Web browser. There are several different Web browser choices available, and all of them are free to download and use. The real cost of the Internet is the monthly fee for getting access to the ISP servers. The most popular available Web browsers include the following:

- **Microsoft Internet Explorer:** Built into Windows, this browser is the most popular among Windows users.

- **Netscape Navigator:** Owned by AOL, this browser includes special features for AOL users. You can download Netscape from `http://browser.netscape.com`.

- **Opera:** This Web browser is available for all systems and can be used on cell phones and PDAs also. You can download the latest Opera Web browser at `www.opera.com`.

- **Mozilla Firefox:** The Firefox Web browser provides security and the ability to add on new features. You can download Firefox for free at `www.mozilla.com`.

It's true that Internet Explorer is by far the most popular Web browser, but if you are having trouble with Internet Explorer or just don't like some of its features, you can always switch without any trouble.

On all Web browsers, users can enter a Web address (also known as a URL, which stands for Uniform Resource Locator) in the address bar at the top of the browser window. Entering a URL causes the browser to download and display the Web pages located at that address. Browsers also include Forward and Back buttons for navigating between recently visited pages.

The Favorites feature lets you save your favorite Web pages to a list that can be easily revisited. If you don't know an exact URL for the topic you want to research or the item you want to find, Web browsers also let you search the Web for sites by entering specific key words in the address bar. If there's a particular site that you want to access frequently, such as your e-mail package or an online shopping catalog, you can save its URL to a Favorites list. This list provides easy access by keeping the URLs of your favorite sites at your fingertips. Figure 32.1 shows Internet Explorer, where you can select these features from a toolbar at the top of the browser window.

FIGURE 32.1

Microsoft Internet Explorer includes a range of common browser features, making it easy to move around the Web.

Choosing an e-mail package

After you're connected to the Internet, you are able to send and receive e-mail using a separate e-mail package, or *client*. This piece of software may be one of the most used on your computer.

Windows includes Microsoft Outlook Express, but other e-mail clients are also available, including the following:

- **Microsoft Outlook:** Bundled with the Microsoft Office suite, Outlook includes a wide range of features including content and time management, a rules-based engine, and features to organize and archive e-mail content.

- **Microsoft Outlook Express:** Built into Windows, the Outlook Express e-mail client is a simplified version of Microsoft Outlook.

- **Netscape Communicator:** Owned by AOL, this e-mail client includes special features for AOL users. Netscape's e-mail client is included as part of the Netscape browser; you can download it from http://browser.netscape.com.

- **Eudora:** This e-mail client provides specialized customization features that make it a favorite of many users. You can learn more about Eudora at www.eudora.com.

■ **Novell GroupWise:** This e-mail package includes a robust e-mail client along with many scheduling and collaboration tools.

■ **Lotus Notes:** Used by large corporations around the world, Lotus Notes includes a suite of contact and communication tools.

■ **Firefox e-mail:** An e-mail client integrated with the Firefox Web browser.

Of all the e-mail client features, finding an e-mail client that is easy to use is one of the most important features to look for. It is also important to have an e-mail client that is secure and reliable. Figure 32.2 shows Microsoft Outlook Express, a relatively simple and easy-to-use e-mail client.

CROSS-REF You can learn more about how to use an e-mail client in Chapter 46.

FIGURE 32.2

Microsoft Outlook Express is simple and easy to use.

E-mail clients both send and receive e-mails. They also include an Address Book that makes it easy to select and recall the e-mail addresses of frequent contacts.

The more complex e-mail clients offer e-mail along with several integrated features for scheduling and planning your time. For example, Microsoft Outlook includes a Calendar feature, Tasks list, journal, and Contact list. All of these features are integrated to work hand-in-hand with the e-mail client, as shown in Figure 32.3. For example, the Calendar feature lets you add in important dates such as birthdays and anniversaries, and Windows notifies you on these dates with a reminder.

A common collaboration feature available in most e-mail clients is instant messaging. This feature opens a text window where you can connect to other users that are online at the same. The text that you type and send is instantly relayed to the connected user and their response can be immediately returned.

One feature that is becoming more important is the e-mail client's ability to handle spam. *Spam* is any unsolicited message sent to your e-mail client. These e-mails, in addition to being annoying, can be a security risk. E-mail clients handle spam by searching for specific text phrases and routing these e-mails to a quarantined folder where they can be isolated and deleted. Most of the higher-end e-mail clients include these features.

NOTE Most e-mail servers have a limit on the size of attachment that can be sent via an e-mail. If the e-mail size is too large, the server typically sends a response to the sender's e-mail detailing the problem.

FIGURE 32.3

Microsoft Outlook includes calendaring, scheduling, and collaboration features.

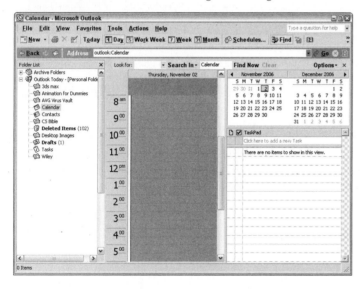

E-mails can include attached files. To attach a file to be sent with an e-mail, simply select the Insert ⇨ File menu or click the Attach File button (the actual command depends on the e-mail client that you're using). This opens a window where you can browse for the file that you want to send. The attached e-mail is listed at the top of the new e-mail.

If the attached file is one that Windows recognizes, then the icon for the application that opens the attachment is displayed along with the attachment's file name. If the file is one that Windows recognizes, you can double-click to open it using the identified application or you could right click on the file name and select an option to save the file.

CAUTION   Attached files can be a risk if you don't know the source of the attachment. The best practice is to never open an e-mail attachment unless you know the sender and the file he or she is sending. If a harmful e-mail is sent to you and you delete it without opening any of its attachments, it can't do your system any harm.

Some e-mail attachments, such as pictures, can be embedded within the e-mail. Embedded files don't require a separate application to open and view them; you can view them from within the e-mail client.

Using Web mail

When an e-mail client is installed, it is typically placed and configured for the local machine only (the exception is for network installations). So if you're on a business trip and stop at an Internet café to check your e-mail, you won't have the same e-mail client available. Most ISPs include a Web mail client that works within a Web Browser. You can access Web e-mail clients by simply entering the ISP's Web address and logging into the client.

Once logged in, you can check for and send new e-mails. Checking e-mails using a Web browser makes the e-mails visible, but doesn't download them to the local computer. This way, when you get back home, the e-mails are still available for downloading to your personal computer's e-mail client.

Using firewall, antivirus, and other security software

When your computer is connected to the Internet, others connected to the Internet have access to your computer and data unless you've installed and configured software to protect your data. To help keep your computer and data safe, you need to install some software that makes it difficult for other users to get access to your files.

Enabling Windows Firewall

A firewall is a piece of software (or hardware in some cases) that monitors all programs running on a computer and prevents any outside programs from running on the local system. The latest version of Windows includes a firewall, or you could install a separate firewall package that has additional features.

To see the Windows Firewall settings, open the Control Panel and double-click the Windows Firewall option. This opens the Windows Firewall dialog box, shown in Figure 32.4, where you can enable and configure the firewall application.

To enable the Windows Firewall, simply select On. If the Don't allow exceptions option is enabled, every time you run a program a warning dialog box appears stating that the application is blocked from running. The warning dialog box includes an option to allow the program to run, but it can be annoying to see this warning every time you run a program.

FIGURE 32.4

The Windows Firewall dialog box lets you enable the firewall for your system.

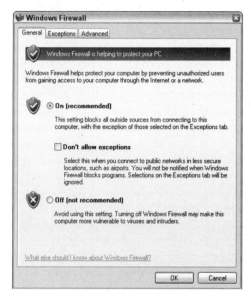

The Exceptions panel of the Windows Firewall dialog box, shown in Figure 32.5, includes a list of local programs allowed to run without any warning. To add a program to the Exceptions list, click the Add Program button and select the program that you want to run.

If you need to communicate with a single computer on the Internet or over the Internet (such as when playing a network game), you can open up a port to that specific computer using the Add Port button. This button opens the Add a Port dialog box, where you can name the connection and identify a *port number*. A port number is like an address to where the external program or computer can connect. If you're playing a network game, the game tells you which port it is looking to connect to.

CAUTION Many malicious computer users scan for open ports on your system as a way to get access. If you open a port, be sure to close it back up when you're finished or unwanted visitors could access your system.

Although enabling Windows Firewall is a good start, computer hackers are always looking for new ways to penetrate current security solutions. The Windows development team is active in identifying and blocking these security holes. The new security blocks are delivered as updates after they have been developed and tested. In order to keep your computer and data safe, you should regularly install these new updates.

CROSS-REF   Information on finding and installing updates is covered in Chapter 31.

FIGURE 32.5

The Exceptions tab of the Windows Firewall dialog box lets you identify programs that can run without any warning.

Protecting against virus threats

A computer virus is a small program intended to harm the data on a computer. Some viruses are created as pranks, but others are intended to destroy all the data on your system. Antivirus software can detect and eliminate potentially dangerous viruses and are necessary to keep a system safe.

There are different types of viruses, but they are typically categorized by their purpose and the way they propagate. Of all the various types of viruses, the more common viruses include the following:

- **Virus:** Any program that attaches itself to other files or to the computer's framework (boot sector) to avoid detection and replicates itself to insure its survival.

- **Worm:** A program that copies itself and spreads throughout the computer and to other computers using Internet and network connections or e-mail.

- **Trojan Horse:** A file disguised as a valid file that acts harmfully when opened. Trojan horses often come through e-mail as attachments.

- **Hoax:** An e-mail that instructs you to delete a dangerous file from your system, but the file that you are deleting is actually a needed system file.

- **Phishing e-mail:** Another dangerous e-mail type states that there is a problem with your bank account or credit card account and asks you to log in, but the login is to a different site where the sender can steal your bank login information or credit card information, thereby getting access to your account.

NOTE The short list above is not a complete list of the possible threats to your system. New types of viruses are developed and launched all the time. To be safe, keep your security programs up-to-date and be skeptical of any unknown e-mails.

Although Windows includes a rudimentary antivirus offering, you want to purchase and install a full antivirus package. When looking for an antivirus package, look for one that has regular updates using the Internet. This insures that your system remains safe from new viruses that appear all the time.

NOTE Just as with all types of software, some antivirus packages are excellent and others are essentially junk. If you're concerned about the quality of the software package you are considering, look for reviews and ratings on various Web sites to find a quality package that fits your particular needs.

Another feature to look for is an antivirus package that can integrate with your e-mail client, providing security from viruses and spam coming through as e-mails.

The following list of antivirus software vendors includes offerings that are up-to-date and easy to integrate.

- **Symantec:** One of the most popular antivirus packages is Norton Antivirus created by Symantec. You can learn about this package at `www.symantec.com`.

- **Grisoft:** Makers of the popular AVG antivirus package. You can find more information about their products at `www.grisoft.com`.

- **McAfee:** McAfee offers a suite of antivirus offerings, including an online antivirus solution that works by simply logging onto their site. Visit `www.mcafee.com` to learn more.

- **Computer Associates:** CA's Antivirus suite offers protection from multiple virus attacks. You can learn more about CA's antivirus software at `www.ca.com`.

NOTE The above list is by no means comprehensive. Many Internet sites include lists of available antivirus software vendors.

Antivirus software such as Grisoft's AVG package, shown in Figure 32.6, includes control centers where you can search for new updates, scan the entire system, or configure the protection features.

FIGURE 32.6

Antivirus features are typically controlled using a command center interface.

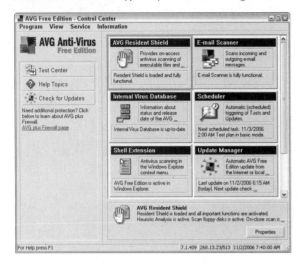

CROSS-REF You can learn more about using antivirus software in Chapter 48.

Pop-up blocker

Another piece of security software that has become necessary is a pop-up blocker. This software prevents annoying advertisement Web pages from launching. Although there is nothing wrong with a single Web page being loaded to show some product that you may be interested in, some Web sites go way overboard, causing these Web page ads to launch faster than you can close them, bringing the system to a standstill.

Pop-up blockers can be installed as separate applications, or you can install them as a Web browser add-on. The latest version of Internet Explorer includes an integrated pop-up blocker. You can enable this feature using the Tools ⇨ Pop-up Blocker ⇨ Turn On Pop-up Blocker menu.

You can access the Pop-up Blocker Settings dialog box, shown in Figure 32.7, using the Tools ⇨ Pop-up Blocker ⇨ Pop-up Blocker Settings menu command in Internet Explorer. Using the Settings dialog box, you can set the Filter Level to Low, Medium, or High. The Settings dialog box also lets you enter Web sites where pop-ups are allowed.

TIP If the Filter Level is set to High, you can temporarily disable it by holding down the Ctrl key.

FIGURE 32.7

The Pop-up Blocker Settings dialog box lets you specify Web sites where pop-ups are allowed.

Adobe Reader and Flash

The Web is a text-based tool that displays information in its limiting format, but there are other data formats that display a more richly designed format. Two such products are Adobe Portable Document Format (PDF) and Adobe Flash.

Both of these formats require that you install a special piece of software within the browser before you can view them, the Adobe Reader opens PDF files and Flash files are viewed with the Flash player. Downloading and installing these viewers is as easy as clicking on a link; the Web browser doesn't even need to be restarted to work. You can download Adobe Reader and Flash Player for free from the Adobe site at www.adobe.com.

Viewing PDF files

Adobe Reader produces documents using the PDF format. You can view PDF files on a Web page or transmit them using e-mail, but you can only view them when using a freely available, specialized reader that can open and view these files.

Once you install Adobe Reader, you can open and view PDF files using the stand-alone reader, shown in Figure 32.8, or within a Web browser. You can search, print and zoom PDF files as needed. The key benefit of PDF files is that their formatting is retained just as the designers intended; once a PDF is created, it is a read-only document. Other viewers cannot alter it.

 Many software manuals are sent out as PDF files.

FIGURE 32.8

The Adobe Reader can view PDF files as a stand-alone application or within the Web browser.

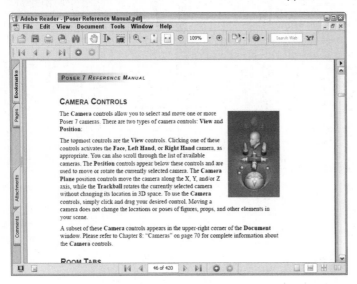

To create PDF files, you need to purchase a separate application, Adobe Acrobat, which can save documents using this format. Other Adobe products including Photoshop, Illustrator, and InDesign can also save files as PDFs. Microsoft Office can export documents with special add-on software installed.

Viewing Flash files

Another rich format type is Flash. Flash files are vector-based graphics, which create images using mathematically based lines and shapes instead of rows and columns of pixels, and can include interactivity. Flash provides a simple way to create animated sequences and video that can play on Web sites. Many Web sites use Flash content to spice up their site with games, animation, video, and interactive elements, as shown in Figure 32.9.

Flash files, like PDF files, need a special piece of software installed in order to display and view Flash files. Although the Flash Player is free, you need to purchase the Flash Professional product in order to create Flash files.

FIGURE 32.9

Flash files can add animation, video, and interactivity to Web pages.

Other Utilities

Utilities software is designed to enhance and extend the features that are part of the operating system. Although Windows includes a broad set of utilities, you can purchase other utility packages that enhance the available Windows utilities.

 **Many freely available utilities that add simple, useful features to Windows are available on the Internet.**

Screen savers

When a computer is sitting idle, you can set it to have a screen saver run across the screen to provide something interesting to look at. Screen savers were originally intended to prevent screen burn-in caused when the same pixels on a CRT screen were highlighted over a long period of time. LCD monitors don't have this problem, and these days screen savers are simply intended to provide some animated color in the room.

Whether you choose to display photos of your children or grandchildren, or a tranquil setting of swimming fish, screen savers can act like a dynamic image hanging on the wall of your office.

To access available screen savers, including all the screen savers that come with Windows, right-click on the Desktop and select the Screen Saver panel from the Display Properties dialog box. This panel, shown in Figure 32.10, lets you choose the screen saver and how long to wait before the screen saver appears.

FIGURE 32.10

The Screen Saver panel of the Display Properties dialog box lets you choose which screen saver to use and how long to wait before it appears.

The Settings button lets you configure the selected screen saver, and the Preview button shows the selected screen saver in full screen.

Along with a configured screen saver, you can click the Power button to configure the power saving settings, shown in Figure 32.11.

CROSS-REF   You can learn more about the various power saving features in Chapter 17.

FIGURE 32.11

The Power Options Properties dialog box lets you set the monitor and hard disks to turn off after a specified amount of time.

Backup

Another common utility that speeds the process of backing up critical files in case of crash is backup software. Backup software can save designated files to an external device, to the network, or directly to a CD-ROM or DVD. By backing up critical data files, you can protect the important data in case of disaster or system crashes.

CROSS-REF Backing up critical software and data is covered in Chapter 49.

File compression

If you plan on sending files through the Internet, you can take advantage of a file compression utility. These utilities reduce a file's size by compressing the file. The compressed file then needs to be uncompressed using the same software on the recipient's computer, but for transporting files through the Internet, the reduced file size is worth the effort.

There are several different compression formats available, including:

- **Zip:** Zip compressed files are one of the most popular compression formats. You can create zip files using WinZip, located at `www.winzip.com`.
- **Arc:** Arc stands for "archiving" and is another common compression option for older DOS-based systems.

- **Rar:** Rar files are cross-platform and provide a good compression ratio.
- **Tar:** Unix systems use tar files to compress files.
- **Sit:** Macintosh systems use sit files to compress files using the StuffIt application.

Application Programs

The major applications that your computer can access are another key reason for getting a computer in the first place. These packages are intended to solve a specific task and are focused on letting you produce and manipulate data. You can install these packages by default onto your system when the computer is purchased, or you can add them at a later time.

Most application software packages come with an installation CD that launches automatically when you insert it into the computer's CD-ROM drive. If the CD doesn't launch the installation application, you can usually go to the root of the CD using Windows Explorer and double-click the Setup icon to manually run the installation program. Or you could use the Start ➪ Run command to locate and run the Setup.exe program from the software's CD.

You can purchase and install some software directly from the Internet without dealing with a shipping product. This can be convenient if you need immediate access to a program. Online software purchases typically include an online manual.

TIP If you purchase online software, be sure to archive the downloaded files and print a copy of the license agreement along with any license keys, so that you can reinstall the software in case your system ever crashes.

Word processor

Another very popular computer application is the word processor. This software makes it possible to write and save text files with formatting. Word processor files can include images, bulleted lists, and other typical text elements. Word processors also include powerful features such as spell-checkers and auto-formatting.

Two popular word processors are Microsoft Word and Corel WordPerfect. Figure 32.12 shows a resume being written in Microsoft Word. These two packages are similar in their features and are usually included along with a suite of products including spreadsheets and presentations packages.

NOTE Word processors are commonly integrated with the system's e-mail client, allowing you to use advanced formatting features as you create e-mails.

FIGURE 32.12

Microsoft Word uses wizards and templates to automate the creation of certain documents.

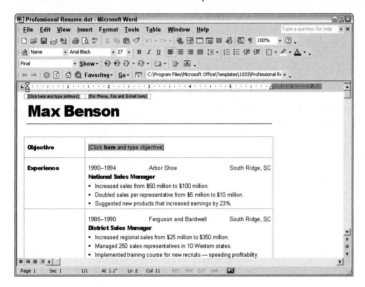

Spreadsheets

Computers are very good at performing calculations, and spreadsheets are good at automating this process. Spreadsheets consist of rows and columns of data that you can manipulate to calculate results. You can also create spreadsheets to automatically calculate solutions to preset formulas.

For example, if you need to create a report of the amount of money spent in the last month as compared to the family budget, you could use a spreadsheet to organize all the data, compute the averages and totals for each category and present the data using several different graphs.

Two popular spreadsheets are Microsoft Excel and Corel Quattro Pro. These products are complex and can take some time to learn to use effectively. Excel is endowed with wizards that guide you through some of the more complex features. Figure 32.13 shows a sample spreadsheet created in Excel.

Presentations

You can use presentation packages to create business presentations or a slide show of your last vacation. Presentation software can include images, text, and even audio and video. Two common presentation packages include Microsoft PowerPoint and Corel Presentations. Figure 32.14 shows a sample slide from a PowerPoint presentation.

CROSS-REF You can learn more about using presentation software in Chapter 36.

FIGURE 32.13

Microsoft Excel lets you manipulate numbers and formulas.

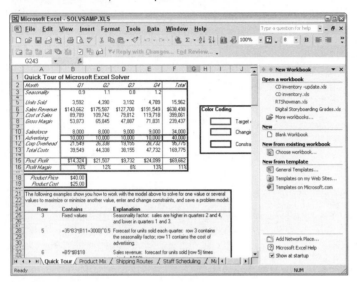

FIGURE 32.14

Microsoft PowerPoint lets you easily create multi-page presentations.

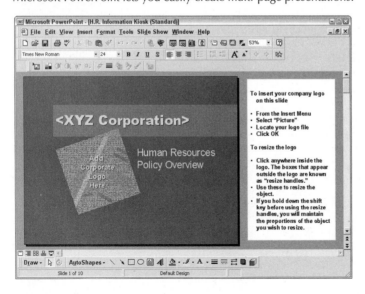

Databases

Database packages allow you to store, manipulate, and recall specific data from a set of data. Whether the data includes product numbers for a business or lists of clients, database software is another command application used extensively. Databases include form editors that are created for inputting data and specialized search tools for locating relationships between data.

Microsoft produces a database product known as Access, Corel has a database product called Paradox, and even OpenOffice includes a database module. Database packages come in several different versions depending on the set of features you need.

Office suites

Word processors, spreadsheets, and presentation software are typically bundled and sold as part of a suite of common applications that work together. Purchasing an office suite lets you get several popular office packages at a price that is less than the total of all three individually.

Microsoft develops the most popular office suite package. Microsoft Office includes Word, Excel, and PowerPoint, and all are integrated to work well together. Microsoft also produces a professional-level office suite that includes the Access database and an office suite for the home market called Microsoft Works that includes a smaller set of features.

Other office suites are available from Corel. WordPerfect Office includes WordPerfect, QuattroPro, Presentations, and Paradox.

Another office suite option was developed by an open source group sponsored by Sun Microsystems that collaborated to produce the entire product. OpenOffice, as shown in Figure 32.15, is available as a free download from www.openoffice.org, but donations are encouraged.

OpenOffice includes six different components: Math, Calc, Draw, Base, Writer, and Impress.

Finance and tax

Several personal finance packages are available that can help keep your finances organized. Quicken is a popular choice for managing finances, and Microsoft offers a similar package called Money. These applications can help you establish a budget and keep track of all your finances. They also show you how to bank online.

Another common software package that helps every year is tax preparation software. One common choice is TurboTax, created by the same company that makes Quicken. Tax software guides you through the tax preparation process by asking you a series of questions using standard wizards. Another popular choice is TaxCut.

FIGURE 32.15

OpenOffice's Calc application is a freely available spreadsheet.

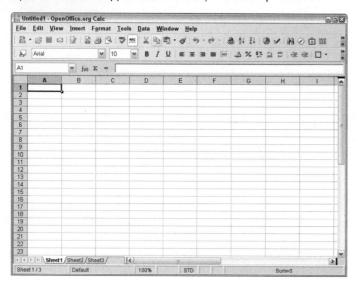

 Because tax laws change year to year, you need to purchase a new version of tax software every year.

The software can help inform you of deductions that you can claim, saving you money on the taxes you need to pay. Once completed, the software can print the documents you need to submit, or you can submit your taxes via the Internet. Most tax packages include modules for paying both federal and state taxes.

TIP Even if you submit your taxes online, be sure to print a copy for your records.

Graphics

Multiple software packages are available for creating graphics. These packages include software for editing photographs, drawing illustrations, creating multimedia, desktop publishing, and even creating animation.

Adobe and Corel are popular companies producing graphics software. For editing and printing photographs Adobe Photoshop is a popular choice. Photoshop, shown in Figure 32.16, is a professional-level product used by design professionals, but a home version of Photoshop with the major features, called Photoshop Elements, is also available.

FIGURE 32.16

Adobe Photoshop is used to edit and create images.

For drawing illustrations, Adobe offers Illustrator, shown in Figure 32.17. This package lets you draw pictures using a variety of lines and brushes. For creating newsletters and printed material, desktop publishing software is available. To meet this need, Adobe has created a product called InDesign.

NOTE Most word processors include a rudimentary set of graphics features that are used to create newsletters and brochures. The Abode products are professional level tools that can produce the same quality documents that publishers do. For simple graphics tasks, the word processor might be enough, but for serious graphics work look into these advanced graphics products.

Besides the offerings from Adobe, Microsoft has a desktop publishing package called Publisher, and Corel makes an illustration product called CorelDraw and a desktop publishing product called Ventura. Another very popular professional-level desktop publishing package is QuarkXPress.

TIP Many Web sites offer product reviews of the various graphics software. If you are having trouble deciding which package is right for you, look into one of these Web sites.

Following the lessons learned from the office products, many companies such as Adobe have begun bundling common graphics packages together into a suite of products. Adobe has developed Creative Suite that includes Photoshop, Illustrator, InDesign, Acrobat, and GoLive, which is used to create Web sites.

FIGURE 32.17

Adobe Illustrator lets you draw images using lines and brushes.

Audio and video

If you plan on using your computer to work with audio or video files, you need to install the software that makes this possible. If you simply want to download music to your media player, you can use the software that ships with your media player.

If you want to edit or create audio and video files, you can look into purchasing a separate product. There are several professional-level audio-editing tools, including Adobe Audition.

For editing videos, you can use Adobe's Premiere. There is also a version of Premiere Elements for the home market. Another popular video editor choice is Ulead's VideoStudio.

CROSS-REF The various audio and video options are covered in Chapter 42 and Chapter 43.

Games and Other Entertainment

The computer isn't all about software intended to make businesses productive. You can also use your computer for entertainment. Computers provide a strong alternative to console game systems like Sony's PlayStation, Microsoft's Xbox, and Nintendo's Wii.

Windows games

Even if you're not an avid gamer, you can still take advantage of games on your computer. Windows comes by default with several pre-installed games, including the immensely popular Solitaire card game, shown in Figure 32.18.

FIGURE 32.18

Windows Solitaire provides a welcome break from working on a computer.

Other Windows games include FreeCell, Minesweeper, and Spider Solitaire. You can find these games in the Start ⇨ All Programs ⇨ Games menu.

Casual games

Casual games can be played in a relatively short period of time; this type of game is common on many different Web sites; they're great for those times you need just a quick break from serious work.

If you're connected to the Internet, you can find casual game sites all over the Web, including the following:

- **PopCap Games:** This site, located at www.popcap.com, offers a large assortment of online games, including the popular Bejeweled game.
- **Shockwave:** Shockwave.com is a repository of games created using Flash and includes a large number of different categories.
- **GameTap:** GameTap.com is a nostalgic site that features many of the older video games from bygone years. The site requires a fee to sign up for their service.

- **Yahoo Games:** Located at `games.yahoo.com`, this site features many games you can play against other people onlines.
- **MSN Games:** Another popular site featuring multiplayer games. This site is found at `games.msn.com`.

Many of these games are Flash-based and require that you download and install the latest Flash player.

PC games

For many gamers, the PC is the game platform of choice. For many years, video games were developed for the PC before they were released on to the various console systems. Even though many games are developed only for a specific console systems, PC games are still quite common and allow features such as playing over local networks. Many players still prefer PC games over console because of the high resolution that is possible via the video cards.

The speed and resolution of PC games is controlled directly by the video card. Expensive video cards that include built-in graphics processors can accelerate game play at high resolutions. Video cards accelerate the game display using specialized graphics instruction sets that are optimized for performance. The two common display drivers used in games are DirectX and OpenGL. Depending on the game, the latest version of DirectX or OpenGL need to be installed before the game works. The game installation discs will check for the appropriate display drivers and install them if necessary during the installation process.

CROSS-REF   You can learn more about video cards and graphic controllers in Chapter 10.

LAN games

Although all the various video game consoles support multiple players simultaneously, PC games played over a Local Area Network (LAN) can include tens or even hundreds of players. Each player sits at their own computer, which they don't need to split between the other players and all the action, statistics, and updates to the game are relayed over the network to the other players.

Many first person shooter games such as Doom, Quake, and Half-Life are popular network games, but strategy games such as Warcraft and Age of Empires are also common. One of the key benefits to network games is that the opponents are actual reasoning players instead of the pre-programmed opponents that built into the game. Actual players provide more of challenge to expert players.

Built into most networked games is the ability to chat and send messages to the other players, which can be a useful strategy between team members or a way of taunting the other team. LAN games provide a social experience that is unlike the small room gatherings common for console games.

CROSS-REF   Networking and establishing a network is covered in Chapter 44.

Online multiplayer games

LAN games are great if you're looking for a challenge after beating all of the game's enemies, but if you don't have access to a network or other players, you can use the Internet to connect to hubs where online players gather to play. Most online gaming hubs provide several different rooms for players of different skill levels and all are closely monitored to prevent abuse.

NOTE The latest consoles also offer methods for connecting to online gaming hubs.

The Internet has also give rise to an entirely new type of game. Massively Multiplayer Online Games (MMOG) are games where hundreds or thousands of users play simultaneously in an alternate reality where the players can communicate, interact and play together using an avatar or a virtual character in the game. Several popular MMOG games include Runescape, World of Warcraft, Guild Wars, and Everquest.

Gaming hardware

For avid game players, you can install custom hardware such as joysticks and driving wheels that deepen the gaming experience. This additional hardware is typically connected using the USB port. The game must support these devices before you can use them.

Summary

The computer is only a platform for storing and running software, but the software that you install on your computer depends on your needs. Some software is designed to help your computer run better, and other applications are designed for producing specific files like text documents, graphics, or videos.

If you intend to use your computer to connect to the Internet, you need to install and configure a Web browser and an e-mail client. This software lets you surf Web pages and send and receive e-mails. In addition to the common Internet software, it is a good idea to install software such as a firewall and antivirus software to help keep your data and system safe. Other utility packages don't deal with the Internet but can keep your system working properly and protected.

The core applications installed on your system enable you to work productively on your computer. This application software may include programs like word processors, spreadsheets, presentation packages, and databases. These packages are commonly collected together into a suite of products. Other applications can include finance, tax, graphics, and audio/video solutions.

Chapter 33

Alternatives to Windows

The vast majority of personal computers use some version of Microsoft Windows, but that's not the only option. In addition to the Apple Macintosh, which used a quite different architecture until recently, several other operating systems can use the same hardware that supports Windows. These include the most recent incarnation of DOS, the Disk Operating System that was widely used before Windows replaced it as the dominant operating system, and several versions of Unix, Linux, and BeOS.

This chapter briefly describes each of these alternate operating systems and explains where to find them and how to load them. If you are reading this book, it's a safe bet that your primary interest is in using your computer with Windows, but it can be helpful to know that other operating systems are out there, and how to recognize them. If you're serious about using a computer with Unix or Linux, you might want to look for one or more books that describe them in more detail, such as *Linux Bible* by Christopher Negus or *Beginning Unix* by Paul Love et.al.

Because Windows is the most widely used operating system, it's also the most popular target for the bad guys who distribute viruses and spyware. Linux and Unix viruses are not unknown, but they are extremely uncommon; keeping Windows off your computer is one very effective way to improve your system's security.

Other users choose to install Unix or Linux because they don't like or don't trust Microsoft, or as a political act in favor of *open source* software that isn't controlled by one giant corporation. This book and its authors do not take sides in this debate; we're glad the choices are out there.

Obviously, this is not a book about how to install and use Linux or any other version of Unix. But even if you are a satisfied Windows user, you should know that other operating systems are available that work on your desktop or laptop computer. If you want to try one of those alternatives, this chapter provides enough information for you to make an informed choice and tells you where to obtain them.

DOS

Most users gave up the command-line MS-DOS operating system (IBM called it PC-DOS) a decade or more ago, after Microsoft introduced increasingly sophisticated versions of Windows. But DOS is still around, and it still has its uses. If you have a 10-year-old computer collecting dust in the attic, you can return it to service as a limited Internet client, or for use with the old programs that were written for DOS. Those programs may not be as pretty as the latest Windows applications, and they don't have all the advanced features that add value to the newest software, but they can still do the jobs they were originally designed to do. For example, a text editor or DOS-based word processor can still be entirely adequate for simple correspondence, note taking, or for writing a personal journal or a manuscript that doesn't require complex formatting. And of course, some businesses have been using the same DOS programs on their original 8086 or 80286-based computer forever because those programs have always done everything they think they need.

It's entirely possible to set up a modern computer with a Pentium or comparable AMD processor to run some version of DOS. Considering that today's processors are many times faster than the ones designed with DOS in mind, a newer system can run many DOS programs at very high speed. But for most us there really isn't any good reason to install DOS on a new computer, except as an exercise in nostalgia.

You might find a few DOS programs on CDs or floppy disks that are designed to load and run without Windows. These include the formatting utilities supplies with many new hard disk drives, and emergency boot disks that can run when the hard drive is damaged on infected by a virus that interferes with normal startup. These disks automatically load DOS and then run one or more specific programs. It's generally not practical to use the versions of DOS on these disks for any other purpose.

NOTE   A computer running Windows can use most DOS programs without the need to install a separate operating system. The Command Prompt utility (Start ⇨ Programs ⇨ Accessories ⇨ Command Prompt) in Windows opens a command-line interface that accepts most important DOS commands and performs exactly like a DOS screen.

Unix

The Unix operating system exists in several versions and in implementations for many different kinds of computers, ranging from desktop personal computers to room-filling mainframes. Each version has a slightly different set of commands and features, but in general, those differences are more important to programmers and network administrators than end users (the final user of a computer, after it has been developed, marketed, and de-bugged — basically, anyone who's not a programmer or engineer). If you understand one version, you should have little trouble using a computer running any other type of Unix. Many Internet file servers, network servers, and other institutional computers use Unix, so a working knowledge of essential Unix commands and concepts can be useful, even if your own computers all use Windows.

Much of the core architecture of Unix should be familiar to a knowledgeable Windows user. It includes a *kernel*, which assigns processing time and memory to programs and maintenance tasks, and defines the file structure and communications processes; one or more *shells* that present a command interpreter to each user; and several optional *graphical user interfaces (GUIs)* that provide a working environment that is easier for non-technical users to understand.

The most common Unix shells are the Bourne shell (sh), the C shell (csh), and the Korn shell (ksh). Most versions of Unix include at least two of the three. Each shell uses a slightly different set of commands, but if you master any one shell, you can probably understand code written in any of them with a bit of guidance from a manual.

There are hundreds of published guides and manuals to Unix, but the official user's manual is supplied as part of the code, like the Help screens in Windows. To find instructions for using any Unix command or program, type man. Man pages are not always clear and easy to understand, but they're easy to find, and they usually include details about the proper syntax for entering a command.

The BSD (Berkeley Software Distribution) family of Unix versions is among the most widely used types. Of these, NetBSD, FreeBSD, and OpenBSD all have active user communities and well-supported software. They are available online from these sources:

NetBSD	www.netbsd.org/Releases
FreeBSD	www.freebsd.org/where
OpenBSD	www.openbsd.org

Many Unix GUIs operate in a similar fashion to the point-and-click design of the Windows desktop. For example, Figure 33.1 shows the DesktopBSD GUI, which is available as a free download from www.desktopbsd.org. DesktopBSD is based on FreeBSD and the KDE (Kool Desktop Environment) graphic environment. Other KDE variations are available from www.spreadkde.org. Two other widely used Unix environments are GNOME, which is included with many Unix distribution packages and available from www.gnome.org/start, and X Window, available from www.x.org. And the latest Macintosh operating system, Mac OS X, is yet another variation on Unix.

Many Unix programs are available as *open source* software that does not require an expensive license. Putting aside the very real costs of upkeep and support, Unix and other open source software are almost always less costly to obtain and install than comparable commercial Windows products.

Many open source programs are just as stable and reliable as their commercial competitors. For example, the Mozilla Firefox Web browser and Thunderbird e-mail client (both available from www.mozilla.com) are comparable to Microsoft's Internet Explorer and Outlook Express, and the OpenOffice.org suite of business software (including a word processor, spreadsheet, presentation software, and other programs that can read and write files that are compatible with Microsoft Office formats) are respectable alternatives to Microsoft's Office programs. Many open source programs, including OpenOffice.org, Firefox, and Thunderbird are also available in versions that run under Windows.

Unix is also the *native language* for much of the Internet because most of its underlying structure is based on Unix. Most of the standard commands and utilities for navigating through the Internet, such as telnet, ftp, ping, and tracert, originated in Unix.

On the other hand, Unix is undeniably an operating system for hardcore computer geeks rather than mainstream end users. The proliferation of Unix versions and environments means that there is no common standard (or a single series of official releases) that applies to every computer using the operating system as there is with Windows, so you have no guarantee that your employees or family know how to use the particular version you have installed. A few businesses and government agencies have adopted some version of Unix or Linux, either as some kind of anti-Microsoft political statement, or because of the lower initial cost, but they are still rare. Many computer professionals can offer convincing arguments that Unix (and Linux) is technically superior to Windows, and many Macintosh users would never consider changing, but in today's marketplace (both the market for operating systems and the market for information workers), Windows is still the default standard.

FIGURE 33.1

DesktopBSD uses a similar graphic environment to Windows Explorer.

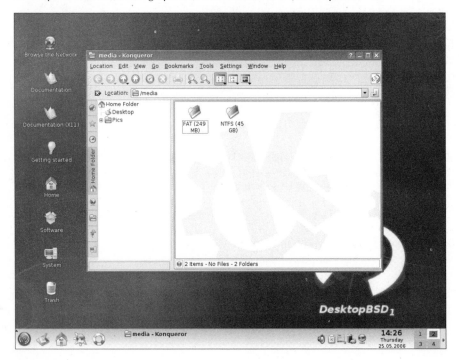

Linux

By the late 1980s, Unix had become a standard operating system in academic computing centers at many colleges and universities; as the students at those schools moved on to jobs in business and government, they continued to use it. This was about the same time that the earliest personal computers were appearing, and naturally, many young computer professionals were among the first wave of home computer users. Many of these people wanted to install Unix on their home computers, but the only available versions were slow and expensive.

Linux was originally created as an open source version of Unix for personal computers. In other words, it looks and feels like Unix, but it doesn't violate the copyrights on the original Unix kernel. Because it's an open source project, many people have contributed drivers, utilities, and application programs that work with the core Linux software, so by now the latest versions support a huge variety of computers and peripherals, including many old and obscure products that don't work with any other modern operating system. Because it doesn't require as much processing power as Windows XP or Vista, Linux can use an old and relatively slow computer as a backup system for word processing, Web browsing, and other applications, long after Windows has declared it obsolete and useless.

Today, Linux is probably the strongest competitor to Windows. It's supported by a huge base of enthusiastic users, and like other Unix versions, the original command-line interface can hide behind any of several desktop environments that are just as sophisticated and easy to use as the Windows desktop. On computers with similar processors and adequate memory, Linux is fast and reliable, and it still carries a certain special status among computer enthusiasts that may set you apart from the silent majority of users who are still tied to Windows.

If you enjoy that sort of thing, you can download and install any of several Linux versions at no cost, and depend on the online documentation and very helpful user community for support. Or if you prefer, you can buy a commercial version on a CD or DVD, complete with dedicated support. Because Linux is an open-source product, the actual software is the same, whether you pay or you get it free (although you might get more add-on programs with a paid version). Each version includes a somewhat different set of additional utilities and other programs, but the core operating system is the same.

The most difficult part of getting started with Linux can be choosing which version to install. There are more than a hundred of them, each with a different set of added features and functions. As you might expect, several Web sites are devoted to discussing the relative merits of different distributions; these include `http://distrowatch.com`, `www.tuxmachines.org`, and `www.tuxs.org/which.htm` (Tux is the nickname for the friendly penguin who has become the Linux mascot and logo). For new users, PCLinuxOS (`www.pclinuxos.com`) and Ubuntu (`www.ubuntu.com`) are both well regarded. Figure 33.2 shows a screen full of overlapping applications in PCLinuxOS.

FIGURE 33.2

PCLinuxOS is known as a beginner-friendly Linux distribution.

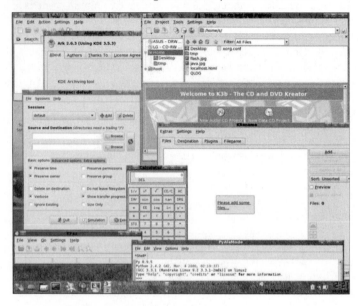

Finding Drivers for Unix and Linux

As in Windows, every storage device, graphics, sound, or network adapter, pointing device, I/O port, and other peripheral device supported by Unix or Linux requires a device driver to convert the operating system's generic commands and data to the specific instructions and formats used by each device. Many of the most commonly used device drivers are included with most operating system software distributions, but others are new enough or obscure enough that you have to find and install them separately.

The first place to look for a Unix or Linux device driver is the Support section of the manufacturer's own Web site. Most hardware developers understand that Unix and Linux users can represent a small but important portion of their potential user base, so they develop and test versions of their own device drivers and control programs for Linux, and sometimes for other versions of Unix, along with the more popular Windows drivers.

If the manufacturer can't provide a driver for the version of Unix or Linux you're using, don't give up. One of the greatest strengths of these operating systems is the community of users and software developers who are anxious to help newcomers and to extend their favorite operating system to every imaginable type of hardware. So there's an excellent chance that somebody, someplace has created the driver you need, or possibly has produced a driver for a similar product that uses the identical controller chip set; if so, it can also work with your obscure device.

To find a device driver, try one of these methods:

- Send a query to the manufacturer's Technical Support center, or ask a question in the User's Forum in the manufacturer's Web site.

- Use Google or some other Web search tool to search for "[*insert make and model here*] Unix driver" or "[*insert make and model here*] Linux driver."

- Look in the appropriate Usenet newsgroup for the version of Unix you are using. The archive of Usenet messages at `http://groups.google.com` contains messages dating back to the 1980s, so it's a valuable tool for searching through other people's requests and announcements. If you can't find what you need, post your own message, wait a day or two, and somebody will probably give you an answer. For Linux, try the `comp.os.linux.hardware` newsgroup. For Unix, look for a newsgroup in the `comp.unix` hierarchy. When you find the appropriate newsgroup, use the Search this group tool with "device driver" in quotation marks, followed by the make and model of the device you want to install.

- Look for a link to sources of device drivers at the home page for your particular variety of Unix or Linux.

Loading a Different Operating System

If you're reading this chapter, you might be thinking, "Maybe I should try one of those other operating systems. But I sure would hate to completely remove Windows and lose all those custom features and options that I spent so much time organizing." The good news is that you can install two or more operating systems on a single computer, and choose the one you want to use each time you turn on the computer. The bad news is that the process is somewhat complex, especially if you don't already have a working knowledge of both operating systems, and the different file systems used by Windows and Unix or Linux can add to the confusion.

So it's generally better to dedicate a separate machine to the new operating system. Remember that Linux and any of the BSD Unix versions can run quite well on a system that Windows XP (let alone Windows Vista) would refuse to even consider. If you (or your friends or relatives) don't already have an old computer that you're no longer using, you can often find one very cheaply at a rummage sale or secondhand computer store. The whole thing, including a secondhand CRT monitor, keyboard, and mouse, and a network interface card shouldn't cost you more than about $50.

Any computer with an early Pentium processor should be entirely adequate to experiment with. If you can find an inexpensive additional memory module or two that fits your new old computer, go ahead and add them. When you decide to use the new OS for general use, you can add more memory and a bigger hard drive later.

CROSS-REF For more information about how to add memory, see Chapter 7. Chapter 9 contains details about how to install hard drives.

If you decide to try setting up a dual boot system that can allow you to load more than one operating system on the same computer (one at a time), look for a specific procedure for the version of Unix you want to install alongside of Windows. Run a Web search for "howto dual boot xp [*insert version here*]" for instructions that apply to your particular choice of Unix or Linux versions.

Windows Services for Unix

Microsoft offers a free package of services, tools, and programs for integrating computers using Windows with network servers that use Unix or Linux, and for using Unix commands and programs on a Windows system. Look for more information at the Windows Services for Unix (SFU) home page at www.microsoft.com/technet/interopmigration/unix/sfu/default.mspx.

SFU includes a C shell, a Korn shell, and a telnet client that all present the same appearance as the same shells in a computer running Unix.

 Microsoft states that Windows Services for UNIX 3.5 doesn't install on Windows 9x or Windows XP Home Edition.

Summary

Alternatives to Windows include the old command-line DOS operating system, Linux, and several versions of Unix. Of these, Linux is the strongest competitor to Windows as a desktop operating system. The three most popular BSD Unix versions are also excellent choices.

Both Unix and Linux are stable and reliable, but Microsoft's success in making Windows the *de facto* standard for desktop computers means that Windows is still the default choice for most users. Unless you have a good reason not to use Windows — for enhanced security and protection against viruses, because it is a local standard, as a protest against Microsoft, or just to set you and your computer apart from the majority — the Microsoft operating system probably does just about everything you need or want. On the other hand, a larger proportion of the world's file servers and Internet servers use some version of Unix, so you could easily justify choosing to install Unix on your own servers.

Chapter 34

Sharing a Computer

Whether your computer is located at home, in an office, or in some other setting, it's not uncommon to share a single computer among two or more users.

There are two ways to share a computer: either let everybody use a single login account, or assign a separate account to each user.

With just one shared account, everybody has access to all the files, and everybody uses the same visual layout. Anybody can turn on the computer and start using it. If there's a password on the shared account, everybody knows what it is; more likely, there won't be any password at all.

With separate accounts, each user can keep separate files and use different choices of desktop background, color schemes, type fonts, and mouse cursors. For example, you can create separate accounts on a home computer for each member of the family. When a young child logs on, the Windows desktop might use a cartoon character as the desktop image, large easy-to-read fonts, and on-screen shortcuts and Start menu programs that are appropriate for the child's age. When an older child uses the same computer, the background is different, and the shortcuts and menu are links to the Web browser, instant messaging program, word processor, and other programs and services that he or she uses regularly. And when Mom and Dad sign in, they each see their own personalized set of screen elements. It's the same computer, but it takes on a different personality for each user.

In an office where two or more users share a single computer, each user can have a separate account. For example, one person might work during the day and another person occupies the same desk on the evening or overnight shift. In another workplace, the computer is not a major part of the worker's

IN THIS CHAPTER

Reasons to share

Assigning an account to each user

Logging in as a different user

Working with the Shared Computer Toolkit

daily routine, so a single computer is adequate for several people; the keyboard and monitor might be on a separate table and not on anybody's desk.

This chapter contains information about creating and using more than one user account on a single computer, and descriptions of several kinds of sharing devices.

Accounts for Multiple Users

If all the users on a computer use the same account (or if only one person uses the computer), it's probably set up to bypass the login requirement; when you turn on the computer, it takes you directly to the Windows desktop.

But when more than one person uses the same computer, it often makes sense to create a separate account for each regular user, and maybe a guest account as well. Each account can have a customized appearance, a different set of programs in the Start menu, and even restricted access to certain files and folders.

Creating a new account

If your computer is connected to a network through a domain, ask your network administrator to create new accounts for you. If you don't use a domain, follow these steps to create a new user account on a computer that is already running Windows XP:

1. **From the Control Panel, choose User Accounts.** The User Accounts window shown in Figure 34.1 appears.

FIGURE 34.1

The User Accounts window offers several options for creating and changing accounts.

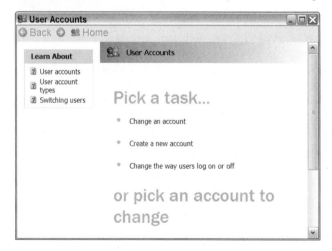

2. **Click the Create a new account option.** The Name the new account window shown in Figure 34.2 appears.

FIGURE 34.2

Use the Name the new account window to assign a username.

3. **Type the new user's name in the New User field and click Next.** The Pick an account type window shown in Figure 34.3 appears.

FIGURE 34.3

Choose the type of account you want to create.

4. **Choose the type of account you want this user to have.** A user with an Administrator account can install and remove hardware and software; create, delete, and change user accounts, and perform other maintenance tasks. Users with Limited accounts can change only the picture, desktop settings, and password assigned to their own accounts.

5. **Click the Create Account button at the bottom of the window.** The User Accounts window reappears, but this time it includes the name of the new account at the bottom of the window. You may have to scroll down the window to see the list of users.

The first time you log on to a new account, Windows opens with the default appearance settings, and it will probably offer to set the mouse options (including tracking speed, use of the middle button and so forth). To change the appearance scheme, including the desktop color, background image, screen saver, and fonts and video display settings, move the cursor to an empty spot on the desktop, right-click, and choose Properties from the pop-up menu. To change the sound scheme (or turn off all sounds) open Control Panel ➪ Sounds and Audio Devices ➪ Sounds.

CROSS-REF   For more details about how to adjust your settings, see Chapter 27.

Changing account settings

To change the name assigned to an account, create or change a password, change the type of account, or change the picture next to this account name in the login screen, either click Change an account and choose the account in the next screen, or scroll down and click the name of the account in the Change an account screen. The What do you want to change screen shown in Figure 34.4 appears.

Click the type of change you want, and follow the on-screen instructions to make that change. If you don't assign a password to an account, it is possible to use that account by leaving the password field in the login screen empty.

Switching between users

To change user accounts, follow these steps:

1. **Open the Start menu and click the Log Off item near the bottom of the menu.**

2. **Windows asks if you're sure you want to log off.** Click the Log Off button. Windows shuts down the current user's session and displays a list of all users with accounts on this computer. This is the same screen you see when you turn on the computer.

3. **Click the name of the account you want to use.** Windows asks for a password.

4. **Enter the password for the new account.** Windows loads the desktop for that account.

FIGURE 34.4

Use the What do you want to change window to edit account settings.

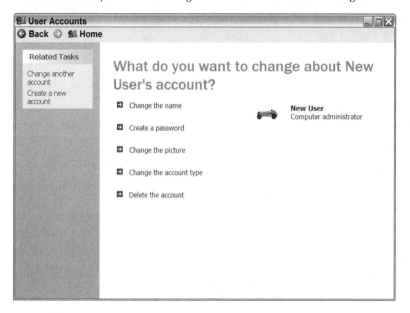

It's only possible to use one user account at a time, but if a second user wants to interrupt, Windows can suspend the current user's activity to allow a new login. For example, if one user is playing a game on the computer that has the household laser printer connected to it, but another user wants to print a document, the first user can suspend the game and use Fast User Switching to open the other account. When the print job is complete, switch users again to resume the first account at the point where it was suspended.

To turn on Fast User Switching, follow these steps:

1. **From the Control Panel, open User Accounts.**

2. **In the Pick a task screen, click Change the way users log on or off.** The Select logon and logoff options window shown in Figure 34.5 appears.

3. **Turn on both the Use the Welcome screen option and the Use Fast User Switching option, and click Apply Options.**

4. **Close the Pick a task window.**

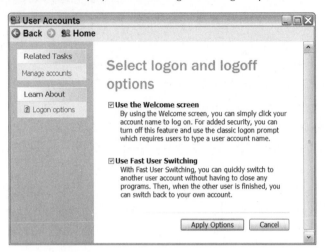

FIGURE 34.5

This window displays the Select logon and logoff options.

When Fast User Switching is active, Windows offers a choice of "Switch Users" or "Log Off" when you choose the Log Off command in the Start menu. Choose the Switch Users option to suspend the current session without closing down any programs.

Using the Microsoft Shared Computer Toolkit

The Microsoft Shared Computer Toolkit is primarily intended for computers in public locations, such as libraries, classrooms, community centers, and Internet cafés, where unsupervised users could change the desktop and other configuration settings, expose the computer to viruses, spyware, and other harmful files, and examine other users' private files, history files, and browser caches. It can also be useful in families where parents want to place time limits on their children's use of the computer or the Internet, limit access to specific programs, and keep the children from changing configuration settings. The Shared Computer Toolkit is a free download from www.microsoft.com/windowsxp/sharedaccess.

The Shared Computer Toolkit is an extremely flexible program that includes dozens of options (and a hundred-page instruction manual), so you can create a different profile for each account or for each class of user, such as students at different grade levels in a school library, or customers, employees, and managers in a corporate reception area.

The Toolkit is a powerful set of tools that can make the difference between possible damage to your computer and an extremely secure system configuration. By restricting each user to an appropriate set of programs and services, it allows you to provide an appropriate level of access to each user without interfering with any other users' experience. Before you install the Toolkit, it's worth the time to skim through the handbook supplied with the program because it includes detailed explanations of each option and feature.

When you install the Toolkit, it offers to run a Getting Started routine that steps through every possible option. If you prefer, you can use the very detailed User Restrictions dialog box shown in Figure 34.6.

FIGURE 34.6

The Shared Computer Toolkit can set restrictions on many Windows features and functions.

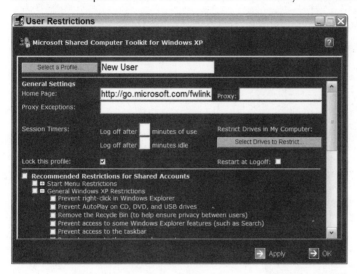

The Shared Computer Toolkit can also provide easy access to many of the Accessibility utilities in Windows, as shown in Figure 34.7. This allows a user with special needs to select one or more of these utilities, without changing things for other users.

CROSS-REF See Chapter 30 for more information about making your computer more accessible to users with limited vision, mobility restrictions, or other special needs.

In order to prevent damage from viruses, spyware, and other unauthorized changes, the Toolkit also includes a set of Disk Protection options, as shown in Figure 34.8. When Disk Protection is active, it discards any changes to Windows or other programs, and it restores the drive partition that contains Windows and other software to its original state every time the computer restarts.

TIP If patrons, students, or other users keep data files on a computer that uses Disk Protection, store those files on a separate disk partition, in order to avoid losing them when Disk Protection discards recent changes to the partition that contains Windows.

FIGURE 34.7

Users can turn on Accessibility utilities for their own accounts, without making system-wide changes.

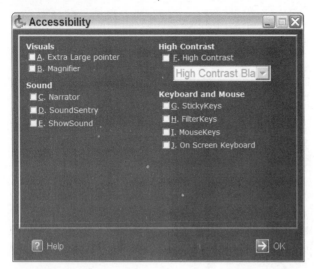

FIGURE 34.8

Disk Protection returns Windows and other programs to their original condition after a user tries to make changes.

Summary

When two or more users share the same computer, it's often useful to establish separate login accounts. In Windows, each user's account can have a distinctive set of configuration settings, and private folders and files that are not accessible to other accounts. When one user is logged on, the Switch Users control can suspend that user's activities without the need to shut down all of his or her open programs.

In public settings like classrooms and Internet cafes, the free Microsoft Shared Computer Toolkit can establish appropriate restrictions and security controls to maintain the privacy of each user and prevent damage from viruses and shareware. The Shared Computer Toolkit is also useful for setting parental controls over a child's use of the computer or access to the Internet.

Chapter 35

Printing from Your Computer

There used to be talk, as computers started to become more popular, that paper and printed objects would become obsolete. Well, computers are more popular than ever and the sale of printers is as strong as ever. The printed page is familiar and comfortable, so you can expect it to be around for some time.

Printers come in many different types. Some are better for printing text and some are better at printing photographs, but all printers connect to the computer and access data files in pretty much the same way.

Understanding how printers work helps keep them working well and available when you need them. This chapter covers all the details you need about printers to use them effectively.

Understanding Printer Types

There are several different types of printers that you can choose from. The one you choose depends on the type of printing you need to do. Some printers are relatively easy to use but limited in the number of pages they can print. Other printers, such as those for offices, can handle large print jobs without having to be refilled with paper or toner as often. Some printers specialize in specific types of documents such as photographs. The technology used to print pages differs with each of these printer types.

Laser printers

Laser printers produce the crispest, cleanest results; they are also among the fastest type of printer, but they can also be the most expensive type of printer. Some time ago, laser printers could print only in black and white, but color laser printers are now available and reasonably priced, making it possible for anyone to print crisp, clean color pages.

Laser printers include a drum cylinder that is initially positively charged with an electrostatic charge. The data sent to the printer is used to control a fine laser light that discharges the areas on the drum where the ink should be. The drum is exposed to the toner, which is like fine powder. This ink sticks to the areas of the drum that are now negatively charged. A page of paper is rolled under the drum, and some heated rollers melt the ink to the page where it is permanently affixed.

Several different manufacturers produce laser printers, including Brother, Hewlett-Packard, Samsung, and Lexmark. Figure 35.1 shows the Dell 5310n laser printer.

FIGURE 35.1

Laser printers are quiet, fast, and available in versions that can print in monochrome or color.

Image courtesy of Dell Inc.

The advantages of buying a laser printer are that they operate quietly and print fairly quickly. Laser printed pages also don't have the problem common with inkjet pages of smearing ink that gets rubbed. Ink cartridges for laser printers can be expensive, but they typically last a long time.

> **NOTE** When considering which printer to buy, you should consider the cost per page, which factors in the initial cost of the printer, the cost of the paper, and ink supplies. Even though laser printers and their ink cartridges are more expensive, they generally have a lower overall cost per page than inkjet printers.

Inkjet printers

Inkjet printers work by spraying ink onto the paper. Inkjet printers are much cheaper than laser printers, but the results can be fuzzy and blurry when printed on normal paper. This can be improved if you use the inkjet printer with a specialized glossy paper.

> **NOTE** Newer technologies have greatly improved the quality of inkjet printers in recent years, but many people still consider them inferior to laser printers.

Even though inkjet printers are fairly inexpensive, they use a lot of ink and their ink cartridges run out fairly quickly. Inkjet printers use two different ink cartridges: a color cartridge that includes magenta, cyan, and yellow ink, and a separate cartridge that holds black ink.

Mixing the three primary ink colors together in differing amounts produces a wide range of colors. However, if you use one color more than the others, then that color may run out before the others, requiring a new color cartridge. Mixing all three colors together can create black, but without the extra black ink cartridge this actually results in a muddy brown color instead of dark black. It also uses three times the amount of ink than just using the black cartridge.

> **TIP** Many companies help reduce the cost of purchasing new cartridges by offering the ability to refill the existing cartridges.

Inkjet printers are also very slow. They work by printing the image in strips, and the ink can smear if they get rubbed soon after being printed.

Impact printers

Impact printers, which are often called dot-matrix printers, work by striking a metal head or pin against a page of paper with an ink ribbon in-between. The result creates a small dot on the page. By controlling the position of the printer head, you can precisely print to a page.

Older impact printers have heads made from 9 pins, but 24-pin heads are also available. The more pins on the head of an impact printer, the better its resolution.

Impact printers are older technology, but they have the advantage of being able to print onto multiple-sheet pages like receipts. One of their major drawbacks is the noise they create. Replacement ink ribbons for impact printers are relatively cheap when compared to inkjet or laser printer cartridges. The quality of impact printers is also inferior to laser and inkjet printers.

Photo printers

You can use photo printers with digital cameras to print photographs that are similar to those produced by a photo lab. However, photo printers are specialized and cannot be used to print data files such as text documents.

There are several different technologies used to print photos. One photo printer technology works just like inkjet printers by combining and spraying dots of ink on the page. These photo printers work best when combined with specialized photo paper that more effectively captures the ink. Photo printers that use this technology also use six unique color cartridges instead of the typical three, including light cyan, light magenta, cyan, magenta, yellow, and black. Using six colors gives a much broader color range.

Other photo printers use a dye sublimation process, which involves melting and combining solid ink blocks together to create the image's colors.

Photo printers can print high-quality images that are comparable to photographs, but the cost is still fairly expensive, equating to roughly 20–40 cents per print. These printers are not very good at printing documents that include a lot of text. Photo printer cartridges are very expensive when compared to inkjet and laser printers, but the quality is excellent.

Some photo printers include slots that allow you to insert a flash memory card directly into the printer and print without connecting the printer to a computer. These printers also include a small LCD screen where you can preview, edit, and even crop the photos before printing them. Figure 35.2 shows a popular Dell photo printer.

 As an alternative to buying a photo printer, many department and drug stores offer photo printing kiosks that accept memory cards.

All-in-Ones (printer/scanner/copier/fax)

If you purchase a printer, a fax machine, and a flatbed scanner separately, they can take up a lot of desk space. You can resolve this issue by getting an All-in-One device that can work as a printer, scanner, copier, and fax machine.

CROSS-REF You can learn more about scanning in Chapter 37 and more about faxing in Chapter 45.

A printer and scanner combined into a single unit can act as a copier without requiring a computer.

The key benefit of these All-in-Ones is cost. A single unit that can print, scan, fax, and copy is much cheaper than buying each individually. These units have the ability to use inkjet or laser technology. The drawback to these units is that they can be complicated. If you never plan on using the fax features, then all the extra buttons may be confusing.

FIGURE 35.2

Some photo printers allow you to print directly from a flash memory card without connecting to a computer.

Image courtesy of Dell Inc.

Connecting a Printer to Your Computer

You can connect a printer to your computer in several different ways. Older computers connect using a parallel port, but newer devices can connect using the USB port.

Parallel port

Windows doesn't automatically recognize many of the older printers that connect through a parallel port. To set up these printers, you can use the Add Printer Wizard. You access this wizard by double-clicking the Printers and Faxes item in the Control Panel, which opens a list of the installed printers along with a link to Add a Printer.

If you click the Add a Printer link, the Add Printer Wizard window opens, as shown in Figure 35.3. The first page of the wizard lets you add a local or a networked printer to your system. There is also an option to automatically detect the connected printer. If you select to automatically detect the connected printer, then Windows searches for a driver to communicate with the printer. If Windows finds a compatible driver, the driver is loaded and configured. If Windows doesn't find a compatible driver, the wizard lets you manually configure the printer.

FIGURE 35.3

You can add connected parallel port printers to your system using the Add Printer Wizard.

In the second page of the Add Printer Wizard, you can select which port the printer is connected to. This may be the parallel port (LPT1, LPT2, or LPT3), a serial port, or an Infrared port, as shown in Figure 35.4. For networked printers, you can create a new port and specify a TCP/IP port, which connects through the connected network.

TIP If you name a printer using its model name and number, the actual printer can be easy to identify. If your network has several of the same type of printer, give each printer a separate name, and label each printer with its name.

In the next page of the Add Printer Wizard, shown in Figure 35.5, you can load the printer driver that lets the printer speak to the computer. You can select the appropriate driver from a list of supported printers, or you can click the Have Disk button to select the driver from the CD that came with the printer. The Windows Update button lets you update the driver list using the Internet.

FIGURE 35.4

The second page of the Add Printer Wizard lets you select the printer's port.

FIGURE 35.5

The next page of the Add Printer Wizard lets you load the printer driver.

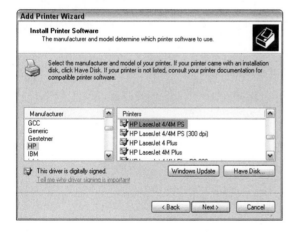

The next pages of the Add Printer Wizard let you name the printer so it can be recognized from within the Print dialog boxes in the various applications. You can also choose to set this printer as the default printer, which makes it appear by default whenever you choose to print.

Then a page appears where you can choose to print a test page to the established printer. The final page of the Add Printer Wizard, shown in Figure 35.6, shows the selected options before closing the wizard.

FIGURE 35.6

The final page of the Add Printer Wizard summarizes the options you've selected.

After the printer is configured, the new printer shows up in the Printers and Faxes page of the Control Panel.

USB port

Most computers that are connected using a USB port are automatically detected when plugged in and the required driver is located and installed. If the correct driver can't be found, Windows opens the Found New Hardware dialog box where you can locate the printer driver.

 **Some USB devices require that the printer's software and drivers be installed before the printer is connected to the computer.**

Through a network

If a printer is attached to your network via another computer, you can use the Add Printer Wizard to connect to the printer if the printer is set up to be shared. Before you can connect to a network printer, you need to enable sharing for the printer. This is a setting that you can enable using the

Network Setup Wizard. Once sharing is enabled for your network, you can turn on sharing across the network for an installed printer using the Sharing panel in the Printer Properties dialog box.

CROSS-REF You can learn more about setting up a network in Chapter 44.

To configure your system to use a shared network computer, follow these steps:

1. **Open the Properties dialog box for the printer using the computer that the network printer is connected to.** In the Sharing panel, enable the Share this Printer option and give the printer a name.

2. **On a computer that you want to use the network printer, open the Control Panel.** Double-click the Printers and Faxes option.

3. **Click the Add a Printer link to open the Add Printer Wizard.**

4. **In the first page of the wizard, select the option to add a network printer and click Next.**

5. **In the next page of the wizard, shown in Figure 35.7, you can browse for the printer, enter the printer's name, or enter the printer's network address.** The easiest method is to browse for the printer, or you could have Windows search the network for the printer's name.

TIP One of the easiest ways to identify a network printer is to print a test page using one of the computers that is already connected. There is a Print Test Page button in the General panel of the Printer Properties dialog box. The test page displays the printer's name, location on the network, and address. You can enter this information into the Add Printer Wizard.

FIGURE 35.7

When connecting to a network printer, the Add Printer Wizard includes several options for locating the printer.

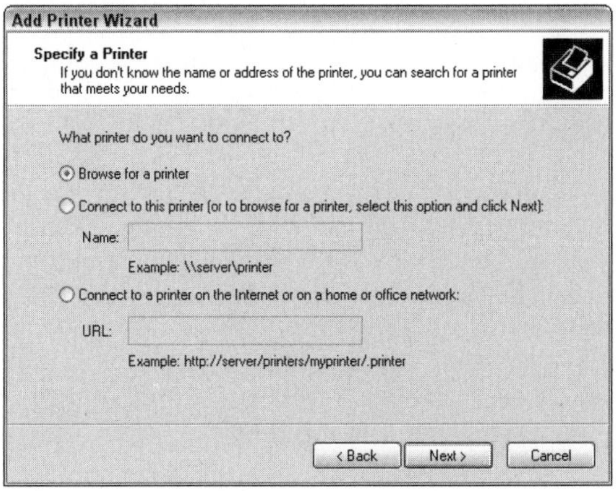

6. **In the next page of the wizard, browse to locate the network printer, select the printer, and click Next.** The new printer is added to the list under Printers and Faxes in the Control Panel.

Accessing printer properties

All new printers added to your system appear in the Printers and Faxes list of the Control Panel. If you select the File ➪ Properties menu from this list, the properties for the selected printer opens, as shown in Figure 35.8.

 The printer's name is the same name entered in the Add Printer Wizard.

FIGURE 35.8

The printer's Properties dialog box includes all the settings for the selected printer.

The General tab of the printer Properties dialog box includes the name of the printer. This same name appears in the Print dialog box when you print from the various applications. This tab also includes details about the selected printer, such as whether it supports color and can print double-sided and stapled, and its rough speed and resolution. It also has a button that can be used to print a test page.

The Sharing tab makes this printer available to other computers over the network. The Ports tab displays the port that this printer is connected to, and includes a button to add a new port or configure the selected port. One of the new port options is a Standard TCP/IP Port, which enables you to send the document to the printer using the same connection that you use to connect to the Internet.

The Color Management tab includes options to manually set the color configuration or to let Windows manage it. If you have some color management software, you can choose the Manual option where you can add a color profile from the configured software. The Driver tab includes a button that downloads the latest driver for this printer from the Internet.

The Advanced tab, shown in Figure 35.9, includes settings for controlling when the printer is available for printing. For example, if the network is shut-down during the night for maintenance, you could set the hours when the printers are available.

Spooling is the process of sending the print job to the printer's hardware. Once a print job is spooled, it resides in the printer's memory waiting to print. The spool options determine how quickly the application that issued the print job gets control again and how quickly the print job starts. For urgent jobs, you can have them print immediately, but lower priority print jobs could bundle the entire print job together before sending it to the printer.

FIGURE 35.9

The Advanced tab of the printer's Properties dialog box lets you set when the printer is available to print.

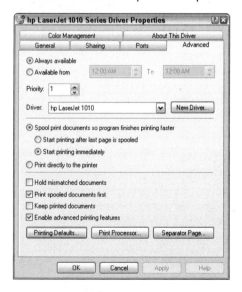

The Printing Defaults button displays a dialog box of settings that are unique to the selected printer. Figure 35.10 shows a sample of this dialog box for the HP LaserJet printer attached to my system. Using this dialog box, you can set the paper size, the print quality, scaling, watermarks, number of copies, and whether the page prints using portrait or landscape orientation.

 The specific settings available in the Printing Defaults dialog box is different for each printer.

The Separator Page button in the Advanced tab of the printer's Properties dialog box lets you include a page that prints at the beginning and end of each print job. If your printer is connected to the network, this option can make it easy to identify the various print jobs and route them to the correct person.

FIGURE 35.10

The Printing Defaults dialog box lets you change specifics about the printer, such as the paper size and orientation.

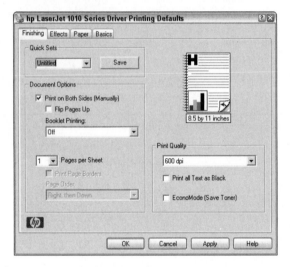

Using Fonts

The first printers that appeared needed to include fonts within the printer, but now software can generate any installed system font on the printer. Windows ships with a huge selection of fonts, but you can add new fonts to your system as needed.

To add new fonts to your system, follow these steps:

1. Download or locate new fonts from a CD.
2. Copy the new fonts into the Windows/Fonts directory or into the Fonts folder in the Control Panel.
3. After the font file is added to the Fonts directory, the new font is automatically available to all applications.

 Many viruses are disguised as downloadable fonts. Be sure to verify the font's source before installing any downloaded fonts on your system.

All the fonts that are installed on a system can be used within the installed applications such as the word processors and desktop publishing packages. The installed Windows fonts are located in a single place that you can access using the Fonts option in the Control Panel, as shown in Figure 35.11.

NOTE You can change the look of the Fonts folder between Large Icons, List, Similarity, and Details using the buttons at the top of the Fonts folder.

FIGURE 35.11

All system fonts appear in the Fonts folder in the Control Panel.

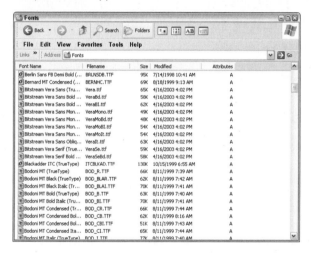

If you want to see what a specific font looks like you can right-click a font from the Fonts folder and select Open to see the font in a sample window, as shown in Figure 35.12, or you could select to print the selected font.

Several different types of fonts are available, but they can all be used within Windows. Early fonts were created from bitmaps, and these fonts required a separate bitmap for each font size to reduce distortion when the font changed sizes. You can still use bitmap fonts, but you shouldn't resize them or the text will appear distorted.

Over time, scalable fonts developed. These fonts were defined using *vectors* (mathematically defined curves) that could be scaled to any size without losing their shape. This resulted in significantly smaller font sizes and fonts that could be printed at almost any resolution while still retaining legibility.

FIGURE 35.12

The Open pop-up menu displays a sample of the selected font.

These different scalable types include the following:

- **Type 1 fonts:** Adobe created Type 1 fonts, which were initially supported on Macintosh systems.

- **TrueType fonts:** TrueType fonts were scalable fonts developed for Windows computers.

- **OpenType fonts**: OpenType is a format that works on both Macintosh and Windows computers.

OpenType fonts also support Unicode, which is an extended set of characters that includes space for characters used in other languages such as Hebrew, Greek, Japanese, Chinese, and so on.

Understanding Printer Memory

Like computers, printers can also use memory. The more memory your printer has, the larger the files it can manage. This doesn't mean that printers with a small amount of memory can't print large files, but the connection between the application and the printer remains open until the entire file is sent to the printer. This process is called *spooling* to the printer.

Printers with more memory can spool more and larger print jobs. If you work in a home office and don't mind waiting for your print job to complete, a low amount of printer memory may be fine, but in an office environment when multiple print jobs are spooled to the printer at a time, it is important to have enough printer memory so the employees don't spend all day waiting for their print jobs to complete.

NOTE Printer memory cannot be upgraded on many inexpensive printers, such as inkjets; however, upgradeable memory is common in laser printers.

The amount of memory that a printer can hold is different for each printer; check with your printer specifications to find out the memory capacity of your printer. If there is room to upgrade your printer's memory, you need to open up the printer and locate the memory slots. The more memory the printer has, the larger the print jobs it can handle.

CROSS-REF Installing printer memory works the same way as installing computer memory. See Chapter 7 for information on how to install memory.

Choosing and Handling Paper

One aspect that determines the size and cost of a printer is how it handles paper. All printers hold a set amount of paper, but larger printers handle great volumes of paper without requiring reloading.

NOTE Most inexpensive inkjet printers don't have a paper tray, but simply load pages from a slot in the back of the printer.

You can specify how the printer handles the loaded paper using the Paper tab of the Printing Preferences dialog box, as shown in Figure 35.13. The options in this dialog box differ for each printer, but this tab gives you options for selecting the Source Tray.

FIGURE 35.13

The Paper tab of the Printing Preferences dialog box lets you select which tray of paper to use.

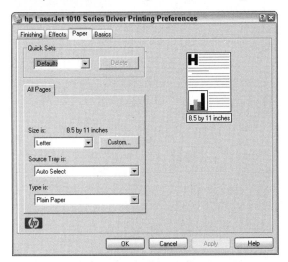

Some printers have multiple trays of paper. For example, an office printer may have one tray loaded with plain white paper and another tray loaded with letterhead paper, or glossy paper for printing photos. Using the Paper Type field you can identify which type of paper is loaded into each tray. You can also select the size of the paper for each tray.

Duplexing is a feature that enables a printer to print on both sides of a page without manual intervention. This can help reduce the amount of paper used, but requires specialized hardware to flip the page.

Another common setting found in the Printing Preferences dialog box is the paper orientation. If the printed page is taller than it is wide, the paper is using Portrait orientation; this is the default setting. You can change the orientation to be wider than it is tall; this orientation is called Landscape, as shown in the Basics tab of the Printing Preferences dialog box, shown in Figure 35.14.

FIGURE 35.14

The Basics tab of the Printing Preferences dialog box lets you change the paper's orientation.

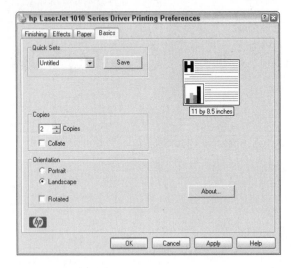

Printing Documents

After a printer is connected to your system, you can use that printer to print documents from the various applications. All applications that include a Print command can print documents. These applications range from word processors and e-mail clients to desktop publishing and image editing packages.

 **NOTE**   Most print commands are found within the File menu. Print buttons, which look like a small printer, are usually found on the application's toolbar.

When a print command is issued, the Print dialog box opens, as shown in Figure 35.15. This dialog box looks different depending on the application where the command was issued, but it always includes similar features.

At the top of the Print dialog box is a drop-down list where you can select the printer to use. A single system could have multiple printers set up: one for color prints, one for laser prints, and another for photographs. The Name field displays the name that was entered when the printer was installed. Underneath the printer's name is information about the printer type and location.

If you click the Properties button to the right of the printer name, the printer's Preferences dialog box covered in the previous section opens.

You can also use the Print dialog box to specify the range of pages to print. The options let you print all the pages in the current file, just the current page, just the current selection, or only the specified pages. You can also set the number of copies to print. If multiple copies of a document are selected, you can use the Collate option to have all the pages in the current document print in turn before another copy of the document is printed. If the Collate option is disabled, page 1 is printed for the specified number of copies before page 2 is printed.

 **If you leave the Collate option disabled, then the print job prints faster and uses less printer memory.**

FIGURE 35.15

The Print dialog box lets you choose which printer to use for the selected print job.

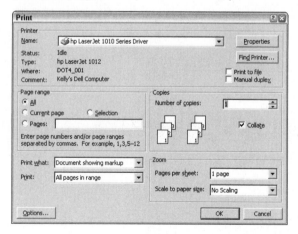

The Zoom option lets you print multiple pages of the current document on a single page. This is helpful if you want to save paper by condensing multiple slides of a presentation to a single page for a handout to accompany a presentation.

Printing to a file

Most applications can also print a document directly to a file instead of to a printer. If you enable the Print to File option in the Print dialog box, a File dialog box opens when you click Print. This saves the file as a PRN file in the location you specify.

These PRN files can then route directly to the printer from the Command Line using the copy MyPrintJob.prn lpt1: command. This textual command routes the file directly to the printer where it is printed. If multiple files are printed, you can write a macro to print an entire directory of files automatically one after another.

 PRN files are printer image files intended for a printer and display as unrecognized characters when opened in a word processor.

Using Page Setup

Another common printer application command is File ⇨ Page Setup, which opens the Page Setup dialog box, shown in Figure 35.16. Using this dialog box, you can change the document's margins and orientation without having to open the Printer Preferences dialog box.

FIGURE 35.16

The Page Setup dialog box lets you set the document's margins and orientation.

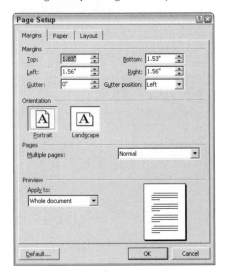

The Paper tab of the Page Setup dialog box, shown in Figure 35.17, includes options for setting the paper size. You can also choose the paper source.

FIGURE 35.17

The Paper tab of the Page Setup dialog box lets you set paper size and paper source.

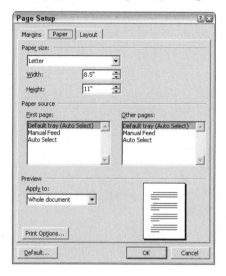

Using Print Preview

Many software applications also include a File ⇨ Print Preview command. This command shows exactly what the document looks like when printed, as shown in Figure 35.18. The Print Preview dialog box includes buttons for opening the Print and Page Setup dialog boxes, as well as for zooming in on the document.

FIGURE 35.18

The Print Preview dialog box shows what the document will look like when printed.

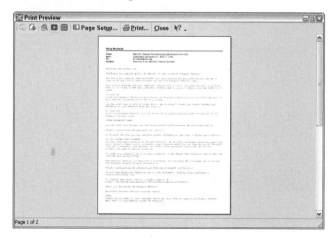

Summary

Before you can print documents from your applications, you first need to install and configure a printer. Understanding the different types of printers can help you purchase the printer that best meets your printing needs. A variety of printers are available, such as laser, inkjet, impact, and photo printers. All-in-One units include the ability to print, scan, fax, and copy documents in one piece of hardware.

You can connect printers directly to a computer using a parallel or USB port. You can also access printers over the network using the New Printer Wizard. The Printer Properties dialog box enables you to configure the selected printer.

Fonts allow you to design and print your documents using different text styles. All the installed system fonts are located in the Fonts folder in the Control Panel.

You can upgrade your printer's ability to spool larger files or multiple print jobs by increasing its memory. Larger printers include multiple paper trays for handling big print jobs.

Documents are printed from applications using the Print dialog box, which lets you choose from the available printers. You can also configure the document using the Page Setup and Print Preview dialog boxes.

Chapter 36

Making Presentations

If you need to make a presentation to a group, you can use the computer to create a presentation. Several software packages, such as Microsoft's PowerPoint, are available that you can use to automate the creation of a presentation. Presentations can include graphics, text, sound, and even video.

Once you have created your presentation, you can connect your computer to an office projector to project the entire presentation onto the wall and step through the pages of the presentation as you speak. This is much easier than having a large crowd grouped around a single computer monitor.

This chapter presents several tips for both creating presentations and connecting a projector to your computer.

Using Presentation Software

There are several different versions of presentation software available. The more popular ones include Microsoft PowerPoint and Corel Presentations. For those that are budget-minded, there is also a freely available presentation package called OpenOffice Impress. Regardless of the package that you choose, they all have roughly the same set of features.

NOTE When purchasing a presentation package, be sure that the software you select can save the file to a standard format that others can read.

PowerPoint

You can purchase Microsoft PowerPoint separately or as part of an office suite. It includes wizards that walk you through creating a presentation step by step, or you can manually build slides by adding images, text, and audio.

When you first open PowerPoint, the program divides the window into three separate panes, as shown in Figure 36.1. The left pane shows a thumbnail of each of the slides in the current presentation. If you click on any of these slides, its content loads into the center pane where you can change its text and load images or sound. The right pane of the PowerPoint window displays links and thumbnails for selecting specific tasks or loading different slide templates and/or designs.

FIGURE 36.1

PowerPoint divides the window into three different panes allowing quick access to each of the slides in the current presentation.

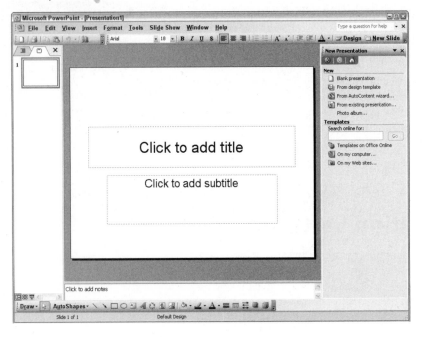

To create a presentation using PowerPoint, follow these steps:

1. **Open PowerPoint and click on the Create a New Presentation link in the right pane.**

2. **Click on the From Design Template link in the right pane.** This causes thumbnails of the available design templates to load in the right panel.

3. **Select a design template and double-click on its thumbnail in the right panel.** The design template automatically applies to all slides in the current presentation, as shown in Figure 36.2.

4. **Click on the box in the center panel that holds the title text. Type the title of the presentation, and then click on the subtitle box and type in its text.** If you drag on the title or subtitle box's corners you can change the size of the box or you can drag on its edge to move the text box.

FIGURE 36.2

The selected design template automatically applies to all slides in the current presentation.

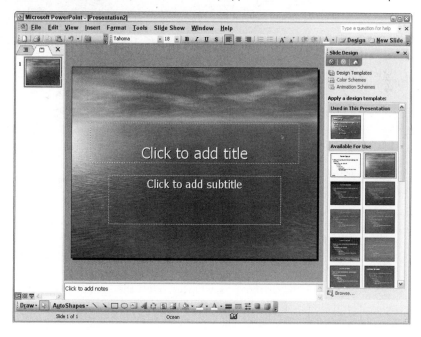

5. **To add a new slide to the current presentation, click on New Slide at the top of the window.** This opens several new slide template thumbnails in the right pane, as shown in Figure 36.3. It also adds a new slide beneath the current slide in the left panel.

6. **Double-click on a slide thumbnail with a bulleted list.** The bulleted list template adds as a second slide. Enter the text for the bulleted list.

7. **Click on New Slide again.** Double-click on a slide thumbnail with an image. A new slide with a box for loading an image is added to the presentation. In the center of the image template's box is a small window that lets you load a Table, a Chart, ClipArt, a Picture, a Diagram, an Organization Chart, or a Media File.

FIGURE 36.3

The New Slide thumbnails let you choose from several different templates.

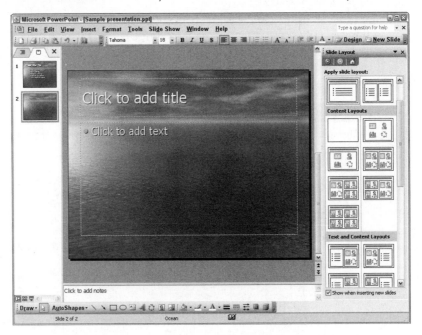

8. **Click on the ClipArt button to open the Select Picture dialog box.** Select an image and click OK. The image is added to the current presentation slide, as shown in Figure 36.4. You can resize the added image, as well as move it and rotate it by dragging on its corner handles.

9. **To preview the current presentation, select the View ⇨ Slide Show menu or press the F5 key.** The first slide of the current presentation fills the screen. Pressing the Spacebar or the arrow keys allows you to move between the various slides.

If you have some elements that need to be added to every page of the presentation, such as the date, page numbers, or a company logo, you can add these elements to a single page called the Master page. All text added to the Master page appears automatically on all slides within the presentation. You can access the Master page in PowerPoint using the View ⇨ Master menu.

 PowerPoint's Insert menu includes options for automatically adding the current Time/Date and Page Numbers to the current page.

To add sound and video files to the presentation page, use the Insert ⇨ Sound and Movies menu command. This opens a submenu of options for opening movies and sound files from several sources. There is even an option to Record Sound directly into the presentation. You can also include charts and graphs created in other applications into the current presentation page.

 Be consistent with the design and font used throughout the presentation. Changing the design and font throughout the presentation shows poor design and destroys consistency.

FIGURE 36.4

You can move images anywhere within the slide by dragging it to its new position.

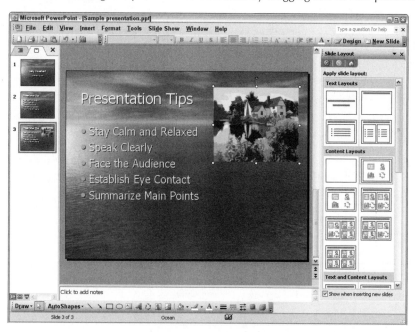

Elements placed on the page can be moved and resized by dragging the elements around the page. There are also alignment features for making the edges or centers of elements line up. The style of the text font and size can also be changed.

PowerPoint also includes several different *transition* options that you can select. A transition is the effect that appears between two slides. Transitions such as fade out and fade in are good for slowly introducing new slides. They also give the audience that is busily taking notes time to see the slide before it completely disappears.

 Before completing the presentation, be sure to use PowerPoint's Spell Check feature. Nothing can damage an effective presentation quicker than misspelled words.

Once the presentation is complete, you can switch between several different view modes. One view lets you see your outline, and another lets you see the entire presentation as thumbnails. This is helpful if you need to reorganize any of the pages. You can also view and create a page of notes, which is helpful for creating handouts for the group. The final view option is Slide Show. This option makes the current page fill the screen and should be used when you present slides.

While presenting, you can press the spacebar to move to the next slide, or you can use the arrow keys to move forward and backward through the presentation pages.

 You can also navigate through the presentation slides using the left mouse button or the mouse's scroll wheel.

OpenOffice Impress

OpenOffice is an office suite with word processor, spreadsheet, database, and presentation modules. The modules are developed by a team of developers that work together over the Internet. It is multiplatform, which means it can work on several different types of computers. The software is free to download and use, but you are encouraged to donate funds. You can download and find more information about OpenOffice at www.openoffice.org.

 If you are considering moving to Linux in the future, then OpenOffice may be an excellent choice because it works the same in Windows and Linux.

The presentation module that comes in OpenOffice is called Impress. In many ways, it is similar to PowerPoint. Impress starts with a wizard that lets you choose specific templates. In the main view, shown in Figure 36.5, you can select from the current set of slides in the left pane and choose a new template to use in the right pane.

FIGURE 36.5

OpenOffice Impress provides an alternative presentation package.

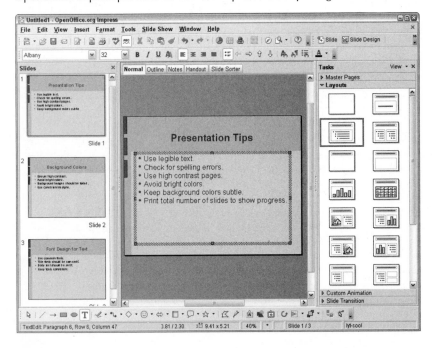

The tabs across the top of the main window let you switch between the various views. To run the presentation, choose the View ➪ Slide Show menu option. The arrow keys let you move through the presentation pages.

> **NOTE** Another key benefit of OpenOffice is that it can import and export files in a format that PowerPoint can read, so files created with PowerPoint can be opened in OpenOffice Impress and vice versa.

Choosing a Projector

Most companies have conference rooms with a projector already set up and ready to use, but there are many factors that are different among the various projectors on the market. Projectors are also coming down in price, making projectors available for home use. If you have the chance to purchase or recommend a projector, then understanding these differences can help with your decision.

There are two technologies used in most projectors today — DLP and LCD. DLP projectors use a mirrored chip to focus the projection, resulting in projectors that are lighter and smaller. DLP projectors are more mobile and generally sturdier than LCD projectors. LCD projectors use three liquid crystal panels to create a projection. These result in a brighter beam that shows up more clearly across a large room. Figure 36.6 shows a sample DLP projector available from Dell, Inc.

> **NOTE** If you intend to use the projector in a room with windows that can let in some external light, then look for an LCD projector that has a brightness value of at least 800 lumens and a DLP projector with a brightness value of at least 1000 lumens.

FIGURE 36.6

Projectors can project a computer image onto the side of a wall so an entire group can view the presentation.

Image Courtesy of Dell Inc.

Each projector has a recommended distance range that the projector can handle. If the distance between the screen and projector is larger than this recommended distance, then you may want to consider a different unit. Trying to use a projector beyond its recommended distance results in an image that isn't clear or in focus.

It is also important to check the resolution that the projector supports. Projectors that support higher resolutions can display more details. For television viewing, an SVGA resolution of 800 x 600 is sufficient, but for connecting to a computer or for high definition (HD) video, a resolution of 1024 x 768 (XGA) is required.

In addition to resolution, watch for the aspect ratios that the projector can handle. Standard aspect ratios for television and standard video are 4:3, but widescreen movies have an aspect ratio or 16:9. If your projector doesn't handle widescreen, then you may be stuck watching movies in standard format.

The final option to check when looking into projectors is the connection method. Common connectors for projectors include standard RCA, S-Video, and component video connections. If you need to connect to a computer, look for a projector that has a monitor port that can connect to a computer. Some projectors require a converter to convert the analog video signal to digital.

Connecting to a Projector

Whether your presentation is installed on your laptop or on a desktop computer, the best way to display your presentation is to connect a computer to a projector that can display the presentation on a large wall or screen.

CAUTION   One of the expensive parts of a projector is the lamp that projects the display. When you turn off the projector, be sure to let the fan run for some time to cool the unit before you disconnect power.

Connecting a projector is slightly different depending on whether you're connecting to a laptop computer or to a desktop computer, but either isn't particularly difficult.

Connecting to a laptop

Arriving one hour early to the conference room can ensure that you get your presentation displaying properly before everyone arrives. You might be happy to know that if the presentation is on your laptop, then connecting it to a projector is as simple as plugging in the projector to the video port and switching the display to the projector.

If you examine the projector closely, you should discover a cable with a video port connector attached to it. This video cable can connect directly to your laptop in the same place where the external monitor connects.

Once the projector is attached, you need to tell your laptop to switch its display to the projector. This is usually accomplished by holding down an option key and pressing the F7 or F8 key (although this may be different depending on your computer). Pressing this key combination toggles the display between your laptop screen and the projector. It is often helpful to have both the laptop screen and the projector visible at once.

Connecting to a desktop computer

The easiest way to connect a projector to a desktop computer is to simply replace the cable going from the computer to the monitor with one that goes to the projector. This causes the projector to use the same display settings as those for the monitor, which may not be correct for the projector.

If the resolution that the projector uses is different from the resolution on your computer, then you need to change the resolution settings on your computer before the computer desktop can correctly display on the projector. You can fix the display setting using the Display Properties dialog box, shown in Figure 36.7. The easiest way to access this dialog box is to right-click on the Desktop, select Properties from the pop-up menu, and then click the Settings tab.

NOTE If you already connected the computer to the projector and are having trouble setting the resolution, then reconnect the video cable to the computer and set the resolution using the computer's monitor before switching back to the projector.

FIGURE 36.7

The Display Properties dialog box lets you change the display resolution.

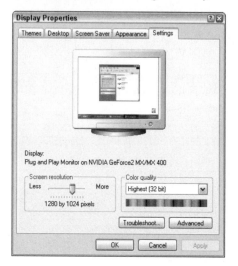

If you need to view the monitor screen while the audience views the projector screen, you may need to configure your graphics card to display on two screens simultaneously. The process for doing this depends on the video card that you are using, but the processes are roughly the same across the board.

From your computer's Control Panel, choose the specific control panel for the graphics adapter that you are using. It can be identified at the NVIDIA or ATI Control Panel. Within this dialog box is a Display tab that lets you select to use two monitors. If you select this option, you can hook the monitor to a single video port and the projector to the second video port. If there is a Clone option (or sometimes called a Mirrored option), select it to see the same display on both screens.

> **NOTE**   The Extended Output option extends the desktop into one extra long screen. This is convenient if you work with a large number of windows.

Some video cards don't support two monitors, but you can still use the projector and a monitor if you purchase a video splitter. This device lets you connect both the projector and the video screen to the computer. Using a splitter lets you face the crowd while looking at your computer monitor.

Summary

Several different software packages are available for creating presentations, including Microsoft PowerPoint and OpenOffice Impress. These packages rely heavily on wizards and templates to make building presentations easy. They also include the capabilities to include images, text, audio, video, simple animations, and page transitions.

Projectors offer a great way to show a presentation to a large crowd. There are several different options available for projectors. Be sure to check the features of the projector you are purchasing so it works for your needs.

Once a presentation is complete, you can connect either a laptop or a desktop computer to a projector to display the presentation to a group. Connecting a projector is a fairly easy process for laptops and requires some simple adjustments for desktop computers.

Chapter 37

Scanning to Your Computer

A scanner lets you transfer printed images, whether photos or printed text, into the computer as digital images. The most common type of scanner looks like a copier with a glass surface where you place the scanned document, and a button to initiate the scanning process. Scanners are typically connected to a computer with a USB cable.

On the computer side is the Scanner and Camera Wizard that lets you preview the document before starting the process. You can also select to scan the document as a color photograph or as a black-and-white page of text.

Using additional software, you can process scanned pages of text and convert them into text documents that can be edited just like any other text document.

Choosing a Scanner

When looking for a scanner, keep in mind why you need it. Do you need to archive your old photos onto CD, do you need to scan hundreds of images for a home business catalog, or do you need to convert pages of type to editable documents? A wide range of scanners is available on the market from very expensive to fairly reasonable depending on intended use.

Scanner types and size

The most common home scanner is the flatbed scanner. This type of scanner is like a small copier with a glass plane where the object to be scanned rests. Once the scanning process starts, a light sweeps across the range of the page and sensors detect the image.

CROSS-REF All-in-One printers, covered in Chapter 35, can also scan documents.

For portable systems, you can get a handheld scanner that is much smaller than the flatbed and works by dragging the device over the page.

CAUTION Handheld scanners can be problematic because they rely on the user dragging the scanner smoothly across the page for a good scan.

Flatbed scanners can be outfitted with a document-handling unit that enables multiple pages to be scanned without manually placing each individual page. An alternative to getting a document-handling unit is to purchase a sheet-fed scanner that has document-handling hardware built into the scanner.

Slide scanners are specialized scanners that can scan images from film negatives and slides.

Print shops and pre-press departments typically use a *drum scanner* that can scan images at very high resolutions, but can also be very expensive. Other expensive specialized scanners include microfilm and slide scanners that can scan rolls of film and transparent slides.

The most common flatbed scanner size is letter-sized, which can scan a normal 8.5 x 11–inch page. Larger scanners that can handle legal-sized documents are also available.

Resolution and bit depth

Another distinguishing feature of scanners is the resolution that they are capable of scanning. Images intended for display on a computer monitor, such as those that appear on Web pages, can be scanned at 72 dots per inch (dpi). This resolution is fairly low and should be handled by most scanners. Images for print should be scanned at 300 dpi. Scanners that are capable of scanning at higher resolutions can capture finer detail.

The maximum resolution capability is determined by the scanner's optical scan resolution value, which can range between 1200 x 1200 to 4800 x 9600 for higher-end scanners. The optical scan resolution is the actual number of dots per inch that can be scanned. Many scanners report higher resolution values as *interpolated scan solution*, which is the number of dots per inch that can be computed.

Scanners also report the number of bits that the scanner can process. This value is the amount of scanned data that is captured by the scanner. Larger bit depths can produce larger data files with more resolution. A 24-bit scanner produces files with half the resolution of a 48-bit scanner.

Most scanners use one of two technologies — Charge Coupled Device (CCD) or Contact Image Sensor (CIS) — to produce a scan. CIS technology is newer and works by converting light into electric signals that can be used to create a digital image. CIS scanners are generally smaller and more compact that CCD scanners and require less power.

Bundled software

Another major factor that influences the scanner cost is the software that is bundled with the scanner. Most scanners come with software that allows users to edit images and to convert scanned text to editable text. The software that allows scanned text to be converted to editable text is called Optical Character Recognition (OCR) software. Less expensive scanners are typically bundled with "light" versions of software, and more expensive scanners include full versions of software.

Setting Up a Scanner

After you've purchased a scanner that meets your needs, the setup process is fairly easy with just a few steps, including connecting the scanner to your computer and installing the scanner software.

Connecting the scanner

One of the biggest differences between the various scanners is how the scanner connects to the computer. Older scanners connect via the computer's parallel port, but new models can use a USB port to efficiently connect. Some higher-end models include a FireWire connection, which enables data to be transferred to the computer at a faster rate.

TIP For the average user, a USB connection is sufficient. But if your computer doesn't have a USB port, you need to look for a parallel or serial port scanner. FireWire scanners can be expensive, but they capture scans much faster than other methods.

Connecting a scanner to the computer is an easy process. Most USB scanners are detected automatically when connected. When it detects a scanner, Windows looks for an available driver that can communicate with the scanner. If it finds one, the scanner is ready to go, but if Windows can't find a driver that will work, it asks you to locate the correct driver. Scanner drivers are included on the CD that ships with the scanner, or you can locate the necessary driver from the manufacturer's Web site.

TIP If you get a used scanner, you can typically find the necessary drivers by visiting the manufacturer's Web site.

Installing the scanner software

Most scanners come with a CD-ROM that includes the scanner device drivers and some bundled software. After you connect the scanner to the computer, insert the CD-ROM and follow the instructions for installing the software.

NOTE Some installations ask you to disconnect the scanner while the software and drivers are installing.

The software included with the scanner is typically proprietary software and cannot be used between scanners by different manufacturers.

The TWAIN standard

The common device driver used by the computer to talk to the scanner hardware is the TWAIN driver. The TWAIN driver has universal support and can be used by almost all scanners. Windows XP uses this driver to read data from the scanner using the Scanner and Camera Wizard.

The TWAIN driver also lets software packages such as Adobe's Photoshop scan images directly into the software where they can be edited and cleaned up.

Testing the scanner

You can use the Control Panel to check the installation of your scanner before you start scanning. To access the Properties dialog box for the installed scanner, open the Control Panel and double-click the Scanners and Cameras icon. This displays a list of all the installed digital cameras and scanners. Choose the scanner and select the File ⇨ Properties menu.

The scanner Properties dialog box, shown for the HP Scanjet scanner that is attached to my system in Figure 37.1, includes several tabs. In the General tab, you can click the Test Scanner or Camera button to test if the scanner works. This button causes the scanner to turn on, and if the communication between the scanner and the computer works, a dialog box appears stating that the scanner is ready.

FIGURE 37.1

The scanner's Properties dialog box lets you test the scanner installation.

The Events tab of the Properties dialog box, shown in Figure 37.2, lets you define what happens when the interface buttons on the front of the scanner are pressed. The Troubleshooting tab includes buttons for testing the document feeder and handling any problems that may exist. The Color Management tab lets you synch the color profile with the other connected devices such as the printer and the monitor.

FIGURE 37.2

The Events tab of the scanner's Properties dialog box lets you define which applications open when the interface buttons are pressed.

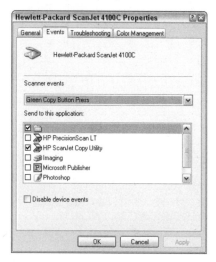

Scanning Images and Documents

If you've ever used a copy machine, you should feel right at home with a scanner. To use a scanner, simply place the image or page you want to scan on the flatbed scanner's glass, close the lid and press Scan on the scanner. This activates the scanner software or the Windows Scanner and Camera Wizard on your computer, as shown in Figure 37.3. The first screen of the wizard lists the scanner's name.

 **NOTE** If the Scanner and Camera Wizard doesn't appear, you can access it directly using the Start ⇨ All Programs ⇨ Accessories ⇨ Scanner and Camera Wizard menu.

FIGURE 37.3

The Scanner and Camera Wizard automatically opens when you press Scan on the scanner.

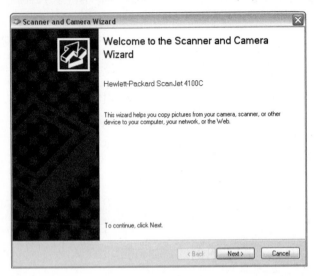

After clicking the Next button, the wizard displays a step where you can select the type of picture that you'll be scanning, as shown in Figure 37.4. The options include Color picture, Grayscale picture, Black and white picture or text, and Custom. Most scans use the Color option, but the Grayscale option is good if you intend to print the scanned image. For pages of text that will convert to text files, the Black and White or Text option works well.

CAUTION Be cautious when scanning copyrighted materials out of books and magazines. A majority of printed material cannot be scanned and used unless you have permission from the publisher.

If the Custom option is selected, you can click the Custom settings button to access a dialog box of options, shown in Figure 37.5. Using this dialog box, you can change the Brightness and Contrast values. These values can be positive or negative with 0 representing no change.

You can also adjust the Resolution (dpi) setting depending on the capabilities of your scanner. Online images are usually only 72 dpi, but you should use 300 dpi or higher for images that will be printed. The file size for the scanned image increases as the dpi value is increased.

FIGURE 37.4

The second screen of the Scanner and Camera Wizard lets you select which type of picture you'll be scanning.

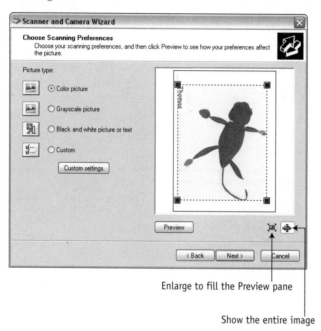

Enlarge to fill the Preview pane

Show the entire image

FIGURE 37.5

The Custom scan settings include an option for setting the resolution of the image to be scanned.

If you click the Preview button shown in Figure 37.4, the scanner activates and the image placed on the scanner appears. At each corner of the preview are square handles that you can drag to mark where the image should be cropped. The two icon buttons below the Preview pane are used to show the entire scan area or to enlarge the crop area to fill the Preview pane.

 Cropping an image before scanning makes the scan go quicker and results in a smaller file.

The third step of the Scanner and Camera Wizard, shown in Figure 37.6, lets you name the scanned image and specify its format and where it saves. The supported file formats include BMP, JPEG, TIF, and PNG. When you click the Next button on this page, the scan begins and its progress is shown in the next wizard page.

FIGURE 37.6

The third step of the Scanner and Camera Wizard lets you name and save the scanned image.

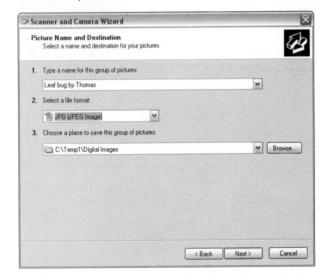

The final page of the wizard gives you options to publish the pictures to a Web site, order prints from a photo-printing Web site, or do nothing. Click the Finish button to close the wizard. Immediately after closing the wizard, a Windows Explorer page opens to where the scanned image was saved.

Using text recognition software

Another common application that is typically bundled with a scanner is Optical Character Recognition (OCR) software. Using this software, you can convert a page of scanned text into a file that can be opened and edited by a word-processing application, saving you the hassle of retyping the document.

 The best results come from a document that has clean, typed words. You should also scan documents at 300 dpi.

The actual OCR software included with your scanner will be different depending on the product that you purchase, but they all work approximately the same. Some OCR packages can even detect and format documents.

My scanner was made by Hewlett-Packard and the bundled software is called PrecisionScan LT, as shown in Figure 37.7. This software allows you to specify the type of file that the scan saves as. One option is to save the scanned document as a text file. This causes the scanned document to automatically convert and save as a text file using OCR technology.

 The Camera and Scanner Wizard doesn't include an OCR scanning option.

FIGURE 37.7

The HP PrecisionScan LT software is an example of the kind of software that ships with a scanner.

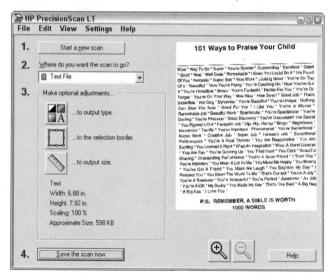

Using your scanner as a copier

Most bundled scanner software also includes a utility that lets your scanner act as a copier. This requires that you connect both a scanner and a printer to your computer. The scanned document routes to the printer using this utility. Figure 37.8 shows an example of the copier utility that ships with HP scanners.

589

FIGURE 37.8

The HP ScanJet Copy Utility lets you use your scanner and printer like a copier.

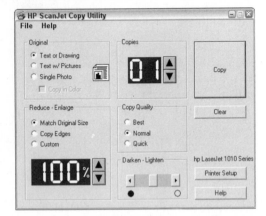

Summary

A scanner can be a valuable piece of hardware, allowing you to input existing images and printed documents into the computer. A wide variety of scanners are available, and understanding what to look for can help as you look for a specific scanner to fit your needs.

Setting up a scanner can be an easy process if you get the right kind of scanner for your system. Scanners are typically connected to a computer using the USB or parallel ports. You also need to install the scanner software, which includes the scanner drivers.

Once installed, you can use the bundled software to scan images or text documents. You can then convert text documents into a format that you can edit using specialized OCR software. If a printer is connected to your computer, the scanner can act like a copier.

Chapter 38

Using Your Computer with a Digital Camera

When you consider the cost of film and film processing, a digital camera is a worthwhile investment, but the trade-off is often made in the quality of the prints.

Digital cameras with higher resolution are appearing all the time and their cost is steadily coming down. Photo printers are now available that can print images comparable to those you'd get at the photo lab.

Before purchasing a digital camera, it is helpful to know what all the various features are for and if you need them. Considerations like how many mega-pixels you want, resolution, and the quality of lenses all add cost to a camera.

Images are saved on the flash memory cards included in the digital camera, where they are stored until you connect the camera to a computer and download the images. Once downloaded, you can use the Windows features to view the images as a slide show.

If the images you've captured have some problems, you can improve them by editing them using an image editing package such as Windows Paint or Adobe Photoshop.

This chapter looks at all the features enabled by using a digital camera with your computer system.

Selecting a Digital Camera

Lots of different digital cameras are available, and understanding the differences among these cameras can make a big difference as you begin to shop.

The most important distinguishing feature in a digital camera is the maximum resolution that it can take. The maximum resolution also affects the price of the camera.

 Don't base your purchasing decision on a single feature such as resolution. A camera with a high resolution and a poor dynamic range may not be the best bet.

Resolution in megapixels

Camera resolutions are measured in the number of megapixels that a camera can shoot. This value is a combination of the number of horizontal and vertical pixels for the image. For example, a digital camera that can capture 2500 horizontal pixels by 1900 vertical pixels can save the image in a 5.0 megapixel camera.

The preferred resolution depends on what you plan to do with the images you capture. The greater the resolution, the clearer the subtle details are. If you plan on simply sending the pictures you take over the Internet to share with relatives, then a lower resolution camera may be sufficient, but if you are planning on printing out your images, then larger resolutions are a must.

NOTE Some digital cameras report the *interpolated resolution,* which is the resolution they can produce after calculating the pixels positioned in between the captured pixels. This value isn't a direct measurement relative to what the camera actually captures.

Dynamic range

Related to the camera's resolution is *dynamic range*, which is the number of discreet grayscale levels that can be captured between the brightest and darkest areas of the image. A digital camera's dynamic range is controlled by the camera's sensor. If a camera has a poor dynamic range, then the images it captures are easily over- or under-developed. If this happens, then the amount of pixels that you can capture doesn't really matter because all the image's details are washed out in the shadows.

One way to check the image's dynamic range is to look at the image's *histogram*, which is a graph that shows the available levels for the image. Some digital cameras show the image's histogram on its LCD screen.

Camera lenses

A camera is only as good as the lens it has. More expensive cameras have finer, higher quality lenses. Most low-end digital cameras include an embedded lens, but for professional photography, look for a digital camera that can change lenses.

Lenses are measured by their *focal length*, which is measured in millimeters. This value determines the range that the camera lens can zoom in on a scene. A 35 mm lens is common for most shots, wide angle lens would be in the 24 mm range, and telephoto lenses would be in the 105 to 200 mm range. Camera lenses are another major expense for digital cameras.

Many high-end digital cameras can switch between different lenses, but lower-end digital cameras can simulate these different lens settings using a zoom feature. Cameras with a 3X zoom can provide wide angle and telephoto shots of the scene without changing position.

Digital cameras deal with zooming in two ways. An optical zoom feature includes a feature that actually moves the lens closer or further from the scene. A digital zoom feature zooms the image using logic programmed by software. Some cameras combine these two features to increase the amount of zoom power that a camera has.

TIP Cameras with an optical zoom feature are more expensive, but offer a greater chance to zoom in on the scene than those cameras with only a digital zoom feature.

Flash memory

The images taken with a digital camera are saved on a flash memory card. Some cameras have built-in memory, but memory cards are more common. You can switch out memory cards to save more images without having to download all the images off a camera. Once the images from a flash memory card are downloaded to a computer, you can clear the memory card and capture new images.

Flash memory cards come in different sizes; the larger the memory card, the more digital images it can hold. You can also alter the quality settings on your camera to take images with a reduced resolution. More smaller-resolution images can fit on a single memory card. For example, a 1GB flash memory card can hold 200 images that are 5MB in size, but the same memory card can hold 500 images if the resolution setting is reduced to capture 2MB images.

A number of different flash memory card formats are available and they aren't interchangeable. Only one type of memory card works with each specific digital camera. The available flash memory card formats include the following:

- Compact Flash
- Smart Media
- xD-Picture
- Secure Digital
- Sony Memory Stick

Image formats

Digital cameras can save captured images in several different formats including RAW, TIF, and JPEG. The RAW format saves the actual data for the image without any digital processing. Photoshop can import RAW image data. The TIFF format works well and saves the image data without any degradation, but the file sizes can be large. Cameras that save images using the JPEG format can fit more images on a single memory card, but JPEG is a *lossy* image format meaning that it throws away some of the image data in order to get the file sizes smaller.

 Although the JPEG image format throws away some image data to compress the image's size, it is very picky in which pixels it throws away so the image quality is retained.

Camera settings

Film cameras typically include several settings that can drastically change the resulting picture. Many digital cameras automatically control these settings for you with their *point and shoot* feature, but for some cases, you want access to manually control these settings.

The aperture setting controls the amount of light let into the camera through an opening, or *aperture,* in the lens; the aperture setting control (or commonly called the f-stop value) defines the size of the lens opening. It can also affect where the camera is in focus. The *shutter speed* controls how quickly the aperture opens and closes. For action shots with very fast moving figures, you want to set the shutter speed to act very quickly in order to capture the motion.

You can adjust an exposure control setting depending on whether you're shooting images inside or outside. Low light conditions need a longer exposure to capture the image. You can use color balance controls to control the tint of the image towards red, green, or blue.

Other features

Other features to consider when looking into the various digital cameras include the following:

- **Size:** Some digital cameras are very small and unobtrusive. Higher-end cameras typically are much larger.
- **Sturdiness:** If you need a digital camera that is waterproof or sturdy enough to take a fall, then look into a camera that is more rugged.
- **Battery power:** Most of the smaller digital cameras use a set of double AA batteries, but they can run out of power quickly. Many cameras run on Lithium batteries providing longer battery life. Purchasing a set of rechargeable batteries is a good investment if you're planning on taking a lot of pictures.
- **LCD screen:** Many people like to share their pictures when they take them and a larger LCD screen on the back of the camera makes this easier to do.
- **Auto Focus:** Most lower-end digital cameras include features that automatically focus on the objects in front of you, but on some cameras, this feature focuses on the wrong items.
- **Flash:** For indoor shots a flash can provide the needed lighting, but a built-in flash can quickly drain battery power. If the flash is disabled, it doesn't drain battery power.

Downloading Pictures

All digital cameras include a small LCD screen that you can use to view the pictures you've recently taken, but to edit and print or even just to view these images on a larger display, you need to download the images to a computer. This process moves the stored images from the memory card within the digital camera to the computer's hard drive.

Connecting the camera to your computer

To download the digital images to the computer, you first need to connect a computer cable from the digital camera to the computer. Digital cameras frequently use the USB port, but the port on the camera's end isn't standardized and often the cables for one camera aren't interchangeable between different cameras.

 Some cameras connect to the computer using a camera dock that makes downloading images and recharging the camera quick and easy.

When you insert the digital camera's cable into the USB port, Windows recognizes the device and a dialog box appears, shown in Figure 38.1, where you can select how to handle the connected device.

 If you enable the Always do the selected action option, then the requested action loads automatically when the camera is connected.

The options included in the dialog box let you copy the picture to the hard drive using the Scanner and Camera Wizard, view the images using the Windows Picture and Fax Viewer, print the images, or view the images using one of the applications installed on your system.

 Remember that the digital camera must be turned on when the USB cable is connected for the camera to be recognized unless the camera uses a camera dock.

FIGURE 38.1

The Removable Disk dialog box opens when a USB device is connected to the computer.

Downloading digital pictures

Some computers and/or printers have flash memory slots that allow you to insert the flash memory cards directly into the computer and/or printer for downloading. Using these devices, you don't need to connect the digital camera to the computer, but the images can download directly off the flash memory card.

 **Even if your computer doesn't have slots for inserting flash memory cards, you can purchase a separate add-on device that connects to a USB port that includes these slots.**

If you select to copy the pictures to your hard drive using the Scanner and Camera Wizard, then the wizard is automatically started as shown in Figure 38.2. Using this wizard, you can download the digital images from the camera.

FIGURE 38.2

The Scanner and Camera Wizard can download images from the camera's memory card.

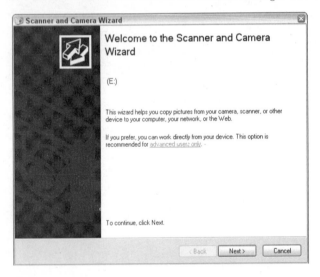

The first page of the Scanner and Camera Wizard queries the camera and displays thumbnails of all the images on the camera's memory card, as shown in Figure 38.3. Using the checkmark above each thumbnail, you can select exactly which images to download. You can use the Clear All and Select All options to select or deselect all thumbnails.

Click on an image thumbnail to select it. The thumbnail becomes surrounded with a border when selected. If you hold down the Ctrl or Shift keys, you can select multiple thumbnails. You can rotate the selected thumbnails clockwise or counterclockwise using the icon buttons under the thumbnails. There is also a Properties icon button that can be used to open a Properties dialog box for the selected image. This dialog box, shown in Figure 38.4, displays the date and time when the image was taken, its format, and size.

FIGURE 38.3

The first page of the Scanner and Camera Wizard displays all the images on the camera's memory card as thumbnails.

FIGURE 38.4

The Properties dialog box shows the date and time when the image was taken.

The next page of the wizard, shown in Figure 38.5, lets you provide a name for the selected images that will download. If multiple images are marked for download, then each of the image files will be named using the specified name followed by a sequential number. You can also choose the location where the image files saves. The Browse button lets you choose a different folder where the images can save. If an image isn't selected to be downloaded, then it remains on the flash memory card.

 It is a good idea to delete the images from the camera's memory as they are being downloaded.

FIGURE 38.5

The next page of the Scanner and Camera Wizard lets you give the images a name and specifies where the images will save.

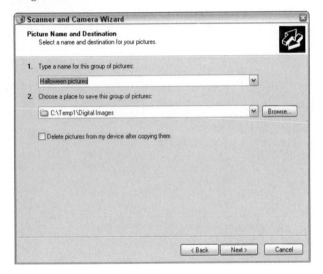

After clicking Next, the images download to the hard drive, and the progress of each of the images is displayed in the wizard, as shown in Figure 38.6. After all images have downloaded, the images are deleted if you selected the delete option.

FIGURE 38.6

The Scanner and Camera Wizard shows the progress of all the images being downloaded.

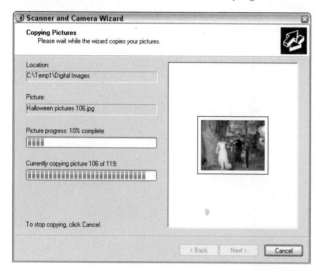

Publishing images to a Web site

The wizard then presents a page, shown in Figure 38.7, with options to publish the downloaded pictures to a Web site, order prints from a photo printing Web site, or do nothing and close the wizard. If you select Publish the images to a Web site, then all the images contained within the folder where the last images were downloaded are displayed as thumbnails; from all the thumbnails contained in this folder you can select which images to upload to a Web site.

You can then choose which Internet account you can publish the images to. If you don't have an account, you can select the MSN Groups option and create a new account. As you complete the wizard, the images upload and become available for viewing on the Web.

If you select to order prints from a photo printing Web site, then you're routed to a Web site that can accommodate this request. If you select the Nothing option, then the wizard closes.

FIGURE 38.7

The next screen in the Scanner and Camera Wizard includes an option to publish the downloaded pictures to a Web site.

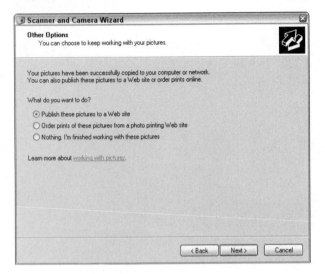

Viewing Pictures

If you open the folder where the images downloaded, you can view a thumbnail of each down-loaded image by simply selecting the image file, as shown in Figure 38.8. Beneath each image thumbnail, the information about the selected image is displayed. This information shows you the format, dimensions, and size of the image.

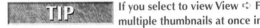

TIP If you select to view View ➪ Filmstrip or the View ➪ Thumbnails options, you can see multiple thumbnails at once in the folder.

At the top of the Windows Explorer folder that holds the images are several picture-specific options you can select to make viewing an entire directory of images easy. There are also options to order prints online, set the selected image as the desktop background, or copy the selected images to a CD.

Viewing images as a slide show

If you select the View as a slide show option from the Picture Tasks section of the Windows Explorer window, then the images in the selected directory are shown at full-screen resolution. In the upper-right corner is a small toolbar of buttons that you can use to Start, Pause and Exit slide show mode. There are also buttons that you can use to move back and forth between the next and previous images.

TIP You can also use the arrow keys to move back and forth through the slide show images. The Ctrl+K and Ctrl+L keys are used to rotate the current image clockwise or counter-clockwise. If you rotate the image, the rotated image saves over the original image.

600

FIGURE 38.8

You can view thumbnail images in Windows Explorer when an image file is selected.

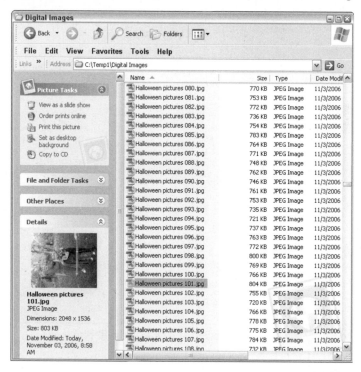

Viewing images as a screen saver

You can also view the downloaded image as a screen saver that appears when the computer is idle for a specified amount of time.

To view a folder of downloaded images as a screen saver, follow these steps:

1. **Right click on the desktop and select the Properties menu option to access the Display Settings dialog box.**

2. **Select the Screen Saver tab, shown in Figure 38.9 and choose the My Pictures Slideshow option.**

3. **Click on the Settings button to access a dialog box of settings for this screen saver, shown in Figure 38.10.** Using these settings you can determine how long the images remain before changing. You can also set the size of the images and whether you can use the keyboard arrows to move back and forth through the displayed images.

FIGURE 38.9

The Screen Saver tab of the Display Properties dialog box lets you set up a screen saver
to view a folder of downloaded images.

FIGURE 38.10

The My Pictures Screen Saver Options dialog box lets you change the directory of
images viewed.

Editing Pictures

If after reviewing your downloaded digital images you find that images aren't exactly what you wanted, you can alter the images using one of many photo-editing applications that are available.

These applications let you change the images in a number of different ways. The results of the image-editing process depend on the skill of the person doing the edits, but several editing techniques are simple enough for any user with even the simplest available application.

The features available in image editing packages vary greatly. Some applications, such as Windows Paint, provide only a basic set of fundamental features, while higher-end applications such as Adobe Photoshop provide complete control over editing all aspects of the image. The following applications are popular choices for editing digital images:

- **Windows Paint:** Even though this provides only a rudimentary set of features, this package still lets you crop, rotate images, and add captions to images.

- **Adobe Photoshop:** This is a professional-level tool that lets you control all aspects of a digital image including the exposure levels and color depth. Photoshop also lets you seamlessly remove or add objects to images.

- **Adobe Photoshop Elements:** If you don't need all the advanced level features of Photoshop, then Photoshop Elements may be just the ticket. Elements includes features for organizing pictures and basic editing.

- **Corel Paint Shop Pro:** This is a popular, easy-to-use editing application.

Rotating images

When using a digital camera, you can rotate the camera so the image is vertical, but when the images download to your hard drive, they appear rotated. Although the Scanner and Camera Wizard includes a feature to rotate the downloading images, you can also rotate images using an editing application such as Windows Paint.

You can access Windows Paint using the Start ➪ All Programs ➪ Accessories ➪ Paint menu. Paint can open images using the File ➪ Open menu or you could simply drag and drop images from Windows Explorer. To rotate the current image, simply select the image and choose the Image ➪ Flip/Rotate menu command. This opens a dialog box where you can Flip horizontal, Flip vertical, or Rotate by 90, 180, or 270 degrees. Figure 38.11 shows an image in Windows Paint that has been rotated to stand upright.

FIGURE 38.11

You can use Windows Paint to rotate images.

Cropping images

Cropping simply means to cut away all the areas of the image that you don't want to keep. By cropping images, you can cut down on the size of the images and subsequently the file size.

To crop an image in Paint Shop Pro, follow these steps:

1. **Open the image that you want to crop in Paint Shop Pro by dragging it from Windows Explorer or by selecting the File ➪ Open command.**
2. **From the toolbar located under the menus, select the Rectangular Select tool.** Drag it over the area of the image that you want to keep, as shown in Figure 38.12.

FIGURE 38.12

You can use the Select tool to choose the area that you want to keep.

Rectangular Select tool

3. **Choose the Image ⇨ Crop menu command.** The image is cropped to include only the selected portion, as shown in Figure 38.13.

4. **Select the File ⇨ Save menu to save the cropped image.** Use the File ⇨ Save As command if you want to save the original file.

FIGURE 38.13

All the unnecessary parts of the image are removed by cropping.

Adjusting brightness and contrast

If you travel all the way to Hawaii on vacation and return to find that the flash on your digital camera didn't work most of the time, you may be frustrated at the pictures you've lost. But, with an image-editing application like Photoshop, you can readjust the brightness and contrast levels to recover the images taken with inadequate lighting.

CAUTION All the editing software in the world can't bring back detail that just wasn't captured to begin with. Try to get your photos right as you take them, as there are limits to what even the best programs can do.

Figure 38.14 shows a digital image that is too dark. Using Photoshop, you can lighten this image while maintaining a strong enough contrast.

FIGURE 38.14

With inadequate lighting, digital images can end up too dark.

Figure 38.15 shows the image after the exposure levels in Photoshop have been adjusted. The adjustment features are found in the Image ➪ Adjustments ➪ Brightness/Contrast menu.

FIGURE 38.15

By adjusting brightness and contrast levels in Photoshop, you can restore the image's clarity.

Removing red eye

Have you ever looked directly at the flash when someone has taken your picture? Not only do you end up seeing dots for the next little while, but when you look at the picture, you notice that your eyes appear an unsightly bright red.

This red-eye phenomenon occurs when the light from the flash bounces off the back of the eye's retina. Although you cannot change this problem on the digital image, you can fix it during the editing process. Photoshop includes a new feature that automatically removes red eyes from characters in a digital image. To use this tool in Photoshop, simply select the Red Eye tool and drag it over the problem area. Photoshop automatically detects the problem area and removes the exposed red color.

Removing objects

Photoshop also includes many specialized tools that remove unwanted sections from an image by covering them up with other sections. This technique works especially well when the areas you're copying are similar in color and texture such as a blue sky or part of a forest.

Using the Clone tool, you can select a point within the image to copy over the area under your brush. The brush then transfers the area you've selected to the area where you're brushing. The results can save a picture from ending up in the trash or being cropped so much it loses its details.

Figure 38.16 shows an excellent picture of a beach, but the shot of the foot in the picture ruins the picturesque beauty.

FIGURE 38.16

Unwanted objects can ruin a good digital picture.

Using Photoshop's Clone brush, you can select an area in the image where the sand is similar to the area where the foot is located. Then by brushing over the foot, you can slowly remove it from the image by replacing it with the sand. Figure 38.17 shows the results after the image of the foot is removed.

FIGURE 38.17

By removing objects, the beauty of the image can be saved.

Storing Pictures

If you take as many pictures as my family and me, in no time at all you end up filling your local hard drive with folders full of images. To free up valuable hard drive space, you can save repositories of digital images to a DVD or print them to a hard copy where they can be saved in photo albums and scrapbooks.

CROSS-REF Saving video segments is likely to be more of a storage problem than photos. You can learn about storing video files in Chapter 43.

Printing images

You can view and print images using many different graphic applications, or you can select the Print this picture option from the top of Windows Explorer. This opens the Photo Printing Wizard. The wizard displays all the thumbnails for the current folder of images and lets you select which ones to print.

The next page of the Photo Printing Wizard lets you specify which printer to use or an option to install a printer. There is also a button for accessing the Printing Preferences dialog box. Following this page in the wizard is a page of layout options, as shown in Figure 38.18. The available options include full page prints and several other layout options including 8 x 10-inch, 5 x 7-inch, 4 x 6-inch, 3.5 x 5-inch, and wallet-sized prints.

 Remember to change the printer quality and the paper when you're ready to print the final copy of your photo.

 You can learn more about printing and printers in Chapter 35.

After selecting a layout and clicking Next, the selected images print and the wizard closes.

FIGURE 38.18

The Photo Printing Wizard lets you select the print size using various layouts.

Backing up images to a DVD

Before you can back up a folder full of digital images to a CD-ROM or DVD, you need to have a CD-ROM or DVD burner attached to your system. These burners are fairly common on newer computers. You need a blank DVD and the software to burn them. If you have a burner attached to your computer, then the needed software should be already installed.

 A single DVD holds 4.7GB of information versus 720MB on a CD-ROM.

You can use the burner's software to identify the images that you want to burn to a DVD or you can select the images in Windows Explorer and choose the Copy to CD option from the top of Windows Explorer.

Using this option copies all the selected images to a temporary folder where they await the command to write them to a DVD. If you open this temporary folder from the System Tray in the lower right corner of the Windows interface, then the folder includes a task to Write these Files to a CD.

Selecting this command opens the CD Writing Wizard. This page also lets you name the CD that you are creating. The next page of the wizard asks you to insert a blank-writable CD that can be used to hold all the selected images.

Summary

Selecting the right digital camera with all the features you need is a wise investment. With the vast assortment of digital cameras to choose from, it is important to select one that has the features that you need.

Even before your digital camera's memory is full, you can download and view the captured images on your computer using the various wizards that come with Windows, but captured digital images can be improved when you begin to edit your images with an image-editing application.

Using these applications you can rotate and crop images to eliminate unwanted areas. You can also improve the image quality of poorly taken photos by adjusting the exposure settings such as brightness and contrast. Finally, you can remove problem areas like red eye and objects that are out of place. You can print your edited images and store them to a CD or DVD for storage.

Chapter 39

Scheduling Software Events

I t is never fun to sit and watch your computer perform maintenance tasks, like clearing deleted files from your hard drive or backing up data, while you're trying to get some work done. Windows includes a useful utility that can schedule these tasks to be performed during a time when the computer is normally sitting idle.

This utility is called the Task Scheduler, and you can set it to run any program or script at a predetermined date and time or whenever the computer is started.

> **TIP** Perhaps the ultimate way to use the Task Scheduler is to write custom batch files that include a specific set of commands and parameters to be executed. You can then set the saved batch file up as a scheduled task.

Using the Task Scheduler

The Task Scheduler is accessed from the Start menu by clicking Start ⇨ All Programs ⇨ Accessories ⇨ System Tools ⇨ Scheduled Tasks. This command actually just opens a folder where the scheduled tasks are stored. Each task has a different icon and name and you can right-click each to access commands for the selected task.

> **NOTE** You can also access the Scheduled Tasks folder from the Control Panel.

The first step in using the Task Scheduler is to create a task, which is accomplished with the Scheduled Task Wizard.

Which tasks should be scheduled?

The Task Scheduler is general enough to be used for just about any type of task, but some of the more common tasks to consider scheduling are maintenance tasks that help to keep your computer running at its best speed. You may want to consider using the Task Scheduler to automate the following tasks:

- **Loading programs at startup:** If you choose to turn off your computer every night, then scheduling Windows to automatically start specific applications that you'd load anyway adds some time to the boot-up cycle but gives you a jump on the day.

- **Backing up your data:** One of the best uses of the Task Scheduler is to back up your critical data files daily.

- **Running Disk Check and Disk Cleanup:** Setting the Disk Check and Disk Cleanup applications to run frequently helps check your hard drives for problems and clears out files that can bog down your system. However, this clears out your Recycle Bin, which permanently removes any files you accidentally deleted.

- **Defragmenting your hard drives:** Scheduling to run the disk defragmenter once a month is a good idea for keeping your hard drive responding quickly. If you're not installing a lot of software, then this can be scaled back to every three months.

- **Updating and running virus checkers:** If you have a virus checker installed, you can schedule it to update its virus data file and to scan your entire system for viruses once a week.

- **Properly shutting down your system:** Using the Shutdown.exe program in the Windows/System 32 directory, you can create a task that automatically logs out the current user, or you could use the shutdown.exe –s command to shut down your computer at the end of the day.

CROSS-REF You can learn more about the Disk Defragmenter, Disk Check, Disk Cleanup, and Back-up utilities in Chapter 49. Antivirus software is covered in Chapter 32.

Using the Scheduled Task Wizard

When the Scheduled Tasks folder is first opened, it contains a single program icon named Add Scheduled Task. Double-clicking this icon begins the Scheduled Task Wizard, shown in Figure 39.1. Click the Next button to continue with the wizard.

 Some installations automatically add tasks to the Scheduled Tasks folder. For example, after installing an iPod, the Scheduled Tasks folder includes an AppleSoftwareUpdate task.

 In addition to programs and scripts, you can also choose a document to be opened; Windows automatically opens the document with its associated application.

FIGURE 39.1

The Scheduled Task Wizard guides you in creating a new task.

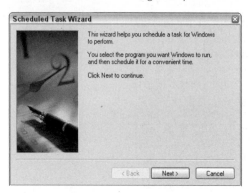

The next step in the wizard presents a list of programs you can choose to run. If you click the Browse button, a file dialog box opens where you can select the specific program or batch script to run, as shown in Figure 39.2. You need to select a program to run before the Next button becomes enabled.

FIGURE 39.2

Step 2 of the Scheduled Task Wizard lets you select a program to run.

The third step of the wizard lets you name the scheduled task and choose how often the task is performed, as shown in Figure 39.3. The options include Daily, Weekly, Monthly, One time only, When my computer starts, and When I log on. Make a selection to activate the Next button in order to continue.

> **TIP** Another useful way to have programs start automatically when a computer is re-booted is to place a shortcut for the program in the Startup folder found in the Documents and Settings\All Users\Start Menu\Startup directory.

The fourth step of the wizard changes depending on how often you've selected to run a task, but for each option you can choose the starting time and the date for the task. If the Daily option is selected, you can set the Start time and Date and whether the task is run every day, only on weekdays, or every specified number of days.

FIGURE 39.3

Step 3 of the Scheduled Task Wizard lets you name the task and decide how often it is executed.

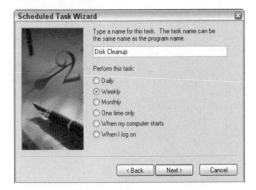

> **TIP** If you leave your computer on during the night, scheduling maintenance tasks to run during the middle of the night is a great idea. Some of these tasks can take a significant amount of time to complete and if scheduled during the day when the computer is likely to be in use, would slow the computer down.

If the Weekly option is selected, then you can set the Start time and whether the tasks run every week or every specified number of weeks. You can also choose specifically which days of the week the task is run, Monday through Sunday. Figure 39.4 shows the fourth step of the wizard for the Weekly option.

If the Monthly option is selected, you can set the Start time along with the day of the month to run the task. You can also select specific days of the month such as the first, second, third, fourth, or last day of the month. You can also choose which months from January through December to include.

If you select the One time only option, you can select a specific Start time and date. Even though this option only runs the task once, the task is still defined and can be restarted at any time using the task's Properties dialog box.

NOTE If your computer is turned off when a task is scheduled to run, a message appears the next time the computer is turned on. The message reminds you that a scheduled task failed to run and gives you the option to run it again.

If you select the When my computer starts or the When I log on options, you don't need to select a time and date, and so this step is skipped.

FIGURE 39.4

Step 4 of the Scheduled Task Wizard lets you specify a time and date for the task.

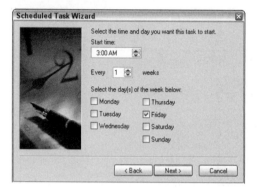

The fifth step of the Scheduled Task Wizard asks you to provide a user name and password, as shown in Figure 39.5. This user name and password is the same information that you use to log in to Windows. By providing the login information, you can use the When I log on option to have specific programs launch only when you log in. This is a useful way to get access to your programs when you share the computer with others.

FIGURE 39.5

Step 5 of the Scheduled Task Wizard requires that you enter the username and password.

 **TIP**   If you don't log into your computer with a username and password, then you can simply leave the fields in the fifth step of the Scheduled Task Wizard blank.

The final step of the Scheduled Task Wizard recaps the settings you've selected, as shown in Figure 39.6. If you enable the Open advanced properties option, the Properties dialog box for the task you've just created appears where you can change the task's settings. After it is created, the new task appears in the Scheduled Tasks folder.

To create a Scheduled Task to run the Disk Cleanup application, follow these steps:

1. **Select the Start ⇨ Control Panel menu command to open the Control Panel.**

FIGURE 39.6

The final step of the Scheduled Task Wizard summarizes the settings.

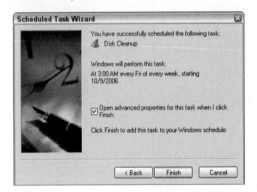

2. **Double-click the Scheduled Tasks icon to open its folder.**
3. **Double-click on the Add Scheduled Task icon to execute it.**
4. **Within the Scheduled Task Wizard, click Next.** In the second panel of the wizard, select the Disk Cleanup application and click Next.
5. **The name Disk Cleanup is automatically added as the task's name.** Select the Weekly option and click Next.
6. **Set the Start time to 3:00 AM, for example, and select the Friday option; then click Next.**
7. **Enter the username and password for your Windows login.**
8. **Click Finish to exit the wizard and to create the new task.**

Working with the Scheduled Tasks

All tasks created with the Scheduled Task Wizard appear in the Scheduled Task folder that you can access using the Start ⇨ All Programs ⇨ Accessories ⇨ System Tools ⇨ Scheduled Tasks menu or by selecting the Scheduled Tasks option in the Control Panel.

 Physically, all tasks are saved into the C:/Windows/Tasks folder with the .job extension.

If you look at the Scheduled Tasks folder with the Details option from the Views menu, the columns show the Schedule, Next Run Time, Last Run Time, Status, Last Result, and Creator, as shown in Figure 39.7.

NOTE **The Status field is left blank if the scheduled tasks run correctly. The Status displays Running when the task is currently being executed, Missed if the task was skipped because the computer was off, and Could Not Run if the task failed for some reason.**

FIGURE 39.7

The Details view shows the last time the task was run and the next time it will run.

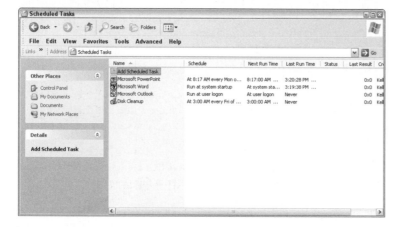

Starting and stopping tasks

The Scheduled Tasks folder also contains an Advanced menu that includes several commands that apply globally to all tasks within the folder. The Advanced ⇨ Stop Using Task Scheduler suspends all scheduled tasks. You can restart the tasks with the Advanced ⇨ Start Using Task Scheduler menu command. An alternative to stopping the scheduled tasks is to use the Advanced ⇨ Pause Task Scheduler command, which pauses all tasks until the Advanced ⇨ Continue Task Scheduler menu is selected.

If you select an individual scheduled task from the Scheduled Tasks folder, you can right-click and select the Run command to immediately execute the selected task. If the task is already running, then the End Task option is available and can be used to stop the current task.

Removing tasks

The right-click pop-up menu also includes a Delete command to permanently remove the selected task. Tasks can be deleted only if they are currently not running.

Troubleshooting scheduled tasks

The Advanced menu includes a toggle option to Notify Me of Missed Tasks. If your computer is turned off when a task is scheduled to run, enabling this option causes a dialog box to appear the next time Windows starts, informing you that a scheduled task was missed.

Every time a scheduled task is created, executed, or tries to run, an entry is made into a log. You can view the log using the Advanced ⇨ View Log command. This log is a simple text file with the most recent entries added to the bottom. This log file is helpful to determine any problems that have occurred with the scheduled tasks.

Some programs such as virus scanners automatically create a scheduled task as part of their installation. Sometimes these installations create tasks that are hidden, but you can view any hidden tasks in the Scheduled Tasks folder using the Advanced ⇨ View Hidden Tasks menu command.

Setting scheduled task properties

Selecting the Properties menu command from the right-click pop-up menu opens the Properties dialog box with three tabs. The Task tab, shown in Figure 39.8, includes a Run line that works exactly like the Start ⇨ Run dialog box. If you click the Browse button, you can change the program or document executed when the task is run.

 **NOTE**   The Run field can also include command-line parameters that are used to configure how the application runs. I cover using these parameters later in this chapter.

The Start in field lets you specify where the program runs, and can be a different folder if you've selected to open a document. For example, if you select to run a Word document, you want to set the Start in directory to be the location of the Word application.

The Comments section lets you enter some notes to help identify the goal of the task. You can also select the user that runs this task.

The Run only if logged on option keeps scheduled tasks from running if another user is logged into the computer. The Enabled option provides another way to disable the task without deleting it.

The Task tab of a task's Properties dialog box lets you change the program and log in info.

Changing the task schedule

The Schedule tab, shown in Figure 39.9, includes settings for specifying the time and date for the task. The options are the same as those found in the wizard: Daily, Weekly, Monthly, Once, At system startup, and At logon. For each option, you can set the Start time and date.

Running tasks when the computer is idle

Along with the schedule options in the Schedule tab is a When Idle option. This option lets you run the scheduled task after the computer has been idle for a specified amount of time. This option is great for running small tasks, such as logging out, when you leave the computer idle for lunch or a break.

Using multiple schedules

The Show multiple schedules option at the bottom of the Schedule tab adds a drop-down list along with New and Delete buttons at the top of the tab, as shown in Figure 39.10. New schedules are added to the list using the New button, and the selected schedule can be deleted with the Delete button. Using this option you can schedule a task to run nightly and also to run when the computer is idle.

FIGURE 39.9

The Schedule tab of a task's Properties dialog box lets you set the task's time and date.

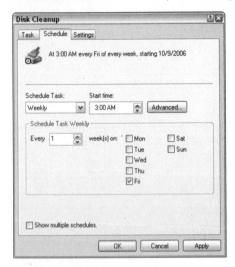

FIGURE 39.10

The Schedule tab lets you include multiple schedules for the selected task.

Making tasks repeat

When a new task is created, you're limited to executing a task only once in a day; but using the Advanced Schedule Options dialog box, shown in Figure 39.11, opened using the Advanced button in the Schedule tab, you can set a task to repeat throughout the day or until a specified time or Duration value is reached. For example, if you receive notification that a particular virus threat will show up on a certain day, then you could enable a task to check for viruses to repeat throughout the day instead of the weekly or daily check.

FIGURE 39.11

The Advanced Schedule Options dialog box lets you set a task to repeat throughout the day.

Using the Properties settings

The Settings tab of the Properties dialog box for the task, shown in Figure 39.12, includes options for controlling how the task is run. The options include the following:

- **Delete the task if it is not scheduled to run again.** This permanently deletes the task after it is run for the last time.

- **Stop the task if it runs for a specified length of time.** This option can keep schedule tasks from running longer than they should. Be careful not to set this value lower than the time it takes for the task to complete.

- **Only start the task if the computer has been idle for at least.** This option keeps scheduled tasks from running if you are using the computer during the scheduled time.

- **Stop the task if the computer ceases to be idle.** This option suspends the task if you start using the computer while a task is running.

- **Don't start the task if the computer is running on batteries.** This option is intended for laptops that aren't connected to an outlet. It keeps tasks from running down a battery completing tasks that can be completed at another time.

- **Stop the task if battery mode begins.** If a task is running when the laptop is disconnected from an outlet, this option stops the task, saving battery power.

- **Wake the computer to run this task.** Most tasks can run in the background without waking the computer, but if you want the computer to wake up to show you the task it is working on, then this option can be used.

FIGURE 39.12

The Settings tab of a task's Properties dialog box lets you set how the task is run.

Suspending all tasks

If you've created a large number of scheduled tasks that run throughout the day and week, then stopping all of them from running can be done with the Advanced ⇨ Stop Using Task Scheduler, but this might cause problems if some tasks are running. Another option is to use the Administrative Tool in the Control Panel to suspend the Task Scheduler service.

To suspend the Task Scheduler service and stop all scheduled tasks as once, follow these steps:

1. **Select the Start ⇨ Control Panel menu command to open the Control Panel.**

2. **Double-click the Administrative Tool icon to launch it.**

3. **Within the Administrative Tools folder, double-click the Services icon.** This opens a tab showing all the active services that are currently running, shown in Figure 39.13.

4. **Right-click the Task Scheduler service and select the All Tasks ⇨ Stop menu option.** This stops all scheduled tasks from running. You can also select to Pause or Restart the service.

FIGURE 39.13

The Services tab of the Administrative Tools folder lets you start and stop running services.

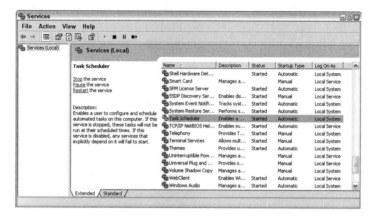

Creating a Batch File

The Scheduled Task Wizard is great for having specific programs run at regular intervals without intervention, but most programs have specific parameters that you can set that change how the program is run. For example, if you run the defrag utility, you can include a –a parameter after the command to cause the utility to run in analysis mode only. Using these parameters, you can control more precisely the type of command that is run.

There are several ways to execute a program with the appropriate parameters attached, including entering the flags in the Run field of the Properties dialog box for the scheduled task, entering the command into the Start, Run dialog box or in the Command Prompt interface, or creating a separate batch file. This last method is particularly useful. By creating a batch file, you can define specific program commands or execute multiple commands at once.

Locating program parameters

Before you can use a program parameter, you need to find the specific parameters for the program that you plan to execute. You can often find these parameters within the Help file for the various utilities, as shown for the Defrag utility in Figure 39.14.

If you have the Command Prompt interface open, you can also get a program's parameters by typing the name of the program followed by the / ? parameter. This retrieves a help list for the given program. You can open the Command Prompt interface with the Start ➪ All Programs ➪ Accessories ➪ Command Prompt menu. Figure 39.15 shows the parameters for the Defrag utility.

FIGURE 39.14

You can find parameters for a specific program within the Help file.

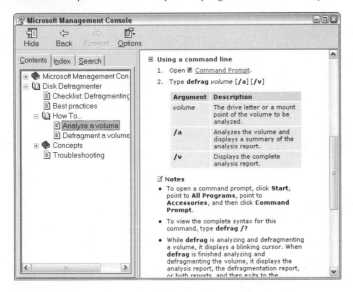

FIGURE 39.15

You can view program parameters by typing the / ? parameter after the program's name.

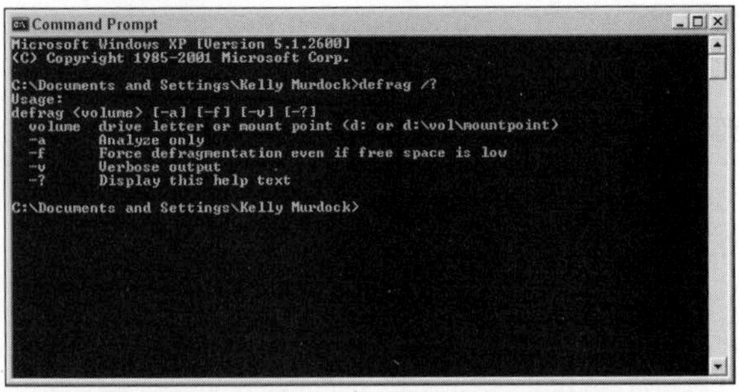

Entering parameters to a scheduled task

The easiest place to add parameters to a scheduled task is in the Properties dialog box for the selected scheduled task. You can simply add the appropriate parameter to the end of the execution command in the Run field, as shown in Figure 39.16.

 You can add multiple parameters to an execution command by separating them with a space.

FIGURE 39.16

You can add parameters to the end of the execution command in the Run field of the task's Properties dialog box.

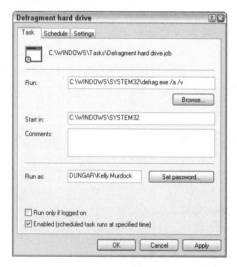

Entering parameters into the Run dialog box

If you select the Start ➪ Run menu, the Run dialog box, shown in Figure 39.17 opens. Using this dialog box you can enter a program to execute along with its parameters. It is important to have the exact program name typed correctly.

FIGURE 39.17

You can add parameters to the end of the execution command in the Run dialog box.

Using the Command Prompt interface

You can also execute program commands and parameters in the Command Prompt interface. This interface hearkens back to the DOS days when all instructions were run using text commands.

The Command Prompt interface opens using the Start ⇨ All Programs ⇨ Accessories ⇨ Command Prompt menu. You can enter DOS commands directly into the interface; you can get a list of DOS commands by entering the command help in the interface. You can perform all of these textual commands within Windows using the various utilities, but the textual commands are helpful when composing batch files.

Writing a batch file

Issuing program commands in the Run dialog box or the Command Prompt runs the command a single time only, but if you enter the commands into a text file and save them as a batch file that can be accessed as a scheduled task, then you have the power to run specific custom tasks regularly.

A *batch file* is simply a text file saved using the .bat file extension. These text files include any textual commands that can be entered in the Command Prompt interface, including program execution commands with parameters and any DOS textual commands. Once you've created the batch file, you can use the Scheduled Task Wizard to make the file into a scheduled task.

 Be sure to test your batch file before making it a scheduled task.

To create a batch file as a scheduled task, follow these steps:

1. **Select the Start ⇨ All Programs ⇨ Accessories ⇨ Notepad menu command to open Notepad.**

2. **Enter the commands to execute in the Notepad window such as** `defrag /a /v`.

3. **Save the file to the hard drive using the .bat extension.**

4. **Locate the saved .bat file and execute it to test its behavior.** If the batch file has any trouble, reopen the file and correct the problems before saving it again.

5. **Once the file is working fine, use the Scheduled Task Wizard to create a new scheduled task that runs the batch file.**

Summary

Windows includes a utility to offload all the boring maintenance jobs (such as loading startup programs, backing up data, running Disk Cleanup and Defragmenter, and scanning for viruses) that you do want to happen, just quietly and in the background. This utility is the Task Scheduler. New tasks can be created using the Scheduled Task Wizard, which walks you through the scheduling process.

Once tasks are created, you can access them from the Scheduled Tasks folder in the Control Panel. Using the Advanced menu and the Properties dialog box, you can change the applications that run and the various settings for the selected task. The Properties dialog box lets you set a task to repeat throughout the day, or to run when the system is idle.

For more specific control over the program's commands, you can add a parameter to the end of the program command. The available parameters for a program are displayed in the various program help files. You can enter these parameters into the Properties dialog box for a selected task, add them to the program execution command in the Run dialog box or in the Command Prompt interface, or save them as part of a batch file. Batch files can include textual program commands and DOS commands. You can then access saved batch files as scheduled tasks.

Chapter 40

Synchronizing Your Data Files

Any time you use two or more computers, you need some way to make sure that you are storing the same information in both of them. Whether it's telephone numbers and appointments or copies of documents and data files, it's essential to have a way to make sure you have the latest versions on all of your computers and computer-like devices such as personal digital assistants (PDAs) and cell phones.

For example, if you use one computer in your office and another at home, and maybe you carry a laptop when you travel, you might work on the same report or spreadsheet on all three machines; if a co-worker is contributing to the same project, there might be even more versions of the same document out there someplace. Unless you have a way to coordinate all those versions, you can eventually find yourself working on an out-of-date copy; every time you add another person to the team, you increase the opportunities for confusion.

Therefore, Windows includes utilities that compare the versions of the same document or other file located on different computers and synchronizes their contents.

This chapter explains how to set up and use the synchronization utilities to keep multiple copies of the same file or document up to date, and how to synchronize data between your computer and a PDA.

IN THIS CHAPTER

Using Briefcase to synchronize files

Moving data between a PDA and Windows

Finding sync software

Synchronizing Files Between Two or More Computers

Windows uses the Briefcase utility to synchronize copies of the same file on more than one computer. When you place a file in a briefcase, the program automatically compares the contents of that file with a master copy of the same file, and synchronizes the two versions.

To use Briefcase, you must identify one computer as the *master computer* that stores the master version of the document or other file. This is the version that every other computer uses to synchronize changes. If your network includes a file server, the server is the logical choice as the master computer. The laptop or other secondary computer is the *slave*. Figure 40.1 shows the relationship between the master computer and the other computers.

FIGURE 40.1

All the secondary computers synchronize their briefcase files with the version stored in the master computer.

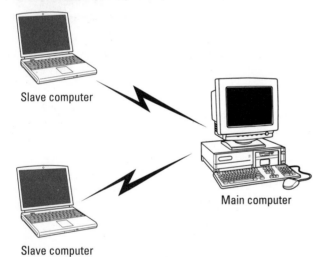

Slave computer

Main computer

Slave computer

CAUTION   Briefcase can replace an older version of a document or file with a new version, but it can't combine changes when both versions have changed. Therefore, it's essential to use Briefcase to synchronize the two versions before you make any additional changes.

For example, if you edit a document on your laptop computer, you must update the version on your desktop to match the one on the laptop before you make any new changes to the document on your desktop.

You can connect slave computers to the master computer through a network, through a direct cable connection, or by physically moving a copy of a file from one computer to the other on a removable drive (such as a floppy disk, a flash drive, or a USB drive).

There are three stages to working with Briefcase:

1. Create a new briefcase on the slave computer.

2. Move the files you want to synchronize into the briefcase.

3. Update the files.

Creating a briefcase

Follow these steps to create a briefcase in the slave computer:

1. **From the Windows desktop or within a folder in My Computer, right-click and select New ⇨ Briefcase from the pop-up menu.** A New Briefcase icon appears.

2. **If you have more than one briefcase, use the right-click Rename command to give each briefcase a unique name.**

Moving a file into a briefcase

To move a file into a briefcase, follow these steps:

1. **Use My Network Places on the laptop or other secondary computer to open the folder that contains the master copy of the document or other file.**

2. **Open the briefcase on the laptop or other slave computer.**

3. **Drag the file you want to edit from the original folder and drop it into the briefcase.**

4. **If the slave is a laptop or other portable you can disconnect it from the network now.**

To edit the document on the slave, open the document from within the briefcase. To edit the version on the main computer, open it from the original folder.

Updating files

To synchronize the edited version on the slave with the master version on the main computer, follow these steps:

1. **Open the briefcase on the slave.**

2. **To synchronize all of the files in the briefcase, choose Update All from the Briefcase menu or the toolbar.** To synchronize one or more specific files, select that file or files and choose Update Selection. The Update window shown in Figure 40.2 appears.

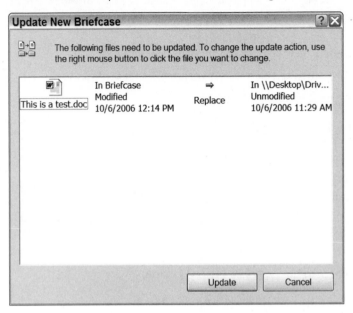

FIGURE 40.2

Briefcase uses this Update window to show the changes that it can make to edited files.

3. **The direction of the arrow in the file listing shows which version replaces the other version.** In this case, the Modified version in the briefcase replaces the Unmodified version in \\Desktop computer. If you want to restore the copy in the briefcase to the unmodified version, right-click the listing and choose the arrow that points in the other direction, as shown in Figure 40.3. To replace a file, click the Update button at the bottom of the window.

You can also use Briefcase to synchronize files on computers that are not connected through a network. For example, if you have been working on a document on your office computer, and you want to take a copy home with you on a floppy disk or a flash drive, you can use Briefcase to keep both versions up to date.

TIP   If you use Briefcase a lot, you might lose track of which computer contains the most recent version of a file or document. To check the status of a file in a briefcase, right-click the icon, choose Properties, and open the Update Status tab. If the two versions are the same, the Properties window shows the status as Up-to-date. If the two versions are different, you can update the unmodified version from within this window.

Follow these steps to use Briefcase with removable media:

1. Insert a floppy disk or connect a flash drive to the computer that contains the documents you want to take with you.

To change an update instruction, right-click the arrow and choose a different command.

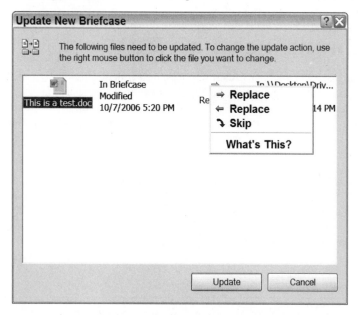

2. Open the floppy disk or flash drive in My Computer and right-click to create a New ⇨ Briefcase from the pop-up menu.

3. Open the briefcase.

4. Use My Computer to open the folder in a second window that contains the file you want to take with you.

5. Drag each file you want to copy from the original folder to the briefcase. An icon for each file will appear in the briefcase window.

6. Remove the floppy disk or disconnect the flash drive from the main computer.

7. When you arrive home (or at some other remote location), insert the floppy disk or connect the flash drive to the second computer.

8. Use the second computer to open the briefcase and edit the document or other file. When you are done, use the Save command to store the file on the removable media.

9. Remove the floppy or flash drive and take it back to the first computer.

10. Insert the floppy or connect the flash drive and open Briefcase.

11. Use the Update All or Update Selection command in Briefcase to synchronize the version of each file on the removable media with the original version on the main computer.

Synchronizing with a PDA

Many people use Palm Pilots, BlackBerry devices, Pocket PCs, and other personal digital assistants or advanced cellular telephones to store important day-to-day details of their lives, including appointment schedules, address books, personal telephone directories, and e-mail. It's often convenient to coordinate these documents with the related versions stored on a desktop computer. Therefore, you may want to synchronize the information on your PDA with files on a desktop or laptop computer.

Most PDA and mobile phone operating systems can use synchronization software to exchange and synchronize data with a computer running Windows XP. Some manufacturers include copies of these programs with their PDAs and phones, but it's always helpful to look for the most recent version on the manufacturer's Web site. Table 40.1 lists programs and sources for the most widely used PDA operating systems and mobile telephones.

TABLE 40.1

Synchronization Software for PDAs

PDA or Mobile Telephone Operating System	Synchronization Software	Download From
Windows Mobile Windows CE Pocket PC	Microsoft ActiveSync	`www.microsoft.com/windowsmobile/ activesync/default.mspx`
BlackBerry	BlackBerry Desktop Software	`www.blackberry.com/products/ software/desktop`
Palm OS	Palm Desktop for Windows	`www.palm.com/us/software/desktop`
Motorola	Motorola Phone Tools	`http://direct.motorola.com/hellomoto/ Motosupport/source/AdvancedMobility_ PhoneTools.asp`

PDA or Mobile Telephone Operating System	Synchronization Software	Download From
Nokia	Nokia PC Suite	`www.nokiausa.com/support/software/main/1,7889,,00.html`
Sony Ericsson	Sony Ericsson PC Suite	`www.sonyericsson.com`
Psion	PsiWin	`www.pscience5.net/psifilessibo.htm`

If your own PDA or wireless telephone is not in this list, consult the manufacturer's Customer Support center for information about synchronization software.

Each of these programs presents a somewhat different appearance, but they all perform similar tasks. After you download and install the program designed for your particular PDA or wireless telephone, it steps you through a connection and initial configuration process. When the configuration is complete, your computer automatically detects a connection between your portable device and your computer. Depending on the specific features of each device, the connection can use a USB cable, a Bluetooth link, or an infrared link to exchange data with your computer.

Every sync program is different, but most of them are similar. For specific instructions, read the help files and other instructions supplied with your program.

To synchronize your files, follow these general steps:

1. **If you are using a USB link between your computer and the PDA or phone, connect the cable to both devices.** If you're using Bluetooth or an infrared link, the computer automatically detects the other device. When the connection is active, you will probably see a full-color icon in the system tray (next to the clock at the bottom of your screen). When no connection is present, the same icon is gray.

2. **Run the Sync program on the computer from the desktop or the Start ⇨ Programs menu.** A program Window like one of the examples in Figure 40.4 opens. Of course, the specific window you see depends on the particular program you are using.

3. **Find the Synchronize or Sync command or shortcut icon and click it.**

4. **Follow the on-screen instructions to choose the data you want to synchronize between the computer and the portable device.** When the setup is complete, the program moves data across the link.

5. **When the data transfer is complete, disconnect the cable if necessary, and close the sync program.**

Many of the same PDA and mobile phone connection programs include many additional features and options. For more details, consult the instructions supplied with your program.

FIGURE 40.4

Each manufacturer's PC interface program uses a different control window layout.

Summary

If you use two or more computers to work on the same documents and files, the Briefcase utility supplied with Windows can eliminate much of the confusion involved in keeping track of updates and changes. By keeping a master copy of each file and using Briefcase to keep all the working copies up to date, you can be certain that you are always working on the most recent version. To synchronize your files, copy the original from the main computer to a briefcase in the second computer, edit the file, and use the Update commands in Briefcase.

Most of the makers of software for BlackBerries, Palm Pilots, and other personal digital assistants and advanced wireless telephones offer synchronization software that allows you to coordinate your contact lists, e-mail directories, appointment calendars, and other personal information between your computer and your PDA. If the synchronization software for your PDA isn't listed in this chapter, look for it on the manufacturer's Web site.

Chapter 41

Using Windows Remote Desktop

As the name suggests, Remote Desktop is a Windows utility that allows you to connect your computer to a second computer through a local network, a virtual private network or a telephone line. You can originate a Remote Desktop connection only through Windows XP Pro or XP Media Center; it's not available in Windows XP Home Edition.

It's also possible to use Remote Desktop through the Internet, but only if there's an exception to your firewall's list of blocked programs for Remote Desktop connections. This opens a possible security breach, so it's best not to try it.

When a Remote Desktop connection is in place, you can use your computer's mouse and keyboard to control the distant system and view activity on the distant computer's screen through your own monitor display. It's almost as if you're reaching through your own computer to operate another computer in another location.

You can use Remote Desktop to open a file and transfer it to the local computer, print a document on a printer connected to the distant computer, view a video or listen to a sound recording stored on the remote system, and perform most of the other tasks that you could run if you were operating the remote system through that system's own keyboard and mouse. The two computers connected through a Remote Desktop link can also share a clipboard, so you can copy text or data from one computer to the other.

Remote Desktop is a powerful tool for business people who are away from their own offices, such as salespeople who need the latest versions of price lists and proposals while they are meeting with customers or clients, people who want to gain access to files and other resources on their office computers from home, and network managers who want to load configuration settings to distant computers without the need for leaving their own offices. If you're operating a help desk, you can also use Remote Desktop to troubleshoot a distant computer.

In order to use Remote Desktop, both the host computer (the one that controls the distant system and the remote computer (the one that has allowed the host to take over control) must have the appropriate software installed and enabled. The host software is part of a standard Windows XP installation, but you must enable the client utility on the remote computer before you can establish a connection. The software for remote computers, called the Remote Desktop Connection client, also works with older versions of Windows including Windows 95, Windows 98, Windows Me, Windows NT, and Windows 2000.

This chapter explains how to set up both host computers and remote clients for Remote Desktop, and how to create and use a Remote Desktop connection.

CAUTION   Because of the potential security risk when an outsider takes control of a local computer, many businesses don't allow their computers to accept Remote Desktop connections. If your computer connects to a network through a domain, or if you are connected to a business network, consult your network manager or help desk before you allow your computer to accept Remote Desktop connections.

In a corporate setting, a virtual private network can offer most of the same benefits as Remote Desktop, without the same security problems.

Setting Up a Computer as a Remote Desktop Client

Before you can use Remote Desktop, you must turn on the program on the distant computer and specify the hosts that can connect.

Follow these steps to enable a Remote Desktop client and specify which users gain remote access:

1. **From the Control Panel, open the System window.** If your Control Panel uses Category View, look for System in the Performance and Maintenance category.

2. **In the System Properties window, choose the Remote tab.** The dialog box shown in Figure 41.1 appears.

3. **In the Remote Desktop box in the bottom half of the window, turn on the Allow users to connect remotely to this computer option.**

Use the Remote tab in System Properties to turn on Remote Desktop.

4. **Click the Select Remote Users button.** The Remote Desktop Users window shown in Figure 41.2 appears. Click the Add button to create a new remote user account.

5. **Click the OK buttons to save your changes and close all the open windows.**

It's also necessary to instruct the Windows Firewall not to block Remote Desktop connections. If you're using a different firewall instead of the one Microsoft includes in Windows XP, consult the firewall manual or your network manager for information about adding Remote Desktop to the firewall's list of exceptions or permitted programs.

Follow these steps to unblock Remote Desktop connections in the Windows Firewall:

1. **From Control Panel, open the Security Center.**

FIGURE 41.2

The Remote Desktop Users window identifies accounts on the host computer that can connect to this client.

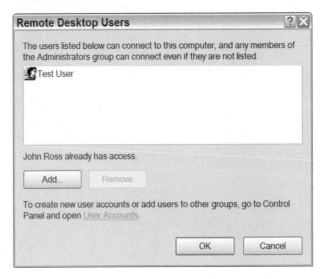

2. Scroll down to the bottom of the Windows Security Center window to see the Manage security settings options shown in Figure 41.3.

FIGURE 41.3

Open the Windows Firewall settings from the Windows Security Center.

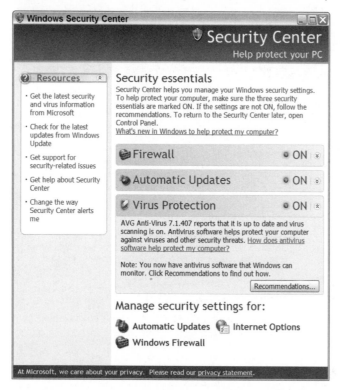

3. **Click the Windows Firewall icon under Manage security settings.** The Windows Firewall window shown in Figure 41.4 appears.

4. **Make sure the Don't allow exceptions option is not active.**

643

FIGURE 41.4

The Don't allow exceptions option should not be active.

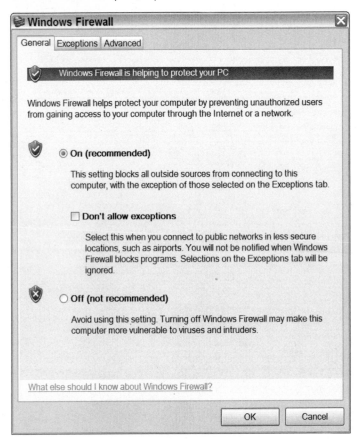

5. Open the Exceptions tab to view the dialog box shown in Figure 41.5.

6. Scroll down the Programs and Services list until you can see the Remote Desktop listing.

7. If it's not already active, turn on the exception for Remote Desktop. Make sure there's a check mark next to the listing.

8. Click OK to save your setting and close the Windows Firewall window, and close the Windows Security Center window.

Remote Desktop only allows connections to User Accounts on the distant computer if the account requires a password. If your account on the distant system doesn't already have a password, follow these steps to assign one now:

1. **On the client computer, open the Control Panel and select User Accounts. The User Accounts Wizard window opens.**

2. **Scroll down to the bottom of the User Accounts window to view the list of accounts, as shown in Figure 41.6.** In this example, the new account name is "Test User."

FIGURE 41.5

The Exceptions list identifies programs that can pierce the Windows Firewall.

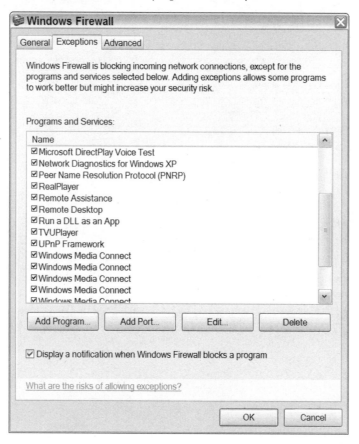

FIGURE 41.6

The User Accounts window enables you to select the account you want to use to connect to a client computer.

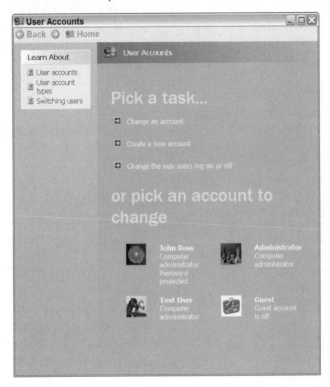

3. **Click the name of the account you plan to use for remote access.** The What do you want to change screen shown in Figure 41.7 opens.

4. **Click the Create a password option.** The dialog box shown in Figure 41.8 appears.

FIGURE 41.7

To assign a password, choose the Create a password option.

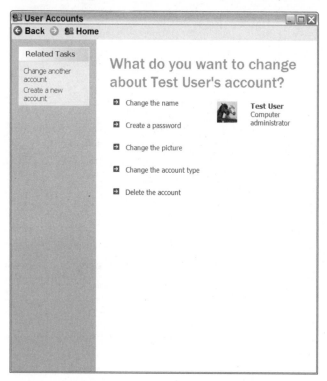

5. **Choose a password and type it in both the Type a new password field and the Type the new password again fields.** If you want, type a hint in the password hint field. Click Create Password to save your new password. The wizard asks if you want to make your files and folders private.

6. **Choose either the Yes or No button, as you prefer.**

7. **Close the User Accounts window.**

FIGURE 41.8

Enter your new password in the Create a password screen.

Finally, make a note of the name assigned to the client computer:

1. **From the Control Panel, open the System window and choose the Computer Name tab.** The dialog box shown in Figure 41.9 appears.

2. **Look for the Full computer name about a third of the way down the window.** That's the name that Remote Desktop uses to identify this host computer through the local area network.

3. **Click Cancel to close the System Properties window without making any changes.**

FIGURE 41.9

Note the Full computer name assigned to the host computer.

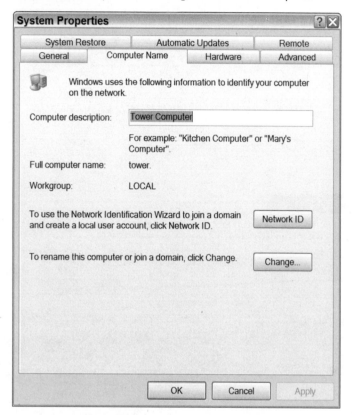

Connecting to a Remote Computer

After you have turned on the client software, you can use Remote Desktop to operate the distant computer from a host on the same network. Follow these steps to set up a connection:

1. **From the Start menu, open Programs (or All Programs) ⇨ Accessories ⇨ Communications ⇨ Remote Desktop Connection.** The Remote Desktop Connection shown in Figure 41.10 appears.

2. **If it's not already visible, type the name assigned to the distant computer (the one you want to control with Remote Desktop) in the Computer field (see the previous section to find the name) and click Connect.** The desktop from the client computer appears on the host's screen, as shown in Figure 41.11.

FIGURE 41.10

Use the Remote Desktop Connection window to set up a link to a client computer.

FIGURE 41.11

When a Remote Desktop link is active, the distant computer's desktop is visible on the host.

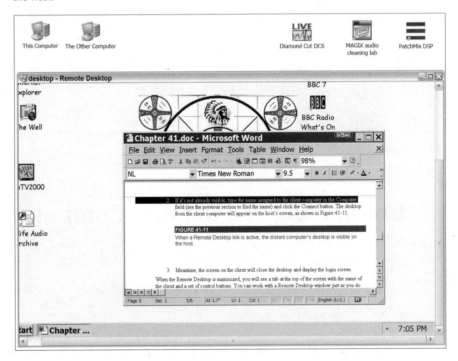

3. **Meanwhile, the screen on the distant computer closes the desktop and displays the login screen.** If a user logs into the distant computer from the keyboard connected to that computer, the Remote Desktop connection closes.

4. **To close a Remote Desktop connection from the computer that is remotely controlling another computer, close the Remote Desktop window.**

When the Remote Desktop is maximized, you see a tab at the top of the screen with the name of the client and a set of control buttons. You can work with a Remote Desktop window just as you do with any other window on the host's screen:

- To reduce the remote desktop to a smaller window, click the Restore button.

- To hide the remote desktop as a button in the taskbar, click the Minimize button.

- To close the Remote Desktop client window and end the connection, click the Close button (the X).

Everything else in the Remote Desktop window works exactly like it would if you were sitting in front of the client computer: You can open desktop shortcuts, use the Start menu, and even use the Control Panel to add, remove, or change most configuration settings.

 Don't forget to save any open documents before you close a Remote Desktop connection. If you don't save your work from the host, you might lose any changes.

Connecting to an Older Version of Windows

Remote Desktop can also connect to client computers that use older versions of Windows, including Windows 2000, Windows NT, Windows 95, Windows 98, and Windows Me, if the client computer has an installed copy of the Remote Desktop Connection software.

To install Remote Desktop Connection software on an older system from a Windows XP CD, follow these steps:

1. **Place the Windows XP CD in the drive.**

2. **If the Welcome to Microsoft Windows XP window doesn't open automatically, open My Computer and then double-click the CD icon.**

3. **From the Welcome window, choose the Perform Additional Tasks option.** The window shown in Figure 41.12 opens.

4. **Click the Set up Remote Desktop Connection option.** The Connection software loads from the CD.

If you can't locate a Windows XP CD, you can also download the Connection software from `www.microsoft.com/windowsxp/downloads/tools/rdclientdl.mspx`.

After you have installed the Remote Desktop Connection software on a client machine, you can connect to that machine from a host, just as you would connect to a computer running Windows XP.

FIGURE 41.12

Choose Set up Remote Desktop Connection to install the client software.

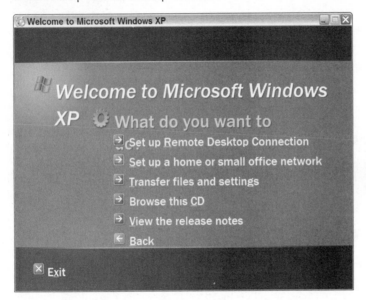

Connecting Through the Internet

As noted earlier in this chapter, Remote Desktop can also work through an Internet connection. However, when you allow Remote Desktop through your firewall, you might also permit intruders to make unwanted attacks on your system through the same path. Therefore, you should not allow remote connections except when you are actually using them.

Because of the security threat, I don't recommend using Remote Desktop through the Internet, even through it can be done. If you want to try it, take a look at the article at `www.microsoft` `.com/windowsxp/using/networking/expert/northrup_03may16.mspx` for detailed instructions.

If you do decide to use Remote Desktop through the Internet, you must also instruct the router connected to the distant computer to accept Remote Desktop connections. Each router has a different layout for its controls, but the procedure is similar to this one, for a Linksys router:

1. **From the Start menu, choose Run and enter** cmd.exe **in the Open field.** Click OK. A command window opens.

2. **Type** ipconfig **and press Enter.** A list of configuration settings similar to the one in Figure 41.13 appears.

3. **Note the numeric addresses listed as the IP Address and the Default Gateway.** Open Internet Explorer or another Web browser and enter the Default Gateway address in the browser's address field. The browser asks for a login name and password.

FIGURE 41.13

The IP Configuration list shows the address of your router as the Default Gateway.

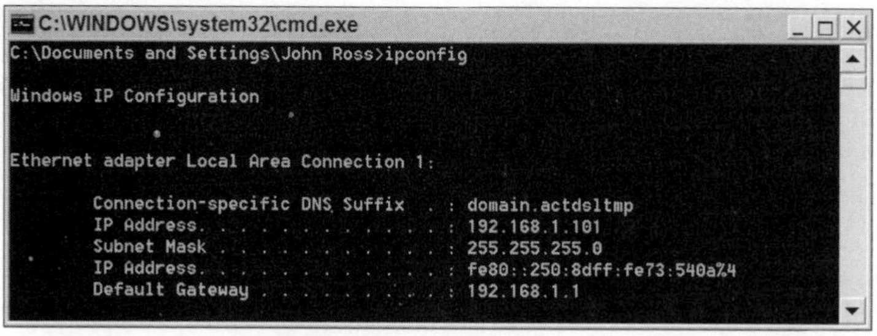

```
C:\WINDOWS\system32\cmd.exe                                    _ □ ×
C:\Documents and Settings\John Ross>ipconfig

Windows IP Configuration


Ethernet adapter Local Area Connection 1:

        Connection-specific DNS Suffix  . : domain.actdsltmp
        IP Address. . . . . . . . . . . . : 192.168.1.101
        Subnet Mask . . . . . . . . . . . : 255.255.255.0
        IP Address. . . . . . . . . . . . : fe80::250:8dff:fe73:540a%4
        Default Gateway . . . . . . . . . : 192.168.1.1
```

4. **Consult your router's manual for the password (hint: try** admin**).** When the router accepts your login, it opens a control home page in the browser.

5. **Look for a link to Forwarding or Port Forwarding on the home page.** If you can't find it, try the Advanced page or link. The Port Forwarding page appears similar to Figure 41.14.

6. **In the External Port field, type** 3389, **which is the port used by Remote Desktop.** If the router asks for a range, use 3389 as both the beginning and end of the range. A port number is the software path used by a specific program or service.

7. **Turn on the TCP protocol option for Port 3389.** Change the IP address for this port to the IP address you noted from the ipconfig report. If there's an Enable option or control, turn it on and click Apply or OK.

8. **Save your changes and close the browser.**

FIGURE 41.14

Your router's Port Forwarding (or Port Range Forwarding) options control access through the firewall.

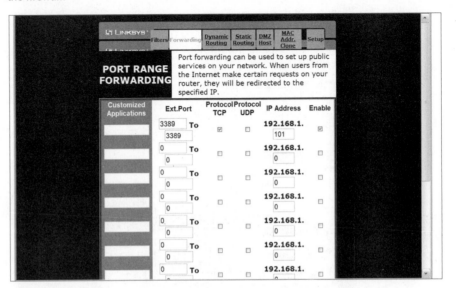

Summary

Remote Desktop is a slick Windows utility that makes it possible to use one computer to control a second computer through a network connection. You can use Remote Desktop to install and delete software on the distant computer; add, move, change, or delete files and folders; and perform remote troubleshooting and repairs. Before you can open a remote desktop, you must enable a Remote Desktop Connection on the client system.

It's possible to use Remote Desktop through an Internet connection, but it's not a good idea, because it won't work unless you create a hole in your firewall that might also provide a point of entry for unwanted intruders.

Chapter 42

Playing, Creating, and Editing Sound

I f you break down a digital audio file, you will find that it is just a series of numbers. Because computers are so good at working with numbers, it isn't surprising that the personal computer can be a powerful audio device.

You can use your PC not only to play audio files, but also to record, create and edit sound files. In fact, many professional studios use computers extensively to mix, edit, and master audio tracks.

You can connect state-of-the-art audio equipment to your computer system, as well as hook your computer to an existing stereo component to create an amazing audio experience.

Listening

If you sit down at the computer to write a letter and your stereo happens to be located in the other room, don't worry. Your computer can meet your musical needs.

From the ability to play standard CDs to downloaded digital music, the computer provides an excellent resource for managing, cataloguing, and playing music.

CROSS-REF There are several critical hardware pieces necessary for sound to play on a computer. Chapter 13 covers the required audio hardware including sound cards, speakers, headphones, and microphones.

Playing CDs

For a simple experience using your computer as an audio listening device, try placing a standard CD into the CD-ROM drive. When you insert an audio CD into a computer, Windows recognizes the CD format and causes the default media player software to load and begin playing the CD.

To hear the CD, you need to have speakers (or headphones) connected to your system and configured properly.

Media players

When you access a media file via an inserted CD or by double-clicking on a media file, Windows automatically loads the default media player. This player enables you to view or listen to the selected media file.

CROSS-REF   Media players can play video as well as audio files. You can find more about video media files in Chapter 43.

Several different media players are available, each with its own feel and look. Most of these media players can play audio files directly from the hard drive or from Internet sources.

Windows Media Player

Windows comes with its own media player installed. You can access Windows Media Player from the Start ➪ All Programs ➪ Accessories ➪ Entertainment menu. If the media player isn't in this directory, then you can install it using the Add New Windows Components button on the Add or Remove Programs window in the Control Panel. However, the installation found on the Windows Setup CD is probably older than the current version available on the Web.

If your computer is already connected to the Web, visit the Microsoft Web site and search for Media Player. The latest version of Windows Media Player is available as a free download. During the installation process, Windows Media Player lets you choose which files are associated with the media player. When a file type is associated with media player, Windows knows which application to open when the file is selected. All files associated with Windows Media Player cause the Windows Media Player application to load when the associated file is opened.

Windows Media Player, shown in Figure 42.1, shows the album cover for the loaded CD along with a track listing of the songs on the CD. The controls at the bottom (or top) of the window let you play, pause, and skip between tracks. There is also a volume control and buttons to repeat the current track or shuffle all the tracks. The progress bar at the bottom edge of the window shows how far the track has progressed. You can fast forward or rewind the current track by dragging this bar.

FIGURE 42.1

Windows Media Player highlights the current track that is playing.

As an alternate to displaying the album art, the Media Player window can display some pre-programmed visualizations that beat in time with the music. You can select the visual effects using the Now Playing ⇨ Visualizations menu. Figure 42.2 shows the player using the Alchemy visualization module.

FIGURE 42.2

Windows Media Player can be set to display colorful visualizations that move with the music.

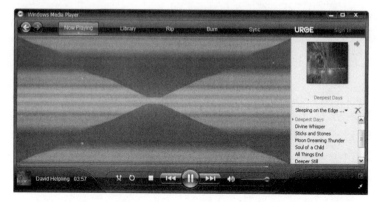

In addition to playing music, the Windows Media Player can also catalog and organize your available music. In the Library window, shown in Figure 42.3, all the music files in the My Music folder load for quick display along with their tracks and album covers where available. By scrolling through the Library, you can quickly select which music albums to listen to.

You can add media files to Media Player's library using the Library ➪ Add to Library command. This menu lets you select a folder to search for audio and video files that you can add to the library. Once specified, any media files dropped into the selected folders automatically add to the library.

FIGURE 42.3

The Library tab of the Windows Media Player displays all the digital albums available on your system.

QuickTime

Apple QuickTime is the default media player for Macintosh computers, but a Windows version of the QuickTime player is also available, as shown in Figure 42.4. The QuickTime player can play video files that use the QuickTime (MOV) video format.

iTunes

When you install an iPod to your system, the software also installs iTunes. This is a software interface for loading MP3 and video files onto an iPod device. iTunes also lets you create and access libraries of media clips and create playlists.

RealOne Player

Another common player that is available is RealOne Player, shown in Figure 42.5. This media player is another portal with music samples, movie trailers, and new reports.

FIGURE 42.4

The QuickTime Player is also available for Windows and provides a portal for the latest samples from the Internet.

FIGURE 42.5

The RealOne Player is yet another popular media player available on the Internet.

MusicMatch

MusicMatch Player is another great media player that includes the ability to catalog and organize music sets into playlists, as shown in Figure 42.6. You can streamline most media players and hide them away in a corner of the Windows interface so they don't take up much space. MusicMatch Player was one of the first players that could read CDs and automatically download song and album titles from the Internet.

 Media players often are included with certain types of software such as an iPod or pre-loaded on the computer.

FIGURE 42.6

MusicMatch Player can display song and album titles from the Internet.

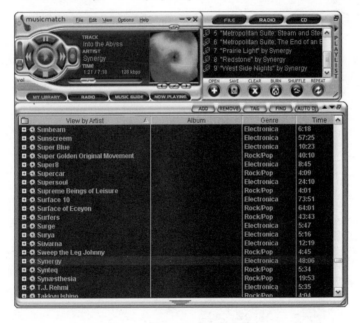

Changing media players

When a media player is installed on your system, it is configured to play the vast assortment of media files that it may encounter. You can switch a specific file type to use a different media player if you wish.

If you select the audio file and open its Properties dialog box, it includes an option to change the media player that opens the specified file type.

To change the media player used to open the selected file type, follow these steps:

1. **Locate a media file type such as MP3 in Windows Explorer.**

2. **Choose the File ⇨ Properties menu or right click on the selected file.** Choose the Properties menu command.

3. **In the Properties dialog box, shown in Figure 42.7, click on Change.**

4. **In the Open With dialog box that appears, select the desired media player.** Close the dialog box. Then click the Apply button on the Properties dialog box.

 Most media players can reset the files associated with their player and some even include regular checks to see if these associations have been switched to another player.

FIGURE 42.7

The media files Properties dialog box lets you change its default media player.

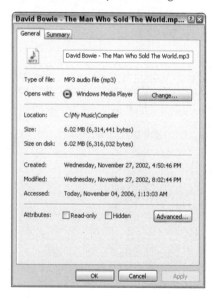

MP3

Digital music is all the rage now with MP3 and media players available from many different manufacturers and songs available for download from many artists.

Each of the media players has the ability to store and play MP3 music your PC downloads from the Internet; most provide access to a music service where you can access and download music files for a nominal fee.

Digital music files can be some of the largest data files on the Web. CD-quality sound is recorded at 44,100 samples per second, which for 16-bit sound in stereo (with two channels) turns out to be a whopping 1,411,200 bits of data for every second of sound. At this ratio, even a simple nursery rhyme would be around 5 to 10 megabytes (MB) in size.

MP3 is a compression format that enables music files to be reduced in size significantly without seriously degrading the sound quality. This format makes it possible to reduce a three-minute song from 30MB down to one that is roughly 3MB when 128KB per second compression is used. You can save better quality sound by using less aggressive compression ratios.

NOTE   The Moving Pictures Experts Group developed the MP3 audio format. It was the third major release of the format, which stands for MPEG audio Layer-3. A newer format called MP3 Pro is available that reduces the compression rates even more, but the new format requires a new encoder to realize these compression rates and a new player to get the best sound quality.

When saving MP3 files, you can set the Bit Rate between 42KB per second to 192KB per second. Lower bit rates compress the audio file to a greater extent but result in lower quality. MP3 files saved at 192KB per second bit rate have the best quality sound.

Downloads

In addition to CDs, downloaded MP3 files are another common source of digital music. Users can download MP3 files ripped from CDs and also upload them to servers. You can add downloaded music files to the media player's library by simply dragging them onto the media player's window.

Many fee-based Web sites let you pay a fee for the ability to download digital music files to your computer. From your computer, you can download the files to an MP3 player for taking your music on the go.

 **CAUTION**   Sharing ripped MP3 files is against copyright laws.

Podcasts

Another way to listen to digital audio is to use a media player to connect to a *podcast*. Podcasts are digital audio programs that you can download and listen to or take with you on your mobile device.

Podcasts are available on every conceived topic and can be searched using a Web browser. The iTunes player includes an online repository of podcasts that are easy to navigate and use.

Streaming Internet audio

Many Internet sites offer streaming audio. These broadcasts, like radio stations, have a continual digital file that isn't downloaded in its entirety. Instead, the program is streamed to your computer's hard drive where a portion of the program is saved. As the program continues, more of the program downloads while you are listening to the section that is already saved. By continually downloading the next section so it can be heard without interruption, the program lasts indefinitely.

Many radio stations broadcast their programs on their Web sites in conjunction with their broadcast over the airwaves. If you do a search for you favorite stations, there is a good chance you can find them online. Streaming audio servers are required in order to be able to set up a streaming audio program, but anyone with a Web browser and the correct add-ons can listen in on a streaming audio program.

Recording

If you have a microphone attached to your computer, you can record sound that you can save to the local hard drive. Another way to save sound files is to rip the music files off a CD, one that you should legally own, into the MP3 format. Most media players can rip music files for you. The process is explained later in this chapter.

Recording sound files

You can record sound files via the attached microphone using the Sound Recorder, shown in Figure 42.8. This simple little utility is found in the Start ➪ All Programs ➪ Accessories ➪ Entertainment ➪ Sound Recorder menu. It works by simply clicking the Record button and speaking into the microphone.

FIGURE 42.8

The Sound Recorder utility can record sound directly into the microphone.

Recorded sound files can be saved using the .WAV file format. The .WAV format is created using the File ➪ Save As menu. This format saves all the data without any compressions, which results in file sizes that are much larger than MP3 audio.

Ripping CDs into MP3 files

When you insert a CD into the computer's CD-ROM or DVD drive, the computer automatically detects an audio CD and loads it into the default media player. Within the media player is a feature that can convert its audio files into MP3 files and save them to the computer's hard drive. This process is called ripping a CD.

Once you rip a CD's audio files, you can play them using the media player without having to insert the original CD again. This is a convenient way to keep your music collection on the computer. It also gives you the chance to shuffle all the songs in your collection into jukebox mode.

CAUTION   Most CDs are protected by copyright laws, and you should rip them only if you own the CD. Copyrighted music files also should not be made accessible where other users can download them.

To rip a music CD into MP3 files using Windows Media Player, follow these steps:

1. Insert a music CD into the computer's CD-ROM or DVD drive.
2. The Windows media player automatically loads and begins to play the music CD.
3. From the Windows Media Player interface, select Rip to open the Rip music tab, shown in Figure 42.9.
4. Click Start Rip to begin the process.
5. Each selected file converts to an MP3 file and copies to a folder with the album's name in the My Music folder. You can use the Rip ➪ Format menu to change the format between Windows Media Audio, MP3, or WAV. The Rip ➪ Bit Rate menu can change the quality/compression rate. The Rip ➪ More Options menu lets you change the folder where the audio files are saved.

NOTE   If you enable the Copy protect music option in the Options dialog box, the ripped files are protected and require media usage rights to load before they are played on a separate computer.

FIGURE 42.9

The Rip window of Windows Media Player includes a button that can begin the ripping process.

Editing Sounds

Once you capture and save an audio file, you can use specialized software to edit the sound files. This software can combine separate sound files together, mix in sound effects, reduce noise, and convert the sound files to other formats.

Software for recording and editing

Several different sound editing packages are available. Some of these are professional-level tools used by music producers; others are intended for home use. If you're looking into editing sound files, consider these products:

- **Sound Forge:** This is a valuable tool for mixing and editing sound clips.
- **Adobe Audition:** Audition integrates well with other Adobe products.
- **Sony's ACID:** Used to make music loops, many DJs use Sony's ACID on the dance floor.
- **Cakewalk:** This is used to integrate MIDI sequencing and multi-track audio.
- **Goldwave:** A simple-to-use Windows audio-editing package.

How to edit sound

Sound-editing software displays sound by showing its relative volume over time, known as its *soundwave*. By looking at the soundwave, you can easily detect where the volume is loud and where the volume is low or pauses between speaking. This makes it easy to separate spoken words into separate sections. By splicing in new words, you can change the resulting sound files.

Editing software can also control the volume of the sound and add special effects, like reverb and reversed sound. You can also convert the sound files to different formats including the compressed MP3 format.

To edit soundwaves, just drag over a section of the soundwave to select it. Once you've selected a portion, you can cut, copy, and paste it to another part of the soundwave. You can also edit the selected section or completely remove it from the sound file.

Connecting Your Computer to Your Stereo System

Even if you have a decent pair of computer speakers with a subwoofer, it still probably isn't up to par with your stereo components. With the correct cables and some patience, you can connect your computer to your stereo system and play your ripped music files on your stereo system. This is where high quality MP3 files with bit rates of 192KB per second are noticeable.

There are several different ways to connect your computer and your stereo including direct cabling, USB audio devices, and wireless transmitters.

If the sound card on your computer has RCA jacks (with red, yellow, and white connectors), then you can use stereo cables to connect the two using these jacks. Be sure to connect the output jack on your computer's sound card to the CD jack on your stereo.

If you plan on recording the stereo output to the computer, then you need to connect the Line-out jack on your stereo receiver to the Line-in jack on your sound card.

You can also use USB cables with audio jacks on the opposite end (called a USB Audio cable) to connect the computer to the stereo. USB cables are less likely to be bothered by noise from the computer components than the standard cables.

In some stores, you can find a wireless transmitter. These transmitters connect to your sound card or to a USB port and transmit up to 300 feet to a device connected to the stereo's headphone jack. These devices are more expensive than cabling and can be susceptible to static interference, but tend to work well if you listen to the stereo from a static position without a lot of moving around.

Summary

One of the joys for new computer users is popping a CD into a computer and having it automatically start playing. Via their PCs installed media players, users can listen to CDs, view videos, and enjoy downloaded digital music files. There are several different types of audio that can play on a computer including MP3 files, podcasts, and streaming audio.

Using the Sound Recorder utility, you can record simple audio. You can create MP3 files by ripping a CD, another feature of media players. You can edit recorded sound or sound files using specialized sound-editing software.

Finally, you can enjoy the convenience of digital audio on state-of-the-art stereo components by connecting your PC to your home entertainment stereo system.

Chapter 43

Viewing, Creating, and Editing Video

When DVDs first started to appear, people were amazed with their picture and sound quality, but they were still tied to the television. The real fun came later when you could play a DVD on a long road trip or entertain a small group in the airport.

DVD drives and their ability to play video DVDs are common on most new laptops and computers. Movie DVDs require a DVD drive to be installed in the computer along with some specialized software that can read and play the DVDs before they can be seen.

A common place to see lower-resolution video is through the Internet using one of the many media players and an Internet connection. Although streaming video can be seen using a dial-up connection, they really require a broadband connection to see the video in any detail.

Most video cameras that are available today are digital and with the right cabling can be connected directly to a computer. By connecting a video camera to a computer, you can download the video sequences to the computer where you can edit them, then store them on a DVD.

This chapter shows how you can use computers to view DVDs and also use them with video cameras to view, create, and edit video segments.

IN THIS CHAPTER

Playing DVDs

Streaming video over the Internet

Using Windows Movie Maker

Capturing video to the computer

Playing DVDs on Your Laptop

When a movie DVD is inserted into a computer's DVD drive, it is automatically detected if the software for viewing the DVD is installed. This software is different depending on the manufacturer of the DVD drive, but the software is designed to work just like a stand-alone DVD player with buttons for playing, pausing, and skipping to the next or previous chapters.

Figure 43.1 shows a DVD loaded into Windows Media Player, which features a list of all the available chapters and an image of the DVD's cover. Clicking the Play button starts the DVD.

FIGURE 43.1

DVDs can load directly on a computer with a DVD drive and the appropriate software.

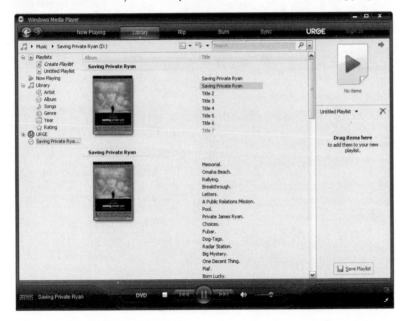

Viewing Streaming Video from the Internet

If you've established a connection to the Internet using a broadband connection, then you should be able to take advantage of the ability to view video segments over the Internet.

 You can still view video sequences if you connect to the Internet using a dial-up connection, but the resolution is so small and pixilated that it is difficult to see.

Viewing video on the Internet

Internet video is made possible using software that runs within the Web browser or in a separate Media Player. One such example is the Flash plug-in that enables a browser to view video segments. Other plug-ins are available and typically installed with their corresponding media player. The following video formats are common on the Web:

- RealOne (RA)
- Microsoft Video (AVI)
- Windows Media Format (WMF)
- Apple's QuickTime (MOV)
- Motion Pictures Export Group (MPEG)
- Adobe Flash (SWF)

> **NOTE** The Flash format can do much more than just play video. It is an interactive format used to create games and applications.

You can download short movie segments in their entirety, but longer segments often are easier to view if the video is streamed to the computer. When a video file is streamed, an initial portion of the file downloads before it starts. The movie then plays while the next section of the file is downloaded. By keeping enough of the file in a buffer to allow the video segment to play continuously, the streaming process stays one step ahead of the viewer.

Once a video segment uploads to a Web server, anyone connecting and viewing the streamed video segment needs only a Web browser with the right software installed and a fast enough connection to view the video.

To view a streaming video segment on the Internet, follow these steps:

1. **Locate a Web site on the Internet that offers video segments, such as** www.apple.com/trailers.

2. **Click on a video link in the Web page.** The video is offered in several different sizes (Small, Medium, Large, and IPod) depending on the speed of your connection.

3. **Click on the size that corresponds to your Internet connection speed.** If the required software isn't available, then a dialog box appears asking if you want to download the software to play the video.

4. **Click Yes to download the required software.** The software downloads and installs automatically and the video segment starts playing.

Downloading video to a mobile media player

Another popular way to view video is to download video files to a portable media player such as an iPod. These devices can hold audio and video files and play them on demand. These portable devices allow you to take media clips with you wherever you go. Figure 43.2 shows a media player created by Creative Labs.

When you select to download a video clip to a media player, the clip saves to a directory where the media player can access it. The clip waits in this directory until the media player is connected and the player is synchronized with the computer. This causes all the downloaded clips to transport over to the media player where they can play on demand.

669

FIGURE 43.2

Media players, like this Creative Labs device, allow you to view video segments on the go.

Image courtesy of Creative Labs

Using Your Computer with a Video Camera

Most modern video cameras store their data digitally. This allows them to download their recorded data to a computer. Handheld video cameras are common today, but smaller Web cameras are also available that can record and allow face-to-face communication between connected users.

Streaming to the Internet

Internet Web cams are popular and readily available. Most connect to the computer using a simple USB port and allow their captured image to be streamed across to the Internet. Figure 43.3 shows a sample Web cam created by Creative Labs. A simple camera such as this one can sit on the top of your monitor and send your image to others as you communicate with them.

FIGURE 43.3

Web cams like this Creative Labs device allow users across the Internet to communicate face-to-face.

Image courtesy of Creative Labs

A Web cam typically doesn't have the best image quality because it has to move the data through the Internet, but you should look for a camera that can capture a high resolution as well as a high frame rate. The frame rate (fps) is the number of frames that can be captured per second. Movies run at 24 fps and television runs at 30 fps, but most Web cams are significantly less than this. It is common for Web cams to run at 12–15 fps, but for smoother video you can find cameras that run higher.

When purchasing a Web cam, you should also watch for the software that is included. This software lets you stream your images over the Internet and edit them.

Making movies

The first step in creating a movie is to use your handheld camera to capture video data. Because the data is digital, it can be transported to the computer where you can edit the results. Several software packages are available for editing video including:

- Adobe Premiere
- Ulead's Video Studio

- Pinnacle Studio
- Windows Movie Maker

 A less-expensive version of Premiere called Premiere Elements is available from Adobe. It includes a strong set of core features for editing videos.

Using Windows Movie Maker

Windows includes a simple utility that can be used to combine video segments, pictures, and audio together to create a movie. Windows Movie Maker is located in the Start ⇨ All Programs ⇨ Accessories ⇨ Entertainment ⇨ Windows Movie Maker menu.

Gathering resources

The interface is simple to use and the steps are listed in a panel to the right, as shown in Figure 43.4. You can drop content including pictures, video, and audio into the collection panel in the center. From these resources, you can create a storyboard along the bottom of the window. The panel to the right in Figure 43.4 shows a preview of the resulting movie.

FIGURE 43.4

Windows Movie Maker lets you combine pictures, video, and audio together.

Adding transitions and effects

You can add transitions between each part of the storyboard. To view the available transitions, select the Tools ➪ Video Transitions menu. You can drop these into the icon positioned between the storyboard images, as shown in Figure 43.5.

The Tools menu also includes a category of Video Effects that can change the way the video segments appear. The options include effects such as fade to black, speed up double time, rotate the frame, add film grain, blur, and ease in and out.

Controlling timing and audio

The Timeline, shown in Figure 43.6, shows how long each resource remains on the screen. You can edit this length and reposition them relative to one another by dragging and dropping the Timeline pictures.

FIGURE 43.5

Transitions can be added between each resource in the storyboard.

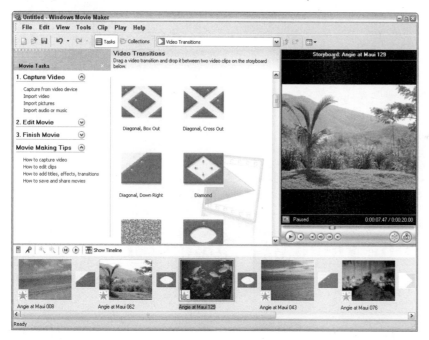

FIGURE 43.6

The Timeline lets you control how long a resource stays on the screen.

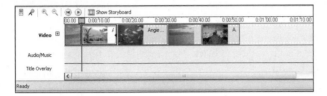

Once the sequence flows together, you can use the Tools ➪ Narrate Timeline menu to enter a recording mode that lets you speak the narrative for the movie as it plays.

Capturing video

You can capture video segments taken with a handheld video camera directly into Windows Movie Maker. Start by connecting the video camera to the computer. If your camera is a Web cam with a USB connector, then connecting is easy; however, if you're using a standard video camera, check out the next section that explains how you can connect video devices to the computer. When a USB Web cam is connected, Windows detects this device and lets the Movie Maker software know that the device is available.

When a connection is established, the next step is to name and tell the video file where it should save. In the Video Settings dialog box, select the settings for this video clip and click the Start Capture button. When the video segment that you want to record has completed, click the Stop Capture button and the file saves.

CAUTION   Video files can take up a lot of space depending on the audio settings and the video resolution. Be sure you have enough room for the file before starting the capture process. If the resolution of your video image takes up 200KB, which is fairly small, and the video is set to run at 15 fps, then 10 seconds of video takes up 30MB of disk space without sound.

Connecting Video to a Computer

Before you can edit video on your computer, you need to load the video data onto your computer hard drive. There are several ways to do this and the way you choose depends on the hardware in your computer and the type of video data that you want to edit.

TIP   Before attempting to capture any video data, make sure you have ample hard drive space. Video data can take up a lot of space depending on the *codec* that you use. Codec stands for compression/decompression software that saves the analog digital video signal into its digital equivalent.

Using FireWire

The easiest method for loading video data onto your hard drive is with a FireWire port. Most digital video cameras have a FireWire port that you can link via cable directly to your computer's FireWire port. Once connected, you can use a command within your video editing software to capture the recorded video data or to capture the live video feed. The specific command that you use to record video differs depending on the software that you use.

 **If you have a choice between FireWire and USB2, choose the FireWire port. It can capture video data at a rate that is two to three times that of USB.**

If the video data you want to capture is from an analog source such as an older VHS tape, then you need to use an external digital video converter. You can link these converters directly to the FireWire port on your computer; the other end hooks into your VHS or DVD player.

 **For more on using FireWire and USB interfaces, check out Chapter 14.**

Capturing video via USB2

If your computer doesn't have a FireWire port, then you can still capture video data to the hard drive using a USB2 connection. To use this connection, you need to get an external USB2 video capture device. These devices connect your VHS or DVD player to the USB2 port.

 **USB2 ports are high-speed and work well for capturing video data. You can still use the older USB1 ports, but the process is much slower and you risk losing much of its audio track.**

Figure 43.7 shows a sample USB connector made by Pinnacle with an attachment that lets you connect to a DVD or VHS unit.

 **If a video or DVD player is connected to the computer, you can use them to load recorded video also.**

To capture a digital video segment from your digital video camera, follow these steps:

1. **Locate the video segment on your digital camera that you want to capture.**

2. **Connect the digital camera to a USB video capture device using an S-Video cable.** Then connect the video capture device to the USB port. Figure 43.8 shows Pinnacle's video capture device.

3. **Open the image editing software that came with your video capture device.** For my system, this software is Pinnacle Studio.

4. **Press the Play button on the digital camera and click the Start Capture button in the editing software.** A dialog box appears showing the progress of the captured video.

5. **Select the Make Movie option to save the captured video clip to the AVI video format.**

FIGURE 43.7

A USB connector can capture video from a variety of sources.

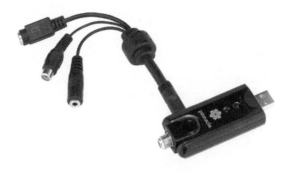

Image courtesy of Pinnacle Systems

FIGURE 43.8

The Pinnacle video capture device lets you connect your digital video camera to your computer.

Image courtesy of Pinnacle Systems

To capture a digital video segment from a DVD or VHS player, follow these steps:

1. **Locate the video segment on a DVD or VHS tape that you want to capture.**

2. **Connect the DVD or the VHS player to a USB video capture device using the red, yellow, and white RCA cables.** Then connect the video capture device to the USB port.

3. **Open the image editing software that came with your video capture device.** For my system, this software is Pinnacle Studio.

4. **Press the Play button on the DVD or VHS player and click the Start Capture button in the editing software.** A dialog box appears showing the progress of the captured video, as shown in Figure 43.9.

5. **Select the Make Movie option to save the captured video clip to the AVI video format.**

FIGURE 43.9

The Pinnacle Studio software lets you capture, edit, and save video segments as movie files.

Capturing video with a Video Capture Card

If your computer is older and doesn't include either a FireWire or USB2 port, then you can still capture video data by installing an internal video capture card. These cards include ports for connecting VHS and DVD machines and are installed internally, so capture speed isn't a problem. Figure 43.10 shows a Dazzle external video capture device.

FIGURE 43.10

External video capture devices can connect directly with video equipment.

Image courtesy of Pinnacle Systems.

Summary

If your computer or laptop has a DVD drive installed, you can play DVDs directly on your computer. Just insert the DVD and it begins playing automatically. The Internet can also be a source for video segments. Videos are streamed when played off the Internet. You can also download videos to a mobile media device.

If you own a digital video camera, then you can use the camera to capture and transport video segments directly to the computer. Windows includes a handy piece of software called the Windows Movie Maker that walks you through the creation of movies. This software includes transitions, video effects, and audio narrative.

To capture video taken with a video camera, you need to connect the camera to the computer. You can do this using FireWire, USB ports, or video capture devices.

Part VII

Using Your Computer for Communications

Chapter 44

Connecting Your Computer to a Network or Another Computer

Any time you have more than one computer in your business, household, or other location, you can see some significant benefits if you connect them together through a network, including file exchange, instant messaging, and shared access to printers, file servers, and the Internet. A computer connected to a network can be a very powerful communications tool.

This chapter explains some of the most important concepts related to computer networks and offers instructions for setting up the most important types of network connections on a computer running Windows.

How Networks Work

A computer network is a set of two or more computers that can exchange commands and data. Successful computer communication requires a physical connection among the computers, using wires, radio, light waves, or some other transmission media, and a common set of data formats, languages, and rules for signaling.

The worldwide community of computer designers and users has established a long list of networking standards for everything from direct cable connections to carrier pigeons. With a few unimportant exceptions, all the networks you're likely to use work in a similar manner — only the physical media that carry the signals are different.

Packet data

The first communications networks, including telegraph and early telephone systems, used direct physical connections between the origin and the destination. When you placed a telephone call, an operator at a switchboard (or later, an automatic switching system) would connect the wires from your telephone to the wires that led to the home or office of the person you wanted to call; for the duration of the call, there was a continuous link between the two telephone sets.

If the two parties were in the same town, or in the same neighborhood in a bigger city, the operator would plug the line from the calling party directly into the line to the person they wanted to reach. But if the two parties were not both connected to the same switchboard, the operator would connect to a second switchboard through one or more *trunk lines,* as shown in Figure 44.1. For as long as the call continued, there was a physical connection between the two parties' telephones, and the lines that connected them could not be used for any other call.

FIGURE 44.1

Early telephone service used a separate physical connection for every call.

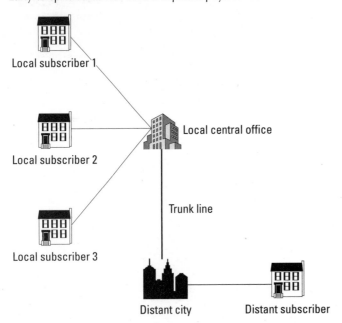

Local subscriber 1

Local subscriber 2

Local central office

Local subscriber 3

Trunk line

Distant city   Distant subscriber

CROSS-REF   Chapter 5 talks about how your computer combines a series of bits into a sequence that corresponds to a specific letter, number, punctuation mark, or other character called a byte, and how it uses those bytes to move data around inside the computer's processor and chipset.

NOTE
Long before computers, that same kind of bit sequence was used by news agencies to send text to Teletype machines through telephone and telegraph wires. That's why the Associated Press, Reuters, and the others are still called *wire services*.

Continuous connections work well for relatively slow, low-volume services, but as the demand for more connections increased, communications engineers developed methods for sharing a single circuit among many users. In a high-speed computer network today, the computer sending a stream of data breaks up the stream into smaller strings of binary data called *packets*, which the computer at the receiving end reassembles into a continuous message. Each packet moves through one or more switching centers that can hold it until it can establish a link to the destination (or to the next switching center). This method provides several benefits:

- It allows the receiving computer to examine the integrity of each packet and ask for another copy when it detects a problem.

- In a complex network with more than one possible route between the originating point and the destination, it permits the network to choose a different path if the first choice becomes unreliable during transmission.

- It can carry packets from more than one message through the same communications channel at the same time.

At any specific point in time, the signal on a communications circuit is either on or off. In order to use a circuit to transmit information, the people or machines at each end of the circuit must agree on these rules:

- The amount of time each bit occupies (the duration)

- The type of signal that is accepted as an "on" signal (also known as a 1 or 0, or a mark or space) rather than random noise

- The exact order of bits that corresponds to each letter, number, or other character

- A sequence of bits that identifies the beginning of each character string

It doesn't matter how you send those bits and bytes from one point to another. You can use flashing lights, smoke signals, two different audio tones, or a series of electrical impulses through a wire. As long as you use the same method to convert between useful information and data bits at both ends, you can use the channel to communicate information. When the communications channel is working properly, the information that goes into the transmitter is exactly the same when it comes out of the receiver.

Unfortunately, almost every kind of communications channel is susceptible to some kind of interference. It could be electrical noise caused by a lightning strike, interference from another communications circuit, dirt on an electrical contact, or fog between the smoke signals and the person reading them. When a modern communications circuit is moving tens of millions of bits every second, it doesn't take much to make some of the data unintelligible.

Therefore, each data packet usually includes some kind of *error checking* along with the original data. This is usually a standard string of bits called a *checksum* attached to each byte or each packet. If the checksum is not correct, the receiver notifies the transmitter, which sends the same byte or packet again.

In a complex network, each packet might move through several different communications channels. For example, you might send a file or an e-mail message from your laptop computer through a Wi-Fi link to the local area network (LAN) in your office, and from there through a series of switching centers on the Internet to the recipient's service provider and onward to their LAN and the recipient's computer. At each stage of this path, the network equipment might add or remove a string of routing information and error checking checksums to or from the beginning or end of each packet. Because the network has to carry all of this *handshaking data* along with the original message, the effective data transfer speed is always somewhat slower than the maximum capacity of a channel.

Fortunately, most of this process of dividing the data stream into packets, and adding error checking and other handshaking information occurs automatically, once you have configured your network interface, modem, router, and other network equipment. All you have to do is assign the right address to each file or message before you send it.

Network connections

Your computer can use several methods to join a network:

- You can connect to another computer as a remote terminal
- You can exchange data directly with a second computer (peer-to-peer networking)
- You can connect to a LAN and exchange data with all of the other computers connected to the same network
- You can connect through a LAN (a local area network in which all the computers and other connected devices are usually close together, and in which all the connected devices can exchange data with one another) to a wide-area network (WAN, a network in which the connected devices are connected through telephone lines or other communications channels) or the Internet

When most people talk about networking, they probably mean connecting a computer to a new or existing LAN, and through that LAN to the Internet. However, remote terminal connections and peer-to-peer networks still have their uses.

Remote terminals

Before everyone had personal computer, most computers used one or more terminals, usually connected to them through a serial data port. A terminal typically included a keyboard that sent data to the computer's input, and either a video display or a printer that received data from the output. A terminal that was located in a different room from the computer was called a *remote terminal*. If both the computer and the remote terminal were located in the same building, they were usually connected through a serial data cable. But it was also possible to use a pair of modems to connect the terminal to the computer through a telephone line.

A remote terminal can work with just about any kind of computer and operating system. Even though your own computer uses Windows, you can send commands through a communications link to machines running Unix, Linux, and most proprietary operating systems; as long as the host recognizes the commands, it accepts and responds to them.

CROSS-REF See Chapter 33 for more on Unix and Linux.

Today, remote terminals are mostly used for access to mainframe computers and time-sharing systems (a shrinking number of library catalogs also require remote terminal access). Most connections to remote computers use the World-Wide Web instead of a remote terminal connection, but you might still need to use a remote terminal when the system doesn't offer any alternative connection method.

When you type a command on the terminal's keyboard, the terminal sends the command to the host computer. For example, Figure 44.2 shows a login screen at The Well, a virtual community that operates on a Unix host. The host treats a connection through a telephone line or through the Internet as if it was receiving commands and returning data to and from a local terminal.

FIGURE 44.2

The Well accepts logins from remote terminals.

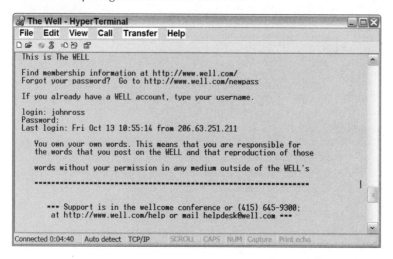

If the host computer is connected to a LAN, you can also use your remote terminal connection to gain access to connect the host to other computers through that network. If the host has an Internet connection, you can run many Internet programs (such as an e-mail client or an FTP file transfer program) from your remote terminal. Because you are using the command-line interface, or *shell*, to use the Internet, this kind of access is called a *shell account*.

Windows uses a utility called a *terminal emulator* to connect to a distant host and present the same appearance as a remote terminal. Most Windows terminal emulators include these features:

- Emulation of common terminal types, including VT-100, Wyse60, and IBM 3278, along with the generic ANSI terminal, among others
- Support for several file transfer protocols that specify the rules for moving data between computers, including Xmodem, Ymodem, Zmodem, and Kermit
- Automatic control of a modem
- Telnet support through a TCP/IP (Internet) connection, explained later in this section
- Preset connection profiles for quick links to frequently used hosts
- Access to the Windows Clipboard to cut, copy, and paste text between the terminal emulator and a text editor or other program
- A method for saving the text of a terminal session as a file or sending the file to a printer

The HyperTerminal program (Start ⇨ All Programs ⇨ Accessories ⇨ Communications ⇨ HyperTerminal) supplied with Windows is entirely adequate for simple connections, text entry, and file transfers. However, there's a better version available at no cost from Hilgraeve, the developer that created the program for Microsoft. You can download HyperTerminal Private Edition from www.hilgraeve.com/htpe.

If you're using a distant computer for more complex work (such as remote access to a Unix host or some other mainframe system), you might want to consider a third-party terminal emulator program with additional features, including scripts and emulation of the specific characteristics of more makes and models of terminals (such as codes produced by function keys and on-screen text in more than one color).

Telnet (short for telecommunications network) is the set of rules that the Internet and other networks use for text-based communication between a terminal and a host computer, or between two computers. When your computer is already connected to the Internet, you can use a telnet utility to log onto a remote host as a terminal, as shown in Figure 44.3. There's a very primitive telnet utility supplied with Windows; most terminal emulator programs (including HyperTerminal) include telnet services and allow you to use them as your default telnet program. To set up a telnet session, open Start ⇨ Run and type `telnet [name of host]`.

Most terminal emulator programs include an option that makes that program the default program that runs when you enter a telnet command. If you can't find that option, you can follow these steps to set your favorite terminal emulator as the default telnet program:

1. **Open My Computer and select Tools ⇨ Folder Options from the menu.**
2. **In the Folder Options dialog box, open the File Types tab.** The window shown in Figure 44.4 opens.

FIGURE 44.3

A terminal emulator (top) normally connects directly to a host computer. A telnet program (bottom) connects to a host through the Internet.

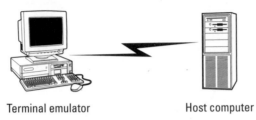

Terminal emulator   Host computer

Telnet client   Telnet host server

3. **Select the (NONE) URL:Telnet Protocol file type from the list.** Click the Advanced button near the bottom of the dialog box.

4. **In the Edit File Type dialog box, select Open in the list of Actions (it's probably the only entry in the list).** Click Edit to open the Editing action dialog box.

5. **In the Editing action dialog box, use the Browse button to open a window where you can select the new default program.** Hyper Terminal is located at C:\Program Files\Windows NT\hypertrm.exe. Most other terminal emulator programs are located in a subfolder with the program name, within the Program Files folder. If you can't find the program, use the Windows Search tool to locate it.

6. **Use the Open button in the Open With window, and the OK buttons in the other open dialog boxes to close the dialog boxes.** Save your choice.

After you have assigned a new default telnet program, that program opens and sets up a connection when you enter telnet [address] in the Start ⇨ Run window.

FIGURE 44.4

Edit the URL: Telnet Protocol setting to set a new default telnet program.

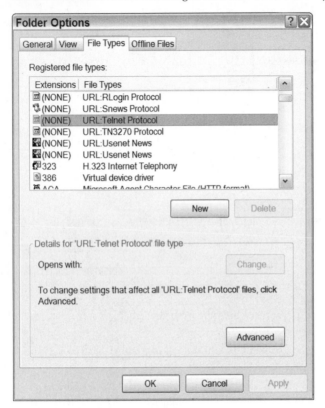

TCP/IP connections

Unless some other kind of network is specifically identified, just about any time people talk about connecting a computer to a network, they're probably using the TCP/IP (Transmission Control Protocol/Internet Protocol) standards that are the core of the Internet and most modern LANs. There are some other network standards out there, but because everybody eventually wants to connect to the Internet, they probably use TCP/IP.

Most Windows connections to a LAN use either a wired connection through an Ethernet adapter and cable, or a wireless connection through a Wi-Fi access point.

Before you start to set up your network connection, you must obtain the following information from your network manager, your Internet service provider, or the installation manual for the network hub or router. Don't worry if you don't know what one or more of these items represents; it's essential to have the names and numbers correct, but the significance of each one doesn't matter unless you're a network manager:

- The name assigned to your computer
- The name of the workgroup that your computer will join
- The name of your domain, if any
- If the network uses static IP addresses, the numeric IP address assigned to your computer
- If the network does not assign them automatically, the numeric addresses of your network's Internet Domain Name Servers
- The numeric address of your network's default gateway to the Internet
- The numeric subnet mask address

If you're connecting to an existing network through an Ethernet cable, follow these steps to set up a network connection:

1. **If a network interface adapter is not already in place, turn off the computer and install one in your computer.** If you're using a desktop computer, use a network card on an internal expansion card or connect an external adapter through a USB port. If you have a laptop, use either a USB adapter or an adapter on a PC Card. Use the software supplied with the adapter to install the device driver.

2. **When you turn on the computer after installing a network adapter, Windows should automatically detect the new hardware and install any device drivers or other software that isn't already in place.** If Windows doesn't automatically find the device driver, use the software supplied with the adapter. If the adapter came with additional software, install it now.

3. **Connect an Ethernet cable from the network interface adapter to the network switch, hub, or gateway router that connects to the other devices in your network.**

If you're connecting through a Wi-Fi link, follow these steps:

1. **Consult the manual or quick start guide supplied with your wireless adapter to learn whether you should install the control software before or after connecting the wireless interface adapter.** If the manual instructs you to load the software first, install it now.

2. **If the wireless network adapter is not built into your computer, install the adapter on a PCI expansion card, a PC Card, or a USB connection.** If the computer is not already on, turn it on now.

3. **Windows automatically detects the wireless adapter and loads the appropriate device driver.** When the Windows installation is complete, load any Wi-Fi software supplied with the adapter that you haven't already installed.

4. **Restart the computer.** If the network interface detects one or more Wi-Fi access points nearby, Windows and the proprietary software asks if you want to connect.

If your network manager or Internet service provider has provided specific instructions for connecting your computer, follow those instructions. If not, run the New Connection Wizard from Control Panel ⇨ Network Connections to assign the necessary addresses.

Hubs, switches, and routers

Your computer connects to the network through either a hub, a switch, or a router.

A *hub* is the least complex type of network connection. All of the networked computers and other devices (such as printers) connected to a hub are linked directly through a common connection point. When a hub receives a data packet from one of the devices connected to it, it sends a copy of that packet to all of its data ports, so every packet that comes into a hub goes back out through all of the hub's ports. The destination device accepts packets that contain its address, and all the other network devices ignore them. Figure 44.5 shows a hub connection.

FIGURE 44.5

A hub is a passive network connection point.

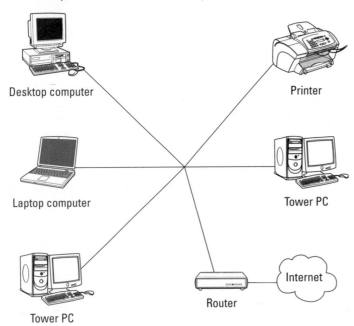

Desktop computer

Printer

Laptop computer

Tower PC

Tower PC

Router

Internet

A *switch* is a more sophisticated connection point. The switch examines the address of each incoming packet and copies the packet to the port connected to the device with that address. Figure 44.6 shows a data switch.

In a low-volume network, there's not much difference between the performance of a hub and a switch. However, when there's a lot of network traffic, the switch moves data through the network more efficiently. The difference in cost between a hub and a switch is often insignificant, so a switch is usually the better choice.

A *router* is a connection point or interface between two networks, such as a LAN and an Internet connection. On each side of the router, it has a different address that identifies it as a member of the network connected to that side. So, for example, it could connect all the computers on a LAN to the Internet through a shared broadband connection to an Internet provider's WAN.

The computers and other devices on the LAN side of the router have addresses that are visible only to other devices on the same LAN. All the devices on the LAN appear to outsiders on the other side of the router with the router's address.

FIGURE 44.6

A switch sends incoming packets to specific destinations.

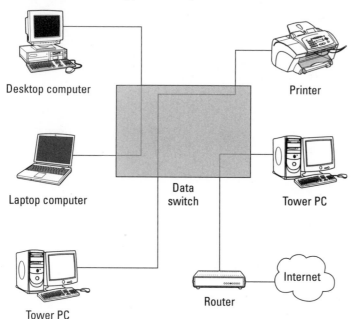

A router that connects a LAN to the Internet is often called a *gateway router*. Figure 44.7 shows the sequence of network devices in a typical small home or office network. A larger network is similar, but it probably has more nodes. The individual computers and printers connect to one or more switches (or hubs) to form a LAN, which connects to an Internet service provider's (ISP) WAN through a router. The WAN connection moves data through a modem that drives either a DSL line or a cable TV line. At the ISP, the WAN connects to the Internet through yet another router. Each switch, router, and modem is a separate logical device, but the switch and router or the router and modem are often combined into a single physical device. Other routers are combined with Wi-Fi access points to allow both wired and wireless connections, or with a DSL or cable modem.

FIGURE 44.7

A small network usually includes a switch, a router, and a modem.

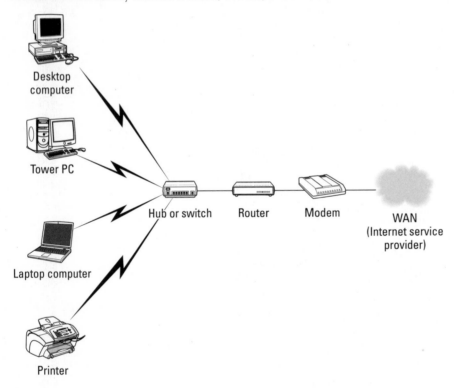

Connecting Through a Network

Your computer can connect to a network through several kinds of communication channels:

- A serial data port (now mostly replaced by faster connection types)
- A modem that communicates through the public telephone network
- An Ethernet connection to a LAN
- A wireless interface that uses one of the 802.11 (Wi-Fi) standards
- A wireless interface that uses one of the 3G mobile telephone standards
- An infrared lightwave connection
- An IEEE 1394 (FireWire) connection

Using a modem

A *modem* is a device that converts computer data to signals that a communication channel can transmit to a second modem that converts the signal back to data. The name is short for modulator-demodulator. The most common modems connect a computer to either a dial-up telephone line, a broadband DSL service or a cable TV system. In most cases, if somebody talks about a *modem* without any other identification, they're referring to a modem that connects to the dial telephone system. A *DSL modem* also connects to a telephone line, but it uses a Digital Subscriber Line service that moves broadband data to and from the Internet at high speed. A *cable modem* connects to the Internet through a cable TV system. A *broadband modem* could be either a DSL modem or a cable modem.

Many new computers and motherboards come with built-in dial-up modems. If your computer does not have a modem, you can add one that mounts inside a desktop computer on a PCI expansion card or fits a laptop computer's PC Card socket. If you prefer, you can connect a modem through a USB port.

In order to connect your computer to another computer or to a network host through a dial-up telephone line, you need to know these items:

- The distant computer's telephone number, including the area code
- Your account name and password on the distant computer
- The type of network host you are calling. The options include PPP (Point-to-Point Protocol), SLIP (Serial Line Internet Protocol), or a remote terminal port.

When you connect via PPP or SLIP, you join a network through your modem. When you connect as a remote terminal, you exchange commands and data with a computer that may already be connected to a network (or the Internet), or it might be a stand-alone computer with no other access to a network.

If you're connecting as a remote terminal, use the Call Setup or New Connection tool in your terminal emulator program to set up the call. The program asks you to specify the data port connected to your modem and the telephone number of the host.

If you're installing dial-up Internet access from your Internet service provider, use the software supplied by the ISP.

If your ISP provided a CD with their own connection software, use the software on that disk to set up your connections. If you don't have a CD, follow these steps to create a connection profile for a PPP or SLIP network connection to the Internet through a modem and a telephone line:

1. **If it's not already in place, connect your computer to a modem.** Your modem might connect to the computer through a USB connection or a serial data port, or it might plug into a PCI slot or a PC Card to.

2. **Install a telephone cable between the modem's telephone line socket and a telephone line wall outlet or connection block.**

3. **From the Control Panel, open Network Connections.**

4. **Run the New Connection Wizard.**

5. **When the wizard reaches the Network Connection Type screen, choose Connect to the Internet and click Next.**

6. **If your ISP did not supply a software disk, choose Set up my connection manually and click next.**

7. **In the How do you want to connect window, choose Connect using a dial-up modem and click Next.**

8. **Continue through the wizard and as the wizard requests them, enter the name of your ISP, the dial-in telephone number supplied by the ISP, and your account name and password.**

9. **At the Completing the New Construction Wizard window, turn on the Add a shortcut option and click Finish.**

When the Wizard completes the setup, you can click the shortcut on your desktop to call your ISP and log into your Internet account, using the Connect window shown in Figure 44.8. When you use a Web browser or other Internet program, your computer automatically makes the connection for you.

To connect through your dial-up account, click the Dial button at the bottom of the Connect window.

To disconnect the call, right-click the Network Status icon in the system tray and choose Disconnect from the pop-up menu.

FIGURE 44.8

Use this connect window to place a call to your dial-up Internet account.

Setting up an Ethernet connection

Most local networks use Ethernet connections between each computer and the hub, switch, or router and the core of the network. The Windows New Connection Wizard that steps you through the initial configuration settings is enough to configure a connection, but it is helpful to understand what the settings mean and how to set or change them from the Properties window.

To open a LAN Properties window, follow these steps:

1. **From the Start menu or the Control Panel, open Network Connections.**
2. **Double-click the name of the LAN connection profile.** It's probably Local Area Connection. A status window like the one in Figure 44.9 opens.
3. **Click Properties near the bottom of the window.** A Properties window opens.

FIGURE 44.9

The status window provides information about an active network connection.

Figure 44.10 shows the General tab of a LAN Properties window. If your LAN connects you to the Internet, click the select the Internet Protocol (TCP/IP) settings item at or near the bottom of the list of clients, services, and protocols and click Properties to configure your connection.

As Figure 44.11 shows, the General tab of the Internet Protocol Properties window specifies the IP address and the Domain Name Servers' addresses that this connection profile uses to connect to the Internet. If a router or the network host uses DHCP (Dynamic Host Configuration Protocol) to assign addresses, choose the Obtain an IP address automatically option. If each computer has a permanent numeric address, your network manager or the manual supplied with the router or the DSL or cable modem provides the range of IP addresses that the device accepts. Your network manager or Internet service provider should supply the DNS server addresses.

FIGURE 44.10

The LAN Connection Properties window provides access to configuration settings for many network clients, services, and protocols.

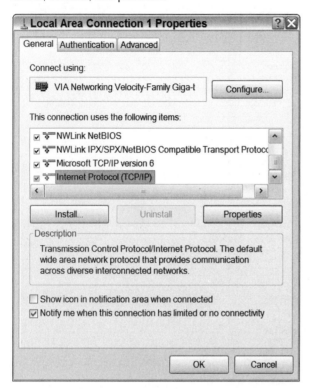

The Advanced button in the General tab opens another dialog box, like the one shown in Figure 44.12. The only setting you're likely to change in this window is the Default gateway, which is the address that the router uses to identify the gateway from the LAN to the Internet. You can obtain the Default gateway address from the manual supplied with your network router or broadband router, or from your network manager.

FIGURE 44.11

Use the Internet Protocol Properties window to set your computer's IP address and the addresses of the ISP's domain name servers.

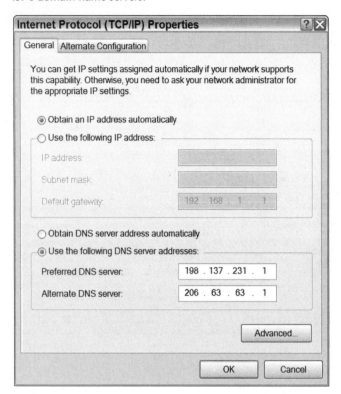

Setting up a 1394 network

It's not commonly used, but Windows also allows you to connect two computers into a small network by running a cable between their IEEE 1394 (FireWire) ports. A 1394 network does not use an Ethernet hub, so it's generally not practical for connecting more than two computers together.

If your computer has a FireWire port, it should automatically accept a 1394 network connection. To install a 1394 network, use a FireWire cable to connect the two computers and open Network Connections from the Start menu or the Control Panel. You should see a 1394 Connection item in the Network Connections window, and your connection should work without any additional action.

FIGURE 44.12

The Advanced button in the General tab opens the Advanced TCP/IP settings dialog box.

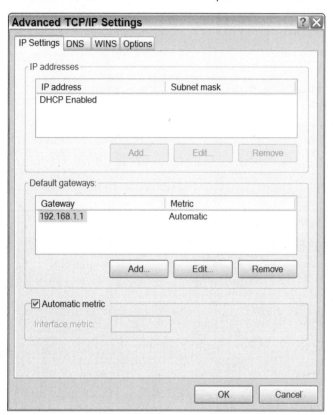

Connecting through an infrared (IrDA) link

Infrared transceivers are very common on laptop computers, where they are often built into the system, and it's also possible to use one with a desktop computer if you install a USB-to-infrared (IrDA) adapter. Infrared links are mostly used to transfer files between two computers, or from a digital camera to a laptop. In most cases, it's probably easier to use a Wi-Fi network connection instead of infrared, but Windows still supports the older technology.

About the only time you're likely to use an IrDA link would be when you're in a meeting where you want to send a file to somebody else's laptop computer across the table. For most other uses, an Ethernet link through a LAN or the Internet is a better method.

In order to use an infrared link, the transceivers on both devices must be enabled. To confirm that your computer's transceiver is enabled, follow these steps:

1. **Right-click My Computer in the Windows desktop.**

2. **Select Properties from the pop-up menu.** The System Properties window appears.

3. **Choose the Hardware tab and click Device Manager near the top of the window.** The Device Manager opens.

4. **Look for the Infrared Devices listing.** If you can't find it, this computer does not have an infrared transceiver. Click the listing to see a list of devices (there might be just one item in the sub-list).

5. **Right-click the item in the sub-list.** A pop-up menu like the one in Figure 44.13 appears.

FIGURE 44.13

The Device Manager shows the current status of your infrared transceiver.

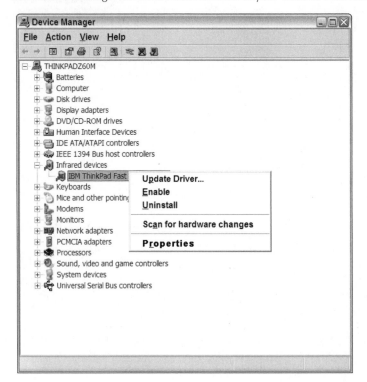

6. **If the second item in the pop-up menu says Enable, click that item to enable the infrared transceiver.** If it says Disable, click an empty space in the window to close the menu; the transceiver is already enabled.

7. **Close the Device Manager and the Properties window.**

To set up an infrared connection to another computer, follow these steps:

1. **From the Start menu or the Control Panel, open Network Connections.**

2. **Open the New Connection Wizard.**

3. **In the Network Connection type window, choose Set up an advanced connection and click Next.**

4. **In the Advanced Connection Options window, choose Connect directly to another computer and click Next.**

5. **In the Host or Guest window, choose Host if you plan to send data to another computer, or choose Guest if the other computer will send data to you.** Click Next.

6. **If you chose Host, choose the infrared port in the Connection Device window and click Next.** In the User Permissions window, choose the users who are authorized to gain access to your computer from the list, or use the Add button to add a new name.

7. **If you chose Guest in step 5, type a name for this link in the Connection Name window, click Next, and then choose the infrared port in the Select a Device window.**

8. **Click Next and Finish to complete the New Connection Wizard.** Windows adds this connection profile to the Guest's Network Connections list.

To make an infrared connection, place the two computers within about 10 feet (3 meters), open Network Connections on the Guest computer, and double-click the name of the connection profile. A link from the Host computer should appear on the Guest's desktop. You can gain access from the Guest to the Host through an infrared link just as you would through any other type of network.

Direct Connections

It's not always necessary to connect to a network when all you really need is a simple connection to one other computer to transfer files or exchange text messages. This kind of connection is sometimes described as an *ad hoc* network because it's usually a temporary link, established for a specific purpose and ended when it is no longer needed.

An ad hoc network can use any of these methods to establish the connection:

- A direct wired connection between serial data ports, using a null modem cable
- A cable connection between the IEE 1394 (FireWire) ports

- A link between USB ports, using a USB-to-serial adapter at each end and a null modem cable
- A connection through the public telephone network, between modems attached to each computer
- An ad hoc Wi-Fi radio link
- A link using infrared lightwaves between IrDA ports

Summary

Connecting a computer to a network makes the computer useful as a communications device as well as a data and text processor. Windows supports many kinds of network connections that allow a user to move data between computers, including Ethernet and IEEE 1394 cables, radio waves, and infrared light. The data that moves through all of these transmission media break the data stream into packets to add error checking, addressing, and other important information to the original data stream.

The information in this chapter explains how to use each type of connection to join your computer to a network. The same rules apply to connecting a computer to a LAN and to the Internet; indeed, when you connect your local network to the Internet through a LAN, both the LAN and your own computer become part of the Internet.

Chapter 45

Sending and Receiving Faxes

Once you have a computer set up and working fine, you need to go out and purchase a fax machine to make your home office complete, to fax legal documents that require signatures, or to have the ability to fax a take-out order to the local pizza place. Or, you could just use your computer to act as a fax machine.

Whether your computer connects to a phone line directly through an internal modem or via the Internet, you can both send and receive faxes through your PC. This capability is integrated directly into most of the major word processors, letting you send a fax as easily as selecting a menu command.

This chapter covers the details to enable your computer to act like a fax machine.

Creating a Fax in Windows

Before you start sending faxes using Windows, you first need to install the fax component. This requires that you install an internal modem that supports faxing on your system. After the fax component is installed, you can configure it to work with your computer.

> **NOTE** The fax component isn't installed by default.

Installing the fax component

Before installing the fax component, you can check your system to see if the component is already installed. Open the Start ⇨ All Programs ⇨

Accessories ⇨ Communications menu and look for the Fax Console option. If the component isn't there, you need to install it from the Windows Setup CD.

To install the Fax Console component from the Windows Setup CD, follow these steps:

1. **Open the Control Panel and click the Add/Remove Windows Components button.** This opens the Windows Component Wizard, shown in Figure 45.1.

FIGURE 45.1

The Windows Component Wizard lets you install additional components to Windows.

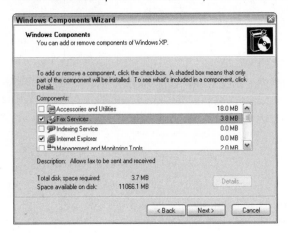

2. **Select the Fax Services button and click Next.**

3. **Some files copy from the Windows directory, but you need to insert the Windows Setup CD to complete the installation.** If you can't find the correct components, browse to the D:\I386 directory.

4. **When the installation is complete, click Finish to close the wizard.**

Configuring the Fax Console

After you've installed the fax component, you can open and configure the Fax Console using the Start ⇨ All Programs ⇨ Accessories ⇨ Communications ⇨ Fax ⇨ Fax Console menu. If this is the first time you've accessed the Fax Console, the Fax Configuration Wizard appears, but if you've already configured your computer for faxes, then this option opens the Fax Console. If you need to change the fax settings, you can revisit them in the Printers and Faxes option in the Control Panel.

NOTE   As the Fax Configuration Wizard opens, it searches your system for a modem installation. If the Fax Configuration Wizard doesn't find a modem installed on your system, you need to install one or run the troubleshooter to make sure the modem is working properly.

CROSS-REF You can learn more about working with modems in Chapter 44.

The first page of the Fax Configuration Wizard, shown in Figure 45.2, lets you enter personal information that is used to automatically create fax cover pages. The wizard then completes the configuration and closes. You can revisit the personal information entered in the wizard by selecting the Tools ➪ Sender Information menu in the Fax Console.

FIGURE 45.2

The Fax Configuration Wizard lets you enter personal information for creating fax cover pages.

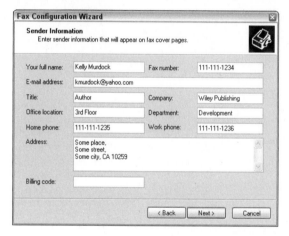

The next step of the Fax Configuration Wizard lets you select the modem that you use to send and receive faxes. If you check the Enable receive box, the modem automatically answers the telephone when faxes are received if the line is available. Sending and receiving faxes requires that the line be available. If someone is using the phone line, then the status for the fax is set to Line Unavailable and faxes cannot be sent or received until the line is cleared.

NOTE Most modems include the ability to handle faxes, but some older modems do not.

The next step of the Fax Configuration Wizard requires that you enter a Transmitting Subscriber Identification (TSID) string. This ID is used to track faxes if any abuse is detected, so you know who to contact when you receive unwanted faxes. It is common to enter some characters to identify the computer followed by your phone number. The TSID also appears on the fax machine of the location where you are sending the fax. If your name is Johnson, then the TSID could be Johnsons followed by your phone number. The receiving fax identifier value can be the same as the TSID.

The final step of the Fax Configuration Wizard lets you specify a folder where the incoming faxes are stored and a printer where the faxes can print.

Changing the fax settings

If you need to revisit any of the configuration settings, you can view all the configured fax devices using the Printers and Faxes option in the Control Panel. If you select a fax device and choose the File ⇨ Properties menu, the Fax Properties dialog box appears, as shown in Figure 45.3.

FIGURE 45.3

The Fax Properties dialog box includes all the settings for the configured fax device.

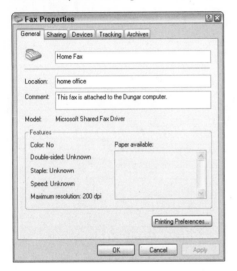

You can change the TSID value in the Devices panel. The Tracking panel includes options for notifying you and opening the Fax Monitor when faxes are sent or received. It can also configure the sounds that are played when these events take place, so you'll be able to hear from the other room when the outgoing fax is completed. The Archives panel includes settings for specifying where the incoming and successful outgoing faxes are stored.

Using the Fax Console

After you install the fax component and configure the fax modem, you are able to use the Fax Console to send and receive faxes from the computer. The Fax Console can also manage all the fax jobs.

You can access the Fax Console, shown in Figure 45.4, by selecting the Start ⇨ All Programs ⇨ Accessories ⇨ Communications ⇨ Fax ⇨ Fax Console menu. The Fax Console, like the e-mail client, includes folders for Incoming faxes, Inbox, Outbox, and Sent Items.

The Fax Console can manage all faxes sent from and received by the local computer.

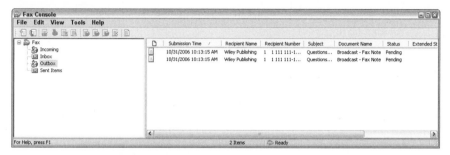

Sending faxes

You can use the Fax Console to send single pages of information included on a cover sheet. To send a fax, simply click New Fax on the Fax Console's toolbar or choose the File ➪ Send a Fax menu. This opens the Send Fax Wizard. For multiple page faxes, you can use the Fax command in the word processor to send the opened document along with a cover page.

Specifying a recipient

The first step in the Send Fax Wizard, shown in Figure 45.5, is to enter the information of the person that will receive the fax. Enter the person's name and phone number. If you click the Address Book button, the same address book used by your e-mail client opens.

The first step of the Send Fax Wizard is to enter the information of the fax recipient.

Establishing dialing rules

If you enable the Use dialing rules option, you can specify how to dial specific numbers. The Dialing rules button opens a dialog box where you can tell the modem to dial specific numbers to reach outside lines or to use a dialing code for long-distance calls. Several different locations can be created for laptops traveling to different locations.

If you click the Edit button for a specific location, you can change the dialing settings for the selected location, as shown in Figure 45.6. There are also tabs for establishing rules for the local area code and for using calling cards.

FIGURE 45.6

By establishing a set of dialing rules for a location, you can tell the modem how to dial to get an outside line.

Back in the Send Fax Wizard, you can select to send the current fax to several recipients at once. Just click Add to select additional people to receive the fax.

Selecting a cover page

The next page of the Send Fax Wizard, shown in Figure 45.7, lets you select and customize a cover page for the outgoing fax. The cover page uses the personal information that you previously entered while setting up the fax. There are four different cover page templates you can choose from, including Confidential, FYI, Generic, and Urgent. You can also enter a subject line and some notes.

FIGURE 45.7

FIGURE 45.7

You can customize the cover page for the outgoing fax with a subject line and some notes.

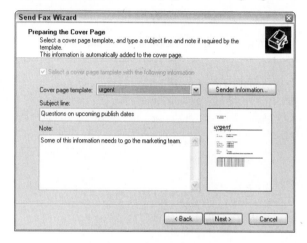

Scheduling the fax

The final page of the Send Fax Wizard, shown in Figure 45.8, lets you schedule when the fax sends. You can choose to send the fax immediately or to send it at a specific time within the next 24 hours. You can also set the priority of the fax to high, medium, or low. If you send multiple faxes at the same time, the fax with the highest priority goes first.

FIGURE 45.8

You can schedule to send the fax anytime during the next 24 hours.

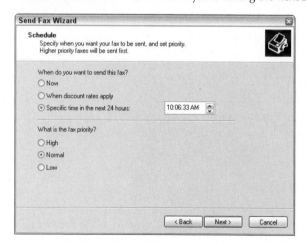

The wizard completes with a summary of the outgoing fax settings. There is also a Preview Fax button you can use to see how the fax will look.

Receiving faxes

When the fax device, or modem, is set up, you can receive faxes using the Fax Console. If the Fax Console is open when an incoming fax is detected, the fax is received and routed to the Inbox folder.

If you know that a fax is coming in, you can enable the Fax Monitor using the Tools ➪ Fax Monitor menu in the Fax Console. This opens the Fax Monitor window, shown in Figure 45.9, which listens for incoming faxes. You can configure Fax Monitor to open automatically whenever an incoming fax is detected. The modem is smart enough to distinguish between fax calls and voice calls.

FIGURE 45.9

The Fax Monitor listens for incoming faxes.

Faxing Documents

The Send Fax Wizard is helpful for those times when you need to send a quick fax containing a limited amount of information; for more detailed information, you can select to send documents created in a word processor or scanned using a scanner.

Faxing scanned documents

Using the installed fax features, you can fax files scanned into the computer. In the scanning software that is initiated to begin the scanning process, there is an option to route the scanned image to a printer. This works by essentially printing the scanned image document to a fax printer. This also works for other software, such as Photoshop, that can print documents.

CROSS-REF You can learn more about scanning and using a scanner in Chapter 37.

When printing, the Print dialog box opens, as shown in Figure 45.10, and you can choose a specific printer to use. Instead of printing to an installed printer, choose the option to print to the fax device.

FIGURE 45.10

When printing a document, you can choose to print to the fax device instead.

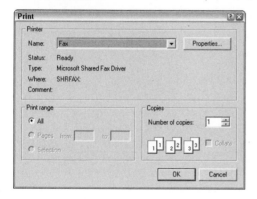

Clicking Print causes the Send Fax Wizard to open, where you can specify a recipient and a cover letter.

Faxing from within a word processor

Using the installed fax device, you can also fax files created with a word processor. Within Microsoft Word, there are two ways you can fax documents. The first is to use the File ⇨ Print command to print the current document to the fax printer, just as you can for scanned documents. The second method uses the File ⇨ Send To ⇨ Fax Recipient menu command to begin Word's Fax Wizard, shown in Figure 45.11. The Fax Wizard lets you add a cover page to the outgoing fax.

Using Word's Fax Wizard, you can select the document to fax and which fax device to use, create a cover sheet, specify a recipient, and enter your personal information. When you want to select a cover sheet, the wizard supplies several different templates to follow, as shown in Figure 45.12.

NOTE Many legal documents require a signature. If digital signatures aren't accepted, then you can print and sign the document and fax the scanned copy that includes the signature instead of sending it from the word processor application.

FIGURE 45.11

Microsoft Word includes its own Fax Wizard for sending out faxes.

FIGURE 45.12

Word's Fax Wizard lets you choose the cover letter style.

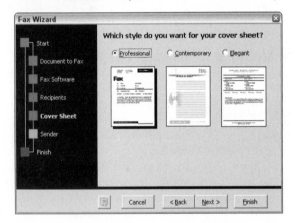

Creating a Custom Cover Page

The Send Fax Wizard includes by default four cover sheet templates, but you can create your own custom cover sheet if you don't like any of the default templates. You can create new cover sheet templates using the Fax Cover Page Editor application, shown in Figure 45.13. You can access this application using the Start ➪ All Programs ➪ Accessories ➪ Communications ➪ Fax ➪ Fax Cover Page Editor menu.

FIGURE 45.13

The Fax Cover Page Editor lets you create custom fax cover pages that include data from the Send Fax Wizard.

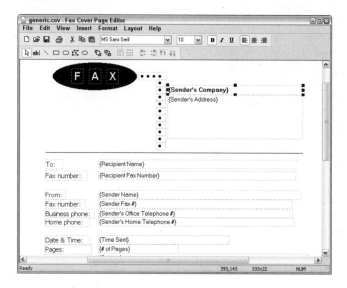

The Fax Cover Page Editor lets you add text and images to the page. To move an element, select and drag it to its new position. Using the Insert menu, you can add information taken from the Send Fax Wizard to the cover page. You can include information from the wizard, such as the sender's information, the recipient's information, the total number of pages, and the date/time that the fax is sent.

When saving the custom fax cover page, save it to the Common Coverpages folder in the MSFax folder. This includes your custom page along with the other cover pages in the Send Fax Wizard.

Faxing Using the Internet

Even if you don't have a modem installed on your computer, you can still use a connection to the Internet via a DSL, cable, or satellite connection to send and receive faxes. Faxing through the Internet requires you to set up an account through a Web site that offers this capability. Several such Web sites exist.

If you look closely at the first page of Word's Fax Wizard, you can see a button labeled Internet Fax Options. If you click this button, a Web page with a link to the eFax service appears, as shown in Figure 45.14. This service costs a fee, but it can deliver faxes directly to your e-mail.

FIGURE 45.14

Several online services, such as eFax, enable you to send and receive faxes through the Internet.

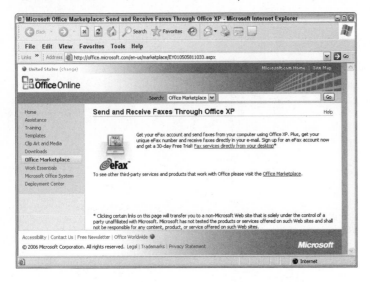

If you're considering using an Internet fax service, consider these vendors:

■ eFax.com

■ MyFax.com

■ JFax.com

Summary

It can be a little work to install and configure the fax features in Windows, but once installed, they can be used just like a printer by all Windows applications. Installing the fax feature makes the Fax Console available. From the Fax Console you can send, receive, and manage all your faxes just like an e-mail client.

The Fax Console includes the Send Fax Wizard, which walks you through defining the fax recipient and cover page. Scanned documents and word processor documents can also be sent via the fax capabilities.

The Fax Cover Page Editor is an application where you can create your own custom cover pages to include with faxed documents.

Finally, if you don't have a modem installed, you can sign up for a service that allows faxing through the Internet.

Chapter 46

Using Your Computer on the Internet

For some people, gaining access to the Internet is the most important reason for buying a computer. Whether used for research, entertainment, or to communicate with others via e-mail, the Internet is an important tool used by millions each day.

Before you can use the Internet, you need to set up access to it. Windows includes a wizard that walks you through this otherwise tricky setup, but there are some tips that can help you along the way.

The two main applications used to interact with the Internet are the Web browser and an e-mail client. Each of these tools needs to be configured before it works properly. This chapter covers setting up and configuring these important tools.

Connecting to the Internet

Before you can connect to the Internet, there are some preliminary tasks that you need to do, such as deciding on an Internet service provider (ISP) and selecting the connection method. Several connection methods are available, including dial-up — Digital Subscriber Line (DSL), cable, wireless, and satellite. Dial-up connections are made possible through standard telephone lines via a modem; DSL connections transmit data over phone lines without interfering with voice service. Cable, wireless, and satellite connections all require specialized hardware. Each of these methods has advantages and disadvantages, and availability differs depending on your geographical area.

Choosing an ISP

Connecting to the Internet is made possible by establishing a connection to a dedicated piece of hardware called a router. Connected to these routers are computers called *servers*, which hold all the content that is accessible via the Internet. The routers and servers are controlled and maintained by various Internet service providers (ISPs).

When researching the available ISPs in your area, keep the following in mind:

- **Availability:** An Internet connection that isn't available for dial-up connections during busy times doesn't help much. A good ISP offering dial-up service should have several connection numbers available that you can use in case one is tied up.

- **Reliability:** Dedicated servers should be up and running at all hours of the day. If an ISP has a reputation of having their servers crash, you should probably look elsewhere.

- **Upgradeability:** If you start with a dial-up connection and find it too slow, does the ISP allow you to upgrade to a faster connection?

- **Cost:** There can be a large difference among the costs of different ISPs. Most ISPs offer a discount if you pay for a year's worth of service rather than a monthly rate.

- **Local Connection Numbers:** If you're using a dial-up connection, make sure that the ISP you select has a local number for accessing the Internet, or you could be subject to long-distance rates while you connect.

- **Speed:** The speed of your connection can differ greatly depending on whether you choose to connect using dial-up or broadband, whether the line conditions cause a drop in speed or whether too many users are connected at once.

- **Virus/Spam filtering:** Many ISPs offer services that check for potential viruses and block unwanted e-mail spam.

Connection options

The speed at which you can surf the Internet depends on the type of hardware that you use to make a connection. Even if you have a fast, top-of-the-line computer, the speed at which Web pages show up is determined by the speed of your connection.

Dial-up configuration

Dial-up connections are accessed through a modem using a telephone line. This type of connection is common, but the speed at which data downloads from the Internet is limited to 56KB per second. The speed of dial-up connections can diminish if the quality of the connection is poor. Dial-up connections are generally less expensive than broadband, and they don't require any additional hardware to connect because most users already have phone service to their homes.

Using a different standard can increase connection speed over standard dial-up lines. Integrated Services Digital Network (ISDN) lines are an international communication standard for sending voice, video, and data over normal phone lines. ISDN lines can range between 64 to 128KB per second.

Broadband configuration

Broadband connections are much faster than dial-up connections, but the extra speed usually comes at an increased cost. Broadband connections don't require you to log on to the Internet like dial-up connections. Instead, broadband connections are always on, which makes it easier to initially open your browser window. The speed of the broadband connection depends on the hardware that is used.

There are several options for connecting at broadband speeds, including the following:

- **DSL:** Digital Subscriber Line (DSL), uses 2-wire cabling telephone line that makes the Internet always on. DSL standards differ in geographical areas. Common DSL lines can download data at 1.5 to 9MB per second and upload data at 16 to 640KB per second.

- **Cable:** Cable connections require special cabling routed to the home through a specialized cable modem. It uses the same cabling that cable television runs through and enables connection speeds that range from 512KB to 20 MB per second. Cable connections allow multiple users to use a larger bandwidth connection to access the Internet, but if too many users access the Internet at once, the connection speed can slow down for all users. If you choose a cable modem, then you can usually get a discount when multiple services (Internet and television) are purchased together.

- **Wireless:** Wireless connections require specialized hardware to connect, and you must be within the broadcast area in order to connect, which is limited in some areas. The connection speed depends on the connection standard that is used. The most common standard includes 802.11b (Wi-Fi), which connects at up to 11 MB per second.

- **Dedicated T1/T3:** T1 and T3 connections are leased lines common in businesses. A single T1 line includes 24 channels that can be configured to carry voice or data at a combine rate of 1.544 MB per second. T3 lines expand the connection to 672 channels which combine for a connection speed of 43 to 45 MB per second. T3 lines are common for ISPs.

- **Satellite:** Satellite connections use orbiting satellites to establish a connection and don't require cabling, but they can be disrupted by weather patterns. Satellite connection run at a speed of 492 to 512KB per second.

Using the New Connection Wizard

An initial step in getting connected to the Internet is to set up your Internet connection. Windows includes a Connection Wizard to help you establish this connection. You can access this wizard using the Start ⇨ All Programs ⇨ Accessories ⇨ Communications ⇨ New Connection Wizard menu.

This wizard can be used to connect to the Internet or to connect to a network. In the first step of the New Connection Wizard, shown in Figure 46.1, you need to select which type of connection you want to create. The options including Connecting to the Internet, Connecting to the network at my workplace, Set up a home or small office network, and Set up an Advanced Connection. To set up an Internet connection, select the first option and click the Next button.

CROSS-REF You can learn more about establishing network connections in Chapter 44.

Before you can connect to the Internet, you need to sign up for service from one of these ISPs. The various ISPs provide different ways for users to sign up for their service and these different methods are integrated into the second page of Connection Wizard, shown in Figure 46.2.

FIGURE 46.1

The first step of the New Connection Wizard lets you choose the type of connection you want to create.

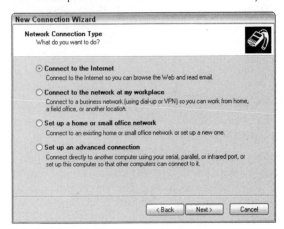

FIGURE 46.2

The second step of the New Connection Wizard lets you choose from different ways to sign up for ISP service.

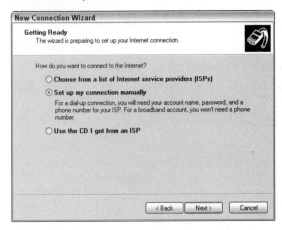

The options for selecting an ISP service included in the Connection Wizard are the following:

- **Choose from a list of ISPs:** If you choose this option, the wizard closes and a folder opens with links to Microsoft's MSN service and another page of preferred ISPs.

- **Set up my Connection Manually:** If you select this option, then you should have already contacted an ISP and you have a username, password, and phone number for the ISP.

- **Use the CD I got from an ISP:** This option also closes the wizard and instructs you to simply insert the ISP CD. AOL frequently sends out signup CDs that can be used.

After clicking the Next button, you can select to setup a connection using a dial-up modem or using a broadband connection.

The third step of the Connection Wizard, shown in Figure 46.3, lets you choose the type of connection to configure. The options include dial-up, broadband using a username and password, or an "always on" broadband connection. The broadband choices can either require login information when you connect or it could be configured to always be on and accessible.

The next step of the Connection Wizard, shown in Figure 46.4, lets you name the connection. It is possible to have several different connections if, for example, you travel with a laptop between different locations, so it is a good idea to give each connection a unique name. This name shows up on the icon for the connection.

If you've selected to use a dial-up connection, the next page in the wizard lets you enter the ISP's connection number. The number you enter should be the same number that you would use to dial the number from your phone directly including any numbers required to access an outside line if needed. Broadband connections do not need a phone number because they connect using a different method.

FIGURE 46.3

The third step of the New Connection Wizard lets you choose the connection type.

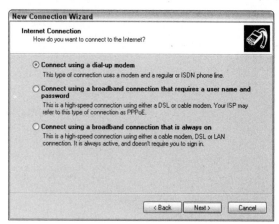

FIGURE 46.4

The next step of the New Connection Wizard lets you give the connection a name.

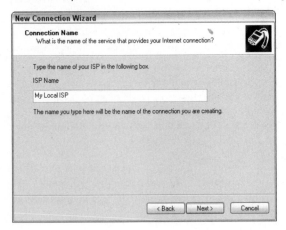

You then need to enter the account information you've received from the ISP into the next page of the wizard, shown in Figure 46.5. This account information includes the username and password used to log into the connection. The username does not include any spaces, and the safest passwords include a combination of letters and numbers.

 When typing the password, the letters are displayed as simple bullets so someone looking over your shoulder cannot copy them.

FIGURE 46.5

Entering your username and password lets you automatically log in to the ISP.

Beneath the password, you can set the option to allow anyone to use this account by logging onto the computer. If you've set up your computer with several accounts, enabling this option lets any of the user accounts use the ISP connection.

If you have several Internet connections, you can enable the default Internet connection option to make this defined connection the default when you choose the Internet icon.

This completes the wizard, and the final page shows a summary of the selected options, as shown in Figure 46.6. There is also an option to create a desktop shortcut.

Once the Connection Wizard has finished, you can access the Internet by double-clicking the shortcut icon on the desktop. If you chose not to create a desktop shortcut, you can access the new ISP connection icon using the Start ⇨ Connect To menu, where all your created connections appear.

If you choose the Start ⇨ Connect To ⇨ Show All Connections option, a folder opens showing all the available connections that you've created. If you select a connection icon and choose the File ⇨ Properties menu, you can access a dialog box of properties for the connection.

FIGURE 46.6

When the Connection Wizard completes, the final page summarizes all the selected options.

Changing dial-up connection properties

When you open the Properties dialog box for a dial-up connection, shown in Figure 46.7, you can configure the modem that you are using for the connection, change the connection phone number, select to use the established dialing rules, and choose to show an icon when the connection is made.

If you click on the Dialing Rules button, you can access a dialog box where you can tell the modem which numbers to dial when using the modem. You can set up several different sets of rules based on your location. For example, you could have a default set of rules for dialing from work, another set for dialing from home and a third set for dialing on the road.

For each rule set, you can define the Area Code to use, a number to access an outside line, and carrier codes for long-distance and international calls. You can also select an option to disable call waiting so the phone line doesn't get interrupted when another call is received. This is also a panel where you can input and use a calling card number.

Next to the phone number field is an Alternates button. If you click this button, a dialog box opens where you can add more phone numbers that can connect to the ISP. There is also an option to try the next number if the current number fails, and another option to move successful numbers to the top of the list. Using these options, you can insure that you connect quickly by having the computer dial a different number if the main one is busy.

CROSS-REF   **Establishing dialing rules is covered in Chapter 45.**

The Options tab of the dial-up connection Properties dialog box, shown in Figure 46.8, includes several options for when the connection is dialing. You can select to display the dialog progress while it is connecting. The Prompt for name and password option is good if you are sharing your computer with other users, but it requires that you enter your username and password each time you connect.

FIGURE 46.7

The dial-up connection Properties dialog box lets you change the connection phone number.

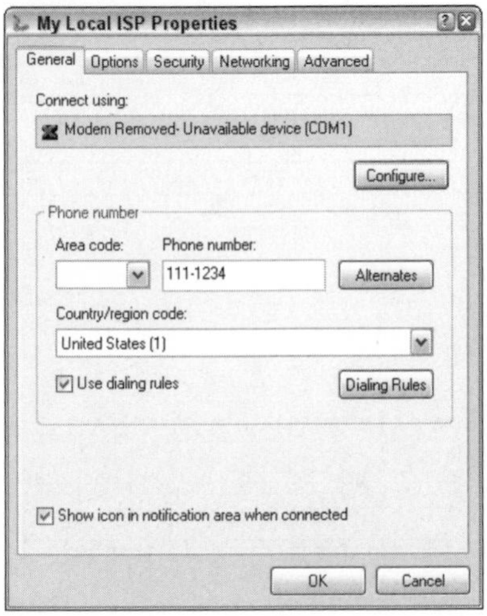

The Include Windows logon domain is required to connect to some networks. You can also select to enter the phone number each time you connect, which is a good option if you're worried about having the kids or your cat accidentally connecting.

The Redial options section lets you specify how often the number is retried if a connection cannot be made. You can also specify the amount of time between redial attempts. These options have the computer keep trying up to the number of times without intervention. The default setting is to attempt 3 redials at 1 minute apart, but you can set this to whatever you'd like.

The Security tab of the dial-up connection Properties dialog box, shown in Figure 46.9, lets you specify how to validate your username and password. For the Typical selection, the options include allowing unsecured passwords, validating using a secured password, or using a Smart Card. These options are different technologies used to keep sensitive information secure.

The standard method is to use an unsecured password, but secured passwords let you add on your Windows logon, password and domain and/or data encryption to connect. Unsecured passwords can be used by any user if they guess your login information. Secured passwords keep your login information safer from people accessing your account because they only work from your designated computer. A Smart Card is like a credit card that holds your login information and is required before you can login.

FIGURE 46.8

The Options tab of the dial-up connection Properties dialog box lets you specify how often the connection redials the number when a connection can't be made.

If you choose the Advanced option, you can require authentication using several different protocols including Extensible Authentication Protocol (EAP), Unencrypted password PAP, Shiva Password Authentication Protocol (SPAP), or Challenge Handshake Authentication Protocol (CHAP). These protocols speak directly with an authentication server, and if they don't match the similar protocol on the server's side, the connection terminates. Some ISP setup discs make this setting automatically.

CROSS-REF You can learn more about network encryption and these protocols in Chapter 48.

FIGURE 46.9

The Security tab of the dial-up connection Properties dialog box lets you specify the encryption options for data on the server.

The Networking tab of the dial-up connection Properties dialog box, shown in Figure 46.10, lets you specify the communication and data transfer method (known as a protocol) between the local computer and the ISP hardware to which you are connecting. The protocol used on the Internet is Transmission Control Protocol/Internet Protocol (TCP/IP). Networks use different protocols to communicate.

CROSS-REF Setting up and configuring a network is covered in Chapter 44.

The Advanced tab of the dial-up connection Properties dialog box, shown in Figure 46.11, lets you enable Windows Firewall, which helps prevent unwanted access to your computer while you're connected. You can also set options for allowing other users access to your computer. If you plan on using a remote connection, enabling these options makes it possible for you to get access to your home computer while at work and vice versa.

FIGURE 46.10

The Networking tab of the dial-up connection Properties dialog box lets you choose the communication protocol used to talk with the Internet servers.

CROSS-REF Enabling and using Windows Firewall is covered in Chapter 48 and the Windows Remote Desktop is covered in Chapter 41.

FIGURE 46.11

The Advanced tab of the dial-up connection Properties dialog box lets you enable the Windows Firewall and configure sharing options.

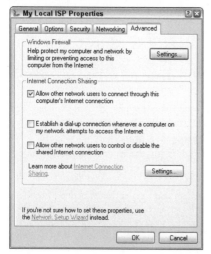

Changing broadband connection properties

Almost all of the various settings in the Properties dialog box for broadband connections are exactly the same as those for dial-up. The only differences are in the General tab where there isn't an option to change the connection phone number because the broadband connection uses a different connection method. Also, in the Networking tab, the connection device is different for broadband connections.

If you are using a broadband connection that is always on, the connection Properties dialog box only includes tabs for selecting the networking protocol, a tab of authentication options, as shown in Figure 46.12, and a tab where the Windows Firewall can be enabled.

FIGURE 46.12

The Authentication tab of the always on broadband connection Properties dialog box lets you specify which authentication options to use.

Browsing the Web

After a connection to the Internet is established, you can open a Web browser, such as Internet Explorer, and begin to view Web pages. When a Web browser opens, it immediately loads the default Web page. You can change which Web page is the default using the Internet Options dialog box, shown later in this chapter.

CROSS-REF There are several different Web browsers that you can use to surf the Internet. The different browsers are presented in Chapter 32.

Each Web page has a unique address that appears in the Address field at the top of the browser, as shown in Figure 46.13. If you enter a new address in the Address field and press Enter, the new Web page loads. Web addresses are technically called Universal Resource Locators or URLs.

Another way to get to new Web pages is to click on links within the current Web page. These links may be images or colored text. When you position your cursor over a link, a new URL for the target Web page appears at the bottom of the browser window.

When you select a link or type in the URL for a new Web page, the new page loads automatically. The speed with which the new page loads depends on the complexity of the page's content and the speed of your connection. The progress of the loading page appears along the bottom of the browser.

After a new Web page loads and appears in the browser, you can quickly navigate back and forth between the recently opened pages using the Back and Forward buttons located at the top of the browser.

If you're waiting for a Web page that is taking too long, you can click Stop on the main toolbar to have the browser stop requesting content from the page. Next to the Stop button is the Refresh button. This button causes the content on the current page to be completely reloaded. If the entire page isn't completely downloaded due to line interference or if the page has new information such as an updated weather report that you want to view, you can click on the Refresh button. Clicking the Home button causes the default home page to load.

FIGURE 46.13

When a Web browser first opens, its default Web page automatically loads.

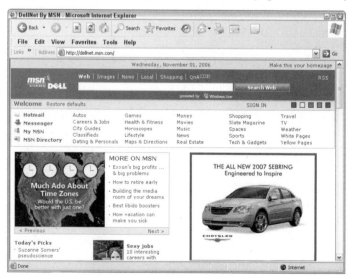

Searching the Web

With millions of Web pages on the Internet, it can be difficult to find the exact information that you are looking for. Throughout the Web are several pages devoted to searching the Web. These *search engines*, such as Google in Figure 46.14, offer different ways to search the Internet from categorized lists to thumbnails of Web pages. Some of the more popular sites for searching the Web include:

- Google.com
- Excite.com
- Yahoo.com
- Altavista.com
- Ask.com

Most search engines index Web pages based on the keywords found throughout the site, but Web pages also contain information contained within the page that isn't visible in the Web browser that describes the page's contents. Search engines can access this non-visible information to catalogue Web sites that don't have good keywords such as a page that includes nothing but pictures.

FIGURE 46.14

Sites like Google.com let you search the Web for specific information.

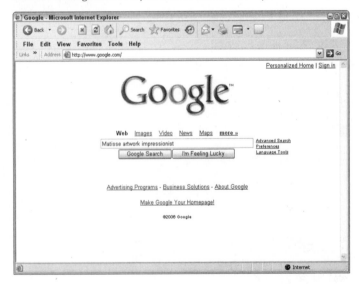

When entering keywords into a search engine, it is important to select and use keywords that are representative of the type of pages you are looking for. Most search engines ignore pronouns and simple adjectives like *it, the, each,* and *for,* so limit your keywords to descriptive nouns like movies, astronomy, and botany. If you include multiple keywords, then the search engine returns Web pages that include both of those key words, such as comedy movies, radio astronomy, and molecular botany.

NOTE   Some search engines such as Ask.com use entire sentences, complete with pronouns, in question form to locate Web pages such as "How do I fix a leaking faucet?"

If you include a set of keywords within a set of quotes, then the search engine returns Web pages that exactly match the words within quotes such as "all-time popular comedy movies," "NASA radio astronomy reports," and "molecular botany morphology."

There is also a Search button at the top of Internet Explorer. If you click this button, a Search sidebar opens to the left of the browser window; this sidebar is powered by MSN Search. If you type a keyword in the Search field, a list of Web pages that include that word or phrase appears. Figure 46.15 shows the results when I searched for the word *Matisse.* Clicking any of these Web page thumbnails takes you to the selected Web page.

FIGURE 46.15

The Search sidebar within Internet Explorer lets you search for Web pages that contain the words you entered.

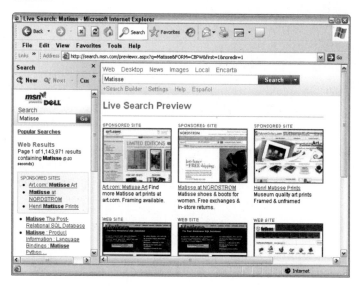

Saving Favorites

As you visit different Web pages, you may find one that you'd like to revisit at a future time. Sites such as this can be added to your Favorites list. The pages in this list can then be recalled using the Favorites menu.

Clicking the Favorites button at the top of the browser opens all your favorite links in a panel to the left of the window, as shown in Figure 46.16. From this list, you simply click an item from the list to revisit the selected page.

FIGURE 46.16

You can recall a list of favorite sites by clicking the Favorites button at the top of the browser.

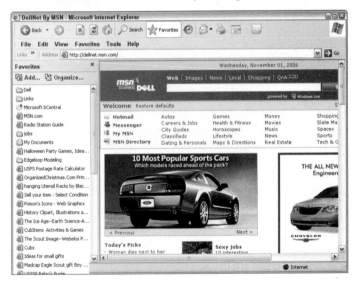

You can add the current Web site to the Favorites list by clicking Add at the top of the Favorites side panel, or by selecting the Favorites ➪ Add to Favorites menu. Either command opens the Add Favorite dialog box, shown in Figure 46.17. Using this dialog box, you can name the current Web page or add it to a specific folder. You can also use this dialog box to create a new folder.

If you accidentally add a favorite Web site to the wrong folder, you can use the Favorites ➪ Organize Favorites menu option to open the Organize Favorites dialog box, shown in Figure 46.18, where you can rename links, create new folders, and move links between folders. This dialog box also lets you drag and drop links into folders.

FIGURE 46.17

The Add Favorite dialog box lets you add the current Web site to your Favorites list.

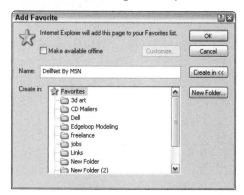

FIGURE 46.18

The Organize Favorites dialog box lets you rename links and move links between folders.

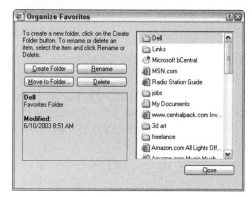

Viewing History

Another way to locate Web pages you've already visited is with the History sidebar, shown in Figure 46.19. You can open this by clicking on History at the top of the browser. The History sidebar displays a list of all the Web sites that you've visited in the last several days.

FIGURE 46.19

The History sidebar keeps track of the Web sites that you've visited over the last several days.

Configuring Internet Explorer

Behind the scenes of the Web browser are several settings that control the look and feel of the browser as well as its security. All of these settings are in the Internet Options dialog box, shown in Figure 46.20. You can open this dialog box by selecting the Tools ➪ Internet Options menu or by double-clicking the Internet Options selection from the Control Panel.

Changing the default Web page

At the top of the General tab of the Internet Options dialog box is an Address field that contains a Web address. This designated page is the default Web page that appears when the Web browser is first opened.

To change the default Web page, follow these steps:

1. **Open Internet Explorer and choose the Tools ➪ Internet Options menu command.**

2. **Type a new Web page address at the top of the dialog box that opens.** Close the dialog box by clicking OK.

3. **Click on Home at the top the Web browser.** The designated Web page opens.

FIGURE 46.20

The Internet Options dialog box lets you configure the settings for Internet Explorer.

TIP An easy way to set your default Web page is to navigate to a Web page and click on the Use Current button in the Internet options window.

Managing cached files

Every time you visit a Web page, the contents of the page download from the server where the content is hosted. At the same time, the content of the Web page also saves to a temporary folder on the hard drive. This saved content is called a *cache*, and by saving a cached copy, the browser can immediately recall any requested content instead of downloading the content again. This is why Web pages appear so quickly when you use the Back button.

If you look at a lot of different Web pages, over time the folder that holds the cached content fills up. You can delete all the cached files at any time using the Delete Files button in the General panel of the Internet Options dialog box.

NOTE If you notice that Web pages aren't coming up as fast as they did before, then it could be that Internet Explorer is spending too much time searching the cache for content that is already download. Clearing the cache could help speed up Web browsing.

There is also a button for deleting cookies. A *cookie* is a file that keeps track of the type of content that you are viewing on a Web site. For example, if you visit an online shopping Web site, the site may save a cookie to your hard drive that remembers the type of items that you viewed while visiting the site. The Web site can then reuse this information to present customized Web pages of the type of items you may be interested in.

CROSS-REF You can also delete all cached Web page files using the Disk Cleanup utility. More on this utility can be found in Chapter 49.

The General tab of the Internet Options dialog box also includes a Settings button for setting the options for the cache folder. This button opens the Settings dialog box shown in Figure 46.21. The top options let you choose if the browser checks for newer versions of a cached Web page. If you select to have the browser look for newer versions every time you visit the page, the browser takes a bit longer to load the Web page; if you choose the Never option, the cached Web page appears almost immediately but may include older content.

NOTE If you notice that Web pages don't seem to ever be updated, such as displaying old dates, then check to see if the Never option is enabled.

The Settings dialog box also lets you specify the size of the cache folder. Larger cache folders can hold more content for immediate recall, but the downloaded content consumes space that could be used for other programs and data. Once the downloaded content fills the available cached space, the newer content overwrites the older content.

The size of your cache really depends on the type of content you regularly view. If you view standard Web pages without any video or audio, then a maximum setting of 50MB should be more than enough. However, if you spend a lot of time viewing videos and listening to online audio programs, then a setting of 250MB is more than enough. If Internet Explorer sets your cache to be 5 percent of your hard drive and you have a large hard drive, you may end up with a cache size of 5GB or more. This is way too big and should be reduced.

The Move Folder button opens a file dialog box where you can specify a new location for the cached folder. The View Files button opens all the cached folders within a Windows Explorer window. The View Objects button opens a folder that includes all the downloaded programs used by the browser.

Managing history

The History section in the General tab of the Internet Options dialog box lets you set the number of days of history to retain. Larger histories let you backtrack to sites visited over the last designated number of days. There is also a Clear History button that clears the history of all the Web pages that have been visited.

FIGURE 46.21

The Settings dialog box lets you change the size of the cache folder.

Changing the browser's colors and fonts

If you click Colors in the General tab of the Internet Options dialog box, the Colors dialog box, shown in Figure 46.22, opens. Using this, you can change the color of text, background, and links in the browser. By changing the text and background colors, you can increase the contrast of the browser text to make it easier to read.

> **NOTE** Web page creators can also specify the colors and fonts used on the pages they create. If the Web page creator specifies a specific color or font, changing the default colors in the Colors dialog box has no effect over these pages.

By default all Web page links appear blue, then purple after they have been clicked on; you can also make them appear red when the mouse cursor is over them. You can change these default colors to something else using the Colors dialog box.

FIGURE 46.22

The Colors dialog box lets you change default browser colors for text and links.

The Fonts button in the General tab of the Internet Options dialog box, shown in Figure 46.23, lets you change the font used for the text in the Web page.

FIGURE 46.23

The Fonts dialog box lets you change the default browser text font.

Changing the browser's text size

If the text displayed within a Web browser is too small, you can increase the text size using the View ⇨ Text Size menu. The options include Largest, Larger, Medium, Smaller, and Smallest. Figure 46.24 shows the browser with the Largest text size setting. Although the Text Size menu changes the text on a Web page, it has no affect on the pictures or any text that is saved as a picture.

 Windows also includes several tools that can make Windows more accessible for people with disabilities. You can learn more about these tools in Chapter 30.

Changing the browser's language

If you stumble across a Web page that has a random mess of characters, it could be that the page is trying to display the text in another language. You can change the language used to display the browser's text using the Language button in the General tab of the Internet Options dialog box.

The Languages button opens the Language Preference dialog box, shown in Figure 46.25. To add another language to the list of available languages, click the Add button and select the desired language from the list. The order in which the languages are listed determines the priority of the language used to display the Web page.

FIGURE 46.24

The View ➪ Text Size menu option can change the size of the Web page's text.

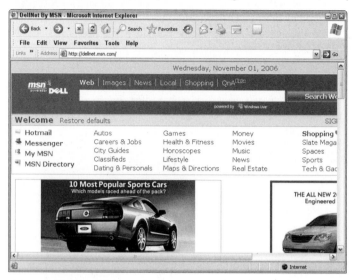

FIGURE 46.25

The Language Preference dialog box lets you add more languages to the list of languages that the Web page can use.

Controlling security settings

The Security tab of the Internet Options dialog box, shown in Figure 46.26, lets you set the security level to use when browsing the whole Internet or when browsing the Local Intranet. You can also specify a list of Trusted and Restricted Sites. By changing the various security levels, you can control which potentially dangerous programs and scripts can be run within the browser.

FIGURE 46.26

The Security tab of the Internet Options dialog box lets you set security settings for your browser.

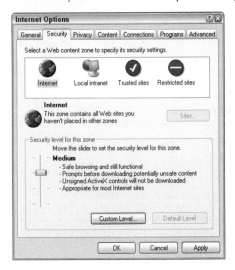

For each of the icons appearing at the top of the Security panel, you can use the slider at the lower half of the tab once a level is selected to change the security level. The options include the following:

- **High:** This security level is the most secure, but it disables all potentially harmful programs.

- **Medium:** This security level prompts for most potentially harmful programs before downloading them.

- **Medium-low:** This security level runs most downloaded programs except for unsigned ActiveX controls without prompting.

- **Low:** This security level runs all downloaded programs, including ActiveX controls, without prompting the user.

 For the Internet option, you shouldn't set the Internet Zone security level lower than Medium or potentially harmful programs could cause damage to your system.

For the selected icon, the Custom Level button sets the specific security options. The Custom Level button opens the Security Settings dialog box, shown in Figure 46.27, where you select to Disable, Enable, or Prompt for specific types of downloadable objects such as ActiveX controls and scripts. At the bottom of the Security Settings dialog box, you can choose to Reset the settings to a High, Medium, Medium-low, or Low security level.

FIGURE 46.27

The Security Settings dialog box lets you enable or disable specific security settings.

For the Trusted and Restricted Sites categories, you can choose which specific sites to add to these categories using the Sites button. This opens a list of sites that are Trusted or Restricted. You can use the Add button to add new sites to the list. If you visit a Web site that has been added to the restricted list, the page still loads, but all potentially harmful programs and scripts are prevented from running.

Controlling privacy settings

Another aspect of security is privacy, which deals with keeping your identity secure. If other users get access to your username and password, they can access the sites you visit as if they were you.

When you visit a Web site that includes a username and password, the site saves a text-based file that includes your personal information, called a cookie, to your hard drive. This cookie is retrieved when you revisit the Web site and logs you in without requiring you to enter your user-name and password every time you revisit the site. Cookies are also used to track your browsing and shopping habits to customize the content that you may be interested in viewing. Although cookies can be helpful, they also represent a potential risk if other users get access to them.

If you open the Privacy tab in the Internet Options dialog box, shown in Figure 46.28, you can set the Privacy setting for all the pages that you visit on the Internet. The privacy levels include the following:

- **Block All Cookies:** This privacy level is the safest, disallowing all cookies from being saved to your hard drive. This can cause problems with some Web sites.

- **High:** This privacy level blocks all cookies without a privacy policy and that contain login information. A privacy policy is a written statement issued by the Web site that explains how they will keep your personal information safe.

- **Medium-High:** This privacy level is similar to the High level, except it allows cookies for the sites that you specify.

- **Medium:** This privacy level prompts for most cookies before saving them.

- **Low:** This privacy level lets most cookies save to your hard drive.

- **Accept All Cookies:** This privacy level lets all cookies be saved and read from Web sites.

CAUTION   Although cookies may seem like a security risk that you'd want to disable, be aware that many Web sites that you probably visit rely on cookies. If you disable all cookies, you may also disable any online banking you may have set up.

FIGURE 46.28

The Privacy tab of the Internet Options dialog box lets you set how the browser handles cookies.

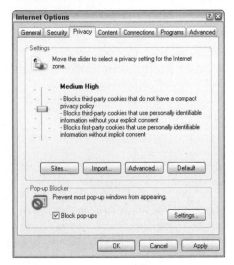

For all privacy levels, you can select to block or allow cookies to save to the hard drive for the specified sites by clicking the Sites button. The Import button lets you import custom cookies to your hard drive.

At the bottom of the Privacy tab of the Internet Options dialog box is an option to Block pop-ups. Pop-ups are those annoying advertising windows that appear at random when you visit certain sites. Using the Settings button in the Pop-up Blocker section, you can select to enable pop-up windows for designated sites.

Blocking inappropriate content

Internet Explorer includes filters that block inappropriate content. These filters only work to block content that has been rated by the Web page creators, so they may miss some content that is incorrectly rated.

You can access the content filters from the Content tab of the Internet Options dialog box, shown in Figure 46.29. This tab also includes options for accepting security certifications and enabling AutoComplete for login usernames and passwords to specific sites.

FIGURE 46.29

The Content tab of the Internet Options dialog box lets you set content filters for blocking inappropriate content.

You can find the content filters in the Content Advisor dialog box, shown in Figure 46.30, which is opened by clicking Enable. In the Ratings tab, you can use the slider to set the appropriate level for Language, Nudity, Sex, and Violence.

FIGURE 46.30

The Content Advisor dialog box lets you set the filter level for inappropriate content in a number of categories.

The Approved Sites tab includes a list of sites that you can view regardless of their ratings. You can also use this panel to create a list of sites that can never be viewed. The General tab of the Content Advisor dialog box, shown in Figure 46.31, includes an option that allows sites with no rating to be viewed. It also includes an option to enter a Supervisor Password so children can't change the filter settings.

FIGURE 46.31

FIGURE 46.31

The General tab of the Content Advisor dialog box lets you set a supervisor password for the content filters.

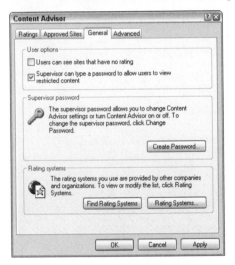

Changing your login information

When the Connection Wizard is used, you can enter your username and password; if the username and password don't exactly match the information on the server, you cannot connect to the Internet. Also, as a security measure, several ISPs require that you change your username and password frequently.

To change your login username and password, follow these steps:

1. **Open Internet Explorer.** Choose the Tools ⇨ Internet Options menu command.

2. **In the dialog box that opens, click Connections.** The Connections dialog box, shown in Figure 46.32, opens.

3. **Select the ISP connection for the account that you want to change.** Click Settings. This opens a dialog box with settings for the current connection selection, as shown in Figure 46.33.

4. **Change the User Name and Password for the selected connection.** Click OK to close the Settings dialog box.

FIGURE 46.32

The Connections tab of the Internet Options dialog box shows you the various ISP connections.

FIGURE 46.33

The ISP Settings dialog box for the selected connection lets you change the username and password.

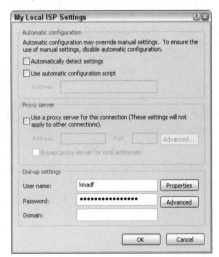

Setting browser programs

Internet Explorer can work as the hub to several other programs that can edit Web pages and access e-mail and newsgroups.

You can specify which programs are connected to Internet Explorer by default using the Programs tab of the Internet Options dialog box, shown in Figure 46.34.

FIGURE 46.34

The Programs tab of the Internet Options dialog box lets you select which programs get opened when their button is clicked in Internet Explorer.

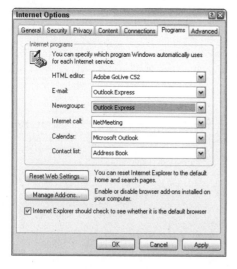

Sending and Receiving E-Mail

In addition to allowing you to browse the Web, an Internet connection also enables you to send and receive e-mails. E-mails are messages with text and graphics sent between users on the Internet. Each user on the Internet with an ISP account is set up with not only a username and password for accessing the Internet, but an e-mail address as well. This address is unique for each user, and all e-mails addressed to that specific e-mail address are routed to the owner's e-mail client.

In order to receive an e-mail, you need to get a piece of software called an e-mail client. This software, like the Web browser, connects to the Internet and retrieves all e-mails addressed to the designated e-mail address from the ISP's server.

CROSS-REF There are several different e-mail clients that you can use to access e-mail. The different e-mail clients are presented in Chapter 32.

Windows includes a bare-bones e-mail client called Outlook Express that you can use to check your e-mail, and if you install the Microsoft Office Suite, you get a more powerful e-mail client called Microsoft Outlook.

Configuring your e-mail client

After your e-mail client software is installed, you need to configure it to access your ISP account and retrieve your e-mails. The precise way to configure your e-mail client differs depending on the e-mail client you're using, but for Outlook Express, you can click the front page link labeled Set up a mail account. This opens the Internet Connection Wizard.

One of the first steps of the Internet Connection Wizard, shown in Figure 46.35, is to enter your name. This is the name that appears in the From section of the e-mails you send out, so it could be an online pseudonym. However, it is best to set it to your own given name.

FIGURE 46.35

The Internet Connection Wizard guides you through configuring your e-mail client.

The next step is to enter your e-mail address, which the ISP should provide. Next, enter the address for the incoming and outgoing mail servers, as shown in Figure 46.36. Located at the ISP are servers for handling all the mail addressed to the ISP's user and for handling all the outgoing e-mail messages that the ISP's user have written. The incoming e-mails stay on the incoming server until they are downloaded by the user and the outgoing e-mail stays on the outgoing e-mail server until it is routed to the appropriate place. E-mails sent to your e-mail address are routed through the Internet and end up on the ISP's server where they sit until you log in to retrieve them.

FIGURE 46.36

The Internet Connection Wizard asks you to enter the names of the mail servers where the e-mails are stored.

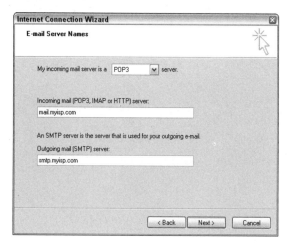

There are three different mail server options for the incoming mail server. Your ISP tells you which option to use. There are slight differences between each: a POP3 account downloads all the e-mails to the local e-mail client when a connection is made, removing the e-mails from the server as they download. POP3 is the most common option. An IMAP account downloads e-mails to the client but keeps a copy of the e-mail on the server. This is helpful if you connect to your mail server using several different computers. Using an IMAP mail account allows you to retrieve your e-mails on your office computer and your laptop computer when on the road. The HTTP account transports e-mails using the same protocol that Web pages use to download Web content.

The final step of the Internet Connection Wizard, shown in Figure 46.37, lets you enter the username and password used to log in to the ISP mail server.

A single mail client can include multiple e-mail accounts. For example, you may have an e-mail account from your ISP that you use as your default, but you may also have a free e-mail account via Yahoo or Hotmail that you want to check periodically. You may also want to check your work e-mail at home. All of these separate accounts can be checked using the same e-mail client.

If you open the Internet Accounts dialog box, shown in Figure 46.38, which you can access using the Mail panel in the Tools ➪ Accounts menu, then you can view all the current accounts that are setup. If you select an account from the list and click the Properties button, you can change the settings for the selected account.

FIGURE 46.37

The final step of the Internet Connection Wizard lets you specify your login information for accessing the ISP's mail server.

To add a new account to the list, click on the Add button and select the type of account that you want to add, then follow the steps to configure the new account using the same dialog boxes presented earlier. E-mail configuration accounts can also be imported and exported from other e-mail clients.

FIGURE 46.38

You can change the settings for each e-mail account using the Internet Accounts dialog box.

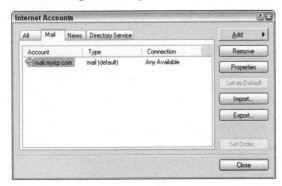

Creating a new e-mail

After your e-mail client is correctly configured, you can try it out by creating and sending a new e-mail. Clicking the Create Mail button opens a window where you can enter the message that you want to send, along with the recipient's address.

To create a new e-mail, follow these steps:

1. **Open Outlook Express.** Click the Create Mail button.

2. **The New Message window opens.** Type the e-mail address of the person you want to send the message to.

NOTE In the CC field, you can enter another e-mail address of a person that you want to be *carbon-copied* on the e-mail. You can also enter multiple e-mail addresses by separating each address with a semicolon (;).

3. **Enter a word or phrase describing the content of the e-mail in the Subject line.**

4. **In the window below the Subject field, type the e-mail message, as shown in Figure 46.39.** This is called the message's body.

5. **When you're finished with the e-mail, click Send to send the e-mail to its recipient.** If you're not connected to the Internet at the time, the e-mail will sit in the e-mail client's Outbox until a connection is made.

The New Message window includes several tools for formatting the e-mail message, including the ability to change the text's font, size, and style. You can also change the alignment and use numbered or bulleted lists. The Create a Hyperlink button opens a dialog box where you can enter a URL to turn the selected text into a live link. The Insert Picture button at the end of the window toolbar opens a file dialog box where you can select and insert a picture where the cursor is located.

By clicking Attach at the top of the e-mail client, you can select a file to attach to the e-mail. Clicking the Spelling button spell-checks the e-mail before it is sent out to let you correct any spelling errors.

CAUTION Never open an e-mail attachment unless you recognize the file and the person who sent it. Viruses can transmit via e-mail and infect your system if you're not careful.

FIGURE 46.39

A new window opens when you create a new e-mail where you can enter the message text.

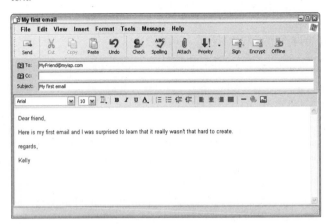

Using the Address Book

It can be tricky to remember the exact e-mail address for all the people you want to keep in contact with, but the Address Book can help. If you don't enter the exact text for a recipient's e-mail address, the e-mail message does not route correctly. The Address Book lets you identify people using their common names or nicknames and correlates that name to their e-mail address, phone number, and other contact information.

 **TIP** You can add to the Address Book by right-clicking on the address of an e-mail you've received.

You can open the Address Book using the Addresses button at the top of the Outlook Express window. The Address Book, shown in Figure 46.40, includes a number of fields for holding a contact's information.

The New button opens a tab that holds the contact's information. Separate tabs, shown in Figure 46.41, can access different categories of information, including Home, Business, Personal, and so on.

FIGURE 46.40

The Address Book can keep track of all the contact information for individuals.

FIGURE 46.41

Creating a new Address Book entry opens a dialog box where you can enter all the contact's information.

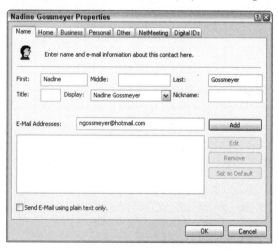

At the top of the Address Book is a field where you can search for specific people. The Address Book also lets you divide your contacts into groups and organize them into folders.

The real power of the Address Book is the way it integrates into other Windows applications such as Microsoft Office. For example, while you're creating a new e-mail message, you can access the Address Book by clicking To or CC to the left of their respective fields. These buttons open the Select Recipients dialog box, shown in Figure 46.42, that displays all the contacts in the Address Book.

FIGURE 46.42

The e-mail client is integrated with the Address Book, enabling e-mail addresses to be automatically added to new e-mail messages.

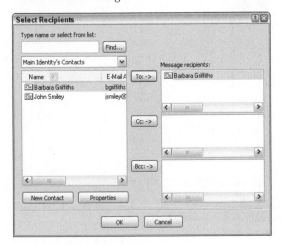

Receiving e-mails

After you've configured your e-mail account, you can click the Send/Receive button at the top of the mail client to receive any e-mails that may be on the ISP's server. Clicking this button opens a dialog box, shown in Figure 46.43, which shows the progress of the e-mails downloading and any new messages being sent out.

 You can test your e-mail account by sending an e-mail to your own e-mail address.

All incoming e-mails route to the Inbox within your e-mail client, and all outgoing e-mails leave the Outbox. You can view the new e-mails by clicking on the Inbox. The e-mail client shows a list of all the new e-mails in the top half of the window and the contents of the selected e-mail in the lower half of the window, as shown in Figure 46.44. Whenever an e-mail is sent, a copy of the e-mail is saved in the Sent Items folder.

FIGURE 46.43

This dialog box appears when you select to send and receive e-mails.

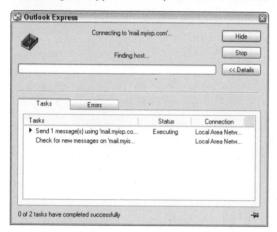

FIGURE 46.44

When reading received e-mails, the top half displays a list of received e-mails and the bottom half shows the contents of the selected e-mail.

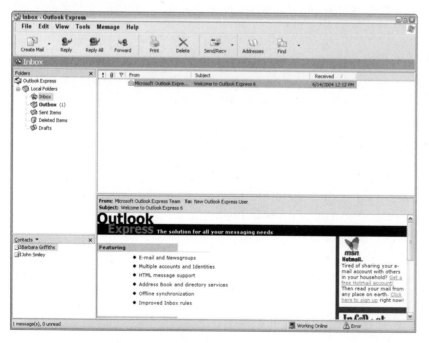

When you select an e-mail in the mail client, several new buttons appear, letting you print the selected e-mail, forward it to another person, or reply to the e-mail. If you select the Reply or Reply All buttons, the sender's e-mail is added to the To field so you can send a response directly to the sender.

Managing e-mails

If you right-click on the Local Folders directory in the left pane, you can choose to create a new folder. You can also drag and drop selected e-mail messages into the folders in the left pane. By creating a specific set of e-mail folders, you can quickly organize all incoming e-mails.

If you don't want to keep an e-mail, you can select it and press Delete to trash the e-mail. All deleted e-mails route to the Deleted Items folder. You can permanently delete these items by right-clicking on the Deleted Items folder and selecting the Empty Deleted Items option.

Using Instant Messaging

If you're comfortable with e-mailing people but frustrated that it takes too long for a response to be returned, you can use Instant Messaging. Instant Messaging is an application that opens a connection between two or more users and lets them converse in real time by typing messages. The messages route directly to the connected person and the results appear immediately.

In order for Instant Messaging to work, both people need to be connected to the Internet and logged in to the application at the same time.

Configuring Windows Messenger

Windows Messenger is a utility that comes with Windows, but it isn't installed by default. You can install it by selecting the Add/Remove Windows Components button in the Add or Remove Programs dialog box, which you can access from the Control Panel.

To install this component, select it from the Windows Components Wizard's list and click Next. After installation, you can select it from the Start ⇨ All Programs menu. Windows Messenger appears with a single link that says "Click here to sign in."

After clicking this link, the application tries to log you in, but if you haven't signed up, you route to a Web page where you can sign up for the messaging service. It only requires a valid e-mail address and a password.

After you're signed in, you can set the Windows Messaging options, which includes your display name, using the Tools ⇨ Options menu command. This opens the Options dialog box, shown in Figure 46.45. The Options dialog box includes the ability to block certain users.

FIGURE 46.45

Windows Messenger's Options dialog box lets you specify how the messaging application works.

Using Windows Messenger

After you've configured Windows Messenger and signed up, you can log in to the application; the result looks like Figure 46.46. From the login page, you can select to Add a Contact, Send an Instant Message, or Send a File or Photo using the links at the bottom of the application.

When you click Add a Contact, a wizard opens where you can locate contacts by typing in their e-mail addresses or contact names. Once a contact is made, a notification is sent to the contacts informing them that you've requested that they be added to your contact list. The contacts then have the choice to accept or block your request. If they accept, you can see when they are online. Contacts that are online appear in green, and contacts that are not appear in red.

When a contact is online, you can select to send him or her an Instant Message by selecting the contact and then choosing the Send an Instant Message option. This opens a separate Conversation dialog box, shown in Figure 46.47, where you can communicate by typing a message and clicking Send.

If you select Send a File or Photo, a file dialog box opens where you can select a file to send to the selected contact. Choosing Voice or Video Conversation starts the Audio and Video Tuning Wizard where you can set up the necessary microphones, speaker, and video cameras required to allow two users to communicate back and forth.

FIGURE 46.46

Once logged in to Windows Messenger you can use the links at the bottom of the application.

FIGURE 46.47

Windows Messenger lets you communicate in real time with connected contacts.

Summary

Connecting to the Internet starts by first choosing an Internet service provider (ISP) and then creating a connection to the ISP's server. There are several different types of connections that are available including dial-up and broadband, but you should check to see which services are available in your area. The Connection Wizard guides you through this process.

Once connected, you can configure your Web browser to surf the endless supply of Web pages available on the Internet. Internet Explorer includes tools that allow you to search for specific Web pages, save your favorite Web sites, and recall the recent browsing history.

An e-mail client allows you to send and receive e-mails, but you can also communicate with others using applications such as Windows Messenger.

Chapter 47

Using Virtual Private Networks

A virtual private network (VPN) is an private extension of a LAN or a link between two networks through a second network or through the Internet. The second network is usually a public network with limited security.

The VPN connects two points on a network through an encrypted channel (sometimes called a *data tunnel*). A VPN can connect a single computer to a network, two computers to one another, or provide a gateway between two networks. Therefore, you can use a VPN to create a secure connection from your home computer to your company's network, securely connect your laptop from a public Wi-Fi access point to your home or office computer, or establish a link between the in-house LANs in two branch offices of a business.

VPNs use these methods to protect the data carried on them:

- They require a password and login account to limit access to legitimate users.

- They use encryption to make the data impossible for intruders to understand.

- They include error checking with each data packet to confirm that the data is not damaged during transmission and to prevent unauthorized access to the VPN.

A VPN operates on top of the existing network connections, so it's not limited to a single network link, or even a single type of connection. If you connect your laptop computer to a LAN through a Wi-Fi link, and connect the Wi-Fi access point to a gateway router through a cable and then to another computer in the next city or halfway around the world through the Internet, you can still create a VPN that connects the two computers together.

The following are the most common uses of VPNs:

■ To connect a user in an isolated location (such as a home office or an Internet café) to a distant LAN with the same kind of access as a local user, as shown in Figure 47.1.

■ To connect the LAN at a branch office to a company's central network resources through a secure link, as shown in Figure 47.2.

FIGURE 47.1

A virtual private network can connect a remote computer to a distant LAN.

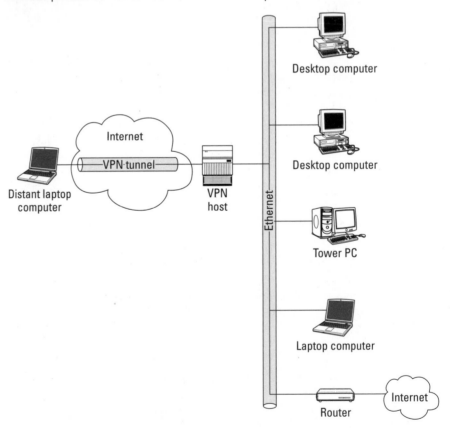

FIGURE 47.2

A VPN can also connect a branch office LAN to a corporate network.

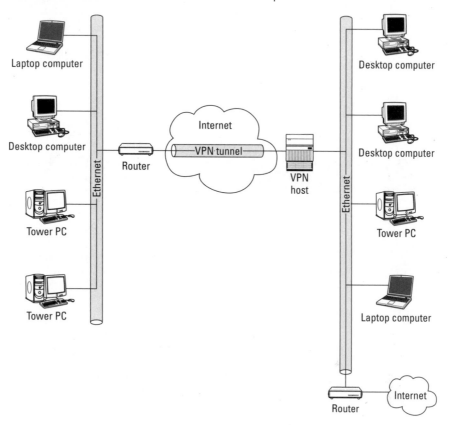

- To add an extra layer of security to a wireless network connection, as shown in Figure 47.3.

- To restrict access to sensitive or confidential information by isolating the computer or server that contains that information in a "hidden network," as shown in Figure 47.4.

TIP For more in-depth information on VPNs, check out *Virtual Private Networking: A Construction, Operation and Utilization Guide* by Gilbert Held (Wiley, 2004) or *Virtual Private Networks For Dummies* by Mark S. Merkow (Wiley, 1999).

VPNs are used primarily in corporate networks, but it's also possible to add a VPN host to a home network. This could allow you to monitor the video cameras and appliance sensors, and operate home automation controls without exposing your home to unwanted attention from outsiders through the Internet.

FIGURE 47.3

VPNs can add security to a wireless link.

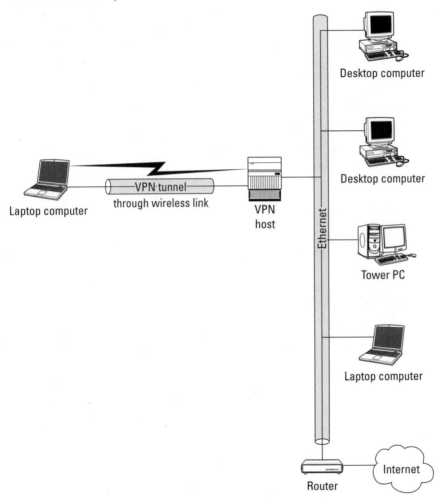

This chapter explains how a virtual private network operates, and it offers instructions for creating and connecting your computer to a VPN. If you're responsible for creating VPN hosts and maintaining VPN services for a business or other organization, you need more detailed information than this chapter supplies, but it should be adequate when you're trying to connect through a VPN to an existing server.

FIGURE 47.4

A hidden VPN can isolate a computer from the rest of a network.

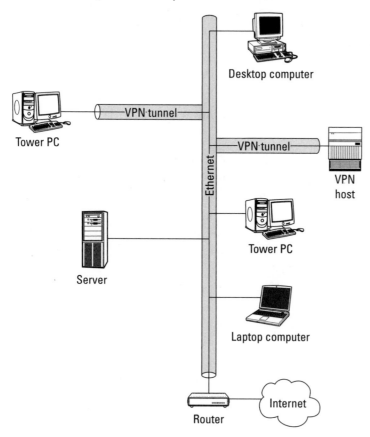

How a VPN Works

A VPN carries data between two end points through one or more networks. The network path between the two end points is called a *route*. At one end, the VPN client isolates data packets (relatively short strings of data, with error checking and address information added) by attaching an additional block of data (a header) to each data packet or frame that contains information about the address of the other VPN end point. At the other end of the route, the VPN server removes the VPN header and treats each packet or frame just like packets and frames that come from local network clients (when the server returns data to the client, the same thing happens in the other direction).

Several formats exist for tunneling headers, so it's essential that the two ends of a VPN link use the same format. The most common *protocols*, or sets of rules, for VPNs are Point-to-Point Tunneling Protocol (PPTP), Layer Two Tunneling Protocol (L2TP), and Internet Protocol Security (IPSec) mode. IPSec tunnels can only operate across TCP/IP networks, but PPTP and L2TP also work with Novell NetWare and NetBEUI connections. In practice, both NetWare and NetBEUI networks are rapidly becoming obsolete.

Both PPTP and L2TP can provide secure VPN connections, but they use slightly different approaches. The relative advantages of each method include:

- L2TP provides more types of security and authentication than PPTP.
- L2TP connections provide stronger authentication.
- L2TP packets are always transmitted in encrypted form.
- PPTP can work with computers using any version of Windows back to Windows 95, but L2TP only works with Windows XP and Windows 2000.

When you add a VPN connection to your own computer, the choice of PPTP or L2TP will depend on the type of connection used by the VPN host. When you set up the connection, Windows detects the type that the network host uses, and automatically set your end of the link to match it. If you're using a manual configuration, your help desk or network manager should tell you which version to use.

For a more technical explanation of each VPN method, look at Microsoft's white paper on Virtual Private Networking (www.microsoft.com/windows2000/docs/VPNoverview.doc).

Setting Up a VPN

In order to establish a VPN connection, you must install a VPN server program on the host computer, and VPN client software on the remote computer. The server can be either a program running on a host computer or a separate switch, router, or gateway. The Virtual Private Network Consortium (VPNC) has established a set of interoperability standards for VPN hardware; if a device is on their list at www.vpnc.org/testing, you can expect it to work with a Windows XP client. The same list includes links to information about specific VPN networking products. Microsoft Windows server products, including Windows NT Server, Windows 2000 Server, and Windows Server 2003 all include VPN host software.

In most cases, you want to set up a new VPN link to an existing host, so we'll leave the process of creating a new server to the network managers and other experts; if you must build your own server, you will want to read one of the books mentioned in the introduction to this chapter.

It doesn't matter to the users of VPN clients whether the host is a stand-alone device or software on a network server, or which operating system the host computer is using. The VPN method does make a difference because both ends of a VPN tunnel must use the same protocol. However, Windows can automatically detect the connection type, so you should be able to make a successful VPN connection to any server.

To configure your computer as a VPN client, follow these steps:

1. From the Control Panel or the Start menu, choose Network Connections.

2. In the Network Connections window, choose the New Connection Wizard.

3. From the Welcome window in the New Connection Wizard, click Next to open the Network Connection Type window shown in Figure 47.5.

FIGURE 47.5

Choose the Connect to my workplace option to set up a VPN client.

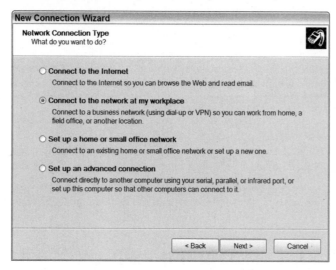

4. Choose the Connect to the network at my workplace option and click Next. The Network Connection window shown in Figure 47.6 appears.

5. Choose the Virtual Private Network connection option and click Next. The Connection Name asks you to assign a name to the VPN connection profile.

6. Type the name of the destination or some other identifier and click Next. The Public Network screen shown in Figure 47.7 appears.

FIGURE 47.6

The Network Connection screen includes a VPN option.

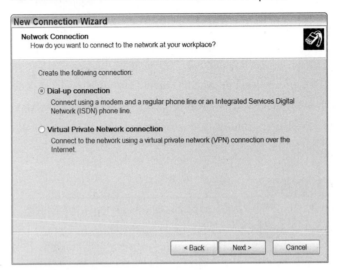

FIGURE 47.7

Choose the type of connection for your VPN end point.

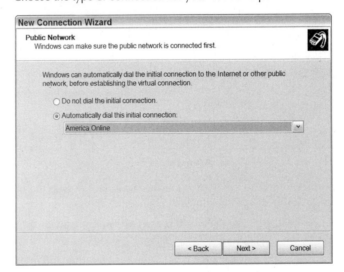

7. **If you're connecting to the Internet through a LAN or a broadband service such as DSL or cable, choose the Do not dial option.** If you have to connect to the Internet through a dial-up service, choose the Automatically dial option. Click Next. The VPN Server Selection screen shown in Figure 47.8 appears.

FIGURE 47.8

Type the name or address of the VPN host.

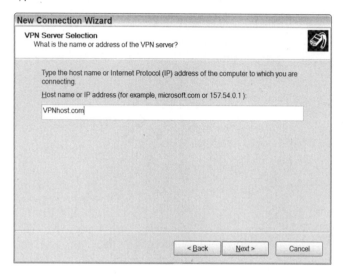

8. **Obtain the name or numeric address of the VPN host from your network manager.** Type either the name (such as VPNhost.com) or the numeric IP address of the host and click Next.

9. **The final screen of the wizard confirms the name of the connection profile and offers to add a shortcut on your desktop.** Click Finish to save the profile and close the wizard. The Connect window shown in Figure 47.9 appears.

10. **Type the account name and password assigned by your network manager in the Connect window, and click the Connect button at the bottom of the window to test your connection.**

If the VPN connection works, you see a login or confirmation screen from the host; you now have a live connection through your VPN to the distant host or network that accepts any command that you could enter from a local computer on the same network.

FIGURE 47.9

The Connect window sets up a VPN link.

Sending a VPN Through a Firewall

Most VPN connections pass through one or more firewalls and routers, which interrupt the data flow unless you tell the firewalls to accept the VPN data. To set your firewall or router to pass a PPTP signal, you must open each firewall and router's configuration tool and change the Port Forwarding settings.

You must enable these ports and protocols:

    Client Ports 1024-65535/TCP

    Server Port 723/TCP

    Protocols PPTP

    IP Protocol 47 (GRE)

The location of these settings is different for each device, so you have to consult the manuals for your own equipment to learn exactly what you must do to change them. Of course, some manuals are better than others, so if the manual doesn't tell you what you need to know, call your network manager and the tech support center for each firewall and router.

If the connection does not work, confirm that your account name and password are correct. If they are, it's possible that your computer did not automatically recognize the connection type. To set your VPN client to a either PPTP or L2TP, follow these steps:

1. **Open your VPN connection profile.** The Connect window opens.

2. **Click the Properties button and choose the Networking tab in the Properties window.** The dialog box shown in Figure 47.10 appears.

3. **Open the drop-down Type of VPN menu near the top of the dialog box, and choose the connection method used by your VPN.** Click OK to save your settings.

4. **Try to open your VPN connection.** If it still doesn't work, consult your network manager.

For more about troubleshooting a VPN connection, see Microsoft Knowledge Base Article No. 314076, "How to configure a connection to a virtual private network (VPN) in Windows XP" at `www.support.microsoft.com/kb/314076`.

FIGURE 47.10

Choose the type of connection in the Properties window.

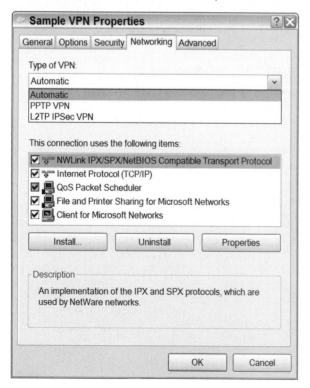

Connecting to a VPN

After you have created a VPN connection profile, you can open the connection by simply clicking a shortcut, either on the Windows desktop or in the Network Connections window.

The connection to the distant network or host computer is exactly the same as it would be if you had a direct connection to a computer or network in the same room as your own computer. If you use particular programs, file shares, or other resources on the host network, you can create additional shortcuts that automatically open the VPN link and connect you to that file, folder, or program. Users of other computers on the same LAN can send and receive messages to you by e-mail, instant messaging, and any other service installed on the network. In all respects, your computer is a fully functional part of the network.

Summary

A Virtual Private Network is a secure connection between a computer and a network, or between two LANs through the Internet or some other network structure that uses packets. Because the VPN link is protected by passwords, encryption, and packet authentication, it provides a way to create a direct tunnel between an isolated user and a distant home or corporate network, or between a portable computer and a wireless access point that is not accessible to network intruders or other unauthorized users.

To set up a link from your computer to a VPN host, use the New Connection Wizard in Start ➪ Settings ➪ Network Connections, and choose the Virtual Private Network connection option. If you connect to the Internet through one or more firewalls or routers, remember to change the Port Forwarding settings.

After you have set up the link, you can connect through a VPN from the Network Connections window; if you use the link frequently, you can save a few mouse clicks by creating a desktop shortcut to the VPN network profile.

Part VIII

Security and Maintenance

Chapter 48

Keeping Your Computer and Data Secure

The most serious threats to your computer include theft of the machine itself, viruses and other forms of software vandalism, and efforts to steal valuable information. If you leave a computer unattended in a public place, it will probably disappear; if you connect the computer to the Internet without some kind of firewall, antivirus program, or other security software in place, you can expect online intruders to find you within minutes.

Therefore, security is not an optional enhancement to your computer; it's an absolute necessity. If you don't take control of your computer, both inside and out, somebody else will take it away from you.

This chapter contains information about the steps you can take to protect your computer against theft, viruses, and software attacks, and how to restore your system to secure operation after an attack has occurred.

IN THIS CHAPTER

Protecting your computer against physical harm

Preventing data loss

Insuring your computer

Protecting against invasion

Preventing the attack of viruses and spyware

Physical Security

Personal computers, especially laptops and other portables, are very attractive targets for thieves. Even if your computer doesn't ever leave your home or office, you should take some practical steps to protect it.

CROSS-REF Chapter 26 includes an extensive discussion about security for laptop computers.

Protecting against theft

It's difficult to discourage a really dedicated thief, but you can often slow him down by making your computer and other personal property more difficult to steal. If your computer is stolen, there are things you can do beforehand to make your property easier to recover.

Obviously, the location where you use your computer makes a difference. In your own home, or in a secure workplace, the risks are different from an office cubicle or some other location where unknown passers-by can easily get to your computer when you're not there.

First, don't leave small and easily removed equipment and parts in plain sight. In an unsecured office, lock your spare parts and loose accessories (including PC Cards) in a cabinet or a desk drawer overnight and when you're away from the computer. If you can, secure larger components like the monitor and the main processor box to a desk or heavy table with a lock and heavy cable or chain, a clamp, or a lockdown plate.

If your computer is in a high-risk area, you can also install an antitheft alarm mounted on a PCI card. When the alarm card is in place inside your computer, it sounds a very loud warning signal if somebody tries to lift the computer, remove the cover, or disconnect cables unless he or she enters a security code first. A battery keeps the alarm card active when the computer itself is turned off.

You should also try to improve the chances that you might retrieve your computer equipment if it is stolen. These techniques can help police and other authorities return your computer to you:

- Keep a list of makes, models, and serial numbers in a secure place separate from the computer.

- Mark some kind of personal ID code on each piece, inside and out (don't try to cut into printed circuit boards or hard drives with your marking tool), and take a photo of each marked item. In many places, you can borrow an electric engraving machine from local libraries, police stations, and fire stations. Copies of your photos are useful when you want to report stolen property to the police, and when you want to make an insurance claim.

- Notify your local police as soon as possible. Law enforcement authorities can distribute a description of your property to pawnshops, used computer stores, and other local resellers. If the thief tries to sell your computer to one of these places, the store's owner may find your equipment listed on a *hot sheet* and notify the police.

- Use security labels with bar codes that are listed with an asset tracking and recovery service. These labels use a permanent adhesive that leaves an indelible "tattoo" that identifies the item as stolen when somebody tries to remove them.

- Install tracking software that can quietly call home to a tracking center with information about the computer's current location (telephone number or Internet address) every time it connects to a telephone line or the Internet. If you advise the tracking center that your computer has been stolen, they can work with police, the telephone company, and Internet service providers to find and recover your property. One tracking program, called LostPC, is available at no cost from Mountain Systems (www.lostpc.com).

Preventing damage

There's not much you can do to completely avoid random accidents and natural disasters such as fires and earthquakes, but there are a few ways to minimize the consequences. If you apply some common sense when you install and use your computer, you can reduce the likelihood of serious damage.

Some of the things you can do to prevent or minimize damage include:

- Don't place your computer in a precarious location where somebody could accidentally knock it off the table or desk to the floor below.

- If you live in an earthquake zone, don't stack the equipment too high.

- If you're using the computer in a basement or some other location where flooding is possible, don't place the processor case on the floor; put it on a table or a riser to keep it up off the floor.

- If you're working in a room with a sprinkler system, cover the computer when you leave or remove the computer from the room.

Protecting your computer from power surges

One more possible source of damage to your computer is a spike or surge from the AC power source. Chapter 17 of this book describes the problems that can be caused by an inconsistent power source, and explains how to protect your computer from them. Most of the same tools and techniques, including a surge protector, can also protect a laptop.

Back Up Your Data!

We all know that unexpected computer glitches happen — hard drives fail, or files become corrupted, or you accidentally delete an essential file, or something else makes it impossible to open and read a file — but most of us don't bother to make regular backup copies of the important files stored on our computers until after we experience a loss. The information on your hard drives — including personnel files, financial records, manuscripts, and accumulated e-mail messages, among other things — is often more valuable than the computer hardware. If you can't find a way to reconstruct your business records, you may no longer *have* a business.

Home computer user can face similar problems. If old tax records, family photos and e-mail are on a failed disk drive, they could be lost forever if you don't have backup copies.

So it's essential to back up your data files. Windows includes a simple utility that can create regular backup copies of selected files and folders; many third-party backup programs offer somewhat more sophisticated solutions to the same problem. You can find more about the Windows Backup program later in this section.

Choosing a backup program is just one of the decisions you must make when you establish a backup plan. The others include:

- What kind of media do you use to store your backup copies?

  If you have a relatively small amount of data to store, one or more recordable CDs might be adequate, but when you need more than four or five CDs to make a complete backup, you should move to DVDs or some other medium that takes less time to record and doesn't force you to juggle a lot of separate disks.

  Other alternatives include an external hard drive connected to your computer through a USB port, or a second computer connected to yours through a network. High-capacity tape drives are another option, but most of them are either too slow or too expensive for home and small business users, or both.

- How often do you need to create backups?

  How much data can you afford to lose? If you're running a business on your computers, you may want to make backups at least once a week — maybe more often than that. It's not uncommon to make automatic backups to a server through your office network every night. Most home computer users can get along with a backup once or twice a month.

  Of course, it's always a good idea to make an additional unscheduled backup whenever you create or revise a very important file or document, such as a tax return, irreplaceable research notes, or the manuscript of your novel or thesis. If it would take a lot of time to reconstruct your work, make frequent backups.

  Data stored on your laptop computer is a special case. Because laptops are always in danger of being stolen, you should make backup copies of new files and documents every day that you use it.

- Where do you plan to keep the backup copies?

  The point of making backups is to have copies of important files after your computer is damaged, lost, or stolen. So it doesn't do much good to store all your backup copies on another computer in the same office, or in the drawer of a desk that will burn up in the same fire that destroys your computer. It's true that viruses and damaged disk drives are more common than fires, but when you're thinking about security, you should anticipate the worst.

  The best approach is to keep two sets of backup data — one near your computer and the other in a secure off-site location. You can use the copy in your desk drawer when a virus destroys your data, and the off-site copy after the house burns down.

  The off-site copies might be another branch office within your company, or the home of one of the owners or managers. The backup copies of data from your home computers can go to the home or office or a trusted friend or relative. The location of your backups isn't as important as your ability to retrieve them on short notice in an emergency.

In most major urban areas, you can find businesses that collect your backup disks or tapes on a regular schedule, store them in a secure location, and return them to you upon request. If you're dealing with a medium-to-large business with a lot of backup media, this kind of service may be a better choice than trying to establish your own, less formal backup storage system.

The Backup utility supplied with Windows is not the fastest or the most flexible backup tool you can use, but it's already installed on your computer, so it's entirely adequate for many users. To create backup copies of your files, follow these steps:

1. **From the Start menu, choose Programs (or All Programs) ⇨ Accessories ⇨ System Tools ⇨ Backup.** The Backup Utility window shown in Figure 48.1 appears.

2. **You can either use the Backup Wizard to step through the process, or open the Backup tab shown in Figure 48.2 to choose the folders whose contents you want to back up.** Either way, select the folders for the backup and the location of the media where you want to store the copies. You can specify another drive on the same computer, a removable drive, or a storage device connected to this computer through your local network.

FIGURE 48.1

Use the Windows Backup Utility to create or recover backup files.

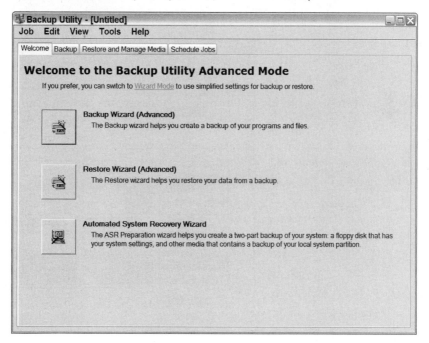

FIGURE 48.2

Choose the folders you want to back up and the media where you want to store the copies.

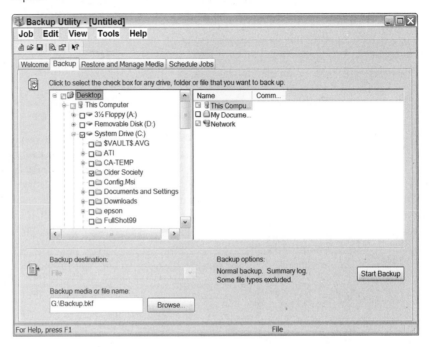

3. **When you're ready to start making backup copies, click the Finish button in the wizard or the Start Backup button in the Backup Utility window.**

To restore files from your backup media, use the Restore and Manage Media tab in the Backup Utility shown in Figure 48.3. Choose the files you want to recover and click the Start Restore button.

To automate your backup process, open the Schedule Jobs tab and click the Add Job button to run the Backup Wizard, where you can choose the type of backup and the interval between backups.

> **TIP** The worst time to discover that your backup disks have a problem is after you have lost the originals. When you make a backup, try restoring your data right away, just to be certain that the backup files are good.

FIGURE 48.3

Use the Restore and Manage Media tab to retrieve files from your backup media.

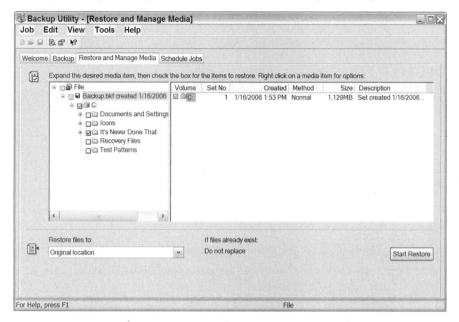

Insurance

Insurance might not protect your computer from loss or damage due to theft, power surges, fires, floods, or other disasters, but it can go a long way toward reducing the pain involved in replacing it. If you're willing to pay for it, you might even find insurance that includes coverage for loss of essential business data.

Coverage in business

The insurance agent who provides coverage for your business should be familiar with the specific risks that are common in your industry. You can also ask trade associations and local chambers of commerce for advice about appropriate coverage. A standard business owner's policy (BOP) is often good enough to cover loss from theft, fire, flood, or vandalism.

Data recovery is sometimes included in a BOP, but if not, it may be worth the additional expense. An Electronic Data Policy (EDP) that picks up where your BOP leaves off might also include coverage against business losses caused by mechanical failure, power surges, and even viruses and spyware.

In some cases, your general business insurance might include computer coverage. However, that's not always enough to replace everything you might lose in a catastrophic event, so it's worth the time and trouble to evaluate the risks in your particular situation. If your basic coverage does not specifically include computer coverage, ask your agent to add a computer equipment rider to the policy.

Homeowner's or renter's coverage

Most homeowners and renters insurance includes coverage for loss or damage to computers and related equipment, up to a specified replacement cost. If you have just one computer, you're probably okay, but if each member of the family has a computer, or if you have an expensive laptop, you should review your policy and make sure you have enough coverage. Your insurance agent can tell you how much computer coverage your existing homeowner's or renter's insurance includes. If it's not enough, ask about a rider or a separate policy. Make sure your insurance covers full replacement value of any lost or damaged equipment.

Laptop computers and other portable equipment might require a special rider on your regular policy, or special coverage called a *floater* that protects property away from your own premises. Some floaters specify the geographic areas that are covered, so it's important to advise your insurer about unusual travel plans.

Making an inventory

Before you talk to your insurance agent, make a complete inventory of your equipment. This is also a good time to create or revisit your plans for making and keeping backup copies of your data.

When you make an inventory, don't forget all the extra bits and pieces inside and outside your computer, including the graphics controller, sound controller and other internal expansion cards, external storage, network switches, routers and modems, the video display monitor, speakers, keyboard, and uninterruptible power supply. Your laptop inventory should include everything in your computer bag, including the power pack, PC Cards, cables, and the bag itself. The inventory should also include the serial numbers for everything including motherboards, cases, and other internal parts, and copies of the receipts or invoices for each piece.

If you have the receipts or invoices for your existing computer equipment, place a copy of each one in your inventory file folder. When you buy new computer equipment, add those receipts to the same folder. That kind of paperwork is the best way to document exactly when you bought an item and how much it cost.

As part of your inventory, keep a list of all the software installed on your computers, including serial numbers and other unique identifiers. Many software companies can provide free or low-cost replacements for lost or stolen products (your insurance claims specialist should be able to help with this).

When the inventory list is complete, make several copies and store at least one away from your own home or office — it does you no good if you lose it in the same fire that destroyed the computer. A safe-deposit box, a branch office, and the home of a family member who doesn't live with you are all good places to store a copy of the list. Your insurance agent might also agree to keep a copy in your account file.

Protecting Yourself against Snoops, Data Thieves, and Eavesdroppers

In order to keep your computer secure, you must be sure that your files are confidential, that intruders can't change them, and that the files are accessible to you and other authorized users on demand.

Any time your computer is connected to the Internet, it may be exposed to attacks from intruders (also known as *hackers* or *crackers*) who want to read your files and e-mail, steal your credit card numbers and financial records, and use your computer for their own nefarious purposes. Some of these creeps are nothing more than simple vandals, whose idea of fun is to alter or destroy your files or damage your hard drive. Obviously, you must protect your computer against this kind of thing.

The same high-speed communications channels that we all use to send and receive messages and retrieve information from all over the world are also available to the hackers and crackers. Whenever somebody discovers a new and better technique for breaking into computers, the news moves around the world within a few days. The battle between the bad guys who want to break into computers and the good guys who want to stop them goes on and on.

Online intruders are not the only kind of threat to your computer. You must also protect your files and data from unauthorized users with physical access to the machine with passwords, encryption, and other tools that allow only legitimate users to operate the system.

Working with access control

To protect your files from unwanted attention by people with physical access to the computer — relatives, co-workers, and visitors to your office who might walk in when you're not there, and even random intruders — you can use several tools to protect your data. These include passwords, encrypted text and data, fingerprint readers, and other devices that a user must operate before the computer starts.

Assigning passwords to Windows users

In Windows, you can easily assign a password to each user account; if a user can't provide the password, the operating system doesn't accept a login to that account. To assign or change an account's password, follow these steps:

1. **From the Control Panel, choose User Accounts.** The User Accounts window shown in Figure 48.4 appears.

2. **Choose the name of the account whose password you want to change.** You might have to scroll down the User Accounts window to see the list of existing accounts.

3. **Under the What do you want to change headline, choose Create (or Change) a Password.** The Create a password for your account window shown in Figure 48.5 appears.

4. **Type the new password in both the new password and the confirm fields.** Add a password hint if you want. Click the Create Password button to save your choice and close this window.

Be sure to assign a password to each account; just one account not protected with a password provides a way for intruders to start the machine.

 **CAUTION** If you leave the computer on when you walk away from it, an intruder doesn't need a password to open your files and steal your data.

FIGURE 48.4

Use the User Accounts utility assigns or changes a password.

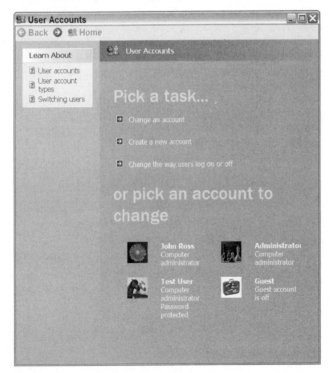

FIGURE 48.5

Use this dialog box to assign a new password to an account.

Using a fingerprint reader

Some new laptop computers include a fingerprint reader as standard or optional equipment. These devices allow a user to pass a finger across a scanner that creates an image of the fingerprint and compare it with the stored images created by authorized users. If the new fingerprint matches one already stored in the computer, the security program sends the user's name and password to Windows or another protected file or program. If there is no match, the computer (or the individual program) does not start.

Using a fingerprint reader is faster and easier than typing a password, and it's also more secure, because it's not possible to guess another person's fingerprint or copy it from a list. It's true that dedicated crackers can still break into a computer with a fingerprint reader, but it takes more time and trouble than breaking into a computer that uses a typed login and password.

Using encryption

When you encrypt the contents of a file, the text or data in that file is impossible to read unless you apply the corresponding un-encryption process first. Intruders who try to read the encrypted version see nothing but gibberish.

No encryption scheme is completely secure because it's almost always possible to decode the text if you throw enough computing power at the file. But even a relatively simple encryption scheme is enough to protect your data from casual thieves and crackers.

In Windows XP, you can use the Encrypting File System (EFS) to encrypt a single file or all of the files in a folder. If an intruder gains access to your computer, either onsite or through a network or the Internet, the encrypted files remain secure.

EFS is particularly useful on laptop computers; even if your computer is stolen, your sensitive or confidential files is still protected.

To encrypt a file, folder, or an entire drive, follow these steps:

1. **Open My Computer.**

2. **Open a drive and drill down to a specific folder or individual file that contains the file or folder you want to encrypt.**

3. **Right-click the file or folder you want to encrypt, and choose Properties from the pop-up menu.** The Properties dialog box shown in Figure 48.6 appears.

FIGURE 48.6

Encryption is an Advanced Attribute of a file or folder.

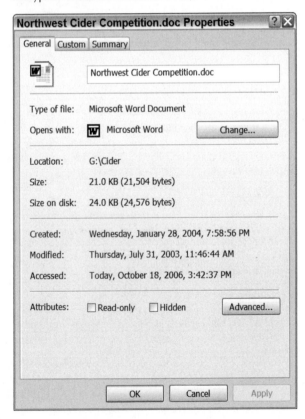

4. **Click the Advanced button to open the Advanced Attributes dialog box shown in Figure 48.7.**

FIGURE 48.7

Turn on the Encrypt contents option to encrypt this file or folder.

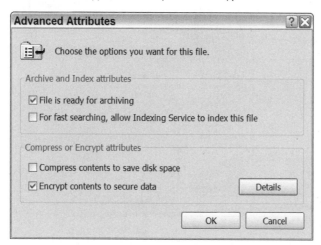

5. **To encrypt a file, enable the Encrypt contents to secure data option near the bottom of the window.** To remove encryption from a previously encrypted file, disable this option.

When a file or folder is encrypted, the name appears in My Computer in green rather than the usual black. You can still open the file, but if another user (either from a different account on the same computer, or from another computer through a LAN) tries to read it, Windows refuses to open the file.

TIP As an alternative to the encryption service supplied with Windows, you might want to try a free open-source encryption program such as TrueCrypt, which is available from www.truecrypt.org/.

Protecting your Wi-Fi connection

When you connect to the Internet through a Wi-Fi access point, you are using radio transmitters to send data between the access point (also called a wireless router) and your computer. Anybody else with a Wi-Fi–enabled computer or a specialized radio receiver can also receive those signals. Unless you protect your Wi-Fi network, anybody with a Wi-Fi network interface can use it to connect to the Internet and possibly open files on your own computers.

In many neighborhoods and business districts, as many as a dozen or more different Wi-Fi signals are floating around. For example, Figure 48.8 shows the Wi-Fi networks within range of my house in Seattle. Most of my neighbors have turned on their access points' security features, so it's a lot more difficult to grab an unauthorized connection from any of them than to break into a network through an unsecured access point.

FIGURE 48.8

Five different Wi-Fi networks are active in this neighborhood.

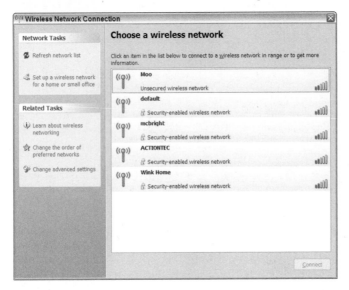

There are methods out there for cracking Wi-Fi encryption, but most intruders look for an unsecured network rather than taking the time to break through encryption. However, no wireless network is totally secure without additional (and expensive) tools, so your best defense is to make your wireless network more secure and more difficult to crack than the one across the street.

Most Wi-Fi access points support two types of security: encryption and access control. The exact procedure for turning on these features is different for each make and model of access point, so you have to consult the manual supplied with your access point to learn how to set them for your network.

CAUTION When you install a Wi-Fi access point, remember to use a network name (the SSID) that doesn't tell a snooper who you are, and to turn off SSID broadcast. And don't forget to change the access point's default password, which is widely known, and often the same on hundreds of thousands of units. The manual supplied with your access point or base station contains the specific instructions for making these changes.

Setting encryption

Wi-Fi encryption uses the same key code on the access point and on each client computer to provide access to encrypted data. To add a key code to a Wi-Fi connection profile in Windows, follow these steps:

1. **From the Control Panel or the system tray, open the Wireless Network Connection Properties window and choose the Wireless Networks tab.** The dialog box shown in Figure 48.9 appears.

Choose an encrypted network from the list of preferred networks.

2. **Find the name of the network in the list of Preferred networks and click the Properties button.** The Properties dialog box shown in Figure 48.10 appears.

3. **Open the drop-down Data encryption menu and choose WEP or WPA.** If the program offers you a choice of key lengths, choose the longest possible number of digits.

4. **Type the same network key that you used to set up encryption on your access point in both network key fields.**

5. **Click the OK buttons in both open Properties windows to save your settings and close the windows.**

FIGURE 48.10

Use the Properties window to enter the network key for this Wi-Fi network.

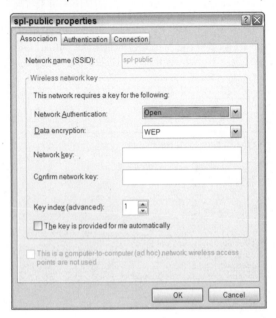

Using Access Control

Many access points also offer an Access Control option that limits the network to computers (and other devices) with specific MAC (Media Access Control) addresses. To turn on Access Control, consult the manual supplied with your access point for specific instructions.

To find the MAC address of your Wi-Fi adapter, look for a label on the back or bottom of your computer, or on the USB or PC Card wireless adapter itself. Figure 48.11 shows the MAC address of a Wi-Fi adapter on a PC Card.

If you can't find a MAC address on the outside of your computer or Wi-Fi adapter, use the Device Manager (Control Panel ⇨ System ⇨ Hardware) to open the Properties window for your wireless adapter. Look in the Advanced tab for a MAC address. Figure 48.12 shows the Properties window for an Intel adapter — the layout of the Advanced tab is different for other makes, but the MAC address is always someplace in the window.

FIGURE 48.11

The MAC address of a Wi-Fi adapter is normally marked on the device.

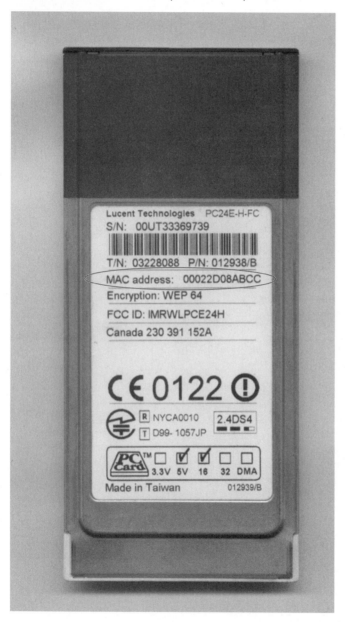

FIGURE 48.12

The MAC address for this Intel adapter appears near the bottom of the Properties window.

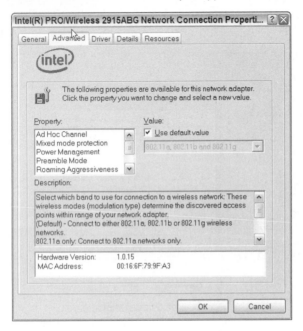

Using a firewall

Every computer or LAN connected to the Internet should include a firewall to protect it from intruders. Firewalls are not 100 percent effective, but they can turn away a lot of unwanted attempts to connect to your computer or network. A firewall can be a software package or a hardware device; either way it filters every incoming and outgoing request for a network connection and rejects the ones that don't match a preset list of security rules. For more effective protection, you can use both software and hardware.

For example, a firewall might accept incoming data that was requested by your Web browser or FTP program, but it rejects packets addressed to other services. Another filter in the same firewall might examine the contents of e-mail files and reject messages from senders that are known to be sources of spam.

A good firewall can protect your computer from many kinds of attacks, including:

■ Remote access to your files and programs.

■ Access to bugs in Windows and other programs.

■ Attempts to use your computer to relay e-mail from an outside source. This can make spam and other unwanted mail difficult or impossible to trace.

■ Denial of service attacks and e-mail bombs. These are two forms of massive attacks that send thousands of messages or requests for connection to the same address, with the hope that the recipient will become overloaded and break down.

The latest versions of Windows XP include firewall software, as do many network gateways and routers (described in Chapter 44). It generally doesn't hurt, and it might be helpful, to use more than one firewall at the same time. If the Windows Firewall isn't already active, Windows will probably harass you until you turn the thing on. Even if you already have a separate firewall in place, go ahead and turn on the Windows Firewall:

1. **From the Control Panel, open Security Center.** The window shown in Figure 48.13 appears.

FIGURE 48.13

The Windows Security Center shows the current state of your security software.

2. **If the firewall is off, scroll down to the bottom of the window and click Windows Firewall under Manage Security Settings.** The Windows Firewall window shown in Figure 48.14 appears.

3. **Click On (recommended) to turn on the firewall software.** Unless you have a reason to change them, keep the default settings in the Exceptions and Advanced tabs.

793

FIGURE 48.14

The Windows Firewall window controls the firewall software.

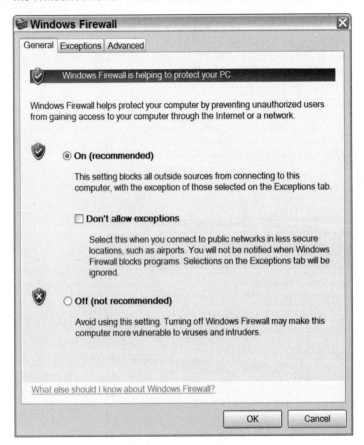

To test the effectiveness of your firewall, you can use one or more of the online security testing Web sites. These programs send harmless probes to your Internet address that test many of the most common gaps in computer security. If your computer fails one or more of these tests, check your existing firewall or install a new one.

These Web sites offer useful security tests:

HackerWatch	www.hackerwatch.org/probe
Shields UP!	www.grc.com/x/ne.dll
PC Flank	www.pcflank.com

Keeping Viruses and Spyware Out of Your Computer

Spyware, viruses, worms, and Trojan horses are among the most common types of computer *malware*, or malicious software. They all use different methods to gain access to your computer, but they're all inherently evil; you must protect yourself against all of them.

A virus is a small piece of computer code that usually enters your computer hidden inside a larger program. The virus runs when you open the file that carries it, and it performs some kind of unwanted (and often damaging) action. Like a biological virus, many computer virus programs also create copies of the virus code and hide them inside other programs and data files; when a user sends a copy of the host file to another user, the virus infects yet another computer.

Boot sector viruses are a sub-category of virus that attacks the section of the hard drive that contains the programs that run when you turn on the computer, before Windows (or some other operating system) loads.

E-mail viruses travel as embedded code or attached files in e-mail messages. When you open an infected message, the virus runs. Many e-mail viruses also copy themselves and send copies to all of the names in the e-mail program's address book.

A worm is a program that attacks computers through security defects in common programs like Windows and Outlook. As they move through the Internet, some worms perform other unwanted tasks, such as altering Web pages and damaging utilities.

A Trojan horse is a program that is disguised as something other than its real identity. For example, you might discover an attractive-sounding game or music file, or even an anti-malware utility on a Web site. But when you download and install the program, it does something entirely different, such as erasing the files on your hard drive, or changing the home page on your Web browser to a site that carries advertising or offensive content.

Many of these programs do an excellent job of camouflaging themselves. It's easy to infect your computer with malware, but it's often extremely difficult to get rid of because the malware has moved in and taken control.

Preventing virus infections

Even if you don't have any visible evidence, it's entirely possible that your computer has been infected. And new attacks are happening all the time. So antivirus software is essential. If your computer doesn't already have an active antivirus program in place, install one now.

A good antivirus program includes both a full-time monitor that detects viruses before they can install themselves on your computer, and a scanning utility that examines your system for previously undetected infections.

Microsoft has tested most of the antivirus programs that are currently available, and posted a list of them at `www.microsoft.com/athome/security/viruses/wsc/en-us/flist.mspx`. Some of these suppliers offer free trial versions of their products, so you can test more than one before you make your choice. At least two, Avast (`www.avast.com`) and Grisoft (`http://free.grisoft.com`) offer free versions for personal use.

To be sure your regular antivirus program hasn't missed anything, you should also run an occasional scan with a second antivirus package from a different supplier. You can run free online virus scans from Trend Micro (`www.trendmicro.com/hc_intro/default.asp`), BitDefender (`http://bitdefender.com/scan8/ie.html`), or Panda Software (`www.pandasoftware.com/activescan/activescan`).

Antivirus programs are usually effective in keeping your system clean, as long as you remember to install updates as soon as they become available (most programs can run automatic updates every couple of days). But to be doubly sure, take these precautions:

- **Don't open files attached to e-mail messages unless you know and trust the person who sent it to you.** If you have already opened a suspicious file, run an antivirus scan as soon as possible. In particular, don't open any file with one of these file extensions:

.bat	.pif
.com	.scr
.eml	.vbe
.exe	.vbs
.js	wmf
.jse	.wsf
.lnk	.wsh

- **If you receive an e-mail with an attached file with one of these extensions from somebody you know and trust, don't open the file.** Send a reply asking the originator to compress the original file and send it as a .zip file.

- **Don't install or run programs you downloaded from unknown sources.** Games, music files, and pornography are especially popular virus carriers.

- **Turn off your computer or unplug the network connection when it's not in use.** Like the proverbial rust, crackers and other online intruders never sleep.

- **Find and install all the available updates and patches for Windows, your antivirus program, and all the other programs installed on your computer.** When software developers discover security threats or other problems, they usually provide fixes or patches through their Web sites. Look in each program's Help menu for an "About" command that displays the address of the developer's Web site.

- **Back up your files!**

Preventing spyware attacks

Spyware is software that collects information about you and your computer and sends it to people who want to use it without your permission. Spyware includes programs that might do any of these unwanted actions:

- Capture and forward your keystrokes

- Copy images of your screen

- Forward lists of the hardware and software installed in your computer

- Replace your Web browser's home page with a page that contains advertising, pornography, or political messages

- Replace the content or banner ads in Web sites with the Spyware author's own advertisements

- Collect account names, passwords, and other personal information

- Track your online activity to send you targeted advertising, either as e-mail, or in unwanted pop-up windows

Spyware usually loads itself into your computer without your knowledge or permission, often hidden inside other programs. Just because an online ad or e-mail offers something like a "free computer tune up," the real program does not always provide a truly useful service.

To protect yourself against the damage that spyware can do, you must find and remove any spyware that has already made its way into your computer, and keep new spyware out. Several anti-spyware utilities can perform all of these functions: Ad-Aware (`www.lavasoft.com`), Spybot Search and Destroy (`www.safer-networking.org`), and Windows Defender (`www.microsoft.com/athome/security/spyware/software`) are all effective against the most common spyware.

For more advice about removing spyware, including specific instructions for killing and removing programs that don't always respond to the all-purpose anti-spyware utilities, consult the list at `www.pchell.com/support/spyware.shtml`.

Summary

Computers are expensive and easy to steal. It's a matter of both common sense and sad experience to protect your computer and related equipment against theft and damage caused by fires, flood, and other natural or human disasters. You should do everything possible to make your computer difficult to steal and to minimize possible damage.

And if some miscreant does steal your computer, you should make the data files stored inside difficult or impossible to open and read. Passwords, fingerprint readers and other biometric systems, and encrypted data are all effective techniques for preventing unwanted access to your confidential information.

Insurance should also be part of your personal or corporate computer security plan. Your own insurance agent and experts at chambers of commerce and professional organizations can all offer helpful advice about the right kind of insurance coverage for you particular needs.

Unfortunately, physical security is not the only threat to your computer. Viruses, spyware, hackers, and crackers are all widespread problems. If you ever connect your computer to the Internet or any other network, or if you install software from sources you can't trust implicitly, it's absolutely essential to use a firewall, antivirus program, and anti-spyware utility.

Chapter 49

Preventing Trouble Through Maintenance

Through regular use, data files are littered all over the hard drive and if not properly cared for, disorganized data files can take longer to find and errors could begin to appear. The results of hard disk problems are slower system performance, corrupt data files, and possibly lost data files.

Windows includes several utilities that can help keep your hard drive clean, organized, and error free. Backing up data files is another important maintenance task that can help you recover from problems.

CROSS-REF The Task Scheduler utility can automate these maintenance applications. You can learn more about scheduling tasks in Chapter 39.

Keep It Clean

When dealing with maintenance issues, it is important to keep your computer clean both inside and out. Keeping the work area around the computer free of dust, grime, and especially water is important. You should also make sure that the computer is well ventilated, with open access to all external vents where the heat generated by the computer can be dissipated.

Another critical aspect of maintenance is keeping the hard drives clean of extraneous data, organized, and in good condition. Windows includes several tools that can help with this task.

IN THIS CHAPTER

Using the Disk Cleanup utility

Defragmenting your hard drive

Checking your hard drive for errors

Backing up data

Every time you delete a file, it automatically goes to the Recycle Bin where the file resides until permanently deleted. The Recycle Bin lets you restore any deleted files, but over time it tends to fill up and take valuable space that could be used to store other data files.

In the Recycle Bin Properties dialog box, you can set the Maximum size of the Recycle Bin as a percentage of the hard drive. Any deleted file that is larger than the space remaining in the Recycle Bin will be immediately and permanently deleted. This Properties dialog box also includes an option to immediately remove all deleted files. There is also an option to skip the annoying delete confirmation dialog box that appears whenever a file is deleted.

> **TIP**   Enabling the Do not move files to the Recycle Bin option or setting the Maximum Size of the Recycle Bin to 0 keeps the Recycle Bin empty.

The Recycle Bin isn't the only place where unneeded files tend to accumulate. Another common place where you can reclaim disk space is the Temp directory. When a new application is installed, the installation files usually copy to a temporary directory during the installation. After the installation has completed, these temporary files are typically deleted automatically, but sometimes they are not. Other programs save temporary back-ups to the Temp directory.

If your computer is connected to the Internet, files are downloaded and saved in a cache directory where they can be quickly recalled if you revisit a page. By retrieving cached images and files from the local hard drive, Web pages can load quicker, but saving all the files you encounter on the Web can fill up a lot of space.

Internet Explorer includes settings in the Internet Options dialog box where you can select to delete all cached files. You can also set the maximum size of the folder that holds cached files.

> **CROSS-REF**   More information on using Internet Explorer is presented in Chapter 46.

Using the Disk Cleanup utility

Hunting down all these temporary and deleted files can be a chore, but there is a Windows utility called Disk Cleanup that can automatically find and permanently delete these unneeded files. You can open Disk Cleanup using the Start ➪ All Programs ➪ Accessories ➪ System Tools ➪ Disk Cleanup menu.

> **TIP**   You can also access the Disk Cleanup utility using a button located on the Properties dialog box for the selected hard drive.

When you first start Disk Cleanup, it begins scanning and analyzing your system to find any temporary files it can delete, as shown in Figure 49.1.

Once the entire system is scanned, the Disk Cleanup utility appears, as shown in Figure 49.2. This utility shows the results of the hard drive scan and lets you select which files to delete. It also computes the total amount of disk space you can gain with your selections.

FIGURE 49.1

Disk Cleanup scans your local hard drives for temp files it can delete.

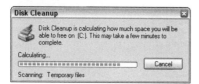

FIGURE 49.2

The Disk Cleanup utility shows you how much disk space you can regain by cleaning the hard drive.

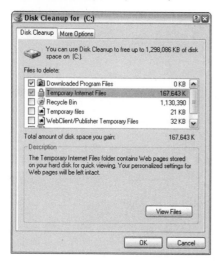

If you click and select a specific category of files from the Files to delete list, the Description pane explains the files that will delete. There is also a View Files button you can click to see the files for the Downloaded Program Files, Temporary Internet Files, and the Recycle Bin. Clicking this button opens the folder containing the selected category where you can move files you don't want to delete.

The category at the bottom of the Files to delete list is Compress Old Files. If you select this option, an Options button appears below the Description pane. If you click this button, the dialog box shown in Figure 49.3 opens; here you can set the number of days to wait before a file is targeted for compression.

After you select the files to delete and click OK, a confirmation dialog box appears. After answering Yes, the selected files are deleted and the disk space is reclaimed.

 Scanning your entire hard drive for files that can be cleaned up and deleting the files can take a long time; it is best to run this utility when the computer is idle.

FIGURE 49.3

If you select the Compress Old Files category, the Options button opens this dialog box.

Accessing more options

The Disk Cleanup utility includes a second tab titled More Options, shown in Figure 49.4. Within this tab are three additional options for cleaning up files and restoring disk space. The options are

■ **Window components:** Clicking this button opens the Windows Components Wizard dialog box where you can select which components to add and remove from your system. Deleted components can be reinstalled at a future time if you need them.

FIGURE 49.4

The More Options tab of the Disk Cleanup utility lets you reclaim even more disk space.

- **Installed programs:** This button opens the Add or Remove Programs utility from the Control Panel. The Add or Remove Programs utility lists all the installed programs. Selecting a program and clicking the Change/Remove button uninstalls the program.

- **System restore:** The System Restore Clean up button presents a warning dialog box asking if you want to delete all but the most recent restore points. Setting a restore point is covered in Chapter 50.

 Permanently deleting all the deleted e-mail messages in your mail client is yet another way to reclaim disk space.

Defragment Your Drive

Whenever data saves to the hard drive, it saves in the available free space on the hard drive; but after weeks and months of saving and deleting files, the free space starts to look like Swiss cheese with a small open area over here and a larger section over there. In extreme cases, this can slow down recalling data from the hard drive because Windows has to move all over the disk drive's surface to find the data you need.

The answer to this problem is to defragment the hard drive. Defragmenting the disk drive collects all the data for a specific file into a continuous area on the hard drive and places the data files back to back in an orderly manner. All the free space then moves together so that future files can be saved all together. The end result of defragmenting a hard drive is quicker access to hard drive data.

Using the Disk Defragmenter utility

The Windows utility that defragments your drive is found in the Start ➪ All Programs ➪ Accessories ➪ System Tools ➪ Disk Defragmenter menu. This opens the Disk Defragmenter utility shown in Figure 49.5.

Analyzing defragmentation

The first step of the defragment process is to analyze the hard drive to see how fragmented the hard drive is. You can begin the analysis phase by clicking the Analyze button. The progress of the analysis is displayed at the bottom of the utility window. When complete, a simple dialog box appears stating that the analysis is complete; there are options to View Report, Defragment, and Close.

After analysis, the top bar in the utility window shows the current state of the hard drive. All blue vertical lines show the areas on the hard disk where the files are packed closely together, the red vertical lines show the areas where the files are fragmented, and the white lines show the areas of free space. There are also some files that cannot be moved. These files include any applications and files that are currently open and any operating system files that are currently in use.

After the hard drive analysis is done, you can select to view a summary report with the View Report button. This report, shown in Figure 49.6, lists the results of the analysis including the amount of fragmentation found. It also lists all the main fragmented files and their size and location. This Analysis Report can be printed or saved.

FIGURE 49.5

The Disk Defragmenter utility shows the amount of Free Space available on the current drive.

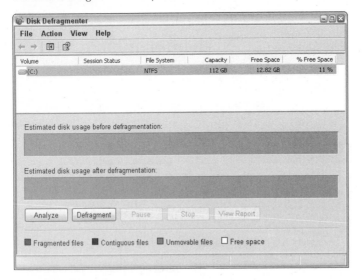

FIGURE 49.6

After the hard drive has been analyzed, you can view a report that shows the fragmented files.

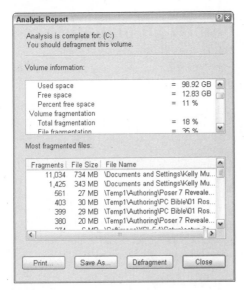

NOTE The key piece of information in the Analysis Report is the Total fragmentation value. If this value is higher than 10 percent, defragmentation helps improve hard drive performance. If defragmentation is less than 10 percent, then the utility doesn't recommend defragmenting the drive.

Starting defragmentation

If you decide to defragment your hard drive, click the Defragment button to begin the process. It is recommended that you have at least 15 percent free space on the hard drive before you begin the defragment process. If you don't have enough free space, a warning dialog box appears before beginning the defragmenting.

NOTE Be aware that defragmenting your hard drive usually takes a long time to complete and is best run at the end of the day when other tasks won't interrupt the process.

As the defragment process continues, you can see its progress in the bottom of the utility window. You can also see the progress in the lower color bar which shows the updated collection of data files. Over time, the red lines are mostly eliminated and the blue and white lines collect into adjoining areas; in Figure 49.7, these lines are shown in grayscale.

FIGURE 49.7

After you've defragmented the hard drive, much of the file data and free space collects together.

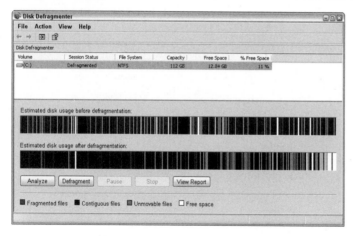

Check the Integrity of Your Drive

Within a hard drive is a dense magnetic cylinder where the data is stored. When data is requested from the hard drive, the cylinder spins around as an arm with a device for reading the data extends to the specific place where the data is stored. This all happens very fast and results in the whirring sound when you access the hard drive.

Hard drive errors

There are several different ways that errors can appear on your hard drive. Hard drive errors manifest as warning dialog boxes that say "An error occurred trying to read a file," or as a dialog box claiming that a file is missing. Hard drive errors could be caused by physical damage to the hard drive surface or when the computer tries to write one file over the top of another, a situation that results in *cross-linked* files. Cross-linked files occurs when two files are written to the same space on the hard drive. Another potential problem occurs when the index to the file gets mixed up.

Physical damage

Current hard drives are built in a way to protect the read/write arm from impacting with the magnetic cylinder, but if the computer gets bumped or dropped during the read/write process, the hard drive could be damaged, making it impossible to save or retrieve data from the damaged area. Power surges are another potential cause of hard drive damage.

 You can help avoid damage to your hard drive by placing the computer in a safe place where it won't be bumped or dropped.

If a hard drive gets damaged, the damaged area produces read errors when the data at the area tries to get read, but the remainder of the hard drive continues to work fine. Using a disk check utility, you can check your entire hard drive for damaged areas. If any damaged areas are found, the utility marks these areas as *bad sectors* on the hard drive so the computer doesn't try to write data to these areas anymore.

Cross-linked files

When the computer tries to save data to the hard drive in a place where a file already exists, the two files become cross-linked. When this occurs, data from both files share the same sector on the hard drive causing both to become corrupt. In some cases, one of the cross-linked files can be saved, but often both must be deleted.

Misaligned indexes

When file indexes get mixed up, they can usually be fixed without having to delete any data. A file index tells Windows where on the hard drive the data is located. It also tells what type of data to expect. Windows sometimes writes the wrong address for the file, but the Error checking tool can fix these problems.

Using the Error-checking tool

To locate and mark damaged areas and fix other problems on your local hard drive, you can use the Error-checking tool. This tool is found in the Tools tab of the Local Disk Properties dialog box, shown in Figure 49.8. The Local Disk Properties dialog box can be opened by selecting the C: drive in Windows Explorer and choosing the File ⇨ Properties menu command, or you could right-click on the C: drive and choose Properties from the pop-up menu.

FIGURE 49.8

The Tools tab of the Local Disk Properties dialog box includes the Error-checking tool.

 **TIP** You can schedule the Error-checking tool, like the other disk maintenance utilities, to run regularly using the Scheduled Tasks utility.

The Error-checking tool cannot fix any errors if any files are currently open. You should close down all applications before running the Error-checking tool. It is also helpful to disconnect your computer from the Internet and/or network before checking the local hard drive so that any automatic process such as checking email aren't running.

To begin the Error-checking tool, simply click the Check Now button. This opens the Check Disk Local Disk dialog box, shown in Figure 49.9, where you can choose the Check Disk options and start the tool. This tool can detect any errors on the hard drive even if neither of the options are selected, and you can choose whether the tool automatically tries to fix the errors or to recover any of the data located in the damaged sectors.

FIGURE 49.9

The Check Disk Local Disk dialog box includes options for how the hard drive is checked.

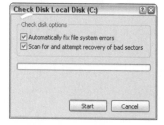

> **TIP** You can use the Error-checking tool to check any hard drive attached to your system including floppy drives, external hard drives, and network drives. However, it cannot check CD-ROM drives.

The Error-checking tool runs in several phases. During the first phase, it verifies the integrity of all files; the second phase verifies all file indexes (which can take a lot longer); the third phase verifies the security descriptors; and the last phase does a hardware scan if the Scan for and attempt recovery of bad sectors option is enabled.

When the Error-checking tool is run, a warning dialog box opens every time an error is found; but if you enable the Automatically fix file system errors option, these dialog boxes are skipped and the tool automatically attempts to fix any errors it finds.

> **NOTE** If you're worried about letting the Error checking tool fix the errors automatically, you can disable this option and all errors are displayed before any action is taken.

The search for cross-linked files and misaligned indexes happens relatively quickly, but checking the entire physical hard drive sector by sector can take a lot of time — up to an hour depending on the hard drive size and speed. If you select the Scan for and attempt recovery of bad sectors option, the Error-checking tool scans the entire physical hard drive sector by sector.

The Error-checking tool can run in read-only mode if none of the options are enabled. But if the tool finds any opened files or any attempts to read or write data to the hard drive when either of the options are enabled, the dialog box shown in Figure 49.10 appears, asking if you want to reschedule the tool to run next time Windows is restarted. If you select Yes, the disk is checked as part of the boot-up process, which may take some time, the next time Windows is restarted.

FIGURE 49.10

If you're having trouble running the Error-checking tool, you can schedule it to run the next time Windows is restarted.

Running the Error-checking tool from the Command Prompt window

The Error-checking tool, called Chkdsk, can also be run from the Command Prompt. To open the Command Prompt, just type cmd in the Run dialog box, shown in Figure 49.11.

FIGURE 49.11

The Command Prompt lets you execute commands such as **chkdsk**.

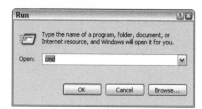

From the Command Prompt console, you can navigate to the hard drive that you want to check by typing its drive letter followed by a colon and pressing enter. Then type the following command:

    chkdsk /F /R

where the /F and /R are the options for automatically fixing errors and scanning for bad sectors. By typing chkdsk /?, you can see the available options for this utility, as shown in Figure 49.12.

FIGURE 49.12

At the Command Prompt are several additional options for setting checking the hard disk.

NOTE   Running chkdsk on large hard drives may take a long amount of time to complete.

Back Up Your Data

It is common for computer users to not ask if a computer will crash, but when. One of the best things you can do to help recover from a system crash is to back up your critical files. Windows includes a Backup utility that can make this process easy.

CROSS-REF Another helpful task that can help you recover from a system crash is to create a restore point, which is covered in Chapter 50.

Making backups

You can access the Backup utility using the Start ⇨ All Programs ⇨ Accessories ⇨ System Tools ⇨ Backup menu command. This opens the Backup or Restore Wizard, shown in Figure 49.13. When the Backup utility is first run, it opens in wizard mode that takes you through the process of configuring the utility. Once configured, you can run the utility in advanced mode, which skips the wizard steps.

FIGURE 49.13

The first step of the Backup or Restore Wizard starts the steps for configuring the Backup utility.

The second step of the Backup or Restore Wizard, shown in Figure 49.14, lets you choose to back up or restore files. Before you can restore a backup, you first need to configure and back up your files.

The organization of Windows makes it easy to locate files that are critical to backup. By default Windows saves all of its setting files that are unique to the current user in the Documents and Settings folder. Windows also encourages users to save all data files in the My Documents folder.

The third step of the Backup and Restore Wizard, shown in Figure 49.15, lets you choose which files to backup. The options include backing up the files in the My Documents folder along with settings for the current user, all the custom files for all users, and all data files, or an option to let you choose which files to backup.

FIGURE 49.14

The second step of the Backup or Restore Wizard lets you choose to back up or restore files.

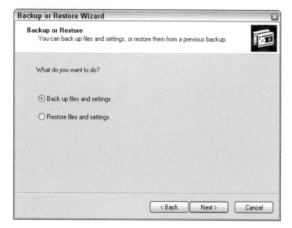

FIGURE 49.15

The third step of the Backup or Restore Wizard lets you choose which files to backup.

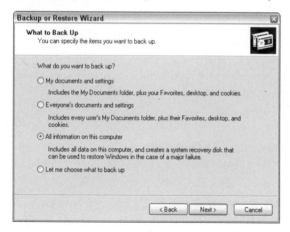

If any of the first three options in the What to Back Up step are selected, the next step is to decide where the backup is saved. If you select the last option, the wizard shows a hierarchical list of the current hard drive, shown in Figure 49.16, where you can select which files to back up. If you place a check mark in the box next to a folder, the files within that folder are marked for back up. All folders are displayed in the left pane and subfolders and files within the current selection are displayed in the right pane.

FIGURE 49.16

The Backup or Restore Wizard lets you select exactly which files to backup.

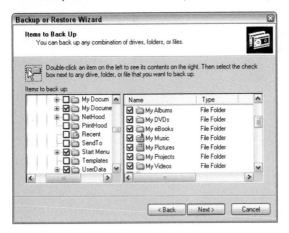

The fourth and final step of the Backup or Restore Wizard lets you choose the backup type, which is discussed below, and specify the location and name of the backup, as shown in Figure 49.17. The backup file is saved with the .bkf file extension. The options available depend on the hardware that you have connected to your computer, and may include the following:

- **Backup to the A: drive:** If your computer includes a floppy drive, then you can back up several small files to a floppy disk.

- **Backup to the hard drive:** Using the Browse button, you can select a specific location on the local hard drive where the entire backup can save as a single file. This file can then write to a CD-ROM using a burner.

- **Backup to a network drive:** Backup files can also save to a location on the network.

- **Backup to a zip drive or external hard drive:** The backup file can be saved to an external hard drive or a zip drive or flash drive connected to your computer. These external storage devices are typically connected to the computer using USB or FireWire cables.

NOTE Although the Backup or Restore Wizard can't save directly to a CD-ROM or DVD drive, you can save the backup file to the local hard drive and then burn the backup file to a CD. To save the backup to the local hard drive, choose the Backup to hard drive option and run the Backup utility. Then select the file and burn it to a CD-ROM.

The final page of the Backup or Restore Wizard recaps all the settings for the current backup configuration, as shown in Figure 49.18.

FIGURE 49.17

The fourth step of the Backup or Restore Wizard lets you select the backup location and its name.

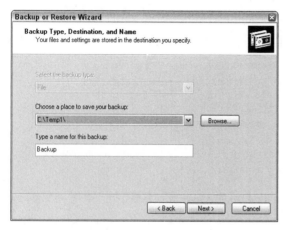

FIGURE 49.18

The final page of the Backup or Restore Wizard summarizes the settings for the current configuration.

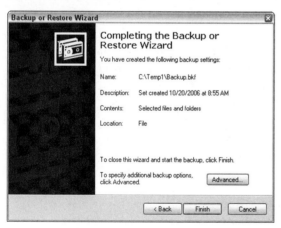

This dialog box also includes an Advanced button for accessing additional options. Clicking on the Advanced button lets you select the type of backup. The options include the following:

- **Normal:** This option backs up the selected files and marks each file as being backed up.
- **Copy:** This option backs up the selected files, but does not mark the files as being backed up.

- **Incremental:** This option only backs up the selected files if they have been modified since being marked as backed up.

- **Differential:** This option only backs up the selected files if they have been modified since being marked as backed up and removes the backed up marker for these files.

- **Daily:** This option only backs up the files that have been modified within the last 24 hours.

 **If you want to keep track of files that have been recently backed up use the Normal backup type for the first time you backup files and the Incremental option thereafter.**

After closing the wizard, the backup process begins and a dialog box shows the progress. All actions save to a log file that you can view using the Report button in the Backup Progress dialog box that appears when the backup is complete. The log file can help if the backup process encounters any errors. Before running the Backup utility, make sure that no files or applications are open or they may corrupt the backup files. The log file reports any writing errors occurring the backup process.

TIP **Once a backup has completed, you should check the integrity of the backed up files.**

Restoring from backups

Once a backup file is saved, it can be recalled and restored to the computer by selecting the Restore option in the second step of the wizard. This opens a dialog box where you can select the backup file to restore.

Once the backup file is selected, a summary page of the restoration process opens. This page includes an Advanced button. If you click Advanced, you can select to restore the files to their Original Location, to an Alternative Location, or to a Single Folder. If you select any of these options, another page of options appears where you can Leave Existing Files, Replace Existing Files if they are Older than the Backup Files, or Replace Existing Files.

NOTE **The Backup utility can also be run in advanced mode, which is different from Wizard mode. Advanced mode displays all the Backup options in one tab and all the Restore options in another tab. Advanced mode also includes a calendar where you can schedule backup tasks.**

Summary

Through regular maintenance tasks, you can keep your hard drives free of clutter and running at their optimal speed. To help with these tasks, Windows includes several helpful utilities and tools. The Disk Cleanup utility can remove temporary files and deleted files from the hard drive in a single step. The Disk Defragmenter utility can organize the hard drive into consecutive free and used areas, which can speed up the time it takes to access saved data.

The Error-checking tool can be used to find and repair any cross-linked files and misaligned indexes. This tool can also scan the entire drive for damaged sectors. Finally, the Backup utility can save critical files to a place where they can be restored at a later time in case of a system crash.

Chapter 50

Restoring Windows

New software can be fickle, especially if it relies on hardware such as the sound card or the CD/DVD drive. If you ever run into a situation where the sound on your computer stops working or inserted CD/DVDs suddenly aren't recognized after installing a program, then you might want to look into using the System Restore utility.

Another reason to use the System Restore utility is to recover from a system crash. A system crash could be caused by a virus attack, by installing new improperly configured hardware or software, or by any number of other system failures or conflicts. A system crash can be devastating, but with proper precautions, you can minimize the damage.

Regardless of what caused the hardware failure, software problems, or a system crash, there are procedures you can follow to recover. Windows includes a utility that can save the state of the system during a time when the system is working. This is called a restore point and it can be recalled after a system crash to return the system to a working state.

Using the System Restore Utility

The System Restore utility can't solve all your hardware and software problems, but it is one of the first steps to try to get your system back to a working state. System Restore doesn't remove any data, application, or email files from the system, but only changes the application settings back to a previous restore point.

If your system is having trouble with an application that was recently installed, you should first try uninstalling the offending program before running the System Restore utility. If a recently installed piece of hardware is causing problems on your system, then you should first try disabling the device using the Device Manager before running the System Restore utility. The Device Manager can be opened from the Hardware panel of the System Properties dialog box.

CROSS-REF You can learn more about device drivers and using the Device Manager in Chapter 31.

The System Restore utility is accessed using the Start ⇨ All Programs ⇨ Accessories ⇨ System Tools ⇨ System Restore menu. The System Restore utility, shown in Figure 50.1, lets you create a restore point or restore the computer to an earlier time. The utility uses step-by-step wizards to walk you through the process of creating and restoring restore points. The restore process is completely reversible if you need to revert back the computer's original state before the restore.

CROSS-REF Although the System Restore utility can restore your Windows setup, it doesn't save or delete any of your data files. To save data files, you can use the Backup utility which is covered in Chapter 49.

FIGURE 50.1

The System Restore utility is used to create and restore existing restore points.

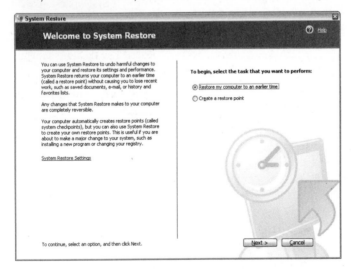

Creating a restore point

A restore point saves the settings of the computer during a time when everything is working properly. By saving a restore point, you can backtrack if the system starts experiencing problems. Some problems to watch for include software behaving erratically; throwing errors or reporting that certain modules are missing or can't be located; hardware that stop working or that throws errors; or when the operating system shows up as a blue screen reporting an error.

Windows automatically creates regular restore points, but you can use the System Restore utility to create restore points at any time.

 If you're planning on installing software that relies on hardware to function properly, it is a good idea to create a restore point just before beginning the installation.

To use the System Restore utility to create a restore point, follow these steps:

1. Select the Start ➪ All Programs ➪ Accessories ➪ System Tools ➪ System Restore menu to run the System Restore utility.

2. Select the Create a restore point option and click Next.

3. **In the next step of the wizard, you can enter a restore point description.** This description identifies and distinguishes the restore points from each other.

 A good restore point description explains the system before any changes, such as "System settings before installing the latest Outlook update."

4. **After naming the restore point, click the Create button to begin the process.** A dialog box listing the restore point is displayed once the process is finished, as shown in Figure 50.2.

FIGURE 50.2

The System Restore utility can create restore points at any time.

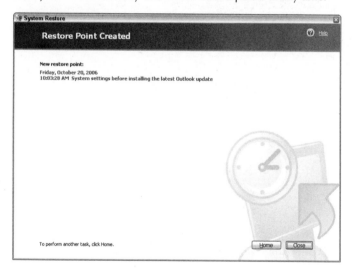

5. Click the Home button to return to the first page of the wizard.

Returning to a restore point

If your computer is acting erratically and you can't troubleshoot the issue, you can sometimes eliminate the problem by using the System Restore utility to return the computer to an earlier restore point when the system seemed to be running just fine.

 **NOTE** Returning the system to an earlier restore point does not delete any files or data that have been saved since the restore point was created.

When the Restore my computer to an earlier time option is selected in the first page of the System Restore wizard, the next page of the wizard shows a calendar for the current month, as shown in Figure 50.3. Every date that includes a restore point is marked in bold.

FIGURE 50.3

All days that include a restore point are shown in bold.

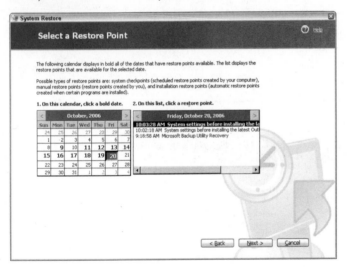

If you select a restore point and click Next, the restoration process begins. During this process, the computer reboots, so you should save any work before beginning the restoration. Returning to an earlier restore point also doesn't change the current time and date.

After you use the Return to restore point command, the wizard includes an option to Undo my last restoration. If returning to a restore point causes more problems than it fixes, you can undo the last restoration. This requires another system reboot.

Accessing the System Restore settings

If you click the System Restore Settings link on the first page of the System Restore utility, the System Restore tab of the System Properties dialog box, shown in Figure 50.4, appears. Using this tab, you can disable the System Restore utility. If restore points are established daily, they could potential use a lot of disk space for a feature that you aren't likely to use very often, especially if you aren't regularly installing new software. If you find that you're getting low on disk space, you may want to disable this utility.

 **NOTE** You can also access the System Properties dialog box by right-clicking the My Computer icon and selecting the Properties menu command.

FIGURE 50.4

The System Restore tab of the System Properties dialog box lets you configure and disable the System Restore utility.

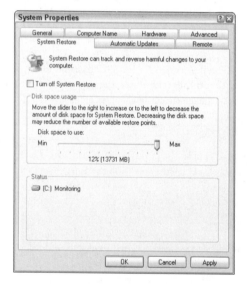

You can also use the System Restore tab to set the amount of disk space that the computer uses to save restore points. The System Restore utility automatically creates restore points before the installation of every application. As the designated disk space limit is approached, the older restore points are overwritten. If the amount of available space on your hard drive falls below 200MB, then the System Restore utility is automatically disabled.

TIP If you need to reclaim disk space after changing the disk space limit used for restore points, open the Disk Cleanup utility and click the More Options tab. Within this tab is an option to free disk space by removing all but the most recent restore point.

Restoring Windows from CDs

For some system crashes and problems, the System Restore utility is sufficient. If it still doesn't fix the problems, the next step is to try something a little more dramatic. System crashes in particular can paralyze a system resulting is a blue error screen. If this screen keeps reappearing even after you've used the System Restore utility several times, then you might need to use the installation CDs to fix the problem. Using the installation CDs that shipped with your computer, you can repair, restore, or even reinstall Windows on your system.

CAUTION Before you continue restoring Windows from the installation CDs, you should try to back up all the data files that you don't want to lose. Reinstalling Windows often requires that you erase all the data on the hard drive.

Using the Windows XP CDs

To access the screen used to repair the current installation of Windows, insert the Windows installation CD into the CD-ROM drive and reboot the computer. This causes a simple text message to appear asking if you want to boot from the CD; press the Enter key to continue. This loads all the necessary files from the CD to boot the computer to a text-based screen.

The options on this page include setting up Windows XP, repairing a Windows XP installation using Recovery Console, and exiting without installing. If you press the R key, the setup loads a DOS-like interface where you can access your data files and execute some diagnostic features, but you'll need to know what you're doing if you go this route. The Recovery Console provides a way to get access to your data files when the computer doesn't boot.

NOTE The installation process for each of the different versions of Windows is different. For example, the installation process for Windows Vista is different from the Windows XP process outlined above.

Repairing a Windows installation

If you press the Enter key, the setup continues by showing you a License Agreement and searching for any existing installations. At this point, you can select the installation (most likely at C:\Windows) and choose to repair the installation by pressing the R key. The setup process then copies all the setup files over the existing installation and reboots the computer. If the repair works, all your applications, data files, and hardware settings remain intact and Windows boots up as normal without the blue screen errors.

After the Windows installation is repaired and working fine, visit the Microsoft site and download and install the latest Service Pack.

TIP If you open the Automatic Updates tab in the My Computer Properties dialog box and enable the Automatic option, Windows automatically downloads and installs the latest updates.

Reinstalling Windows

If you've tried using the System Restore utility and repairing the Windows installation and the problems still persist, then one of the last options to try is to reinstall Windows onto a blank hard drive.

There are several different ways to reinstall Windows. First, you can try renaming the current Windows directory and reinstalling Windows into a new empty Windows directory. If successful, you can retain your data files, but you need to reinstall your software applications.

The second method is to buy and install a new hard drive and set up the old hard drive as a secondary drive. You can then reinstall Windows on the new hard drive and recover the data files from the secondary hard drive.

If you've backed up all the data files and don't mind erasing the current hard drive, you can select to format (a process that erases the hard drive) the hard drive and then reinstall Windows onto the reformatted hard drive. This erases all data and programs from the hard drive, but data files can be restored from a backup copy.

> **NOTE** One common problem that causes system crashes and software problems is when the system files on the hard drive get corrupted. If you format the hard drive, be sure to run the Disk Check utility to identify and block corrupt hard drive sectors before reinstalling Windows.

Summary

Physical abuse or corrupt files can cause a system to crash, but even though a system crash makes a computer behave erratically, there are several solutions you can use to fix the problems.

The System Restore utility saves snapshots of the system when everything is working fine, and these snapshots can be recalled any time a system is having trouble. The utility also lets you manually take these snapshots, called restore points, at any time, so you can preventively protect your system from potential crashes.

If the System Restore utility is unsuccessful, you can use the Windows installation CDs to repair the current Windows installation. Doing so maintains all your current applications, settings, and data files. As a last resort you can reinstall Windows to a blank hard drive folder.

Chapter 51

Troubleshooting: Finding the Problem After It Happens

It would take a book much bigger than this one to describe everything that can possibly go wrong with your computer. From relatively simple problems such as a keyboard that isn't connected to a CPU, to obscure things such as an overheated CPU caused by cat hair accumulated inside the heat sink, it's just not possible to anticipate all the ways your computer can go wrong. And when you add Windows and all the other software installed on your computer, you're facing a tremendous number of potential glitches, hiccups, and massive disasters.

So the best way to deal with a computer problem is to use a systematic troubleshooting routine. This chapter offers instructions for analyzing a problem and finding the specific steps needed to fix it.

General Troubleshooting Techniques

When something on your computer stops working, or when it begins to behave differently, there is always a reason, even if it is not immediately obvious. One of the goals of troubleshooting is to identify the cause of the failure or change.

A problem can be as serious as a complete system failure, or as minor as a different background color in a program window. The first thing to do is to find as much information as you can about the problem. If there's an error message on the screen, read it; even if you don't understand the text, or if it's nothing more than a string of code, you might find an explanation in the Microsoft Knowledge Base or someplace else on the Web.

IN THIS CHAPTER

Taking a systematic approach to troubleshooting

Finding the source of a problem

Understanding blue screen Stop errors

Working around a damaged hard drive

Returning to a restore point

Finding viruses and spyware

Alternatives to replacing a hard drive

If you can set up a second computer with an Internet connection close to the one you're trying to fix, do it; this makes it possible for you to read and apply the information you find on a Web site without the need to move back to the computer with the problem. If you don't have a second computer, you'll have to take careful notes on paper and use a computer at a friend's home or office, at the public library, or an Internet café to search for online information and assistance.

As you analyze a problem, ask yourself these questions:

- **What were you doing, and what was the computer doing just before the problem appeared?** Does the problem appear when you try to turn the computer on or off, or when you run a particular program? What programs were running? Did you try to run one program while another program was already active? Did the computer make a strange noise or display a message you hadn't seen before?

- **Has something changed?** Did you recently install a new program or a new piece of hardware? Has the physical environment around the computer changed? Have you changed any configuration settings, even if they don't seem to be related to the problem?

- **Can you reproduce the problem?** If you turn off the computer and restart it, does the same thing happen again?

- **What have you tried?** Keep track of all the things you try, even if they don't solve the problem. If you have to call a friend, colleague, or a tech support center for help, this information might provide a valuable hint. And if you do find a solution, note what you did; if the same problem occurs again, you want to use the same steps to fix it.

- **Have you ever seen this problem before?** Have you seen something similar?

Your troubleshooting plan

Your troubleshooting plan should include these steps:

Identify the symptoms

Has the mouse stopped moving your on-screen cursor, or does a program take longer to load? Does your Web browser take you to a strange page you didn't ask for? Just exactly what do you see, hear, and smell? Make a list of everything that seems different from normal operation. Sometimes the solution becomes obvious when you look at the symptoms (for example, if the keyboard doesn't work, check for a loose connector). In other cases, you might detect a pattern in a bunch of unrelated problems (for example, if you can't reach any Web sites through your browser and you're not receiving any e-mail, check your Internet connection). If it's not obvious, you should use the information in your list to describe the problem to a support person.

If your computer displays one or more error messages or codes, copy the text, even if you don't understand what the messages mean. The Microsoft Knowledge Base (`http://supportmicrosoft.com/search/?adv+1`) and other online resources contain detailed explanations of many error messages.

Did you hear a series of beeps when you turned on the computer? Look in the manual supplied with your computer or motherboard, or online (www.ami.com/support/doc/AMIBIOS-codes.pdf or www.phoenix.com/en/Customer+Services/BIOS/AwardBIOS/Award+Error+Codes.htm) for an explanation of the specific code you heard.

Does the problem occur during startup, before Windows loads? Look for an error message in the text on your screen.

Open the Event Viewer

The Windows Event Viewer (Start ⇨ Run ⇨ eventvwr.msc, and choose System) shown in Figure 51.1 can often cast more light on the cause of a problem.

FIGURE 51.1

The Windows Event Viewer lists errors and other events that may be related to a system problem.

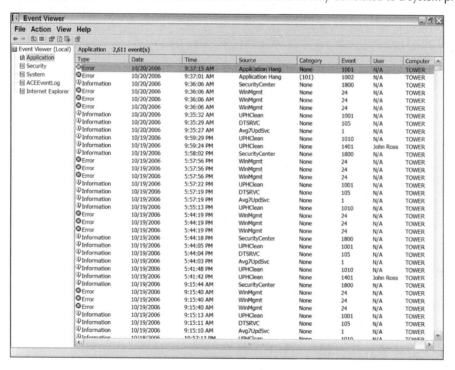

The items in the System section of the Event Viewer are events that have been logged by a component of Windows XP, such as a command to start or stop a particular function. Most of the items in the list are Information listings that describe routine events that are not particularly helpful for troubleshooting. The more interesting events have either a Warning or an Error in the Type column. These include device drivers that failed to load during startup, and minor error messages (a minor error is one that doesn't interfere with normal Windows operation).

To see more details about an event listed in the Event Viewer, double-click the listing to open an Event Properties window like the one shown in Figure 51.2. Like other error messages, the text in the Description section may not mean very much to you, but it can be useful when you talk to a support center. To make a copy of the information in a Properties window before you move on to the next one, click the Copy button under the up and down arrow buttons, and paste the text to Notepad or WordPad.

FIGURE 51.2

Each event listed in the Event Viewer has a related Properties window with more detailed information.

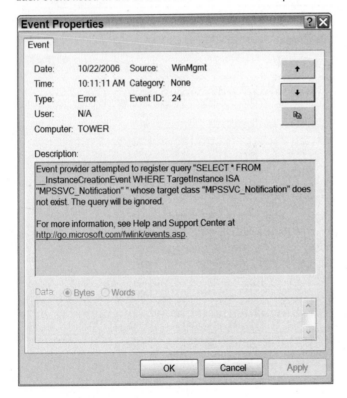

Restart the computer

If there's no other obvious way to fix a problem, try turning off the computer and all the external equipment connected to it (including your network gateway router and modem, if possible, because the problem might be in one of those devices), wait 10 or 15 seconds, and then turn everything back on again. In a surprising number of cases, that's enough to clear a problem, because restarting often resets the configuration options to the default settings.

Remember to copy the text of any error messages and note any other unusual conditions before you shut down the computer.

Look for a simple fix

Before you spend a lot of time searching for complicated solutions to simple problems, try to eliminate the things that are easy to fix:

- Make sure the computer and other devices are plugged into a power outlet and turned on.
- Check all the cables and connectors and confirm that they are firmly seated in their correct sockets.
- Look in the floppy disk or CD drive for a disk that is blocking normal startup.
- If other people use your computer or the LAN connected to your computer, look around to see if somebody else is running a program or has made some kind of change to hardware that could affect your own system.
- If you can't hear anything coming out of the speakers, confirm that the volume isn't turned all the way down. Check both the physical volume control on the speakers and the on-screen Volume settings. Also, make sure that none of the Mute options in the Volume Control window are active.
- Confirm that the printer and the network control devices (the modem, switch and gateway router) are On Line.
- Make sure the printer is not out of paper, ink, or toner.
- Confirm that the fans or blowers on the power supply, case, and motherboard are all operating. If any of them are not turning, use the BIOS Settings utility or a program such as SpeedFan (www.almico.com/speedfan.php) to check the computer's internal temperature.
- If a particular program, group of programs, or specific hardware device is not working the way you expect it to work, check the configuration settings and Properties windows related to that program or device.
- If your laptop won't start on battery power but it runs with AC power, replace the battery.
- Run complete virus and spyware scans. If your regular security programs don't find anything, try one of the online scan services listed in Chapter 48.

Isolate the problem

If you have a hardware problem, try to locate the source by replacing cables, expansion cards, and memory modules one at a time. If the problem disappears, the item you removed probably caused the problem.

If it's a software problem, try shutting down one program at a time. If you recently installed a program or device driver that runs in the background, try uninstalling it. Use the Task Manager (right-click the taskbar to open it from a pop-up menu) to turn off active Applications and Processes.

Sometimes, you won't know whether the source of a problem is hardware or software. In that case, try both type of troubleshooting: check the cables and other hardware, and then try turning off software programs (Applications) and processes, one at a time.

Try restarting the computer in safe mode to run a bare-bones version of Windows. If the problem is still present, you have isolated the problem to the Windows kernel. To run safe mode, restart the computer and press the F8 key several times while Windows begins to load, and choose Safe Mode from the list of startup options.

As a last resort, try reinstalling Windows from the CD or Recovery Disk. If the problem is gone, it's in one of the programs that normally loads with Windows.

CAUTION **Don't re-load Windows until you have tried every other possible way to solve a problem. Re-installing Windows over-writes all of your configuration settings and it could possibly destroy some of your data files. Before you re-load Windows, try as many of the other methods in this chapter (call Tech Support, look for information on the Internet, try System Restore and so forth) first.**

Look for help

If you can't identify and fix the problem yourself, it's time to look for help. It's a safe bet that somebody else has faced the same problem, and there's probably a solution out there someplace. First, try the online Help screens built into Windows and many other programs. The Windows Help and Support Center includes both text files stored on your own computer and links to online resources. Read everything you can about your symptoms — the solution is often buried in the seventh paragraph or hidden in a Related Topic.

Next, ask your local tech support people for help. This might be a formal corporate Help Desk or Computer Support Center, the knowledgeable person in the next cubicle, or a friend or family member who's good with computers. Describe the problem to your support person in as much detail as possible, and try whatever they suggest.

If your computer or a new piece of hardware or software is still under warranty, call or e-mail the technical support center for that product. If it's no longer under warranty, check the Support section of the manufacturer's Web site.

The Microsoft Knowledge Base

If your local support people can't find a solution to the problem, look in the Microsoft Knowledge Base. Even if the problem is not in a Microsoft product, their support people have probably heard about it and they might have prepared a Knowledge Base article with useful information.

To use the Knowledge Base, type the keywords that describe your problem into the search field on the main Support page. If you can't find anything, or if you get more links than you can use, try adding another keyword to describe the problem in more detail. If you see an error message, type the first four or five words of the message inside quotation marks. If there's a code number or error number, search for that number combined with a keyword that identifies the program that produced the error message, such as *XP* or *Outlook*. That's usually enough to narrow the search down to a manageable number of links.

Other manufacturers' tech support centers

If the Microsoft Knowledge Base doesn't contain anything useful and the problem appears to be related to a specific device or program, try the Technical Support section of that manufacturer's Web site. Look for a Knowledge Base or a list of FAQs (frequently asked questions), or a users' forum with answers to specific questions. If you can't find anything, try asking your own questions by telephone or e-mail.

Don't call or e-mail Microsoft's technical support, except as a last resort; unless you're asking about an installation problem, they may charge you a per-incident or per-call fee.

The collective wisdom of the Internet

If the official tech support centers can't provide a solution, move on to the unofficial information sources. If somebody has faced the same problem, he or she might have posted some information on the Internet that can help you. Use the name of the product and the symptoms as the subject of a keyword search in your favorite Web search tool to look for Web sites that might contain an explanation or instructions for fixing the problem. If you have an error message or ID number, try including both the name of the product and the first few words of the message or code in your search.

Unfortunately, some of the information you find online might not be particularly useful. Before you try any fix, read the advice on several different sites. The most promising solution is likely to be the one that appears in more than one place.

Try a solution

When you find a possible solution to your problem — from a tech support center, Web site, or from some other source — go ahead and try it. If it doesn't work, remember to undo whatever change you might have made before you try anything else; otherwise, you might end up with a new and different problem on top of the one you're trying to fix.

Keep notes

Whether a repair technique works or not, it's important to keep track of what you have done and how it affected your system. Don't assume that you will remember what you did, and that you will know how to do it again if the problem ever recurs. You might, but if it happens again six months from now, it's quite possible that you will have forgotten the specific details.

Keep a notebook or log of your computer problems and solutions that you can grab off a shelf and consult when you confront a similar problem in the future. Over time, the same logbook might also give you an idea about patterns of simple problems that might suggest a single, more serious cause.

CAUTION Keep your repair log in a notebook, a file folder, or a loose-leaf binder. Don't store it in an online text file because you might not be able to open and read the file the next time your computer breaks down.

Blue Screen Failures

When Windows detects a problem that is so serious that the computer can't continue to run, but it can still display information on the monitor screen, it halts all other activity and produces a detailed error message on a blue background. Microsoft officially calls this a stop message, but everybody else calls it a blue screen error, or the "blue screen of death."

Many blue screen errors occur during the Windows startup routine because Windows has failed to find a working hardware component (such as a disk drive or a memory module). Others might appear when a component fails after Windows has already started. Still others occur when there's a fatal bug in a program or driver's code, but you probably won't see those errors unless you're testing unreleased software.

Stop messages always present information about the problem that caused them in the same order. Starting at the top of the screen, they include these elements:

At the top of the screen, a unique stop error number or bugcheck code identifies the specific problem that caused the computer to break down, such as:

```
***STOP: 0x00000024 (0x00000000, 0xF73120AE, 0xC0000003,
0xD00000000)
```

The first part of the number identifies the type of failure; in this case a 0x00000024 failure is a problem in the NTFS file system. The numbers inside the parentheses provide more details about the problem. This code is often a pointer to the cause of the failure.

The next two lines of the error message contain generic text:

```
A problem has been detected and Windows has been shut down to
prevent
damage to your computer.
```

After Windows tells you that it has detected a problem, it displays a *symbolic name* that corresponds to a specific stop error number. For example, the symbolic name for a 0x00000024 failure is always:

```
NTFS_FILE_SYSTEM
```

The Microsoft Knowledge Base contains articles that explain each error, so you can usually find a solution by searching the Knowledge Base for the symbolic name or the stop error number that appears in the message.

The next part of the blue screen message is one or more paragraphs that contain Recommended User Action. The quality of these recommendations is uneven; some tell you exactly what to do to fix the problem, but many others were written by people who already understood why the failure happened, so the messages are unintelligible to the rest of us.

Under the Recommended User Action, a line of driver information provides the name and address of the device driver or other file that generated the blue screen. If a tech support person can use this address to identify a specific object or program, that can be a good start toward repairing the problem that caused the failure.

```
*** FILENAME.SYS - Address D62449BD base at B0000001D, DateStamp 35bo72a3
```

Finally, the last few lines of the screen contain Debug port and status information. If a kernel debugger was enabled when the failure occurred, it may be able to use this information to help find the source of the problem. Kernel debugging can be useful when a stop error occurs while a software developer is testing new code, but it's not particularly helpful for fixing an error condition caused by a hardware problem or code that has been distributed to real-world users.

Read the Recommended User Action section carefully and follow its instructions, if you can. But before you restart the computer, be sure to copy the entire stop code, the symbolic name, and the driver information onto a piece of paper or a text file on another computer, or use a digital camera to take a picture of the whole screen.

If you see a blue screen again after you perform the Recommended User Action, or if the message doesn't offer any useful suggestions, use another computer to search the Microsoft Knowledge Base for the stop code or the symbolic name, exactly as it appears in the blue screen message. The knowledge base article that applies to your problem almost always includes a more detailed set of instructions for solving the problem.

However, sometimes the Knowledge Base articles don't tell you very much except "this is a hardware problem." If your search points to one of these articles, try these steps:

1. **Look for obvious signs of damage: broken or missing parts; loose expansion cards, cables, or memory modules; black stains on a circuit board caused by overheated or burned components; or any other indication that something has gone seriously wrong.** If something looks bad, test it or replace it.

2. **Clean the accumulated dust and dirt from the motherboard, the CPU, and all other components.**

3. **Check for blocked fans and air vents that interfere with air flowing through the computer.**

4. Confirm that all the internal and external cables are solidly connected to their sockets.

5. Make sure the CPU, memory, and graphics controller are not overclocked beyond their capacities. If you are intentionally overclocking, restore the settings to the factory specifications and test them.

6. Test the output voltages from the computer's power supply.

If you continue to see stop errors, copy the complete Stop code (the top line of the screen) and use Google or another search tool to search for that code. If somebody has found a solution to the problem or an explanation of its cause, you can probably find information about the problem someplace on the Web.

Bypass the Hard Drive

If Windows does not load, the hard disk that holds the Windows software files may have a problem. To isolate the problem to the disk drive, try restarting the computer with your Windows software CD or an emergency boot disk in the CD drive or the floppy disk drive. If the computer starts and reads startup code from the CD or floppy, look for a problem on your hard disk.

Begin by restarting and using the BIOS Setup utility to see if it can detect the hard drive and identify its characteristics. If not, remove the old drive and install a new one, or move the jumper on the drive to change it from Master to Slave, and install the new drive as the Master and then reinstall Windows on the new drive.

 If the BIOS utility finds and identifies the suspect drive, consult Chapter 8 for more information.

Use the System Restore Tool

If you can't find any other solution to a problem, the System Restore tool included in Windows can often return the computer to its condition before the event that caused the problem occurred. Windows automatically creates *restore points* on a regular schedule and after certain important events (such as upgrades and other software changes).

When a problem appears, you can use System Restore to choose a restore point without affecting your documents, e-mail, favorites list, or other data files. However, it does remove all the changes you might have made since the restore point was created, including automatic updates to Windows and your security programs, so you might want to consider some other methods first.

Specifically, try these things first:

■ Restart the computer. This clears any residual junk from the memory, which is often all it takes to fix a problem.

- If the problem appeared in mid-session, return to the Last Known Good Configuration. Last Known Good Configuration clears out all the changes that might have been made since the last time you started Windows, including new or updated programs and device drivers.

- To return to the previous configuration, restart the computer and immediately press the F8 key, which takes you to the Windows Advanced Options Menu; choose the Last Known Good Configuration from the list of startup options and press Enter to let the computer start up again.

CROSS-REF See Chapter 50 for detailed information about System Restore.

Test for Viruses and Spyware

When everything else seems okay, but you continue to see some kind of evidence that the computer is not working properly, it's possible that it has been infected by one or more viruses or invaded by spyware. So it's always appropriate to perform complete system scans to either find and remove the problem or eliminate those problems from your list of possible causes.

CROSS-REF Chapter 48 provides information about spyware and viruses, as well as pointers to antivirus and anti-spyware programs.

Don't Reformat That Hard Drive — Yet

Many technical support centers put a tremendous amount of pressure on their employees to handle as many calls as they possibly can, so the support people working for those sweatshops often advise callers to reformat the computer's hard drive and reload Windows and everything else that had been installed on it.

This is bad advice. It may fix the problem, unless it's a virus that has infected the BIOS or some kind of hardware failure, but it's almost always overkill — like amputating a foot because of a blister on your heel, or bulldozing your whole house because there's a leak in a water pipe. In almost every case, there are other less destructive things you can do to solve a problem, if you would only take the time to find it.

Reformatting a hard drive should be an absolute last-resort technique because it erases everything — yes, everything — stored on that drive, and it may take you at least half a day to reload the software and restore Windows to the way it was before you started. As for your data files, forget it; they're probably gone forever.

Instead of reformatting the drive, try one of these techniques:

- **Run a complete antivirus scan on your computer.** If the first scan doesn't find anything, try a program from a different maker, or run one or more of the online virus scans described in Chapter 48.

- **Try starting Windows in Safe Mode.** If that works, the problem is probably caused by one of the other programs that load at Startup. Use the System Configuration Utility (Start ⇨ Run ⇨ msconfig) to turn off the programs in the Startup and Services tabs, one at a time, and restart the computer. When Windows starts without the problem, the last item you turned off was probably the source.

- **If Windows doesn't load, use the Recovery Console.** Use the console to copy the NTDETECT.COM and ntldr files from the Windows CD, and to repair the Master Boot Record and the boot sector. To fix a drive that isn't opening, try replacing or repairing all four of these files.

  - To open the Recovery Console, place your Windows CD in the CD drive and restart the computer. When you see the Welcome screen, press the R key. If your computer didn't come with a Windows CD, either borrow one from a friend or colleague, or call your computer maker's support center and ask them how to open the Recovery Console.

  - The Recovery console uses a command line screen similar to the Command Prompt in Windows or the old MS-DOS screen. To replace ntldr, type:

    ```
    Copy c: i386\ntldr
    ```

    To replace NTDETECT.COM, type:

    ```
    Copy c: i386\ntdetect.com
    ```

    To repair the Master Boot Record, type:

    ```
    fixmbr
    ```

    To repair the boot sector, type:

    ```
    fixboot
    ```

  - To close the Recovery Console, type Exit at the C:\ prompt.

- **Try re-installing Windows from the distribution CD.** Remember to install all of the updates, patches and Service Packs from Microsoft's Windows Update site.

- **Remove the suspect drive from your computer and install a new one.** If your computer already has a second hard drive, make it the boot disk and remove the old one, and then install Windows on the new boot drive. Don't forget to move the jumper on the drive.

CROSS-REF For a more thorough discussion on jumpers, see Chapter 9.

After you have installed Windows on the new boot disk, you can get back to work and worry about retrieving your data files later. Consider this: you can buy a new hard drive big enough to install Windows for less than $100 (check the big-box computer stores and office supply places; one brand or another is always on sale). Are your data files worth that much to you?

After you have installed another drive, try a data recovery program such as Runtime Software's GetDataBack (`www.runtime.org`) to retrieve your data files from the damaged drive. This and similar programs can often read data files that Windows can't.

Summary

Computer troubleshooting can be a long and frustrating process unless you apply a systematic approach to your efforts to find and fix problems.

Your standard troubleshooting routine should include these steps:

- Define the problem.
- Try restarting the computer.
- Try the simple fixes first.
- Isolate the problem — try replacing parts or shutting down programs, one by one.
- Look for help. You might find the information you need in this book, or in the online Windows Help and Support pages, or on the Internet. If you're still unable to fix the problem, talk to your local experts or hardware or software manufacturer's technical support center.
- If you see one or more error messages, copy the exact text and search for an explanation on the Internet.
- If a suggested fix doesn't solve the problem, do what you can to restore the system to its condition before you started to work on it.
- Keep track of everything — error messages and other symptoms, and all the things that didn't solve the problem. Even if something didn't solve a problem, that information might be useful to a tech support advisor. And when you do fix it, your notes will be tremendously helpful if the problem returns.

And finally, don't panic. Your computer isn't haunted. Somebody else has seen the same problem, and probably figured it out — the world of formal and informal tech support, and the collective wisdom of the Internet can almost always help you, if you know where to look.

Index